Enforcing Interna
Norms Against Terrorism

Edited by
ANDREA BIANCHI
Graduate Institute of International Studies

with the editorial assistance of
Yasmin Naqvi

·HART·
PUBLISHING

OXFORD AND PORTLAND OREGON
2004

Published in North America (US and Canada) by
Hart Publishing
c/o International Specialized Book Services
5804 NE Hassalo Street
Portland, Oregon
97213-3644
USA

Hart Publishing is a specialist legal publisher based in Oxford, England.
To order further copies of this book or to request a list of other
publications please write to:

Hart Publishing, Salters Boatyard, Folly Bridge,
Abingdon Rd, Oxford, OX1 4LB
Telephone: +44 (0)1865 245533 Fax: +44 (0) 1865 794882
email: mail@hartpub.co.uk
WEBSITE: http//:www.hartpub.co.uk

British Library Cataloguing in Publication Data
Data Available

ISBN 1-84113-566-6 (paperback)

Typeset by Olympus Infotech Pvt Ltd, India, in Palatino 10/12 pt
Printed and bound in Great Britain by
Biddles Ltd, King's Lynn, Norfolk

Foreword

It may be ill advised to start a research project in the wake of a catastrophe, causing an emotional shock. Yet the foundations of this project were laid in the aftermath of the 11 September 2001 attacks in New York and Washington. The sense of bewilderment and dismay at the brutality of terrorist violence, with which most of us were taken, soon yielded to a compelling sense of moral commitment to action. *Oportet ut scandala eveniant*, as the Latin adage goes, although at times one would wish to question its wisdom. It would be preferable indeed if the adjustment of the law to the new challenges and realities of the societal body from which it emanates would materialize regardless of catastrophes. However, it surely is a lesson to be learnt from history that catastrophes frequently act as a catalyst for change.

The prevailing preoccupation, at the time, that international law might not possess adequate means to counter the threat of terrorism seemed unsubstantiated, yet represented a challenge for governments, other international actors and the scholarly community alike. The urge to provide a professional insight was a reflection of a desire to compensate, if not substitute, for the sense of *impuissance* to which many of us felt relegated. When every single colleague I had made contact with, with no exception, gladly accepted to join the project, I realised that my concerns were shared and that they were matched by a general and genuine sense of intellectual commitment within the profession.

To assess the viability and efficacy of the wide array of legal tools available at international law to enforce norms against terrorism is apparently an easy task. The implementation of norms in such different areas as the use of force and the system of collective security, the law of State responsibility, international humanitarian and human rights law and the law of jurisdiction poses different problems and requires specific analysis with regard to each particular regime. This is all the more so, if one wants to preserve the unity of the international legal system and the overarching structure of its general principles and processes as generally understood and applied. Furthermore, the interaction between the different levels of legal authority involved in the process of implementation requires careful consideration.

As I write these few lines, the bloodshed caused by the terrorist attack in Madrid is still a vivid memory. It has not been the only attack since 11 September 2001. Presumably, it will not be the last. We are bound to live under the Damocle's sword of terrorist violence in the years to come.

The feeling that no place can provide a safe shelter has crept its way into the world civil society. Regrettably, this is precisely the effect intended by terrorist groups. Besides the many scenarios it evokes, the 'war on terror' to many human beings is also a personal itinerary of introspection and a cause to pose fundamental questions, bearing on the very essence of life and human nature. The less ambitious task of this book is to assess to what extent international law is well equipped to deal with the resurgence of international terrorism on such a grand scale. Short of providing an answer to the more essential quandaries that international terrorism entails, it is hoped that this collection of essays may help to better understand how the law can complement politics by responding effectively to these types of threats.

Within the framework of the research project, a conference was held at the Catholic University in Milan on 10–11 May 2002, in which the contributors submitted their drafts to the scrutiny of the other participants and the public. There is no doubt that the event was an important contribution to the project, as it provided a forum to discuss our ideas and preliminary findings.

The organisation of an international conference is no easy job and I would like to express my gratitude to all of those who participated in the effort. Silvia Borelli, Anna Gardella and Francesca Tremolada helped me with the endless tasks and practicalities that make the organisation of a conference a multifaceted activity. The administrative staff of the Catholic University was very helpful. Mr L Dioli, Head of logistical services and his deputy, Ms A Patriarchi, put at the organiser's disposal their professional skills and their knowledge of the institution's somewhat complex organisational practices. During the two days of the conference three students, Greta Barbone, Federica Bisol and Nazira Seliman attended to the participants and made sure that what had been planned in advance actually took place. Ms Domenica Cuzzocrea, the Secretary of the Institute of International Studies, provided them with an unrivalled model of kindness and efficiency and supervised their work in a motherly fashion.

I would like to thank also the Dean of the Law Faculty, my colleague and friend Giorgio Pastori for his encouragement and unconditional support. Were it not for him, I doubt I would have ever set out to organise the event. Institutions from the public and private sector showed their sensitivity to our intellectual efforts and manifested particular interest in the research topic. In particular, the substantial financial support of the *Fondazione Cariplo*, the *Regione Lombardia*, and the *Comune di Milano* is gratefully acknowledged.

My heartfelt thanks go also to Professor Alan Boyle of the University of Edinburgh; Professor Giorgio Gaja of the University of Florence and to Judge Theodor Meron, President of the International Criminal Tribunal for the former Yugoslavia for having masterfully chaired the three sessions in which the Conference was divided. Overall, my recollection of the Conference is that of an intellectually stimulating atmosphere coupled with the pleasant sensation that everyone felt well at ease in the fairly diverse group, which the participants made. Junior colleagues were encouraged and cheerfully admitted into the club, less junior ones submitted their views and constructively engaged into the debate that followed their presentations. In the highly confrontational and hierarchically structured academic world where egos more than intellectual constructs often come to clash, the Conference stood out as a comforting exception.

Finally, I would like to express my gratitude to my editorial assistant, Yasmin Naqvi, assistant to the International Law Section and doctoral candidate at the Graduate Institute of International Studies in Geneva. Yasmin joined the project at a much later stage, but her contribution has been invaluable. She relentlessly worked on the manuscripts and even found the time and energy to co-author one of the pieces that appear in the volume. Her cheerful disposition and full commitment to the project deserve my appreciation and gratitude.

It is customary to stress the difficulties inherent in the editor's job. Indeed, to undertake the editing of a collection of essays on a highly politicised topic, with events unfolding so rapidly that no one could reasonably aspire to including them all in their contributions, may well have appeared to many as a particularly unprofitable business. At the end of the exercise, while not at all denying the many hurdles that have stood in the way, one feeling definitely prevails over the others. If the time and energy this project has taken was the price to ensure that a group of distinguished colleagues could work together in a spirit of utter intellectual freedom, mutual respect and sympathy, it surely was a fair one for me to pay. As usual, only the reader will tell if it was worth the effort.

AB
Geneva, March 2004

List of Contributors

Georges Abi-Saab
Chairman, Appellate Body of the World Trade Organization; Emeritus Professor of International Law, Graduate Institute of International Studies, Geneva.

Eyal Benvenisti
Professor of International Law, Tel Aviv University, Faculty of Law.

Andrea Bianchi
Professor of Public International Law and Director of Graduate Studies, Graduate Institute of International Studies, Geneva; Professor of International Law, Catholic University of Milan.

Silvia Borelli
PhD candidate in International Law, University of Milan; Research Fellow, British Institute of International and Comparative Law, London.

Antonio Cassese
Professor of International Law, University of Florence.

Andrew Clapham
Professor of Public International Law, Graduate Institute of International Studies, Geneva.

Paul Clarke
Solicitor of the Supreme Court of New South Wales, Australia.

Luigi Condorelli
Professor of Public International Law, Faculty of Law, University of Florence; Honorary Professor, Faculty of Law, University of Geneva.

Ugo Draetta
Professor of International Law, Faculty of Political Science, Catholic University of Milan.

Pierre-Marie Dupuy
Professor of International Law, the University of Paris II and the European University Institute, Florence.

Bardo Fassbender
Assistant Professor of Law, Institute of International and European Law, Humbolt University; Lecturer in Public International Law, University of St Gallen, Switzerland.

Anna Gardella
Research Fellow in International Law, Faculty of Law, Catholic University of Milan.

Richard Garnett
Associate Professor of Law, University of Melbourne, Australia.

Robert Kolb
Professor of International Law, Universities of Neuchatel, Berne and Geneva (University Centre of International Humanitarian Law).

Mauro Megliani
Research Assistant in International Law, Catholic University of Milan.

Madeline Morris
Professor of Law, Duke Law School; Director, Duke/Geneva Institute in Transnational Law.

Yasmin Naqvi
PhD candidate in International Law and Assistant to the International Law Section, Graduate Institute of International Studies, Geneva.

Luca G Radicati di Brozolo
Professor of Private International Law, Catholic University of Milan; Partner, Bonelli, Erede, Pappalardo.

August Reinisch
Professor of International and European Law, University of Vienna; Professorial Lecturer, Bologna Center of SAIS/John Hopkins University, Bologna.

Natalino Ronzitti
Professor of International Law, LUISS University G Carli, Rome.

Michelangela Scalabrino
Professor of International Law, Catholic University of Milan and University of Urbino.

Ruth Wedgwood
Professor of Law at Yale Law School and at SAIS, John Hopkins University, Washington.

Contents

Introduction

*The Proper Role of International Law in Combating Terrorism**

GEORGES ABI-SAAB

WHAT IS THE proper role of international law in combating terrorism? Has it been affected by the 11 September 2001 events, and if so how and how far? And has this effect gone, as some contend, to the very foundations of the international legal system?

In this, as in any other respect, whoever tries to deal with the September 11 events is daunted by the avalanche of writings and opinions on the subject that has swamped the world since, to the point of making whatever one may say or write seem rather trite and "déjà vu". Yet, reiterating the obvious, however banal it may sound, can still be useful as a reminder of basic premises, particularly when they are ignored by some, not to say by many.

In what follows, an attempt is made, by successive approximations, to answer some of these queries, with a view to delineating the area where international law can really play a useful role in combating terrorism, without prejudicing its structures and other functions. But before turning to these queries, it is necessary to address briefly their general context.

I. THE SPECIFICITY OF THE SEPTEMBER 11 EVENTS

Obviously, by their scale and design, the September 11 events were horrendous and they precipitated spectacular reactions; all of which will undoubtedly leave an indelible mark on the international legal system. Still, one has to keep a sense of proportion.

In the United States, one keeps hearing by reference to these events such qualifications as "a defining moment", "a turning point" or

* A shorter version of this paper is published in the first issue of I (2002) *Chinese Journal of International Law*, No 1.

"a system change". But were these events so unique and conceptually unimaginable as to deserve such qualifications?

In fact, they were not.

A foretaste of these tragic events was provided by the earlier attack against the World Trade Center, by the uncovered conspiracy to blow up the New York tunnels and the UN building, as well as by the Oklahoma City (McWeigh) terrorist attack. Each of these events or planned event could have led, under different circumstances, to a catastrophe of a magnitude similar to that of September 11.

Moreover, we have been reading for decades about the possibility of nuclear terrorism, of groups of terrorists or mercenaries hijacking States (as happened recently for a short while in the Comoros islands) and other such scenarios. But these scenarios were perceived as moot intellectual hypotheses, because of their very low statistical probabilities. We know, however, that an event with a statistical probability, as infinitesimal as it can be, will occur at one point or another, however distant it may be. Still once it happens, it gives a "shock of recognition". One recognises in his guts what one may have intellectually perceived, but has not palpably visualized and realized what it actually signifies. A shock of recognition is very important in that it literally "brings home" to the collective psyche, as an immediate reality, what may have been barely perceived until then as an esoteric hypothesis verging on science fiction.

Another such shock of recognition — where the parallels are striking, and can help us put the long term effects of the September events in perspective — is "Chernobyl". Everyone knew that a nuclear catastrophe could happen, but only when it happened did the shock of recognition take place, and everybody thought that it would beget a serious system change. More than fifteen years later, has it done so?

Coming back to September 11, these events, however tragic and traumatic, have, like Chernobyl, to be put in perspective; and for us this means that they have to be put in legal perspective, in other words they have to be situated within or in relation to the international legal system.

Can they be processed through the system, i.e. apprehended, comprehended and dealt with by the system? This would still be the case even if these events, by their specificities and scale constituted an important precedent in the course of evolution of the system. Or, and this the other alternative, are these events so unique as to be indigestible by the system as it stands and hence call for a "system change"; not in the details of implementation and specification, but in the parameters of the system as a whole?

One gets the impression in the US that it is the latter case that obtains; that everything, including all the rules and institutions of international law, have to be reconsidered and reconfigured through the prism of September 11, even if this radical revisionism is represented sometimes in the guise of interpretation.

I personally take strong exception to this latter attitude, first and foremost because the solutions it comes up with ride roughshod over the international legal system so as to render it — this system, which is already imperfect and frail enough — completely unworkable, almost installing the very anarchy that one of the declared purposes of combating terrorism is to repel. The more so as there is no need for such a reconfiguration. The September 11 events, if characterized and handled correctly within the system, not only can receive a better response or remedy, but would also contribute to strengthening and perfecting the system as it stands and would favour its development for the future.

We should not go off on the wrong tangent. It is submitted that even what took place in terms of response to these events, in spite or perhaps because of the ambiguity which surrounded its legal justification, can withstand different legal interpretations; and that international lawyers, as a corporation, should adopt those interpretations which cohere with the international legal system and tend to strengthen it or, minimally, which would do least damage to its structure, rather than play with so-called "inventive" or "imaginative" new solutions, which would undermine the system and ultimately bring down its whole structure.

II. THE LEGAL CHARACTERIZATION OF THE SEPTEMBER 11 EVENTS

Turning to the specific queries, the first concerns the legal characterization of the September 11 events. There are here two contending approaches, with two consequent regimes of response: The first characterization is that these events constitute a criminal enterprise calling for a "law enforcement" approach in the sense of criminal prosecution and repression of the individual perpetrators. The other characterization is that they are "acts of war", bringing into play the law of war, with both its branches the *jus ad bellum* and the *jus in bello*.

Of course, the legal consequences of these two characterizations are very different, and particularly as concerns the role of international law in both. The first situates the events in a micro analytical setting, dealing with individuals or groups of individuals, calling on the appropriate institutions of national law in the first place, with the back up of those of international law which go with them: crime prevention and prosecution, social defense, respect of human rights, judicial cooperation, etc.; while the second situates them in a macro analytical setting of belligerent relations between collectivities, calling directly on the institutions of the international law of war. Obviously, when one deals with micro settings, one has to use a microscope and be very precise in directing repressive action to particular individuals, while dealing with macro settings, calls for a telescope and opens the way to large scale military action.

Can we really call these events or the reaction to them "war" as they are rhetorically called in the US? One can perceive "war against terrorism", the same as "war on poverty", as an exceptional rhetorical call for national mobilisation to counter an impeding scourge. But is it war in the legal technical sense? Michael Howard, who is not a lawyer but a military historian, has shown very eloquently in a short article in *Foreign Affairs* entitled "What's in a name?", all the fallacy and great dangers with which such a misnomer is fraught.[1]

"War" or "armed conflict", in the sense of international law, necessarily involves internationally recognizable entities which are capable of being territorially defined (whether States or peoples struggling for self-determination over a particular territory), even if their territorial confines are not completely determined. Non-international armed conflicts are also territorially defined, albeit negatively, as taking place on the territory of one State and between belligerents belonging to that State. If the armed conflict spills over to other States, either territorially or by their direct military engagement in the armed conflict, the conflict is automatically internationalized.

In this respect, the scale of an illegal act is not determinative of its legal characterization. It cannot by itself transform a criminal act under municipal law into an "act of war", initiating a "state of war", under international law.

Can there be a war, in the formal legal sense, between a State and a transnational criminal group or organization? Doesn't this confer on such a group the dignity of subject of international law? And with what implications? If criminals are considered subjects of international law, the law of war becomes applicable to them in its entirety, including the fundamental principle of the *jus in bello* which is that of the equality of the parties, as well as the status of prisoners of war for captured combatants and their impunity for the mere participation in hostilities and their acts of war which are not prohibited by the law of armed conflict. Moreover, wouldn't that privatize war, and take us back to the days before Grotius? Would the international legal system survive such a reconfiguration or are we to invent a completely new one?

It is submitted that it is both legally not possible to consider the September 11 events in themselves as war or acts of war; and, as a matter of policy, very damaging for the international legal system to stretch the interpretation of its rules beyond recognition in this manner, with incalculable

[1] (2002) 81 *Foreign Affairs*, no 1, 8. See also the excellent and more legally elaborate article of F Mégret, "War? Legal Semantics and the Move to Violence", (2002) 13 *European Journal of International Law* (2002), no 2, 361.

consequences for its future development. But the legal characterization of the US reaction is another matter, to which we now turn.

III. THE LEGAL BASIS OF INTERNATIONAL ACTION AND THE US REACTION

The second query is, if the September 11 events are not considered war in the technical legal sense, what is the legal basis of international action and the US reaction to these events?

The sense of outrage that was felt throughout the world was reflected in the Security Council resolution of 12 September 2001, the day following these events, and later on Resolution 1373 of 28 September, both of which characterize these events as constituting a "threat to international peace and security", opening the way to the application of collective measures under Chapter VII of the UN Charter (art 41 and 42). And a real threat it was indeed. In this respect, I totally agree with the depiction of these resolutions by Michael Reisman[2] as "the shared perception of a common danger, not simply to individual States, but to a system of world public order". But Michael Reisman falls into contradiction when he concludes from this shared perception of common danger that the proper reaction to it is a "war of self defense", meaning an individual reaction rather than a collective, i.e. social, measure; self-defense, including collective self-defense, being an individual rather than a social use of force, which defends an individual victim rather than society as a whole.

Of course, a State is at liberty — and is even bound if it is to discharge properly its functions — to take all measures, within its territory, to defend and ensure its security and the security of its citizens against criminal pursuits. Call this self-defense if you will, but it is not self-defense in the meaning of international law. It is part and parcel of the State function of maintaining law and order within the realm.

But how and where else, beyond State boundaries can this "self-defense war" or "borderless war" be waged against transnational terrorism? Apart from the high seas (and attendant airspace), this can only be on the territory of other States. If the other State or States concerned are willing, this would be merely a species of administrative and judicial cooperation in preventing and prosecuting transnational crime. If, however, the other State or States do not cooperate, there is no way of extending the fight against transnational terrorism to their territories in the name of self-defense, unless they — *ie* the territorial State or States — can be held legally responsible for the acts of terrorists according to the rules of

[2] "In Defense of World Public Order", (2001) 95 *American Journal of International Law*, no 4, 833 at 834.

attribution of responsibility in international law. In this latter case, the acts of terrorism would constitute an "aggression" in the sense of international law, committed (whether as principal or complicit) by that territorial State. Only then would it be permissible to use force in the exercise of self-defense against that State, and only within the limits of that concept in international law. Otherwise, such forcible action would itself constitute an aggression against the territorial State on whose territory it takes place.

This is because self-defense in international law is an exception from the comprehensive prohibition of individual resort to force, controlled and limited to the specific circumstances which justify it; while social defense, in the sense of criminal law, is a standing option and indeed a permanent function of organized society. This is why the threshold of coercive intervention in the name of social defense by the collectivity is much lower than that in case of self-defense by the victim of aggression and its allies, which is an exception from a general peremptory rule, enshrined both in the UN Charter and general international law.

The reference to the right of individual or collective self-defence in the preamble of the Security Council resolutions does not imply an espousal or ratification by the Council of the US characterization of these events as an "armed attack" in the meaning of Article 51; and how could it have been on 12 September, the date of the first resolution, before it was known who had perpetrated those acts and with what help or on whose instigation? This reference was merely a without prejudice clause, in case the conditions of exercising self-defense were subsequently revealed to be fulfilled. On 12 September this was not yet the case; nor was it on the 28th, in spite of growing suspicions. So the right of self-defense was preserved for such an eventuality. That's all.

The increasingly revealed evidence of Al-Qaeda's role and of the Taliban regime's involvement, in fact its instrumentalization by Al-Qaeda (thus permitting the attribution of the attack to a State, assuming that the proof of attribution of the acts to Al-Qaeda and of the complicity of the Taliban is sufficient), renders this debate rather moot (*ie* whether we are dealing with an armed attack in the meaning of Article 51 of the Charter or with a common threat to international peace and security). But it is not totally moot when it comes to examining the limits of permissible action: against whom (*ratione personae*)? Where and how far (*ratione loci*)? And for how long (*ratione temporis*)?

Self-defence is contextual, exercised against a specific "armed attack" emanating from a State or a subject of international law, and it ends with the repelling of that attack and the prevention of its continuation, if it has a continuous character. Self-defence cannot go beyond that.

There is a great difference between repelling an attack against the US from Afghanistan and preventing its continuation or its threatened imminent repetition, on the one hand, and fighting terrorism or terrorist groups in general, on the other. The use of force in pursuing the latter task cannot be justified as self-defence under any interpretation of that concept, however stretched it may be. And after all, is force, whether individual or social, the first best way of combating terrorism? I do not think so.

Of course, once the harm is done and the crime perpetrated, repression — in the criminal law sense of pursuit, prosecution and punishment, as well as prevention — has to follow suit, by resort to legal force if need be. The immediate reaction to the September 11 events can be seen within this context. Indeed, Security Council resolution 1373 of 28 September 2001 comes nearest to a declaration of an "international state of emergency" to face up to these events, establishing a temporary regime under Chapter VII to take measures against terrorism in this particular emergency. But it should not be seen as doing more than that, notwithstanding contrary contentions. Particularly, this temporary regime is not sustainable for the duration, for at least two reasons, one of a general nature relating to the limits of Security Council powers, the other particular to "terrorism":

1) The Security Council cannot act under Chapter VII in the abstract. In other words, it cannot impose obligations on States and create subsidiary organs to monitor and assist in their fulfillment except as measures for the maintenance or the reestablishment of international peace and security in a specific situation which it would have characterized beforehand as "a threat to peace, a breach of peace or an act of aggression". This characterization is indispensable for opening the way to the application of mandatory collective measures. Such measures have thus always to be pegged to a particular crisis or situation.

   Notwithstanding the seemingly general language of the resolutions, we have to recall that the crisis situation initiated by the events of September 11, and characterized by the Security Council as constituting "a threat to international peace and security", was not limited merely to their aspect of being attacks against the United States, but stemmed more from the reach and capacity for harm of international terrorism that was revealed by these events, and which poses an acute generalised threat to world public order at large. The measures taken by the Security Council were intended to respond to this larger aspect of the crisis, with a view to containing and eventually eliminating this overall threat, which probably accounts for the generalised language of the resolutions.
2) More particularly, all international efforts for decades, starting with the League of Nations and continuing in the United Nations,

to draw a comprehensive convention criminalizing terrorism in general (and not merely specific acts of terrorism) have hitherto failed, absent a generally accepted and shared legal definition of what is terrorism, a terrorist act or a terrorist group. This is not because of any logical or technical impossibility to formulate such a definition, but because of the lack of universal *opinio juris*, particularly about the ambit of the proposed crime *ratione personae*. Roughly speaking, the major powers insist on limiting the crime to private actors, excluding from it State actors; small powers on the contrary insist on including State actors, while some of them would like to exclude "freedom fighters".

Without a universally shared definition of the crime, how can there be a coherent and permanent regime for its prevention and suppression? Resolution 1373 itself reveals the same flaw. For while it provides for numerous measures against terrorists and terrorist organizations and for the prevention of terrorist acts and plots, nowhere does it indicate who or what those individuals, groups or acts are, or how they can be identified.

IV. THE PROPER ROLE OF INTERNATIONAL LAW IN COMBATING TERRORISM

What is then the proper role of international law in combating terrorism? I submit that first of all, we should discard the approach of the law of war, which is totally wrong in this context, relying as it does on large scale unilateral use of force, which goes against the fundamental principles and ethos of contemporary international law.[3]

The first task for international law is to bring to a successful conclusion the long term efforts of producing a comprehensive convention against terrorism. It is true that up to now these decades of efforts have remained fruitless. But the shock of recognition produced by the September 11 events

[3] My criticism of a "law of war" approach to combating terrorism should not be taken as implying that the *jus in bello* (or international humanitarian law) should not apply if an "armed conflict" breaks out as a result of acts of terrorism. For what counts in this case is the materialisation of the objective conditions of the existence of an armed conflict, whether of an international or an non-international character, and not the reasons or the circumstances that led to it. In such a case, international humanitarian law applies fully, particularly the principle of the equality of the parties, and full protection has to be afforded to all the victims of the armed conflict whether civilians or combatants (including their entitlement to prisoners of war status in case of capture). From either side, as prescribed by the norms of that law. But as the applicability of international humanitarian law and the international law of human rights in these conflicts is amply treated by other contributors to this book, I need not pursue the issue any further.

has created a new situation and provided the psychological mobilisation for overcoming the obstacles to reaching a generally acceptable definition. Preferably, such a definition should be exclusively pegged to the acts and their consequences, together with the accompanying intent, regardless of the status or the quality of the actor, as is the case of crimes against humanity and genocide.

The convention would then establish tighter networks of international cooperation for preventing, suppressing and prosecuting the newly defined crime of terrorism, not only in terms of obligations of best efforts (*obligations de moyen*), but also of obligations to achieve certain results (*obligations de résultat*), once we know what we are speaking about. This entails as well the creation of the institutional arrangements indispensable for the effective management and implementation of what would necessarily be a very dense and involved network of collaborative legal relations, and vesting them with the necessary powers to do so. The International Criminal Court is the prime example of such an institution. Its jurisdiction could be extended to cover the crime of terrorism once it is clearly defined. Countries that want to strengthen the role of international law in fighting terrorism should support the Court, rather than working to undermine it, as the United States is now doing.

Such measures would contribute to perfecting the budding system of individual international criminal responsibility and would tighten the obligations of States in the field of judicial cooperation and assistance. And that would in turn help push international law further from the concepts and methods of "the international law of coexistence" (as the traditional international law was called by Wolfgang Friedmann) which purports to maintain the coexistence between antagonistic units, assumed to have contradictory interests, playing a zero sum game through unilateral actions and reactions by the individual States (self-help) — towards the more collaborative vision and model of "the international law of cooperation", based on the ideas of common interests and values and of a common enterprise or action in defending and promoting them.

Finally, it is necessary to recall that even if all these measures are taken, they will not suffice, by themselves, to form an effective strategy for combating terrorism. It is banal to say that we live in a globalized world, and that globalization creates new threats that cannot be contained and controlled within one State. They call for responses at their own level, meaning that of the international community at large. These threats and entropies are, however, the pathological aspects of globalization. International cooperation in devising repressive strategies within the framework of criminal law deals mainly with the symptoms. But we have to go to the root causes of these symptoms, in other words we have also to increase cooperation in addressing the root causes of terror. What are these? Deep feelings of injustice and oppression, of loss of hope and prospects, resulting from misery, exploitation, denials of human rights, and great inequalities between and within peoples.

To illustrate by a similar example, there has been no international agreement at all for the last thirty years on a minimum price of cocoa, which led to the ruin of many cocoa growing latin-american farmers. Some of them ended up cultivating coke. Fighting drugs is all very well, but at the same time, something has to be done to make it possible for farmers to earn a living on what they would otherwise produce, like cocoa.

In other words, a coherent legal strategy for combating terrorism requires a complementary and mutually re-enforcing set of measures — from tightening international cooperation in the prevention, criminal prosecution and repression of terrorist activities, to long term cooperative schemes to remedy or at least attenuate their root causes — if it is to lead to a better containment and eventual eradication of terrorism.

This is why it is vital, in my submission, that the September 11 events and the reactions to them past and particularly future, by the US as well as by the international community, be perceived along the lines, and kept within the confines of the interpretation suggested above, which is consistent with the structure of international law and the role it can usefully play in combating terrorism. By so doing, we would strengthen that role as well as the role of law in the international community in general.

The alternative course of resort to unilateral force (whether by one State or a coalition of States), pressuring and threatening other States and even acting on their territory without their consent, in the name of combating terrorism — apart from its blatant violation of some of the most fundamental principles of international law — can only lead to disastrous results. It would nurture a widening and increasingly destructive cycle of violence on a global level, of which nobody can foresee the end or the full consequences, apart from the total erosion of the international legal order, and a gradual descent into anarchy at the hands of those who are supposedly trying to defend world order.

Part I

Terrorism and the International Legal System: The Alleged Inadequacy of International Law and the Quest for an Effective Response

1

State Sponsors of Terrorism: Issues of International Responsibility

PIERRE-MARIE DUPUY

THE ATTACKS OF 11 September 2001 led President Bush to dramatically declare "war" on terrorism. But what exactly does that mean?[1] War on individual criminals and non-State terrorist entities only? Or does it also mean war on the States sponsoring terrorist actions? Does this issue deserve a different answer in 2003 than in 2002? In other words, does the American-British decision of March 2003 to attack Saddam Hussein's regime in Iraq shed any more light on this question? This seems quite doubtful if one accepts the official justifications given by the two Allies for using force against Iraq, which primarily were based on the reputed "threat of arms of mass destruction" Iraq was supposed to present to the international community, there having been no evidence at the time of any substantial link between Saddam Hussein's regime and Al-Qaeda.

Whatever the case may be, it is clear that the President of the United States George Bush's declaration of "war on terrorism" amounted to a "shift in perspective", since the President thereby refocused "the nation's strategic posture from one that targeted terrorists as criminals to one that treats terrorists and supporting States capable of threatening the US and its allies, as threats to national security".[2]

[1] See in particular A Cassese, "Terrorism is also Disrupting Some Crucial Legal Categories of International Law", (2001) 12 *European Journal of International Law*, 993 ff; C Greenwood, "International Law and the 'War against Terrorism'", (2002) 78 *International Affairs*, 78 ff; C Tomuschat, "Der 11 September 2001 und seine rechtlichen Folgen", (2001) 21–23 *EuGRZ*, 535 ff; L Condorelli, (2001/4) 105 "Les attentats du 11 septembre et leurs suites: où va le droit international?", *RGDIP*, 829 ff; N Schrijver, "Responding to International Terrorism: Moving the Frontier of International Law for 'Enduring Freedom'", (2001) 48 *Netherlands International Law Review*, 371 ff; AM Slaughter and W Burke-White, "An International Constitutional Moment, (2002) 43 *Harvard International Law Journal*, 1 ff.

[2] A Sofaer, "On the Necessity of Pre-emption", (2003) 14 *European Journal of International Law*, at 209.

The dramatic and highly charged context in which the political debate concerning terrorism is situated and the actual reactions by States to the perceived universal threat that international terrorism presents make it nevertheless necessary to attempt to define the terms in which the issue of the responsibility of States accused of sponsoring terrorism are legally raised.

Two sets of questions seem, in this regard, to be of primary importance: (1) the issue of acts of terrorism as *wrongful acts*, primarily considered from two perspectives, being those of qualification and attribution; and (2) the question of the *victim States*: how should these States be classified if not identified and what responses to terrorism may they legally resort to?

I. WRONGFUL ACTS

As clearly affirmed by the International Law Commission's Articles on Responsibility of States for Internationally Wrongful Acts[3] in Article 2, wrongful acts consist of two elements, one being "objective" and the other "subjective". This Article follows the terminology already introduced in 1970 by Roberto Ago, the first Special Rapporteur to the Commission on this topic.[4] In order to define an act of terror as a wrongful act within the terms of State Responsibility, one must first assess a substantial definition of terrorism as an act contrary to international law and second, decide whether the act may be attributed to a subject of public international law.

A. Definition of Terrorism as a Wrongful Act

How should terrorism be defined? A significant amount of academic literature has already been devoted to this issue.[5] Most authors raise the difficulty of defining "terrorism" in a simple way, although specialists of humanitarian law, like Antonio Cassese or Luigi Condorelli rightly make

[3] See J Crawford, *The International Law Commission's Articles on State Responsibility, Introduction, Text and Commentaries* (Cambridge University Press, Cambridge, 2002), at 81 ff.
[4] Second Report, *Yearbook of the International Law Commission* 1970, Vol II at 176 ff.
[5] See in particular JM Sorel, "Existe-t'il une definition universelle du terrorisme?" in CEDIN University of Paris I, *Le droit international face au terrorisme* (Paris, Pedone, 2002) at 35–68.; C Stahn, *International Law at a Crossroads? The Impact of September 11*, ZaöRV (Heidelberger Journal of International Law, 2002, 62/1–2, 182 ff, at 186. See also UN GA Res "Measures to Eliminate International Terrorism" of 30 January 2001, UN Doc 1/Res/55/158; J Murphy, "Defining International Terrorism: A Way Out of the Quagmire", (1989) 19 *Israel Yearbook of Human Rights* 13 ff.

the point that the prohibition of clearly identified acts of terrorism may be found in the "law of Geneva".[6] Judge Rosalyn Higgins nevertheless asks:

> Does the theme of "terrorism" really constitute a distinct topic of international law? ... Is there an international law of terrorism; or merely international law about terrorism? Is our study about terrorism the study of a substantial topic or rather the study of the application of international law to a contemporary problem?[7]

What seems at least evident is the absence of any universally accepted definition of terrorism; but this does not necessarily raise a major issue for identifying the rules of international law applicable for combating terrorism, this including the pertinent secondary rules of State Responsibility.

United Nations Security Council Resolutions 1368 and 1373 both contain references to "terrorism" without providing any definition of the term. This absence of a legal definition, however, does not prevent the identification of the attacks of 11 September 2001 as terrorism, as they clearly were aimed at causing terror among a civilian population for political or ideological reasons. Terror exercised on a civilian population as a political weapon is evidently at the core of any definition of terrorism, the international element being provided by the physical origin of the action and/or the nationality of wrongdoers.

These features are shared by any type of specific acts of terror as covered by a series of international conventions, such as the 1963 Tokyo Convention on Offences and Certain Other Acts Committed on Board Aircraft, the 1970 Hague Convention for the Suppression of Unlawful Seizure of Aircraft, the 1971 Montreal Convention for the Suppression of Unlawful Acts Against the Safety of Civil Aviation, the 1979 New York Convention Against the Taking of Hostage or the 1988 Convention for the Suppression of Unlawful Acts Against the Safety of Maritime Navigation.

National legislation in regard to acts of terror also helps one to identify the fundamental elements of terrorism. For example, the 1984 United Kingdom legislation on terrorism states that it consists of "the use of violence for political ends and includes any use of violence for the purpose of putting the public or any section of the public in fear".[8] In the United States of America, a 1987 law sets out the following definition: "the term 'terrorist activity' means the organizing, abetting or participating in a

[6] See in this book A Cassese, "Terrorism as an International Crime" and L Condorelli and Y Naqvi, "Wars against Terrorism and *Jus in Bello*: Are the Geneva Conventions out of date?".
[7] R Higgins, "The General International Law of Terrorism" in R Higgins and M Flory (eds) *Terrorism and International Law* (Sweet and Maxwell/Routledge, London and New York, 1997) at 13.
[8] Cited by G Guillaume, "Terrorisme et droit international", *Recueil des cours* (Academy of International Law, The Hague, 1989) 215, 291–416 at 304–5.

wanton or indiscriminate act of violence with extreme indifference to the risk of causing death or serious bodily harm to individuals not taking part in armed hostilities".[9]

In his lecture at The Hague Academy of International Law, the President of the International Court of Justice Guillaume proposed the following definition:

> *le terrorisme implique l'usage de la violence dans des conditions de nature à porter atteinte à la vie des personnes ou à leur intégrité physique dans le cadre d"une entreprise ayant pour but de provoquer la terreur en vue de parvenir à certaines fins.*[10]

This definition provides a concise understanding of what constitutes terrorism, in particular if one adds the precision that the civilian population is the primary target of such acts. The Common Position of the European Union's Council adopted on 27 December 2001 does take account of this latter element, and then lists possible acts of terror ranging from murder, hostage-taking, massive destruction of various types of infrastructure, hijacking of planes or ships, production, possession, transport or supply or explosives, and various other weapons, setting fires, and so on.[11]

The fact of being able to identify such a generic definition of terrorism, together with the existence of treaties prohibiting specific terrorist acts, makes it evident that the "objective" element of terrorism as a legally wrongful act, contrary to the writings of many commentators, does not really raise a difficulty.

This leaves the question of the "subjective" element of a wrongful act, ie can one attribute an act meeting the criteria indicated above to a subject of international law?

B. Attribution

Acts of terror are for the most part committed by non-State actors, either persons acting individually or, more frequently, non-State armed groups acting through a transnational network of agents. The difficulty, at least for keeping within the classical framework of public international law, lies with the fact that these groups do not at first glance appear to be subjects of international law, thereby not fulfilling the "subjective" element. If a wrongful act cannot be attributed to a subject of international law, there

[9] *Ibid*.
[10] *Ibid* at 306.
[11] Common Position of the Council, 2001/931/PESC, OJEC 28.12.2001, L 344/93. See also EC Règlement n°2580/2001 of 27.12.2001, OJEC 28.12.2002, L 344/70.

is no wrongful act of public international law and no responsibility for blatant acts of terrorism.[12]

Were the reasoning to be confined within the narrow boundaries of traditional notions of State responsibility, the result would be hardly satisfactory. This is why one needs to analyze the actual evolution of international practice in order to come to a more reasonable solution. As noted elsewhere,[13] there are basically two ways to ensure respect of certain rules of international law by non-State actors, particularly in those areas such as international human rights, humanitarian law and terrorism, where compliance with international law standards by these actors is most needed. The first technique consists of expanding the range of subjects of international law, thus including non-State entities, the second one of broadening the criteria of attribution for the purpose of triggering State responsibility.

As regards the possibility of broadening the notion of subjects, one may notice that terrorism has for a number of years been described as amounting to a "threat to international peace and security" in the sense of Article 39 of the Charter of the United Nations. This was expressly stated in September 2001 in UN Security Council Resolutions 1968 and 1973; but it had been previously asserted in earlier UN Security Council resolutions, such as in Resolution 1267 (1999) and 1333 of 2000, both dealing with the situation in Afghanistan.[14]

One may view this series of resolutions in conjunction with those dealing with other situations, such as those existing at one stage in Angola or in Sierra Leone, in which the Security Council referred to the international duties not only of States but also of non-State armed factions, thereby delineating them as subjects of international law. From this perspective, it could be argued that, for the sake of maintaining international peace and security, Security Council practice may provisionally establish an entity as a subject of international law, indicating that this entity is endowed with specific obligations deriving from the substantial body of classical international (inter-State) law. As this author explains elsewhere, the theory concerning the subjects of international law should be reviewed in the light of the ICJ's Advisory Opinion on *Certain Reparations* (1949) essentially from *functional* and *teleological* perspectives.[15] This viewpoint supports the argument that, even when not committed by States, acts of terrorism, such

[12] See J Wolf, *Die Staatenhaftung für Privatpersonen nach Völkerrecht* (1997), at 387ff.

[13] PM Dupuy, "Quarante ans de codification du droit de la responsabilité internationale des Etats. Un bilan", (2003) *Révue Générale de Droit International Publique*, 2003, 318.

[14] International terrorism as practiced on 11 September has also been assimilated to an "armed attack" by common reference of NATO Member States to Art 5 of the North Atlantic Treaty.

[15] See P Dupuy, "Cours general de droit international public", *Receuil des cours* (Hague Academy of International Law, The Hague, 2003) vol 297, 106–18.

as those perpetrated on 11 September 2001, fall under the scope of Chapter VII of the Charter of the UN.

In terms of the attribution of acts or terror, they are at least two conclusions to be drawn from the above-mentioned remarks. Firstly, the very fact that terrorism is usually committed by transnational non-State actors should not raise any major technical difficulty in legal terms. The Security Council acting as the main international UN body responsible for collective security might attribute this wrongful act to any specifically identified terrorist group. This group might then be held internationally responsible for the act of terror it committed, with all the legal consequences attached to this attribution.

With respect to State responsibility, it can be triggered at the occasion of the commission of acts spreading terror throughout a civilian population for political purposes, either on the basis of commonly accepted principles of attribution (because the act was committed by State agents) or because the State may be harbouring terrorist groups. Here, it becomes necessary to define more precisely what may be meant by States *sponsoring* international terrorism in legal terms. The expression may cover a diverse range of State involvement in terrorism, from ex-post facto approval or endorsement of terrorist acts to direct participation of State organs in the perpetration thereof.

In 1980, in the case of *United States Diplomatic and Consular Staff in Tehran (Hostage Case)*, the ICJ made the distinction between acts committed by entities "having been charged by some competent organ of the Iranian State to carry out a specific operation" from the private initiative taken by Islamic students.[16] After the official support was given to the students by the Iranian Government, the Court states that they then became "agents of the Iranian State".[17]

In 1986, in the *Military and Paramilitary Activities in and against Nicaragua* case, the Court had to define the way in which a State could be held responsible for sponsoring the terrorist activities of a non-State armed group, namely the *contras*. As it is well known, the Court espoused a strict conception of control, that is, it had to be shown that the United States had "effective control" over the actions of the *contras*. The attribution of some of the activities carried out by the *contras* on the territory of Nicaragua to the United States depended on whether or not the relationship between the individuals participating in the *contra* groups and the State was "one of dependence on the one side and control on the other". In this case, the Court found that it had not been proved that "the US had actually exercised such a degree of control in all fields as to justify treating the contras as acting on its behalf".[18]

[16] ICJ Reports 1980, at para 58.
[17] *Ibid* at para 74.
[18] ICJ Reports 1986, at para 115.

On the contrary, in the 1999 *Tadic* case, the Appellate Chamber of the International Criminal Tribunal of the former Yugoslavia (ICTY) having as its aim the need to qualify the conflict in this territory as either international or internal, adopted a less stringent test of attribution, that of "overall control" which made it possible for the Court to attribute some of the crimes perpetrated by the Bosnian-Serbs to the Federal Republic of Yugoslavia (and thus qualify the conflict as international).

If one turns now to more recent State practice, in particular, the events which took place immediately after 11 September 2001, two elements are striking: first, the initial universal and quasi-spontaneous assertion that terrorism amounts to a threat to international peace and security; and second, the prompt assimilation of Afghanistan with Al-Qaeda, the former having been judged by the international community as being responsible for harbouring the relevant terrorist group and helping in the preparation of some of the terrorist acts committed by Al-Qaeda.[19] The Security Council apparently endorsed the view of John Negroponte, the US Permanent Representative to the UN, when stating that:

> The attacks on 11 September 2001 and the ongoing threat to the United Sates and its nationals posed by the Al-Qaeda organization have been made possible by the decision of the Taliban regime to allow the parts of Afghanistan that it controls to be used by this organization as a base of operation.[20]

To identify the rules attributing responsibility to a State in this context, acts of terrorism *directly* perpetrated by a State's organs should be distinguished from those acts which were carried out by private persons, but with the support and/or control of a State.[21] A further possibility for attributing responsibility to a State could, under certain rather restrictive conditions, be argued on the fact that the territorial State did not display a sufficient degree of diligence for preventing terrorist acts from being actively prepared or performed on or from its territory.

In the first case, if there is strong evidence of a State organ directly perpetrating the terrorist act, this conduct is attributable to the State wherever such act had taken place; this is so even if the act was committed by the organ *ultra vires*. Such acts may, for example, be carried out by members of the armed forces, provided that the organ was acting in this capacity.

[19] As raised by Michael Byers in his article "Terrorism, The Use of Force and International Law after 11 September" (2002) 51 *International and Comparative Law Quarterly*, 401–14 at 403: "this raises the question whether Afghanistan could have been considered a 'failed State'". See D Thürer, "The 'Failed State' and International Law" (1999) 81 *International Review of the Red Cross*, at 731.

[20] UN Doc S/2001/946. See also C Wren, "US Advises UN Council More Strikes Could Come", *New York Times*, 9 October 2001, 5.

[21] See P-M Dupuy, "Quarante ans de codification du droit de la responsabilité internationale des Etats, un bilan", (2003) 2 *Revue Générale de Droit International Public*, 305–48.

In times of war, as pointed out by Luigi Condorelli, Article 91 of the First Additional Protocol to the Geneva Conventions codifies the rule according to which a State Party "shall be responsible for all acts committed by persons forming part of its armed forces".[22] This attribution of responsibility for acts of the members of armed forces to the State goes beyond the acts performed in the exercise of their functions and includes acts *ultra vires*; it also covers "non official acts" such as acts committed by individual soldiers in a private capacity.[23]

International law undoubtedly prohibits States to send "armed bands, groups, irregulars or mercenaries which carry out acts of armed force against another State". According to UN General Assembly Resolution 3314 of 1974, such conduct would amount to an act of aggression if of substantial gravity; a rule which was already embodied in UN General Assembly Resolution 2625, the oft-cited "Friendly Relations" Declaration adopted by the General Assembly in 1970.

As for the possibility to attribute acts committed by private persons to a State, in its Articles on Responsibility of States for Internationally Wrongful Acts of 2001, the International Law Commission seems to have adopted a definition of attribution which is in between the two approaches referred to above. Article 8 sets out the following rule of attribution:

> The conduct of a person or group of persons shall be considered an act of a State under international law if the person or group of persons is in fact acting on the instructions or under the direction or control of that State in carrying out the conduct.

This formulation leaves much room for interpretation. In particular, it is not quite clear whether "acting on the instructions" of a State is considered by the ILC as being exactly on the same level as being "under the direction or control" of the State. This ambiguity was most probably left purposely in order to maintain some flexibility for different possible interpretations.

One should also consider Article 11 of the ILC's Articles. This provision states that:

> Conduct which is not attributable to a State under the preceding articles shall nevertheless be considered an act of that State under international law if and to the extent that the State acknowledges and adopts the conduct in question as its own.

[22] See L Condorelli, "Imputation à l'Etat d'un fait internationalement illicite" *Recueil des cours* (Hague Academy of International Law, The Hague, 1984/VI) at 146.
[23] L Condorelli, "The Imputation to States of Acts of International Terrorism", (1989) 19 *Israel Yearbook on Human Rights* at 233 ff.

In its commentary to that provision, the ILC refers to the 1980 *Hostages Case*. It distinguishes between the "approval" given by a State to the conduct of a non-State actor from the case when a State provides support to terrorist attacks. It may be argued that the position taken by the Taliban government in Afghanistan in relation to the acts of Al-Qaeda was similar to that foreseen in Article 11 of the ILC Articles.

Under treaty law, State Parties have particular obligations to prevent the financing and perpetration of some specific acts of terrorism, for example, hijacking under the Hague Convention of 1971.[24] They also have the duty of prosecuting or extraditing individual perpetrators of such acts.[25] Notwithstanding the several differences of the legal regimes of the various conventions, in general international law, States are under an obligation to prevent and combat acts of terrorism. As pointed out by Luigi Condorelli, "in the case of terrorist activities taking place on one State's territory, this situation plays the role of a catalyst, an expression used by Ago in his reports."[26] To paraphrase the ICJ in the 1980 *Hostages Case*, the acts of individuals are a catalyst for the State's international responsibility when the State authorities: (a) were "aware of the need for action on their part"; (b) had "the means of their disposal to perform their obligations"; and (c) "failed to use the means which were at their disposal".[27]

II. WHAT RIGHTS DO VICTIM STATES HAVE?

The legal regime of the responsibility of States sponsoring terrorism, whatever the specificity of the primary obligations it sanctions, is not a self-contained one. This means in other terms that the general customary law of the international responsibility of States for committing any wrongful act may be applied to a "terrorist State". As far as the secondary obligations of State Responsibility are concerned, a State guilty of committing a wrongful act is obliged, according to Article 30(a) of the ILC Articles, to cease the said act if it is continuing. An appropriate example would be the harbouring and supporting of terrorist groups on its territory. The obligation may also comprise giving appropriate assurances and guarantees of non-repetition (Article 30(b)) and providing reparation proportionate with the damage caused, including, if need be, restitution or compensation.[28]

[24] See JM Sorel, "Some Questions About the Definition of Terrorism and the Fight Against Its Financing", (2003) 14 *European Journal of International Law*, no 2, 365–378.
[25] See D Vagts, "Which Courts Should Try Persons Accused of Terrorism?" 2003 14 *European Journal of International Law*, no 2, 313–326.
[26] L Condorelli, "The Imputability to States of Acts of International Terrorism", (1989) 19 *Israeli Yearbook on Human Rights*, 233–246.
[27] 1980 *Hostages Case*, above n 13, para 68.
[28] See ILC Articles 35 and 36.

A more complex problem is that concerning the rights of the victim State(s). This question directly puts in issue the legal effects of acts of terrorism and the scope of their impact. Do terrorist acts only affect the individual State where the act took place, the State whose nationals have been killed or injured or whose national interests have otherwise been directly threatened? Or, if the terrorist act is of such a scale or gravity as to amount to a crime against humanity under international law, does such an act of terror exercised against a specific target create at the same time an objective legal interest in any State, as part of the international community, to invoke the responsibility of the wrong-doing State? If one accepts the latter contention, as it seems a large majority of nations does, expressed, among others, in UN Security Council Resolutions 1368 and 1373, then the concept of "victim" State can arguably be enlarged to all States. Grand scale terrorist attacks attributable to a State may constitute a "serious breach of obligations under peremptory norms of general international law"[29] and therefore allow all States to resort to legal responses.

Notwithstanding this argument, a clear distinction should be maintained between two categories of victim States: on the one hand, the "injured States" (Article 42 ILC Articles) and on the other, "any State other than an injured State" (Article 48 ILC Articles).

A. Rights of the "Injured State"

1. *Self Defence*

The precedents set by State practice following the attacks of 11 September 2001 are of special interest in this context. In particular, UN Security Council Resolutions 1368 and 1373 have been almost unanimously interpreted, at least during the months following the destruction of the Twin Towers, as amounting to an indirect authorisation for the exercise of self-defence by the United States. Such an interpretation raises a series of legal questions dealing, in particular, with the definition of "armed attack" for the purpose of invoking the right to self defence and the proper role of the Security Council. This issue is related to the question of the content of the right to self-defence under customary international law as compared to the rule laid down in Article 51 of the UN Charter. According to the latter rule, the Security Council is supposed to retain full control over the response to the "armed attack".[30]

[29] The specific definition of this phrase still needs to be agreed upon by States.
[30] See in particular O Corten and F Dubuisson, "Opération 'Liberté Immuable': une extension abusive du concept de légitime défense ?", (2002) 1 *Revue General de Droit International Public*, 51 ff; N Krisch, *Selbstverteidigung und kollektive Sicherheit* (Berlin, Springer, 2001);

The classical conditions for invoking self-defence are well known and do not need here more than a very brief review[31]: the necessity for resorting to armed force must be "instant, overwhelming, leaving no choice of means and no moment for deliberation" according to the famous Webster Doctrine in the *Caroline Case*.[32] The use of force is to be exclusively directed to repel the armed attack and be proportionate to this purpose; moreover, it must be terminated as soon as possible and stay within the limits imposed by fundamental principles of humanitarian law; and armed reprisals are forbidden.

The dangers of any loose interpretation of these rules, even if perceived as justified in the name of the "war" on terrorism, are extremely serious. The idea that self defence might be invoked against any activity unilaterally qualified as "terrorist" would undoubtedly lead to the weakening of the whole collective security system established by the UN Charter. This would particularly be the case if States began to automatically accept that an act of terrorism could legitimise unilateral self-defensive action by the injured State, outside the UN framework. But this does not at present seem to be the case.

The same conclusion may also be drawn from international practice with regard to "preventive" self-defence. American President Georges W. Bush, appearing to acknowledge the classically restrictive rules of international law in regards to the use of force, stated in his presentation of the US National Security Strategy that:

> Legal scholars and international jurists often conditioned the legitimacy of pre-emption on the existence of an imminent threat — most often a visible mobilization of armies, navies and air forces preparing an attack.[33]

But then went on to say:

> We must adapt the concept of imminent thereat to the capabilities and objectives of today's adversaries ... The greater the threat, the greater the risk

D Greig, "Self-Defence and the Security Council: What Does Article 51 Require?" (2002) 40 *International and Comparative Law Quarterly* at 366; T Franck, "Terrorism and the Right of Self-Defense", (2001) 95 *American Journal of International Law*, 839ff; C Stahn, "International Law at a Crossroad? The Impact of September 11", (2002) 62 *ZaöRV*, 1–2, at 214 ff. Compare M Travalio, "Terrorism, International Law and the Use of Force", (2000) 18 *Wisconsin International Law Journal*, 145ff; MF Brennan, "Avoiding Anarchy: Bin Laden Terrorism, the US Response and the Role of Customary International Law", (1999) 59 *Louisiana Law Review*, 1195.

[31] See for instance C Gray, *International Law and the Use of Force*, (Oxford University Press, Oxford, 2000), at 111–15.
[32] See the letter addressed by Mr Webster to Mr Fox on 24 April 1841 (29 Brit & For St Papers 1137–38).
[33] National Security Council, *National Security Strategy of the United States of America*, at 15 available at <http://www.whitehouse.gov/nsc/nss.html>.

> of inaction — and the more compelling the case for taking anticipatory action to defend ourselves, even if uncertainty remains as to the time and place of the enemy's attack.

The negative reaction by the majority of States in response to the United Kingdom's and the United States" recourse to force against Saddam Hussein's regime may be interpreted as a continuance of earlier refusals by the international community to approve the use of preventive armed attacks in breach of the law of collective peace and security, for example those perpetrated by Israel against the Palestinian authority or resistance groups.[34] As rightly observed by Professor Bothe, "*De lege lata,*... the expansion of the right of anticipatory self-defence proposed in the National Security Strategy is not acceptable".[35] Evidently, it does not meet with the restrictive conditions set forth in the *Caroline* case outlined above. Neither is it consistent with the UN regime of collective security. The present international legal order obliges States to restrict the use of force within the limits defined in the UN Charter, which may be regarded as the "constitution of the international legal system". [36]

2. *Countermeasures*

Injured States cannot respond to terrorism by resorting themselves to terrorism. For example, States cannot engage in the systematic destruction of civilian houses in order to exercise massive pressure on the population to which the perpetrators of terrorist attacks belong. Illegal measures of response of this type are clearly prohibited by Article 50 of the ILC Articles which may be said to codify a rule of customary law preventing States from adopting certain types of countermeasures, in particular as regards "obligations for the protection of fundamental human rights" and "obligations of a humanitarian character prohibiting reprisals" (Article 50(c)).[37]

[34] See for instance UN Security Council Resolution 487 (1981) adopted unanimously. See also Byers, above n 16, at 410; M Bothe, "Terrorism and the Legality of Pre-emptive Force", (2003) 14 *European Journal of International Law*, no 2, at 232.
[35] Bothe, *ibid*.
[36] See in particular B Fassbender, "The United Nations Charter as Constitution of the International Community", (1998) 36 *Columbia Journal of Transnational Law*, no 3, 531–619; AL Paulus, *Die internationale Gemeinschaft im Völkerrecht* (Beck, Munich, 2001), in particular at 285–329.
[37] Countermeasures are dealt with in Chapter 11 of Part III of the ILC Articles. The "injured State" may resort to countermeasures only "in order to induce the responsible State to comply with its obligations" (Art 49). The customary condition of "proportionality" is articulated in Art 51 ("Countermeasures must be commensurate with the injury suffered, taking into account the gravity of the internationally wrongful act and the right in question"). Although there is no doubt that suicide attacks against a civilian population are illegal and may even amount to crimes against humanity, under international law, this provides no

B. Rights of "Any State Other than an Injured State"

Under Article 48(1)(b) and (2) of the ILC's Articles on State Responsibility, the responsibility of a State for breach of obligations *erga omnes* may be invoked by "any State", which may claim from the responsible State: (a) cessation of the internationally wrongful act and assurances or guarantees of non-repetition and (b) performance of the obligation of reparation in the interest of the injured State or of the beneficiaries of the obligation breached.

It is widely accepted that there is at least a presumption that most acts of terrorism, if not all of them, amount to breaches of peremptory norms, as they violate basic principles of human rights and/or humanitarian law.[38] Regrettably, however, Article 54 in its final version only allows non-injured States to take "lawful measures" against the wrongdoing State in the interest of the injured State or of the beneficiaries of the obligation which has been breached. At this point one may wonder whether the ILC simply confined itself to stating the obvious, ie that States may take measures, which are lawful by their very nature, or, rather, it actually meant that States may take countermeasures to protect the general interests of the international community, which by their being adopted in reaction to a prior wrongful act have to be regarded as lawful. As rightly noted,[39] nowhere in the text nor in the commentary is the latter possibility directly or indirectly envisaged.

The anomaly lies in entrusting the task of protecting the public order of the international community to such instruments as countermeasures, which in many ways can be considered as the legacy of the international law of coexistence. Countermeasures are by their very nature decentralised, whereas violations of the international public order and reactions thereto need, respectively, to be evaluated and managed by a centralised authority,

legal basis for the injured State to exercise similar types of countermeasures. Compare F Kirgis, "Israel's Intensified Military Campaign Against Terrorism", *ASIL Insight*, December 2001; A Sofaer, "On the Necessity of Pre-emption", (2003) 14 *European Journal of International Law*, no 2, 209–27; G Neuman, "Humanitarian Law and Counter-terrorist Force", (2003) 14 *European Journal of International Law*, no 2, 265–83; J Klabbers, "Rebel with a Cause? Terrorists and Humanitarian Law", (2003) 14 *European Journal of International Law*, no 2, 299–313.

[38] See in particular, Art 33 Geneva Convention IV and Art 4 Statute of the International Criminal Tribunal for Rwanda. See also the Rome Statute of the International Criminal Court which has jurisdiction over the crime against humanity under Art 7(1)(a): "when committed as part of a widespread or systematic attack directed against any civilian population with knowledge of the attack." Acts amounting to crimes against humanity include murder and "other inhumane acts of a similar character intentionally causing great suffering or serious injury to body or to mental or physical health".

[39] D Alland, "Les contremesures d'intérêt général", in PM Dupuy (ed), *Obligations multilateral, droit imperatif et responsabilité internationale* (Pedone, Paris, 2003), 167.

legitimately representing the community. This is why international reactions to terrorism remain bound by the framework of the United Nations, as the sole structure securing collective interest of States "other than the injured one". It is evident that the widespread use of terror poses new challenges to the world community. Clearly, in tackling the international problem of terrorism, the UN is confronted with a number of challenges of a political nature. However, the institutionalised cooperation of States for combating the common threat of terror must rest with (or return to) the United Nations, in accordance with the substantial and procedural rules set out in its Charter. This has been recently demonstrated by the evolution of the situation in Iraq after the non-UN authorised use of force against a political regime which, no doubt, had committed massive breaches of fundamental rules of international law. However, leaving the choice of how to react unilaterally to States, independently of the general will of the members of the organised community risks undermining the foundations of the international public order which the reaction intends to protect.

2

The Legality of Covert Operations Against Terrorism in Foreign States

NATALINO RONZITTI

I. INTRODUCTION

COVERT OPERATIONS CAN involve many kinds of intervention in a foreign country, ranging from non-violent activities to military coercion. The list is long. A non-exhaustive list encompasses propaganda, political action, intelligence gathering, paramilitary action and fomenting a *coup d'Etat* aimed at overthrowing the regime in power.[1] In this contribution, only those activities which imply the use of force are taken into consideration.

The environment in which covert activities take place can also vary. They may be carried out in peacetime, in time of crisis, as a part of low intensity operations, during a non-international armed conflict or in wartime, i.e during an inter-State conflict.

The target of covert activities can be a State or its government (for instance, in the situation of a *coup d'Etat*) or an objective within a State, such as property or individuals. Covert activities are adopted for several reasons. They could, for example, be part of a counter-terrorism policy. Practice shows that covert activities have been employed both when States resort to military force to combat international terrorism and as an instrument of a law enforcement policy.

The aim of this contribution is to provide a survey of relevant State practice with a view to identifying certain basic principles which might be of guidance in evaluating the legality of these operations.

[1] See generally WM Reisman & JE Baker, *Regulating Covert Action: Practices, Contexts, and Policies of Covert Coercion Abroad in International and American Law* (Yale University Press, New Haven, 1992); ME Bowman, "Secrets in Plain View: Covert Action the US Way", *The Law of Military Operations, Liber Amicorum Professor Jack Grunawalt, 72 International Law Studies* 1998 (Naval War College, Newport, Rhode Island), 1 ff.

II. COVERT OPERATIONS AND SELF-DEFENCE

The strike against the Twin Towers on 11 September 2001 was qualified by the United States as an armed attack, giving the aggrieved State the right to respond in self-defence. This view was supported by several countries and international organizations, in particular NATO which considered the strike an armed attack on a member State, realizing the *casus foederis* and triggering the mechanism under Article 5 of the North Atlantic Treaty.[2]

Covert operations could also be part of a policy of self-defence. Here the problem is to reconcile "the covert" aspect with the openness of defence measures required under Article 51 of the Charter of the United Nations 1945. Article 51 establishes a duty to report measures taken in self-defence to the Security Council. Such a duty should be "immediately" discharged. The test was considered by the International Court of Justice (ICJ) in the *Nicaragua* case, since the operations by the United States in the Central American republic were carried out "covertly", through the CIA and other US agencies, in support of anti-Sandinist forces. The US action was a classical intervention in a civil war on the side of the insurgents, an activity forbidden by international law. Since the US claimed that they intervened in self-defence, the Court had to tackle the question of whether the US had infringed the duty to report measures taken in self-defence to the Security Council. The Court stated that the duty to report belongs to treaty law; it is not part of customary international law. Since the Court was tasked with adjudicating the case according to customary international law, no violation of the obligation to report was attributed to the US, even though the Court found that the US' failure to report was in contradiction with its claim to have acted in self-defence.[3] In his dissenting opinion, Judge Schwebel pointed out the following:[4]

— if an aggression is covert, the reaction in self-defence might also be covert;

[2] The Atlantic Council, in its meeting held in Brussels on 12 September 2001, stated as follows: "The Council agreed that if it is determined that this attack was directed from abroad against the United States, it shall be regarded as an action covered by Article 5 of the Washington Treaty, which states that an armed attack against one or more of the Allies in Europe or North America shall be considered an attack against them all". Evidence was brought by the US; the Atlantic Council, with a subsequent resolution of 4 October, decided to support the US action against terrorism. The statement by the Atlantic Council on 6 December 2001 reaffirmed the previous position. In its para. 3 it said: "We consider the events of 11 September to be an armed attack not just on one ally, but on us all, and have therefore invoked Article 5 of the Washington Treaty. Accordingly, we have decided to support, individually and collectively, the ongoing US-led military operations against the terrorists who perpetrated the 11 September outrages and those who provide them sanctuary".

[3] *Military and Paramilitary Activities in and against Nicaragua (Nicaragua v. United States of America), Merits, Judgment*, ICJ Reports 1986 14, at 121–122.

[4] *Ibid*, Dissenting Opinion of Judge Schwebel, at 373–377.

— it is not clear that the intent of the Charter was to oblige member States to take action "openly";
— domestic policy reasons (for instance, Congressional authorization) can suggest the use of covert actions.

State practice does not support the view that States feel obliged to abide by the duty to report.[5] Nor do authors view the duty to report as an ingredient of the legitimacy of acts of self-defence. For example, Lamberti Zanardi states that the duty to report is not a real obligation. Its infringement does not carry any legal consequences.[6] Combacau, in reviewing State practice, finds that States "rarely" report to the Security Council.[7] Usually the issue of self-defence is raised at a later stage, when the intervening State is accused of having unlawfully employed armed force. Dinstein observes that failure to report to the Security Council is not evidence of the State not acting in self-defence, if all the other conditions under Article 51 are met.[8] According to Randelzhofer, "... the restriction envisaged by the reporting duty ... has so far been almost devoid of practical significance".[9]

One can thus conclude that "reporting" acts taken in self-defence to the Security Council is only a procedural matter. It can also be argued that covert action is a lawful countermeasure against a State resorting to a policy of terrorism.[10] Therefore, covert action in self-defence is allowed under international law, provided that all substantive conditions required under the law of self-defence are met.

III. COVERT OPERATIONS CARRIED OUT WITH THE CONSENT OF THE TERRITORIAL SOVEREIGN

If a covert operation is carried out with the consent of the territorial State, the principle *volenti non fit iniuria* applies and the intervening State does not commit any infringement of the territorial integrity of the territorial State. However, the consent of the territorial State cannot excuse a serious

[5] But see C Gray, *International Law and the Use of Force* (Oxford University Press, Oxford, 2000), at 91, who observes that since the *Nicaragua* case States are abiding by the duty to report.
[6] PL Lamberti Zanardi, *La legittima difesa nel diritto internazionale* (Giuffrè, Milano, Dott A, 1972), at 275–76.
[7] J Combacau, "The Exception of Self-defence in UN Practice", in A Cassese (ed), *The Current Regulation of the Use of Force* (Martinus Nijhoff Publishers, Dordrecht, Boston, Lanchaster, 1986), at 15.
[8] Y Dinstein, *War, Aggression and Self-Defence*, 3rd ed, (Cambridge University Press, Cambridge, 2001), at 189–91.
[9] A Randelzhofer, "Article 51" in B Simma (ed), *The Charter of the United Nations: A Commentary* (Oxford University Press, Oxford, 2002), at 804.
[10] On the "secret wars" see JN Moore, "The Secret War in Central America and the Future of World Order" (1986) 80 *American Journal of International Law*, 89 ff.

violation of human rights such as assassination, torture or other kinds of inhumane treatment. Should such a violation of human rights take place, the responsibility of the territorial State could arise in addition to that of the intervening State.[11] If a norm of peremptory international law is violated, the consent of the territorial State is invalid and the covert operation would constitute an infringement of the territorial State's sovereignty — a violation that is also committed if the intervening State is not acting within the limits established by the territorial State.

IV. COVERT OPERATIONS AND THE LAW OF ARMED CONFLICT

The law of armed conflict does not forbid singling out an individual for the purposes of killing, provided the attack is carried out by lawful combatants wearing uniforms.[12] However, assassination carried out by spies behind enemy lines, even if the individual is a military target, is forbidden. The law of war prohibits treacherous killing and assassination, which should be considered acts of perfidy.[13]

Article 23(b) of the Regulations annexed to the 1907 Hague Convention IV respecting the Laws and Customs of War on Land prohibiting treacherous killing is construed by the US Army Field Manual, *The Law of Land Warfare* 1956, as forbidding assassination. The British Manual (*The Law of War on Land*, 1958) states that "assassination, the killing or wounding of a selected individual behind the line of battle by enemy agents or partisans ... are not lawful acts of war".[14] However, according to the British Manual, the killing of an enemy by uniformed men is not assassination.

This rule has to be reconciled with modern means of warfare. Practice shows that singling out and killing an enemy combatant behind enemy

[11] Article 16 of the Final Draft Articles on the State Responsibility adopted by the International Law Commission (ILC) addresses the question of aid or assistance in the commission of an internationally wrongful act. In its commentary, the ILC makes the example of facilitating the abduction of a person on foreign soil: GAOR, 56th session, Suppl 10 (A/56/10), *Report of the International Law Commission*, 53rd session (23 April–1 June and 2 July–10 August 2001), 155.

[12] See Y Dinstein, "Legitimate Military Objectives under the Current *Jus in bello*" (2002) 31 *Israel Yearbook on Human Rights*, 15.

[13] Art 37 of the Protocol Additional to the Geneva Conventions of 12 August 1949, and Relating to the Protection of Victims of International Armed Conflicts (Protocol I), of 8 June 1977, affirms the rule prohibiting perfidy. It defines perfidy as constituting "[a]cts inviting the confidence of an adversary to lead him to believe that he is entitled to, or is obliged to accord, protection under the rules of international law applicable in armed conflict, with intent to betray that confidence".

[14] See also ICRC, *Model Manual of the Law of Armed Conflict for Armed Forces* (ICRC, Geneva, 1999), rule 1013.

lines may be now carried out by unmanned aircraft.[15] Destruction of military objects in enemy territory (sabotage) is not forbidden.

However, combatants operating in civilian disguise are at the mercy of the enemy, if captured.[16]

V. COVERT OPERATIONS IN PEACETIME

Assassination is illegal in wartime. *A fortiori* it should be considered illegal in peacetime. Recently, one author[17] put forward the thesis that assassination of terrorist leaders is a kind of anticipatory self-defence. However, this type of argumentation blurs the difference between self-defence against State or a terrorist organization and law enforcement.

It should be recalled that the 1982 US Executive Order No 12333, related to US intelligence activities, prohibits assassination:

> ... no person employed by or acting on behalf of the United States Government shall engage in, or conspire to engage in, assassination. No agency of the Intelligence Community shall participate in or request any person to undertake activities forbidden by this order.

The 1982 Executive Order was not abrogated during the recent campaign against terrorists belonging to Al-Qaeda. Nonethless, the United States regards terrorists as lawful targets. As a consequence, the United States adopted National Security Presidential Directive No 18 in December 2002, which in an annexed list singles out the most dangerous terrorists and authorizes their killing. The Presidential Directive is not considered inconsistent with the 1982 Executive Order, since it is the US view that the Directive is not intended to regulate matters belonging to the law of war.

[15] For instance, a US unmanned aircraft penetrated into Yemen on 4 November 2002 and killed six terrorists belonging to Al Qaeda: *Washington Post*, November 5, 2002. The operation in Yemen is to be considered legal in so far as it is to be deemed as a part on "war on terrorism" and thus regulated by the law of armed conflict.

[16] See ex parte *Richard Quirin et al.* (Supreme Court of the United States, 29 October 1942), in HS Levie (ed) *Documents on Prisoners of War* (1979) Vol 60 *International Law Studies* (Naval War College, Newport, Rhode Island, 1979), at 229. In explaining the opinion of the Court, Chief Justice Stone stated: "The spy who secretly and without uniform passes the military lines of a belligerent in time of war, seeking to gather military information and communicate it to the enemy, or an enemy combatant who without uniform comes secretly through the lines for the purpose of waging war by destruction of life or property, are familiar examples of belligerents who are generally deemed not to be entitled to the status of prisoners of war, but to be offenders against the law of war subject to trial and punishment by military tribunals".

[17] DB Pickard, "Legalizing Assassination? Terrorism, The Central Intelligence Agency, and International Law", (2001) 30 *Georgia Journal of International and Comparative Law*, 1 ff.

Other international instruments confirm the prohibition of assassination in times of peace. For instance, Article III, para 5, of the 1963 Charter of the Organization of African Unity states an "unreserved condemnation, in all its forms, of political assassination". Likewise, the 1973 UN Convention for Prevention and Suppression of Crimes Against Internationally Protected Persons condemns the assassination and kidnapping of internationally protected persons (Article 2). Article 4 obliges States parties to take the necessary measures to prevent the assassination of such persons, within or outside their territory.

Operations aimed at singling out and killing an enemy have also been considered by the UN Security Council. On 16 April 1988, an Israeli commando landed in Tunisia, where the PLO Headquarters were hosted. The commando stormed the private home of Abu Jihad, a military chief and PLO "number two", and killed him. Security Council Resolution 611 (1988) condemned the Israeli raid as an act of aggression, and implicitly took a stance on the unlawfulness of the Abu Jihad killing. As a matter of fact, the word "assassination" appears in the preamble of the resolution, notwithstanding the fact that the operation was carried out by men wearing military uniforms.[18]

Sabotage in time of peace is obviously also forbidden. The leading example in this regard is the *Rainbow Warrior* affair.[19] In 1985, the Rainbow Warrior, a ship belonging to Greenpeace which tried to protest against and stop the French nuclear tests in the South Pacific, was sunk in Auckland, New Zealand, by two French agents belonging to the French Directorate General of External Security (Secret Service). The case was referred to the UN Secretary General for a ruling.[20] The French government recognized their violation of New Zealand's sovereignty and offered an apology and compensation. Pursuant to the Secretary General's ruling, the two French agents, who had been arrested by New Zealand authorities and sentenced to ten years of prison, were subsequently transferred to France and assigned to an island outside Europe for a period of three years.

VI. COVERT OPERATIONS AND ABDUCTION

Covert operations in a foreign State are often carried out to abduct a person and bring him/her to justice. There does not seem to be any law authorizing transfrontier kidnapping and establishing a procedure for taking the kidnapped into custody. However, the principle *male captus*

[18] See MN Schmitt, "State-Sponsored Assassination in International and Domestic Law" (1992) 17 *Yale Journal of International Law*, 634.
[19] *Rainbow Warrior (New Zealand/France)*, *RIAA*, vol XX, 217 (1990).
[20] See (1987) 26 *International Legal Materials*, at 1346 ff.

bene detentus is usually applied and courts retain their jurisdiction on the basis that the individual is under the custody of the territorial State. The United States has a long record of foreign abductions. This issue was also reviewed by the US Supreme Court in the case of the *United States v Alvarez-Machain* (1992)[21] concerning a Mexican national suspected of having killed a US drug enforcement agent. Alvarez was abducted in Mexico and brought to trial in the United States. The Court held that kidnapping an individual in a foreign State constitutes a violation of international law; however, the Court upheld the rule *male captus bene detentus* for the purpose of exercising criminal jurisdiction.

Louis Henkin correctly affirms that the principle *male captus bene detentus* is antecedent to the age of human rights.[22] In particular, he views it as a violation of both Articles 7 and 9 of the 1966 International Covenant on Civil and Political Rights, since international kidnapping constitutes "cruel, inhuman, or degrading treatment" and a violation of the prohibition of arbitrary arrest or detention. Article 9(1), of the Covenant clearly states that "no one shall be deprived of his liberty except ... in accordance with such procedures as are established by law".

VII. THE STATUS OF AGENTS CARRYING OUT COVERT OPERATIONS

The status of agents carrying out covert operations must be evaluated according to the rules applicable both in time of peace and in time of war.

In time of peace, clandestine agents can be submitted to the criminal jurisdiction of the territorial State.[23] In the *Rainbow Warrior* affair, France sought release of the two French agents implicated in the sinking of the ship because they had acted under order of the government.[24] This jurisdictional claim, however, was contested by New Zealand.

Diplomats enjoy a special status. The leading case, in this context, is *United States Diplomat and Consular Staff in Tehran*.[25] In 1979 US diplomat

[21] 60 USLW 4523 (U.S. June 15, 1992) (No 91–712).
[22] L Henkin, "Correspondence", (1993) 87 *American Journal of International Law*, 100–1; see also J Paust, "Correspondence", (1993) 87 *American Journal of International Law*, 252–56. For a contrary view, see M Halberstam, "In Defence of the Supreme Court Decision in Alvarez-Machain" (1992) 86 *American Journal of International Law*, 736 ff; M Halberstam, "Correspondence", (1993) 87 *American Journal of International Law*, 256–57; MJ Glennon, "State-Sponsored Abduction: A Comment on *United States v Alvarez-Machain*", (1992) 86 *American Journal of International Law*, 746 ff. In the United Kingdom, the rule *male captus bene detentus* seems no longer applied by the British courts: see the paper by S Borelli in this volume.
[23] R Jennings and A Watts (eds) *Oppenheim's International Law*, 9th edn, Vol 1, (Longman, London and New York, 1996), at 1176–77.
[24] See the Memorandum of the Government of the French Republic to the Secretary-General of the United Nations, (1987) 26 *International Legal Materials*, 1358 ff.
[25] ICJ Reports 1980, 3.

and consular staff suspected of carrying out covert operations against Iran were held hostage by rioters who seized the US embassy and consular premises. The ICJ held that any act of violence against diplomats is forbidden. Article 50(2)(b) of the ILC Articles on State Responsibility prohibits any countermeasure against diplomatic and consular personnel in contravention with the duty to protect the physical safety and inviolability of diplomatic agents. Nor can diplomatic staff be submitted to any form of criminal proceedings by way of reprisal. Diplomatic law provides a remedy against clandestine operations carried out by diplomats, since they can be declared *personae non gratae* and obliged to leave the country.

As discussed above, in time of armed conflict, saboteurs in civilian disguise and spies are at the mercy of the captor State. Any act of belligerency committed while not carrying arms openly implies forfeiture of the status of prisoner of war.[26] The agents may be tried and punished for the offence committed, as can be inferred from Article 44(4) of Additional Protocol I to the Geneva Conventions.

VIII. CONCLUSION

The following principles can be adduced by way of conclusion and could serve as a broad legal guide for any covert anti-terrorist policy:

- An action that is illegal under international law remains illegal, whether carried out openly or covertly (for instance, assassination);
- Conversely, a lawful operation remains lawful, whether carried out openly or covertly;
- In certain cases, however, the law requires that an action be carried out openly: for instance, in order to keep their legal combatant status, combatants must distinguish themselves from the civilian population or at least must carry arms openly when engaged in a military operation;
- An action in self-defence, covertly carried out, is not, as a rule, contrary to international law. The only infringement is non-respect of a procedural duty: reporting to the UN Security Council, provided that covert self-defence can be justified as a lawful countermeasure.

[26] Unlawful combatants, however, remain under the shield of Additional Protocol I (Article 75) and, according to an opinion, they also qualify as protected persons under the Geneva Convention Relative to the Protection of Civilian Persons in Time of War of 12 August 1949 (Fourth Geneva Convention, Article 5): see K Dörmann, "The legal situation of 'unlawful/ unprivileged combatants'", 85 (2003) *International Review of the Red Cross*, no. 849, 45.

3

The War Against Terrorism and Jus in Bello: *Are the Geneva Conventions Out of Date?*

LUIGI CONDORELLI AND YASMIN NAQVI

I. INTRODUCTION

EVER SINCE THE "War on Terror" began in earnest following 11 September 2001, international lawyers and policy-makers have been debating whether or not the range of international legal instruments existing in each particular field is adequate to meet the challenges of international terrorism. There has been an underlying assumption by many commentators that this may not be the case and that the current legal framework may turn out to be insufficiently developed or even counterproductive. In this particular context, the object of this chapter is that of determining whether international humanitarian law is well equipped to effectively regulate and to punish acts of terrorism or whether a substantial reform of the existing regime ought to be envisaged.

This question is all the more relevant and timely if one considers that, in the aftermath of the September 11 attacks, many, particularly in the United States, have voiced the concern that the Geneva Conventions are out of date. The perceived obsolete character of many of its provisions as well as their being primarily addressed to States, would make their application, in the view of many commentators, utterly unfit to face the challenges of the "world fight against terrorism". The controversial and highly politically charged debate that has ensued calls for an objective evaluation of the suitability of international humanitarian law to effectively counter the terrorist threat.

To properly delimit the boundaries of our enquiry a preliminary remark is in order. At closer scrutiny, the above-mentioned debate reveals that what is at stake is not the suitability of international humanitarian law to face the challenge of terrorism but rather its being a potential hurdle in the fight against it. In other words, international humanitarian law rules and principles are perceived as hampering the enforcement of anti-terror policies. This is why some have suggested that these rules should be temporarily set aside, awaiting for reform or, at least, reconsidered in the light of the changed international context. Yet, it should be acknowledged that not the whole of international humanitarian law is called into question. Only the rules pertaining to the determination of the status to be granted to members of enemy forces are seriously contested. In particular, the United States has objected to the applicability of the rules laid down in the Geneva Conventions to individuals apprehended in the course of the armed conflict in Afghanistan and ever since detained in Guantanamo Bay, Cuba, or elsewhere.

This paper is taken up with two main questions. The first concerns the normative standards laid down in international humanitarian law for acts of terrorism perpetrated in time of armed conflict. Second, the issue will be broached of whether the respect for humanitarian standards in armed conflict is likely to undermine the effectiveness of the fight against terrorism.

II. EXTANT RULES OF INTERNATIONAL HUMANITARIAN LAW RELATING TO TERRORISM

It might be opportune at the outset to refer to the well-known distinction between *jus ad bellum* and *jus in bello*. In short, the reason why an armed conflict takes place must not affect the obligation of the parties to the conflict to respect the rules of international humanitarian law.[1] Given their exclusively humanitarian character, these obligations are not owed bilaterally from one State to another but, rather, to the international community as a whole. In other words, they are obligations *erga omnes*. All parties to the conflict, be they aggressor or victim, equally must respect civilians, protect captured enemy combatants, avoid recourse to means and methods of warfare which are prohibited, ensure the safety of women and children and so on. As is known, this fundamental concept is expounded in the fourth paragraph of the preamble of the 1977 Protocol I additional to the Geneva Conventions.[2] The utmost concern must be expressed at any stance taken by a State on the application of

[1] For a discussion, see F Bugnion, "Guerre juste, guerre d'agression et droit international humanitaire", (2002) 84 *International Review of the Red Cross*, no 847, 523–546.

[2] Paragraph 4 of the preamble to the Protocol Additional to the Geneva Conventions of 12 August 1949, and Relating to the Protection of Victims of International Armed Conflicts (Protocol I), of 8 June 1977, 1125 UNTS 3, provides: "*Reaffirming* further that the provisions of the Geneva Conventions of 12 August 1949 and of this Protocol must be fully applied in all circumstances to all persons who are protected by those instruments, without any adverse distinction based on the nature or origin of the armed conflict or on the causes espoused by or attributed to the Parties to the conflict".

humanitarian law which risks undermining the whole edifice of international humanitarian law. This may occur by way of a violation of the rules that affects the fundamental principles that lie at the very foundation of the humanitarian legal regime.

A. International Armed Conflicts

International humanitarian law seeks to regulate the use of armed violence in wartime firstly by restricting the right to use armed force to combatants, these being members of armed forces of the parties to the conflict. Secondly, certain categories of persons such as civilians and those not or no longer taking part in conflict must be protected from attacks and the worst effects of the conflict. Both these means of regulating violence in times of war imply the prohibition of the activities of terrorists, who may not be members of armed forces and whose attacks are by definition aimed at causing terror among civilians.

As regards international humanitarian law provisions applicable in international armed conflicts that expressly refer to terrorism, their number is relatively scant. In particular, mention must be made of Article 51(2) of Additional Protocol I to the Geneva Conventions. This provision reads:

> The civilian population as such, as well as individual civilians, shall not be the object of attack. Acts or threats of violence the primary purpose of which is to spread terror among the civilian population are prohibited.

International humanitarian law lays down a precise obligation, of a general scope, to exempt the civilian population from acts of war. In this context, it is spelt out that acts of terrorism, or even their threat, against the civilian population, are prohibited. It is notable that the actual term "terrorism" is not expressly used. This is due to the fairly ambiguous character if the term, which, as is known, has so far prevented the adoption of a comprehensive international legal instrument on this very matter. To hold, as is done in Article 51, that *any* act or *any* threat directed to spread terror in the civilian population is prohibited is tantamount to saying that the nature and scale of the act or threat is immaterial to its prohibition. Furthermore, the rule in Article 51 does not take into account at all either the motive inspiring such acts or threats or the legitimacy — or lack thereof — of the causes in the name of which the perpetrators may act. What matters in order to trigger the prohibition is intent to spread terror in the civilian population. Therefore, not only is a direct attack against the civilian population absolutely prohibited, regardless of motive and circumstances, but also any threat or act of violence aimed at spreading terror among the civilian population, short of a direct attack.

Incidentally, it would be desirable that such an approach to a rule prohibiting terrorist acts, which forbids the act or threat of terror against the civilian population regardless of scale or motive, also influenced the attempts to define terrorism outside the domain of *jus in bello*.

Article 51 is part and parcel of the so-called "Geneva law" concerning the protection of civilians and civilian objects in times of armed conflict. However, in the so-called "Hague law", regulating the means and methods of warfare, one can also find rules that can aptly be applied to terrorist activities. The law of armed conflict makes it clear that in any armed conflict the right of the parties to the conflict to choose the means and methods of warfare is not unlimited.[3] In particular, it is prohibited to use weapons or methods of warfare causing unnecessary suffering or superfluous injury.[4] Resort to means and methods of warfare that do not allow the distinction between military and civilian targets are also prohibited.[5] Furthermore, parties to armed conflicts are obliged to limit as much as possible collateral damage to civilian targets in the course of an attack against a military objective.[6] Of particular relevance to terrorist acts is the prohibition of perfidy (codified in Article 37 of Protocol I) that forbids the feigning of a protected status (such as a civilian or non-combatant status) with intent to betray the confidence of the enemy in order to kill, injure or capture an adversary. Mention may also be made of the rule prohibiting the denial of quarter (Article 40 of Protocol I).

Violations of the aforementioned rules and principles which result in death or serious injury to civilians may amount to war crimes, under Article 147 of the Fourth Geneva Convention and Article 85 of Protocol I. This means that perpetrators must be prosecuted by domestic courts and punished where found guilty. Terrorist acts carried out in the context of an armed conflict which are classed as war crimes would also fall under the jurisdiction of the International Criminal Court (ICC).[7]

Finally, with regard to international armed conflicts mention should be made of Article 33 of the Fourth Geneva Convention, the only provision in the 1949 Geneva Conventions in which the word terrorism appears. According to this Article, protected persons under the Convention (persons in the hands of a party to the conflict of which they are not nationals)

[3] This fundamental principle, first expounded by Grotius in his work *"De iure belli ac pacis,"* published in 1625, demonstrated the necessity of *"temperamenta belli,"* of imposing limitations on the destructive power of weapons to be used. The principle was codified in Art 22 of the Hague Regulations, Annex to the Convention (IV) respecting the Laws and Customs of War on Land of 18 October 1907, 187 Consol TS 277 and reaffirmed in Art 35(1) of Protocol I, above n 2.

[4] Art 35(2) Protocol I, above n 2.

[5] See Articles 48 and 51(4) and (5) Protocol I, *ibid*.

[6] See in particular Articles 51(5)(b), 52, 54, 57 and 58 Protocol I, *ibid*.

[7] Art 8 Rome Statute of the International Criminal Court, 18 July 1998, UN Doc A/CONF 183/9.

must be protected from acts of terrorism.[8] Although the word "terrorism" in Article 33 may have a more restricted meaning than in the contemporary understanding of the term[9], it is, however, clear that wilful killing, torture or inhuman treatment, the taking of hostages or extensive destruction of property are all grave breaches of the Fourth Geneva Convention, and therefore those carrying out these war crimes must be prosecuted.[10]

The question arises as to whether members of armed forces are also protected against terrorist acts under international humanitarian law. Clearly, soldiers directly participate in armed warfare and therefore are legitimate targets of attack. Nevertheless, it is equally apparent that the rules limiting the choice in the means and methods of warfare apply to attacks carried out on military personnel. Therefore, any attack which causes superfluous injury or unnecessary suffering would be unlawful, as would be a perfidious attack on the members of armed forces. These prohibitions indicate that certain terrorist acts would certainly still be prohibited if committed against military personnel.

B. Non-International Armed Conflicts

Turning to internal armed conflicts, the minimum standards laid down in Article 3 common to the four Geneva Conventions, although not expressly prohibiting acts of terrorism, could nonetheless be interpreted as to cover them.[11] General principles such as the principle of humane treatment as well as more specific prohibitions such as that relating to cruel treatment could well be applied to acts of terrorism. Additional Protocol II to the Geneva Conventions relating to non-international armed conflicts affirms and develops these legal standards. In particular, Article 4 of

[8] Art 33 of the Geneva Convention Relative to the Protection of Civilian Persons in Time of War of 12 August 1949, 75 UNTS 287 (Fourth Geneva Convention) provides: "No protected person may be punished for an offence he or she has not personally committed. Collective penalties and likewise measures of intimidation or of terrorism are prohibited."

[9] See H-P Gasser, "Acts of terror, 'terrorism' and international humanitarian law", (2002) 84 *International Review of the Red Cross*, no 847, 547 at 558.

[10] Articles 146–147 Fourth Geneva Convention, above n 8.

[11] Article 3 common to the Geneva Conventions applies in "the case of an armed conflict not of an international character occurring in the territory of one of the High Contracting Parties". Each party to the conflict is bound to apply, as a minimum, the following rules: (1) persons taking no active part in the hostilities must be treated humanely, without any adverse distinction; (2) violence to life and person, in particular murder of all kinds, mutilation, cruel treatment and torture are prohibited; (3) the taking of hostages is prohibited; (4) outrages upon personal dignity, in particular, humiliating and degrading treatment are prohibited; (5) the passing of sentences and the carrying out of executions without previous judgment pronounced by a regularly constituted court are prohibited; and (5) the wounded and sick shall be collected and cared for.

Protocol II, in laying down the fundamental guarantees which all those who do not or who no longer participate in the hostilities should enjoy, expressly provides that acts of terrorism are prohibited at any time in any place. Furthermore, Article 13 repeats the rule of Article 51 of Protocol I and expands the scope of application of the prohibition not to spread terror among the civilian population to internal armed conflicts.

It is well-accepted that serious violations of such prohibitions can be characterized as war crimes under customary international law. This is a recent development, as such qualification was envisaged neither in the codification of 1949 nor in the 1977 Protocols. However, it is generally uncontested that since the 1990s, particularly with the adoption of the Statute of the International Criminal Tribunal for Rwanda (ICTR)[12] which gave the Tribunal specific competence over serious violations of common Article 3 and Additional Protocol II, the jurisprudence of the ICTY in the *Tadic* case[13] and, more recently, the adoption of the Rome Statute which expressly qualifies such violations as war crimes within the ICC's jurisdiction,[14] this classification has made its way into customary international humanitarian law.

Overall, the rules we have highlighted should be sufficient to meet the challenge of international terrorism. They prohibit, without exception, terrorist acts committed in either international or non-international armed conflicts. Where such acts amount to war crimes, humanitarian law dictates that suspects must be prosecuted and punished accordingly.

III. APPLICABILITY OF INTERNATIONAL HUMANITARIAN LAW TO THE "WAR ON TERROR"

The terrorist attacks of 11 September 2001 and the subsequent military operations in Afghanistan and elsewhere have raised certain problematic aspects to the question of the applicability of international humanitarian law to the "War on Terror". The fact that the September 11th attacks were carried out by civilians of different nationalities who formed part of an internationally affiliated terrorist group with no fixed territorial base, using a civilian object (though turned into a weapon), upon civilian targets within a State (although the Pentagon could arguably count as a

[12] ICTR Statute, Art 4, Annex to Security Council Res. 955 (1994), S/RES/955 (1994), 8 November 1994.

[13] Although the ICTY was not given the specific subject matter jurisdiction over serious violations of common Article 3 of the Geneva Conventions, the Tribunal decided that customary international law imposes criminal liability for such violations and that it had jurisdiction over them: *Prosecutor v. Dusko Tadic*, IT–94–1, Decision on the Defence Motion for Interlocutory Appeal on Jurisdiction, 2 October 1995, para 137.

[14] Rome Statute, above n 7, Art 8(2).

military objective), does not easily fit into the definition of an "act of war" because it is not directly attributable to a State, nor does it fulfil the criteria necessary to trigger the application of the Geneva Conventions, apart perhaps from common Article 3.[15]

These aspects concern the critical date at which international humanitarian law became or might have become applicable. Was it 11 September 2001 or, rather, 6 October 2001, when the military operation against Afghanistan began? As some have argued, in the aftermath of the attack it seems fair to assume that the former date was the trigger for the application of the law of armed conflict. If one accepts that on 11 September the United States was the victim of an armed attack in violation of international law and the Charter of the United Nations and that, consequently, the military response by the United States in Afghanistan could be qualified as an act of self defence — whether legitimate or not — it may be logically argued that this is the date which marked the beginning of the armed conflict.

This submission has been criticized on the basis that an "armed attack" for the purposes of triggering the right to self-defence under the Charter of the United Nations is something that only States may carry out. Furthermore, it has been pointed out that an isolated attack by non-State actors upon a State, despite the horrific number of casualties, may not in itself be sufficient to be considered the beginning of an armed conflict. Countering this argument is the view that September 11th was part of a continuing armed terrorist campaign against western (especially American) targets which started many years ago, thereby fulfilling the criteria of being a "protracted" armed conflict necessary (according to the ICTY in the 1995 *Tadic* case[16]) to trigger the application of common Article 3 to the Geneva Conventions.

Notwithstanding the correctness or not of these arguments, to identify the date of 11 September 2001 as the critical date at which time hostilities actually began has the advantage of characterizing the terrorist acts as war crimes. From the perspective of ensuring the criminal prosecution of those responsible for the attacks this may indeed be a factor supporting this characterization.

In terms of the application of international humanitarian law to the conflict in Afghanistan, one should note that no State party to the conflict objected to applicability of international humanitarian law as a whole.

[15] Prior to the US military intervention in Afghanistan, an international armed conflict did not exist, as there was no armed conflict between two High Contracting Parties, as required by common Art 2 of the Geneva Conventions to trigger their application. Neither of the two additional Protocols were applicable, because of their respective scope of application and because the US is not a party to the instruments.

[16] *Prosecutor v Dusko Tadic*, above n 13, para 70. Art 8(2)(f) of the Rome Statute, above n 7, also adopts the criterion that the armed conflict be "protracted" for the application of Art 8(2).

One may even go as far as saying that its applicability has been endorsed at the highest level by the allied force. In its Memorandum of 24 October 2001, the International Committee of the Red Cross (ICRC) reminded the parties to the conflict of their obligations under the applicable rules of international humanitarian law. This Memorandum was never challenged. It is true that, in contrast to the general practice of the ICRC which forwards such memoranda, as much as possible, before the actual waging of hostilities, the Memorandum was circulated relatively late. According to press sources the two weeks delay could be attributed to the rejection by the United States of an earlier version on the basis that this text declared that the threat or use of nuclear weapons is absolutely prohibited under international humanitarian law, a position the United States does not consider as reflecting the current state of the law. Be that as it may, the remaining substantive parts of the document were not protested against, from which one can infer that the United States accepted that the main body of international humanitarian law was applicable. This is unsurprising given that, despite the asymmetrical character of the conflict and despite the fact that the Taliban was an unrecognized government, the war was essentially one between two High Contracting Parties of the Geneva Conventions, thereby automatically triggering Article 2 thereof.

The occasional disputes concerning the legality of specific military operations do not undermine the above presumption. In fact, several situations in the course of the Afghan conflict have given rise to heated disputes over the legality of certain conducts on the part of the allied forces. It suffices to mention the aerial bombing of ICRC warehouses, the arguably disproportionate amount of collateral damage which occurred at the occasion of attacks against military targets, the dubious characterization of certain targets as military and the use of cluster bombs. The disputes over these facts mainly revolved around the issue of whether or not a violation of specific rules of international humanitarian law had occurred. No party to the conflict claimed that these rules were not applicable.

With regard to Afghanistan one should notice that both the international humanitarian legal regime applicable to international armed conflicts and that applicable to internal armed conflicts operated jointly or were often intermingled. The violent struggle between Afghan factions surely remained an internal conflict even after the allied forces' military intervention. This intervention, however, caused an international armed conflict to arise between the United States and Afghanistan. Practically all commentators agree on the fact that the armed forces of different States were involved. To complicate the picture even more, there seemed to be at the time a complete integration of Taliban fighters (who must be regarded as governmental forces even if they belonged to a non-internationally recognized government[17]) and Al-Qaeda members. President Bush at the occasion of his speech before the UN General Assembly on 10 November 2001 stated that the two components of enemy forces were "now virtually indistinguishable". These types of considerations have significant implications for the applicability of humanitarian law. Could, for example, Al-Qaeda members be considered as "members of other militias and members of other volunteer corps ... belonging to a Party to the conflict and operating in or outside their own territory" for the purposes of prisoner-of-war status and treatment?[18] While the United States has flatly rejected such arguments, preferring to consider Al-Qaeda members and even Taliban fighters as "unlawful combatants", this interpretation stands in contrast to the United States' acceptance of the application of all the other relevant provisions of the Geneva Conventions to the Afghan conflict.

An even more blurry picture in terms of the applicability of international humanitarian law emerged after the fall of the Taliban and the setting up of the new government of Afghanistan on 19 June 2002. The armed struggle against Al-Qaeda and remnant forces of the Taliban continued, but this could not be classed as an inter-State conflict by virtue of common Article 2 of the Geneva Conventions. Neither of the additional Protocols applied due to their respective scopes of application and the fact that the US is not a party to either. Even the application of common Article 3 is difficult to maintain in the ongoing "War on Terror" during which the US has maintained a military presence in Afghanistan and has made military strikes on terrorist targets in other States, such as Yemen. This is due to the fact that this provision requires the conflict to be taking place on the sole territory of one of the High Contracting Parties. It is unclear if the localisation of the conflict and its parties on the territory of one State is an essential criterion for the application of common Article 3. Furthermore, must the non-State actors be strictly of one national group with a territorial base, or may they be part of a transnational organisation with no definite link to territory? One could argue that in the light of globalization and the increased phenomenon of trans-border conflicts, geographical localisation is no longer essential for the application of common Article 3. The International Court of Justice's characterization of common Article 3 as reflective of "elementary standards of humanity" would seem to reinforce this view.[19]

[17] See Art 4(A)(3) of the Geneva Convention Relative to the Treatment of Prisoners of War of 12 August 1949, 75 UNTS 135 (Third Geneva Convention).

[18] This is one of the listed categories of those entitled to prisoner-of-war status under the Third Geneva Convention, *ibid*: Art 4(A)(2).

[19] See *The Corfu Channel Case (Merits)*, ICJ Reports 1949, at p 22 and the case concerning *Military and Paramilitary Activities in and against Nicaragua (Nicaragua v United States of America)*, ICJ Reports 1986, at p 112, para 215.

IV. DOES RESPECT FOR INTERNATIONAL HUMANITARIAN LAW HAMPER THE FIGHT AGAINST INTERNATIONAL TERRORISM?

Considering the general and specific rules pertaining to the prohibition of terrorism under international humanitarian law and the lack of sweeping objections to the adequacy of international humanitarian law to counter terrorist acts perpetrated in time of armed conflict, one should be careful not to over-emphasize the claim that the current regime of *jus in bello* is unfit to meet the challenge of terrorism. After all, the only rules which are perceived as inadequate, out of date, or unsuitable, according to some commentators close to the US administration, would be those which concern the legal status and treatment of apprehended enemy combatants. According to this view, if these rules were duly enforced, they would present an obstacle to effectively fight against terrorism. Strict observation of the rules would hamper investigations of terrorist suspects and lead to the overly early release and repatriation of prisoners and other individuals detained once the active hostilities have ended.

In fact, these are not the official reasons given by the US government. Despite ambiguities and often contradictory versions, the official position seems to be that detainees, captured in Afghanistan during the armed conflict are not entitled to the status of "protected persons" under the Geneva Conventions. Although members of the Taliban army are "in principle" protected persons under the Third Geneva Convention, the position taken by the US administration is that they are not entitled to such protection as they had failed to comply with the necessary requirements that the same Convention demands of enemy combatants.[20] As regards members or affiliates of the Al-Qaeda terrorist organisation, the US view is that they should be qualified as "unlawful combatants" and no provision of international humanitarian law is therefore applicable to them.

Much criticism has been raised against this stance taken by the US. In particular, many have viewed the US refusal to accord any legal status to the detainees as being counter to the fundamental principles of international humanitarian law. While more detailed examinations of possible violations of specific provisions of humanitarian law have been done elsewhere, it is worth recalling some general principles of international humanitarian law which may be relevant to the case at hand.

First, as previously noted, the application of international humanitarian law cannot be made dependent on the legality of the armed conflict. The fact that one of the belligerent parties may have resorted to armed

[20] These requirements, listed in Art 4(2) of the Third Geneva Convention, above n 17, are: (1) being commanded by a person responsible for his subordinates; (2) having a fixed distinctive sign recognizable at a distance; (3) carrying arms openly; and (4) conducting operations in accordance with the laws and customs of war.

force contrary to the *jus ad bellum* does not exempt any of the parties to the conflict from respecting international humanitarian law rules, which by their very nature have an *erga omnes* character.

Second, all individuals, without exception, who are apprehended by the enemy in the course of an armed conflict do benefit from the status of protected persons under the Geneva Conventions, either as prisoners of war (Third Geneva Convention) or as interned civilians (Fourth Geneva Convention). The ICTY made this clear when it affirmed that "there is no gap between the Third and Fourth Geneva Conventions. If an individual is not entitled to the protection of the Third Convention as a prisoner of war … he or she necessarily falls within the ambit of [the Fourth Convention], provided that its art. 4 requirements [defining a protected person] are satisfied".[21]

Third, where the prisoner-of-war status of an individual is uncertain, or where the person does not appear to fit within the categories of prisoners of war, the detaining power has the obligation to have the person's status decided by a "competent tribunal" according to Article 5 of the Third Geneva Convention. So far the United States has refused to comply with this obligation. Despite the obvious glaring legal difference that prisoner-of-war status would have for the detainees (given the fact that it is an offence to illegally participate in armed conflict), it seems that the US is planning to go straight to the prosecution stage by the use of military commissions. These commissions established pursuant to the Military Order of 13 November 2001, issued by the President of the United States, have been set up specifically to try terrorist cases. Given these commissions' direct link with the executive branch of government and their military composition and functioning, it is doubtful that these commissions would meet the requirements of independence and impartiality required by international humanitarian law.[22]

Fourth, at the end of the hostilities, all detained persons, provided that they have not committed crimes and that, consequently, they are not prosecuted in compliance with the due process of law, must be promptly released.[23] This issue will not be dealt with in detail, given the panoply of contributions which have exhaustively explored these particular aspects.[24] For the purposes of this paper, however, what matters is not to

[21] *Celebici*, Case IT–96–21, Trial Chamber, judgment of 16 November 1998, para 271.

[22] Fair trial standards are required in common Art 3(1)(d) to the Geneva Conventions, Articles 84 and 99–108 of the Third Geneva Convention, Articles 70–76 of the Fourth Geneva Convention, Art 75 Protocol I, above n 2 and Art 6 of the Protocol Additional to the Geneva Conventions of 12 August 1949, and Relating to the Protection of Victims of Non-Intenational Armed Conflicts (Protocol II), of 8 June 1977, 1125 UNTS 609.

[23] Art 118 Third Geneva Convention, above n 17; Art 133 Fourth Geneva Convention, above n 8.

[24] See, eg, L Vierucci, "Prisoners of War or Protected Persons qua Unlawful Combatants? The Judicial Safeguards to Which Guantanamo Detainees are Entitled", (2003) 1 *Journal of International Criminal Justice*, 284–314.

establish that serious violations of international humanitarian law principles and rules may have been committed by the US by refusing to apply certain provisions of the Geneva Conventions. The question to address is rather if the respect for such principles and rules may hamper the effective fight against terrorism. Should this be the case, it could be argued that the violation of these rules would be somewhat justified or even compelled by the necessity to win the "War against Terror".

The answer to the above query cannot be but a negative one. Respecting international humanitarian law creates no further hurdle than respecting the "hard core" of international human rights law. The status of prisoner of war does not prevent a person from being prosecuted for war crimes or for other crimes committed independently of the conflict at any point in time. What is excluded is prosecution for acts of violence committed as a lawful combatant in conformity with the *jus in bello*. In other words, international humanitarian law neither hampers the criminal prosecution of individuals for acts of terrorism nor prevents — as superficially maintained by some — the interrogation of prisoners of war. The latter contention is often based upon Article 17 of the Third Geneva Convention which provides that every prisoner of war is bound to give only his surname, first names and rank, date of birth, and army, regimental, personal or serial number, or equivalent information. Importantly, the provision forbids any physical or mental torture, nor any other form of coercion to secure from them information of any kind. In particular, prisoners of war who refuse to answer "may not be threatened, insulted, or exposed to any unpleasant or disadvantageous treatment of any kind." These rules are clearly designed to prevent any ill-treatment of prisoners of war and merely reiterate standards of interrogative conduct in any civilized nation. They do not impose any more restrictions on interrogations than are already provided for in human rights treaties[25] and most domestic legislation.

What international humanitarian law does do is prevent the detaining power from arresting and putting into custody apprehended individuals in an arbitrary way, particularly at the end of the hostilities. It allows their detention only in relation with violations or crimes personally committed by them and always in conformity with the judicial guarantees imposed by the applicable rules of armed conflict. Incidentally, human rights law provides for analogous guarantees. Hence, the legal limbo in which individuals being held in Guantanamo and elsewhere, having no access either to lawyers or judges, and thus not enjoying basic judicial guarantees, amounts to a violation of both international human

[25] See in particular Articles 7, 9 and 14 International Covenant on Civil and Political Rights, 23 March 1976, GA res 2200A (XXI), 21 UN GAOR Supp (No 16) at 52, UN Doc A/6316 (1966), 999 UNTS 171.

rights and humanitarian law.[26] Nor can such a violation be justified on the grounds that these measures are necessary to fight international terrorism. Non-compliance with such fundamental standards of humanity in blatant disregard of international obligations stands in contrast to the legacy of our civilization and fosters the interests of those who would like to undermine its very foundation.

V. CONCLUSION

By way of conclusion one may say that international humanitarian law unequivocally condemns acts of terrorism committed in both international and internal armed conflicts. Furthermore, it provides a system for the prosecution and punishment of those who perpetrate such acts.

The concern that the respect for international humanitarian law may represent a hurdle in the fight against international terrorism does not seem to be founded. In terms of the dispute over the granting of prisoner-of-war status, it is apparent that international humanitarian law does not set limits to State conduct which differ markedly from those already provided by international human rights law.

While the loose parameters of the "War on Terror" present challenges for the straightforward application of international humanitarian law to all the multi-dimensional contexts of the fight, it is clear that where an armed conflict arises, parties to the conflict generally accept the application of humanitarian rules. If States are really fighting for a humane world of democracy and freedom free from terrorist threats, the broad application of the Geneva Conventions could never seem less out of date.

[26] In response to the complaint concerning the Guantanamo prisoners the Inter-American Commission on Human Rights stated that where there are circumstances connected to an armed conflict individual's "fundamental rights may be determined in part by reference to international humanitarian law as well as international human rights law", emphasising that "no person under the authority and control of a state, regardless of his or her circumstances, is devoid of legal protection for his or her fundamental and non-derogable rights." Decision of 12 March 2002, precautionary measures, reproduced in (2002) 23 *Human Rights Law Journal* at 15–16.

4

The Treatment of Terrorist Suspects Captured Abroad: Human Rights and Humanitarian Law

SILVIA BORELLI

I. INTRODUCTION

THIS CHAPTER EXAMINES the situation of terrorist suspects captured during the conflict in Afghanistan and currently detained by US authorities. In particular, it will address the issue of the guarantees under international humanitarian law and human rights norms that US authorities are obliged to grant to those detainees (and accordingly will attempt to assess the compatibility of US conduct with internationally accepted standards).

A large proportion of the alleged members of Al-Qaeda who have been apprehended by the United States were captured during the military operations in Afghanistan. Most of the captured combatants are in the custody of the new post-Taliban Afghan authorities, but the US military has been screening and interrogating detainees in Afghan custody in order to identify individuals whom the United States wishes to prosecute or to detain, or who may have useful intelligence information. Thus, the US military has taken custody of several hundreds detainees held by Afghan forces and has transferred them to its own detention facilities. Moreover, US military forces have directly taken custody of persons apprehended during the military operations in the Afghan territory. From January 2002 the US government began transferring some of the detainees from the detention facilities in Afghanistan to a more permanent detention facility at the US military base at Guantanamo Bay, Cuba.[1]

[1] Up until 18 July 2003, the total number of detainees at Guantanamo Bay is of approximately 660. See US Department of Defense, News Release, 18 July 2003, available at <http://www.defenselink.mil/releases/2003/nr20030718–0207.html>. In the discussion that follows, only the position of those held at Guantanamo Bay who were captured in Afghanistan will be considered.

In order to determine the guarantees that the Guantanamo detainees enjoy under general international law or under relevant treaty provisions, some preliminary questions must be answered. The first question regards the legal qualification of the situation in Afghanistan. On the basis of this, one must determine which international law regime applies to such a situation. It is only on the basis of those norms that the issue of the status of the individuals apprehended during the Afghan conflict, and consequently what guarantees they enjoy under international law, can be addressed.

II. APPLICABILITY OF THE *IUS IN BELLO* TO THE AFGHAN CONFLICT

As to the question of the legal qualification of the events that took place in Afghanistan, the relevant issue is whether the military operations in Afghanistan can be considered an *armed conflict*[2] under international law.[3] International law does not provide a definition of armed conflict: thus, the existence of an armed conflict is essentially determined by the behaviour of the States or belligerents involved. In order to determine the existence of an armed conflict, a factual determination has to be made: a state of generalised hostilities persistent enough or of a sufficient magnitude to rise to the level of armed conflict in the view of the international community is *ipso facto* an armed conflict. On the basis of such a "factual determination", the Afghan conflict can undoubtedly be considered an armed conflict, due to both the magnitude of the military operations and the duration of the conflict. As for the character — internal or international — of such a conflict, military action conducted by the regular forces of

[2] After the Second World War, the traditional concept of *state of war* proved no longer adequate to describe the situations of conflict involving the use of armed force that could arise in the international community: the increase in the number of military conflicts that cannot be characterised as "wars" in the technical sense, and the need for limitation of the use of force and for the respect of the dignity and the fundamental rights of individuals even in those contexts, have brought about the new concept of *armed conflict*, be it internal or international. The concept of state of war has been abandoned by recent doctrine, and superseded by the notion of armed conflict. See, E David, *Principes de droit des conflits armés* (Bruylant, Brussels, 1994), at 63 ff; I Detter, *The Law of War*, 2nd edn (Cambridge University Press, Cambridge, 2000), at 17–20; N Ronzitti, *Diritto internazionale dei conflitti armati*, 2nd edn (Giappichelli, Torino, 2001), at 121; E Lauterpacht, "The Legal Irrelevance of the State of War", (1968) *Proceedings of the American Society of International Law* at 58; C Greenwood, "The Concept of War in Modern International Law", (1987) 36 *International and Comparative Law Quarterly* 283. Compare M Bothe, "War", in *Encyclopaedia of Public International Law* (1982), 282–90.

[3] The more controversial question of the qualification of the attacks of September 2001 as acts of war is not relevant in this context. As the individuals held in Guantanamo were apprehended during the military operations conducted by US forces in the Afghan territory, in order to determine the status of those detainees one can focus on the situation arising from the beginning of those military operations.

sovereign States in the territory of another sovereign State constitutes, by definition, an international armed conflict.[4]

The law applicable to international armed conflicts is codified principally in the Hague Convention of 1907 and the annexed Regulations Concerning the Law and Customs of War on Land[5] (which codify what is properly defined as the law of war, ie the rules governing the conduct of hostilities), and by the four Geneva Conventions of 1949[6] (which codify what is generally referred to as international humanitarian law). Additional Protocol I of 1977 contains provisions developing the law in both of these areas.[7]

Both the US and Afghanistan are parties to the Geneva Conventions; accordingly, the status of the individuals apprehended during the military operations in Afghanistan must be established having regard to the relevant provisions of the Conventions, and in particular of the Third Geneva Convention, relative to the treatment of prisoners of war, or of the Fourth Geneva Convention, on the treatment of civilians.

III. LEGAL STATUS OF THE GUANTANAMO DETAINEES

A. The US Position

The first prisoners arrived in the US base at Guantanamo Bay, Cuba on 11 January 2002. On the same day, the United States government

[4] Given that the Taliban regime had only been recognised by three States (Pakistan, Saudi Arabia and the United Arab Emirates) prior to the conflict, there is an (extremely weak) argument that the conflict was an internal armed conflict between the Taliban and the Northern Alliance, which was subsequently "internationalised". However, given that the United States and its allies at no point relied upon an invitation by the latter as a justification for its use of force, preferring to characterise it as an exercise of the right of self defence (see the letter from the US to the Security Council, UN Doc S/2001/496, 7 October 2001), a characterisation seemingly supported by Security Resolution 1368 of 12 September 2001, this argument does not seem at all tenable.

[5] Convention (IV) Respecting the Laws and Customs of War on Land, The Hague, 18 October 1907 (in force 26 January 1910).

[6] Geneva Convention for the Amelioration of the Condition of the Wounded and Sick in Armed Forces in the Field, 12 August 1949, 75 UNTS 31 (entered into force 21 October 1950); Geneva Convention for the Amelioration of the Condition of Wounded, Sick and Shipwrecked Members of Armed Forces at Sea, 12 August 1949, 75 UNTS 85 (entered into force 21 October 1950); Geneva Convention Relative to the Treatment of Prisoners of War, 12 August 1949, 75 UNTS 135 (entered into force 21 October 1950); Geneva Convention Relative to the Protection of Civilian Persons in Time of War, 12 August 1949, 75 UNTS 287 (entered into force 21 October 1950) (hereinafter referred to, respectively, as "First, Second, Third and Fourth Geneva Conventions").

[7] Protocol Additional to the Geneva Conventions of 12 August 1949, and relating to the Protection of Victims of International Armed Conflicts, 8 June 1977, 1125 UNTS 3 (entered into force 7 December 1978) (hereafter "Additional Protocol I"); Additional Protocol I has not been ratified by the US, but the US accepts that many of the principles enshrined in it reflect customary international law: see J Matheson, "Remarks on The United States Position on the Relation of Customary International Law to the 1977 Protocols Additional to the 1949 Geneva Conventions", (1987) 2 *American University Journal of International Law and Policy* 419.

announced that it would not apply the Third Geneva Convention on the treatment of prisoners of war in relation to the treatment and internment of those taken prisoner in Afghanistan or Pakistan by the United States; the United States explained that the prisoners were not actually prisoners of war, but were in fact "unlawful combatants", and therefore not entitled to "any rights under the Geneva Convention."[8]

After this first declaration, the US authorities have taken a more nuanced position, distinguishing between soldiers of the Taliban army, and members of Al-Qaeda. The distinction is on the basis that, although Afghanistan is a party to the Geneva Conventions, Al-Qaeda is an international terrorist group; "as such, its members are not entitled to POW status."[9] However, even though the Taliban soldiers are covered by the Geneva Convention, the position of the US authorities is that they still do not qualify as prisoners of war.[10] The justification given for this determination is that "they failed to meet the criteria for POW status" by failing to wear uniforms that distinguish them from the civilian population, failing to be organised in units with an identifiable chain of command,[11] and failing to conduct their operations in accordance with the laws and customs of war, as they "knowingly adopted and provided support to the unlawful terrorist objectives of the Al-Qaeda."[12]

B. Assessment of the US position

The protection and the treatment of captured combatants during an international armed conflict is detailed in the Third Geneva Convention relative to the treatment of prisoners of war. The Convention defines the category of prisoners of war and provides specific guidelines for the treatment of enemy combatants who have been taken prisoners.

[8] See News Briefing, Department of Defense, Secretary Rumsfeld, 11 January 2002, available at <http://www.defenselink.mil/news/Jan2002/t01112002_t0111sd.html>.

[9] See Fact Sheet, White House Press Office, 7 February 2002, available at <http://www.whitehouse.gov/news/releases/2002/02/20020207–13.html>. See also Press Conference, Department of Defense, Secretary Rumsfeld, 8 February 2002, available at <http://www.defenselink.mil/news/Feb2002/t02082002_t0208sd.html>: the Geneva Convention "does not apply to the conflict with al Qaeda, whether in Afghanistan or elsewhere."

[10] See Fact Sheet, White House Press Office, 7 February 2002, above n 9. The US however insisted that all detainees at Guantanamo would be treated humanely, and in a manner consistent with the principles of the Third Geneva Convention, and would be granted a number of POW privileges as a matter of policy.

[11] See Press Conference, Department of Defense, Secretary Rumsfeld, 8 February 2002, above n 9.

[12] Statement of the Press Secretary on the Geneva Conventions, available at <http://www.whitehouse.gov/news/releases/2003/05/20030507–18.html>. [The link is to a page which gives the date as 7 May 2003; however, it is quite clear from exact quotations elsewhere that the statement was made in February 2002. See, for instance, the press release on the web site of the US Embassy in Venezuela at <http://embajadausa.org.ve/wwwh1628.html>].

According to Article 4A of the Third Geneva Convention, individuals in the following categories who have fallen into the power of the enemy are entitled to the *status* of prisoners of war:

— members of the armed forces of a party to the conflict or of militias or volunteer corps forming part of such armed forces;
— members of other militias and members of other volunteer corps, including those of organised resistance movements;
— members of regular armed forces who profess allegiance to a government or an authority not recognised by the detaining power; and
— inhabitants of a non-occupied territory who have spontaneously taken up arms to resist an invading force, provided that they carry arms openly and respect the laws and customs of war.[13]

Quite clearly, the members of the Taliban Army apprehended during the military operation in Afghanistan belong to the first category enlisted in Article 4. The language of Article 4A refers simply to "the armed forces of a party to the conflict". The Taliban undoubtedly constituted a party to the conflict; the fact that the US did not recognise the Taliban as the government of Afghanistan is irrelevant.[14] Further, with regard to the argument that members of the Taliban did not wear uniforms, it is clear from the drafting of the Convention that the condition that combatants must wear "fixed distinctive sign recognizable at a distance"[15] is only applicable to the category of "members of other militias and members of other volunteer corps, including those of organised resistance movements", contained in Article 4A(2), as is the requirement of "conducting operations in accordance with the laws and customs of war".[16] The argument that soldiers must be organised in "military units, as such, with identifiable chains of command",[17] finds no parallel in

[13] Art 4A(1), (2), (3) and (6), Third Geneva Convention. In addition there are two minor additional categories covering persons travelling with armed forces without being part thereof (para. 4) and members of the merchant marine and crews of civil aircraft not benefiting from a more favourable status under other rules of international law (para. 5).

[14] See Art 4A(3), Third Geneva Convention and Art 43(1), Additional Protocol I: "The armed forces of a Party to a conflict consist of all organized armed forces, groups and units which are under a command responsible to that Party for the conduct or its subordinates, *even if that Party is represented by a government or an authority not recognized by an adverse Party*" (emphasis added). See also the Fact Sheet, White House Press Office, 7 February 2002, above n 9: "Although we never recognized the Taliban as the legitimate Afghan government, Afghanistan is a party to the Convention, and the President has determined that the Taliban are covered by the Convention".

[15] Art 4A(2)(b), Third Geneva Convention.

[16] Art 4A(2)(d), Third Geneva Convention. The fact that the members of the armed forces qualify for prisoners of war status would not preclude them being tried for violations of the laws and customs of war; see Art 4A(2)(b), Third Geneva Convention.

[17] See Press Conference, Department of Defense, Secretary Rumsfeld, 8 February 2002, above n 9.

either the Third Geneva Convention, or in Additional Protocol I. The closest that these two instruments come is the requirement in Article 4A(2)(a) of the Third Geneva Convention "of being commanded by a person responsible for his subordinates", and Article 43(1) of the Protocol which provides that "armed forces shall be subject to an internal disciplinary system which, *inter alia*, shall enforce compliance with the rules of international law applicable in armed conflict." Finally, the argument that the Taliban violated the laws and customs of war because they "knowingly adopted and provided support" for the terrorist attacks of Al-Qaeda seems to be a further distortion of the provision of Article 4A(2)(d); apart from the fact that the provision is not applicable to the regular forces of a Party to a conflict, it provides that troops must *conduct their operations* in accordance with the laws and customs of war. Referring back to the actions of a group which, on the US hypothesis, is not even part of the Taliban, to prove a failure in this regard is, to say the least, strained.

The US reading of the Geneva Convention is a severe misinterpretation of the text of Article 4, and is at odds with the generally accepted conception of the category of prisoners of war; although it may be that "the war on terrorism is a war not envisaged when the Geneva Convention was signed in 1949",[18] this does not justify the US in unilaterally rewriting the rules. Further, the interpretation may have unintended consequences, in that other States in the future may attempt to employ the same reasoning, using the US position as a precedent. Moreover, groups such as the US Special Forces do not always wear "fixed and distinctive signs [of allegiance] recognisable from a distance", nor do they always carry their arms openly as required by Article 4A(2)(c).[19]

Turning to the position of the members of Al-Qaeda captured in Afghanistan, the US position that the Geneva Conventions do not apply to them at all because they are "a foreign terrorist group"[20] is entirely inconsistent with the scheme of the Geneva Conventions, which aims at ensuring that no-one is left without protection.[21] From a systematic reading of all of the Geneva Conventions, the position of the US is untenable. The protection of the Geneva Conventions does not only extend to prisoners of war; all individuals captured during an international armed conflict are entitled to some protection under the Geneva system. The whole

[18] See, Statement of the Press Secretary on the Geneva Conventions, above n 12.
[19] See, however, Art 44(3), Additional Protocol I.
[20] Fact Sheet, White House Press Office, 7 February 2002, above n 9.
[21] Further, it is inconsistent with the attempt to link the actions of Al-Qaeda to the Taliban, noted above.

system aims at guaranteeing that "nobody in enemy hands can fall outside the law."[22] Accordingly,

> [e]very person in enemy hands must have some status under international law: he is either a prisoner of war and, as such, covered by the Third Geneva Convention, a civilian covered by the Fourth Convention, [or] a member of the medical personnel of the armed forces who is covered by the First Convention. There is no intermediate status … .[23]

While it is indisputable that the members of Al-Qaeda did not belong to the regular army of the Taliban, and therefore do not qualify as prisoners of war on that basis, they nevertheless formed a hierarchically organised militia which took an active part in the hostilities, had a connection with a State or a group that was Party to the conflict and therefore would seem, at least *prima facie* to fall within the provisions of Article 4A(2) of the Third Convention which covers "[m]embers of other militias and members of other volunteer corps, including those of organised resistance movements, belonging to a Party to the conflict and operating in or outside their own territory". However, if one were to interpret the conditions contained in Article 4A(2) narrowly, it would certainly be possible to deny the members of Al-Qaeda the status of prisoners of war.

The concepts of "unlawful combatants" and of "battlefield detainees" that the US authorities have used to define the Al-Qaeda members held in Guantanamo, and which according to them mean that the detainees fall entirely outside the protection of the Conventions,[24] appear nowhere in the Geneva Conventions or in Additional Protocol I. Nevertheless, the term is used in legal literature and in military manuals to indicate "all persons taking a direct part in hostilities without being entitled to do so and who therefore cannot be classified as prisoners of war when falling into the power of the enemy".[25] Those individuals still enjoy some protection

[22] ICRC, *Commentary: IV Geneva Convention Relative to the Protection of Civilian Persons in Time of War* (Pictet (ed), Geneva, 1958), at 51. The International Criminal Tribunal for the Former Yugoslavia has explicitly affirmed the principle of the complementarity of the Geneva Conventions, stating that "there is no gap between the Third and Fourth Geneva Conventions. If an individual is not entitled to the protection of the Third Convention as a prisoner of war … he or she necessarily falls within the ambit of [the Fourth Convention], provided that its art. 4 requirements [defining a protected person] are satisfied", *Celebici*, Case IT–96–21, Trial Chamber, judgment of 16 November 1998, para. 271.

[23] ICRC, *Commentary: IV Geneva Convention Relative to the Protection of Civilian Persons in Time of War*, above n 22, at 51.

[24] See News Briefing, Department of Defense, Secretary Rumsfeld, above n 8: "They will be handled not as prisoners of wars, because they're not, but as unlawful combatants. The — as I understand it, technically unlawful combatants do not have any rights under the Geneva Convention." See also Statement of the Press Secretary on the Geneva Conventions, above n 12.

[25] K Dormann, "The Legal Situation of 'Unlawful/Unprivileged Combatants'", (2003) 85 *International Review of the Red Cross* 45, at 46. See also R Baxter, "So-called 'Unprivileged Belligerency': Spies, Guerrilla and Saboteurs", (1951) 28 *British Yearbook of International Law*

under the Geneva system, and in particular under the Fourth Geneva Convention. According to Article 4, which defines the personal scope of application of the Convention:

> Persons protected by the Convention are those who, at a given moment and in any manner whatsoever, find themselves, in case of a conflict or occupation, in the hands of a Party to the conflict or Occupying Power of which they are not nationals.[26]

The protection of the Fourth Geneva Convention extends also to non-Afghani citizens captured in the territory of Afghanistan during military operations, unless they are nationals of one of the belligerents in the conflict or of a State that is not a party to the Geneva Conventions.

That active participation in the hostilities does not deprive individuals which are in the hands of a Party to the conflict of their status of protected persons under the Fourth Geneva Convention is confirmed by Article 5 of the Convention. That Article states that where "an individual protected person is definitely suspected of or engaged in activities hostile to the security of the State, [he] shall not be entitled to claim such rights and privileges under the present Convention ... as would be prejudicial to the security of the State". The fact that only those rights and privileges that would be "prejudicial to the security of State" are curtailed, demonstrates that an individual is entitled to the status of protected person even if he or she commits belligerent acts. Such an individual must "nevertheless be treated with humanity, and in case of trial, shall not be deprived of the rights of fair and regular trial prescribed by the present Convention" and must "be granted the full rights and privileges of a protected person under the present Convention at the earliest date consistent with the security of the State."

Such an interpretation is confirmed also by the International Committee of the Red Cross (ICRC), which has made absolutely clear its position that failure to meet the conditions necessary to qualify as prisoners of war does not exclude members of irregular forces totally from protection under the Geneva Conventions. To the contrary, the ICRC

323, at 328; G Aldrich, "The Taliban, Al Qaeda and the Detention of Illegal Combatants", (2002) 96 *American Journal of International Law* 892; J Klabbers "'Rebel with a Cause?' Terrorists and Humanitarian Law," (2003) 14 *European Journal of International Law* 299.

[26] Art 4 further specifies that "Nationals of a State which is not bound by the Convention are not protected by it. Nationals of a neutral State who find themselves in the territory of a belligerent State, and nationals of a co-belligerent State, shall not be regarded as protected persons while the State of which they are nationals has normal diplomatic representation in the State in whose hands they are" (para. 2) and "Persons protected by the [First, Second and Third] Geneva Convention[s] shall not be considered as protected persons within the meaning of the present Convention" (para. 4).

Commentary to the Fourth Geneva Convention explains that such people must be protected as civilians.[27]

Finally, quite apart from dubious qualifications made by the US, the unilateral classification of an entire group of individuals captured during an armed conflict as not being entitled to prisoner of war status is in conflict with the provisions of Article 5(2) of the Third Geneva Convention. According to that provision, in case of doubt a competent tribunal should make any determination about the *status* of the detainees on an individual basis.[28] The principle set forth by Article 5(2) has in the past been recognised by the United States, which established tribunals to determine the status of captured individuals, in conflicts from Vietnam to the first Gulf War.[29] In 1997, a Regulation issued by military authorities set out detailed procedures for tribunals that could be established to determine the status of individual apprehended during military operations.[30] Indeed, the Regulation seems to extend the guarantees set forth in Article 5 of the Third Convention to a wider group of subjects, in that it establishes that a person having committed a belligerent act or engaged in hostile activities in aid of enemy armed forces is entitled to have his or her status determined by

[27] See ICRC, *Commentary: IV Geneva Convention*, above n 22, at 50: "If members of a resistance movement who have fallen into enemy hands do not fulfil [the conditions for POW status] they must be considered to be protected persons within the meaning of the present Convention."

[28] Art 5(2), Third Geneva Convention reads: "Should any doubt arise as to whether persons, having committed a belligerent act and having fallen into the hands of the enemy, belong to any of the categories enumerated in Art 4, such persons shall enjoy the protection of the present Convention *until such time as their status has been determined by a competent tribunal*" [emphasis added]. See Art 45, Additional Protocol I: (1) A person who takes part in hostilities and falls into the power of an adverse Party shall be presumed to be a prisoner of war, and therefore shall be protected by the Third Convention, if he claims the status of prisoner of war, or if he appears to be entitled to such status … . Should any doubt arise as to whether any such person is entitled to the status of prisoner of war, he shall continue to have such status and, therefore, to be protected by the Third Convention and this Protocol until such time as his status has been determined by a competent tribunal. (2) If a person who has fallen into the power of an adverse Party is not held as a prisoner of war and is to be tried by that Party for an offence arising out of the hostilities, he shall have the right to assert his entitlement to prisoner-of-war status before a judicial tribunal and to have that question adjudicated.

[29] See MO Lacey and BJ Bill (eds), *US Military Judge Advocate General Operational Law Handbook* (Judge Advocate General's School, Charlottesville, 2000), at 7. See also the statement made in 1987 by the Deputy Legal Advisor to the US State Department: "[the US] do support the principle that, should any doubt arise as to whether a person is entitled to combatant status, he be so treated until his status has been determined by a competent tribunal, as well as the principle that a person who has fallen into the power of an adversary is not held as a prisoner of war and is to be tried for an offence arising out of the hostilities, he should have the right to assert his entitlement before a judicial tribunal and to have that question adjudicated", Matheson, above n 7, at 425–26.

[30] Army Regulation 190–8, Enemy Prisoners of War, Retained Personnel, Civilian Internees and Other Detainees (1 October 1997). On the regulation and on the relevant practice of the United States, see Y Naqvi, "Doubtful Prisoner-of-War Status", (2003) 84 *International Review of the Red Cross* 571, at 584–87.

a competent tribunal not only where "any doubt arises as to the whether he belongs to one of the categories enumerated in Article 4 GPW",[31] but also in cases where such person, "although not appearing to be entitled to prisoner of war status, asserts that he or she is entitled to treatment as prisoner of war."[32]

While US authorities have recently assured that the US will respect its obligations under Article 5 of the Third Geneva Convention in relation to those apprehended during the conflict in Iraq, by treating all belligerents captured during the conflict as prisoners of war until a competent tribunal determines that they are not entitled to prisoner-of-war status,[33] until now no tribunal of this kind has been called upon to determine the status of the individuals captured during the Afghan conflict.[34] The US determination that the Third Geneva Convention simply does not apply to those captured in Afghanistan not only is in contradiction with its earlier approach and its stated intentions in Iraq, but also seems to preclude any judicial consideration at all of its qualification of the detainees.

The US authorities do not seem particularly concerned by the fact that the first consequence of the denial of the status of prisoners of war to those apprehended in Afghanistan, and their inevitable qualification as protected persons under the Fourth Geneva Convention, is the characterisation of the transfer of those individual to Guantanamo as a blatant violation of international humanitarian law. Such transfers constitute a grave breach of the Fourth Geneva Convention.[35] Article 49 contains an absolute ban on forcible transfers, providing that "Individual or mass forcible transfers, as well as deportations of protected persons from occupied territory to the territory of the Occupying Power or to that of any other country, occupied or not, are prohibited, *regardless of motive*".[36]

[31] Section 1–6(a), Army Regulation 190–8.

[32] Section 1–6(b), Army Regulation 190–8.

[33] See Briefing on Geneva Conventions, EPW's and War Crimes, Department of Defense, 7 April 2003, available at <http://www.defenselink.mil/news/Apr2003/t04072003_t407genv.html>.

[34] The non-compliance of US authorities with the procedural guarantees established by Art 5(2) of the Third Geneva Convention has been criticized by the UN High Commissioner for Human Rights, who in a statement issued on January 2002 recalled that "the legal status of the detainees, and their entitlement to prisoner-of-war status, if disputed, must be determined by a competent tribunal, in accordance with the provisions of Art 5 of the [Third] Geneva Convention", *Statement of High Commissioner of Human Rights on detention of Taliban and Al-Qaeda prisoners at US base in Guantanamo Bay, Cuba*, 16 January 2002 (available at <http://www.unchr.ch>).

[35] See Art 147, Fourth Geneva Convention. If the detainees had been qualified as prisoners of war, then transfer would not be a grave breach, although see Articles 46 and 48, Third Geneva Convention.

[36] Emphasis added.

IV. CONSEQUENCES OF QUALIFICATION OF THE DETAINEES AS PROTECTED PERSONS

The qualification of the individuals apprehended during the Afghan conflict as prisoners of war under the Third Geneva Convention or as protected persons under the Fourth Convention has relevant consequences for the standard of treatment they should be granted. While the basic principles on the respect of human dignity have to be respected regardless of the classification under one or the other category, the qualification of the detainees as unlawful combatants deprives them of some guarantees, which are envisaged exclusively for prisoners of war.

A. Humane treatment and non discrimination

Both the Third and the Fourth Geneva Convention state the principle that protected persons who have fallen in enemy hands should be humanely treated at all times[37] and that they should enjoy the protection of the Conventions "without any adverse distinction based, in particular, on race, nationality, religion or political opinion".[38] In particular, the Third Geneva Convention specifies this principle, providing that prisoners of war must be kept in facilities in conditions as favourable as those of the forces of the detaining power in the same area,[39] they should be protected against acts of violence or of reprisal, they should be granted respect for persons and honour[40] and must be afforded complete latitude in the exercise of religion, including attendance at services, on condition they comply with disciplinary routine.[41] As already noted, Article 5 of the Fourth Geneva Convention specifies that, at a minimum, humane treatment shall be granted even to those people who have engaged in hostile activities.

B. Interrogation

One of the main consequences of the qualification of the detainees as prisoners of war by the US would be that those individuals would enjoy

[37] Art 13, Third Geneva Convention; Art 27, Fourth Geneva Convention.
[38] Art 16, Third Geneva Convention; Arts 13 and 27, Fourth Geneva Convention.
[39] Art 25, Third Geneva Convention.
[40] Art 13, Third Geneva Convention: "prisoners of war must at all times be protected, particularly against acts of violence or intimidation and against insults and public curiosity. Measures of reprisal against prisoners of war are prohibited"; Art 14: "Prisoners of war are entitled in all circumstances to respect for their persons and their honour .... Prisoners of war shall retain the full civil capacity which they enjoyed at the time of their capture. The Detaining Power may not restrict the exercise, either within or without its own territory, of the rights such capacity confers except in so far as the captivity requires".
[41] Art 34, Third Geneva Convention.

the protection of Article 17 of the Third Convention, which provides that prisoners of war are required only to give their name, rank, date of birth and army serial numbers to interrogators and sets forth the prohibition of physical or mental torture and of coercion to obtain information. The same Article establishes that prisoners who decline to provide information may not be threatened, insulted or exposed to unpleasant or disadvantageous treatment.[42] Thus, the administration presumably thought that, by not classifying the detainees as prisoners of war, it could enjoy a wide discretion in questioning them.

C. Criminal Prosecution

As for the prosecution of terrorist suspects apprehended during the Afghan conflict, the qualification of the detainees at Guantanamo as prisoners of war would not undermine the effectiveness of criminal prosecution. As noted also by the International Committee of the Red Cross,[43] the Third Geneva Convention, while providing for the return of prisoners of war at the end of the conflict,[44] expressly sets out an exception to this rule: the detaining State can hold the prisoners of war if they have been accused of war crimes or of other crimes.[45] Moreover, the Convention clearly implies that prisoners of war can be tried for offences committed before capture, *provided that they are granted all the guarantees set forth in the Convention.*[46] Consequently, US authorities could indict the detainees of Guantanamo for the war crimes, if any, committed during the armed conflict in Afghanistan and for other crimes with which they could be committed *during or before* the conflict in Afghanistan.

Assuming that the members of Al-Qaeda captured in Afghanistan are prisoners of war, the problem is that of determining what crimes they could be indicted for. Prisoners of war may not be tried for having

[42] Art 17, Third Geneva Convention: "Every prisoner of war, when questioned on the subject, is bound to give only his surname, first names and rank, date of birth, and army, regimental, personal or serial number, or failing this, equivalent information. If he wilfully infringes this rule, he may render himself liable to a restriction of the privileges accorded to his rank or status.... No physical or mental torture, nor any other form of coercion, may be inflicted on prisoners of war to secure from them information of any kind whatever. Prisoners of war who refuse to answer may not be threatened, insulted, or exposed to any unpleasant or disadvantageous treatment of any kind [...] The questioning of prisoners of war shall be carried out in a language which they understand".

[43] See "Geneva Convention on Prisoners of War", ICRC Press Release, 9 February 2002.

[44] Art 118(1), Third Geneva Convention.

[45] Art 119(5), Third Geneva Convention.

[46] Art 85, Third Geneva Convention provides: "Prisoners of war prosecuted under the laws of the Detaining Power for acts committed prior to capture shall retain, even if convicted, the benefits of the present Convention". The relevant fair trial guarantees are set out in Articles 84, 86–88, 99–108.

committed acts of war against other combatants. However, they may be prosecuted for the same offences for which the forces of the detaining power could be tried, including common crimes unrelated to the conflict, war crimes and crimes against humanity. The Third Geneva Convention provides that "[n]o prisoner of war may be tried or sentenced for an act which is not forbidden by *the law of the Detaining Power* or *by international law*, in force at the time the said act was committed".[47] Acts of international terrorism, and in particular the acts of which some members of Al-Qaeda are accused, are criminal both under international law[48] and under US domestic legislation. Thus, the qualification of acts of terrorism as *indictable offences* under Article 119(5) of the Third Geneva Convention and the prosecution of members of Al-Qaeda by US authorities do not represent an issue under international humanitarian law. If adequate evidence can be collected, the US would be perfectly entitled to charge the Guantanamo detainees with war crimes, crimes against humanity or other violations of US domestic criminal law, regardless of their status as prisoners of war, and it could legitimately detain and prosecute them even after the end of the military operations in Afghanistan.[49] Moreover, instead of conducting the prosecution itself, the US could choose to extradite some suspects, in cases where sufficient incriminating evidence exists, to another State party of the Geneva Convention interested in the prosecution.[50] Thus, if their home countries wanted to prosecute Al-Qaeda members, the US could consider handing over the suspects, although the modalities of rendition would depend on the terms of any extradition treaty with the country involved.[51]

[47] Art 99, Third Geneva Convention [emphasis added].

[48] The killing of thousands of civilians might possibly qualify as a crime against humanity. Under the definition of Art 7 of the ICC Statute (Statute of the International Criminal Court (Rome, 17 July 1998, UN Doc. A/CONF.183/9 (1998), entered into force 1 July 2002), a crime against humanity is defined as, *inter alia*, murder or "other inhumane acts of a similar character intentionally causing great suffering, or serious injury to body or mental and physical health", provided that such act is "committed as a part of a widespread or systematic attack directed against any civilian population, with knowledge of the attack."

[49] Art 103, Third Geneva Convention provides that "Judicial investigations relating to a prisoner of war shall be conducted as rapidly as circumstances permit and so that his trial shall take place as soon as possible. A prisoner of war shall not be confined while awaiting trial unless a member of the armed forces of the Detaining Power would be so confined if he were accused of a similar offence, or if it is essential to do so in the interests of national security. In no circumstances shall this confinement exceed three months."

[50] Art 45, Third Geneva Convention.

[51] The US has already declared that in most cases it would like to send suspects back to their own countries, if prosecution can be guaranteed. However, the US cannot stipulate how other countries should operate their criminal justice system. Most European States have an independent prosecution service, and cannot say whether suspects will be prosecuted before having seen the evidence and issued charges. As regards European countries, the European Convention on Human Rights (Convention for the Protection of Human Rights and Fundamental Freedoms, Rome, 4 November 1950, ETS No. 5, in force 3 September 1953) stipulates that suspects are entitled to a "fair and public hearing ... by an independent and

D. Trials

The Third Geneva Convention sets out guarantees regarding the trial of captured combatants: according to the Convention

> [I]n no circumstances whatever shall a prisoner of war be tried by a court of any kind which does not offer the essential *guarantees of independence* and *impartiality* as generally recognised, and, in particular, the procedure of which does not afford the accused the rights and means of defence provided for by Article 105.[52]

Such rights and means of defence consist, *inter alia*, of assistance by a qualified advocate or counsel of the prisoner's own choice, the calling of witnesses, and the services of an interpreter. Moreover, the first part of Article 84, which states that "prisoners of war shall be tried only by a military court, unless the existing laws of the Detaining Power expressly permit the civil courts to try a member of the armed forces of the Detaining Power in respect of the particular offence alleged to have been committed by the prisoner of war", has to be read to mean that prisoners of war have to be tried by the courts — whether civil or military — which would have jurisdiction over the members of the Detaining Power's own armed forces.[53] If such a rule was to apply, Guantanamo detainees could only be tried by US court martial procedures and not by military tribunals set up under emergency legislation, let alone military commissions like the ones envisaged by the Presidential Military Order of November 2001.[54] The idea of subjecting terrorist suspects to the jurisdiction of military commissions was

impartial tribunal established by law" (Art 6); however, some human rights groups have expressed concern that trials in countries such as Saudi Arabia and Pakistan would not be fair and might be used as political showcases.

[52] Art 84(2), Third Geneva Convention [emphasis added].

[53] Such an interpretation is supported also by Art 81, which, in disciplining the application of penal and disciplinary sanctions to prisoners of war, sets forth the so-called *principle of assimilation*. See also ICRC, *Commentary: III Geneva Convention Relative to the Treatment of Prisoners of War*, (J Pictet (ed), Geneva, 1960), 406–9 and 411–19.

[54] Presidential Military Order on Detention, Treatment, and Trial of Certain Non-Citizens in the War Against Terrorism, issued by President George W. Bush, November 13, 2001 (66 FED REG 57833 (2001)) (hereafter 'Presidential Order'). The Presidential Order has been further implemented, in accordance with section 4(b), by regulations and instructions emanating from the Department of Defense: Department of Defense, Military Commission Order No 1, 21 March 2002 (hereafter 'Military Commission Order'); Department of Defense, Military Commission Instructions No 1–8, April 30, 2003 (hereafter 'Military Commission Instructions'). All documents are available at <http://www.dfenselink.mil>. For further discussion of the fucntioning and of the compatibility of the proposed Military Commissions with internationally accepted human rights standards, see, in this volume, S Borelli, 'The Rendition of Terrorist Suspects to the United States: Human Rights and the Limits of International Cooperation'.

to put the suspects on trial faster and in greater secrecy than in ordinary criminal courts. The decision has, however, been widely criticised by human rights groups and by some of the close allies of the United States, who fear that suspects would lack the legal protection offered in criminal courts and that trials might be conducted in secret without outside scrutiny. Even after the disclosure of the modalities of their operation, the legality of the military commissions and their consistency with international human rights standards remains questionable. From the perspective of humanitarian law, the legality of such commissions is also doubtful. Some of the requirements of a "regular" trial — such as the right of a defendant to appoint his own lawyer and that proceedings be held mainly in public — may possibly be met. But whether a military commission set up by executive order can possibly guarantee the independence and impartiality of a regular trial — as required by Article 84 — is another matter.

Suspects should be brought before regular military tribunals, usually reserved for the court martial of soldiers of the US Army. These would be less controversial than the military commissions being proposed under the Presidential Order, as they are governed by well-established procedural rules, which provide for adequate guarantees for the defendant, thus meeting the requirements of fair trials established by international humanitarian and human rights norms.

The US authorities have claimed that the qualification of terrorist suspects apprehended in Afghanistan as prisoners of war would seriously jeopardise the fight against terrorism. This contention is clearly unfounded. Indeed, as the International Committee of the Red Cross restated in relation to the treatment of the individuals held at Guantanamo, "compliance with international humanitarian law in no manner constitutes an obstacle to the struggle against terror and crime", since "[i]nternational humanitarian law grants the detaining power the right to legally prosecute prisoners of war suspected of having committed war crimes or any other criminal offence prior to or during the hostilities."[55] The above considerations show that in qualifying the Guantanamo detainees as prisoners of war, the US would not only behave in conformity with its international obligations, but would also in no way jeopardise the fight against international terrorism. Prisoners of war status does not shield captured combatants against criminal prosecution. Moreover, by treating prisoners as prisoners of war, the US would not automatically prejudice its security concerns.

Finally, from a pragmatic point of view, the denial of the humanitarian law protection to detainees from Afghanistan could result in a mistreatment of captured American soldiers at some future point. The Hague and Geneva Conventions have provided a general framework of protection

[55] "Geneva Convention on Prisoners of War", ICRC Press Release, above n 43.

for combatants and civilians in time of war. The US has always argued for a broad interpretation of these conventions in particular regarding prisoners of war, both to set an example and to ensure a fair treatment of American soldiers when captured.

IV. THE INTERPLAY OF HUMANITARIAN LAW AND HUMAN RIGHTS LAW

It is often said that the rules of humanitarian law are complementary to the provisions of human rights law, in that the former apply to situations of armed conflict, while the latter provide principally for the protection of fundamental rights in peacetime.[56] However, care needs to be taken; the two areas do not live completely distinct lives.[57] While it is true that some human rights guarantees can be derogated from or limited in times of armed conflict or of national emergency,[58] certain core guarantees apply in all circumstances,[59] including situations of conflict and therefore, "in situations of armed conflict, the protections under international human rights and humanitarian law may complement and reinforce one another, sharing as they do a common nucleus of non-derogable rights and a common purpose of promoting human life and dignity."[60] Of note also in this context is the "Turku Declaration" which attempted to codify minimum standards "applicable in all situations, including internal violence, disturbances, tensions, and public emergency, and which cannot be derogated from under any circumstances".[61] Article 2 of the Declaration provides

[56] See the Advisory Opinion delivered by the International Court of Justice on the *Legality of the Threat or Use of Nuclear Weapons,* ICJ Reports 1996, p 226, at 239, para 24: some States "suggested that the [ICCPR] was directed to the protection of human rights in peacetime but that question relating to unlawful loss of life in hostilities were governed by the law applicable in armed conflict."

[57] See R Kolb, "The Relationship between International Humanitarian Law and Human Rights Law: A Brief History of the 1948 Universal Declaration of Human Rights and the 1949 Geneva Conventions", (1998) 324 *International Review of the Red Cross* 409; R Quentin-Baxter, "Human Rights and Humanitarian Law: Confluence or Conflict?", (1985) 9 *Australian Yearbook of International Law* 101; L Doswald-Beck and S Vité, "International Humanitarian Law and Human Rights Law" (1993) 293 *International Review of the Red Cross* 94.

[58] Art 15, ECHR; Art 27, ACHR; Art 4, ICCPR.

[59] See, however, the ICJ in *Legality of the Threat or Use of Nuclear Weapons,* above n 56, at 240, para 25, which observed that although "the protection of the [ICCPR] does not cease in time of war", except in accordance with the derogation provision of art. 4, with regard to the non-derogable right not to be arbitrarily deprived of one's life, the applicable standard of arbitrariness "falls to be determined by the applicable *lex specialis,* namely, the law applicable to armed conflict."

[60] Inter-American Commission of Human Rights, *Abella v Argentina,* Case No 11.137, Report No 5/97, Annual Report of the IACHR 1997, para 160–61. See also *Coard et al v the United States,* Inter-American Commission on Human Rights, Case 10.951, Report No 109/99, 29 September 1999, para 39.

[61] Art 1, Declaration of Minimum Humanitarian Standards, Turku/Åbo, 2 December 1990, available at <http://www.abo.fi/instut/imr/publications_online_text.htm>.

that these standards "shall be respected by, and applied to all persons, groups and authorities, irrespective of their legal status and without any adverse discrimination".

Therefore, even if the United States refuses to recognise that terrorist suspects detained in Guantanamo are entitled to the status of protected persons under the relevant instruments of international humanitarian law, the treatment of these individuals must nevertheless be in conformity with non-derogable international human rights standards deriving both from customary international law and from the human rights treaties to which the US is a party.[62]

In several recent decisions relating to the issue of the indefinite and incommunicado detention of foreign citizens at Guantanamo, US courts have held that the detainees were seized and all times have been held outside the sovereign territory of the United States. The courts have relied on the fact that the agreement between the US and Cuba on the lease of Guantanamo to the United States declared that "sovereignty" over Guantanamo Bay remained with Cuba, and held that the Constitution does not apply to territories and people which are not under the sovereign power of the United States.[63] As a consequence, those detained at Guantanamo are not entitled to invoke the rights guaranteed by the US Constitution before any US court.[64]

[62] The United States is a party to the International Covenant on Civil and Political Rights (New York, 16 December 1966, 999 UNTS 171, entered into force 23 March 1976 (hereinafter "ICCPR"), ratified by the United States on 8 June 1992); the United Nations Convention against Torture and Other Cruel, Inhuman or Degrading Treatment and Punishment (New York, 10 December 1984, UN Doc. A/39/51 (1984), entered into force 26 June 1987, ratified by the United States on 21 October 1994) and it is a signatory of the American Convention of Human Rights (San José, 22 November 1969, *OAS Treaty Series* No 36, in force 18 July 1978 (hereinafter "ACHR"), signed by the United States on 6 January 1977). Being a Member of the Organization of American States, the US is also bound by the American Declaration of the Rights and Duties of Man, OAS Res. XXX, adopted in 1948 by the Ninth International Conference of American States. The Declaration is technically not a legally binding agreement under international law; however, it is a source of legal obligations for OAS Member States: see, *Interpretation of the American Declaration on the Rights and Duties of Man within the Framework of Article 64 of the American Convention on Human Rights*, Advisory Opinion OC-10/90 of 14 July 1989, IACtHR, *Series A*, No 10 (1989), para 45.

[63] *Al Odah v United States*, 321 F3d 1134 (DC Cir, 2003). The Supreme Court has since granted *certiorari* to hear the appeals on the narrow question of whether the US courts have jurisdiction to determine the legality of the detention; see further n 77 *infra*. See also *Coalition of Clargy v Bush*, 189 FSupp 2d 1036, 1046 (CD, Cal, 2002), aff'd *Coalition of Clergy v Bush*, 310 F3d 1153 (9th Cir 2002). Note, however, that the Court of Appeals for the Ninth Circuit, while affirming that the coalition lacked standing to seek a writ of *habeas corpus*, vacated "the district court's determination that there was no jurisdiction in the Central District of California and its far-reaching ruling that there is no United States court that may entertain any of the habeas claims of any of the detainees" (at 1165).

[64] Commenting on the decision of the United States' Court of Appeals for the District of Columbia Circuit in *Al Odah*, above n 63, the UN Special Rapporteur on the independence of judges and lawyers, stated that it "appears to imply that a government of a sovereign State could lease a piece of land from a neighbouring State, set up a detention camp, fully operate

Quite apart from any consideration of the legitimacy of such decisions in the light of US constitutional law, the qualification of the military base of Guantanamo as an area outside the sovereign territory of the United States does not relieve the US of its obligation to respect internationally recognised human rights standards.

Many of the major human rights instruments, including those binding on the United States, oblige States to ensure to everyone *within their territory* or *subject to their jurisdiction* the rights contained therein.[65] The concept of "individual subject to the jurisdiction" has been interpreted widely by human rights monitoring organs for the purpose of determining the personal scope of application of those treaties, to include individuals within the power or under the control of a State party even if not situated within the territory of the State Party.[66] Under the relevant jurisprudence, it is clear that States" human rights obligations can extend to their extraterritorial treatment of non-nationals.

The case law of the European Court of Human Rights demonstrates that, even though the recognition of the exercise of extra-territorial jurisdiction by a Contracting State for the purpose of determining the reach and the scope of application of the Convention is exceptional, such jurisdiction has to be recognised "when a State, through the effective control of the relevant territory and its inhabitants abroad as a consequence of military occupation or through the consent, invitation or acquiescence of the Government of that territory, exercises all or some of the public powers normally to be exercised by that Government."[67] Similarly, in 1999 the Inter-American Commission of Human Rights held that although the expression "person subject to a State's jurisdiction" "most commonly refers to persons within a state's territory, it may, under given circumstances, refer to conduct with an extraterritorial locus where the person concerned is present in the territory of one state, but subject to the

and control it, arrest suspects of terrorism from other jurisdictions, send them to this camp, deny them their legal rights — including principles of due process generally granted to its own citizens — on grounds that the camp is physically outside its jurisdiction" and that "[b]y such conduct, the Government of the United States, in this case, will be seen as systematically evading application of domestic and international law so as to deny these suspects their legal rights": see Press Release, "US Court Decision on Guantanamo Detainees has Serious Implications for Rule of Law, says UN Human Rights Expert", 12 March 2003, available at <http://www.unhchr.ch>.

[65] See, eg, Art 1, ECHR; Art 2, ICCPR; Art 1, ACHR.

[66] T Meron, "Extraterritoriality of Human Rights Treaties", (1995) 89 *American Journal of International Law* 78, at 81.

[67] *Bankovic and others v Belgium and 16 other contracting States* (Application no. 52207/99), decision on admissibility of 12 December 2001, para. 71. See also *Loizidou v Turkey* (Preliminary Objections), judgment of 23 March 1995, ECHR, *Series A*, no. 310, para. 62 and *Drodz and Janousek v France and Spain*, judgment of 26 June 1992, ECHR, *Series A*, No. 240, para. 91.

control of another state."[68] Therefore, according to the Commission, "the inquiry turns not on the presumed victim's nationality or presence within a particular geographic area, but on whether, under the specific circumstances, the State observed the rights of a person subject to its authority and control."[69]

In early 2002, the Inter-American Commission expressly recognised that individuals detained at Guantanamo are "within the jurisdiction" of the United States and that therefore the US is under an obligation to respect the obligations laid down in the relevant international instruments with respect to those people.[70] After noting that individual detainees at Guantanamo "remain wholly within the authority and control of the United States government", the Commission underlined that no person under the authority and control of a State, regardless of his or her circumstances, can be deprived of legal protection for his or her fundamental and non-derogable human rights and invited the United States to take the necessary steps in order to ensure that the legal status of each of the detainees was clarified and that they were afforded the legal protections, which should not fall below the minimum standards of non-derogable rights.[71]

Another firm reaction to the position of US authorities on Guantanamo detainees can be found in the practice of the Human Rights Committee which is in the process of adopting a General Comment on "The Nature of Legal Obligations Imposed on States Parties to the Covenant". The latest draft of May 2003 expressly declares that, under Article 2(1) of the Covenant, "a State Party must respect and ensure the rights laid down in the Covenant to anyone *within the power or effective control* of that State Party, even if not situated within the territory of the State Party", including "those within the power or effective control of the forces of a State party acting outside its territory."[72] It seems clear that the drafters had in mind the situation of the detainees held at Guantanamo.

The practice of regional and universal human rights monitoring organs lends support to the proposition that the human rights obligations of a State apply with respect to its treatment of non-nationals outside the sovereign territory of the State if such individuals find themselves under its control and therefore that, in the present case, the US is obliged to respect its human rights obligations in relation to those detained at Guantanamo.

[68] *Coard*, above n 60, para. 37.
[69] *Ibid.*
[70] Inter-American Commission of Human Rights, *Precautionary Measures in Guantanamo Bay, Cuba*, 13 March, 2002. See also Annual Report of the Inter-American Commission on Human Rights 2002, Chapter III, para. 80, available at <http<www.cidh.oas.org>.
[71] *Precautionary Measures in Guantanamo Bay*, above n 70.
[72] Human Rights Committee, "Draft General Comment on Article 2, The Nature of the General Legal Obligations Imposed on States Parties to the Covenant", UN Doc. CCPR/C/74/CRP.4/Rev.3, 5 May 2003, para. 9.

Quite apart from the question of the respect of the right to fair trial in the unfortunate but extremely probable event the US administration decides to try terrorist suspects before the commissions envisaged by the Military Commission Order issued by the Department of Defense,[73] and the consistent pattern of allegations that detainees at Guantanamo are subjected to inhuman and degrading treatment, serious questions about the compatibility of the US conduct with internationally accepted human rights standards arise from the choice of the US administration to detain suspected terrorist in Guantanamo indefinitely, without indicting them with any specific crime. On 19 February 2002 a petition for *habeas corpus* was commenced before the District Court for the District of Columbia on behalf of three prisoners detained at Guantanamo Bay.[74] A similar action based, *inter alia,* on violation of due process was brought by relatives of other Guantanamo detainees.[75] As already noted, after joining the cases, the Court of Appeals, affirmed the decisions of the District Court, and ruled that the military base at Guantanamo Bay was outside the sovereign territory of the United States and that, in consequence of this fact and the fact that the claimants were aliens, the Court had no jurisdiction to entertain their claims, thus denying the possibility for foreign citizens detained at Guantanamo to question the legality of their detention before any court of the United States.[76] The United States Supreme Court has recently granted certiorari in the *Rasul* and *Al Odah* cases, although only on the narrow question of "Whether United States courts lack jurisdiction to consider challenges to the legality of the detention of foreign nationals captured abroad in connection with hostilities and incarcerated at the Guantanamo Bay Naval Base, Cuba."[77] However, should the Supreme Court decide that the US courts do have jurisdiction to rule on the legality of the detention, it is to be expected that the merits of the cases will be remitted to the DC District Court.

Moreover, the Presidential Order on Detention, Treatment, and Trial of Certain Non-Citizens in the War Against Terrorism expressly declares that "any individual subject to [the] order ... shall not be privileged to seek any remedy or maintain any proceeding, directly or indirectly, or to have any such remedy or proceeding sought on the individual's behalf, in

[73] Military Commission Order No 1, above n 54. On the legality of the Military Commissions under internationally accepted standards on fair trial, see, S Borelli, 'The Rendition of Terrorist Suspects to the United States', above n 54, in particular at 75–81.
[74] *Rasul v Bush,* Civil Action No 02–299, filed before the District Court for the District of Columbia by the families of an Australian and two British citizens held by US forces in Guantanamo Bay.
[75] See *Al Odah,* above n 63, filed by the families of twelve Kuwaiti nationals detained at the US Naval Base at Guantanamo Bay.
[76] *Al Odah,* above n 63.
[77] *Rasul v Bush, Al Odah v United States* (Cases 03–334 and 03–343), 10 November 2003. See also "Justices to Hear Case of Detainees at Guantánamo", *New York Times,* 11 November 2003.

(i) any court of the United States, or any State thereof, (ii) any court of any foreign nation, or (iii) any international tribunal,"[78] and thus seems to seek to oust jurisdiction of any court on persons indicated under the Order.

While the detention of terrorist suspects in Guantanamo may to a certain extent be justified as a measure strictly necessary in time of national emergency[79] (although the time period that has now elapsed renders this improbable), and the incompatibility of the condition of detention with internationally accepted human rights standards on human treatment has to be assessed on a case by case basis, the fact that individuals detained at Guantanamo have no means of challenging the legality of their detention renders their detention an "arbitrary detention" *per se* contrary to the fundamental norms of international human rights law, as well as international humanitarian law.[80]

Article 9 of the International Covenant of Civil and Political Rights, to which the United States is a party, affirms "the right to liberty and security of person". In particular, paragraph 4 provides "anyone who is deprived of his liberty by arrest or detention shall be entitled to take proceedings before a court, in order that a court may decide without delay on the lawfulness of his detention and order his release if the detention is not lawful."[81] In its General Comment No 8, the Human Rights Committee underlines that "the important guarantee laid down in paragraph 4, ie the right to control by a court of the legality of the detention, applies to *all persons* deprived of their liberty by arrest or detention" and that "also if so-called preventive detention is used, for reasons of public security, it must be controlled by these same provisions, ie it must not be arbitrary, and must be based on grounds and procedures established by law (para 1), information of the reasons must be given (para 2) and *court control of the detention must be available* (para 4)."[82]

The right of every individual deprived of his liberty to challenge the legality of his arrest is recognised also in Article 7 of the American Convention of Human Rights, paragraph 6 of which provides "Anyone who is deprived of his liberty shall be entitled to recourse to a competent court, in order that the court may decide without delay on the

[78] Sec 7 (b) (2), Presidential Military Order, above n 54.
[79] The President of the United States declared a national emergency in the immediate aftermath of the attacks of September 2001 (Proclamation No 7453, Declaration of a National Emergency by Reason of Certain Terrorist Attacks, 66 Fed Reg 48, 199 (14 Sept 2001)). Surprisingly, however, no formal notification of any derogations has been deposited by the US under the "emergency clauses" of any of the treaties to which the US is a party.
[80] See J Paust, "Judicial Power to Determine the Status and Rights of Persons Detained Without Trial", (2003) 44 *Harvard International Law Journal* 503.
[81] Art 9(4), ICCPR.
[82] Human Rights Committee, General Comment 8 on Article 9 (Sixteenth session, 1982), UN Doc HRI\GEN\1\Rev 1 at 8 (1994), paras 1 and 4 [emphasis added].

lawfulness of his arrest or detention and order his release if the arrest or detention is unlawful".[83] The right to *habeas corpus* is one of the judicial guarantees that cannot be derogated from even during a state of emergency, in that it is "essential for the protection of various rights whose derogation is prohibited ... and serve[s] to preserve legality in a democratic society."[84]

The position of the US on the Guantanamo detainees has been the object of strong criticism by many States, by international organisations, human rights monitoring bodies and NGOs.[85] In the *Abbasi* case,[86] the British Court of Appeal recognized that "in apparent contravention of fundamental principles recognised ... by international law, Mr Abbasi is at present arbitrarily detained in a 'legal black-hole'"[87] and took the unusual step of expressing its "deep concern that, in apparent contravention of fundamental principles of law, Mr Abbasi may be subject to indefinite detention in territory over which the United States has exclusive control with no opportunity to challenge the legitimacy of his detention before any court or tribunal."[88] However, on the narrow point before it, the Court affirmed the orthodox view that a State is under no obligation as a matter of international law to make diplomatic representations regarding the treatment of its nationals by another State, and that no such duty exists as a matter of British constitutional law. However, the decision of the court is striking for its oblique criticism of the position taken by the courts in the United States in the *Al Odah* and *Rasul* cases. One of the considerations expressly taken into account by the Court of Appeal in reaching its decision was that the Supreme Court had not yet refused to hear the cases;[89] however the court

[83] In its Advisory Opinion on the right to *habeas corpus*, the Inter-American Court declared that such a right is the necessary corollary of the possibility to impose limitation on the right to personal liberty in emergency situations. In the words of the Court "in a system governed by the rule of law it is entirely in order for an autonomous and independent judicial order to exercise control over the lawfulness of ... measures [taken to face a state of emergency] by verifying, for example, whether a detention based on the suspension of personal freedom complies with the legislation authorized by the state of emergency. In this context, habeas corpus acquires a new dimension of fundamental importance", *Habeas Corpus in Emergency Situations (Arts. 27(2) and 7(6) of the American Convention on Human Rights)*, Advisory Opinion OC-8/87 of 30 January 1987, IACtHR, *Series A*, No 8 (1987), para 40.

[84] *Habeas Corpus in Emergency Situations*, above n 83, para 42; *Judicial Guarantees in States of Emergency (Arts 27(2), 25 and 8 of the American Convention on Human Rights)*, Advisory Opinion OC-9/87 of 6 October 1987, IACtHR, *Series A*, No 9 (1987), para 42. See also Articles VII and VIII of the *Guidelines on Human Rights and the Fight Against Terrorism* adopted by the Committee of Ministers of the Council of Europe on 15 July 2002. For further discussion of the *Guidelines*, see S Borelli, "The Rendition of Terrorist Suspects to the United States: Human Rights and the Limits of International Cooperation", in this volume, n 177.

[85] See, *inter alia*, Amnesty International, Report 2003, at <http://web.amnesty.org/report2003>.

[86] *R (Abbasi & Another) v Secretary of State for Foreign Affairs* [2002] EWCA Civ. 1598.

[87] *Ibid*, para 64.

[88] *Ibid*, para 107(iii).

[89] *Ibid*, paras 15, 107(iii). The court also took account of the fact that the Inter-American Commission was seized of the matter: paras 21, 107(iv).

stated that "we find surprising the proposition that the writ of the United States courts does not run in respect of individuals held by the government on territory that the United States holds as lessee under a long term treaty."[90]

Quite apart from the issue of the qualification of Guantanamo detainees as protected persons under either the Third or the Fourth Geneva Convention, even where "only" ordinary human rights laws norms were deemed to apply to the situation in Guantanamo, the attitude of US authorities seems to be inconsistent with several fundamental norms of international human rights law. The US administration's refusal to abide by humanitarian laws and by the norms of international human rights law stands in stark contrast with the justifications advanced for the US military action. The war against terrorism has been presented as a war necessary to defend the values of "civilization" against "evil."[91] The Geneva Conventions, together with international human rights law are undoubtedly a bulwark of civilisation, one of the main achievements of the "civilisation" that needs to be safeguarded. To disregard their basic principles in the name of "civilisation" seems not only a contradiction in terms, but also, and above all, a surrender to the barbarity of terrorism.

[90] *Ibid*, para. 15.

[91] See George W. Bush, Address to a Joint Session of Congress and the American People on 20 September 2001: "This is not, however, just America's fight. And what is at stake is not just America's freedom. This is the world's fight. This is civilization's fight. This is the fight of all who believe in progress and pluralism, tolerance and freedom. We ask every nation to join us. We will ask, and we will need, the help of police forces, intelligence services, and banking systems around the world". In a televised speech on 8 November 2001, President Bush declared the bombing of Afghanistan to be "a war to save civilization itself"; see also Bush's speech to the Warsaw Conference on Combating Terrorism, 6 November 2001; all available at <http://www.whitehouse.gov>.

5

Arresting Terrorism: Criminal Jurisdiction and International Relations[*]

MADELINE MORRIS

INTERNATIONAL TERRORISM SITS at the cusp of crime, the domestic politics of States and international relations. Precisely because terrorist offences are poised at that volatile intersection, significant practical, legal, and political difficulties attend the exercise of criminal jurisdiction over terrorist crimes in any forum. Prosecutions in the domestic courts of affected States pose one set of concerns, while prosecutions in an international criminal court, or in the domestic courts of third-party States under universal jurisdiction, pose others. This essay will examine the factors underlying the jurisdictional difficulties in this field and will consider the implications of those factors for future policy.

I. THE IMPETUS TO INTERNATIONALIZE ENFORCEMENT

Most crime is prosecuted at the national, not the international, level. This is true even of cross-border crime. For the most part, States criminalize conduct domestically. Where States need to cooperate with other States to enforce their domestic criminal law, they do so through mutual legal assistance agreements, extradition treaties, coordination of investigations, and the like.

But terrorism is not ordinary crime. It is not even ordinary cross-border crime. Although the term "terrorism" has no international legal definition, the term would seem to indicate, at a minimum, an unlawful violent

[*] This essay develops ideas earlier presented in M Morris, "Prosecuting Terrorism: The Quandaries of Criminal Jurisdiction and International Relations" in W Herre (ed), *Terrorism and the Military*, 2003.

act committed for a political purpose. Unsurprisingly, since terrorism has political motives, States are typically the targets and, not infrequently, the sponsors of terrorism. This fact enormously complicates the issue of criminal jurisdiction over terrorism. The likely involvement of States as targets or sponsors of terrorism creates an impetus to resort to some authority above the State for the handling of terrorist offences.

It is easy to understand this impulse to seek an authority above the State for the handling of terrorist offences when the alternative would be to rely for law enforcement on the very State that has sponsored the terrorist act. Take, for instance, the bombing of Pan Am flight 103, the flight that exploded over Lockerbie, Scotland. It appears that the bombing was in fact sponsored by the government of Libya.[1]

The Montreal Convention for the Suppression of Unlawful Acts Against the Safety of Civil Aviation criminalizes and provides for the prosecution of aircraft bombing.[2] Libya, the United Kingdom and the United States of America each were parties to that treaty at all times relevant to the Lockerbie case.[3] The Montreal Convention provides that whenever an individual suspected of aircraft bombing is found on the territory of a State party to the treaty, that State must either prosecute the suspect or extradite him for prosecution elsewhere.[4] This provision for *"aut dedere, aut judicare"* is quite standard in the several multilateral treaties dealing with what would generally be thought of as "terrorist offences."[5]

[1] Libya has formally accepted responsibility for the bombing. See Letter of 15 August 2003 from the Representative of the Libyan Arab Jamahiriya to the President of the UN Security Council; see also UN Security Council Res. 731, Preamble (1992) (in which the Security Council States that it is "[d]eeply concerned over the results of investigations, which implicate officials of the Libyan government" in the bombing of Pan Am flight 103).

[2] Montreal Convention for the Suppression of Unlawful Acts Against the Safety of Civil Aviation, 23 September 1971, 24 UST 564, 974 UNTS 177 (hereinafter "Montreal Convention").

[3] (1992) 46 *UN Yearbook* 52.

[4] Specifically, Art. 7 of the Montreal Convention, above n 2, provides: "The Contracting State in the territory of which the alleged offender is found shall, if it does not extradite him, be obliged, without exception whatsoever and whether or not the offence was committed in its territory, to submit the case to its competent authorities for the purpose of prosecution".

[5] See Convention for the Suppression of Unlawful Seizure of Aircraft, 16 December 1970, 22 UST 1641, 860 UNTS 105; Montreal Convention, above n 2; Protocol for the Suppression of Unlawful Acts of Violence at Airports Serving International Civil Aviation, supplementary to the Convention of 23 September 1971, 24 February 1988, S. Treaty Doc. No. 100-19; Convention and Protocol on the Suppression of Unlawful Acts Against the Safety of Maritime Navigation, 10 March 1988, 27 I.L.M. 668; International Convention Against the Taking of Hostages, 17 December 1979, TIAS No. 11,081, 1316 UNTS 205; Convention on the Prevention and Punishment of Crimes Against Internationally Protected Persons, Including Diplomatic Agents, 14 December 1973, 28 UST 1975, 1035 UNTS 167; Convention on the Safety of United Nations and Associated Personnel, 15 December 1995, UN GAOR 49th Sess., Supp. No. 49, Vol. 1, at 299, UN Doc. A/49/49 (1994), 34 I.L.M. 482 (1995); International Convention for the Suppression of Terrorist Bombings, 37 I.L.M. 249 (1998); International Convention for the Suppression of the Financing of Terrorism, 10 January 2000, 39 I.L.M. 270 (2000).

The two suspects in the Lockerbie case were Libyan nationals living in Libya. Libya indicated that it would prosecute the suspects in its own national courts. Since there was evidence that Libya had sponsored the bombing, this posed a problem. The UK and the US insisted that Libya not prosecute the suspects but, rather, extradite them to the US or the UK for prosecution. The issue was presented to the UN Security Council. Based on the evidence that Libya itself was implicated in the crime, the Security Council issued resolution 748, under Chapter VII of the UN Charter, effectively requiring the extradition of the suspects.[6]

Libya took the position that the Security Council lacked the authority to issue that resolution. This dispute resulted in cases, brought by Libya against the UK and the US,[7] before the International Court of Justice (ICJ).

At the base of that dispute is the legal problem posed by State sponsorship of terrorism. Libya, which would ordinarily be responsible for the enforcement of the law against aircraft sabotage in this case, hardly can be relied upon for that purpose if the government of Libya is in fact responsible for the crime. In this respect, the terrorism treaties, with their "prosecute-or-extradite" systems for jurisdiction, have a built-in limitation: they do not provide for the foreseeable circumstance in which the crime was in fact sponsored by the State that has custody of the suspect.

State-sponsored terrorism has led logically to an impetus toward some form of supra-national authority for the handling of terrorist offences. Resort to a supra-national authority is sought to safeguard against perpetrators being shielded from justice by the States that have sponsored their terrorist acts.

The US and UK resorted to a supra-national authority in responding to State sponsorship of terrorist crimes in the Lockerbie bombing case. In that instance, the authority resorted to was the UN Security Council acting under Chapter VII of the UN Charter. To be sure, the purpose of recourse to the Security Council was to gain custody of the defendants for criminal prosecution in the domestic criminal courts of the US or UK. But the route through which that outcome was sought to be attained was the supra-national authority of the Security Council.

Another supra-national mechanism that some have advocated for the handling of terrorism cases is the International Criminal Court (ICC).[8]

[6]See UNSC Res 748, para 1 (1992).

[7]Application Instituting Proceedings, ICJ Gen List No 88, filed 3 March 1992 [*Libya v UK*]; Application Instituting Proceedings, ICJ Gen List No 89, filed 3 March 1992 [*Libya v US*].

[8]The ICC is intended to be a permanent international criminal court. It was established pursuant to a multilateral treaty, the Rome Statute of the International Criminal Court, adopted on 17 July 1998, UN Doc A/Conf 183/9 [hereinafter ICC Treaty]. The ICC had not been established at the time of the Lockerbie bombing. However, the use of an ad hoc international criminal tribunal was proposed, though ultimately rejected at that time, as a jurisdictional resolution for the Lockerbie dispute. See J Crawford, "The ILC Adopts a Statute for an International Criminal Court", (1995) 89 *American Journal of International Law*, 404, at 408.

The ICC would both provide the supra-national authority to assure that the case would be pursued and also constitute the criminal forum in which the case would actually be tried.

The prospect of the ICC serving as an international forum for the prosecution of terrorism presents a number of questions. The next Section will examine the broad policy issues concerning international jurisdiction over terrorism that arise from the political nature of terrorist offences. The final Section of the Essay will then consider particular legal questions concerning the ICC's capacity to adjudicate international terrorism cases.

II. IS INTERNATIONALIZING ENFORCEMENT GOOD POLICY?

It is fairly easy to understand the impulse to internationalize law enforcement — for example, through recourse to the UN Security Council or to the ICC — where the State that would otherwise be relied upon for law enforcement is itself implicated in terrorist offences. Enforcement by an international authority impedes the capacity of implicated States to shield perpetrators from justice. It is somewhat more difficult, however, to understand the impulse to internationalize law enforcement where the State that would otherwise exercise jurisdiction is not the perpetrator State but, rather, the State that was the target or "victim" of the crime.

Why is it, then, that, when the United States suffered terrorist attacks on 11 September 2001, there were suggestions that prosecutions should be conducted outside of the courts of the United States, in third-party States or in an international tribunal? A major reason appears to be that the US was viewed, in effect, as a "party to the conflict". The courts of the United States, it was argued, could not be relied upon to be neutral or, in any case, might be perceived to be non-neutral. Accordingly to this view, therefore, the case should be handled by an entity outside of the principally-affected State: an international court or a third-party State exercising universal jurisdiction.

In fact, this was essentially the same argument as was made by Libya before the ICJ in the *Lockerbie* case, and the same concern as was expressed by several of the ICJ judges dissenting from the ICJ's 1992 opinion denying provisional measures in that case. Judge Shahabuddeen questioned whether the accused could receive an impartial trial in the United States.[9] Judge *ad hoc* El-Kosheri stated that the accused "could not possibly

[9] *Questions of Interpretation and Application of the 1971 Montreal Convention Arising from the Aerial Incident at Lockerbie (Libyan Arab Jamahiriya v United States of America)*, Provisional Measures, Order of 14 April 1992, ICJ Reports 1992, 114, at 141 (separate opinion of Judge Shahabuddeen).

receive a fair trial, neither in the United States or in the United Kingdom, nor in Libya".[10]

The impulse to internationalize justice processes in this area is an understandable and, perhaps, logical response to the recognition that crimes of terrorism have a political component. Because of the political aspect of international terrorism cases, the reasoning goes, States (be they perpetrator States *or* target States) are interested parties in these cases. And, as interested parties, States — perpetrator States or target States — cannot be permitted to stand as judges in their own causes.

Internationalization of justice in this field might be a tidy solution to this problem if there were an international institution that States trusted sufficiently to decide these matters. The problem is that this sort of confidence in international institutions frequently is lacking, and for comprehensible reasons.

States accused of sponsoring terrorism question the legitimacy and the neutrality of the international institutions that would assert authority. Certainly, Libya has challenged the Security Council's action on both of those grounds in the *Lockerbie* case.

Significantly, States that are the targets of terrorism also have been unwilling to rely upon international handling of those cases. A targeted State may question the effectiveness of international investigative and prosecutorial mechanisms, particularly if the targeted State has highly developed investigative and prosecutorial systems domestically and has substantial resources to devote to the cases. Targeted States are also aware that different States have different interests; not all States are similarly situated relative to terrorism. Targeted States may therefore be unwilling to relegate the handling of terrorism cases to an international court that may have different priorities from those of the targeted State. In addition, a targeted State may question whether the international institution that would handle the cases will share the State's view of the law in this field in which there remain so many differences of interpretation and so many open legal questions.[11] The US, certainly, declined any suggestion of an international tribunal for prosecution of the crimes of 11 September 2001. Precisely because terrorist crimes do pose a threat to the national security of targeted States, and precisely because terrorist crimes do have volatile political and foreign-relations dimensions, States are particularly wary of relinquishing control over these cases to international bodies.

[10] *Ibid*, at 216 (Judge *ad hoc* El-Kosheri, dissenting).

[11] The definition of "terrorism" has itself remained highly controversial. Certainly, there is no accepted international legal definition of the term. The General Assembly debates following 11 September 2001 reflected the highly contentious nature of this question, with Middle East politics virtually assuring that no international consensus on a definition will be arrived at in the near future. See C Miller, "US Strikes Back", *Los Angeles Times*, 11 October 2001, at 3.

Having identified some of the difficulties that attend international jurisdiction over crimes of terrorism, it quickly becomes clear that a similar set of weaknesses affects the option of holding terrorist trials in third party States under universal jurisdiction. Under the international law doctrine of universal jurisidiction, any State may prosecute individuals for certain international crimes without regard to the territory where the crimes were committed or the nationality of perpetrators or victims.[12] Universal jurisdiction is thus distinguished from other internationally recognized bases for jurisdiction by the fact that universal jurisdiction is not based on a particular nexus between the offence and the prosecuting State.[13]

Two distinct arguments are put forward in favor of universal jurisdiction over terrorism cases. The first is that terrorist crimes are of concern to all States. The second is that third-party States may be relied upon to be more impartial in terrorism cases than the principally-affected States. Neither of those arguments withstands scrutiny.

The first argument for universal jurisdiction over terrorism, that all States have an interest in ensuring accountability for terrorist crimes, is belied by the very existence of State-sponsored terrorism. But, even if we were to accept, *arguendo,* the existence of such a unity of interest at least among States that do not themselves sponsor terrorist crimes (a point which certainly could be debated), the interests of States obviously diverge on a great number of other matters. Because criminal trials for terrorism do not exist in isolation from those other aspects of inter-State relations, we may anticipate that universal jurisdiction would sometimes be used as a tool for achieving other political ends. For this reason, third party States may not be consistently relied upon to be impartial in the handling of terrorism-related cases.

Thus, the second argument for universal jurisdiction over terrorism cases — that third party States can be relied upon as neutral adjudicators in relation to terrorist acts — is simply unrealistic. Precisely because terrorism has a political component — and international terrorism has an international political component — it would be naive to assume that the State that would step forward to exercise universal jurisdiction would reliably be more neutral or impartial than the principally affected State.[14]

[12] See *Restatement (Third) of Foreign Relations* (1987), §§ 404, 423.

[13] Universal jurisdiction is one among the five bases for jurisdiction comprising the standard list of internationally recognized forms of jurisdiction. Each of the other four jurisdictional bases (territoriality, nationality, passive personality, and protective principle) is founded on a particular nexus between the offence and the State asserting jurisdiction. See generally K Randall, "Universal Jurisdiction Under International Law", (1988) 66 *Texas Law Review,* 785, 785–88.

[14] For a fuller consideration of the political implications of universal jurisdiction, see M Morris, "Universal Jurisdiction in a Divided World", (2001) 35 *New England Law Review* 337.

The fundamental quandary posed by the position of States as interested parties in terrorism cases lies at the base of the political debate concerning the best configuration of criminal jurisdiction over terrorism. The terrorism treaties, with their "extradite-or-prosecute" clauses, have fallen far short of resolving the difficulties concerning jurisdiction over terrorist offences. Because international terrorism implicates volatile issues of international politics and inter-State relations, the extradite-or-prosecute regime for jurisdiction over terrorism is flawed insofar as it relies on States: non-neutral perpetrator States, or non-neutral targeted States, or third party States that, in fact, cannot be presumed to be — or will not be perceived to be — neutral. Similarly, because of the political features of international terrorism, utilizing international fora for the prosecution of terrorist crimes also does not satisfactorily fulfil the complex requirements for effective enforcement in this field. The inherent political impediments to effective use of international fora for the prosecution of terrorist offences are well exemplified in the context of the ICC.

III. THE ICC AS AN INTERNATIONAL ENFORCEMENT MECHANISM

The political difficulties surrounding the use of international fora for the prosecution of terrorist crimes are reflected in a number of legal constraints on the powers of the ICC. These limitations concern the ICC's jurisdictional structure, its complementarity regime, and the international law of immunities. Unsurprisingly, these legal limitations, which reflect States' political concerns, also in practice place constraints on the ICC's capacity to effectively prosecute crimes of international terrorism.

A. Limitations Arising from the ICC's Jurisdictional Structure

As the subject-matter jurisdiction of the ICC is currently defined, terrorist crimes come within the subject-matter jurisdiction of the ICC only if the particular terrorist acts also constitute genocide, war crimes, or (as is more likely) crimes against humanity. Those are the three crimes currently within the subject-matter jurisdiction of the ICC.[15] Therefore, only if a terrorist act comprised the elements of one of those three crimes would that

[15] See ICC Treaty, above n 8, Art. 5. While the ICC Treaty also provides for jurisdiction over the crime of aggression, see *ibid* Art 5(1)(d), the treaty further provides that the ICC shall not exercise that part of its subject-matter jurisdiction until such time as the treaty is amended to include provisions defining the crime of aggression and setting out the conditions under which the court will exercise jurisdiction over that crime. *See ibid*, Art 5(2).

terrorist act come within the jurisdiction of the ICC.[16] Proposals to include terrorism *per se* within ICC jurisdiction were defeated in the ICC treaty negotiations process, in part because of politically charged disagreements between States as to the appropriate definition of "terrorism".

In addition to limitations on ICC powers based on subject-matter jurisdiction, there are also limitations on the ICC's exercise of jurisdiction that are based on nationality and territoriality. By the terms of the ICC Treaty, unless the UN Security Council refers a case to the ICC, the ICC may exercise jurisdiction *only* if the crime was committed by the national of or on the territory of a State party to the ICC treaty (or by the national of or on the territory of a non-party State that has consented to ICC jurisdiction *ad hoc* for the matter in question).[17] Consequently, crimes committed on the territory of a non-consenting, non-party State by the national of a non-consenting, non-party State may not be prosecuted before the ICC. In the course of the ICC treaty negotiations, some States advocated that the ICC should be accorded universal jurisdiction (that is, jurisdiction without regard to the territory where the crime occurred or to the nationality of the perpetrator or victim). However, other States prevailed in their view that ICC jurisdiction should be limited, absent Security Council referral, to cases in which a State party to the treaty had territorial or nationality-based nexus to the crime in question (or in which such a State consented *ad hoc* to ICC jurisdiction.) These limitations on the ICC's exercise of jurisdiction preclude ICC prosecution of terrorist acts committed by a non-consenting, non-party State's national within his own State and also terrorist acts committed by a non-consenting, non-party State's national in a different non-party State. Based on the current number of ICC ratifications, these limitations would, for instance, have precluded ICC prosecution of any of the nineteen hijackers responsible for the attacks of 11 September 2001 (had they survived, and had the ICC been established at that time).

In addition to those limitations on the ICC's exercise of jurisdiction that are based on the terms of the ICC Treaty itself, there is also a question about whether the ICC may lawfully exercise jurisdiction when the defendant is a national of a non-consenting, non-party State — even if the crimes were committed on the territory of a State party. Such an exercise of jurisdiction over a non-party national is permitted under the terms of the ICC Treaty. But some States — notably, the US — have argued that such ICC jurisdiction over non-party nationals would be unlawful.[18]

[16] Concerning the possibility of future expansion of the ICC's jurisdiction to include terrorism crimes that do not constitute genocide, war crimes, or crimes against humanity, see *infra* Part III(D).

[17] ICC Treaty, above n 8, Art. 12.

[18] For a comprehensive treatment of concerns regarding ICC jurisdiction over non-party nationals, see M Morris, "High Crimes", above n 5. The arguments in that article formed the

This issue remains unresolved, as a political as well as a legal matter. Since State sponsors of terrorism are unlikely to become parties to the ICC Treaty, this issue may be of particular significance in relation to ICC jurisdiction over terrorism offences.

B. Limitations Arising from the ICC's Complementarity Regime

An additional set of impediments to effective ICC jurisdiction over terrorism offences is posed by the ICC's "complementarity" regime, encompassed in Articles 17–19 of the ICC Treaty. Under Article 17, a case is admissible before the ICC only if the States that would otherwise have jurisdiction are unable or unwilling genuinely to investigate and, where appropriate, to prosecute the case in question. The complementarity regime was designed to reflect the position, arrived at in the course of the ICC treaty negotiations, that States should retain primary authority and control over prosecutions for international crimes, with the ICC serving as a fail-safe enforcement mechanism of last resort.

The apparatus for implementing the complementarity regime, laid out in Articles 18 and 19 of the ICC Treaty, may allow State sponsors of terrorism opportunities to forestall, if not to prevent, terrorism prosecutions before the ICC. Under Article 18, the ICC prosecutor is required to publicize his or her intention to proceed with an investigation. Notice must be sent to all States parties and to all States that would ordinarily exercise jurisdiction over the crimes in question. At a minimum, this provision would require notice to the State where the crime was committed and to the suspect's State of nationality. This means that, where State-sponsored terrorism is involved, that State sponsor is likely to be among the States entitled to early notice of the prosecutor's intentions. The ICC Treaty does provide that the prosecutor may make such notice confidentially, and may limit the scope of information provided in order to prevent the destruction of evidence or the absconding of suspects. But, where a notified State is complicit with the suspects, those provisions cannot obviate the potential disadvantage to the prosecution.

The obstacles to effective terrorism prosecutions that are posed by Article 18 do not end there. Within one month of receiving notice of investigation from the ICC prosecutor, a State may inform the prosecutor that the State itself is investigating or has investigated the crime in question, and may request that the ICC prosecutor defer to the State's investigation. Having been so requested by a State, the prosecutor may not proceed further with an investigation unless he receives authorization to do so from

legal basis of the US position on this issue. See D Scheffer, "Staying the Course with the International Criminal Court", (2002) 35 *Cornell International Law Journal*, 47, at 66, note 68.

the ICC's Pre-Trial Chamber.[19] Article 18 applies to all cases except those referred by the UN Security Council.

An additional determination of the admissibility of a case before the ICC may also be made through a proceeding under Article 19 of the treaty. The Article 19 procedure is applicable to all cases before the ICC, including those based on a referral by the UN Security Council. Article 19 permits challenges based on jurisdiction or admissibility. Those challenges may be brought by the accused, by a State with jurisdiction over the case, or by a State whose consent would be required for the ICC to exercise jurisdiction over the case. If a challenge is made by a relevant State, then "the Prosecutor shall suspend the investigation until such time as the Court makes a determination in accordance with Article 17".[20]

The pre-trial proceedings provided for under Articles 18 and 19 of the ICC Treaty then provide opportunities for a State to forestall an investigation or prosecution. The Treaty does provide that the Court may give exceptional authorization to the prosecutor to continue an investigation "where there is a unique opportunity to obtain important evidence or there is a significant risk that such evidence may not be subsequently available".[21] But, once again, that safeguard, while ameliorating the problem, cannot eliminate it.

Cumulatively, the complementarity provisions of the ICC Treaty would allow a State sponsor of terrorism to impede ICC prosecution of a case. The ICC might, nevertheless, ultimately succeed in concluding an effective and appropriate prosecution. While Article 17 provides that a case shall not be admissible before the ICC where that case is being investigated or prosecuted by a State with jurisdiction over it, an exception is made where that State is determined by the ICC to be unable or unwilling genuinely to carry out the investigation or the prosecution. If the ICC determines that a State is unable or unwilling "genuinely" to proceed, then the ICC, by the terms of the Treaty, *may* exercise jurisdiction even over the objection of that State. But much time will have passed between the moment when the prosecutor informed a State of his intention to investigate and the time when that State is determined to be — contrary to its protestations — unwilling genuinely to investigate or to prosecute. Perhaps in some cases the outcome will nevertheless, ultimately, be desirable. In other cases, very likely, the ICC's effectiveness will be limited by the exigencies of complementarity.[22]

[19] Under Art 18, if the Pre-Trial Chamber declines to authorize the continuation of investigation by the ICC prosecutor, the prosecutor may re-apply subsequently based on new facts or evidence. A determination by the Pre-Trial Chamber on this issue may be appealed by the prosecutor or by the relevant State. The prosecutor may apply for provisional measures in order to preserve evidence during the course of Art 18 proceedings.

[20] ICC Treaty, above n 8, Art 19(7).

[21] ICC Treaty, above n 8, Art 19(6); see also *ibid*, Art 95.

[22] See WA Schabas, *An Introduction to the International Criminal Court*, (2001), 101–3.

C. Limitations Arising from the International Law of Immunities

The international law of diplomatic, sovereign, and Head of State immunities embodies the principle of the sovereign equality of States (by prohibiting one State from standing in judgment on the official acts or the head of State of another State) and facilitates diplomatic relations (by prohibiting one State from bringing legal process against a foreign diplomat present on its territory). The law of immunities is, thus, intended both to reflect the fundamental structures of international law and to facilitate peaceful inter-State relations.

If a high governmental official bears responsibility for the perpetration of a terrorist crime (as may often be the case), that individual may be immune from ICC jurisdiction under the international law of immunities. This problem is not at all evident on the face of the ICC Treaty. Indeed, the Treaty clearly states that immunities will not be recognized for the crimes now within the jurisdiction of the court.[23] However, the international law of immunities cannot in fact be dispensed with so quickly. The problem becomes clear upon examination.

The best starting point for examination of this issue is the 2002 decision of the International Court of Justice (ICJ) in the case of the *Arrest Warrant of April 11th 2000 (Democratic Republic of the Congo v Belgium)*.[24] The case concerned an international warrant, issued by Belgium, for the arrest — of the then foreign minister of the DRC for crimes including crimes against humanity. The DRC claimed that the international law of immunities was violated by the issuance of that warrant.

The ICJ concluded that:

> ... the functions of a Minister for Foreign Affairs are such that, throughout the duration of his or her office, he or she when abroad enjoys full immunity from criminal prosecution and inviolability. That immunity and inviolability protect the individual concerned against any act of authority of another State which would hinder him or her in the performance of his or her duties.[25]

However, the ICJ majority went on to say that, even though a foreign minister would be immune from criminal proceedings before the courts of another State,

> an incumbent or former Minister for Foreign Affairs may be subject to criminal proceedings before certain international criminal courts, where they have jurisdiction. Examples include ... the future International Criminal Court

[23] See ICC Treaty, above n 8, Art 27.

[24] *Case Concerning the Arrest Warrant of 11 April 2000 (Democratic Republic of Congo v Belgium)*, ICJ General List No 121, 14 February 2002.

[25] *Ibid* at para 54.

> created by the 1998 Rome Convention. The latter's Statute expressly provides, in Article 27, paragraph 2, that "[i]mmunities or special procedural rules which may attach to the official capacity of a person, whether under national or international law, shall not bar the Court from exercising its jurisdiction over such a person.[26]

The ICJ appears to have spoken too broadly in this respect. In fact, if the question is analyzed consistently with the ICJ majority's own holding on immunities, the conclusion must be that the ICC would have the power to prosecute an incumbent foreign minister (or other covered official) of a State that *is* a party to the ICC Treaty, but would *not* be empowered to prosecute a covered official of a State that is *not* a party to the treaty. This point becomes clear when we consider the basis for the ICC's purported jurisdiction over nationals of States that are not parties to the ICC Treaty.

The ICC Treaty provides that, under certain circumstances, the ICC may exercise jurisdiction even over nationals of States that are not parties to the treaty and have not otherwise consented to the court's jurisdiction. Article 12 provides that, in addition to jurisdiction based on Security Council referral and jurisdiction based on consent by the defendant's State of nationality, the ICC will have jurisdiction to prosecute the national of any State when crimes within the Court's subject-matter jurisdiction are committed on the territory of a State that is a party to the treaty or that consents ad hoc to ICC jurisdiction for that case.[27] That territorial basis would empower the Court to exercise jurisdiction even in cases where the defendant's State of nationality is not a party to the treaty and does not consent to the exercise of jurisdiction.[28]

Advocates of ICC jurisdiction over non-party nationals argue that the foundation for the ICC's jurisdiction over non-party nationals when the crime is committed on the territory of a State party is that the territorial State has delegated its territorial jurisdiction to be exercised by the ICC.[29] The reasoning is that, since the territorial State would have the right to prosecute for offences committed on its territory, the territorial State also has the right to delegate that jurisdiction to be exercised by an international court.[30]

Offering a variant on this rationale, some proponents have contended that ICC jurisdiction over the nationals of non-party States is based upon

[26] *Ibid* at para 61.
[27] ICC Treaty, above n 8, Art. 12.
[28] The issue of ICC jurisdiction over non-party nationals is addressed briefly above.
[29] See, eg, M Scharf, "The ICC's Jurisdiction Over the Nationals of Non-Party States: A Critique of the U.S. Position", (2001) 64 *Law and Contemporary Problems*, 67.
[30] For full and contrasting treatments of the issue of ICC jurisdiction over non-party nationals, see Morris, "High Crimes", above n 5 and Scharf above n 29.

the principles of universal jurisdiction pursuant to which the courts of any State may prosecute the nationals of any State for certain international crimes. Since any individual State could prosecute perpetrators regardless of their nationality, it is argued, a group of States may create an international court empowered to do the same. Under this theory, each State party, in effect, delegates to the international court its universal jurisdiction.[31] Under either theory (delegated territorial jurisdiction or delegated universal jurisdiction), the ICC's jurisdiction over nationals of non-party States rests on the *delegated* jurisdiction of one or more States.

The overbreadth in the ICJ's reasoning concerning immunity before the ICC now becomes clear. Obviously, States (the territorial State or, under the delegated universal jurisdiction theory, any or all States parties) can delegate to the ICC only such jurisdiction as those States have. If States are obliged to recognize a certain immunity, as the ICJ's decision in the *Arrest Warrant* case implies, then those States' delegated jurisdiction logically must carry that immunity with it. The consequence is that, if States would be legally required to afford immunity from prosecution to sitting heads of State, foreign ministers, and perhaps other high officials, then the ICC (when acting without Security Council referral and without the consent of the officials' State of nationality) would be similarly constrained.

This immunity before the ICC would apply only to non-party nationals; it would not apply to officials of States parties to the ICC Treaty. States parties waive the immunity of their officials under Article 27 of that treaty, which States that "immunities ... which may attach to the official capacity of a person ... shall not bar the Court from exercising its jurisdiction over such a person". But that treaty provision constitutes a waiver of immunity only by States parties. The Head of State or foreign minister of a non-party State would maintain immunity.[32] So where an individual responsible for a terrorist crime is a Head of State, foreign minister or, perhaps, other high official of a non-party State, the ICC cannot lawfully exercise jurisdiction over that individual, at least not consistent with international immunity principles as articulated in the ICJ's decision in the *Arrest Warrant* case.

[31] See, eg, Scharf, "The ICC's Jurisdiction Over the Nationals of Non-Party States: A Critique of the U.S. Position", above n 29 at 77. For a critique of this view, see Morris, "High Crimes", above n 5, at Part III.

[32] This conclusion is consistent with the thrust of Article 98(1) of the ICC Treaty, which provides that: "[t]he Court may not proceed with a request for surrender or assistance which would require the requested State to act inconsistently with its obligations under international law with respect to the State or diplomatic immunity of a person or property of a third State, unless the Court can first obtain the cooperation of that third State for the waiver of the immunity."

D. Additional Limitations Affecting the ICC's Capacity to Adjudicate Crimes Added by Amendment to the ICC Treaty

The ICC Treaty limits the ICC's subject-matter jurisdiction to genocide, war crimes and crimes against humanity.[33] However, in the negotiations leading up to the adoption of the ICC Treaty, extensive debate focused on the possibility of encompassing within the jurisdiction of the ICC certain "treaty crimes" — including the terrorism crimes defined in the treaties on hijacking and aircraft sabotage,[34] crimes against internationally protected persons,[35] hostage-taking,[36] sabotage of marine navigation,[37] and the like. In the course of the negotiations, the decision ultimately taken was to exclude those treaty crimes from the jurisdiction of the Court.[38] But Resolution E, adopted at the last moments of the Rome Conference at which the ICC Treaty was adopted, provides for reconsideration of the inclusion of the "treaty crimes". Resolution E states that the Rome Conference, "Affirm[s] that the Statute of the ICC provides for a review mechanism, which allows for an expansion in future of the jurisdiction of the Court, [and] [r]ecommends that a Review Conference ... consider the crimes of terrorism and drug crimes with a view to arriving at an acceptable definition and their inclusion in the list of crimes within the jurisdiction of the Court".[39] Therefore, crimes of terrorism — even when they do not constitute genocide, war crimes, or crimes against humanity — may be brought within ICC jurisdiction in the future.

If the ICC Treaty is amended in the future to include terrorist crimes that do not constitute genocide, war crimes, or crimes against humanity,

[33] See above n 9 and accompanying text.

[34] See Convention for the Suppression of Unlawful Seizure of Aircraft, above n 5; Montreal Convention for the Suppression of Unlawful Acts Against the Safety of Civil Aviation, above n 2; Protocol for the Suppression of Unlawful Acts of Violence at Airports Serving International Civil Aviation, above n 5.

[35] Convention on the Prevention and Punishment of Crimes Against Internationally Protected Persons, Including Diplomatic Agents, above n 5.

[36] International Convention Against the Taking of Hostages, above n 5.

[37] Convention and Protocol on the Suppression of Unlawful Acts Against the Safety of Maritime Navigation, above n 5.

[38] There were a number of reasons for excluding terrorist offences (as well as drug trafficking and other "treaty crimes") from the jurisdiction of the ICC under the Rome Treaty. In part, the attempt to include terrorist offences failed because of States' disagreement over the proper definition of "terrorism." See above n 11. In addition, those who advocated exclusion of terrorism argued that the ICC would be unable to investigate terrorism cases as efficiently and effectively as national governments would be able to do and, also, that the inclusion of terrorism and drug trafficking within ICC jurisdiction would overburden the limited investigative and prosecutorial resources of the ICC. See, eg, *Comments of the United States of America Pursuant to Paragraph 4 of General Assembly Resolution 49/53 on the Establishment of an International Criminal Court, Report of the Secretary General*, at 10–13, UN Doc. A/AC.244/1/Add. 2 (1995).

[39] Final Act of the United Nations Diplomatic Conference of Plenipotentiaries on the Establishment of an International Criminal Court, Annex I, Resolution E, adopted 17 July 1998, UN Doc. A/CONF. 183/10.

the limitations on the ICC's capacity to prosecute those additional offences will be greater than those that affect the ICC's jurisdiction over the crimes currently within its jurisdiction. In addition to the existing limitations based on jurisdictional structure, complementarity, and immunities that affect prosecutions for genocide, war crimes, and crimes against humanity, there is a further significant limitation that will apply to offences added to the jurisdiction of the ICC through amendment of the ICC Treaty. Article 121(5) of the treaty states that: "In respect of a State Party which has not accepted the amendment, the Court shall not exercise its jurisdiction regarding a crime covered by the amendment when committed by that State Party's nationals or on its territory."[40] The ICC treaty amendment process is based on the vote of a super-majority of ICC States parties.[41] The limiting provision in Article 121(5) was included because States parties were not prepared to relegate future decisions concerning ICC jurisdiction over crimes committed on their territories or by their nationals to a super-majority of ICC States parties. Consequently, with regard to States parties, the ICC would have jurisdiction over terrorist crimes added by amendment *only* if the crime were committed by the national of a State *and* on the territory of a State that had accepted the addition of that particular crime to the jurisdiction of the ICC.

The implications of Article 121(5) are less clear for States that are *not* parties to the ICC Treaty. While the Treaty allows States parties to opt out of ICC jurisdiction over added offences, the Treaty appears, ironically, to assert ICC jurisdiction over non-party nationals for those same added offences. The US has proposed language, to be included in the Rules of Procedure for the ICC Assembly of States Parties, which would provide that,

> [w]ith respect to a crime added by amendment to the Statute pursuant to article 121, paragraph 5, the court may exercise jurisdiction only if the amendment has entered into force for both the State of nationality of the alleged perpetrator and the State in whose territory the crime was committed.[42]

That proposal has not been adopted to date, and this issue remains the subject of controversy.[43] What is clear, at a minimum, is that, if terrorism offences are added to the jurisdiction of the ICC, States parties may decline to accept this jurisdiction. This opt-out provision represents a

[40] ICC Treaty, above n 8, Art. 121(5).
[41] ICC Treaty, above n 8, Art. 121.
[42] Working Group on Rules of Procedure and Evidence, Proposal Submitted by the United States of America Concerning Rules of Evidence and Procedure Relating to Part 13 of the Statute (Final Clauses) 2, UN Doc. PCNICC/2000/WGRPE(13)/DP.1 (2000).
[43] See Scheffer, above n 18, at 81.

significant additional limitation that would affect the ICC's capacity to prosecute terrorist crimes added to the ICC's jurisdiction through amendment of the ICC Treaty.

E. The Potential for ICC Terrorism Prosecutions in Conjunction with Action by the UN Security Council

In sum, when the ICC acts in the absence of a Security Council referral, its ability to exercise jurisdiction over terrorist crimes is limited in a variety of ways reflecting underlying international political concerns. Those constraints may be substantially circumvented in the event that the UN Security Council, acting under Chapter VII of the UN Charter, refers the case in question to the ICC.

Under the terms of the ICC Treaty, when the Security Council refers a case, it is not a precondition to the exercise of the ICC's jurisdiction that the territorial State or the defendant's State of nationality be a party to the treaty.[44] Complementarity likely also can be circumvented through the use of a Chapter VII resolution (though this is less clear).[45] (The reasoning here is that, acting under Chapter VII, the Security Council could effectively require a State to forego domestic handling of a case in order for the ICC to handle the matter.) Immunities, evidently, can be abrogated by Chapter VII resolutions, as was done in the Chapter VII resolutions that established the International Criminal Tribunals for the former Yugoslavia and Rwanda.[46]

If the Security Council were to refer a case to the ICC, and thereby to use its Chapter VII powers to augment the powers of the ICC[47] (or, for that matter, if the Security Council were to create a separate *ad hoc* international criminal tribunal to address some particular situation or were to use its Chapter VII powers to augment or supplement the authority of national courts), we would return, full circle, to the situation of the *Lockerbie* case, where resort was made to the UN Security Council as the authority "above" the State. In this way, as in so many others, the Security Council wields superior powers within the international legal system.

[44] See ICC Treaty, above n 8, Arts 12(2) and 13.

[45] See RB Philips, "The International Criminal Court Statute: Jurisdiction and Admissibility", (1999) 10 *Criminal Law Forum*, 61, at 73 and 81.

[46] See Statute of the International Criminal Tribunal for the former Yugoslavia, Art 7(2), in Report of the Secretary-General Pursuant to Paragraph 2 of Security Council Resolution 808, Annex UN Doc S/25704 (1993); Statute of the International Criminal Tribunal for Rwanda, Art 6(2), Security Council Res 955, UN SCOR, 345d mtg, Annex, UN Doc S/RES/955 (1994).

[47] The present essay will not consider the actual likelihood of Security Council referrals to the ICC, which may be remote given the relevant political factors including US objections to provisions of the ICC Treaty. See generally, Morris, "High Crimes", above n 5 (regarding US objections to the ICC Treaty).

IV. CONCLUSION

The likely involvement of States as targets or sponsors of terrorism has created an impetus to internationalize law enforcement in this field through the use of international criminal courts, universal jurisdiction, or UN Security Council powers. But the international political features of international terrorism significantly limit the potential scope and efficacy of such internationalizing mechanisms. Consequently, the prosecution of terrorism cases to date is pursued at the national level, largely in the targeted State. Given the underlying factors shaping this practice, this arrangement, as imperfect as it is, likely will, and quite probably should, remain in place for the foreseeable future.

Part II

Global, Regional and National Responses to Terrorism: The Interplay between Different Layers of Legal Authority

6

The UN Security Council and International Terrorism

BARDO FASSBENDER

I. INTRODUCTION

NOT LONG AFTER the First World War had passed, Hans Kelsen referred to his time as a transitional period in the history of international law, and saw this character reflected in the "contradictions of an international legal theory which in an almost tragic conflict aspires to the height of a universal legal community erected above the individual states but, at the same time, remains a captive of the sphere of power of the sovereign state".[1] More than forty years later, Wolfgang Friedmann arrived at a very similar conclusion when, in his famous book *The Changing Structure of International Law*, he wrote:

> In terms of objectives, powers, legal structure and scope, the present state of international organisation presents an extremely complex picture. It reflects the state of a society that is both desperately clinging to the legal and political symbols of national sovereignty and being pushed towards the pursuit of common needs and goals that can be achieved only by a steadily intensifying degree of international organisation.[2]

It is likely that both Kelsen and Friedmann, were they still alive, would have regarded the way the international community reacted to the terrorist attacks of 11 September 2001 as evidence for the little progress the world has made in terms of its political and legal organisation since they

[1] See H Kelsen, *Das Problem der Souveränität und die Theorie des Völkerrechts: Beitrag zu einer Reinen Rechtslehre* (JCB Mohr–Paul Siebeck, Tübingen, 1920, 2nd unchanged edn 1928), at 320 (translation by the present author).
[2] W Friedmann, *The Changing Structure of International Law* (Stevens & Sons, London, 1964), at 293 f.

wrote their respective books. In particular, it is likely that they both would have been disappointed about the role played, or not played, by the United Nations in that crisis, an organisation — and more: the embodiment of an idea — in which they had placed their hopes for a more just and less violent world. The Charter of the United Nations of 1945 was indeed a bold effort to end Kelsen's transitional stage in favour of a lasting international constitutional order no longer dependent on the capriciousness of sometimes well-meaning, sometimes egoistic States and nations. But, alas, at the beginning of the twenty-first century the contradictions Kelsen and Friedmann described have still not disappeared. To see this very length of the struggle of mankind can also help us avoid rushed accusations. It is surely not one State or one government alone which is to blame for the world's unwillingness to organise itself in a way commensurate with its vital needs and the dangers it is facing.

In regard to the UN Security Council and international terrorism, three propositions may be advanced:

(1) In the present "war against terrorism", which the United States declared after the attacks of 11 September 2001, the UN Security Council is not going to play any major role, irrespective of its mandate under the United Nations Charter and a concomitant expectation or hope on the side of the international community. Today, the United States considers itself to be at war. For the time being, it will lead that war as it sees fit. It will perhaps take advice from nations which it holds in esteem as friends and allies, but it will certainly not accept binding directives from a multilateral institution.

(2) It is unlikely that in the future the Council will play a significant role in responding to single terrorist acts. However, the Council's work is essential and promising in the area of the prevention of terrorism. In particular, the Council must identify and aim at solving certain problems and conflicts which are a fertile soil for terrorist activities. The Council is also called upon to continue its work of international standard-setting which is has begun in the wake of the September 11th attacks.

(3) While the United States decided to react unilaterally to the attacks directed against it, and while accordingly at this time unilateralist rhetoric and action dominate the scene, in the increasingly interdependent world of the twenty-first century even the most powerful State cannot, in the long run, go without engaging in multilateral dialogue and coordination. It is,

> however, not clear whether the Security Council will be the forum of that renewed dialogue when the United States is ready for it. The Council can only, and must, prepare for that hour to come.

So far, the United States has maintained the course it had set immediately after the September 11th attacks, described in the first proposition. Whether the other two estimations will also prove right, only time can tell. With the war against Iraq in the spring of 2003, the first phase of the post-9/11 "war against terrorism" of the United States ended. In the fast-moving world of ours, the attacks in New York City, Washington and Pennsylvania are already beginning to enter the space of history. It will be increasingly difficult to rely on them as a basis of legitimisation for future forceful action against (potential) terrorists or States harbouring them. This means that the approval by the Security Council of the action taken by the United States after the attacks is gradually losing its force, notwithstanding the American efforts to carry on the war declared in September 2001.

In the following text, I shall discuss, in the first section, the Council's reaction to the attacks of 11 September 2001. After taking a closer look at resolutions 1368 and 1373, I shall address the claim to "pre-emptive self-defence" which was brought forward by the United States in the wake of the attacks. The second section of the chapter takes up the above proposition no. 2 and ventures to make some prognoses in relation to future Council action against acts of international terrorism. A concluding section tries to relate the specific problems the Security Council was confronted with after September 11th to the larger question of the Council's present standing in the organized international community.

If the reader permits me to emphasize a point we all know, the following remark may be expedient here: When we say that "the Security Council" did this or did not do that, that it felt compelled to do something, or refrained from doing something else, we really insinuate or suggest an autonomy which the Council does not possess. It would be more correct to follow the Articles of Confederation of 1777 which, as it is known, referred to the new union as "the United States, in Congress assembled". So we should not speak of "the Security Council", as if it had a true life of its own, but of "fifteen states, in Council assembled". For it is really fifteen governments agreeing, or disagreeing, on something — according to what they perceive to be their respective "national interest" (and sometimes also according to the interest of the international community), and always under the shadow of the veto power of five of them.

II. THE SECURITY COUNCIL'S REACTION TO THE ATTACKS OF SEPTEMBER 11TH AND ITS CONSEQUENCES FOR INTERNATIONAL LAW

A. Self-Defence Versus Collective Security: Security Council Resolutions 1368 and 1373

In response to the attacks in New York, Washington DC, and Pennsylvania, the United States immediately claimed its right to self-defence under international law. The Security Council basically accepted that position. However, it did not do so in an unequivocal manner.

Resolution 1368, unanimously adopted on the day after the attacks, is a highly interesting text. It is a combination of traditional and new answers of the Council to the phenomenon of international terrorism, the new answers understandably, but still regrettably, being very ambiguous. Traditional was the condemnation of the attacks and the Council's expression of sympathy for the victims, their families and the people and government of the United States (operative paragraphs 1 and 2). The Council also followed a traditional path when it called on all States "to work together urgently to bring to justice the perpetrators, organizers and sponsors of these terrorist acts", as well as on the international community "to redouble their efforts to prevent and suppress terrorist acts including by increased cooperation and full implementation of the relevant international anti-terrorist conventions and Security Council resolutions" (operative paragraphs 3 and 4). It is important to note that in these paragraphs the Council continued to view terrorist acts as primarily criminal offences committed by individuals or groups of individuals who must be brought to justice in accordance with national and international criminal law. It is not by chance that the Council expressly mentioned its resolution 1269 of 19 October 1999 which is a summary of the traditional ways and elements of fighting terrorism.

Although it would perhaps have been preferable, it seemed impossible for the Council on 12 September 2001 to stop right here and not leave the well-trodden path. The Council felt that it was necessary to offer the United States a stronger form of support than sympathy. Accordingly, it recognized in resolution 1368 "the inherent right of individual or collective self-defence in accordance with the Charter". This was done in a general way in the third preambular paragraph, without referring to a specific State and before mentioning the events of the previous day. Separated from its context, this recognition would not have been new either, because it simply repeated the words of the Charter and stated the obvious and uncontested — the existence of a right of self-defence in accordance with the UN Charter. However, this was the first time that the Council brought up the subject of self-defence in connection with an act of terrorism. This Chapter VII language corresponded to that used in the resolution's first operative paragraph in which the Council said that it regarded the September 11th terrorist attacks "like any act of international terrorism, as a threat to international peace and security". It is not that the Council had not established before a connection between terrorism and the topos of "international peace and security".[3] But it seems that here, in resolution 1368, it used for the first time pure and simple the expression of Article 39 of the Charter, "threat to the peace", with reference to a specific terrorist act.[4] However, the Council intentionally refrained from defining the attacks as an "armed attack", knowing perfectly well that according to Article 51 of the Charter the existence of such an attack is an indispensable precondition for self-defence.[5]

While the Council thus responded to the American expectations, it expressed, in operative paragraph 5 of the resolution, "its readiness to take all necessary steps to respond to the terrorist attacks of 11 September 2001 ... in accordance with its responsibilities under the Charter of the United Nations".[6] With this paragraph, the Council took up and specified what it had already expressed in the preamble of the resolution, namely its determination "to combat by all means threats to international peace and security caused by terrorist acts".

Very rightly Professor Antonio Cassese called resolution 1368 ambiguous and contradictory: "[T]he Security Council wavers between the desire

[3] See especially resolutions 748 of 31 March 1992 and 883 of 11 November 1993 (Lockerbie case), 1054 of 26 April 1996 (Sudan), 1267 of 15 October 1999 and 1333 of 19 December 2000 (the Taliban), and 1269 of 19 October 1999 (international terrorism in general). For a discussion of the *Lockerbie* case in the present context, see R Higgins, "The general international law of terrorism", in R Higgins and M Flory (eds), *Terrorism and international law* (Routledge, London and New York, 1997), 13, at 20 ff.

[4] This has since become an established practice of the Council. See resolutions 1438 of 14 October 2002 (bomb attacks in Bali, Indonesia), 1440 of 24 October 2002 (act of taking hostages in Moscow), 1450 of 13 December 2002 (bomb attack in Kikambala, Kenya) and 1465 of 13 February 2003 (bomb attack in Bogota, Colombia). See also the Council's "Declaration on the Global Effort to Combat Terrorism", resolution 1377 of 12 November 2001, para 3: "*The Security Council ... Further declares* that acts of international terrorism constitute one of the most serious threats to international peace and security in the twenty-first century". Para 10 speaks of "the scourge of international terrorism", in a language reminiscent of the preamble of the UN Charter ("to save succeeding generations from the scourge of war"). See, in contrast, the earlier practice of the Council (resolutions 748, 883, 1054, 1267 and 1333) according to which the failure of a government to comply with certain requests of the Council was said to constitute a threat to international peace and security.

[5] See, by contrast, Security Council resolution 661 of 6 August 1990, preambular para 6: "*The Security Council ... Affirming* the inherent right of individual or collective self-defence, in response to the armed attack by Iraq against Kuwait, in accordance with Article 51 of the Charter".

[6] See also Press Statement by the President of the Security Council of 11 September 2001, SC/7141, last para: "Members of the Security Council express their readiness to take urgent further steps in accordance with their responsibilities under the Charter of the United Nations."

to take matters into its own hands and resignation to the use of unilateral action by the US."[7] However, we should not fail to see the legal craftsmanship of those who drafted the resolution in the turmoil and shock caused by the attacks in the very proximity of the UN headquarters. They tried to create a balance between the conflicting ideas of collective security and self-defence in which the first would carry somewhat more weight than the latter. They chose a language which could be interpreted in line with what the United States called for, and expected from, the Council in the given situation.[8] But while accommodating the United States in this unparalleled situation, they carefully avoided statements from which general and far-reaching conclusions could be drawn. In particular, the Council did not sanction the view that "private" (i.e. non-State) acts of violence may be answered with acts of self-defence under Article 51 of the UN Charter.[9] No such approval can be inferred from the resolution, for the reason alone that on 12 September it was not clear at all that the terrorist attacks of the previous day had not been organised or sponsored by a State government.

In the light of these findings, the Security Council meeting on 12 September 2001[10] was characterized by a noteworthy opposition between two conflicting ideas: On the one hand, representatives of the fifteen member States of the Council all agreed that — to quote Sir Jeremy Greenstock speaking for the United Kingdom — the acts of September 11th "are an attack not only on the United States but against humanity itself" or, as the representative of Ukraine said, "a direct challenge not only to the United States, but to the entire civilized world", or, in the words of the

[7] A Cassese, "Terrorism is Also Disrupting Some Crucial Legal Categories of International Law", (2001) 12 *European Journal of International Law* 993, at 996. See also C Tomuschat, "Der 11. September und seine rechtlichen Konsequenzen", (2001) 28 *Europäische Grundrechte-Zeitschrift* 535, at 543, and EPJ Myjer and ND White, "The Twin Towers Attack: An Unlimited Right to Self-Defence?", (2002) 7 *Journal of Conflict and Security Law* 5, at 10 ff. ("a position of deliberate ambiguity to satisfy the competing political demands").

[8] See also Tomuschat, above n 7, at 544. See further the remarks by Ambassador John D. Negroponte, United States Permanent Representative to the United Nations, at the Security Council Stake-Out, 8 October 2001; US Mission to the UN Press Release no 136 (01) of 8 October 2001, about the effects of Security Council resolutions 1368 and 1373: "[W]e and others who have been involved in this military action continue to enjoy strong understanding of the actions we have taken and, I think, a clear understanding that we are acting in our inherent right of self-defence. *I think that has been understood and anticipated all along*" (Emphasis added).

[9] In this respect, I disagree with Professor Dinstein who refers to the resolution in support of his theory of "extra-territorial law enforcement", according to which a State may take forcible countermeasures in the territory of another State if that State fails to use force against terrorists using its territory "as a springboard of attacks against" the former State. See Y Dinstein, "Comment" in C Walter *et al* (eds), *Terrorism as a Challenge for National and International Law: Security versus Liberty?* (Springer, Berlin and Heidelberg, 2003), and Y Dinstein, *War, Aggression and Self-Defence* (Cambridge University Press, Cambridge, 3rd edn 2001), at 213–21.

[10] Security Council, 4370th meeting, UN Doc S/PV.4370.

representative of the People's Republic of China, "an open challenge to the international community as a whole". This seemed to suggest that it was up to the Security Council, as the organ of the international community responsible for the maintenance of peace and security, to take the necessary action.[11] But actually this assessment went hand in hand with a readiness to allow the United States a unilateral military response in the name of self-defence. Perhaps only the United States was considered to be able effectively to defend by military means the values of the international community as a whole.

The ambiguity of resolution 1368 was not eliminated by the subsequent resolution 1373, adopted on 28 September 2001. In the preamble, the Council reaffirmed both the view that the attacks of September 11th "constitute a threat to international peace and security", and the existence of "the inherent right of individual or collective self-defence as recognized by the Charter of the United Nations as reiterated in resolution 1368 (2001)". The Council also reaffirmed "the need to combat by all means ... threats to international peace and security caused by terrorist acts". However, it did not repeat its statement of 12 September 2001 about "*its* readiness to take all necessary steps to respond to the terrorist attacks".[12] Instead, it restricted itself to a specifically legal measure by making obligatory for all States most of the provisions of the International Convention for the Suppression of the Financing of Terrorism of 9 December 1999.[13] By that time, it had become clear that the United States was not willing to subject its military response to the terrorist acts to the rules and procedures of the Security Council. Thus the Council stepped back from assuming its responsibility under Chapter VII of the UN Charter. This implied a support of the United States view that its impending military actions against targets abroad could be based on the self-defence argument.[14]

The Council was again confronted with that argument a bit later after the United States had begun its military actions against the Al-Qaeda organisation and the Taliban regime in Afghanistan. A letter dated 7 October 2001

[11] See the statements of the representatives of Bangladesh ("It is important that a unified Security Council now take appropriate steps") and France ("A global strategy is needed. The Security Council is the principal organ entrusted with international peace and security"), *ibid*, at 6 and 7, respectively.

[12] Emphasis added. Instead, and more narrowly, the second last para. of resolution 1373 said: "*The Security Council ... Expresses* its determination to take all necessary steps in order *to ensure the full implementation of this resolution ...*" (last emphasis added).

[13] For text, see General Assembly resolution 54/109.

[14] An interesting ambiguity could already be observed in the press statement of the President of the Security Council, Ambassador Jean-David Levitte, of 11 September 2001 (UN Press Release SC/7141): "Members of the Security Council [in their individual capacity? Or as constituent members of the Council as an institution?] express their readiness to take urgent further steps in accordance with their responsibilities under the Charter of the United Nations."

from the Permanent Representative of the United States to the UN addressed to the President of the Security Council said, *inter alia*:

> In accordance with Article 51 of the Charter of the United Nations, I wish, on behalf of my Government, to report that the United States of America, together with other States, has initiated actions in the exercise of its inherent right of individual and collective self-defence following the armed attacks that were carried out against the United States on 11 September 2001.... [M]y Government has obtained clear and compelling information that the Al-Qaeda organization, which is supported by the Taliban regime in Afghanistan, had a central role in the attacks.... We may find that our self-defence requires further actions with respect to other organizations and other States.[15]

A day later, on 8 October 2001, the US Permanent Representative explained that "what was intended by that statement in our letter was simply that we reserved the right to exercise our right of self-defence in the future if we thought that was necessary and the circumstances warranted."[16]

There is no indication that a majority of Council members was willing to discharge the Council's responsibilities under the Charter instead of simply taking note of the American declarations. But even if there had been such an intention, it could not have been realized because the United States would have vetoed any decision restricting its unilateral action.

When assessing the performance of the Security Council after the September 11th attacks, one must bear in mind that the options available to the Council were limited indeed. For this, there is first and foremost a reason one may call systemic. When the United Nations Organization was founded in 1945, it was generally understood that a war waged by one of the so-called Great Powers would remain outside the boundaries of UN control. To fend off any undesired UN intervention in such a conflict was one of the main functions of the right of veto of the five permanent members of the Security Council. As Professor Michael Reisman once remarked, because of the veto the Organization would not be able to "confront directly one of the major power centres or, in more general terms, the effective power process. That seem[ed] necessary for, in such a confrontation, the Organization would be the casualty".[17] Whether or not one agrees from a legal point of view with the US notion of being "at war"

[15] UN Doc S/2001/946 of 7 October 2001. In the address of President Bush to the American people of the same day the term "self-defence" did not appear. Instead, the President said, *inter alia*: "We are supported by the collective will of the world.... This military action is part of our campaign against terrorism". See "Presidential Address to the Nation", 7 October 2001, released by the White House, Office of the Press Secretary.

[16] Remarks by Ambassador John D Negroponte, above n 8.

[17] WM Reisman, "The Constitutional Crisis in the United Nations", (1993) 87 *American Journal of International Law* 83, at 98.

with terrorism in general or the Al-Qaeda organisation,[18] in terms of the real "power process" Professor Reisman's finding certainly applied to the situation of September and October 2001.

More specifically, one must say that it is unlikely that the United States would have accepted any resolution which did not include at least a reference to the right of self-defence. Accordingly, if a majority of Council members, or one of the other permanent members, had insisted on leaving out that reference, the Council would have been forced to remain silent altogether — which would have removed it from the scene right from the start. And even if the United States had accepted "less" than a recognition of its right to self-defence, namely the Council's "authorization" to use military force in response to the terrorist attacks, this would in effect not have amounted to any greater role of the Council. It is only in retrospect that some would have preferred a silent Council to one giving the United States its seal of approval for actions the Council would not be able to influence in any meaningful way. Partly it was this experience which in the months preceding the war against Iraq of March 2003 caused a majority of the members of the Council to refuse the United States the approval and support it sought.

It must be emphasized that the self-restraint displayed by the Council was not motivated by any sense of a lacking of legal competence. There was no doubt that the Council could have taken action on the basis of Chapter VII of the UN Charter. The respective mandate given to the Council is broad enough to cover acts of international terrorism as possible threats to international peace and security. It is obvious that a terrorist crime of a certain gravity which was possibly perpetrated from abroad can easily lead to international friction and a danger that military force is used by the victim State against the possible foreign source of terrorism. Such an international conflict may arise whether or not the terrorist act can be considered as sponsored, or supported, or not prevented from being committed, by a State. A determination of the existence of a threat to the peace under Article 39 of the Charter does not require a responsibility of a State as determined by the international law of State responsibility.

The Council's self-restraint rather followed from the determined position immediately adopted by the United States Government, according to

[18] For US domestic legislation based on that notion, see, eg, Declaration of National Emergency by Reason of Certain Terrorist Attacks, Proclamation of the President, 14 September 2001 (Proc. 7463); Presidential Executive Order on Terrorist Financing, 24 September 2001; USA Patriot Act of 2001, 26 October 2001; Homeland Security Act of 2002; Military Order: Detention, Treatment, and Trial of Certain Non-Citizens in the War Against Terrorism, 66 Fed. Reg. 57, 833, 16 November 2002. The last mentioned order opens with the words, "International terrorists, including members of al Qaida, have carried out attacks on United States diplomatic and military personnel and facilities abroad and on citizens and property within the United States on a scale that has created *a state of armed conflict* that requires the use of the United States Armed Forces" (emphasis added).

which on September 11th the United States had been attacked so that it was up to it unilaterally to decide on necessary measures of defence. This American position found a perfect expression in the State of the Union Address delivered by President George W Bush on 29 January 2002 from which a few sentences may be quoted:

> As we gather tonight, our nation is at war.... [W]e are winning the war on terror. The men and women of our Armed Forces have delivered a message now clear to every enemy of the United States: ... you will not escape the justice of this nation.... Our cause is just, and it continues.... [O]ur war against terror is only beginning.... My hope is that all nations will heed our call... But some governments will be timid in the face of terror. And make no mistake about it: If they do not act, America will....And all nations should know: America will do what is necessary to ensure our nation's security.[19]

The phrase "if they do not act" referred to individual action by certain States suspected by the US of supporting, or at least not actively suppressing, terrorist groups. The phrase did not refer to multilateral action in the form of a Security Council resolution. The United Nations was not mentioned once in the President's speech.

B. The Claim to "Pre-Emptive Self-Defence"

Although, for the reasons discussed above, the course steered by the Council under such difficult circumstances can be regarded as reasonable and appropriate, its willingness to accept the right of self-defence as a legal basis for a use of military power the scope and intensity of which could not be foreseen represented a further stepping back of the Council from exercising its powers under the UN Charter. It is well known that already resolution 678 of 29 November 1990, authorizing "Member States co-operating with the Government of Kuwait...to use all necessary means" in order to free Kuwait from the Iraqi troops, met with some criticism regarding the degree to which the Council relinquished its control over the following military and also political events. This method of "contracting out", it was said, "leaves individual states with wide discretion to use ambiguous, open-textured resolutions to exercise control over the initiation, conduct and termination of hostilities".[20] The then

[19] See "The President's State of the Union Address", The United States Capitol, Washington, DC, 29 January 2002, as released by The White House, Office of the Press Secretary.

[20] See J Lobel and M Ratner, "Bypassing the Security Council: Ambiguous Authorizations to Use Force, Cease-Fires and the Iraqi Inspection Regime", (1999) 93 *American Journal of International Law* 124, at 125. For a pointedly critical view, see J Quigley, "The "Privatization" of Security Council Enforcement Action: A Threat to Multilateralism", (1996) 17 *Michigan Journal of International Law* 249.

Secretary-General of the United Nations Pérez de Cuéllar remarked that the way in which resolution 678 was implemented showed "that there is a need for an improved and more institutionalized mechanism for reporting to the Council by the concerned states". The Council, he said, "needs to preserve for itself the authority to exercise guidance, supervision or control with respect to the carrying out of actions authorized by it".[21]

When the Council limits itself to acknowledging an exercise of the right of self-defence, it adopts an even more detached attitude, even if it fully retains the right "to take at any time such action as it deems necessary in order to maintain or restore international peace and security" (Article 51 of the UN Charter). Clearly, such a policy is not what the drafters of the UN Charter had in mind. Article 51 is based on the assumption that self-defence is a short-term action by a State to repel an armed attack of an aggressor State — in other words, that it is action necessitated by circumstances, only lasting, and only tolerable, until the moment in which the Security Council steps in to restore peace in accordance with the UN Charter. In the case under discussion, the Council would have been perfectly able to take the matter into its own hands, at least at the moment Afghanistan and the Taliban emerged as the (first) principal target of US action. For the Taliban regime and its support of terrorism had since long been a subject-matter the Council had seized.[22] One cannot reproach the Council for having been negligent or blind before the appalling attacks of September 11th. All the threats and problems identified by the United States after the attacks — terrorism in general, the proliferation of weapons of mass destruction, Afghanistan, Iraq, the Middle East, Somalia — had long been on the Security Council's agenda.

Early on, academic observers drew attention to the dangers inherent in the wide understanding of the concept of self-defence that resulted from the events of September 11th — a wide understanding regarding the target of armed action in self-defence, the point of time at which such action is initiated, the duration of the action, and the means to be used.[23] In a "traditional" inter-State war it would at least be certain who the enemy is, and there would be a number of generally accepted rules about the admissibility and proportionality of measures of defence. In contrast, the "war against terrorism" takes place in a largely unchartered territory where most legal questions are open. Only one thing is sure: The easier a

[21] J Pérez de Cuéllar, Address delivered at the University of Bordeaux, 22 April 1991, UN Press Release SG/SM/4560, quoted in D Sarooshi, *The United Nations and the Development of Collective Security* (Clarendon Press, Oxford, 1999), at 184 fn 62.

[22] See especially resolutions 1267 of 15 October 1999, 1333 of 19 December 2000, and 1363 of 30 July 2001. For later resolutions concerning the Taliban and the "Al-Qaeda network" in Afghanistan, see resolutions 1378 of 14 November 2001, 1388 of 15 January 2002, 1390 of 16 January 2002, 1452 of 20 December 2002, and 1455 of 17 January 2003.

[23] See especially Cassese, above n 7, at 997 ff.

recourse to self-defence (as to every form of unilateral use of force) is made, the greater is the danger of an abuse of military power by a strong State against the weaker. For these reasons, a retreat of the Council into the passive role of the observer is particularly problematic.

The following developments fully testified to the correctness of the concerns voiced by Professor Cassese and others. The military actions of the United States in Afghanistan[24] (a country which, in the absence of an internationally recognized government and because of a worldwide detestation of the Taliban, was an unusually easy target) were merely registered by the Security Council.[25] It was only after these actions had essentially been completed that the Council, acting under Chapter VII of the Charter, authorized member States "participating in the International Security Assistance Force to take all necessary measures to fulfil its mandate", this mandate being "to assist the Afghan Interim Authority in the maintenance of security in Kabul and its surrounding areas".[26] Nevertheless, the United States continued bombing targets in other parts of the country, presumably still regarding this as an exercise of its right of self-defence.[27]

In September 2002, the Administration of President Bush proclaimed a new "National Security Strategy"[28] based on a broadly defined right of "pre-emptive self-defence" which considerably goes beyond the controversial "anticipatory self-defence" that in the past some States claimed to be entitled to in the face of an imminent and evident attack. Part III of the paper includes the following statements:

> The United States of America is fighting a war against terrorists of global reach. The enemy is not a single political regime or person or religion or ideology. The enemy is terrorism — premeditated, politically motivated violence perpetrated against innocents. ... We will disrupt and destroy terrorist organizations by: ... defending the United States, the American people, and

[24] For a provisional legal analysis of the campaigns of the "Coalition" forces and the "Northern Alliance/United Front" supported by them in Afghanistan, see R Cryer, "The Fine Art of Friendship: *Jus in Bello* in Afghanistan", (2002) 7 *Journal of Conflict and Security Law* 37.

[25] For Security Council resolutions on Aghanistan after the removal from power of the Taliban, see resolutions 1383 of 6 December 2001, 1386 of 20 December 2001, 1401 of 28 March 2002, 1413 of 23 May 2002, 1419 of 26 June 2002, and 1444 of 27 November 2002.

[26] See resolution 1386 of 20 December 2001, operative paras 1 and 3.

[27] See Myjer and White, above n 7, at 13.

[28] See The National Security Strategy of the United States of America (document issued by the White House, 17 September 2002). See also the National Strategy to Combat Weapons of Mass Destruction (document issued by the White House, December 2002) which, in comparison, is phrased more cautiously: "U.S. military forces and appropriate civilian agencies must have the capability to defend against WMD-armed adversaries, *including in appropriate cases through preemptive measures*. This requires capabilities to detect and destroy an adversary's WMD assets *before these weapons are used*" (p 3, emphasis added).

> our interests at home and abroad by identifying and destroying the threat before it reaches our borders. While the United States will constantly strive to enlist the support of the international community, we will not hesitate to act alone, if necessary, to exercise our right of self-defense by acting preemptively against such terrorists, to prevent them from doing harm against our people and our country....

In accordance with this strategy, President Bush declared in his State of the Union Address of 28 January 2003:

> All free nations have a stake in preventing sudden and catastrophic attacks. And we're asking them to join us .... Yet the course of this nation does not depend on the decisions of others. Whatever action is required, whenever action is necessary, I will defend the freedom and security of the American people. ... Some have said we must not act [against Iraq] until the threat is imminent. Since when have terrorists and tyrants announced their intentions, politely putting us on notice before they strike?

The strategy, covering States and non-State actors alike, was put into practice when in March 2003 the United States attacked Iraq, in spite of the fact that the Security Council had refused to approve that action.[29] Among the various reasons the Bush Administration put forward to justify its going to war "the continuing threat posed by Iraq" because of the country's alleged possession of weapons of mass-destruction and its connection with terrorist groups figured most prominently.[30] "Before the day of horror can come, before it is too late to act, this danger will be removed", President Bush said on 17 March 2003. "We are now acting because the risks of inaction would be far greater. In one year, or five years, the power of Iraq to inflict harm on all free nations would be multiplied many times over."[31]

How can the Bush Administration's "pre-emptive self-defence" be defined in legal terms? According to Professor Reisman, it is a strategy "that claims to use, unilaterally, and without prior international authorisation, high levels of violence to arrest an incipient development that is not yet operational and is not yet directly threatening but, in the view of the prospective 'victim', if permitted to mature could then be neutralised

[29] For a discussion of earlier, small-scale preemptive actions of states, see Y Daudet, "International action against State terrorism", in R Higgins and M Flory, above n 3, 201, at 203 ff, and WM Reisman, "International Legal Responses to Terrorism", (1999) 22 *Houston Journal of International Law* 3, at 17 ff.

[30] See U.S. Congress: Joint Resolution (Authorization for Use of Military Force Against Iraq), 107th Congress, 2nd Session, H.J. RES. 114 (10 October 2002), in particular paras 6, 12, and 13.

[31] See "President Says Saddam Hussein Must Leave Iraq Within 48 Hours: Remarks by the President in Address to the Nation", The White House, Office of the Press Secretary, 17 March 2003.

only at a higher, and possibly unacceptable cost". Very rightly concerned about the future of world order, Michael Reisman added:

> If this doctrine is writ large, the generalised opportunity for attack would simply raise the expectation of violence and press virtually all states to attack sooner rather than later. That is hardly in the interest of international law, one of whose essential functions is to lower the expectation of violence so that real violence will not eventuate.[32]

It is indisputable that such a broad notion of self-defence, apart from being irreconcilable with the general understanding of Article 51 prevailing up to now, seriously erodes the ban on the threat or use of force as laid down in Article 2(4) of the UN Charter and might indeed result in an abolition of that prohibition altogether.[33] The United States does not seem fully to appreciate that international law is a reciprocal system of rules, and that a freedom of action claimed by it cannot be denied other States now or in the future. While one can only agree with the observation that the rules of 1945 about the initiation of the use of force did not foresee the dramatic changes of weapons (the dissemination of ABC weapons) or the nature of adversaries,[34] it is far from clear that the law must be changed in the direction of a higher degree of freedom of unilateral action and less collective responsibility. Instead of discarding the rules of Chapter VII of the Charter, one could eventually try seriously to put them into practice.

III. PROSPECTS FOR FUTURE SECURITY COUNCIL ACTION AGAINST ACTS OF INTERNATIONAL TERRORISM

Apart from the reaction to the terrorist attacks of September 11th which we have witnessed in the past two years, will the Council in the future play a significant role in combatting acts of international terrorism which it called "one of the most serious threats to international peace and security in the twenty-first century"?[35] To this writer, several aspects suggest a rather limited role as regards an immediate response to such acts.

Firstly, other countries which are the victim of a terrorist crime will be inclined to refer to the precedent of resolutions 1368 and 1373 and to claim

[32] See WM Reisman, "Comment" in Walter *et al*, above n 9.

[33] For an expression of the latter view, with which I agree, see, eg, M Bothe, "Terrorism and the Legality of Pre-emptive Force", (2003) 14 *European Journal of International Law* 227. For a discussion of earlier efforts aimed at an expansion of the concept of self-defence, see A Cassese, "Return to Westphalia? Considerations on the Gradual Erosion of the Charter System", in A Cassese (ed), *The Current Legal Regulation on the Use of Force* (Martin Nijhoff, Dordrecht, 1986), 505, at 512 ff.

[34] See Reisman, above n 32.

[35] See resolution 1377 of 12 November 2001, para 3.

a right of self-defence — provided, of course, that they have the necessary military resources at their disposal and are willing to use them unilaterally.

Secondly, the Council was so far unable to agree on a definition of "terrorist acts",[36] and it is unlikely that it will in the foreseeable future. The consequence is a sort of "I know it when I see it" approach, even more unreliable and unpredictable than the Council's reaction to "traditional" violations of the ban on the use of force.[37] Terrorism is a form of political violence, and in the sphere of domestic and international politics it will remain controversial which cause or objective ranks so high that it possibly deserves to be supported by a use of physical force. By way of example, it is sufficient to recall the sympathy of a large part of the international community for the liberation of peoples from colonial and foreign domination. Since 1970, the UN General Assembly recognized a right of colonial peoples and peoples under alien domination to use "all necessary means" in their struggle for self-determination and independence.[38] In the so-called Friendly Relations Declaration of 1970, the General Assembly recognized that peoples are entitled to "actions against, and resistance to" any forcible action by States depriving them of their "right to self-determination and freedom and independence", and that they have a right to seek and to receive support from other States.[39] Some national

[36] For a very careful discussion of the problem of defining international terrorism, see the contribution of R Kolb to this volume. The principal obstacle to a comprehensive convention on international terrorism is the question of who would be entitled to exclusion from the treaty's scope (Art 18 of the draft convention). Correspondingly, agreement on the preamble, Art 1 (definition of phrases used in the convention) and Art 2 (definition of terrorism) is still outstanding. See Report of the Ad Hoc Committee established by General Assembly resolution 51/210 of 17 December 1996, Sixth Session (28 January–1 February 2002), UN Doc A/57/37.

[37] With reason, Professor Falk criticized "a failure to articulate principled lines of distinction when a UN response [to threats to international peace and security] is appropriate". See RA Falk, "The United Nations and the Rule of Law" in SH Mendlovitz and BH Weston (eds), *Preferred Futures for the United Nations* (Transnational Publishers, Irvington-on-Hudson, New York, 1995), 301, at 318 ff.

[38] See General Assembly resolutions 2621 (XXV), para 2, and 2708 (XXV), para 5: "*The General Assembly* ... 5. *Reaffirms* its recognition of the legitimacy of the struggle of the colonial peoples and peoples under alien domination to exercise their right to self-determination and independence *by all the necessary means at their disposal* and notes with satisfaction the progress made in the colonial Territories by the national liberation movements, both through their struggle and through reconstruction programmes" (emphasis added). For discussion, see, eg, LC Green, "The Legalization of Terrorism", in Y Alexander *et al* (eds), *Terrorism: Theory and Practice* (Westview Press, Boulder, Colorado, 1979), at 175–97; C Tomuschat, "The right of resistance and human rights", in UNESCO (ed), *Violations of human rights: possible rights of recourse and forms of resistance* (UNESCO, Paris, 1984), 13, at 18, 21, 26 ff.

[39] Declaration on Principles of International Law concerning Friendly Relations and Co-operation among States in accordance with the Charter of the United Nations, Annex to resolution 2625 (XXV) of 24 October 1970, "The principle of equal rights and self-determination of peoples", para 5, (1970) *United Nations Year Book* 788. For the right of secession in the absence of a "government representing the whole people belonging to the territory without distinction as to race, creed or colour", see *ibid* para 7.

constitutions provide for a right to resistance,[40] and a targeted State authority is likely to label any action based on that right "terrorist acts".[41]

When in 1972 the General Assembly passed its first general resolution on the phenomenon of international terrorism, the resolution bore the complicated but telling title:

> Measures to prevent international terrorism … and study of the underlying causes of those forms of terrorism and acts of violence which lie in misery, frustration, grievance and despair and which cause some people to sacrifice human lives, including their own, in an attempt to effect radical changes.[42]

Although later this title was replaced with a shorter one, it is still widely accepted that in certain situations a use of force is legitimate and lawful. For instance, in a letter addressed to the UN Secretary-General of 17 September 2002 Lebanon insisted that, contrary to the view of the Israeli Government, "the acts of legitimate resistance against the Israeli occupation" in the Lebanese areas occupied by Israel "do not fall under Security Council resolution 1373 (2001) on counter-terrorism", and that a distinction must be made "between terrorism, which we condemn, and the right of peoples to struggle against foreign occupation".[43]

Thirdly, the Security Council lacks the administrative means, or machinery, successfully to deal with a phenomenon so complex like international terrorism. It only knows what it is officially told by governments. It does not have the apparatus of a national government, in particular police forces and secret services, and therefore cannot engage in day-to-day activities with the aim of identifying, locating, and arresting individual terrorists. This situation has not been changed by the existence of the committee established to monitor the implementation of resolution 1373, the so-called

[40] See, eg, Art 20(4) of the Basic Law (Constitution) of the Federal Republic of Germany of 1949: "All Germans shall have the right to resist any person seeking to abolish this constitutional order, if no other remedy is available."

[41] One cannot but agree with the following recent findings of a working group established by the UN Secretary-General: "While terrorist acts are usually perpetrated by subnational or transnational groups, terror has also been adopted by rulers at various times as an instrument of control. The rubric of counter-terrorism can be used to justify acts in support of political agendas, such as the consolidation of political power, elimination of political opponents, inhibition of legitimate dissent and/or suppression of resistance to military occupation. Labelling opponents or adversaries as terrorists offers a time-tested technique to de-legitimize and demonize them. The United Nations should beware of offering, or be perceived to be offering, a blanket or automatic endorsement of all measures taken in the name of counter-terrorism." See Report of the Policy Working Group on the UN and Terrorism, Annex to UN Doc. A/57/273 – S/2002/875 of 6 August 2002, para 14.

[42] General Assembly res. 3034 (XXVII) of 18 December 1972. See Tomuschat, above n 7, at 538.

[43] See letter dated 17 September 2002 from the Chargé d'affaires a.i. of the Permanent Mission of Lebanon to the United Nations addressed to the Secretary-General, UN Doc. A/57/415 – S/2002/1038.

Counter-Terrorism Committee. It shall comprehensively review all member states' counterterrorism capacity and, if necessary, support their efforts to strengthen this capacity. At the time of this writing, it is still too early to try to assess the Committee's novel and ambitious work.[44]

However, if for those reasons I assume that the Council will only exceptionally control a State's military response to a terrorist act, this does not mean that the Council must sit idle. Just the contrary is true. The Council's principal task with regard to international terrorism follows from its role as the primary guardian of international peace and security. In that role, the Council must remind States and peoples everywhere of the general principles of the constitution of the international community designed to ensure a peaceful co-existence and co-operation of the peoples of the world. One of these principles is the duty to refrain from having resort to armed violence, and another the duty to settle disputes by peaceful means. In the latter regard, the Council must steadily remind States of the various multilateral fora available to them, including the International Court of Justice.

The Council further is called upon to devote itself more intensely to the identification and prevention of international conflicts, situations of civil war, and situations of grave violations of human rights.[45] That these conflicts and situations are a fertile soil for terrorist crime and violence was expressed by the Council itself when it emphasized

> that continuing international efforts to enhance dialogue and broaden the understanding among civilizations, in an effort to prevent the indiscriminate targeting of different religions and cultures, ... and to address unresolved regional conflicts and the full range of global issues, including development issues, will contribute to international cooperation and collaboration, which by themselves are necessary to sustain the broadest possible fight against terrorism.[46]

The Council can also engage in setting general norms and standards with the aim of fighting terrorism, following the example of its resolution 1373

[44] For an informative overview of the first stage of the Committee's work, see E Rosand, "Security Council Resolution 1373, the Counter-Terrorism Committee, and the Fight Against Terrorism", (2003) 97 *American Journal of International Law* 333.

[45] For a similar plea of the UN Secretary-General see, eg, his report "Prevention of armed conflict" of 7 June 2001, UN Doc. A/55/985 – S/2001/574, which includes the following recommendation (p 12, following para 39): "I encourage the Security Council to consider innovative mechanisms ... to discuss prevention cases on a continuing basis, particularly with regard to periodic regional or subregional reports that I intend to submit to the Council, as well as other early warning or prevention cases brought to its attention by Member States."

[46] See resolution 1456 of 20 January 2003 (declaration on the issue of combatting terrorism), para 10. This paragraph is based on para 10 of resolution 1377 (2001), above n 4. *Inter alia*, the expression "fight against international terrorism" was replaced with "fight against terrorism".

about the prevention and suppression of the financing of terrorist acts.[47] Today, the respective competence of the Council under Chapter VII of the Charter is widely accepted.[48]

IV. THE PRECARIOUS AUTHORITY OF THE SECURITY COUNCIL

It has rightly been said that the powers of the Security Council "are a precious, but at the same time precarious trust of the international community, certainly the greatest achievement of the new world order that emerged after the catastrophe of the Second World War". "Each and every state should be aware of the enormity of the progress that Chapter VII of the Charter embodies compared with the earlier system of unbridled coexistence of national sovereignties."[49] The Security Council is the principal organ of the international community. It has been entrusted with the task of defending "the interests and values regarded by the same community as being fundamental for the maintenance of its own integrity".[50] The Council represents a centerpiece of the post-1945 constitution of the international community.[51] If the authority and legitimacy of the Council[52] are seriously impaired by a further erosion of its powers under Chapter VII of the Charter, this will inevitably have a direct and negative impact on the international constitution as a whole, and hence the edifice of international law which rests upon that constitution. In other words, the price members of the international community will have to pay for their prolonged neglect of, and indifference to, the standing of the Security Council in the international security system may be much higher than they seem to imagine today.

[47] See PC Szasz, "The Security Council Starts Legislating", (2002) 96 *American Journal of International Law* 901.

[48] For an early recognition of that competence, see C Tomuschat, "Obligations Arising for States Without or Against Their Will", (1993) 241 *Recueil des Cours* 195, at 344. For further references, see B Fassbender, *UN Security Council Reform: A Constitutional Perspective* (Kluwer Law International, The Hague, 1998), at 211 fn 149, and JD Aston, "Die Bekämpfung abstrakter Gefahren für den Weltfrieden durch legislative Massnahmen des Sicherheitsrats: Resolution 1373 (2001) im Kontext", (2002) 62 *Zeitschrift für ausländisches öffentliches Recht und Völkerrecht* 257.

[49] C Tomuschat, "Using Force against Iraq", (1997) 73 *Die Friedens-Warte* 75, at 81.

[50] See PM Dupuy, "The Constitutional Dimension of the Charter of the United Nations Revisited", (1997) 1 *Max Planck Yearbook of United Nations Law* 1.

[51] See especially B Fassbender, "The United Nations Charter as Constitution of the International Community", (1998) 36 *Columbia Journal of Transnational Law* 529, at 574–76, and B Fassbender, "Quis judicabit? The Security Council, Its Powers and Its Legal Control", (2000) 11 *European Journal of International Law* 219.

[52] For the notion of legitimacy as applied to the Security Council, see Fassbender, above n 48, at 315 ff, and B Fassbender, "Uncertain Steps into a Post-Cold War World: The Role and Functioning of the UN Security Council after a Decade of Measures against Iraq", (2002) 13 *European Journal of International Law* 273, at 292–95.

This neglect has not only become apparent in the sidelining of the Council, which is put out of action from what is supposed to be its main activity, that is the safeguarding of international peace and security, but also in the inability of the international community to adapt the Council to the conditions and needs of the world of today.[53] In a September 2002 report, UN Secretary-General Kofi Annan spoke of the "stalled process of Security Council reform". He stated that after nearly a decade of discussions in the UN "a formula that would allow an increase in Council membership is still eluding Member States", notwithstanding the fact that "in the eyes of much of the world, the size and composition of the Security Council appear insufficiently representative".[54] Indeed, today prospects for a comprehensive reform of the Council, which would encompass both the body's composition and its decision-making process, are dim, and the pressure for such a reform, still strong in the early nineties, has given way to a certain ennui or resignation of the interested governments and NGOs. The famous "momentum for reform" was lost. It is true that it is extremely difficult to adapt to the present situation provisions of the Charter so closely, and intrinsically, associated with the international power structure of 1945 or, from a somewhat different perspective, with the specific stage of development that the international system had reached at the end of World War II. However, there is no viable alternative to facing that challenge, and to facing it soon. The difficulties of building a new order on the ruins of the UN Charter would certainly be much greater.

At present, many observers are of the opinion that the general international situation drastically changed in the aftermath of the terrorist attacks of September 11th, and that we witness a fundamental reorganization of the international system characterized by a United States pursuing its national interests, and in particular its security interests, much more resolutely and determinedly than before, and paying less attention to multilateral rules and procedures. If this assessment is correct, the question ensues whether in this new international order there will be a meaningful place for the United Nations and the Security Council. Will the internationalist project that began with the League of Nations and was continued with the UN of 1945 survive? It is almost forgotten that this project was promoted by two great American presidents, Woodrow Wilson and FD Roosevelt.

At the time this chapter is written, unilateralist rhetoric and action dominate the scene. But different from the past the call for international

[53] See B Fassbender, "All Illusions Shattered? Looking Back on a Decade of Failed Attempts to Reform the UN Security Council", (2003) 7 *Max Planck Yearbook of United Nations Law 783*.
[54] See "Strengthening of the United Nations: An Agenda for Further Change", UN Doc. A/57/387 of 9 September 2002, para 20.

cooperation in the fight against violence and terrorism is not simply the call of a few idealists. Multilateralism has effectively come to govern most aspects of the life of nations. It is a truism that the entire environment of States and nations today is characterized by transborder processes and actions. In the long term, even the most powerful State cannot isolate a certain aspect of its life from this environment. A hegemonic or neo-imperial system does not appear to be a viable alternative, if only for the reason that none of the potential hegemonic powers has the resources to enforce such a rule against the rest of the world for long.[55]

In the world of today, no State can guarantee its security only by unilateral means and actions. International cooperation, open discussion and joint action are indispensable, whether it is the Security Council or another body or forum through which they are implemented.[56] This is especially true with regard to the threat posed by terrorism. Military force can be used by one powerful State alone, but such force alone surely cannot put an end to terrorism.[57] More than such force is needed, and can only be achieved in a cooperative effort.[58] As Wolfgang Friedmann said, the world is being pushed towards the pursuit of common needs and goals, whether we want it or not. We may not remain captives of ideas of the past.[59] Hopefully, this will be understood rather sooner than later.

[55] For a dispassionate sketch of what a "hegemonic international law" of our days could look like, see DF Vagts, "Hegemonic International Law", (2001) 95 *American Journal of International Law* 843.

[56] See also JI Charney, "The Use of Force Against Terrorism and International Law", (2001) 95 *American Journal of International Law* 835, at 838: "Over the long term the interests of the United States and the international community will be best served by the Charter-based system of world order. If international terrorists have a coherent goal, it is to undermine this system — an objective the United States is perhaps unwittingly promoting by its actions. Despite the flaws of the United Nations, no one has proposed a better system for serving the interests of peace and security in the face of the agenda of international terrorist groups."

[57] In 1986, Adam Roberts concluded: "The record of what might be termed cross-border, military-punitive responses to terrorist actions is not a particularly encouraging one.... [T]here is a risk that such actions ... will make violence worse, not better." See A Roberts, "Terrorism and International Order", in L Freedman *et al*, *Terrorism and International Order* (Routledge & Kegal Paul, London, 1986), 7, at 20. This statement still appears correct.

[58] For an overview of non-military measures the United States has taken against terrorism, see SD Murphy, "International Law, the United States, and the Non-military 'War' against Terrorism", (2003) 14 *European Journal of International Law* 347.

[59] See above text accompanying notes 1 and 2.

7

Countering Catastrophic Terrorism: An American View

RUTH WEDGWOOD

THE EVENTS OF 11 September 2001 irrevocably changed the American understanding of the dangers of international terrorism. The extraordinary acts of violence and destruction undertaken by Al-Qaeda on that autumn morning were aimed at the virtues of a liberal society. The attacks killed thousands of innocent civilians arriving at work at the centre of international commerce in New York City. The dead included the citizens of more than 80 countries. The hijacked planes from Boston's Logan Airport, filled with civilian passengers, were used to ram the buildings at the tip of Manhattan Island. The jet fuel burned with furious heat, trapping workers on the upper stories of the buildings, causing many to jump to their deaths, melting the towers' structural support until the 100-story buildings collapsed. Other hijacked planes with civilians aboard were used by the Al-Qaeda guerrillas to attempt the decapitation of the American national government. A jet from Dulles Airport flew into the south wing of the Pentagon, killing more than two hundred workers, barely missing the offices of the Secretary of Defense and the National Command Authority. Passengers on a fourth plane struggled with their captors and heroically crashed the plane into the ground in rural Pennsylvania. This last plane was slated to fly to Washington, to destroy either the US Capitol or the White House.

The attacks showed Al-Qaeda's single-mindedness and spectacular ambition. Al-Qaeda has been interested in the cultural symbolism of the World Trade Center for a decade, attacking it with a truck-bomb in 1993, and then returning in 2001 for the deadly assaults from the air. The plan from the first was to topple the buildings across lower Manhattan, to stun a society, to use the heedlessness and pointlessness of the destruction as a method to create panic and insecurity.

Al-Qaeda knows how to exploit the civic virtues of democratic life. The group has organised effectively in the confidence that liberal governments would not look closely at their finances, or follow their travels between Europe, Afghanistan and North America, or restrain their passionate political and religious propaganda recruiting young men for violence. Events that should have triggered alarm, such as flight training by young men who had no involvement in the aviation industry but obvious associations with radical Imams, did not receive due attention in a society that values privacy and deliberately keeps government at arms-length. By constitutional design, American police powers are divided between federal, state and local governments. And in the reforms of the 1970's, additional firewalls were created to divide the activities of intelligence and police agencies. Thus, US government agencies following Al-Qaeda, onshore and off-shore, could not pool their knowledge, even as the terrorist recruits travelled easily between continents. The testimony from criminal grand juries could not be shared with intelligence agencies, and in turn, intelligence collection was not given to criminal investigators. Only after September 11, with Congressional legislation, were these firewalls taken down, so the government could synthesise its available information.[1] So, too, prior to September 11, the government could conduct an intelligence wiretap of a foreign government, but not of a foreign terrorist group. This was also changed by the Congress only after the attacks of September 11.[2]

Al-Qaeda also has challenged the benign assumptions of globalisation. In an integrated world economy, before September 11, borders and citizenship seemed less important than the economic drivers of prosperity, the marketplace forces of innovation, adaptation and resourceful investment decisions. The spread of manufacturing and the diffusion of technology around the world seemed one possible way to lift poor economies out of their long-standing misery. The journeys of enterprising people to the First World as economic migrants has been a central part of contemporary history, making problems such as public health and human rights a matter of global concern. But the misuse of globalisation is now evident as well. The freedom of movement prized in a Schengen ethos can be used to fly couriers, paymasters, and bomb-makers in and out of a country. The technology available on a world market can be purchased by a private group and married to a violent and atavistic worldview. In its adaptive style of warfare, Al-Qaeda is willing to use the scientific fruits of a free society and harness them, in a dangerous syncretism, to the purposes of

[1] The change was made by Congress in the Patriot Act. See "The Uniting and Strengthening America by Providing Appropriate Tools to Intercept and Obstruct Terrorism Act of 2001" (USA PATRIOT ACT), Public Law 107–05, 115 Stat. 2721, at s 203.

[2] *Ibid*, s 218. The Patriot Act also clarified the standards for a wiretap of a foreign terrorist group under the Foreign Intelligence Surveillance Act. The wiretap must be aimed at intelligence collection as a "significant purpose", but a possible criminal referral can also be contemplated. Formerly, the government had to warrant that intelligence was "the purpose" of the interception.

destruction. Al-Qaeda is also skilled at modern dress camouflage, giving its members indulgences to adapt to secular dress and habits, in order to pose as civilians who can mingle without notice while they choose targets, acquire munitions, infiltrate airport staffs and attack without warning.

Until 11 September 2001, the United States was relatively reticent in its method of confronting the challenge posed by Al-Qaeda, using mainly the device of criminal prosecution in individual cases, coupled with co-operating with other States to draft multi-lateral anti-terrorist conventions,[3] imposing civil sanctions against bin Laden's funds and companies[4] and, in an isolated case, using military force against targets associated with the bin Laden network in Afghanistan and Sudan.[5]

The group's attacks escalated in intensity throughout the 1990s. Thousands of young men passed through Al-Qaeda training camps in Afghanistan and Sudan. Alliances were created linking Al-Qaeda's financial and logistical capacity to local personnel from radical Muslim groups. Saudi Arabia gave billions of dollars to subsidise the building of mosques and *madrassas* around the world. Many of these have been used to propagate a radical and violent religious philosophy, teaching the Wahhabist doctrine that non-Muslims are not entitled to human respect, and that *jihad* means a commitment to violence. This incitement to hatred has threatened to displace the moderate traditions of Islam in West Africa and Central Asia with a mercenary propaganda that inclines young men to a madman's death.

The actual incidents of violence escalated, but were largely ignored in American politics — perhaps because the events were far away or claimed as their victims fellow citizens who had volunteered for service abroad. American military personnel serving as peacekeepers and transiting Aden were targeted by Al-Qaeda in 1992.[6] American peacekeepers deployed in Somalia to support the United Nations mission of famine

[3] For example, the US took part in drafting the Convention on the Safety of United Nations and Associated Personnel, 9 Dec 1994, GA Res 49/59, UN GAOR, 49th Sess Supp No 49, Vol 1, at 299, UN Doc A/49/49 (1994) and the International Convention for the Suppression of Terrorist Bombings, 15 Dec 1997, GA Res 52/164, UN GAOR, 52nd Sess, Supp No 49, Vol 1, at 389, UN Doc A/52/49.

[4] On 20 Aug 1998, an executive order froze the US assets of bin Laden and forbade any financial transactions between US companies and his associates: Exec Order No 13,099, 63 Fed Reg 45,167 (1998). Sanctions have been imposed against countries that have supported terrorist cells: Determination Sudan, 58 Fed Reg 52,523 (1993); 50 USC App para 2405(j) (1998).

[5] See below for a discussion. The Afghan targets were training camps used for logistical support and coordination, and also identified as the venue for a top-level meeting of bin Laden's leadership. The Sudan target was an industrial plant in Khartoum—the al Shifa pharmaceutical plant—believed to be a manufacturing or trans-shipping facility for chemical weapons. See Address to the Nation on Military Action Against Terrorist Sites in Afghanistan and Sudan, 34 *Weekly Comp Press Doc*, 1543, 20 Aug 1998.

[6] See, eg, S Barr, "U.S. Stops Using Yemen Support Base", *The Washington Post*, 3 Jan 1993, A18.

relief were ambushed by Al-Qaeda trained guerrillas in 1993. The Mogadishu shoot-out cost the lives of 18 Army Rangers, with the mutilation of several soldiers' corpses, and the loss of two Black Hawk helicopters.[7] Then, in 1993, the World Trade Center was attacked with a truck bomb, killing eight people and causing the evacuation of thousands of workers with serious cases of smoke inhalation and other injuries.[8] In 1995, the Riyadh military training centre in Saudi Arabia was attacked, killing five Americans and wounding 60.[9] In 1996 the Khobar Towers military barracks was truck-bombed, killing at least 19 Americans and wounding more than 300.[10] Incredibly enough, the reconstruction contract for the barracks was awarded by the Saudis to the construction firm run by Osama bin Laden's brothers.

In 1995, Al-Qaeda planned to bomb 11 American civilian jetliners over the Pacific, and did a successful trial run with an "undetectable" nitroglycerin bomb made by smuggling the parts on board a Philippines aircraft, resulting in the grisly death of a Japanese passenger.[11] The project was named "*Bojinka*" ("loud bang" in Serbo-Croatian), and the moniker may have been a souvenir of *mujahedeen* fighting in Bosnia. It was interrupted only perchance when a fire broke out in the Manilla apartment of Al-Qaeda member Ramzi Yousef, and responding firemen found the group's equipment and plans. So, too, Al-Qaeda made grandiose plans to bomb the Lincoln and Holland Tunnels in Manhattan, seeking to trap and flood hundreds of cars and their passengers under the East and Hudson Rivers. They planned as well to blow up the United Nations in New York, by driving a truck-bomb into the UN garage. These projects were intercepted only by the successful infiltration of informants into the groups.

The escalation of Al-Qaeda's plans and attacks was accompanied by missed opportunities. In 1996, the government of Sudan reportedly made an offer to Washington to surrender bin Laden to the Saudis or

[7] See M Gordon with T Friedman, "Details of US Raid in Somalia: Success so Near, A Loss so Deep", *New York Times*, 24 Oct 1993, A1.

[8] See eg, "Explosion at the World Trade Center: Death and Fear Rock a Landmark", *The New York Times*, 27 Feb 1993, 21: "An explosion apparently caused by a car bomb in an underground garage shook the World Trade Center in Lower Manhattan with the force of a small earthquake ... plunging the city's largest building complex into a maelstrom of smoke, darkness and fearful chaos."

[9] See M Sheridan, "Riyadh Blast a Declaration of War, Says Dissident", *The Independent* 15 Nov 1995, 14.

[10] See eg, B Graham, "Bomb Kills 23 Americans at Saudi Base", *The Washington Post*, 26 June 1996, A1.

[11] See "Philippines Charges Militant in Jet Bombing", *The New York Times*, 31 March 1995, A 9: "The Muslim militant [Ramzi Ahmed Yousef] accused of being the main planner of the World Trade Center bombing was charged with murder today in the bombing of a Philippine jet in December".

perhaps to the United States directly. The offer was not pursued, and bin Laden simply relocated his base of operations to Afghanistan[12]. One published account states that the White House declined the Sudanese offer because FBI director Louis Freeh said there was insufficient evidence admissible in federal criminal court to permit the arrest and indictment of bin Laden. (The former United States Attorney in the Southern District of New York has said that she was not informed of the offer and would have scrambled to cobble together a case). Washington was not yet willing to consider the prerogatives of the law of war, even though Al-Qaeda had already declared a *fatwa* against American soldiers. The idea that the US could hold bin Laden as a combatant in an ongoing conflict, was therefore not contemplated.[13]

Then, in 1998, Al-Qaeda mounted horrific truck-bomb attacks against the American embassies in Tanzania and Kenya, leaving more than 200 dead and 4500 people grievously wounded. Most victims were Africans, and many were Muslim.[14] The United States responded by sending in the Federal Bureau of Investigation to gather forensic evidence in the rubble of Dar es Salaam and Nairobi. President Clinton also mounted a symbolic military operation—dubbed "Operation Infinite Reach"—attacking Al-Qaeda training camps in Afghanistan, and leveling the al Shifa pharmaceutical plant in Khartoum, Sudan, thought to be a trans-shipment point for VX nerve gas. The al Shifa plant owner had financial links to bin Laden and was reportedly in telephone contact with the former chief of the Iraqi VX chemical weapons programme.[15] But the al Shifa target choice was widely disputed, and the attacks on the Afghan training camps were ineffectual, delayed for several hours in order to avoid collateral damage in the coordinate strike in Khartoum, thus losing the chance to strike bin Laden.[16] An indictment for bin Laden was subsequently issued in the US for the bombing of the embassies.[17]

[12] See R Wedgwood, "The Law at War: How Osama Slipped Away", (Winter 2001/2002) *National Interest* 69–73.

[13] See R Wedgwood, "Al Qaeda, Terrorism and Military Commissions", (2002) *96 American Journal of International Law*, 328, at 330.

[14] See G Young and L Hannan, "Clinton in tears as embassy dead return", *The Guardian*, 14 Aug 1998, 1.

[15] See "Sudanese Factory Was Working with Iraq on VX Nerve Agent, US Intelligence Says; Assessment Based in Part on Intercepted Phone Calls", *Baltimore Sun*, 26 Aug 1998, at 18A ("Telephone intercepts by the National Security Agency included contacts between senior Shifa officials and Emad al-Ani, the reputed creator of Iraq's chemical weapons program ... "); J Diamond, "US Cites Iraqi Tie to Sudan Plant, *AP*, 26 Aug 1998.

[16] See R Wedgwood, "Responding to Terrorism: The Strikes Against bin Laden", (1999) 24 *Yale Journal of International Law* 559.

[17] Indictment, *United States v Usama bin Laden et al*, S(2) 98 Cr 1023 (LBS) (SDNY 4 Nov 1998). The indictment charged bin Laden with conspiracy, bombing US embassies, and 224 counts of murder.

In October 2000, the *USS Cole*, a guided-missile destroyer with the Fifth Fleet, was also bombed, while on a refueling port call in Aden.[18] A local small craft was filled with shaped C-4 explosives, came alongside and blew a 40-foot hole in the hull, nearly sinking the destroyer and killing 17 sailors. This was Al-Qaeda's second attempt at targeting US military vessels in Aden. An earlier try in January 2000 targeted the USS *Sullivans*, with a dhow loaded with explosives. The craft was overloaded and sank, and the United States never learned of the attempt, continuing Aden port calls. After the Cole attack, FBI agents were again dispatched, though the Yemeni government did not facilitate the investigation. Washington vetoed any immediate military retaliation against Al-Qaeda while the criminal investigation was completed.

And then, of course, came the horrendous attacks of 11 September 2001, in Washington and New York. The original plan, according to the published reports of a captured Al-Qaeda informant, was to hijack 10 passenger jets for synchronised attacks on the East and West Coasts of the United States. But with visa difficulties, the operation was scaled back to four planes.

In three major criminal trials in the 1990's, the federal government successfully convicted the captured operatives of the 1993 World Trade Center bombing and the East African embassies bombing.[19] The trials were held in federal court in the Southern District of New York, and were brilliantly run. But the prosecutions were thought of as "multiple homicides", notes a former head of the FBI Terrorist Task Force. What America did not understand in the 1990's was the importance of disrupting and dislodging the infrastructure of international terrorism. The US treated Al-Qaeda's terrorist attacks as isolated criminal incidents, with the prosecution of expendable operatives. The tools of diplomacy, economic sanctions and military power were not used to disrupt Al-Qaeda's network of safe houses and support personnel, constrain its financing and transfers of cash and break apart its relationships with the rogue elements of some governments. Instead the US insisted on using the reactive stance of criminal law, which punishes and restrains a perpetrator after the fact, when a criminal deed is complete and over, rather than preventing and intercepting the action beforehand.[20] That stance is appropriate in a peacetime world, where even a serious crime will cause only limited damage to

[18] See H Schneider and R Suro, "Death Blast Put at 17 in *USS Cole* Blast", *Washington Post*, 14 Oct 2000, A1.

[19] See *United States* v *Salameh et al*, 152 F 3d 88 (2d cir 1998); *United States* v *Rahman et al*, 189 F3d 88, 103–111 (2d Cir 1999); *United States* v *Salameh et al*, 261 F 3d 271 (2d cir 2001) (1993 World Trade Center bombing). See also *United States* v *Bin Laden et al*, 2001 US Dist LEXIS 15484 (SDNY 2001) (1998 Embassy bombings).

[20] See R Wedgwood, "Cause for Alarm: Legal Action Can Bring Victories, But Preventing Terrorism Calls for Tougher Tactics", *Washington Post*, 3 June 2001, B1.

others. It is not sufficient when an ideological network is targeting military assets in a worldwide campaign, or trying to kill civilians *en masse,* or actively seeking weapons of mass destruction. Courtroom victories did not shut down Al-Qaeda's network of recruitment or its training camps. Nor did judicial verdicts quell Al-Qaeda's appetite for violence. The guilty verdict in the East African embassy bombings case was delivered in a courtroom six blocks away from the World Trade Center, three months before the towers were toppled.

In the common law tradition of Anglo-American criminal law, the government would never act to detain a suspect unless and until there was probable cause to believe that a specific criminal act had been committed or was about to be committed. In the structure of criminal law enforcement, before an arrest can be made, there has to be a good faith belief that "proof beyond a reasonable doubt" can be assembled within 30 to 60 days, to meet the demands of the speedy trial guarantee. And this proof has to pass the hurdles of the technical rules of courtroom evidence, limiting what the fact-finder can consider, excluding hearsay or informant information, calling only first-hand eyewitnesses, and authenticating seized evidence with carefully documented chains of custody and records custodians. If such proof is not available, the government is simply supposed to wait, and hope that enough witnesses will later be found to offer new testimony so that an admissible case can be assembled. In ordinary civil society, the working premise is that no great harm will come to pass from this, for even criminals are members of society, and their ambition is rarely to cause the maximum possible harm. The supposition of ordinary criminal law is that general deterrence is sufficient, bringing the perfected cases that are amenable to courtroom proof, dissuading other potential offenders by the severity of punishment. One doesn't have to solve every crime. But this paradigm crashes against the shoals of a militant group that sees itself as engaged in a world war against the West, urging suicide attacks, experimenting with weapons of mass destruction, and plotting the deaths of innocent civilians in order to achieve the effects of maximum shock and disruption. Al-Qaeda has undertaken tactics discarded by the most sanguinary European terrorist groups. Al-Qaeda leaders have publicly proclaimed interest in a "Hiroshima-style" attack, and in a world awash with weapons, it is well to heed their words.

What changed after September 11 was the understanding of Al-Qaeda's commitment to catastrophic terrorism and the scope of its ambition. No political terrorist network has ever sought to acquire nuclear weapons, build dirty bombs, let loose biological weapons or cause civilian casualties on the scale seen on September 11. The death toll of 3,000, with thousands more seriously injured, could have ranged far higher if the buildings had not been rapidly evacuated; as many as 15,000 people were at work in the complex during the mid-morning attacks. The scale may seem almost genocidal, seeking to annihilate thousands in a flash. Osama bin Laden's *fatwa* in 1998 pronounced all men, women and children, all Christians, Jews and apostate Muslims, to be valid targets for murderous attack.[21] It is a moral nihilism without parallel since the doctrines of the Nazis.

So, too, the fireball over lower Manhattan imparted a new understanding of the limits of deterrence — both in criminal law and international strategy. Until then, the US had supposed that the capture, trial and punishment of a limited number of Al-Qaeda recruits could deter the others. It had also been supposed that a technical demonstration of the ability to mount retaliatory military attacks with stand-off weapons could dissuade Al-Qaeda and the Taliban host. But deterrence cannot work when a non-State actor is unencumbered by worldly commitments, when it lacks any commitment to a people or a territory, and seeks only supernatural reward. Deterrence cannot work when a religion is hijacked and its interpreters prescribe an Islamic duty to use violence against innocents, or when a regime has become dependent on Al-Qaeda's money and armaments to remain in power.

This failure of deterrence creates a dangerous vulnerability. Even during the Cold War, with the overflowing nuclear arsenals of the West and the Soviets, there was some rugged stability provided by "mutually-assured destructive capability" — the unavoidable knowledge that any use of nuclear weapons would bring devastating retaliatory strikes against one's own population and territory. But "MAD" will not work against the asymmetric strategy of a non-State actor.

After September 11, there was agreement that criminal prosecutions would no longer suffice as a stand-alone strategy. Only military intervention, not criminal law, could shut down the training camps in Afghanistan used by Al-Qaeda to train young men in the fine arts of wiring explosives and the "jihadist" philosophy. The methods of financial intermediation used to resupply the coffers of Al-Qaeda could be disrupted only with a new financial transparency prescribed by national governments.[22] Prosecutors alone could not dissuade the Saudis from subsidising the proselytisation of Wahhabist doctrines. And criminal law alone could not interrupt attacks before they were mounted.

The conclusion that the law of armed conflict may have some applicability in the fight against Al-Qaeda is thus founded in the immediate

[21] The text of Osama bin Laden's *fatwa* was published in *Al-Quds al-'Arabi* on 23 Feb 1998, available at: <http://www.ict.org.il/articles/fatwah.htm>.

[22] One report notes that bin Laden allegedly managed a US $ 8 billion fund for the Taliban movement. See "Afghanistan: Report on bin Laden's Activities, Wealth", *Al Watan Al'Arabi* (Paris), 4 Sep 1998.

landscape of the September 11 attacks, which were considered as acts of war against the United States in Al Qaeda's continued campaign against American targets.[23] This conclusion, based on the gravity of the September 11 attacks, was not peculiar to Washington. The United Nations Security Council, NATO, the members of the Rio Treaty, and the ANZUS Pact partners all passed resolutions indicating that Al-Qaeda's attacks shared the scale and scope of war.[24] For the first time in 50 years, the North Atlantic Council invoked the powers of Article 5 of the NATO treaty in a pledge of mutual self-defence.[25] The UN Security Council authorised the use of armed force in a resolution immediately after the attacks,[26] followed two weeks later by resolution 1373 which set rigorous new standards demanding that States refrain from offering any asylum, financial assistance, logistics or intelligence to international terrorist groups.[27]

After the attacks of September 11, the Security Council renewed its demand that the Taliban regime in Afghanistan surrender bin Laden.[28]

[23] See Wedgwood, "Al Qaeda, Terrorism ..." , above n 13, 330: "In an intellectual shift, the Bush order announced that the paradigm of war fit the case after all".

[24] SC Res 1368 of 12 Sep 2001 stated that the September 11 terrorist attacks, "like any act of international terrorism" constituted a "threat to international peace and security": para 1. The OAS invoked Art 3(1) of the Inter-American Treaty of Reciprocal Assistance, of 2 Sep 1947, 62 Stat 1681, 1700, 21 UNTS 77, 95 ("Rio Treaty") following 11 September ("an armed attack against an American State shall be considered as an attack against all the American States"). See "Terrorist Threat to the Americas", Meeting of Consultation of Ministers of Foreign Affairs, Organization of American States, available at: <www.oas.org/OASpage/crisis/RC.24e.htm>. Art IV of the Security Treaty Between Australia, New Zealand and the United States of America of 1 Sep 1951, 3 UST, 3420, 3423, 131 UNTS 83, 86 was invoked by Australia. See Fact Sheet, White House Office of Communications, *Campaign Against Terrorism Results* (1 Oct 2001), available at WL 21898781, 1 (noting that "Australia offered combat military forces and invoked Article IV of the ANZUS Treaty, declaring September 11 an attack on Australia").

[25] Statement by the North Atlantic Council, 12 Sep 2001, in Press Release 124 (2001), 40 ILM 1267 (2001).

[26] SC Res 1368 (12 Sep 2001). Preambular para 2 stated that the Security Council recognised "the inherent right of individual or collective self-defence in accordance with the Charter".

[27] SC Res 1373 (28 Sep 2001): "all States shall: (a) Refrain from providing any form of support, active or passive, to entities or persons involved in terrorist acts, including by suppressing recruitment of members of terrorist groups and eliminating the supply of weapons to terrorists; (b) Take the necessary steps to prevent the commission of terrorist acts, including by provision of early warning to other States by exchange of information; (c) Deny safe haven to those who finance, plan, support, or commit terrorist acts, or provide safe havens; (d) Prevent those who finance, plan, facilitate or commit terrorist acts from using their respective territories for those purposes against other States or their citizens;". *Ibid*, para 2.

[28] In SC Res 1378 of 14 Nov 2001, the Security Council condemned: "the Taliban for allowing Afghanistan to be used as a base for the export of terrorism by the Al-Qaida network and other terrorist groups and for providing safe haven to Usama Bin Laden, Al-Qaida and others associated with them ...". SC Res 1378 (14 Nov 2001), preambular para 4. The Council had earlier imposed sanctions against the Taliban and "the territory of Afghanistan under Taliban control", demanding the surrender of bin Laden. See SC Res 1333 (19 Dec 2000) and SC Res 1267 (15 Oct 1999).

When it refused, the United States deployed military forces to Northern Afghanistan, and fought alongside the Northern Alliance to dislodge Al-Qaeda and the Taliban regime from Afghan territory.[29] Bin Laden was not caught, nor was Taliban leader Mullah Omar, and the Pakistani border has proved difficult to police against continued infiltration. But Al-Qaeda lost its immediate base of operations, and has apparently shifted from a vertical to a horizontal model of operations. The United States has become active in tracing Al-Qaeda's financing, dislodging Al-Qaeda operatives from other locations around the world, and starkly saying to allies and friends that they have the responsibility to police their own territories effectively.

The war against Al-Qaeda has posed some new legal questions. The Geneva Conventions of 1949 were not designed for wars against non-State actors, or regimes that refuse to apply any part of the law of war in their own operations. The Geneva Conventions assume that adversaries upon capture will identify their name, rank and serial number, rather than attempting to feign civilian status. Geneva law also assumes that the adversary will not try to use the protections of the humanitarian legal regime as a means to kill their captors. The fighters captured and detained in Afghanistan were carefully screened by American military and intelligence personnel in an attempt to discern who was a member of Al-Qaeda or a high-level member of the Taliban.[30] Members of Al-Qaeda were not classified as lawful combatants, for they do not fight for a State, and have deliberately cast aside the laws of war. Accordingly, they fail to fit into the categories of prisoners of war listed in Article 4 of the Third Geneva Convention.[31]

[29] US military strikes began against Taliban and Al Qaeda targets in Afghanistan on 6 Oct 2001. See, "Bush announces opening of attacks", CNN, 7 Oct 2001: "Bush said the action was taken after the Taliban refused to meet several non-negotiable American demands. 'More than two weeks ago, I gave Taliban leaders a series of clear and specific demands: Close terrorist training camps. Hand over leaders of the al Qaeda network, and return all foreign nationals, including American citizens unjustly detained in your country,' Bush said." Report available at: <http://www.cnn.com/2001/US/10/07/ret.attack.bush/>.

[30] The screening and review process for combatants has involved four layers of assessment and review *before* a person may be transferred to Guantanamo, and three levels of review thereafter. See Secretary Rumsfeld's Remarks to Greater Miami Chamber of Commerce, 13 February 2004, transcript available at <http://www.defenselink.mil/transcripts/2004/tr20040213-0445.html>, and Briefing by Paul Butler, Principal Deputy Assistant Secretary of Defense for Special Operations and Low Intensity Conflict, and Army Major General Geoffrey D Miller, Commander. Joint Task Force Guantanamo, 13 February 2004, transcript available at <http://www.defenselink.mil/transcripts/2004/tr20040213-0443.html>.

[31] Under Art 4 of the Geneva Convention Relative to the Treatment of Prisoners of War, 12 Aug 1949, 6 UST 3316, 75 UNTS 135 (hereafter Third Geneva Convention) to qualify as prisoners of war, members of Al Qaeda would essentially have to show that they either formed part of the armed forces of Afghanistan or were members of a militia or volunteer corps belonging to a Party to the conflict and which fulfilled the following conditions: (1) being commanded by a person responsible for subordinates; (2) having a fixed distinctive sign recognisable at a distance; (3) carrying arms openly; and (4) conducting operations in accordance with the laws and customs of war. See Art 4A(2) *ibid*.

Members of the Taliban, as hosts to Al-Qaeda and as a side that failed to respect the laws of combat, were also determined not to qualify as lawful combatants.[32] This position is based on the view that "members of regular armed forces who profess allegiance to a government or an authority not recognized by the Detaining Power" as listed under Article 4A(3) of the Third Geneva Convention are not exempted from the requirement of distinguishing themselves from civilians and obeying the laws of war.[33] In fact these "material characteristics" are inherent in the notion of a "regular armed force", as noted by the *Commentary* to the Third Geneva Convention.[34] Protocol I Additional to the Geneva Conventions also appears to require armed groups to generally observe the laws and customs of war in order to qualify as an "armed force".[35]

Nonetheless, the failure of the members of the Taliban and Al Qaeda to qualify as prisoners of war does not exclude them from humanitarian protections.[36] They are allowed to write regularly to their families and receive letters in return, and they are visited regularly by the

[32] A Fleischer, White House Spokesman, Special White House Announcement Re: Application of Geneva Conventions in Afghanistan (7 Feb 2002), available in LEXIS, Legis Library, Fednews File; See also *White House Fact Sheet: Status of Detainees at Guantanamo* (7 Feb 2002), available at <http://www.whitehouse.gov/news/releases/2002/02/>.

[33] This is based *inter alia* on the language of Art 1 of the Regulations Respecting the Laws and Customs of War on Land, Annex to the Hague Convention IV Respecting the Laws and Customs of War on Land, 18 Oct 1907, 36 Stat 2277, 1 Bevans 631 and Art 9 of the 1874 Brussels Declaration: Project of an International Declaration Concerning the Laws and Customs of War, 27 Aug 1874, 65 *British and Foreign St Papers* 1105 (1873–74), reprinted in D Schindler and J Tomans (eds), *The Laws of Armed Conflicts* 3rd edn, (1988), 27 ("The laws, rights, and duties of war apply not only to armies, but also to militia and volunteer corps fulfilling the following conditions: 1. To be commanded by a person responsible for his subordinates; 2. To have a fixed distinctive emblem recognizable at a distance; 3. To carry arms openly; and 4. To conduct their operations in accordance with the laws and customs of war. In countries where militia or volunteer corps constitute the army, or form part of it, they are included under the denomination 'army'").

[34] The *Commentary* states, "These 'regular armed forces' [under Third Geneva Convention Article 4(A)(3)] have all the material characteristics and all the attributes of armed forces in the sense of [Article 4(A)(1)]: they wear uniform[s], they have an organized hierarchy and they know and respect the laws and customs of war. The delegates to the 1949 Diplomatic Conference were therefore fully justified in considering that there was no need to specify for such armed forces the requirements stated in [Article 4(A)(2)]." J de Preux (ed), *Commentary to the Geneva Convention Relative to the Treatment of Prisoners of War*, (International Committee of the Red Cross, Geneva, 1960), 63.

[35] See Art 43(1) of the Protocol Additional to the Geneva Conventions of 12 Aug 1949, and Relating to the Protection of Victims of International Armed Conflicts, 12 Dec 1977, 1125 UNTS 3.

[36] For a general discussion of the legal regime applicable to internees of Guantanamo, see Brief *Amicus Curiae* of Law Professors, Former Legal Advisers of The Department of State and Ambassadors, Retired Judge Advocates General and Retired Military Commanders, and other International Law Specialists in Support of Respondents, in *Ràsul et al v Bush, et al*, and *Al Odah et al v United States et al*, Nos 03-334 and 03–343, Supreme Court of the United States, October Term 2003 (Ruth Wedgwood, Charles Fried, and Max Kampelman, Counsel for *amicus curiae*), available at <http://www.jenner.com/gitmo>.

International Committee of the Red Cross as a monitoring agency. They have received first-class medical care, access to Muslim religious advisers, and religiously appropriate food, with accoutrements for religious observance. But they are combatants captured in armed conflict, and so can be interned for the duration of the conflict in order to prevent their return to the fight.[37] It is a preventive regime of war, not a criminal proceeding.[38] A parallel may be seen in the internment of 400,000 Axis prisoners during the Second World War. Though held on American soil, they were not entitled to appointed legal counsel or a criminal trial, for it was an internment under the laws of war rather than criminal law. Governments often do communicate with the United States on the behalf of nationals captured in the Afghan fighting,[39] but the applicable regime remains the law of armed conflict, not peacetime criminal arrest.

The war crimes committed against American civilians and military personnel may ultimately be prosecuted in military commissions established by the President. On repeated occasions, Congress has recognised the President's constitutional authority as commander-in-chief to establish tribunals under the common law of war.[40] The Supreme Court has also recognised the role of military commissions in cases deriving from World War II.[41] The fact that there has been no formal declaration of war makes no difference to the President's power to establish military commissions due to the fact that the law of war (also known as international humanitarian law) applies in any international state of

[37] Art 118 of the Third Geneva Convention, above n 31, provides that: "Prisoners of war shall be released and repatriated without delay after the cessation of hostilities".
[38] The main principle on which the Third Geneva Convention is based is that captivity in war is "neither revenge, nor punishment, but solely protective custody, the only purpose of which is to prevent the prisoners of war from further participation in the war". This assertion, made in 1941 by German Admiral Canaris, was approved as legally correct by the International Military Tribunal at Nuremburg. HMSO Cmd 6964 (1946) p, 48, reprinted in (1947) 41 *American Journal of International Law*, 228–29.
[39] One example is the discussion between Australia and the United States in relation to the planned military commission trial of Australian nationals detained in Guantanamo Bay. See "Ministerial Statement: Government Accepts Military Commissions for Guantanamo Detainees," *Joint News Release*, Attorney-General Philip Ruddock and Minister for Foreign Affairs Alexander Downer, 25 Nov 2003.
[40] See War Crimes Act of 1996, Report of the Committee on the Judiciary, US House of Representatives, H Rep 104–698, 104th Cong, 2nd Sess (24 July 1996); Uniform Code of Military Justice, 10 US Code 361, cited in President Bush's order of 13 Nov 2001. See also Art 15 of the Articles of War, in Chapter 227, Public Law No 242, 66th Cong, 2d Sess (1920) ("The provisions of these articles conferring jurisdiction upon courts-martial shall not be construed as depriving military commissions ... of concurrent jurisdiction in respect of offenders or offenses that by statute *or by the law of war* may be triable by such military commissions ... ".) (emphasis added).
[41] See *Ex parte Quirin*, 317 US 1 (1942), *In re Yamashita*, 327 US 1 (1946) and *Johnson v Eisentrager*, 339 US 763 (1950).

"armed conflict" as noted by the 1949 Geneva Conventions.[42] In any case, it is clear that Congress has authorised the president's use of force against Al Qaeda and the Taliban.[43]

The rules established for commission trials and appeals were crafted over a lengthy period, with the advice of a group of distinguished leaders of the American bar, and draw from the human rights reform jurisprudence of the last 50 years.[44] Indeed, the military commission rules embody all fundamental procedural guarantees. These include the presumption of innocence, burden of proof on the government, proof beyond a reasonable doubt, the right to cross-examine prosecution witnesses and to call defence witnesses and the mandatory production of exculpatory evidence by the government. Defendants can choose their military defence counsel and retain a civilian counsel, and have the right of appeal from any conviction to an independent review panel, which has the autonomous power to reverse and remand a conviction for any serious errors of law.[45] The first four appointees to the appellate review panel were recently announced, and each was a civilian, including former Clinton Administration Attorney General Griffin Bell, and the Honorable William Coleman, a distinguished African-American cabinet secretary under the Ford Administration and a prominent leader of the American bar.

A military venue is preferred in international law, to the surprise of some observers. The Third Geneva Convention states that lawful combatants *must* be tried in a military tribunal rather than a civilian court, unless the detaining power's own military personnel would also be tried in a civilian court.[46] The two major adaptations of the commissions stem from the exigencies of trying cases in wartime, and the sources of proof available in the hurly-burly of military operations. First, the trial judges sitting as fact-finders are entitled to consider any evidence that a reasonable person would find to be probative. This does not change the standard for sufficiency of proof, and evidence will be considered only for the weight it deserves. It is the same standard of admissibility used in the United

[42] See Art 2 common to the Geneva Conventions of 12 Aug 1949.

[43] *Joint Resolution to Authorize the Use of United States Armed Forces Against Those Responsible for the Recent Attacks Launched Against the United States*, 18 Sep 2001, Pub L No 107–40, 115 Stat 224, reprinted in 40 ILM 1282 (2001).

[44] See R Wedgwood, "Al-Qaeda, Military Commissions, and American Self-Defense", (2002) 117 *Political Science Quarterly*, No 3, 357.

[45] See Procedures for Trials by Military Commissions of Certain Non-United States Citizens in the War Against Terrorism, Department of Defense Military Commission Order No 1, 21 March 2002, available at <http://www.defenselink.mil/news/Mar2002/d20020321. ord.pdf>.

[46] See Third Geneva Convention, above n 31, Art 84 ("A prisoner of war shall be tried only by a military court, unless the existing laws of the Detaining Power expressly permit the civil courts to try a member of the armed forces of the Detaining Power in respect of the particular offence alleged to have been committed by the prisoner of war").

Nations war crimes tribunals,[47] and resembles European law as well. It is different from common law civilian rules,[48] but it is not unfair. Second, there may be some circumstances where the courtroom will be temporarily closed. This is permitted under the Geneva Conventions[49] and will be kept to a minimum, with the guarantee that the military defence counsel will always be present to counter any contested evidence. In addition, the military commissions, like American civilian courts, may in principle impose the death penalty, though one would expect the scrupulousness of fact-finding appropriate to any grave penalty. For a case eligible for the death penalty, a seven-member military commission would have to be appointed, and return a unanimous verdict.[50]

In addition, over time, we may have to find a way to confine the limitless character of the new war against Al-Qaeda. The young men captured on the battlefield are subject to internment until the war is over, and at the moment we are only two years past the fierce fighting in Afghanistan. The Taliban are mounting new attacks from across the Pakistani border, seeking to recapture the south-eastern region. The war, even in a conventional sense, is certainly not over. But we may wish to employ, for the medium term, a more formal structure for the periodic re-evaluation of the dangerousness of combatants.[51] Some may remain committed to *jihad*, but others may persuasively argue that they have re-thought their purpose and would not return to the fight. These reviews are already accomplished through sophisticated intelligence screening. But it may be advisable to have a formal structure that is more visible, rather like the periodic reviews given to mental health patients and repeat sexual offenders. The Secretary of Defense has recently announced that quasi-parole hearings will be conducted

[47] See Rule 89(C) of the Rules of Procedure and Evidence of the International Criminal Tribunal for the former Yugoslavia, 11 Feb 1994, as amended: "A Chamber may admit any relevant evidence which it deems to have probative value." Available at: <http://www.un.org/icty/legaldoc/index.htm>.

[48] In federal courts, for example, only eyewitness testimony can generally be heard. While this may not pose an obstacle in ordinary domestic trials in which citizens are presumed willing to obey the order of the court to give evidence, it is a more difficult hurdle to surmount in the context of legal action against a transnational and powerful terrorist group. Federal court rules governing physical objects and documentary searches may also exclude probative evidence. In particular, the "exclusionary rule" would exclude any evidence taken in a criminal law search conducted without probable cause — a standard inappropriate on the battlefield. For further discussion, see Wedgwood, "Al Qaeda, Terrorism ...", above n 13, 331.

[49] See Art 105 Third Geneva Convention, above n 31, ("The representatives of the Protecting Power shall be entitled to attend the trial of the case, unless, exceptionally, this is held *in camera* in the interest of State security.").

[50] See above n 45.

[51] To date, more than 100 detainees out of approximately 660, including 3 juveniles, have been released by US authorities from the naval base in Guantanamo Bay, Cuba.

periodically to assess whether Guantanamo internees are still dangerous and whether, if released, they would return to the fight.[52] The pity of Al-Qaeda's recruitment is that there is no regime or responsible government that can end the war by surrender.

Democratic governments are now asked to accomplish the unprecedented and confounding tasks of anticipation and protection, rather than reaction and punishment after the fact. Potential targets can be safeguarded to some degree, and societies will pay more attention to commercial and human traffic across borders. But it is hard to design a global economy and social community that does not have significant vulnerability to spoilers. This leaves the challenge of anticipation — seeking to identify the recruits to a diffuse compartmentalised network of actors, and seeking to intercept their plans before a catastrophic attack is actually launched. The adversary speaks a different language, travels from continent to continent, and operates within societies that value personal privacy and restraints on government data collection. It uses counter-surveillance — employing technology to coordinate plans, avoiding electronic means of communication when an event is near at hand. Despite its stringent account of Islam, it has taught its actors to assume secular habits in order to blend into civil society. Indeed, many of its recruits have come from semi-assimilated communities in Western Europe.

The lesson of September 11 is that the control of catastrophic terrorism may require measures beyond criminal law, including military action against Al-Qaeda's unpoliced places of repose, a new system of financial controls, and a new standard of State responsibility for controlling private activity within national territory. Prior to September 11, most observers assumed that vigorous efforts to mount criminal prosecutions could succeed in quelling any private source of violence. But it was not within contemplation that the diffusion of technology means that a non-State actor could exert the destructive power of a State. The controversies that have accompanied the American response to Al-Qaeda's terrorism were probably unavoidable. But one worries, on this side of the Atlantic, that Europe does not appreciate the gravity of Al-Qaeda's ambition, even now.

[52] See Secretary Rumsfeld Remarks to Greater Miami Chamber of Commerce, 13 February 2004, transcript available at <http://www.defenselink.mil/transcripts/2004/tr20040213.0445.html>, and Briefing by Paul Butler, Principal Deputy Assistant Secretary of Defense for Special Operations and Low Intensity Conflict and Army Major General Geoffrey D Miller, Commander, Joint Tank Force Guantanamo, 13 February 2004, transcript available at <http://www.defenselink.mil/transcripts/2004/tr90040213-0443.html>.

8

*The Action of the European Union to Combat International Terrorism**

AUGUST REINISCH

I. INTRODUCTION

IN RESPONSE TO the terrorist attacks on 11 September 2001 in the United States of America, the international community reacted swiftly. The victim State showed a clearly discernible political will to act not only unilaterally but also, at least to some extent, within the framework of international organisations. The United Nations, regional security organisations such as NATO, OSCE and others immediately took steps to increase their efforts in the "fight against terrorism".

The US and its allies focused on military measures involving the use of force following a "declaration of war on terrorism".[1] However, the UN's immediate reaction was not limited to "[r]ecognizing the inherent right of individual or collective self-defence in accordance with the Charter"[2] but also clearly stressed the criminal justice aspect of fighting terrorism.

On 12 September 2001, the day after the terrorist attacks, the UN Security Council adopted Resolution 1368 condemning the terrorist acts of the previous day and called upon all States:

> to work together urgently to bring to justice the perpetrators, organizers and sponsors of these terrorist attacks and *stresses* that those responsible for

* This chapter was finalised in July 2002 and updated in May 2003.

[1] See the White House Questions and answers about the "War on Terrorism" available under <http://www.whitehouse.gov/response/faq-what.html>. See also the documents available under "AMERICA'S WAR AGAINST TERRORISM", <http://www.lib.umich.edu/govdocs/usterror.html>.

[2] Preambular para 3 UN Security Council Resolution 1368, <http://www.un.org/Docs/scres/2001/res1368e.pdf>.

> aiding, supporting or harbouring the perpetrators, organizers and sponsors of these acts will be held accountable;[3]

It also called upon the international community

> to redouble their efforts to prevent and suppress terrorist acts including by increased cooperation and full implementation of the relevant international anti-terrorist conventions and Security Council resolutions, in particular resolution 1269 (1999) of 19 October 1999;[4]

On 28 September 2001, the Security Council adopted Resolution 1373.[5] This resolution contains in 18 sub-paragraphs a list of specific measures against terrorism States are required to take. Among these are the prevention and suppression of the financing of terrorist acts, the freezing of funds, the criminalisation of the financing of terrorism and the criminalisation of other acts supporting terrorism. It also established a Counter-Terrorism Committee (CTC)[6] to monitor implementation of Resolution 1373 and to receive State reports on the measures taken to implement this resolution.

What is particularly interesting about this resolution is the fact that the Security Council clearly ventures into the field of general law-making activity. It should be noted that Resolution 1373 does not contain any specific reference to 11 September 2001, to Osama Bin Laden or to Al-Qaeda.

[3] *Ibid.*

[4] In Resolution 1368 the SC "*Calls upon* all States to implement fully the international anti-terrorist conventions to which they are parties, *encourages* all States to consider as a matter of priority adhering to those to which they are not parties, and *encourages also* the speedy adoption of the pending conventions;" (op. para. 2) and "*Calls upon* all States to take, *inter alia*, in the context of such cooperation and coordination, appropriate steps to

- cooperate with each other, particularly through bilateral and multilateral agreements and arrangements, to prevent and suppress terrorist acts, protect their nationals and other persons against terrorist attacks and bring to justice the perpetrators of such acts;
- prevent and suppress in their territories through all lawful means the preparation and financing of any acts of terrorism;
- deny those who plan, finance or commit terrorist acts safe havens by ensuring their apprehension and prosecution or extradition;
- take appropriate measures in conformity with the relevant provisions of national and international law, including international standards of human rights, before granting refugee status, for the purpose of ensuring that the asylum-seeker has not participated in terrorist acts;
- exchange information in accordance with international and domestic law, and co-operate on administrative and judicial matters in order to prevent the commission of terrorist acts;" (op. Para. 4).

[5] <http://www.un.org/Docs/scres/2001/res1373e.pdf>.

[6] <http://www.un.org/Docs/sc/committees/1373/>.

Rather, it imposes very general obligations on States to legislate and take other measures in the fight against terrorism.[7]

On a European regional level, the participation in the fight against terrorism has proven to be a challenge for the European Union (EU). This has mainly technical, legal reasons. Politically, there is no question that the EU is willing to support the measures decided upon by the Security Council. However, most of these measures relate to the field of justice and police matters — core issues of national sovereignty — wherein the Union only slowly attains powers according to the complicated architecture of the Maastricht Treaty on the European Union (EU Treaty). The Treaty's allocation of competences in the Justice and Home Affairs (JHA) pillar only sparingly conceives of genuine EU powers to combat terrorism. With the Treaty of Amsterdam the new Third Pillar, now referred to as Police and Judicial Cooperation in Criminal Matters (PJCC),[8] provides for certain harmonisation powers, such as the possibility to adopt framework decisions under Article 34 of the EU Treaty.[9]

On the other hand, the awareness of the need to combat terrorism on a European level is not new to the EU. Rather, the fight against terrorism is one of the intergovernmental policy areas since the 1992 Maastricht Treaty. The Amsterdam EU Treaty expressly states that "preventing and combating crime, organised or otherwise, in particular *terrorism*," is one of the tasks of the Union in order to achieve the union's objective "to provide citizens with a high level of safety within an area of freedom, security and justice".[10]

Article 29 EU Treaty identifies three specific areas of closer co-operation: closer co-operation between police forces, customs authorities and other competent authorities, including Europol; closer co-operation between judicial and other competent authorities of the Member States; as well as approximation, where necessary, of rules on criminal matters.

Work on measures against all forms of cross-border organised crime, including terrorism, was pursued by the EU already before 11 September 2001.[11] It even goes well beyond the Maastricht Treaty-created co-operation in the field of JHA and partly dates back to the intergovernmental

[7] See J Finke and C Wandscher, "Terrorismusbekämpfung jenseits militärischer Gewalt" (2001) 49 *Vereinte Nationen* 168–73.

[8] See generally S Peer, *EU Justice and Home Affairs Law* (Harlow, Longman, 2000); J Monar, "Institutionalizing Freedom, Security, and Justice" in J Peterson and M Shackleton (eds), *The Institutions of the European Union* 186–209 (Oxford, Oxford University Press, 2002).

[9] According to Art 34 para 2 (b) EU Treaty the Council may "unanimously on the initiative of any Member State or of the Commission": "adopt framework decisions for the purpose of approximation of the laws and regulations of the Member States. Framework decisions shall be binding upon the Member States as to the result to be achieved but shall leave to the national authorities the choice of form and methods. They shall not entail direct effect;".

[10] Art 29 para. 2 (ex Art K.1) EU Treaty.

[11] See generally T Stein and C Meiser, "Die Europäische Union und der Terrorismus" (2001) 76 *Die Friedens-Warte* 33.

cooperation developed through the European Political Co-operation in the 1970s. An important step was the formation of the TREVI (French acronym for: Terrorisme, Radicalisme, Extremisme et Violence Internationale) Group in 1975 in which the Interior Ministers met in order to combat terrorism through increased police co-operation.

But it is obvious that the Maastricht Treaty on European Union elevated the co-operation to new levels: In 1996 the Council decided by a Joint Action of 15 October 1996[12] to create and maintain a directory of specialised counter-terrorism competences, skills and expertise to facilitate counter-terrorism co-operation between the EU Member States.

With respect to judicial co-operation, Article 31 (b) EU Treaty expressly mentions the facilitation of extradition between Member States. In the 1990s the EU adopted a number of treaties in this field, supplementing the 1957 Council of Europe sponsored European Extradition Convention[13] and the 1977 European Convention on the Suppression of Terrorism[14]: among these are the Convention of 10 March 1995 on simplified extradition procedure between the Member States of the European Union[15] and the Convention of 27 September 1996 relating to extradition between the Member States of the European Union.[16]

The Union also adopted in 1998 a Joint Action on the creation of a European Judicial Network[17] and a Joint Action on making it a criminal offence to participate in a criminal organisation in the Member States of the European Union.[18]

At the October 1999 European Council meeting in Tampere, the concept of extradition law, whether traditional or simplified, was abandoned in favour of a "mutual recognition" approach taken over from the supranational pillar of the EC. Very broadly, the European Council declared that the principle of "mutual recognition" should become the cornerstone of

[12] Joint Action 96/610/JHA of 15 October 1996, adopted by the Council on the basis of Article K.3 of the Treaty on European Union, on the creation and maintenance of a Directory of specialized counter-terrorist competences, skills and expertise in the Member States of the European Union, OJ L 273/1, 25 October 1996.

[13] Paris, 13 December 1957, ETS No. 24, available under <http://conventions.coe.int/Treaty/en/Treaties/Html/024.htm>.

[14] Strasbourg, 27 January 1977, ETS No. 90, available under <http://conventions.coe.int/Treaty/EN/Treaties/Html/090.htm>.

[15] OJ C 78/1, 30 March 1995.

[16] OJ C 313/11, 23 October 1996.

[17] Joint action 98/428/JHA of 29 June 1998, adopted by the Council, on the basis of Article K.3 of the Treaty on European Union, on the creation of a European Judicial Network, OJ L 191/4, 07/07/1998. Available under <http://europa.eu.int/eur-lex/pri/en/oj/dat/1998/l_191/l_19119980707en00040007.pdf>.

[18] Joint action 98/733/JHA of 21 December 1998 adopted by the Council on the basis of Article K.3 of the Treaty on European Union, on making it a criminal offence to participate in a criminal organisation in the Member States of the European Union, OJ L 351/1, 29/12/1998. Available under <http://europa.eu.int/eur-lex/pri/en/oj/dat/1998/l_351/l_35119981229en00010002.pdf>.

judicial co-operation in both civil and criminal matters within the Union and that "the formal extradition procedure should be abolished among the Member States as far as persons are concerned who are fleeing from justice after having been finally sentenced, and replaced by a simple transfer of such persons".[19]

With regard to the harmonisation of criminal law, Article 31(e) EU Treaty contains a clear legislative mandate calling for the adoption of measures establishing minimum rules relating to the constituent elements of criminal acts and to penalties in the field of, among others, terrorism. Thus, the issue of defining terrorism as a criminal offence has become an unavoidable legal problem for the EU.

As will be discussed further below, the EU prepared two basic legal instruments for these purposes: a Council Framework Decision on combating terrorism[20] and a Council Framework Decision on the European arrest warrant.[21] These two are by far the most important legislative measures taken in response to the challenge of terrorism.[22] The following contribution will focus on these framework decisions together with the EU legislation on freezing "terrorist" assets. It should not be overlooked, however, that a host of other measures have been taken or initiated by the EU under the title of "fighting terrorism" in response to the 11 September attacks, such as humanitarian relief for Afghanistan, flight security measures, emergency preparedness, air transport insurance, etc.[23]

II. IMMEDIATE AND GENERAL FOREIGN POLICY RESPONSES OF THE EU TO 11 SEPTEMBER 2001

A. Declaration by the EU

On 12 September 2001, the day after the attacks on the World Trade Center and the Pentagon, the EU Foreign Ministers reaffirmed in the General

[19] Tampere European Council 15 and 16 October 1999, Presidency Conclusions, para 35. Available under <http://ue.eu.int/Newsroom/LoadDoc.asp?BID = 76&DID = 59122& LANG = 1>.

[20] See below text at n 111.

[21] See below text at n 150.

[22] These legislative responses stand in a long tradition of law-making against terrorism. See Y Alexander and AS Nanes (eds), *Legislative Responses to Terrorism* (Dordrecht, Martinus Nijhoff Publishers, 1986); M Cherif Bassiouni (ed), *Legal Responses to International Terrorism: US Procedural Aspects* (Dordrecht, Martinus Nijhoff Publishers, 1988); D Charters (ed), *Democratic Responses to International Terrorism* (London, Cavindish Publishers,1991); N Gal-Or, *International Cooperation to Suppress Terrorism* (Australia, Croom Helm Ltd, 1985).

[23] See for an overview of EU measures: <http://europa.eu.int/news/110901/>. See also C Churruca Muguruza, "The European Union's Reaction to the Terrorist Attacks on the United States" (4/2001) 14 *Humanitäres Völkerrecht* 234–43; T Müller, "Der Kampf gegen den Terror" (12/2001) *Internationale Politik* 47–53.

Affairs Council the Union's "complete solidarity with the government of the United States and the American people".[24]

Already at this early stage, a two-fold purpose of EU action can be observed: On the one hand, immediate action against the attackers of 11 September. In the words of the General Affairs Council which are clearly reflective of US diction:

> The Union and its Member States will spare no efforts to help identify, bring to justice and punish those responsible: there will be no safe haven for terrorists and their sponsors.[25]

On the other hand, the broader intention to fight against terrorism and its future threats by taking preventive action:

> The Union will work closely with the United States and all partners to combat international terrorism. All international organisations, particularly the United Nations, must be engaged and all relevant instruments, including on the financing of terrorism, must be implemented.[26]

B. The EU Action Plan

On 21 September 2001 at the Extraordinary European Council Meeting in Brussels the European heads of State and government adopted an ambitious Action Plan, listing measures from enhancing police and judicial co-operation, developing international legal instruments, putting an end to the funding of terrorism, strengthening air security, to co-ordinating the European Union's global action.[27] This Action Plan contains, *inter alia*, the following precise legal agenda:

1. The introduction of a European arrest warrant and the adoption of a common definition of terrorism "as a matter of urgency" and at the latest at its meeting on 6 and 7 December 2001,
2. The identification of presumed terrorists in Europe and of organisations supporting them in order to draw up a common list of terrorist organisations,
3. Member States sharing with Europol, systematically and without delay, all useful data regarding terrorism,
4. A call for the implementation of all existing international conventions on the fight against terrorism (UN, OECD, etc),

[24] Special Council Meeting, General Affairs, 12 September 2001, 11795/01 (Presse 318) <http://europa.eu.int/news/110901/september.htm>.
[25] *Ibid.*
[26] *Ibid.*
[27] Conclusions and Plan of Action of the Extraordinary European Council Meeting on 21 September 2001, Press Release 21/9/2001 No 140/01. Available under <http://ue.eu.int/en/Info/eurocouncil/index.htm>.

5. Combating the funding of terrorism as a decisive aspect of the fight against terrorism,
6. Measures to strengthen air transport security among them: classification of weapons; technical training for crew; checking and monitoring of hold luggage; protection of cockpit access; quality control of security measures applied by Member States,
7. The General Affairs Council to assume the role of co-ordination and providing impetus in the fight against terrorism.

C. The EU Common Position on Combating Terrorism

On 27 December 2001 the Council acting under Articles 15 and 34 EU Treaty finally adopted the Common Position of 27 December 2001 on combating terrorism.[28] The text of this Common Position basically reiterates the measures listed in Security Council Resolution 1373. A Common Position[29] both in the CFSP and the PJCC area does not have any immediate legal effect. Rather, it requires the Member States or — where the EU/EC has powers — the Union/Community to take action. To a large extent the measures discussed hereinafter can be viewed as action implementing the Common Position.

III. MAIN ISSUES FOR EU ACTION ACCORDING TO SECURITY COUNCIL RESOLUTION 1373

As already mentioned, Security Council Resolution 1373 provides for a very broad array of measures to be taken by UN Member States. For the purposes of the following analysis, Security Council Resolution 1373 shall serve as an analytical framework in order to provide a first brief analysis of the measures actually taken by the EU, their effectiveness and the legal problems involved in their adoption.

Of the numerous obligations contained in Security Council Resolution 1373, the most important and controversial ones will be discussed in more detail:

a. Freezing of terrorist assets,
b. Preventing funds from being made available to terrorists,
c. Punishing and prosecuting terrorist offences.

[28] 2001/930/CFSP, OJ L 344/90, 28 December 2001, Available under <http://europa.eu.int/eur-lex/pri/en/oj/dat/2001/l_344/l_34420011228en00900092.pdf>.

[29] According to Art 15 EU Treaty "[c]ommon positions shall define the approach of the Union to a particular matter of a geographical or thematic nature. Member States shall ensure that their national policies conform to the common positions."

Similarly, Art 34 para. 2 (b) EU Treaty provides that the Council may "adopt common positions defining the approach of the Union to a particular matter."

A. Freezing Accounts and Assets

1. *The Security Council Mandate*

Security Council Resolution 1373 provides that all States shall:

> Freeze without delay funds and other financial assets or economic resources of persons who commit, or attempt to commit, terrorist acts or participate in or facilitate the commission of terrorist acts; of entities owned or controlled directly or indirectly by such persons; and of persons and entities acting on behalf of, or at the direction of such persons and entities, including funds derived or generated from property owned or controlled directly or indirectly by such persons and associated persons and entities.[30]

2. *EU Action*

In order to comply with this provision the EU amended its existing freezing legislation with respect to the Taliban to target Bin Laden and Al-Qaeda. In addition, it drafted new legislation providing a legal basis for the freezing of assets of other terrorists and terrorist groups.

a) Amendments to the Existing Legislation in order to Specifically Target Al-Qaeda On 11 September 2001 far-reaching sanctions, including financial sanctions and the freezing of assets, had already been in force targeting Osama Bin Laden and Al-Qaeda.

In February 2000 — following the adoption of and with a view to implement Security Council Resolution 1267 (1999) — the EU had adopted a flight ban to Afghanistan and a freeze of Taliban funds through Council Regulation (EC) 337/2000[31] which was broadened in March 2001 by Council Regulation (EC) 467/2001[32] providing for the freezing of all funds and other financial resources belonging to any natural or legal person, entity or body designated by the "Afghanistan Sanctions Committee" (established under Security Council Resolution 1267) and listed in one of the annexes to the Regulation.

[30] SC Resolution 1373 para 1 (c).

[31] Council Regulation (EC) No 337/2000 of 14 February 2000 concerning a flight ban and a freeze of funds and other financial resources in respect of the Taliban of Afghanistan, OJ L 043/1, 16/02/2000, available under <http://europa.eu.int/eur-lex/pri/en/oj/dat/2000/l_043/l_04320000216en00010011.pdf>.

[32] Council Regulation (EC) No 467/2001 of 6 March 2001 prohibiting the export of certain goods and services to Afghanistan, strengthening the flight ban and extending the freeze of funds and other financial resources in respect of the Taliban of Afghanistan, and repealing Regulation (EC) No 337/2000, OJ L 67/1, 09/03/2001. Available under <http://europa.eu.int/eur-lex/pri/en/oj/dat/2001/l_067/l_06720010309en00010023.pdf>.

These sanctions have been amended repeatedly: Once in July 2001 by Regulation (EC) No 1354/2001[33] and twice in October 2001 by Regulation (EC) No 1996/2001[34] and Regulation (EC) No 2062/2001[35] and again in November 2001 by Regulation (EC) No 2199/2001.[36] Following a number of other changes, the last amendment dates from February 2002.[37] This legislation was replaced in May 2002 by Regulation (EC) No 881/2002.[38] Starting in June 2002[39] this new Taliban Sanctions Regulation has been repeatedly amended.[40]

[33] Commission Regulation (EC) No 1354/2001 of 4 July 2001 amending Council Regulation (EC) No 467/2001 as regards the persons and entities covered by the freeze of funds and the organisations and agencies exempted from the flight ban in respect of the Taliban of Afghanistan, OJ L 182/15, 05/07/2001, available under <http://europa.eu.int/eur-lex/pri/en/oj/dat/2001/l_182/l_18220010705en00150023.pdf>.

[34] Commission Regulation (EC) No 1996/2001 of 11 October 2001 amending, for the second time, Council Regulation (EC) No 467/2001 prohibiting the export of certain goods and services to Afghanistan, strengthening the flight ban and extending the freeze of funds and other financial resources in respect of the Taliban of Afghanistan and repealing Regulation (EC) No 337/2000, OJ L 271/21, 12/10/2001, available under <http://europa.eu.int/eur-lex/pri/en/oj/dat/2001/l_271/l_27120011012en00210022.pdf>.

[35] Commission Regulation (EC) No 2062/2001 of 19 October 2001 amending, for the third time, Council Regulation (EC) No 467/2001 prohibiting the export of certain goods and services to Afghanistan, strengthening the flight ban and extending the freeze of funds and other financial resources in respect of the Taliban of Afghanistan and repealing Regulation (EC) No 337/2000, OJ L 277/25, 20/10/2001, available under <http://europa.eu.int/eur-lex/pri/en/oj/dat/2001/l_277/l_27720011020en00250026.pdf > .

[36] Commission Regulation (EC) No 2199/2001 of 12 November 2001 amending, for the fourth time, Council Regulation (EC) No 467/2001 prohibiting the export of certain goods and services to Afghanistan, strengthening the flight ban and extending the freeze of funds and other financial resources in respect of the Taliban of Afghanistan and repealing Regulation (EC) No 337/2000, OJ L 295/16, 13/11/2001, available under <http://europa.eu.int/eur-lex/pri/en/oj/dat/2001/l_295/l_29520011113en00160018.pdf>.

[37] Commission Regulation (EC) No 362/2002 of 27 February 2002 amending, for the ninth time, Council Regulation (EC) No 467/2001 prohibiting the export of certain goods and services to Afghanistan, strengthening the flight ban and extending the freeze of funds and other financial resources in respect of the Taliban of Afghanistan and repealing Regulation (EC) No 337/2000, OJ L 58/6, 28/02/2002.

[38] Council Regulation (EC) No 881/2002 of 27 May 2002 imposing certain specific restrictive measures directed against certain persons and entities associated with Usama bin Laden, the Al-Qaida network and the Taliban, and repealing Council Regulation (EC) No 467/2001 prohibiting the export of certain goods and services to Afghanistan, strengthening the flight ban and extending the freeze of funds and other financial resources in respect of the Taliban of Afghanistan, OC L 139/9, 29/05/2002. Available under <http://europa.eu.int/eur-lex/en/dat/2002/l_139/l_13920020529en00090022.pdf>.

[39] Commission Regulation (EC) No 951/2002 of 3 June 2002 amending Council Regulation (EC) No 881/2002 imposing certain specific restrictive measures directed against certain persons and entities associated with Usama bin Laden, the Al-Qaida network and the Taliban, and repealing Council Regulation (EC) No 467/2001, OJ L 145/14, 04/06/2002. Available under <http://europa.eu.int/eur-lex/en/dat/2002/l_145/l_14520020604en00140015.pdf>.

[40] See the most recent Commission Regulation (EC) No 742/2003 of 28 April 2003 amending for the 17th time Council Regulation (EC) No 881/2002 imposing certain specific restrictive measures directed against certain persons and entities associated with Usama bin Laden, the Al-Qaida network and the Taliban, and repealing Council Regulation (EC) No 467/2001, OJ L 106/16, 29/04/2003. Available under <http://europa.eu.int/eur-lex/en/dat/2003/l_106/l_10620030429en00160017.pdf>.

These specific first pillar regulations are mirrored in the CFSP pillar by a number of common positions in which the EU repeatedly laid down its general policy.[41]

b) General Asset Freezing As already indicated above, Security Council Resolution 1373(1)(c) is not narrowly targeted at those responsible for the 11 September attacks. Rather, it is aimed at a general freezing of assets of terrorists. In order to comply with this broader purpose the EU prepared legislation to provide the legal basis for such asset freezing.[42] In order to accomplish this, the EU followed the usual practice of first reaching political agreement within the framework of the CFSP and then taking specific action under the EC Treaty. Thus, the Council first adopted the Common Position of 27 December 2001 on the application of specific measures to combat terrorism.[43] On this basis it voted on Regulation 2580/2001 of 27 December 2001 on specific restrictive measures directed against certain persons and entities with a view to combating terrorism.[44]

The Common Position is a CFSP (and PJCC) act on the basis of Article 15 and 34 EU Treaty applying to "persons, groups and entities involved in terrorist acts" which are listed in an annex. Among the individuals listed there are mainly ETA activists and Arab suspects. Among the 13 groups listed one finds ETA and IRA related ones as well as the Palestinian Islamic Jihad and the terrorist wing of Hamas.[45] The Common Position of 27 December 2001 further contains definitions of "terrorist acts" and "terrorist groups" and provides that the EC "shall order the freezing of

[41] See only Council Common Position of 27 May 2002 concerning restrictive measures against Usama bin Laden, members of the Al-Qaida organisation and the Taliban and other individuals, groups, undertakings and entities associated with them and repealing Common Positions 96/746/CFSP, 1999/727/CFSP, 2001/154/CFSP and 2001/771/CFSP, OJ L 139/4, 29/05/2002. Available under <http://europa.eu.int/eur-lex/pri/en/oj/dat/2002/l_139/l_13920020529en00040005.pdf>.

[42] In its report to the UN CTC the EU stated: "In order to adapt to the wider scope of measures covered by UNSCR 1373, and in order to be able to reach those persons who commit, attempt to commit, participate in or facilitate terrorist acts, but are not linked to any one State, the Council of the European Union, at its meeting on 10 December, reached agreement on a common position and a Regulation which together constitute a legal requirement to freeze and withhold the availability of funds, other financial assets and economic resources, to any previously identified natural or legal person, group or entity figuring in lists annexed to the legislation. It is expected that this legislation will enter into force early in 2002." Report of the European Union to the Security Council Committee established pursuant to resolution 1373 (2001) concerning counter-terrorism, 28 December 2001, UN Doc. S/2001/1297 (hereafter EU Report).

[43] 2001/930/CFSP, OJ L 344/93, 28 December 2001, Available under <http://europa.eu.int/eur-lex/pri/en/oj/dat/2001/l_344/l_34420011228en00930096.pdf>.

[44] OJ L 344/70 28. 12. 2001, Available under <http://europa.eu.int/eur-lex/pri/en/oj/dat/2001/l_344/l_34420011228en00700075.pdf>.

[45] The Common Position of December 2001 listed 29 persons and 13 groups and entities.

the funds and other financial assets or economic resources of persons, groups and entities listed in the Annex".[46]

The Council Regulation 2580/2001[47] is an EC act which provides for the freezing of "all funds, other financial assets and economic resources belonging to, or owned or held by, a natural or legal person, group or entity included in the list referred to in paragraph 3" of the Regulation. Potentially affected assets are very broadly defined.[48] The targets list, established by a separate Council Decision,[49] contains only "EU external" terrorists;[50] it does not apply to Bin Laden and Al-Qaeda who are already covered by earlier legislation.[51]

These lists were updated in early May 2002 by a Common Position[52] and a Council Decision.[53] The Common Position list has been extended and contains now 23 groups including the PKK (the Kurdish Workers Party) and the Peruvian Sendero Luminoso. The list of individuals has grown to 36. The additions to the Common Position list of "EU external" terrorists and terrorist groups have also been made with regard to the Council Decision. In June 2002 the Council again amended the list by a

[46] Art 2 Common Position of 27 December 2001 on the application of specific measures to combat terrorism, above n 43.

[47] Most recently the list of competent authorities in the Member states was partially amended by Commission Regulation (EC) No 745/2003 of 28 April 2003 amending Council Regulation (EC) No 2580/2001 on specific measures directed against certain persons and entities with a view to combating terrorism, OJ L 106/22, 29/04/2003. Available under <http://europa.eu.int/eur-lex/en/dat/2003/l_106/l_10620030429en00220023.pdf>.

[48] According to Art 1 para. 1 Regulation 2580/2001: "'Funds, other financial assets and economic resources' means assets of every kind, whether tangible or intangible, movable or immovable, however acquired, and legal documents or instruments in any form, including electronic or digital, evidencing title to, or interest in, such assets, including, but not limited to, bank credits, travellers' cheques, bank cheques, money orders, shares, securities, bonds, drafts and letters of credit."

[49] Council Decision of 27 December 2001 establishing the list provided for in Article 2(3) of Council Regulation (EC) No 2580/2001 on specific restrictive measures directed against certain persons and entities with a view to combating terrorism (2001/927/EC), OJ L 344/83 28. 12. 2001, lists eight individuals and two groups. Available under <http://europa.eu.int/eur-lex/pri/en/oj/dat/2001/l_344/l_34420011228en00830084.pdf>.

[50] On the reason of this differentiation see below text at note 57.

[51] See Reg. 2580/2001 Preambular para 15: "The European Community has already implemented UNSCR 1267(1999) and 1333(2000) by adopting Regulation (EC) No 467/2001 freezing the assets of certain persons and groups and therefore those persons and groups are not covered by this Regulation."

[52] Council Common Position of 2 May 2002 updating Common Position 2001/931/CFSP on the application of specific measures to combat terrorism (2002/340/CFSP), OJ L 116/75, 3. 5. 2002, Available under <http://europa.eu.int/eur-lex/en/dat/2002/l_116/l_11620020503-en00750077.pdf>.

[53] Council Decision of 2 May 2002 implementing Article 2(3) of Regulation (EC) No 2580/2001 on specific restrictive measures directed against certain persons and entities with a view to combating terrorism and repealing Decision 2001/927/EC (2002/334/EC), OJ L 116/33, 3. 5. 2002, basically added six other groups to the list. Available under <http://europa.eu.int/eur-lex/en/dat/2002/l_116/l_11620020503en00330034.pdf>.

decision which now contains eight individuals and 20 groups.[54] The latest amendment to this list dates from December 2002.[55] It repeals an update of the October 2002 list[56] and now contains 26 individuals and 22 groups.

3. *Controversial and Problematic Issues of the Specific Measures to Combat Terrorism*

a) Distinction Between "EU internal" and "EU external" Terrorists According to the List in the Annex One of the obvious differences in the two lists of terrorists and terrorist groups lies in the fact that the one annexed to the Common Position on the application of specific measures to combat terrorism contains both "EU external" terrorists and "EU internal" terrorists (mainly ETA suspects), while the Council Decisions of 2 May 2002 and 17 June 2002 implementing Article 2(3) of Regulation (EC) No 2580/2001 comprise only "EU external" terrorists.

The EU reasons that this results from the limited powers of the EC: the freezing of assets of "EU internal" terrorists remains within the competence of the Member States.[57] While this may be correct as a result of the complex structure of the EU, it leads to the strange result that the EC is considered to be empowered to take (trade) measures against "EU external" terrorists, not, however, against "EU internal" ones.

b) Procedure and Legal Protection Against Being Included in the List of Persons and Groups Whose Assets Are to be Frozen The freezing of financial assets of individuals or legal persons is a draconian measure. It has a long-standing tradition in US national security law and was also used extensively after 11 September 2001.[58] It can fully deprive those affected

[54] Council Decision of 17 June 2002 implementing Article 2(3) of Regulation (EC) No 2580/2001 on specific restrictive measures directed against certain persons and entities with a view to combating terrorism and repealing Decision 2002/334/EC, (2002/460/EC), OJ L 160/26, 18/06/2002, available under <http://europa.eu.int/eurlex/en/dat/2002/l_160/l_16020020618en00260027.pdf>.

[55] Council Decision of 12 December 2002 implementing Article 2(3) of Regulation (EC)No 2580/2001 on specific restrictive measures directed against certain persons and entities with a view to combating terrorism and repealing Decision 2002/848/EC, (2002/974/EC), OJ L 337/85, 13/12/2002, available under <http://europa.eu.int/eur-lex/en/dat/2002/l_337/l_33720021213en00850086.pdf>.

[56] Decision 2002/848/EC implementing Article 2(3) of Council Regulation (EC) No 2580/2001 on specific restrictive measures directed against certain persons and entities with a view to combating terrorism and repealing Decision 2002/460/EC, OJ L 295/12, 30/10/2002.

[57] See Reg 2580/2001 Preambular para 14: "The list referred to in Article 2(3) of this Regulation may include persons and entities linked or related to third countries as well as those who otherwise are the focus of the CFSP aspects of Common Position 2001/931/CFSP. For the adoption of provisions in this Regulation concerning the latter, the Treaty does not provide powers other than those under Article 308."

[58] See for US freezing measures, HE Sheppard, "US Actions to Freeze Assets of Terrorism: Manifest and Latent Implications for Latin-America", (2002) 17 *American University*

of their means of subsistence. Since a freezing of assets will be brought about without any prior legal proceedings convicting persons of criminal offences, it is particularly important to ensure that freezing orders are imposed on the basis of sufficient evidence. It is against this background that the recent EU legislation has to be read.

Article 2(3) of Council Regulation 2580/2001 provides that the

> Council, acting by unanimity, shall establish, review and amend the list of persons, groups and entities to which this Regulation applies, in accordance with the provisions laid down in Article 1(4), (5) and (6) of Common Position 2001/931/CFSP.

Article 1(4) of the Common Position on the application of specific measures to combat terrorism (2001/931/CFSP) provides:

> The list in the Annex shall be drawn up on the basis of precise information or material in the relevant file which indicates that a decision has been taken by a competent authority in respect of the persons, groups and entities concerned, irrespective of whether it concerns the instigation of investigations or prosecution for a terrorist act, an attempt to perpetrate, participate in or facilitate such an act *based on serious and credible evidence or clues, or condemnation for such deeds*. Persons, groups and entities identified by the Security Council of the United Nations as being related to terrorism and against whom it has ordered sanctions may be included in the list.

It is unclear how one is protected against being included in this list. For instance, the decision to include the PKK in May 2002,[59] a move that followed an earlier decision by the UK, has aroused substantial controversy.[60] The PKK has formally renounced its military struggle against Turkish troops and has been operating lawfully for years in many European countries.

Whether the "credible clues" are sufficient to justify the harsh measures of freezing is questionable and one might be reminded of the succinct concern expressed in the House of Lords debate with regard to similar provisions found in UK anti-terrorism legislation: "[T]here is something distasteful about a process which begins by convicting someone and then proceeds to inquire whether there is a case against them."[61]

International Law Review, 625–639; PD Trooboff, 'September 11: Legal and Practical Implications for the US Practitioner', (2002) 4 *International Law Forum*, 59–68.

[59] See above notes 52 and 53.

[60] See Statewatch News online, EU adds the PKK to list of terrorist organisations, story filed 4.5.02, available under <http://www.statewatch.org/news/index.html>.

[61] Lord Archer of Sandwell, cited in UK Terrorism Act: 21 new proscribed organisations, available under <http://www.statewatch.org/news/2001/oct/01proscribed.htms>. On recent UK legislation see also A Tomkins, "Legislating Against Terror: The Anti-Terrorism, Crime and Security Act 2001", (2002) *Public Law* 205–20.

The procedure of freezing assets clearly raises concern about such fundamental rights as the presumption of innocence[62] and the criminal fair trial guarantees[63] enshrined in Article 6 European Convention for the Protection of Human Rights and Fundamental Freedoms (ECHR).[64]

However, one has to be aware of the rather restrictive interpretation of the scope of Article 6 para 2 ECHR by the Strasbourg organs. According to this view, the European Commission of Human Rights regarded Italian anti-Mafia legislation providing for the confiscation of criminal proceeds as a preventive measure, not a penal one. As a result, it considered the presumption of innocence not applicable.[65]

For the same reason, also the criminal fair trial guarantees of Article 6 para 3 ECHR are likely to be considered inapplicable. However, since the European Court of Human Rights has held that measures of confiscation of property relate to civil rights,[66] at least

[62] Art 6 para 2 ECHR provides: "Everyone charged with a criminal offence shall be presumed innocent until proved guilty according to law."

[63] Art 6 para 3 ECHR provides: "Everyone charged with a criminal offence has the following minimum rights:

a. to be informed promptly, in a language which he understands and in detail, of the nature and cause of the accusation against him;
b. to have adequate time and facilities for the preparation of his defence;
c. to defend himself in person or through legal assistance of his own choosing or, if he has not sufficient means to pay for legal assistance, to be given it free when the interests of justice so require;
d. to examine or have examined witnesses against him and to obtain the attendance and examination of witnesses on his behalf under the same conditions as witnesses against him;
e. to have the free assistance of an interpreter if he cannot understand or speak the language used in court."

[64] European Convention for the Protection of Human Rights and Fundamental Freedoms, 4 November 1950, ETS No. 5, 213 UNTS 221, entered into force 3 September 1953.

[65] *M. v Italy*, European Commission of Human Rights, 15 April 1991, Application No. 12386/86: *"Dans ces circonstances et à la lumière de la jurisprudence de la Cour, la Commission conclut que la confiscation litigieuse ne comporte pas un constat de culpabilité, qui suit une accusation, et ne constitue pas une peine. Dès lors, les griefs tirés de la violation des articles 6 par. 2 et 7 (art. 6–2, 7) de la Convention sont incompatibles 'ratione materiae' avec ces dispositions et doivent être rejetées conformément à son article 27 par. 2 (art. 27–2)."*
See also *AGOSI v United Kingdom*, European Court of Human Rights, 24 October 1986. Available under <http://hudoc.echr.coe.int/Hudoc2doc/HEJUD/sift/3.txt>.

[66] *Raimondo v Italy*, European Court of Human Rights, 22 February 1994, para 44: "The Court shares the view taken by the Government and the Commission that special supervision is not comparable to a criminal sanction because it is designed to prevent the commission of offences. It follows that proceedings concerning it did not involve 'the determination ... of a criminal charge' (see the Guzzardi judgment cited above, p. 40, para. 108). On the matter of confiscation, it should be noted that Article 6 (art. 6) applies to any action whose subject matter is 'pecuniary' in nature and which is founded on an alleged infringement of rights that were likewise of a pecuniary character (see the Editions Périscope v. France judgment of 26 March 1992, Series A no. 234-B, p. 66, para. 40). That was the position in the instant case." Available under <http://hudoc.echr.coe.int/Hudoc2doc/HEJUD/sift/455.txt>.

the guarantees of Art 6 para 1 ECHR[67] would appear to be applicable.

The freezing of assets may also be problematic with regard to the right to property protected by Protocol No 1 to the ECHR.[68] The relevant case-law of the European human rights organs demonstrates, however, considerable deference to the discretion of States as regards freezing or forfeiture or similar orders affecting property rights which are mostly considered to be mere regulations of the use of property.

But it is important to note that the Strasbourg organs have held that even such interferences require adequate judicial remedies.[69]

This has been recently reaffirmed by the Council of Europe Committee of Ministers with particular regard to anti-terrorism measures. In their Guidelines on human rights and the fight against terrorism[70] the Committee stated:

> The use of the property of persons or organisations suspected of terrorist activities may be suspended or limited, notably by such measures as freezing orders or seizures, by the relevant authorities. The owners of the property have the possibility to challenge the lawfulness of such a decision before a court.[71]

c) Legal Remedies Against Incorrect Freezing? Neither the Common Position nor the Regulation make any provision for remedies against incorrect freezing of assets as a result of erroneously being included in the relevant lists. Thus, one has to inquire whether general principles of EU/EC law do provide legal remedies.

A Council decision can be challenged by an annulment action according to Article 230 EC Treaty. The procedural problem of standing usually encountered by "non-privileged" claimants[72] does not arise in the case of

[67] Art 6 para 1 first sentence ECHR provides: "In the determination of his civil rights and obligations or of any criminal charge against him, everyone is entitled to a fair and public hearing within a reasonable time by an independent and impartial tribunal established by law."

[68] Art 1 Protocol No. 1 to the ECHR provides "Every natural or legal person is entitled to the peaceful enjoyment of his possessions. No one shall be deprived of his possessions except in the public interest and subject to the conditions provided for by law and by the general principles of international law. The preceding provisions shall not, however, in any way impair the right of a State to enforce such laws as it deems necessary to control the use of property in accordance with the general interest or to secure the payment of taxes or other contributions or penalties."

[69] See the cases *Raimondo* and *AGOSI*, above notes 66 and 65.

[70] <http://www.coe.int/T/E/Communication_and_Research/Press/Theme_Files/Terrorism/CM_Guidelines_20020628.asp#TopOfPage>.

[71] Art XIV Guidelines of the Committee of Ministers of the Council of Europe on human rights and the fight against terrorism.

[72] See TC Hartley, *The Foundations of European Community Law*, 4th edn (Oxford, Oxford University Press, 1998), 350. See also A Ward, *Judicial Review and the Rights of Private Parties in EC Law* (Oxford, Oxford University Press, 2000).

challenges to decisions which are addressed to the claimants. As far as the substantive illegality is concerned, affected parties will try to argue infringements of fundamental rights on the part of the Community. According to the ECJ's well-established case-law, the EC is bound to respect "fundamental rights, as guaranteed by the European Convention for the Protection of Human Rights and Fundamental Freedoms signed in Rome on 4 November 1950 and as they result from the constitutional traditions common to the Member States, as general principles of Community law."[73]

An alternative route of legal recourse against incorrect freezing of assets might lie in the extra-contractual liability avenue opened by Article 288 EC Treaty. According to this provision damages may be asked of the Community institutions if there is harm as a result of their unlawful acts.

In this context it is interesting to note that the Taliban Freezing Regulations[74] have actually been challenged before the Court of First Instance in a number of actions for annulment brought by affected individuals.[75] Some of these actions expressly challenge the lack of procedural safeguards in making a freezing decision.[76]

B. Measures to Prevent Funds From Being Made Available for Terrorist Acts

An important aspect of combating terrorism lies in putting a hold on the funding of terrorism. As has been clearly demonstrated by the 11 September attacks, terrorists increasingly have control over large

[73] See now also Art 6 (2) EU Treaty.

[74] See above text at n 31.

[75] See eg Case T-315/01 *Yassin Abdullah Khadi v Council and Commission*, 5656/02, 21.2.02; *Action brought on 10 December 2001 by Abdirisak Aden and Others against the Council of the European Union and the Commission of the European Communities* (Case T-306/01), OJ C 44/27, 16.2.02; Case T-318/01 - *Omar Mohammed OTHMAN v Council and Commission*, 6763/02, 27.2.02.

[76] See Case T-306/01 *Abdirisak Aden and Others against the Council of the European Union and the Commission of the European Communities*, OJ C 44/27, 16 Feb 2002:

"The applicants submit further that the Council and Commission have not examined the reasons why the Taliban Sanctions Committee included the applicants in its list. Nor were the applicants given any opportunity to apprise themselves of and refute the allegations on which the decision to include them in Annex I was based. The applicants have thus had onerous sanctions imposed on them without any opportunity to defend themselves. The fundamental legal principle of the right to a fair and equitable hearing has thus been disregarded."

On 7 May 2002 the Court of First Instance rejected the applicants' request for provisions measures. See Case T-306/01 R *Abdirisak Aden and Others against the Council of the European Union and the Commission of the European Communities* [2002] ECR II-2387. The main case is still pending.

amounts of financial resources. It is these resources which support and sometimes even enable them to commit their acts.

1. *The UN Security Council Mandate*

In line with the stated purpose of preventing funds from being made available for terrorist acts the Security Council in Resolution 1373 decided that all States shall:

> Prevent and suppress the financing of terrorist acts;[77]
>
> Criminalize the wilful provision or collection, by any means, directly or indirectly, of funds by their nationals or in their territories with the intention that the funds should be used, or in the knowledge that they are to be used, in order to carry out terrorist acts;[78] and
>
> Prohibit their nationals or any persons and entities within their territories from making any funds, financial assets or economic resources or financial or other related services available, directly or indirectly, for the benefit of persons who commit or attempt to commit or facilitate or participate in the commission of terrorist acts, of entities owned or controlled, directly or indirectly, by such persons and of persons and entities acting on behalf of or at the direction of such persons;[79]

2. *EU Action*

Already in the Action Plan of 21 September 2001 the EU had identified combating the funding of terrorism as a decisive aspect of the fight against terrorism and called for the completion of work on the following measures:

> adopting in the weeks to come the extension of the Directive on money laundering and the framework Decision on freezing assets. It calls upon Member States to sign and ratify as a matter of urgency the United Nations Convention for the Suppression of the Financing of Terrorism. In addition, measures will be taken against non-cooperative countries and territories identified by the Financial Action Task Force.[80]

Well before the 11 September events, the EU had identified the importance of taking measures against the financing of terrorism. In the Council Recommendation of 9 December 1999 on cooperation in combating the financing of terrorist groups[81] the Council recommended that national

[77] SC Resolution 1373 para 1 (a).
[78] SC Resolution 1373 para 1 (b).
[79] SC Resolution 1373 para 1 (d).
[80] Conclusions and Plan of Action of the Extraordinary European Council Meeting on 21 September 2001, Press Release 21/9/2001 No. 140/01. available under <http://ue.eu.int/en/Info/eurocouncil/index.htm>.
[81] Council Recommendation of 9 December 1999 on cooperation in combating the financing of terrorist groups, OJ C 373/1, 23/12/1999. Available under <http://europa.eu.int/eur-lex/pri/en/oj/dat/1999/c_373/c_37319991223en00010001.pdf>.

security services, with the cooperation of EUROPOL, should exchange information on a regular basis on the structures and modus operandi used for financing terrorist groups operating in more than one Member State with a view to take measures against these groups.

The 19 October 2001 European Council in Ghent reaffirmed the importance of effective measures to stop the funding of terrorism.[82] To this end it envisaged the formal adoption of an amendment to the EU Money Laundering Directive and the speedy ratification by all Member States of the United Nations Convention for the Suppression of the Financing of Terrorism.

In its report to the UN CTC, the EU vaguely stated:

> The Special Recommendations on terrorist financing adopted at the Extraordinary Plenary Meeting of the Financial Action Task Force on Money Laundering on 29–30 October 2001 relate to a number of the issues covered in Operative Paragraphs 1 and 2 of the Resolution. It is intended that these recommendations be at least partly implemented by measures taken within the framework of the Treaty on European Union (EU) and the Treaty establishing the European Community (EC).[83]

a) Amendment to the 1997 Money Laundering Directive Concerning the obligation to prevent funds from being made available for terrorist acts the EU stated in its report to the UN CTC:

> The 1991 Directive was amended on 19 November 2001. The new directive extends the prohibition of money laundering to most organised and serious crime. It also extends the coverage of the earlier directive to include a number of non-financial activities and professions which are vulnerable to misuse by money launderers. The EU Member States have agreed that all offences linked to the financing of terrorism constitute a serious crime under the directive.[84]

In December 2001 the Council adopted pursuant to the co-decision procedure of Article 251 EC Treaty Directive 2001/97/EC of the European Parliament and of the Council of 4 December 2001 amending Council Directive 91/308/EEC[85] on prevention of the use of the financial system

[82] Ghent: Informal Meeting of Heads of State or Government: Declaration by the Heads of State or Government of the European Union and the President of the Commission, Press Release: Ghent (19/10/2001), SN 4296/2/01 REV 2 (OR. fr), available under <http://ue.eu.int/en/Info/eurocouncil/ index.htm>.

[83] EU Report, above n 42, 4.

[84] EU Report, above n 42, 5.

[85] Council Directive 91/308/EEC of 10 June 1991 on prevention of the use of the financial system for the purpose of money laundering, OJ L 166/77, 28/06/1991.

for the purpose of money laundering.[86] Because some of the amendments introduced by the European Parliament were not accepted by the Council a conciliation procedure had to be convened on 18 September 2001 to seek a compromise. This compromise was agreed by COREPER on 10 October and by a parliamentary delegation on 17 October 2001.

The amended Directive,[87] which has to be implemented by 15 June 2003, extends the obligations to report suspicious transactions to the authorities responsible for combating money laundering to certain non-financial professions and sectors, among them accountants, auditors and lawyers.[88] It also widens the definition of laundering to the proceeds of all serious crime, including activities of criminal organisations as defined in Article 1 of Joint Action 98/733/JHA,[89] fraud against the EU budget and corruption.[90] The original money laundering legislation applied only to the proceeds of drug offences.

Requirements as regards client identification, record keeping and reporting of suspicious transactions would therefore be extended to external accountants and auditors, real estate agents, notaries, lawyers, dealers in high value goods such as precious stones and metals or works of art, auctioneers, transporters of funds and casinos.[91]

According to the Directive, Member States have to ensure that the covered professions and sectors "require identification of their customers", "cooperate fully" with the authorities in case of suspected money laundering, and "refrain from carrying out transactions which they know or suspect to be related to money laundering", and "establish adequate procedures of internal control" to prevent money laundering.

b) Ratification of the United Nations Convention for the Suppression of the Financing of Terrorism The EU has recommended that all member States ratify the United Nations Convention for the Suppression of the Financing of Terrorism.[92] This treaty entered into force on

[86] OJ L 344/76, 28.12.2001. Available under <http://europa.eu.int/eur-lex/pri/en/oj/dat/2001/l_344/l_34420011228en00760081.pdf>.

[87] See also S Armati, "Services financiers. Lutte contre la criminalité organisée et le terrorisme: prévention de l'utilisation du système financier aux fins du blanchiment de capitaux" (2001) *Revue du droit de l'Union européenne* 769.

[88] Art 2(a) and 6 of the amended Money Laundering Directive.

[89] See above n 18.

[90] Art 1 of the amended Money Laundering Directive.

[91] Art 2(a) of the amended Money Laundering Directive.

[92] Adopted by the General Assembly of the United Nations in resolution 54/109 of 9 December 1999. Available under <http://untreaty.un.org/English/Terrorism/Conv12.pdf>. See also A Aust, "Counter-terrorism — a new approach. The International Convention for the Suppression of the Financing of Terrorism" (2001) 5 *Max Planck Yearbook of United Nations Law* 285–306; R Lavalle, "The International Convention for the Suppression of the Financing of Terrorism" (2000) 20 *Zeitschrift für ausländisches öffentliches Recht und Völkerrecht* 491–510.

10 April 2002,[93] but it has not yet been ratified by all EU Member States. It triggers far-reaching obligations of contracting parties to outlaw the intentional financing of terrorist activities. The financing of terrorism as defined in Article 2 para 1 of the Convention contains also the core of a terrorism definition that may serve as a basis for future negotiations:

> Any person commits an offence within the meaning of this Convention if that person by any means, directly or indirectly, unlawfully and wilfully, provides or collects funds with the intention that they should be used or in the knowledge that they are to be used, in full or in part, in order to carry out:
>
> (a) An act which constitutes an offence within the scope of and as defined in one of the treaties listed in the annex;[94] or
>
> (b) Any other act intended to cause death or serious bodily injury to a civilian, or to any other person not taking an active part in the hostilities in a situation of armed conflict, when the purpose of such act, by its nature or context, is to intimidate a population, or to compel a government or an international organization to do or to abstain from doing any act.

The Convention requires States to take appropriate measures, in accordance with their domestic legal principles, for the detection and freezing, seizure or forfeiture of any funds used or allocated for the purposes of committing the offences described.[95] The offences referred to in the

[93] See UN Press Release available under <http://www.un.org/News/Press/docs/2002/LT4366.doc.htm>.

[94] The annex contains the following conventions:

1. Convention for the Suppression of Unlawful Seizure of Aircraft, done at The Hague on 16 December 1970.
2. Convention for the Suppression of Unlawful Acts against the Safety of Civil Aviation, done at Montreal on 23 September 1971.
3. Convention on the Prevention and Punishment of Crimes against Internationally Protected Persons, including Diplomatic Agents, adopted by the General Assembly of the United Nations on 14 December 1973.
4. International Convention against the Taking of Hostages, adopted by the General Assembly of the United Nations on 17 December 1979.
5. Convention on the Physical Protection of Nuclear Material, adopted at Vienna on 3 March 1980.
6. Protocol for the Suppression of Unlawful Acts of Violence at Airports Serving International Civil Aviation, supplementary to the Convention for the Suppression of Unlawful Acts against the Safety of Civil Aviation, done at Montreal on 24 February 1988.
7. Convention for the Suppression of Unlawful Acts against the Safety of Maritime Navigation, done at Rome on 10 March 1988.
8. Protocol for the Suppression of Unlawful Acts against the Safety of Fixed Platforms located on the Continental Shelf, done at Rome on 10 March 1988.
9. International Convention for the Suppression of Terrorist Bombings, adopted by the General Assembly of the United Nations on 15 December 1997.

[95] Art 8 United Nations Convention for the Suppression of the Financing of Terrorism 1999.

Convention are deemed to be extraditable offences and the contracting parties have obligations to establish their jurisdiction over the offences described, make the offences punishable by appropriate penalties, take alleged offenders into custody, prosecute or extradite alleged offenders, co-operate in preventive measures and countermeasures, and exchange information and evidence needed in related criminal proceedings.

c) EU Co-operation within the Financial Action Task Force On the international level, the so-called Financial Action Task Force (FATF)[96] is the leading institution in the fight against money laundering and the financing of terrorism. It was established in 1989 at the G-7 Paris Summit Meeting and was given the responsibility of examining money laundering techniques and trends, reviewing the action which had already been taken at a national or international level, and setting out the measures that still needed to be taken to combat money laundering.

In October 2001 FATF's mission was enlarged to cover terrorist financing. At the October meeting FATF adopted a series of recommendations to combat the financing of terrorism.[97] These recommendations include ratification and implementation of UN instruments, criminalising the financing of terrorism and associated money laundering, the reporting of suspicious transactions linked to terrorism, strengthening customer identification measures in international wire transfers, etc. The EU has expressed its willingness to support these recommendations.

d) Work on a Directive to Counter Insider Dealing and Market Manipulation Also EU amending legislation on insider dealing is frequently portrayed as a specific anti-terrorism measure. In early 2003 a Commission Proposal for a Directive of the European Parliament and of the Council on insider dealing and market manipulation (market abuse) (Insider Dealing Directive)[98] was adopted. On the official Europa homepage the then proposal[99] was described as one of the key elements of legislation fighting the financing of terrorism:

> The Finance Council of 13 December 2001 reached unanimous orientation agreement on [the] proposed Directive to counter insider dealing and market manipulation: The Council unanimously reached an orientation agreement on the proposal for a Directive on market abuse (see IP/01/758

[96] See <http://www1.oecd.org/fatf/AboutFATF_en.htm>.
[97] <http://www1.oecd.org/fatf/TerFinance_en.htm>.
[98] Directive 2003/6/EC of the European Parliament and of the Council of 28 January 2003 on insider dealing and market manipulation (market abuse), OJ L 96/16, 12/04/2003 (hereafter Insider Dealing Directive). Available under <http://europa.eu.int/eur-lex/en/dat/2003/l_096/l_09620030412en00160025.pdf>.
[99] COM(2001) 281 final, 30.5.2001. OJ C 240/265 E, 28/08/2001. Available under <http://europa.eu.int/eur-lex/en/com/pdf/2001/en_501PC0281.pdf>.

> and MEMO 01/203). The proposed Directive is based on the principles of transparency and equal treatment of market participants. It aims to reinforce protection against insider dealing and market manipulation by building one set of rules for all the EU's financial markets, thus reducing potential inconsistencies, confusion and loopholes. It would heighten investor protection and make European financial markets more attractive. It was identified by the 16 October joint Finance/Justice Council as a key measure in the fight against the financing of terrorism.[100]

The proposed Insider Dealing Directive imposes on EU Member States an obligation to

> prohibit any person ... who possesses inside information from using that information by acquiring or disposing of, or by trying to acquire or dispose of, for his own account or for the account of a third party, either directly or indirectly, financial instruments to which that information relates.[101]

Article 2(1) second subparagraph of the Directive defines as insiders any person

> who possesses that information:
>
> (a) by virtue of his membership of the administrative, management or supervisory bodies of the issuer; or
> (b) by virtue of his holding in the capital of the issuer; or
> (c) by virtue of his having access to the information through the exercise of his employment, profession or duties; or
> (d) by virtue of his criminal activities.

In addition to outlawing insider trading, the directive prohibits other "market manipulation".[102]

A closer look at this directive, however, makes the observer wonder where the specific anti-terrorism aspect of this legislation is hidden. The Commission Proposal — which dates back to May 2001 — does not mention terrorism even once. Rather, the proposal looks like the "normal" market protection legislation one would expect under its title. It is true that the EP suggested in its opinion to add to the proposed directive's preamble the statement that "[t]his Directive meets also the concerns expressed by the Member States following the terrorist attacks on 11 September 2001 as regards the fight against financing terrorist activities".[103] However,

[100] <http://europa.eu.int/news/110901/emu.htm>.
[101] Art 2 para. 1 Insider Dealing Directive.
[102] See Art 1 para. 2 Insider Dealing Directive.
[103] EP Report on the proposal for a European Parliament and Council directive on insider dealing and market manipulation (market abuse) (COM(2001) 281, C5-0262/2001,

whether this has been effectively accomplished by the minor change proposed by the EP in extending the definition of "primary insiders"[104] to "... any person who possesses that information by virtue of his criminal activities" remains doubtful at least.

3. *Is the Prohibition of the Financing of Terrorist Activities Sufficiently Addressed by the EU Action?*

Despite the repeated assurances of the EU that the above-mentioned action adequately provides against the financing of terrorism,[105] it is highly questionable whether any of the actions discussed above are sufficient to comply with the requirements under Security Council Resolution 1373 concerning the prevention, suppression and prohibition of the financing of terrorist activities. It was rightly noted that terrorist financing may occur not only through money-laundering and other illegal activities but also by lawful methods, such as soliciting funds via charitable and educational organisations, etc.[106] Therefore even the FATF experts on money-laundering in addressing a typology of terrorist financing could not agree on "whether anti-money laundering laws could (or should) play a direct role in the fight against terrorism".[107]

The new money laundering legislation prohibits only the use of criminally obtained proceeds (which now include proceeds of terrorist crimes). However, it still does not criminalise the provision of legally obtained funds for terrorist purposes. Also the new Insider Dealing Directive does not really address the problem of intentional financing of terrorist acts. Rather, the new legislation, as currently proposed, will only address the specific insider market abuse of taking advantage of knowledge as a result of criminal activities. The financing itself cannot be punished on this basis.

This should be contrasted with US legislation which makes it a criminal offence to "knowingly provide[s] material support or resources to a foreign terrorist organization."[108] Both the obligations under the 1999 UN Convention for the Suppression of the Financing of Terrorism and the FATF recommendations aim at outlawing the financing of terrorism,

2001/0118(COD)), A5-0069/2002, 27 February 2002; now preambular paragraph 14 Insider Dealing Directive.

[104] Art 2, paragraph 1, second subparagraph proposed Insider Dealing Directive.
[105] See the EU Action Plan of 21 September 2001 and the EU report to the UN CTC, above notes 80 and 83.
[106] MS Navias, "Finance Warfare and International Terrorism" in Lawrence Freedman (ed), *Superterrorism. Policy Responses* (Oxford, Blackwell Publishing, 2002), 57–79, at 70.
[107] Financial Action Task Force on Money Laundering, *FATF-XII Report on Money Laundering Typologies (2000–2001)*, 20; <http://www.fatf-gafi.org/pdf/TY2001_en.pdf>.
[108] 18 USC Sec 2339 B. See also the chapter by A Gardella, "The Fight Against the Financing of Terrorism between Judicial and Regulatory Cooperation" in this book.

regardless of the legal or illegal origin of funds. Thus, formal adherence to the UN Convention as well as observance of the FATF recommendations require additional action.

C. Establishing Terrorist Acts as Serious Criminal Offences and Ensuring that Terrorists are Brought to Justice

1. *The Security Council Mandate*

Security Council Resolution 1373 decides that all States shall:

> Ensure that any person who participates in the financing, planning, preparation or perpetration of terrorist acts or in supporting terrorist acts is brought to justice and ensure that, in addition to any other measures against them, such terrorist acts are established as serious criminal offences in domestic laws and regulations and that the punishment duly reflects the seriousness of such terrorist acts;[109]

2. *EU Action*

Criminal law issues addressed by this subparagraph of Security Council Resolution 1373 are largely within the sphere of the Member States. However, where and to the extent that the EU has powers under the Third Pillar of the EU Treaty, it has taken action in order to ensure compliance with UN law. Specifically, it prepared the adoption of framework decisions on combating terrorism as well as on a European arrest warrant and it reached agreement on the definitive creation of EUROJUST, the co-operation between national judicial authorities.[110]

a) Framework Decision on Combating Terrorism The report of the EU to the UN CTC contains the following terse passage:

> On 6 December 2001, the Council reached political agreement on a Framework Decision on combating terrorism. This legislation includes a common definition of various types of terrorist offences and serious criminal sanctions. The legal text will be adopted shortly, and EU Member States have until the end of 2002 to implement the measures in their own criminal law.[111]

Behind this matter-of-fact account lies a fierce debate about the appropriate definition of terrorist offences that has aroused fears among civil rights

[109] SC Resolution 1373 para 2 (e).

[110] See also generally E Barbe, "Une triple étape pour le troisième pilier de l'Union Européenne — mandat d'arrêt européen, terrorisme et EUROJUST", (2002) 454 *Revue du marché commun et de l'Union Européenne*, 5.

[111] EU Report, above n 42, 6.

groups that freedom of expression and other fundamental rights might be unduly restricted.

In fact, it took another six months until 13 June 2002 to formally adopt the Council Framework Decision on combating terrorism.[112]

The original Commission Proposal for a Council Framework Decision on combating terrorism[113] of 19 September 2001 stated that the purpose of the Framework Decision on combating terrorism is "to establish minimum rules relating to the constituent elements of criminal acts and to penalties for natural and legal persons who have committed or are liable for terrorist offences which reflect the seriousness of such offences".[114]

But the issue of defining terrorist offences was not new after the 11 September attacks. Rather, it was already raised at the Tampere European Council in 1999 which identified terrorism as one of the most serious violations of fundamental freedoms, human rights and of the principles of liberty and democracy. Thus, in order to create a genuine area of freedom, security and justice in the sense of Title VI of the EU Treaty, it was felt necessary to take action, including legislative action against terrorism.

The Framework Decision on combating terrorism defines "terrorist offences"[115] as well as the notion of a "terrorist group". According to the framework decision a "terrorist group" is a "structured group of more than two persons, established over a period of time and acting in concert to commit terrorist offences".[116] The Framework Decision provides that, among others, the following intentional acts should be punishable: directing and certain forms of participating in "terrorist groups".[117] Further, inciting/instigating, aiding or abetting and attempting to commit terrorist offences will be punishable.[118]

There was an extensive debate about the issue of criminal sanctions. The Commission proposal of 19 September 2001 contained a detailed

[112] 2002/745/JHA, OJ L 164/3, 22 June 2002. Available under <http://europa.eu.int/eur-lex/en/dat/2002/l_164/l_16420020622en00030007.pdf>.

[113] European Commission proposal for a Council Framework Decision on combating terrorism, 19/9/2001, COM(2001) 521 final, <http://europa.eu.int/comm/justice_home/unit/terrorism/terrorism_sg_en.pdf>.

[114] Art 1 Commission Proposal Framework Decision on combating terrorism. Preambular para. 6 of the Framework Decision now provides: "The definition of terrorist offences should be approximated in all Member States, including those offences relating to terrorist groups. Furthermore, penalties and sanctions should be provided for natural and legal persons having committed or being liable for such offences, which reflect the seriousness of such offences."

[115] See below text starting at n 121.

[116] Art 2 para. 1 Framework Decision on combating terrorism.

[117] Contrast Art 2 para 2 Framework Decision on combating terrorism with the broader original Art 3 para 1 (l) and (m) Commission Proposal Framework Decision on combating terrorism. See in more detail below text at n 144.

[118] Art 4 Framework Decision on combating terrorism and Art 4 Commission Proposal Framework Decision on combating terrorism.

list of prison sentences, ranging from two to twenty years maximum penalties that Member States should adopt as a bottom line. The text politically agreed upon within the Council in December 2001,[119] and maintained in the final version of June 2002, simplified this by providing — in addition to the standard phrase that the offences should be "punishable by effective, proportionate and dissuasive criminal penalties" — that terrorist offences "are punishable by custodial sentences heavier than those imposable under national law for such offences in the absence of the special [terrorist] intent."[120]

Central Issue: Definition of Terrorism and Terrorist Acts

The most difficult legal and political issue concerning a Framework Decision on combating terrorism was the definition of terrorist acts. This is not surprising since, also on the global level, to date no consensus has been found. On the EU side, the cumbersome procedure to find agreement on an acceptable definition of terrorism mirrors the difficulty the EU had with defining "organized crime".[121]

It is remarkable in this context that — although Security Council Resolution 1373 requires of States that "terrorist acts are established as serious criminal offences in domestic laws"[122] — the definition of what can be qualified a "terrorist act" is left open in Resolution 1373. This uncertainty is not accidental. On the universal level there is a distinct lack of definition mainly due to the controversy about the role of "state terrorism" and a possible exception for "freedom fighters". This clearly has to do with the common wisdom that one State's "terrorist" is another State's "freedom fighter".[123]

The question of a definition of terrorism has a long history.[124] A first attempt to arrive at an internationally acceptable definition was made

[119] Proposal for a Council Framework Decision on combating terrorism, 14845/1/01, REV 1, 7 December 2001, <http://register.consilium.eu.int/pdf/en/01/st14/14845-r1en1.pdf>.

[120] Art 4 Penalties. Proposal for a Council Framework Decision on combating terrorism, 14845/1/01, REV 1, 7 December 2001, now Art 5 Framework Decision on combating terrorism.

[121] See M Valsamis, "Defining organized crime in the European Union: The limits of European law in an area of 'freedom, security and justice'" (2001) 26 *European Law Review* 565.

[122] SC Resolution 1373 para. 2 (e).

[123] See RA Friedlander, "Terrorism" in Rudolf Bernhard (ed), *Encyclopedia of Public International Law*, vol. IV (2000), 845, at 846.

[124] On the problem of defining terrorism in general, see J Dugard, "International Terrorism: Problems of Definitions" (1974) 50 *International Affairs* No.71, 68; RA Friedlander, "Terrorism and International Law: Recent Developments" (1984) 13 *Rutgers Law Journal* 493–511; R Higgins and M Flory (eds), *Terrorism and International Law* (London, Routledge, 1997).

See also A Obote-Odara, "Defining International Terrorism" (1999) 6 *E Law - Murdoch University Electronic Journal of Law*, available under <http://www.murdoch.edu.au/elaw/issues/v6n1/obote-odora61nf.html>.

under the League of Nations,[125] but the draft Geneva Convention for the Prevention and Punishment of Terrorism of 1937[126] never came into existence.

To date, UN Member States have no universally agreed-upon definition. Terminological consensus would, however, be necessary for a single comprehensive convention on terrorism, which some countries favour instead of the present 12 piecemeal conventions and protocols.[127]

The UN General Assembly has stepped in to provide at least partial guidance in resolutions such as GA Resolution 51/210 (1999) on Measures to eliminate international terrorism in which the General Assembly:

1. *Strongly condemns* all acts, methods and practices of terrorism as criminal and unjustifiable, wherever and by whomsoever committed;
2. *Reiterates* that criminal acts intended or calculated to provoke a state of terror in the general public, a group of persons or particular persons for political purposes are in any circumstance unjustifiable, whatever the considerations of a political, philosophical, ideological, racial, ethnic, religious or other nature that may be invoked to justify them.

A further step towards a more general definition was taken in the 1999 International Convention for the Suppression of the Financing of Terrorism[128] which prohibits the financing of acts prohibited by existing special anti-terrorism conventions listed in an annex[129] plus of other terrorist acts. These other terrorist acts are generally circumscribed in Art 2 (b) of the UN Convention which reads as follows:

> Any other act intended to cause death or serious bodily injury to a civilian, or to any other person not taking an active part in the hostilities in a situation of armed conflict, when the purpose of such act, by its nature or

[125] The draft Convention provided: "All criminal acts directed against a State and intended or calculated to create a state of terror in the minds of particular persons or a group of persons or the general public."

[126] Convention for the Prevention and Punishment of Terrorism, 16 November 1937, C.546.M.383.1937.V., *série de publications de la Société des Nations, Questions Juridiques*, 1937, V.10.

[127] In addition to the UN Convention for the Suppression of the Financing of Terrorism and the Conventions listed in its annex (see above n 94) there are: the Convention on Offences and Certain Other Acts Committed on Board Aircraft, signed at Tokyo on 14 September 1963 and the Convention on the Marking of Plastic Explosives for the Purpose of Detection, signed at Montreal on 1 March 1991.

See also the list provided by the UN available under <http://untreaty.un.org/English/Terrorism.asp>.

[128] See above n 92.

[129] See above n 94.

> context, is to intimidate a population, or to compel a government or an international organization to do or to abstain from doing any act.

However, this does not yet solve the issue of defining terrorism. It is therefore on the agenda of current negotiations within the UN for a "Comprehensive" or "Global Terrorism Convention".[130]

On the regional level, there are also important steps to respond to the challenge of defining terrorism. The 1977 Council of Europe Convention on the Suppression of Terrorism[131] basically tries to eliminate the political offence exception for the purpose of extradition.[132]

More relevant to what appears to become an acceptable international definition of terrorism is the description used by the European Parliament in its 1996 Resolution on combating terrorism in the European Union.[133] In this resolution the European Parliament spoke of terrorism as:

> any act committed by individuals or groups, involving the use or threat of violence, against a country, its institutions or people in general or specific individuals, which is intended to create a state of terror among official agencies, certain individuals or groups in society or the general public, the motives lying in separatism, extremist ideology, religious fanaticism or subjective irrational factors;[134]

It is against this background that the proposed Framework Decision on combating terrorism should be read.

[130] See Report of the Ad Hoc Committee established by General Assembly resolution 51/210 of 17 December 1996, Sixth session (28 January–1 February 2002), General Assembly Official Records Fifty-seventh Session Supplement No 37 (A/57/37), available under <http://www.un.org/law/terrorism/english/a_57_37e.pdf>. See also the Working document submitted by India on the draft comprehensive convention on international terrorism, available under <http://www.indianembassy.org/policy/Terrorism/draft_convention.htm>.

[131] Strasbourg, 27 January 1977, ETS No. 90, available under < http://conventions.coe.int/Treaty/EN/Treaties/Html/090.htm>.

[132] Art 1 of the 1977 Convention provides: "For the purposes of extradition between Contracting States, none of the following offences shall be regarded as a political offence or as an offence connected with a political offence or as an offence inspired by political motives:

a. an offence within the scope of the Convention for the Suppression of Unlawful Seizure of Aircraft, signed at The Hague on 16 December 1970;
b. an offence within the scope of the Convention for the Suppression of Unlawful Acts against the Safety of Civil Aviation, signed at Montreal on 23 September 1971;
c. a serious offence involving an attack against the life, physical integrity or liberty of internationally protected persons, including diplomatic agents;
d. an offence involving kidnapping, the taking of a hostage or serious unlawful detention;
e. an offence involving the use of a bomb, grenade, rocket, automatic firearm or letter or parcel bomb if this use endangers persons;
f. an attempt to commit any of the foregoing offences or participation as an accomplice of a person who commits or attempts to commit such an offence."

[133] EP Resolution on combating terrorism in the European Union, OJ C 55/27, 24/02/1997.

[134] Preambular para C EP Resolution on combating terrorism in the European Union.

Article 3(1) of the original European Commission proposal for a Framework Decision on combating terrorism provided under the title "Terrorist Offences":

> Each Member State shall take the necessary measures to ensure that the following offences, defined according to its national law, which are intentionally committed by an individual or a group against one or more countries, their institutions or people with the aim of intimidating them and seriously altering or destroying the political, economic, or social structures of a country, will be punishable as terrorist offences:
>
> (a) Murder;
> (b) Bodily injuries;
> (c) Kidnapping or hostage taking;
> (d) Extortion;
> (e) Theft or robbery;
> (f) Unlawful seizure of or damage to state or government facilities, means of public transport, infrastructure facilities, places of public use, and property;
> (g) Fabrication, possession, acquisition, transport or supply of weapons or explosives;
> (h) Releasing contaminating substances, or causing fires, explosions or floods, endangering people, property, animals or the environment;
> (i) Interfering with or disrupting the supply of water, power, or other fundamental resource;
> (j) Attacks through interference with an information system;
> (k) Threatening to commit any of the offences listed above;
> (l) Directing a terrorist group;
> (m) Promoting of, supporting of or participating in a terrorist group.[135]

This clearly constituted an approach different from the one pursued by the UN Convention for the Suppression of the Financing of Terrorism. The draft Framework Decision lists specific "ordinary crimes" which become "terrorist" if committed with a specific intent — the intent to intimidate and to seriously alter or destroy the political, economic and social structures of a country.

Overly Broad Suppression of Political Dissent?

Civil rights groups in particular have been worried that such a broad definition of terrorist acts might include acts of political dissent as expression of democratic rights.

[135] Commission proposal framework decision on combating terrorism, 19/9/2001, COM(2001) 521 final.

For instance, Article 3(1)(f) of the original Commission proposal refers to "[u]nlawful seizure of or damage to state or government facilities, means of public transport, infrastructure facilities, places of public use, and property". This could embrace a wide range of types of demonstration and protests. It would thus depend upon the intent with which these acts are committed. According to the 19 September Commission Proposal a terrorist act requires both the aim of intimidation and of seriously altering certain structures of a country. Even the Commission in its explanatory note expressly stated that "[t]his could include, for instance, acts of urban violence".[136]

It is not surprising that this has provoked harsh criticism.[137] Apparently, part of this criticism was taken into account by the Council. In December 2001 the Justice and Home Affairs Council concluded:

> When defining terrorist aims, the Council opted for a wording that strikes a balance between the need to punish terrorist offences effectively and the need to guarantee fundamental rights and freedoms, ensuring that the scope could not in any circumstances be extended to legitimate activities, for example trade union activities or anti-globalisation movements.[138]

The Commission proposal was repeatedly changed in the Council. In the version finally adopted, which in turn largely corresponds to the one politically agreed upon on 6 December 2001,[139] Article 1(1) runs as follows:

> Each Member State shall take the necessary measures to ensure that the intentional acts referred to below in points (a) to (i), as defined as offences

[136] Commission proposal framework decision on combating terrorism, 19/9/2001, COM(2001) 521 final, 9.

[137] See the comment by T Bunyan, Statewatch editor: "The European Commission proposal on combating terrorism is either very badly drafted, or there is a deliberate attempt to broaden the concept of terrorism to cover protests (such as those in Gothenburg and Genoa) and what it calls 'urban violence' (often seen by local communities as self-defence). If it is intended to slip in by the back door draconian measures to control political dissent it will only serve to undermine the very freedoms and democracies legislators say they are protecting." Available under <http://www.statewatch.org/news/2001/sep/14eulaws.htm>.

See also the Open Letter to the President of the EU by Human Rights Watch, dated September 26, 2001, stating that the Commission Proposal "provides a broad definition of terrorism that threatens to quell legitimate dissent. Human Rights Watch is concerned that public demonstrations and protests-such as those against nuclear weapons and those in favor of more transparent procedures governing international financial institutions-could be subject to the provisions of the proposal, thus infringing on the rights to freedom of association and assembly." Available under <http://www.hrw.org/press/2001/09/eu-0927-ltr.htm#security>.

[138] 2396th Council meeting, Justice, Home Affairs and Civil Protection, Brussels, 6 and 7 December 2001, 14581/01 (Presse 444), 7. Available under <http://ue.eu.int/newsroom/makeFrame.asp?MAX = 1&BID = 86&DID = 69187&LANG = 1&File = /pressData/en/jha/DOC.69187.pdf&Picture = 0>.

[139] The definition finally agreed upon by the Council in December 2001 and adopted in June 2002 is now also largely in line with the definition of "terrorist acts" in the Council Common

under national law, which, given their nature or context, may seriously damage a country or an international organisation where committed with the aim of:

— seriously intimidating a population, or
— unduly compelling a Government or international organisation to perform or abstain from performing any act, or
— seriously destabilising or destroying the fundamental political, constitutional, economic or social structures of a country or an international organisation, shall be deemed to be terrorist offences:
  (a) attacks upon a person's life which may cause death;
  (b) attacks upon the physical integrity of a person;
  (c) kidnapping or hostage taking;
  (d) causing extensive destruction to a Government or public facility, a transport system, an infrastructure facility, including an information system, a fixed platform located on the continental shelf, a public place or private property likely to endanger human life or result in major economic loss;
  (e) seizure of aircraft, ships or other means of public or goods transport;
  (f) manufacture, possession, acquisition, transport, supply or use of weapons, explosives or of nuclear, biological or chemical weapons, as well as research into, and development of, biological and chemical weapons;
  (g) release of dangerous substances, or causing fires, floods or explosions the effect of which is to endanger human life;
  (h) interfering with or disrupting the supply of water, power or any other fundamental natural resource the effect of which is to endanger human life;
  (i) threatening to commit any of the acts listed in (a) to (h).

Further, Article 1(2) which was inserted at the 6 December 2001 Council meeting states that

> This Framework Decision shall not have the effect of altering the obligation to respect fundamental rights and fundamental legal principles as enshrined in Article 6 of the Treaty on European Union.

In addition, the Council in December 2001 added a "Draft Council Statement" to the draft Framework Decision that runs as follows:

> The Council states that the Framework Decision on the fight against terrorism covers acts which are considered by all Member States of the European Union as serious infringements of their criminal laws committed by individuals whose objectives constitute a threat to their democratic

Position of 27 December 2001 on the application of specific measures to combat terrorism (2001/931/CFSP). OJ L 344/93, 28 December 2001, Available under <http://europa.eu.int/eur-lex/pri/en/oj/dat/2001/l_344/l_34420011228en00930096.pdf>.

> societies respecting the rule of law and the civilisation upon which these societies are founded. It has to be understood in this sense and cannot be construed so as to argue that the conduct of those who have acted in the interest of preserving or restoring these democratic values, as was notably the case in some Member States during the Second World War, could now be considered as "terrorist" acts. Nor can it be construed so as to incriminate on terrorist grounds persons exercising their fundamental right to manifest their opinions, even if in the course of the exercise of such right they commit offences.[140]

The text finally adopted is still open to criticism. The remaining lack of precision leaves uncertainty about what conduct is prohibited. Viewed against the background of criminal law guarantees, such as legal certainty, *nullum crimen sine lege stricta/certa*, etc, the very vague and largely subjective notions used in Art 1 of the Framework Decision[141] raise concern with regard to the standard required under Article 7 ECHR.
Article 7 ECHR provides:

> No one shall be held guilty of any criminal offence on account of any act or omission which did not constitute a criminal offence under national or international law at the time when it was committed. Nor shall a heavier penalty be imposed than the one that was applicable at the time the criminal offence was committed.

This non-retroactivity provision has been interpreted by the European Commission and Court of Human Rights to include a prohibition on the extensive interpretation of criminal law provisions, eg by analogy, and thus to require a certain minimal precision and clarity.[142] The European Human Rights bodies do, however, accept that an established case-law

[140] 2396th Council meeting, Justice, Home Affairs and Civil Protection, Brussels, 6 and 7 December 2001, above n 138, 14.

[141] "Les termes « *graves* » ou « *indûment* » sont purement subjectifs et n'apportent aucune précision objective pour qualifier l'acte." J-C Paye, "Faux-semblants du mandat d'arrêt européen", *Le Monde diplom*atique 2002, 49e année, n 575, February, at 4, <http://www.monde-diplomatique.fr/2002/02/PAYE/16172>.

[142] For instance, in *Kokkinakis v Greece*, 25 May 1993, Series A No 260-A, available under <http://hudoc.echr.coe.int/Hudoc1doc/HEJUD/sift/412.txt>, the Court held that "Article 7 para 1 (art 7–1) of the Convention is not confined to prohibiting the retrospective application of the criminal law to an accused's disadvantage. It also embodies, more generally, the principle that only the law can define a crime and prescribe a penalty (nullum crimen, nulla poena sine lege) and the principle that the criminal law must not be extensively construed to an accused's detriment, for instance by analogy; it follows from this that an offence must be clearly defined in law. This condition is satisfied where the individual can know from the wording of the relevant provision and, if need be, with the assistance of the courts' interpretation of it, what acts and omissions will make him liable."

See also the recent judgement in *EK v Turkey*, 7 February 2002, Application No 28496/95, finding a violation of the prohibition to construe criminal law extensively by way of analogy.

and legal doctrine might render an otherwise vague criminal law provision sufficiently clear and precise to satisfy the requirements under Art 7 ECHR.[143]

With regard to the controversial provisions of the European Framework Decision such practice is necessarily lacking. Thus, the danger of an overly vague and insufficiently accessible and foreseeable criminal law prohibition is clearly pertinent.

Further, in a strict sense, it will depend upon the implementation legislation adopted on the level of the Member States. Third pillar framework decisions — comparable to EC directives — are not directly applicable in the EU Member States. Rather, they require national implementation measures. Thus, technically, the language of framework decisions never has to meet the *nullum crimen* requirements of precision and clarity as long as the national implementing measures do. One has to realise in this context, however, that the level of detail achieved in this Framework Decision — similar to what frequently happens in the case of EC directives — does not give much room for implementation discretion to the Member States. Thus, it is likely that the EU Member States will adopt the wording of the Framework Decision on combating terrorism. Therefore, any lack of precision of the definition of terrorist offences in the Framework Decision will be immediately relevant for the corresponding national legal provisions.

Other Problematic Aspects of the Commission Proposal

(a) The Issue of "Status Crimes" or "Guilt by Association" Another highly controversial point concerned the breadth of the Commission Proposal's criminalisation of activities related to terrorist acts. According to the initial wording of Art 3 of the Framework Decision not only the directing, but also "promoting of, supporting of or participating in a terrorist group" would have entailed criminal responsibility punishable by a maximum

143 In *Hans Jörg Schimanek v Austria*, Admissibility, 1 February 2000, Application No. 32307/96, available under <http://hudoc.echr.coe.int/Hudoc1doc2/HEDEC/200002/32307di.chb1_ 010200e.doc> the Court held: "As regards the alleged lack of precision of Section 3a (2) of the Prohibition Act, it is true that the notion of 'activities inspired by National Socialist ideas' appears rather vague. However, the Court follows the line of reasoning of the European Commission of Human Rights in 12774/87 (quoted above, at p. 220), where a similar provision of the Prohibition Act which contains exactly the same term, was found to be in conformity with Article 7 on the following grounds: 'The legislator intended to outlaw any kind of National Socialist activities. Furthermore, the scope of the provision is limited to the national socialist concept as a historical ideology, frequently referred to in Austria and elsewhere, which is a sufficiently precise concept. In addition to this background, the case-law and legal doctrine in Austria have developed further criteria making the applicable law sufficiently accessible and foreseeable and enabling the jury to distinguish clearly between the applicant's activities which could and which could not be considered as National Socialist activities'."

penalty of up to seven years.[144] It was pointed out that by such sweeping language the expression of political sympathy and understanding for groups could be made a criminal offence contrary to the requirements of legal precision and the guarantees of freedom of expression.[145]

The broad language contained in the initial draft was narrowed by the December 2001 Council agreement which dropped the incrimination of mere support of and participation in "terrorist groups" and replaced it by the more stringent wording of intentionally

> participating in the activities of a terrorist group, including by supplying information or material resources, or by funding its activities in any way, with knowledge of the fact that such participation will contribute to the criminal activities of the terrorist group.[146]

Further, the Council tried to make explicit its intention to safeguard fundamental freedoms by including the following clause in the Framework Decision's preamble:

> Nothing in this Framework Decision may be interpreted as being intended to reduce or restrict fundamental rights or freedoms such as the right to strike, freedom of assembly, of association or of expression, including the right of everyone to form and to join trade unions with others for the protection of his or her interests and the related right to demonstrate.[147]

(b) The Broadening of Anti-terrorism Legislation by Including International Organizations Another change made by the Council is the insertion of "international organizations" as potential targets of terrorist activities. While it is certainly a legitimate aim to protect international organizations in the same way as States against terrorism, the chronological coincidence of increased public uneasiness about anti-globalization protests

[144] Art 3 (l) and (m) in conjunction with Art 5 para 2 (d) Commission proposal framework decision on combating terrorism, 19/9/2001, COM(2001) 521 final, 9.

[145] See the Open Letter to the President of the EU by Human Rights Watch, dated September 26, 2001: "Human Rights Watch is concerned that broad, undefined terms such as 'promoting' and 'supporting' could result in findings of 'guilt by association' of persons sharing the same political ideology, nationality, or ethnicity as persons who commit acts of terrorism. Indeed, with mere expressions of sympathy for terrorists one could run afoul of such provisions." Available under <http://www.hrw.org/press/2001/09/eu-0927-ltr.htm#security>.

See also the general criticism by Amnesty International that the "lack of precision creates uncertainty about what conduct is prohibited" and that such legislation may "criminalize peaceful activities and infringe unduly upon other rights such as freedom of expression and association." Amnesty International's concerns regarding security legislation and law enforcement measures, AI-index: ACT 30/001/2002 18/01/2002, 15, available under <http://www.web.amnesty.org/ai.nsf/recent/ACT300012002?OpenDocument>.

[146] Art 2 para. 2 (b) Framework Decision on combating terrorism.

[147] Preambular para. 10 Framework Decision on combating terrorism.

and attempts to outlaw such demonstrations has been interpreted to indicate that States are willing to use the proposed anti-terrorism legislation for broader purposes than only anti-terrorism in a strict sense.[148] However, there may be also a more harmless explanation lying in the EU's attempt to find a formulation that parallels that of the UN Convention for the Suppression of the Financing of Terrorism.[149]

(c) Framework Decision on the European Arrest Warrant Work on measures against all forms of cross-border organised crime, including terrorism, was pursued by the EU already well before 11 September 2001. With regard to a European arrest warrant, already the conclusions of the October 1999 European Council in Tampere contained this as an important item.[150]

Already on 19 September 2001 the Commission submitted a Proposal for a Council Framework Decision on the European arrest warrant and the surrender procedures between the Member States which was published in the Official Journal.[151] On 29 September 2001 the Commission presented a final proposal.[152] In its Action Plan of 19 October 2001, the European Council in Ghent emphasised the importance of the approval of the practical details of the European arrest warrant. Political agreement on the European arrest warrant was largely reached at the Justice and Home Affairs Council on 6 December but partly delayed until 11 December 2001. The Framework Decision on the European arrest warrant was finally adopted on 13 June 2002.[153]

As of 1 January 2004, the Framework Decision will replace the existing legal instruments, such as the 1957 European Extradition Convention[154]

[148] See Statewatch critique in The Council of the European Union proposes a wider definition of "terrorism" and extends it to those who aim to "seriously… affect… an international organisation", available under <http://www.statewatch.org/news/2001/oct/08counterr.htm> that "such a broad definition would clearly embrace protests such as those in Gothenburg and Genoa."

[149] See text above at n 92.

[150] Tampere European Council 15 and 16 October 1999, Presidency Conclusions, para 35. Available under <http://ue.eu.int/Newsroom/LoadDoc.asp?BID = 76&DID = 59122&LANG = 1>.

[151] Proposal for a Council Framework Decision on the European arrest warrant and the surrender procedures between the Member States, (2001/C 332 E/18), COM(2001) 522 final Š 001/0215(CNS), OJ C 332 E/305, 27 November 2001, <http://europa.eu.int/eur-lex/pri/en/oj/dat/2001/ce332/ce33220011127en03050319.pdf>. On the arrest warrant see also Jean-François Kriegk, "Le mandat d'arret européen et les projets de lutte contre le terrorisme" (2002) 391 *Les Petites affiches: La Loi* 12–15.

[152] <http://europa.eu.int/eur-lex/en/com/pdf/2001/en_501PC0522.pdf>.

[153] Council Framework Decision of 13 June 2002 on the European arrest warrant and the surrender procedures between the Member States (2002/584/JHA), OJ L 190/1, 18/7/2002, available under <http://europa.eu.int/eur-lex/en/dat/2002/l_190/l_19020020718en00010018.pdf>.

[154] See above n 13.

and the 1977 European Convention on the Suppression of Terrorism,[155] the 1995 Convention on the simplified extradition procedure,[156] the Convention of 27 September 1996 relating to Extradition between the Member States of the European Union[157] and the relevant provisions of the Schengen agreement.[158]

The December 2001 EU report to the UN CTC stated:

> Political agreement has also been reached on a framework decision for a European arrest warrant. This is designed to supplant the current procedures of extradition between EU Member States and enable wanted persons to be surrendered to judicial authorities in other EU Member States without verification of the double criminality of the act for a wide range of offences, subject to agreed swift judicial review procedures.[159]

The main purpose of a European arrest warrant is to avoid formal extradition procedures which are usually a cumbersome and complex process leading to considerable delays and uncertainties in the administration of criminal justice. This clearly reflects the law-enforcement point-of-view. On the other hand, important, in some Member States even constitutional law guarantees are intended to protect individuals from being extradited or otherwise surrendered or handed over to the criminal justice system of other States. Only where "full faith and credit" can be given to other criminal legal systems is a dispensation of extradition feasible. The EU has reached the conclusion that this was the case with regard to all Member States.[160]

General Principles

The Framework Decision is intended "to establish the rules under which a Member State shall execute in its territory a European arrest warrant issued by a judicial authority in another Member State."[161]

The Framework Decision defines the "European arrest warrant" as "a judicial decision issued by a Member State with a view to the arrest

155 See above n 14.
156 See above n 15.
157 See above n 16.
158 Art 31 para 1 Framework Decision on the European arrest warrant.
159 EU Report, above n 42, 6.
160 "A high level of mutual trust and cooperation between the member states who share the same highly demanding conception of the rule of law, has made it possible to simplify and improve the surrendering procedure. In doing so, they are developing the European Union into a single European judicial area." Commission homepage under "Agreement on a European arrest warrant" Available under <http://europa.eu.int/comm/justice_home/news/laecken_council/en/mandat_en.htm>.
161 Art 1 September 2001 Draft European Arrest Warrant Framework Decision.

and surrender by another Member State of a requested person, for the purposes of conducting a criminal prosecution or executing a custodial sentence or detention order."[162]

It will apply to cases of 1) immediate imprisonment of four months or more; or 2) an offence carrying a term of more than a year.[163] The Member States designate the competent judicial authorities and the central authority responsible for assisting them (administrative support, translations, etc.). The European arrest warrant contains information on the identity of the person concerned, the issuing judicial authority, whether there is a final judgement or other enforceable judicial decision, the nature of the offence, the penalty, etc.[164] A specimen form is attached to the Framework Decision in an annex.

Procedures

As a general rule, the issuing authority in a Member State transmits the European arrest warrant directly to the executing judicial authority in another Member State.[165] Provision is made for co-operation with the Schengen Information System (SIS). When an individual is arrested, he/she must be made aware of the contents of the arrest warrant and is entitled to the services of a lawyer and an interpreter. In all cases, the executing authority may decide to keep the individual in custody or to release him/her under certain conditions.[166]

The European arrest warrant must be examined as a matter of urgency. In cases where the requested person consents to his or her surrender, the final decision on the execution of the European arrest warrant should be taken within a period of 10 days after consent has been given. The decision must be taken no later than 60, exceptionally 90, calendar days after the arrest of the requested person.[167]

Any consent by an arrested person to his or her surrender must be in accordance with the national law of the executing judicial authority. Consent may not be revoked and must be voluntary and in full knowledge of the consequences. In certain specific cases consent is not required.[168]

[162] Art 1 para 1 Framework Decision on the European arrest warrant. See, however, the broader definitions of "issuing judicial authority", "executing judicial authority", "judgment *in absentia*", "detention order", and "requested person" in the original Art 3 September 2001 Draft European Arrest Warrant Framework Decision.
[163] Art 2 Framework Decision on the European arrest warrant.
[164] Art 8 Framework Decision on the European arrest warrant.
[165] Art 9 para 1 Framework Decision on the European arrest warrant.
[166] Articles 11–12 Framework Decision on the European arrest warrant.
[167] Art 17 Framework Decision on the European arrest warrant.
[168] Art 13 Framework Decision on the European arrest warrant.

Grounds for Refusal to Execute a Warrant and Refusal to Surrender and the Issue of Double Criminality

One of the central political issues in the course of negotiating the Framework Decision was the scope of its application. In principle, the European arrest warrant will apply to all kinds of offences of a certain gravity. As a result of the wide scope laid down in Art 2 of the Framework Decision, any 4 months conviction or prosecution for an offence punishable by more than 12 months may trigger a European arrest warrant. In effect, this breadth was, however, severely limited through the initial proposal of a negative list system.

The September 2001 Commission Draft provided for the following system: Each Member State was to draw up an exhaustive list of cases in which the judicial authorities may refuse to execute a European arrest warrant.[169] In addition, the Commission draft provided that the judicial authorities were entitled to refuse to execute a warrant if:

— the act in question was not considered an offence under their national law and which did not occur on the territory of the issuing Member State;[170]
— final judgment had already been passed upon the requested person in respect of the same offence (*ne bis in idem principle*) in the executing Member State;[171]
— the offence was covered by an amnesty in the executing Member State;[172]
— the requested person had been granted immunity in the executing Member State;[173]
— the warrant did not contain all the requisite information.[174]

One of the core aspects of the European arrest warrant legislation is the abolition of the traditional extradition requirement of double criminality according to which criminal offences are only "extraditable" if they are also a criminal offence under the law of the requested State. In the original Commission proposal double criminality was abolished in principle.[175] However, according to Art 27 of the September 2001 Commission Draft of

[169] Art 27 September 2001 Draft European Arrest Warrant Framework Decision.
[170] Art 28 "Principle of Territoriality" September 2001 Draft European Arrest Warrant Framework Decision.
[171] Art 29 "Ne bis in idem" September 2001 Draft European Arrest Warrant Framework Decision.
[172] Art 30 "Amnesty" September 2001 Draft European Arrest Warrant Framework Decision.
[173] Art 31 "Immunity" September 2001 Draft European Arrest Warrant Framework Decision.
[174] Art 32 "Lack of necessary information" September 2001 Draft European Arrest Warrant Framework Decision.
[175] See also Preambular para. 14 September 2001 Draft European Arrest Warrant Framework Decision.

the European arrest warrant Framework Decision Member States were able to draw up an exhaustive list of crimes to which they would not apply the European arrest warrant. Art 27 initially provided:

> Without prejudice to the objectives of Article 29 of the EC (sic!) Treaty, each Member State may establish an exhaustive list of conduct which might be considered as offences in some Member States, but in respect of which its judicial authorities shall refuse to execute a European arrest warrant on the grounds that it would be contrary to fundamental principles of the legal system in that State.
>
> The list and any change to it shall be published in the *Official Journal of the European Communities* at least three months before a Member State may invoke the first paragraph in respect of the conduct concerned.

This "negative list" had been very controversial[176] and was changed by the JHA Council in early December 2001. Instead of the "negative list" of Article 27, a positive list was designed by the Justice and Interior Ministers. This list contains 32 serious offences, punishable by deprivation of liberty of at least 3 years. In these cases, the surrender of persons does not require the verification of the double criminality of the act.[177]

The agreed upon list was incorporated into Art 2 para 2 of the finally adopted Framework Decision which reads as follows:

> The following offences, if they are punishable in the issuing Member State by a custodial sentence or a detention order for a maximum period of at least three years and as they are defined by the law of the issuing Member State, shall, under the terms of this Framework Decision and without verification of the double criminality of the act, give rise to surrender pursuant to a European arrest warrant:
>
> — participation in a criminal organisation,
> — terrorism,
> — trafficking in human beings,
> — sexual exploitation of children and child pornography,
> — illicit trafficking in narcotic drugs and psychotropic substances,

[176] See Bulletin EU 12-2001, Area of freedom, security and justice (11/28), available under <http://europa.eu.int/abc/doc/off/bull/en/200112/p104011.htm>: "Following rejection by the Council on 6 December, due to Italy's opposition to the draft text, an agreement was finally reached. The European arrest warrant could be issued to implement a court judgment carrying a prison sentence of four months or more, or where the facts giving rise to the prosecution carried a prison sentence of at least one year in the Member State issuing the warrant. Furthermore, verification of double criminality was removed for a list of 32 offences carrying a sentence of at least three years in the issuing Member State. Unlike extradition, the procedure for executing the arrest warrant is entirely judicial, and grounds for refusing to execute a European arrest warrant are strictly limited."

[177] 2396. Council — Justice, Home Affairs and Civil Protection, Brussels (7/12/2001) — Press: 444 Nr: 14581/01, p 6. See also http://europa.eu.int/comm/justice_home/news/laecken_council/en/mandat_en.htm>.

- — illicit trafficking in weapons, munitions and explosives,
- — corruption,
- — fraud, including that affecting the financial interests of the European Communities within the meaning of the Convention of 26 July 1995 on the protection of the European Communities' financial interests,
- — laundering of the proceeds of crime,
- — counterfeiting of the euro,
- — computer-related crime,
- — environmental crime, including illicit trafficking in endangered animal species and in endangered plant species and varieties,
- — facilitation of unauthorised entry and residence,
- — murder, grievous bodily injury,
- — illicit trade in human organs and tissue,
- — kidnapping, illegal restraint and hostage-taking,
- — racism and xenophobia,
- — organised or armed robbery,
- — illicit trafficking in cultural goods, including antiques and works of art,
- — swindling,
- — racketeering and extortion,
- — counterfeiting and product piracy,
- — forgery of administrative documents and trafficking therein,
- — forgery of means of payment,
- — illicit trafficking in hormonal substances and other growth promoters,
- — illicit trafficking in nuclear or radioactive materials,
- — motor vehicle crime,
- — rape,
- — arson,
- — crimes within the jurisdiction of the International Criminal Tribunal,
- — unlawful seizure of aircraft/ships,
- — sabotage.[178]

This result of Council negotiations in December 2001 clearly goes beyond combating terrorism, being only one among many criminal offences now subject to the European arrest warrant system.

Evaluation

The most important issue with regard to the abolition of extradition and the introduction of the new European arrest warrant system will be the ability of the criminal justice systems to maintain individual rights in the fight against serious crime. While certainly less apparent than in the case

[178] See also List of offences giving rise to surrender without verification of the double criminality of the act, provided they are punishable in the issuing Member State by a custodial sentence of a maximum of at least 3 years, in 2396. Council — Justice, Home Affairs and Civil Protection, p 19, above n 177.

of the freezing of assets and the harmonisation of terrorist offences, the rights of European and non-European citizens are at stake also in the field of simplified surrender procedures in the course of criminal proceedings.

Traditional obstacles to intra-Union transfer of suspects and convicts by such venerable legal principles as the requirement of double criminality, the principle of speciality or non-extradition for political offences have been abolished. There is no question that there have been instances of misuse of these principles in the past and that there cannot be any principled justification for their maintenance in a European Union built on the principle of mutual trust.

It has to be seen whether the guarantees incorporated into the new draft Framework Decision on the European arrest warrant will sufficiently protect individual citizens.

(d) Eurojust The December 2001 EU report to the CTC stated:

> On 6 December 2001, the Council reached political agreement on a text setting up the judicial co-operation unit Eurojust. Its objective is to improve and encourage cooperation between the competent national authorities, in particular by facilitating mutual legal assistance and the implementation of extradition requests.[179]

In February 2002 the Council formally created Eurojust[180] which replaced the Provisional Judicial Cooperation Unit of December 2000.[181] Eurojust is a separate EU institution, enjoying its own legal personality, composed of national members (prosecutors, judges, police officers) seconded by the Member States. It is intended to improve the judicial cooperation between EU states, "in particular in combating forms of serious crime often perpetrated by transnational organisations."[182] Though not limited to terrorism, judicial cooperation and legal assistance with regard to fighting terrorism is clearly part of Eurojust's powers.

VI. CONCLUSION

There are two main problem areas concerning the EU action taken to combat terrorism. Both go to the heart of European values as expressed in

179 EU Report, above n 42, 6.

180 Council Decision of 28 February 2002 setting up Eurojust with a view to reinforcing the fight against serious crime, 2002/187/JHA, OJ L 63/1, 06/03/2002, available under <http://europa.eu.int/eur-lex/pri/en/oj/dat/2002/l_063/l_06320020306en00010013.pdf>.

181 Council Decision of 14 December 2000 setting up a Provisional Judicial Cooperation Unit, (2000/799/JHA), OJ L 324/2, 21/12/2000.

182 Preambular para 1 Council Decision of 28 February 2002 setting up Eurojust.

Art 6 para 1 EU Treaty: One, whether the EU will manage to respect fundamental rights and freedoms of individuals as well as the rule of law in its asymmetrical fight against terrorism. The other: whether the Union will be able to adopt effective measures in a fashion that does not forgo the basic demands of participatory democracy.[183]

This paper addressed the potential fundamental rights frictions in various pieces of the new post-11 September EU legislation. The fight against terrorism surely requires that in certain situations tough choices are made. But the EU and its Member States must not lose sight of their human rights achievements. A difficult balancing of interests will have to take place. Fundamental procedural guarantees with regard to a fair trial must not be sacrificed for a perceived higher good. Otherwise terrorism may have already achieved — part of — its aim of "seriously destabilising or destroying the fundamental political, constitutional, economic or social structures of a country".

For the EU's fight against terrorism the old maxim that "the aims do not justify the means" remains valid. This insight should not be restricted to the agenda of moralists and NGOs. It must be the fundamental principle of a EU seeking political legitimacy in the project of European integration. It is incumbent upon the EU to demonstrate that the repeated invocation of fundamental rights guarantees in the new anti-terrorism legislation is more than a mere lip-service.

In this context it should also be recognised that any attempt to legitimise the disregard for human rights on the basis of superior UN Charter obligations, is not only politically unwise but also legally untenable. In this respect the UN General Assembly's call to respect human rights standards when combating terrorism[184] as well as the call by leading UN, Council of Europe and OSCE human rights officials[185] are exemplary.

[183] See also generally I Almeida/L Lipsett, "Promoting Human Rights and Democracy in the Context of Terrorism and the Security State", Prepared for Rights & Democracy's Think Tank — May 30, 2002, available under <http://www.ichrdd.ca/english/commdoc/ publications/intHRadvocacy/thinkTank2002Eng.html>.

[184] See UN GA Measures to eliminate international terrorism, 24 January 2002, A/RES/56/88, op. para. 3: "*Reiterates its call* upon all States to adopt further measures in accordance with the Charter of the United Nations and the relevant provisions of international law, including international standards of human rights, to prevent terrorism and to strengthen international cooperation in combating terrorism ..."

[185] See the joint press statement by Mary Robinson, the United Nations High Commissioner for Human Rights, Walter Schwimmer, Secretary-General of the Council of Europe, and Ambassador Gérard Stoudmann, Director of the Organization for Security and Cooperation in Europe's (OSCE) Office for Democratic Institutions and Human Rights, press release, 29 November 2001: "While we recognize that the threat of terrorism requires specific measures, we call on all governments to refrain from any excessive steps which would violate fundamental freedoms and undermine legitimate dissent. In pursuing the objective of eradicating terrorism, it is essential that States strictly adhere to their international obligations to uphold human rights and fundamental freedoms." See < http://press.coe.int/cp/2001/910a(2001).htm> and <http://www.osce.org/news/generate.php3?news_id = 2183>.

A signal pointing in the same direction was given through the Guidelines of the Committee of Ministers of the Council of Europe on Human Rights and the Fight against Terrorism[186] adopted on 15 July 2002.[187] In theses Guidelines the Foreign Ministers of the 44 Member States of the Council of Europe, including all 15 EU Member States, recalled:

> that it is not only possible, but also absolutely necessary, to fight terrorism while respecting human rights, the rule of law and, where applicable, international humanitarian law.[188]

and reaffirmed

> states' obligation to respect, in their fight against terrorism, the international instruments for the protection of human rights and, for the member states in particular, the Convention for the Protection of Human Rights and Fundamental Freedoms and the case-law of the European Court of Human Rights.[189]

Art II of the Guidelines is very explicit by stating:

> All measures taken by states to fight terrorism must respect human rights and the principle of the rule of law, while excluding any form of arbitrariness, as well as any discriminatory or racist treatment, and must be subject to appropriate supervision.

In addition to the very specific and detailed problems that result from the legislative plans of the EU and from the actual adoption of various freezing measures that may infringe upon fundamental rights of suspects there is a more general concern with regard to the democratic decision-making within the EU that arises from the action taken. It may still be less visible behind the controversial debates about the pros and cons of specific legislative choices. And it relates less to the action itself than to the way by which the action is taken. But it may well be that we will soon find out that the price we paid for more effective EU action against terrorism was very high.

The price may ultimately lie in a further aggravation of the democratic deficit problem in the EU. The intensified recourse to framework decisions in order to harmonise criminal law may contribute to worsen

[186] <http://www.coe.int/T/E/Communication_and_Research/Press/Theme_Files/Terrorism/CM_Guidelines_20020628.asp#TopOfPage>.
[187] See <http://press.coe.int/cp/2002/369a(2002).htm>.
[188] Preambular para d) Guidelines of the Committee of Ministers of the Council of Europe on human rights and the fight against terrorism.
[189] Preambular para i) Guidelines of the Committee of Ministers of the Council of Europe on human rights and the fight against terrorism.

the still fragile democratic legitimacy of the Union. While a less than perfectly democratic decision-making process may be acceptable in more technical fields, be it the creation of a customs union or environmental protection, core political matters such as legislative choices in the field of criminal law do not belong behind closed doors.

Absurdly, the introduction of more effective — less intergovernmental and more quasi-supranational — legal instruments by the Amsterdam Treaty, such as framework decisions, has reinforced the democratic deficit issue for the Union. Since framework decisions — as opposed to Conventions, the traditional instruments of intergovernmental co-operation in the field of JHA, — do not require approval by national parliaments and since they are adopted by merely consulting the European Parliament, neither indirect nor direct democratic legitimacy can be recognised. As a result, the introduction of Council framework decisions by the Amsterdam Treaty has further widened the "democratic deficit" of the EU. What has already been a feature of EU-decision making in general for a long time now reaches into a field that is as politically sensitive as criminal law. Thus, it should not come as a surprise that some national parliaments have reacted negatively to the proposed anti-terrorism legislation. One should not simply dispel this criticism as anti-European sentiment but rather take the challenge seriously and open a more transparent and participatory chapter of European criminal law legislation.

Finally, the big question for the future remains whether the relatively homogeneous EU with only 15 Member States, largely common values, and clearly shared interests in fighting terrorism, etc., will be able to do so effectively. One may hope so. However, the danger of an overly legalistic approach to the problems involved, coupled with the dilatory and compromising outcome of the many skirmishes in the national interest in the course of EU law-making, is as present as in other areas of EU legislation. It remains to be seen whether the impressive legal architecture of the EU action to combat terrorism will provide a real "fortification".

9

Fighting Against International Terrorism: The Latin American Response

MICHELANGELA SCALABRINO

I. A DEFINITION OF TERRORISM — LATIN AMERICAN FEATURES: INTERNAL WAR, GUERRILLA TERRORISM

NO COMMON OR widespread consensus exists on a legal definition of terrorism,[1] both *per se* and/or in relation to other forms of violent, armed conduct, carried out against domestic or non-domestic targets.

In the League of Nations Draft Convention on Terrorism of 1937,[2] terrorism was identified as "all criminal acts directed against a State and intended or calculated to create a state of terror in the minds of particular persons or a group of persons or the general public". Under resolutions of the United Nations,[3] terrorism is described as "activities wherever and

[1] The question of a definition of terrorism has haunted the debate among States for decades. The UN Member States still have no agreed definition. However, terminological consensus would be necessary if, as some countries favour, a single comprehensive convention on terrorism were to replace the present 12 piecemeal conventions and protocols. See in general, J Trahan, "Terrorism Conventions: Existing Gaps and Different Approaches", (2002) 8 *New England International and Comparative Law Annual*, 215 ff and M Cherif Bassiouni, "Legal Control of International Terrorism: A Policy-Oriented Assessment", (2002) 43 *Harvard International Law Journal*, 83 ff.

[2] The first attempt to arrive at an internationally acceptable definition was made under the League of Nations, but the convention never came into existence.

[3] Recalling previous resolutions and existing international conventions relating to various aspects of the problem of international terrorism, on 9 December 1985 the General Assembly (GA) adopted Res 61/40 with the aim of finding measures to prevent acts of international terrorism that endanger or take innocent human lives or jeopardise fundamental freedoms, and studying the underlying causes of those forms of terrorism and acts of violence, such as poverty, frustration, grievances and despair, which cause some people to sacrifice human life (including their own) in an attempt to effect radical changes. Almost six years later, in Res A 46/51 of December 1991 concerning measures aiming at eliminating international terrorism, the GA revisited the problem and noted that a definition of international terrorism which meets general approval would render the fight against terrorism more efficient. "However, on closer examination, one discovers that this resolution reaffirms the ongoing contradictions within the UN, reflecting the division between developed and developing

by whomsoever committed,[4] aimed at the destruction of human rights, fundamental freedoms and democracy, threatening the territorial integrity and security of States, destabilizing legitimately constituted governments, undermining pluralistic civil society and having adverse consequences on the economic and social development of States";[5] as well as "all acts, methods and practices wherever and by whomsoever committed, criminal[6] and unjustifiable, intended or calculated to provoke a state of

countries. While the resolution condemns all forms of terrorism, it also simultaneously affirms the legitimacy of liberation wars. Bridging the gap between the views of the developed and developing countries on the one hand, and finding an acceptable compromise between legitimate acts of war carried out during liberation struggle, and terrorist acts directed against civilians, non-combatants and non-military targets on the other, continue to be difficult": A Obote-Odora, "Defining International Terrorism", (1999) 6 *Murdoch University Electronic Journal of Law*, <http://www.murdoch.edu.au/elaw/issues/v6n1/obote-odora61.html> . See also Kofi Annan's statement, "people who are desperate and in despair become easy recruits for terrorist organizations". Transcript of press conference of President Jacques Chirac of France and UN Secretary-General Kofi Annan, 19 September 2001, available at <http://www.un.org/News/Press/docs/2001/sgsm7964.doc.htm> quoted by A Cassese, "Terrorism is also Disrupting Some Crucial Legal Categories of International Law", <http://www.ejil.org/forum_WTC/ny-cassese.html>.

[4] M Halberstam, "The Evolution of the United Nations Position on Terrorism: From Exempting National Liberation Movements to Criminalizing Terrorism Wherever and by Whomever Committed", (2003) 41 *Columbia Journal of Transnational Law*, 573 ff.

[5] GA Res 48/122, 1993 "Human Rights and Terrorism".

[6] According to Raimo, classifying international terrorism as a crime creates a dilemma because a criminal act of terrorism to some will embody a legitimate act of self-determination to others. T Raimo, "Winning at the Expense of Law: The Ramifications of Expanding Counter-Terrorism Law Enforcement Jurisdiction Overseas", (1999) 14 *American University International Law Review*, at 1482–85: "At times, the US, like other nations, has not strictly applied the definition of international terrorism to foreign acts, recognizing some terrorist acts as legitimate claims of groups seeking self-determination. This method of defining terrorism is based on a political standard that leaves American foreign policymakers the discretion to decide which violent acts are acceptable and allows for the subjective definition of some terrorist groups as revolutionaries. Currently, US law defines international terrorism as a criminal act, classifying acts of violence objectively rather than rendering subjective and potentially arbitrary political decisions. This objective test for defining terrorist acts abroad is not applied in every case, however, resulting in the inconsistent classification of terrorism as a crime". The American Central Intelligence Agency — Directorate of Central Intelligence — Counterterrorist Center, is officially guided by the definition of terrorism contained in Title 22 of the US Code, Section 2656 f (d): "The term terrorism means premeditated, politically motivated violence perpetrated against noncombatant targets by subnational groups or clandestine agents, usually intended to influence an audience. The term international terrorism means terrorism involving the territory or the citizens of more than one country. The term terrorist group means any group that practices, or has significant subgroups that practice, international terrorism." B Ganor, "Terrorism: No Prohibition Without Definition", *The International Policy Institute for Counter-terrorism*, 7 October 2001, stresses that "The US State Department has put forward a definition according to which terrorism is the deliberate use of violence against non-combatants, whether civilian or not. However, this definition of terrorism will not work in practice, as it designates attacks on non-combatant military personnel as terrorism. Despite the natural tendency of those who have been harmed by terrorism to adopt this broad definition, terror organizations and their supporters can justly claim that they cannot be expected to attack only military personnel who are armed and ready for battle. If they were held to such a standard, they would lose the element of surprise and be quickly defeated. By narrowing the definition of terrorism to include only

terror[7] in the general public, a group of persons or particular persons for political purposes, whatever considerations[8] of a political, philosophical,

deliberate attacks on civilians, we leave room for a fair fight between guerillas and State armies. Thus we set a clear moral standard that can be accepted not only by Western countries, but also by the Third World and even by some of the terrorist organizations themselves. When such a moral distinction is internationally applied, terrorist organizations will have yet another reason to renounce terrorism in favor of guerilla actions."

[7] LR Beres, "The Meaning of Terrorism — Jurisprudential and Definitional Clarifications", (1995) 28 *Vanderbilt Journal of Transnational Law*, 239 ff and "The Legal Meaning of Terrorism for the Military Commander" (1995) 11 *Connecticut Journal International* Law, 11: "Little more than an ambiguous threshold exists to differentiate the level of violence distinguishing terrorist acts from acts of war. This ambiguity results in inconsistent definitions of international terrorism that can potentially complicate uniform law enforcement responses to terrorist threats abroad". Raimo, above n 6 at 1483 writes: "When, exactly, is the threat sufficient to argue convincingly for the presence of terrorism? In the absence of settled, unambiguous thresholds, inclusion of threat within the definition can serve propagandistic and/or geopolitical purposes."

[8] According to Beres, *ibid* at 2–9, "Indeed, the standard definitions of terrorism now in professional use offers little or no operational benefit for tactical commanders. The term has become so comprehensive and vague that it sometimes embraces even the most discrepant and unintended activities ... First, each definition is unclear regarding whether national or international law criteria should be analysed to determine the unlawfulness of a particular action. Second, definitions of terrorism which make no explicit reference to legality omit the essential elements of just cause and just means. Third, definitions of terrorism which include the threatened use of force fail to identify necessary threshold levels of force. Fourth, definitions not limited to the actions of insurgent organizations are too broad and therefore unmanageable. Finally, definitions which refer to political violence fail to demarcate the essential boundaries of politics. Under national law, pertinent penal provisions (murder, assault, theft, illegal detention of persons, hostage-taking, arson, etc) normally contain no actual reference to terrorism, and are applicable regardless of any such reference. Under international law, criteria of lawfulness are more or less present in pertinent treaty provisions, but these criteria are one step removed from judgments regarding terrorism; the analyst must first understand that terrorism is a conglomerate crime under international law and must then determine which particular penal components comprise this crime. Even with such an understanding, analysis may still be confounded by authoritative contradictory expectations, especially in regard to standards of just cause. The definitions of terrorism which make no explicit reference to legality also omit the essential elements of just cause (*jus ad bellum*) and just means (*jus in bello*). These indispensable elements distinguish permissible from impermissible insurgencies under international law. Moreover, in view of the supremacy of certain international law over national or domestic law, the elements of just cause and just measure are relevant, whichever realm of law or combination of realms is implicitly under consideration. Lacking these elements, a definition of terrorism necessarily includes both permissible and impermissible forms of insurgency. Hence, it is an altogether useless definition. Under international law, of course, not all resorts to insurgent force are terroristic. Just cause is an integral part of customary and conventional norms and may exist when insurgents fight for the inalienable right to self-determination and for the enjoyment of peremptory human rights. But insurgency is unlawful, regardless of just cause, whenever the means used fail to satisfy *jus in bello* criteria (*ie*, whenever the use of force is indiscriminate, disproportionate and/or beyond the codified boundaries of military necessity). There is an important flip side to the matter of just means. Not only is this standard essential to the identification of terrorism (every insurgency that violates this standard is terroristic), it applies as well to the permissible limitations of effective counter terrorism. Like the insurgents themselves, military forces opposed to terrorists are constrained by certain restrictions of the laws of war. Failure to comply with such restrictions does not convert these military forces into terrorists, but it does make them guilty of war crimes and possibly even crimes against humanity."

ideological, racial, ethnic, religious or other nature ... may be invoked to justify them".[9]

A general debate was also conducted within the Sixth Committee[10] on measures to combat international terrorism, but it moved away from any attempt to define terrorism itself. This term therefore continues to mean different things to different States. The failure of the international community, acting through the UN, to define terrorism is in fact a mainly political problem.[11]

[9] GA Res 49/60, [1994 "Measures to eliminate international terrorism"; GA Res 49/158, 1994 "Strengthening the United Nations crime prevention and criminal justice programme, particularly its technical cooperation capacity", where terrorism is defined as drug-related crime; GA Res 50/53, 1995 "Measures to eliminate international terrorism"; GA Res 51/210,] 1999 "Measures to eliminate international terrorism". According to the "Declaration on Measures to Eliminate International Terrorism", Annex II to GA Res 49/60, para 5: "... States must fulfil their obligations under the UN Charter and other provisions of international law with respect to combating international terrorism and are urged to take effective and resolute measures in accordance with the relevant provisions of international law and international standards of human rights for the speedy and final elimination of international terrorism, in particular: (a) to refrain from organizing, instigating, facilitating, financing, encouraging or tolerating terrorist activities and to take appropriate practical measures to ensure that their respective territories are not used for terrorist installations or training camps, or for the preparation or organization of terrorist acts intended to be committed against other States or their citizens; (b) to ensure the apprehension and prosecution or extradition of perpetrators of terrorist acts, in accordance with the relevant provisions of their national law; (c) to endeavour to conclude special agreements to that effect on a bilateral, regional and multilateral basis, and to prepare, to that effect, model agreements on cooperation; (d) to cooperate with one another in exchanging relevant information concerning the prevention and combating of terrorism; (e) to take promptly all steps necessary to implement the existing international conventions on this subject to which they are parties, including the harmonization of their domestic legislation with those conventions; (f) to take appropriate measures, before granting asylum, for the purpose of ensuring that the asylum seeker has not engaged in terrorist activities and, after granting asylum, for the purpose of ensuring that the refugee status is not used in a manner contrary to the provisions set out in sub para a; 6. In order to combat effectively the increase in, and the growing international character and effects of, acts of terrorism, States should enhance their cooperation in this area through, in particular, systematising the exchange of information concerning the prevention and combating of terrorism, as well as by effective implementation of the relevant international conventions and conclusion of mutual judicial assistance and extradition agreements on a bilateral, regional and multilateral basis; 7. In this context, States are encouraged to review urgently the scope of the existing international legal provisions on the prevention, repression and elimination of terrorism in all its forms and manifestations, with the aim of ensuring that there is a comprehensive legal framework covering all aspects of the matter; 8. Furthermore States that have not yet done so are urged to consider, as a matter of priority, becoming parties to the international conventions and protocols relating to various aspects of international terrorism referred to in the preamble to the present Declaration". See also M Mofidi and AE Eckert, " 'Unlawful Combatants' or 'Prisoners of War': The Law and Politics of Labels", (2003) 36 *Cornell International Law Journal*, 68–70.

[10] M Halberstam, "The Evolution of the United Nations Position on Terrorism: From Exempting National Liberation Movements to Criminalizing Terrorism Wherever and by Whomever Committed", (2003) 41 *Columbia Journal of Transnational Law*, 573 ff; E Rosand, "Security Council Resolution 1373, the Counter-Terrorism Committee, and the Fight Against Terrorism", (2003) 97 *The American Journal International Law*, 333 ff.

[11] Obote-Odora, above n 3 writes: "The political reasons are many and diverse. Among the members of the UN, there are states that are frustrated because they are disempowered.

In its turn, the International Court of Justice (ICJ)[12] has successfully avoided pronouncing any definition of terrorism.[13] The Organization of American States (OAS) has explicitly admitted[14] that "the line between terrorism and other types of crimes is not always clear, but terrorist acts do have certain things in common, including motivations that may transcend the crime itself".[15]

There are also states that consider themselves victims of economic and social wrongs, imposed on them by the developed countries. However, the central point is not whether the allegations made by developing countries against the developed ones are true or false, right or wrong. What is relevant is that these allegations form the political basis for terrorist actions and subsequently serve to justify it. Significantly, these states refuse to accept a legal order that, according to their perception, perpetrates such real or perceived inequalities. Consequently these states tend to refuse to embrace factual definition of terrorism that do not include the root causes of their backwardness and disempowerment. They are therefore disinclined to sign, let alone ratify, a definition which would restrict their freedom of action". PM Dupuy, "The Law After the Destruction of the Towers, in "The Attack on the World Trade Center: Legal Responses", <http://www.ejil.org/forum_WTC/ny-dupuy.html>, and V Nanda, "The Role of International Law in Combatting Terrorism, (2001) 10 *Michigan State University-DCL Journal of International Law*, 603 ff, stress that the existing conventional arsenal, whilst not negligible, remains piecemeal, incomplete, and full of gaps.

[12] See *Military and Paramilitary Activities in and against Nicaragua (Nicaragua v. United States of America)*, Merits, ICJ Reports 1986, 14. A strong criticism on the decision can be found in JN Moore, "The Nicaragua Case and the Deterioration of World Order" (1987) 81 *American Journal International Law* 151–59, as well as in FL Kizgis jz, "Appraisals of the ICJ's Decision: Nicaragua v. United States (Merits)", (1987) 81 *American Journal International Law*, 151 ff.

[13] According to Obote-Odora, above n 3, "It is interesting to note that the ICJ did not use the term terrorism in this very long case notwithstanding that claims advanced by Nicaragua against the US were of a category frequently included in the concept of terrorism under international law. The central claim by Nicaragua included, among other things, that the US was recruiting, training, arming, financing, supplying and otherwise encouraging, supporting aiding and directing military and paramilitary actions in and against Nicaragua and killing, wounding and kidnapping citizens of Nicaragua. These claims were carefully articulated by Nicaragua as substantive charges against the US, each claim accurately reflecting in prohibitive norms of international law, and the ICJ dealt with them as such. Throughout the proceedings, from the beginning to the end, there was no use made of the concept of terrorism by counsels and the ICJ. This omission is all the more striking, as for jurisdictional reasons the ICJ was precluded from applying the Charter of the UN. Even if the Charter was not applicable, the ICJ could, and indeed did, find sufficient authority in customary international law to deal with both the substance of what conduct is or is not permitted in what circumstances; and with the attendant questions of US responsibility, or the lack of it, for prohibited acts where they were carried out by those it financed and encouraged. Almost the only reference to terrorism was in the factual references to US legislation whereby aid was conditional upon the recipient country not "aiding, abetting or supporting acts of violence or terrorism in other countries".

[14] <http://www.oas.org/OASNews/1999/English/Nov-Dec/art2.htm>.

[15] See also point 5 of the Recommendation 1426 (1999) of the Council of Europe's Assembly "European democracies facing up to terrorism", 23 September 2001: "The Assembly considers an act of terrorism to be any offence committed by individuals or groups resorting to violence or threatening to use violence against a country, its institutions, its population in general or specific individuals which, being motivated by separatist aspirations, extremist ideological conceptions, fanaticism or irrational and subjective factors, is intended to create a climate of terror among official authorities, certain individuals or groups in society, or the general public".

The intrinsic difficulty in defining domestic, as well as international terrorism, no matter whether through a negative, *per exclusionem* approach, or in a direct way, may explain why, according to some academics, there would be no point in searching for logic-based definitions of a term which belongs to the realm of political or social science, especially when the term in question carries a negative emotional connotation.[16]

On the other hand, other researchers[17] realise that it is necessary to differentiate between various conditions of violence and to distinguish between diverse modes of conflict, if we want to gain a better understanding of their origins, the factors which affect them, and how to cope with them. If the definition of terrorism is equally applicable to conventional war and guerrilla warfare, the term loses any useful meaning: it simply becomes a synonym for violent intimidation in a political context and is reduced to an unflattering term, describing an ugly aspect of violent conflicts of all sizes and shapes.[18] Thus, a first distinction is attempted: the concept of terrorism is most commonly associated with a

[16] A Merari, "Terrorism as a Strategy of Insurgency" (1993) 4 *Terrorism and Political Violence,* 213–51.

[17] See eg B Ganor, "Defining Terrorism: Is One Man's Terrorist Another Man's Freedom Fighter?", *The International Policy Institute for Counter-terrorism,* 25 June 2001: "A correct and objective definition of terrorism can be based upon accepted international laws and principles regarding what behaviours are permitted in conventional wars between nations. These laws are set out in the Geneva and Hague Conventions, which in turn are based upon the basic principle that the deliberate harming of soldiers during wartime is a necessary evil, and thus permissible, whereas the deliberate targeting of civilians is absolutely forbidden. These Conventions thus differentiate between soldiers who attack a military adversary, and war criminals who deliberately attack civilians. This normative principle relating to a state of war between two countries can be extended without difficulty to a conflict between a non-governmental organization and a State. This extended version would thus differentiate between guerilla warfare and terrorism. Exactly in parallel with the distinction between military and civilian targets in war, the extended version would designate as 'guerilla warfare' the deliberate use of violence against military and security personnel in order to attain political, ideological and religious goals. Terrorism, on the other hand, would be defined as the deliberate use of violence against civilians in order to attain political, ideological and religious aims."

[18] RB Bilder, "A Commentary on the Hostages Convention 1979 by JJ Lambert", (1996) 90 *American Journal International Law,* 346 ff: "One way of protecting humanity against terrorism is to penalize terroristic conduct. If the criminal sanction is to be used, we need to provide a satisfactory legal definition providing the elements of the crimes condemned as terrorism. This requires distinguishing justifiable violence (self-defence or that perpetrated against an enemy combatant in war) and excusable violence (accident or duress) from war crimes and terrorism. And it may require determining the general ambit of the crimes deemed to constitute it, including defenses. This might be done by combining elements of the laws of war with general principles of substantive criminal law. Terrorism during peacetime might be considered analogous to war crimes during war. Thus, one of the weaknesses of most of the conventions is that they fail to satisfy sufficiently essential requirements of criminal law; indeed, where a definition and elements have developed, it has been primarily through domestic enabling legislation and prosecution". Compare JJ Lambert, *Terrorism and Hostages in International Law: A Commentary on the Hostages Convention 1979* (Cambridge, Grotius Publications, 1990) at 418 who argues that a comprehensive, universal approach to the elimination of terrorism will, at least in the near future, remain elusive and that the only way to

certain kind of violent action carried out by individuals and groups rather than by States, and which take place in peacetime rather than as part of conventional warfare. Terrorism is therefore connotes insurgent non-State violence.

Within this scheme, terrorism has subsequently been construed[19] as "an anxiety-inspiring method of repeated violent action, employed by clandestine or semi- clandestine individuals or groups, for idiosyncratic, criminal or political reasons, whereby, in contrast to assassination, the direct targets of violence are not the main targets. The immediate human victims of violence are generally chosen randomly (*targets of opportunity*) or selectively (*representative or symbolic targets*) from a target population, and serve as message generators".[20] Yet, the ground to distinguish between terrorism and other forms of violent conflict, such as guerrilla warfare, is still not evident in the above analysis, whereas such a distinction is most

go forward in the search for international co-operation in the suppression of terrorism is in the piecemeal fashion already begun. Both the promulgation and ratification of treaties dealing with terrorism on a piecemeal basis is preferable from a lawyer's point of view and that definitions of terrorism seem irrelevant to lawyers and legislators, who are concerned with making and enforcing rules to limit all political (or any other) violence, whether the victim is a primary target or merely a means of attacking a different protected interest".

[19] AP Schmid, "Political Terrorism" (Amsterdam, North Holland Publishing Company, 1983), *passim;* R Higgins, "The General International Law of Terrorism", in R Higgins and M Flory (eds) *Terrorism and International Law* (London, Routledge, 1997) *passim* and AP Schmid and AJ Jongman, "Political Terrorism" (Amsterdam, North Holland Publishing Company, 1988) 5–6.

[20] Beres, above n 7at 11–12: "A complementary way to operationalize threats within the definition of terrorism would be to focus on the degree of anticipated harm. Thus, for example, threats above a particularly specified level of destructiveness could be construed as terroristic while those below this level would not necessarily be expressions of terrorism. But here too, regardless of the level of expected harm, a threat would be terroristic only where it was directed at "soft" targets and where the *jus ad bellum* argument was manifestly political". Merari, above n 16 at 21–22: "The essentials of the psychological basis of a terrorist struggle have changed little since last century, when anarchist writings first formulated the principles of this strategy. The basic idea was phrased as 'propaganda by the deed'. This maxim meant that the terrorist act was the best herald of the need to overthrow the regime and the torch which would show the way to do it. The revolutionary terrorists hoped that their attacks would thus turn them from a small conspiratorial club into a massive revolutionary movement. In a way, the original concept of propaganda by the deed, as explained and exercised by nineteenth century revolutionaries, was more refined than its modern usage in the post -World War II era. Whereas the earlier users of this idea were careful to choose symbolic targets, such as Heads of State and infamous oppressive governors and ministers, in order to draw attention to the justification of their cause, the more recent brand has turned to multi-casualty indiscriminate attacks. In doing so, they have exchanged the propaganda value of justification for a greater shock value, ensuring massive media coverage. This change seems to reflect the adaptation of the strategy to the age of television. Anyway, this basic concept of the nature of the terrorist struggle does not constitute a complete strategy. Like some other conceptions of terrorism, in the idea of propaganda by the deed terrorism is only meant to be the first stage of the struggle. It is a mechanism of hoisting a flag and recruiting, a prelude which would enable the insurgents to develop other modes of struggle. In itself, it is not expected to bring the government down".

important in respect of situations such as that prevailing in many parts of Latin America.[21]

As strategies of insurgency, terrorism and guerrilla warfare are quite distinct.[22] Guerrilla warfare is a diffuse type of war,[23] fought in relatively small formations, against a stronger enemy; it avoids direct, decisive battles, opting for a protracted struggle, which consists of many small clashes instead. Terrorism is also a strategy of protracted struggle; guerrilla warfare, however, is primarily a strategy based on a physical encounter. Tactically, guerrillas conduct warfare in a manner similar to conventional armies;[24] on the contrary, terrorist strategy does not vie for a tangible control of territory.

Other practical differences exist between the two forms of warfare, which further accentuate the basic distinction of the two strategies. These differences are actually an extension of the essentially divergent strategic concepts: they relate to unit size, arms, and types of operations. Guerrillas usually wage war in platoon or company size units and sometimes even in battalions and brigades; terrorists tend to operate in very small units,[25] ranging for example from the lone assassin or a single person who makes and plants an improvised explosive device, to a five members'

[21] M Whine, "The New Terrorism", *Annual Report of the Stephen Roth Institute for the Study of Contemporary Anti-Semitism and Racism at Tel Aviv University: "Antisemitism Worldwide 2000/1"*, writes: "The terrorism which prevailed in Latin America during the 1970s and 1980s tended to be an outgrowth of national liberation struggles, or of anti-capitalist movements. It was therefore often possible to observe the ideological steps through which the players passed in their conversion from political activism to terrorism. Generally, this transformation would include several of the following elements: opposition to the State or to perceived injustice expressed through democratic means; a lack of response, or an inappropriate response, by authority; extreme, but not necessarily violent, opposition to the authority; repression by that authority; terrorism against a specific target seen as a symbol of that authority; further repression".

[22] According to Ganor, "Defining" above n 17, "The aims of terrorism and guerilla warfare may well be identical; but they are distinguished from each other by the means used — or more precisely, by the targets of their operations. The guerilla fighter's targets are military ones, while the terrorist deliberately targets civilians".

[23] This is why the Inter-American Court of Human Rights (IACHR) applied Art 3 common of the Geneva Conventions of 12 August 1949 in respect to the Guatemalan insurgency (see *Bámaca Velásquez* case, Merits, below).

[24] Merari, above n 16 at 30: "*Guerrilla* warfare requires a terrain that would be advantageous for the small bands of insurgents and disadvantageous for mechanized and airborne government forces. In Western Europe this kind of terrain, thick jungles or extensive, rugged mountains inaccessible by motor transportation, cannot be found. Guerrillas can sometimes compromise for a less than perfect terrain, providing that other conditions are met, in particular inefficient and poorly-equipped government forces on the one hand and massive popular support for the insurgents on the other hand. In twentieth century Western countries none of these conditions exists and terrorism is the only strategic option for insurgents who are determined to resort to violence to advance their cause".

[25] *Ibid*, at 29, the author reports the largest terrorist teams which have been employed in barricade-hostage incidents. For example, 50 members of the 28th of February Popular League participated in the takeover of the Panamanian Embassy in San Salvador on 11 January 1980 and 41 members of the Colombian M-19 group took over the Palace of Justice in Bogota on 6 November 1985.

hostage-taking team. Thus, in terms of operational units' size, the upper limits of terrorists are the lower limits of guerrilla warfare.[26]

Differences in weaponry used in these two types of warfare are also easily noticeable: whereas guerrillas mostly use ordinary military-type arms, typical terrorist weapons include home-made bombs, car bombs and sophisticated barometric pressure-operated devices, designed to explode on board airliners in mid-air.[27] The differences in unit size and arms are merely corollaries of the fact that tactically guerrilla actions are similar to regular army's mode of operation. On the contrary terrorists, unlike guerrillas, have no territorial base; therefore, they must immerse among the general civilian population, and this is why they ordinarily cannot allow themselves to wear uniforms, while guerrillas ordinarily do.[28]

For the purpose of this article, we assume these points as the basic distinctions between terrorism and guerrilla warfare, bearing in mind that terrorist actions, when carried out systematically, constitute a distinct strategy of insurgency.[29] As far as Latin America is concerned, no other difference appears to exist between the psychological basis of guerrilla warfare and terrorism[30] — terrorism is meant to be the first stage of the struggle,[31] "a mechanism of hoisting a flag and recruiting, a prelude which could enable the insurgents to develop other modes of struggle".[32]

[26] Beres, above n 7 at 17: "Indeed, the very essence of terrorism is the capacity to inflict harms, even catastrophic harms, with extremely small forces. Hence, the military commander assessing correlations of forces in the fight against terrorism will have to look beyond number, to far more subtle sources of power."

[27] Merari, above n 16 at 20: "In practice, the terrorist operational inventory is rather limited. They place explosive charges in public places, assassinate political opponents or carry out assaults by small arms on the public at large, take hostages by kidnapping, hijacking, or barricading themselves in buildings. In most cases, their capability is rather slim."

[28] *Ibid*, 10–13.

[29] *Ibid*, at 18: "Terrorism is not different from other forms of warfare in the targeting of non-combatants. Yet terrorism, more than any other form of warfare, systematically breaches the internationally accepted rules of war. In guerrilla warfare and conventional war, the laws of engagement are often ignored, but terrorism discards these laws altogether in refusing to distinguish between combatants and non-combatants and, with regard to international terrorism, in rejecting the limitations of war zones as well. Unlike conventional and guerrilla wars, terrorism has no legal standing in international law."

[30] Ganor, above n 17, writes "Does this definition of terrorism legitimize guerilla warfare? The answer is that, yes, the definition does make a moral distinction between terrorism and guerilla warfare. Countries forced to deal with ongoing attacks on their military personnel will obviously perceive these attacks as acts of war, which must be thwarted. These countries cannot expect to enlist the world in a struggle against 'legitimate' guerilla warfare, but they can justifiably demand that the international community assist them were they fighting against terrorism."

[31] *Ibid*, at 29–30: "There are several examples in history which show quite clearly what happens when a group of insurgents aims too high in its choice of strategy. The most dramatic in the second half of this century is, probably, Ernesto (Che) Guevara's Bolivian venture."

[32] Merari, above n 16 at 21–22 and 24: "Like the earlier users the original concept of propaganda by the deed, Latin American terrorists carefully choose symbolic targets in order to draw attention to the justification of their cause. Yet, some insurgent groups have viewed terrorism as a strategy designed to wear out the adversary. In fact, this is the only conception of terrorism which viewed this mode of struggle as a complete way of achieving victory, rather than as a supplement or prelude to another strategy. The insurgents were fully aware

In fact, an important constituent in terrorist strategy typical of Latin America is the idea of provocation. Terrorist attacks tend to draw repressive responses by political regimes, which necessarily affect also parts of the population which are not associated with the insurgents. These measures, in turn, make the government more unpopular, thus increasing public support of the terrorists and their cause. When government counter-terrorist actions are not only draconian but also ineffective, anti-government sentiment is bound to be even more prevalent.[33]

Domestic armed violence commonly termed terrorism is far from being unknown to Latin America. On the other hand, international terrorism, in the sense of acts planned and carried out by people of non-OAS States[34] or against foreigners or foreigners' assets, has been, and still is, a statistically less relevant phenomenon.[35] The OAS has recognized this.[36] In fact, only a few infra-Latin American episodes[37] and sporadic attacks against US and/or Japanese corporations' assets and personnel[38] are publicly known, with the sole exception of continuing attacks in Colombia.[39]

of their inferiority as a fighting force compared to the strength of the government and they did not expect that they would ever be strong enough to defeat the government by a physical confrontation. Nevertheless, they assumed that they had a greater stamina than the government and that, if they persisted, the government would eventually yield."

[33] Merari, above n 16 at 23.

[34] According to the US Department of State, Office of the Coordinator for Counter-terrorism, "Patterns of Global Terrorism, 1996 to 2001, there has been a strong suspicion that the two attacks brought against the Argentine — Jewish Mutual Association in 1994, and possibly the 1992 bombing of the Israeli Embassy in Buenos Aires — were carried out by the Iran-backed Lebanese Hezbollah's members or agents coming from or through the Iguazu region. Iguazu is the region where Paraguay, Argentina, and Brazil all touch, near the Paraná River. A Lebanese exiled community settled in this region during the civil war in Lebanon. *Cf* CC Harmon, "Terrorism and Geographical Bridges", (2000) 6 *Journal of Counterterrorism and Security International*.

[35] <http://www.emergency.com/cntrterr.htm#Question-8 - 7April 2001>.

[36] <http://www.oas.org/OASNews/1999/English/Nov-Dec/art2.htm>.

[37] See *Castillo Petruzzi et al v Peru*, IACHR C 41 on Preliminary Objections; C 52 on the merits and Resolution C 59 on the compliance with the sentence. Francisco Sebastián Castillo Petruzzi, Lautaro Enrique Mellado Saavedra, Alejandro Luis Astorga Valdés and María Concepción Pincheira Sáez, were in fact Chilean and members of the MRTA. They were captured in October 1993, when police broke into a house in Lima where the MRTA was holding a Peruvian businessman. They were accused of having killed another five hostages whose families had not paid ransom.

[38] See US Department of State, Office of the Coordinator for Counter-terrorism, "Patterns of Global Terrorism, years 1996 to 2001". In Peru, on 17 December 1996, a MRTA commando made up of 22 guerrillas took the Japanese Embassy in Lima by assault. More than 600 individuals were taken hostage. The MRTA's main demand was the release by the Peruvian Government of MRTA members imprisoned in Peru. On 22 April 1997, Peruvian military forces stormed the residence of the Japanese Ambassador, bringing to an end the hostage. One hostage, two Peruvian soldiers, and all 14 of the MRTA terrorists were dead. For details on the attack, see RKL Panjabi, "Terror at the Emperor's Birthday Party: An Analysis of the Hostage-Taking Incident at the Japanese Embassy in Lima, Peru", (1997) 16 *Dickinson Journal of International Law*, 1 ff.

[39] Foreign citizens often are targets of Revolutionary Armed Force of Colombia (FARC) kidnapping for ransom. US companies suffered severe economic damages due to terrorist

Nevertheless, the decades 1970–90 have been characterised by a number of internal wars,[40] guerrilla insurgencies[41] and terrorist

attacks against oil pipelines. The National Liberation Army (ELN) annually conducts hundreds of kidnappings for ransom, often targeting foreign employees of large corporations, especially in the petroleum.

[40] Internal war is still savaging Colombia, according to the IACHR Resolutions dated 14 September and 12 November 2000 in the case *Comunidad de Paz de San José de Apartadó* (*"La región del Urabá antioqueño, es uno de los epicentros del conflicto armado interno que se desarrolla en la República de Colombia"*) and according to the data provided for by the Institute on Terrorism.

See MC Cardenas, "Colombia's Peace Process: The Continuous Search for Peace", (2002) 15 *Florida Journal International Law*, 273 ff ; LE Cuervo, "Colombia 2025 — Heaven or Hell?", (2003) 77 *Tulane Law Review*, 1049–52; A De La Asunción, "Colombia: The Ignored Humanitarian Crisis", (2000) 31 *University of Miami Inter-American Law Review*, 447–53; FI Dominguez, "An Obsession With Failure?", *Foreign Affairs*, January 1997, 100 ff; JE Esquirol, "Can International Law Help? An Analysis of the Colombian Peace Process", (2000) 16 *Connecticut Journal International Law*, 23–92; P Hakim, "The Uneasy Americas", *Foreign Affairs*, April 2001; W Laqueur, *Guerrilla: An Historical and Critical Study*, (Boston, Little, 1976) Chap 6; A Khan, "A Legal Theory Of International Terrorism", (1987) 19 *Connecticut Law Review*, 945–72; R Pardo, "Colombia's Two-Front War", *Foreign Affairs*, August 2000; RM Latore, "Coming Out of the Dark: Achieving Justice for Victims of Human Rights Violations by South American Military Regimes", (2002) 25 *Boston College International and Comparative Law Review*, 419 ff; KR McGhee, "The Rising Number of Internally-Displaced Persons in Colombia and the United Nations's Response", (2003) 19 *New York Law School Journal of Human Rights*, 843 ff; M Shifter, "Colombia on the Brink — There Goes the Neighbourhood", *Foreign Affairs*, August 1999 and TC Wright, "Human Rights in Latin America: History and Projections for the Twenty-First Century", (2000) 30 *California Western International Law Journal*, 303 ff. As to the links between terrorism and drug-trafficking, see A Arana, "The New Battle for Central America", *Foreign Affairs*, December 2001, Essays, 88 ff; G Díaz Dionis, "Deuda externa, narcotráfico y militarismo", Ko'aga Roñe'eta se.vii (1999) <http://www.derechos.org/vii/dionis1.html> ; LE Nagle, "U.S. Mutual Assistance to Colombia: Vague Promises and Diminishing Returns", (2000) 23 *Fordham International Law Journal*, 1235 ff and FE Thoumi, "Illegal Drugs in Colombia: From Illegal Economic Boom to Social Crisis", (2002) 582 *The Annals of The American Academy of Political and Social Science*, 102 ff.

[41] Eg in Guatemala, ended by the Oslo Peace Agreement of 23 June 1994 and the subsequent Historical Truth Commission's Report published on 25 February 1999, paras 17–20 and 24–25: *"La magnitud de la respuesta represiva del Estado, absolutamente desproporcionada en relación con la fuerza militar de la insurgencia, sólo puede entenderse en el marco de los profundos conflictos sociales, económicos y culturales del país ... En ningún momento del enfrentamiento armado interno los grupos guerrilleros tuvieron el potencial bélico necesario para constituir una amenaza inminente para el Estado. Los contados combatientes no pudieron competir en el plano militar con el Ejército de Guatemala, que dispuso de más efectivos, muy superior armamento, así como mejor entrenamiento y coordinación. También se ha constatado que durante el enfrentamiento armado, el Estado y el Ejército conocían el grado de organización, el número de efectivos, el tipo de armamento y los planes de acción de los grupos insurgentes. De esta forma, fueron conscientes de que la capacidad militar de la insurgencia no representaba una amenaza concreta para el orden político guatemalteco ... La CEH concluye que el Estado magnificó deliberadamente la amenaza militar de la insurgencia, práctica que fue acreditada en su concepto del enemigo interno. Incluir en un solo concepto a los opositores, demócratas o no; pacifistas o guerrilleros; legales o ilegales; comunistas y no comunistas, sirvió para justificar graves y numerosos crímenes. Frente a una amplia oposición de carácter político, socioeconómico y cultural, el Estado recurrió a operaciones militares dirigidas a aniquilarla físicamente o amedrentarla por completo, a través de un plan represivo ejecutado principalmente por el Ejército y los demás cuerpos de seguridad nacional. Sobre esta base la CEH explica por qué la vasta mayoría de las víctimas de las acciones del Estado no fueron combatientes"*. On Truth Commission Reports in Latin America, see T Farer, "Consolidating Democracy in Latin America: Law, Legal Institutions and Constitutional Structure", (1995) 10 *American University Journal of*

attacks,[42] involving large scale fear amongst the civilian population in many States,[43] with Latin American insurgent groups

International Law & Policy, 1302–10; AN Keller, "To Name Or Not To Name? The Commission for Historical Clarification in Guatemala, its Mandate, and the Decision not to Identify Individual Perpetrators", (2001) 13 *Florida Journal of International Law*, 289 ff; GL Smith "Immune To Truth? Latin American Truth Commissions and US Support For Abusive Regimes", (2001) 33 *Columbia Human Rights Law Review*, 241 ff. and M Vasallo, "Truth and Reconciliation Commissions: General Considerations and a Critical Comparison of the Commissions of Chile and El Salvador", (2002) 33 *The University of Miami Inter-American Law Review*, 153 ff. See also GVan Harten, "Guatemala's Peace Accords in a Free Trade Area of the Americas", (2000) 3 *Yale Human Rights & Development Law Journal*, 116–27.

[42] Eg the Shining Path and MRTA attacks in Peru; the Manuel Rodriguez Popular Front's, the Lautaro Youth Movement's, and the Lautaro faction of the United Popular Action Movement's or Lautaro Popular Rebel Forces' in Chile; the Farabundo Marti National Liberation Front's in El Salvador.

[43] The US Department of State, Office of the Coordinator for Counter-terrorism, "Patterns of Global Terrorism, 1997", April 1998, at 53–79 and "Patterns of Global Terrorism, 2000", April 2001, has identified the following list of Latin American terrorist movements and observations relating thereto: Bolivia — National Liberation Army (ELN): Strength: unknown; probably fewer than 100. External aid: none; Chile — Manuel Rodriguez Patriotic Front (FPMR): founded in 1983 as the armed wing of the Chilean Communist Party. Now believed to have between 50 and 100 members. External aid: none. Removed from the State Department's list of international terrorist groups due to the lack of terrorist activities; Chile — The Lautaro faction of the United Popular Action Movement (MAPU/L) or Lautaro Popular Rebel Forces (FRPL): Strength: unknown. Location-area of operation: mainly Santiago. External Aid: none; Colombia — National Liberation Army (ELN): Marxist insurgent group formed in 1965 by urban intellectuals inspired by Fidel Castro and Che Guevara. Activities: kidnapping, hijacking, bombing, extortion, and guerrilla war. Modest conventional military capability. Annually conducts hundreds of kidnappings for ransom, often targeting foreign employees of large corporations, especially in the petroleum industry. Frequently assaults energy infrastructure and has inflicted major damage on pipelines and the electric distribution network. Now believed to have approximately 3,000 to 6,000 armed combatants and an unknown number of active supporters. Location-area of operation: mostly in rural and mountainous areas of north, northeast, and southwest Colombia and Venezuela border regions. External aid: Cuba provides some medical care and political consultation; Colombia — Revolutionary Armed Forces (FARC): Established in 1964 as the military wing of the Colombian Communist Party, the FARC is Colombia's oldest, largest, most capable, and best-equipped Marxist insurgency. Organized along military lines, it includes several urban fronts. Activities: bombings, murder, kidnapping, extortion, hijacking, as well as *guerrilla* and conventional military action against Colombian political, military, and economic targets. Now believed to have approximately 9,000 to 12,000 armed combatants and an unknown number of supporters, mostly in rural areas. External aid: Cuba provides some medical care and political consultation; Colombia — United Self-Defence Forces (AUC-*Autodefensa Unidades de Colombia*): The AUC, commonly referred to as *autodefensas* or paramilitaries, is an umbrella organization formed in April 1997 to consolidate most local and regional paramilitary groups, each with the mission to protect economic interests and combat insurgents locally. The AUC, supported by economic *élites*, drug traffickers, and local communities lacking effective government security, claims its primary objective is to protect its sponsors from insurgents and asserts itself as a regional and national counter-insurgent force. It is adequately equipped and armed and reportedly pays its members a monthly salary. Combat tactics consist of conventional and guerilla operations against main force insurgent units. In early 2001, the government estimated there were 8,000 paramilitary fighters, including former military and insurgent personnel. AUC forces are strongest in the north and northwest. External aid: none; Honduras — Morazanist Patriotic Front (FPM): A radical, leftist terrorist group that first appeared in the late 1980s. Attacks made in

systematically using a mixture of both the strategies described above.[44]

II. LATIN AMERICAN GENERAL INSTRUMENTS

When "terrorism" became a large scale phenomenon in Latin America, the members of the OAS had already agreed on two international conventions relating to possible State, armed or unarmed attacks, and to major criminal offences brought against persons to whom States have a duty to give special protection according to international law. These conventions are the Inter-American Treaty of Reciprocal Assistance (Treaty of Rio) of 9 February 1947,[45] and the Convention to Prevent and Punish the Acts of Terrorism Taking the Form of Crimes Against Persons and Related Extortion that Are of International Significance, signed in Washington DC on 2 February 1971.[46] The Preamble of the former instrument clearly

protest of US intervention in Honduran economic and political affairs. The organization has not recently engaged in terrorist activity. Strength: unknown, probably relatively small. External aid: had ties to former Government of Nicaragua and possibly Cuba. Removed from the State Department's list of international terrorist groups due to the lack of terrorist activities; Peru — Shining Path (*Sendero Luminoso*): Former university professor Abimael Guzman formed Sendero Luminoso in the late 1960s. In the 1980s, SL became one of the most ruthless terrorist groups. Its stated goal was to destroy existing Peruvian institutions and replace them with a communist peasant revolutionary regime. It also opposed any influence by foreign governments, as well as by other Latin American *guerrilla* groups, especially the Tupac Amaru Revolutionary Movement. SL's strength has been vastly diminished by arrests and desertions. Location-area of operation: Peru, with most activity in rural areas. External aid: none; Peru — Tupac Amaru Revolutionary Movement (MRTA): Traditional Marxist-Leninist revolutionary movement formed in 1983 from remnants of the Movement of the Revolutionary Left. Aimed to establish a Marxist regime and to rid Peru of all imperialist elements, primarily US and Japanese influence. Peru's counter-terrorist program has diminished the group's ability to carry out terrorist attacks, and the MRTA has suffered from infighting, the imprisonment or deaths of senior leaders, and loss of leftist support. Activities: previously conducted bombings, kidnappings, ambushes, and assassinations, but recent activity has fallen drastically. Strength: believed to be no more than 100–150 members, consisting largely of young fighters who lack leadership skills and experience.External aid: none.

[44]Merari, above n 16 at 213–51. According to Patterns of Global Terrorism — 2000: "In Colombia, leftist guerilla groups abducted hostages and attacked civil infrastructure, while rightwing paramilitary groups abducted congressional representatives, killed political candidates, and massacred civilians in an attempt to thwart the guerillas. Despite ongoing peace talks, Colombia's two largest *guerrilla* groups, the FARC and the ELN, continued to conduct terrorist acts, including kidnapping private US and foreign citizens and extorting money from businesses and individuals in the Colombian countryside. In Ecuador, organized criminal elements with possible links to terrorists and terrorist groups abducted 10 oil workers and also claimed responsibility for oil pipeline bombings that killed seven civilians."

[45]Treaty Series OAS No B-29, entered into force on 3 December 1948.

[46]Treaty Series OAS No A-49 which from September 2003, is in force among 14 States (Bolivia, Colombia, Costa Rica, Dominican Republic, El Salvador, Grenada, Guatemala, Mexico, Nicaragua, Panama, Peru, US, Uruguay and Venezuela).

states that the treaty was concluded in order to assure peace, to provide for effective reciprocal assistance to meet armed attacks against any American State, and to deal with threats of aggression against any of them.

In Article 3(1), the signatories agree that "an armed attack by any State against an American State shall be considered as an attack against all the American States"; consequently, each of them undertakes to assist the other in repelling the attack, in the exercise of the inherent right of individual or collective self-defence recognized by Article 51 of the UN Charter.[47]

In case of aggression other than an armed attack, but which is capable of affecting the inviolability or the integrity of the territory, or the sovereignty or political independence of any American State, or in case of any other fact or situation which might endanger the peace of America (Article 6), the Organ of Consultation established by the treaty should meet immediately, in order to "agree on the measures which must be taken to assist the victim of the aggression or, in any case, the measures which should be taken for the common defence and for the maintenance of the peace and security of the Continent".

According to the preamble and Article 1 of the latter treaty, terrorism is identified with, but not solely, "kidnapping, as well as extortion in connection with this crime, murder and other assaults against the life or physical integrity of those persons to whom the State has the duty according to international law to give special protection". Article 2 considers the above as common crimes of international significance, regardless of motive, and so the contracting States undertake to include these crimes among the punishable acts giving rise to extradition in any treaty on the subject to which they might agree among themselves (Article 7), as well as in their penal laws, if not already so included (Article 8(d)).

Nonetheless, the right to asylum is still guaranteed,[48] and the principle of non-intervention is affirmed.

At the beginning of the terrorism decades, the Inter-American Convention on Extradition (Treaty of Caracas) was agreed upon, on 28 February 1981.[49] As in all similar conventions, extradition is not granted when, as determined by the requested State, the offence for which the person is sought is a political offence, an offence related thereto, or an ordinary criminal offence prosecuted for political reasons (Article 4(4)).[50] The

[47] According to Art 9, in addition to other acts which the Organ of Consultation may characterize as aggression "unprovoked armed attack by a State against the territory, the people, or the land, sea or air forces of another State" is also considered as such an act.

[48] Art 6 provides: "None of the provisions of this convention shall be interpreted so as to impair the right of asylum."

[49] Treaty Series OAS No B-47, entered into force on 28 March 1992.

[50] *Ibid*: "The requested State may decide that the fact that the victim of the punishable act in question performed political functions does not in itself justify the designation of the offence as political." On the other hand, "No provision of this Convention shall preclude extradition regulated by a treaty or Convention in force between the requesting State and the requested

right to asylum is reaffirmed, when its exercise is appropriate (Article 6).[51] Subsequently, the Inter-American Convention on Mutual Assistance in Criminal Matters was signed in Nassau on 23 May 1992.[52] According to Article 9, the requested State may refuse assistance when it determines that: " ... b) the investigation has been initiated for the purpose of prosecuting, punishing, or discriminating in any way against an individual or group of persons for reason of ideology; c) the request refers to a crime that is political or related to a political crime, or to a common crime prosecuted for political reasons; d) the request has been issued at the request of a special or *ad hoc* tribunal".[53]

However, it was only in 1996 that the Declaration of Lima to Prevent, Combat and Eliminate Terrorism[54] became the real starting-point of more pertinent, if still hesitant, agreements concerning terrorism in Latin America. Its background can be traced to OAS GA/Res 1350 (XXV-O/95), which had resolved to convene an Inter-American Specialized Conference on Terrorism, to be held in the first half of 1996. Accordingly, in February 1995 the Committee on Political and Juridical Affairs of the Permanent Council of the OAS established a Working Group on Terrorism,[55] and the Ministers and heads of delegation agreed on 26 April 1996 on a subsequent Plan of Action on Hemispheric Cooperation to Prevent, Combat, and Eliminate Terrorism. A few months

State whose purpose is to prevent or repress a specific category of offences and which imposes on such States an obligation to either prosecute or extradite the person sought" (Art 5).

[51] "No provision of this Convention may be interpreted as a limitation on the right of asylum when its exercise is appropriate."

[52] Treaty Series OAS No A-55, entered into force on 14 April 1996. An Optional Protocol (Protocol of Managua) Treaty Series OAS No 59 was adopted on 11 June 1993 referring to tax crimes. As of writing, it has not yet come into force.

[53] Meanwhile, Costa Rica, El Salvador, Guatemala, Honduras, Nicaragua and Panama had signed (December 1995) the Framework Treaty on Democratic Security in Central America, in which the parties had undertaken to prevent and combat, without exception, all types of criminal activity with a regional or international impact, such as terrorism, and Argentina, Brazil, and Paraguay had signed (March 1996) a Tripartite Agreement to implement effective measures in response to the criminal phenomenon of terrorism.

[54] Adopted at the second plenary session, held on 26 April 1996 by the Ministers and the heads of delegation of the OAS Member States, meeting for the Inter-American Specialized Conference on Terrorism.

[55] Where the Ministers and heads of delegation resolved: "... 6. To cooperate fully on matters of extradition, in conformity with their domestic law and treaties in force on the subject, without prejudice to the right of States to grant asylum when appropriate; ... 10. To increase cooperation among Member States in combating terrorist acts, while fully observing the rule of law and international norms, especially with regard to human rights; 11. That it is essential to adopt all bilateral and regional cooperation measures necessary to prevent, combat, and eliminate, by all legal means, terrorist acts in the Hemisphere, with full respect for the jurisdiction of Member States and for international treaties and conventions; 9. That it is important for OAS Member States to ratify or accede to international instruments on terrorism as soon as possible and, when necessary, to implement them through their domestic laws; 8. To study, on the basis of an evaluation of existing international instruments, the need for and advisability of concluding a new inter-American convention on terrorism".

later, GA Res 1399 (XXVI-O/96)[56] reiterated its strongest condemnation of all forms of terrorism by whatever agent or means, resolved to repudiate the grave consequences of such acts which constitute a systematic and deliberate violation of the rights of individuals and requested the OAS Permanent Council to consider convening a meeting of government experts to examine ways to improve the exchange of information and other measures for cooperation in order to prevent, combat, and eliminate terrorism. A meeting of government experts was held in Washington DC on 5–6 May 1997,[57] formulating a few final proposals, among which the most relevant was the establishment of a directory of competences, aimed at improving cooperation among Member States. Shortly after, GA Res 1492 (XXVII-O/97) urged Member States that had not yet done so to sign, ratify, and/or accede to the international conventions related to terrorism referred to in the UN GA Res 51/210.[58]

In the meantime, upon the initiative of the States belonging to the Rio Group, the Inter-American Convention on Fabrication and Illicit Trafficking in Firearms, Ammunition, Explosives, and Other Related Materials had been adopted in Washington DC on 14 November 1997, and entered into force on 1 July 1998.[59] According to Article XXI of the Convention, the Consultative Committee provided for in Article XX[60] was established and met for its first session on 9–10 March 2000.[61]

[56] Adopted at the eighth plenary session, held on 7 June 1996.

[57] See GA/Res 1492 (XXVII-O/97) adopted at the seventh plenary session convened by CP/Res 700 (1108/97) and held on 5 June 1997.

[58] The following year, GA Res 1553/98 (XXVIII-O/98), adopted at the twenty-eighth regular session (Caracas, June 1998), reiterated the same decisions and urged Member States to sign, ratify, and/or accede also to the International Convention for the Suppression of Terrorist Bombings, opened for signature on 12 January 1998 at UN headquarters. It also instructed the Permanent Council to carry out the preparatory work for a Second Inter-American Specialized Conference on Terrorism, with a view to convening it.

[59] Treaty Series OAS No A-63.

[60] "1. In order to attain the objectives of this Convention, the States Parties shall establish a Consultative Committee responsible for: a. promoting the exchange of information contemplated under this Convention; b. facilitating the exchange of information on domestic legislation and administrative procedures of the States Parties; c. encouraging cooperation between national liaison authorities to detect suspected illicit exports and imports of firearms, ammunition, explosives, and other related materials; d. promoting training and exchange of knowledge and experience among States Parties and technical assistance between States Parties and relevant international organizations, as well as academic studies; e. requesting from non-party States, when appropriate, information on the illicit manufacturing of and trafficking in firearms, ammunition, explosives, and other related materials; and f. promoting measures to facilitate the application of this Convention". See WG Sharp sr, "The Use of Armed Force Against Terrorism: American Hegemony or Impotence?", (2000) 1 *Chicago Journal International Law*, 37–47, stresses the need of co-operation within States in order to avoid that "in the absence of any State sponsorship of terrorist or criminal activities, a use of force by a State against those non-State actors in the sovereign territory of another State without that State's consent may very be estimated as an unlawful use of force against that territorial State".

[61] See also OEA/Ser. P - GA/Res 1750 (XXX-O/00) of 5 June 2000.

III. THE INTER-AMERICAN COMMITTEE AGAINST TERRORISM (CICTE)

Following the 1996 Lima Conference, a Second Specialized Conference on Terrorism[62] held on 23–24 November 1998 adopted the Commitment of Mar del Plata,[63] which called for the establishment within the OAS of an Inter-American Committee Against Terrorism (CICTE) consisting of competent national authorities of the Member States, and for the adoption of Guidelines for Inter-American Cooperation Regarding Terrorist Acts and Activities.[64] The subsequent meeting of the General Assembly endorsed the recommendations and decisions contained in the Commitment of Mar Del Plata and established the CICTE (*Comité Inter Americano Contra el Terrorismo*).[65]

The basic objectives of the CICTE are: "a) to enhance the exchange of information *via* the competent national authorities, including the establishment of an Inter-American database on terrorism issues; b) to formulate proposals to assist Member States in drafting appropriate counter-terrorism legislation in all States; c) to compile the bilateral, sub regional, regional and multilateral treaties and agreements signed by Member States and promote universal adherence to inter-national counter-terrorism conventions; d) to enhance border cooperation and travel documentation security measures, (e) to develop activities for training and crisis management and ... (h) to design technical cooperation programmes and activities for training the staff assigned to tasks

[62] The Second Inter-American Specialized Conference on Terrorism originated in the Plan of Action of the Second Summit of the Americas (Santiago, Chile, April 1998), at which the Heads of State and government had expressed their willingness to take measures as agreed in the Declaration and Plan of Action of Lima, in order to prevent, combat, and eliminate terrorism and to convene the Second Specialized Inter-American Conference to define future courses of action for the prevention, combat, and elimination of terrorism.

[63] "The Ministers and heads of delegation of the OAS Member States decide to adopt the following Commitment: '(i) To reiterate the most emphatic condemnation and repudiation of all terrorist acts, which they recognize as serious common crimes ... ; (ii) To strengthen cooperation among the Member States to combat terrorism, with full respect for the rule of international law and for human rights and fundamental freedoms, respect for the sovereignty of States and the principle of non-intervention, and strict compliance with the rights and duties of States embodied in the Charter of the OAS; ... (iv) To improve the exchange of information and other measures for cooperation among Member States to prevent, combat, and eliminate terrorism; (vii) To recommend to the GA that it establish an appropriate institutional framework, in keeping with the Charter of the OAS and bearing in mind respect for State sovereignty and the principle of non-intervention, that shall be called Inter-American Committee on Terrorism (CICTE). It shall be formed by the competent national authorities in the Member States of the Organization and it shall hold at least one session a year ...'.

[64] Contained in Appendix I to the Commitment and aimed at establishing effective mechanisms for cooperation among the Member States to prevent, combat, and eliminate terrorism.

[65] See GA/Res 1650 (XXIX-O/99) adopted at the first plenary session held on 7 June 1999, point 3 and E Lagos and TD Rudy, "Preventing, Punishing, and Eliminating Terrorism in the Western Hemisphere: a Post-9/11 Inter-American Treaty", (2003) 26 *Fordham International Law Journal*, 1622–24 .

related to preventing, combating and eliminationg terrorism in each of the member States requesting such assistance".

Nonetheless, at the end of its first regular session held in Miami on 28–29 October 1999,[66] the Committee stressed that although the Second Inter-American Specialized Conference on Terrorism had decided to transmit to it the proposals on the directory of competences and the database, the Member States had not yet circulated any concrete official proposals[67] and that there was not yet a consensus on the exact content of the same. Therefore, it concluded, "for the moment, the type of work the Comité should carry out can not be determined".[68]

As far as the ratification of existing international treaties is concerned, the Committee stated that Member States should be encouraged to support the passage, adoption, and implementation of the international conventions on terrorism referred to in UN Resolution 51/210. Member States should also be encouraged to coordinate and cooperate with the OAS Inter-American Drug Abuse Control Commission (CICAD) to ensure that the Model Regulations Concerning Laundering Offenses Connected to Illicit Drug Trafficking and Other Serious Offenses were best utilized to address the problem of terrorist financing. A second regular session of CICTE was planned to take place in Bolivia in 2000 but had to be cancelled at the last moment. No session was scheduled for 2001.

[66] Doc. OEA/Ser.L/X/2/1 - CICTE/doc.5/99 rev. 2, 28–29 October 1999.
[67] *Ibid*: "Consequently, the CICTE asks for collaboration of Member States on: 1. Preparation of a directory of competent authorities in the Member States on the following items: an updated compilation of bilateral, subregional, regional, or multilateral treaties and agreements entered into by the Member States to prevent, combat, and eliminate terrorism. An updated compilation of legal and regulatory norms on preventing, combating, and eliminating terrorism in force in the Member States. Evaluation of the mechanisms for implementing the international legal norms set forth in conventional instruments in force in the Member States: the preparation of an analytical study on all aspects of the relevant legal cooperation, with a view to strengthening that cooperation. 2. Preparation and implementation of technical assistance programs for Member States that request such assistance in drafting of domestic laws and in staff training ... 3. Compilation of the bilateral or multilateral agreements in force in the Member States on the detection of forged documents. Compilation of mechanisms existing in the Member States on cooperation among migration authorities. Organization of workshops and training courses on priority topics, to include, *inter alia*, cooperation among migration authorities, preparation of a hemispheric diagnosis on terrorism, and strengthening of inter-American cooperation. Design and development of the inter-American network for compiling and transmitting data, including the creation of an inter-American database on terrorism. Implementation of the guidelines for inter-American cooperation regarding terrorist acts and activities. Proposal of coordination mechanisms with other international organizations with competence in the area".
[68] *Ibid*: "Given this, it would be opportune for the delegations to conduct the appropriate consultations in order to more accurately define the content of the directory. Within this context, it will be necessary to specify the type of information that can be included taking into account the publicity it could receive. This in turn will affect the directory's data control systems."

IV. POST 11 SEPTEMBER 2001 ACTIVITIES

The events of 11 September 2001 brought renewed focus to the Inter-American efforts to confront terrorism. The attacks were immediately condemned by the General Assembly, which coincidentally was meeting in Special Session in Lima, to approve the Inter-American Democratic Charter. In addition Resolution RC 23/1/01 ("Strengthening Hemispheric Cooperation to Prevent, Combat, and Eliminate Terrorism") and Resolution RC 24/1/01 ("Terrorist Threat to the Americas") were adopted by the Ministers of Foreign Affairs at their 23rd and 24th Meeting of Consultation held on 21 September 2001 in Washington DC, the latter with the Ministers acting as Organ of Consultation in application of the Treaty of Rio.[69] Paragraph 9 of Resolution RC 23/1/01 calls upon Member States to entrust the Permanent Council with preparing a draft Inter-American Convention Against Terrorism,[70] while paragraph 6 of Resolution RC 24/1/01 resolves that "the terrorist attacks against the US are attacks against all American States and that in accordance with all the relevant provisions of the Rio Treaty, all States Parties to this Treaty shall provide effective reciprocal assistance to address such attacks and the threat of any similar attacks, and to maintain the peace and security of the continent".[71]

Of particular relevance was the decision to support fully the measure applied by the US and other States in the exercise of their inherent right of individual and collective self-defence, thus creating a moral coalition parallel to the US military campaign.[72]

[69] See CP/RES 797 (1293/01), 19 September 2001, of the Permanent Council of the OAS acting as Provisional Organ of Consultation of the Rio Treaty which called for a Meeting of Ministers of Foreign Affairs to serve as the Organ of Consultation under the Rio Treaty, in connection with terrorist attacks in the US. AE Montalvo, "Inter-American Regional Security Against Terrorism: A Shield and a Sword", *ASIL Insight-OSA and Terrorism*, 30 November 2001, notes that some diplomats and international lawyers have not only questioned the effectiveness of the Rio Treaty to combat terrorism, but have also contested its legal applicability. They point out that Art 3 refers to attacks by any State against an American State, and Art 6 refers to an aggression which is not an armed attack. Consequently, they argue that Art 3 is not useful because the suspect terrorist organization that attacked US soil is not a State and, furthermore, Art 6 is not applicable as the aggression was in fact an armed attack.

[70] Montalvo, *ibid*, stresses that "one must also consider Art 9, bestowing the Organ of Consultation with the competence to characterise what constitutes an act of aggression. Therefore, one may conclude that RC 24, adopted under the Rio Treaty, exercises such competence in response to what the Meeting of Ministry of Foreign Affairs, acting as Organ of Consultation, considered to be an attack to all American States".

[71] The Resolution further resolves that "[i]f a State Party has reason to believe that persons in its territory may have been involved in or in any way assisted the 11 September 2001 attacks, are harbouring the perpetrators, or may otherwise be involved in terrorist activities, such State Party shall use all legally available measures to pursue, capture, extradite, and punish those individuals and that the States Parties shall render additional assistance and support to the US and to each other, as appropriate, to address the 11 September attacks, and also to prevent future terrorist acts".

[72] "Support for the Measures of Individual and collective self-defence established in Resolution RC.24/Res1/01", OEA/Ser.F/II.24, CS/TIAR/Res1/01, 16 October 2001.

In its turn, the Permanent Council of the OAS expressed its deep concern under a different perspective in CP Resolution 799 (1298/01) dated 31 October 2001.[73] Subsequently, the CICTE held two special sessions (on 15 October[74] and 29 November 2001)[75] and some Latin American States participated in the works of the Financial Action Task Force on Money Laundering (FATF) and its Recommendation adopted on 31 October 2001.[76]

[73] "Considering that the terrorist acts of 11 September 2001 have had an adverse impact on the economies of Member States and that the continuing threats have discouraged economic activity, consumption, investment, air travel and tourism and have created dislocations in the financial markets in the hemisphere and reverberations worldwide; and that the development prospects of Member States, especially those of smaller size, have been severely affected", it resolved: "1. To request the Inter-American Council for Integral Development to intensify efforts to assist Member States in confronting the adverse economic effects of the terrorist acts of 11 September 2001 and in the implementation of measures aimed at improving economic and social conditions, reducing poverty and facilitating high quality education within the Hemisphere ... 3. To instruct the Secretary General to convene, at the earliest possible opportunity, a meeting of the Committee to Coordinate the Cooperation Programs established by GA Res 1666 (XXIX-0/99), in order to promote the development of a package of socio-economic assistance for the recovery of Member States ... 5. To seek the support of the inter-American agencies, particularly the Inter-American Development Bank, the Pan American Health Organization, the Inter-American Institute for Cooperation in Agriculture and of the UN Economic Commission for Latin America and the Caribbean for the purpose of facilitating a swift economic recovery of Member States; ... 7. To request Member States to engage in increased horizontal cooperation among themselves in order to ensure more rapid economic growth".

[74] See OEA/Ser.L/X.2.2 — CICTE/doc.4/02.

[75] The latter insisting on the aim to begin implementation of the OAS commitment to counter-terrorism, as resolved by the Foreign Ministers. See also HE Sheppard, "US Actions to Freeze Assets of Terrorism: Manifest and Latent Implications for Latin America", (2002) 17 *American University International Law Review*, 625 ff.

[76] " ... II. Each country should criminalise the financing of terrorism, terrorist acts and terrorist organizations. III. Each country should implement measures to freeze without delay funds or other assets of terrorists, those who finance terrorism and terrorist organizations in accordance with the UN resolutions relating to the prevention and suppression of the financing of terrorist acts. Each country should also adopt and implement measures, including legislative ones, which would enable the competent authorities to seize and confiscate property that is the proceed of, or used in, or intended or allocated for use in, the financing of terrorism, terrorist acts or terrorist organizations; IV. If financial institutions, or other business or entities subject to anti-money laundering obligations suspect or have reasonable grounds to suspect that funds are linked or related to, or are to be used for terrorism, terrorist acts or by terrorist organizations, they should be required to report promptly their suspicions to the competent authorities. V. Each country should afford another country, on the basis of a treaty, arrangements or other mechanism for mutual legal assistance or information exchange, the greatest possible measure of assistance in connection with criminal, civil enforcement and administrative investigations, inquiries and proceedings relating to the financing of terrorism, terrorist acts and terrorist organizations. Countries should also take all possible measures to ensure that they do not provide safe havens for individuals charged with the financing of terrorism, terrorist acts or terrorist organizations, and should have procedures in place to extradite, where possible, such individuals. VI. Each country should take measures to ensure that persons or legal entities, including agents, that provide a service for the transmission of money or value, including transmission through an informal money or value transfer system or network, should be licensed or registered and subject to all the FATF Recommendations that apply to banks and non-bank financial institutions. Each country

Subsequently (December 2001–January 2002), the Special Group on Justice entrusted with preparing the Fourth Meeting of Ministers of Justice or of Ministers or Attorneys General of the Americas (REMJA-IV),[77] proposed legal and judicial cooperation in fighting transnational organized crime and terrorism as the central topic for the dialogue of Ministers or Attorneys General, and asked the Secretariat for Legal Affairs, Department of Legal Cooperation and Information, to prepare a base document that would endeavour to clarify the possible scope of the dialogue on this topic.[78]

V. THE INTER-AMERICAN CONVENTION TO PREVENT AND PUNISH TERRORISM (3 JUNE 2002 – 10 JULY 2003)[79]

At the request of the Inter-American Juridical Committee (CJI), a preliminary draft of an Inter-American Convention for the Prevention and Elimination of Terrorism was first prepared in December 1995[80] by the Department of Development and Codification of International Law

should ensure that persons or legal entities that carry out this service illegally are subject to administrative, civil or criminal sanctions. VII. Countries should take measures to require financial institutions, including money remitters, to include accurate and meaningful information (name, address and account number) on funds transfers and related messages that are sent, and the information should remain with the transfer or related message through the payment chain. Countries should take measures to ensure that financial institutions, including money remitters, conduct enhanced scrutiny of and monitor for suspicious activity funds transfers which do not contain complete originator information … ".

[77] See OEA/Ser.GE/REMJA/doc.69/01 add., 18 January 2002.

[78] In REMJA I, Ministers of Justice and Attorneys General concluded that there is a need to promote mutual legal assistance in a flexible and effective manner, in particular with respect to extradition, requests for delivery of documents and other forms of evidence, the establishment of secure and prompt channels of communication and strengthening of the role of the Central Authorities. At the same time, they recommended reinforcing the fight against corruption, organized crime and transnational criminal activity, and adopting new legislation, procedures, and mechanisms as necessary to combat these scourges. In REMJA II, they concluded and recommended that steps should be taken to strengthen international cooperation, in the framework of the OAS and other institutions, in areas of special concern, such as the struggle against terrorism, combating corruption, money laundering, drug trafficking, forgery, illicit trafficking in firearms, organized crime, and transnational criminal activity. They also decided to continue working in an effective and flexible manner to strengthen mutual legal and judicial assistance among the OAS Member States, particularly with respect to extradition, requests for delivery of documents and other forms of evidence, the establishment of secure and prompt channels of communications between central authorities. In REMJA III, they considered issues like these once again, urging states to submit information requested on extradition and mutual legal assistance and deciding to strengthen cooperation and mutual confidence in this field by establishing an information network composed of competent authorities and mandated to prepare specific recommendations in the area of extradition and mutual legal assistance.

[79] Lagos and Rudy, above n 65, 1628–37.

[80] As highlighted by the Explanatory Note attached to Doc. CJI/SO/I/doc.5/96 dated 30 January 1996, the topic of terrorism had been occupying the attention of the CJI since 1994,

(now the Department of International Law) of the OAS Secretariat of Legal Affairs.[81]

It consisted of fifteen articles, the most important being the following:*

— *Objectives and purposes of the future Convention:* the States parties "agree to adopt any measures [of a legislative or other nature] (*the necessary measures*) {necessary} to prevent, punish, and eliminate terrorism" {and to "define acts of terrorism as offences and to establish severe penalties therefore"}.

— {*Definition of act of terrorism*: "any unlawful [*and systematic*] threat or use of violence, regardless of motive, means, or scope, that is intended to generate widespread fear, intimidation, or alarm in all or part of the population, and which, owing to its impact and means of perpetration, seriously jeopardizes the life, the physical, material, or moral well-being, or the freedom of individuals. Said acts must be of international relevance, *ie* they must possibly affect other States parties and be intended for perpetration outside the territory of the State in which they are prepared,organized, or planned"}.

— {*Application of the future convention*: the convention shall apply to any [*threat of, or*] attempt at, complicity in, direct or indirect participation in, or extortion related to the acts described above}.

— *Consideration of acts of terrorism*: "the acts described in the convention shall be considered to be included among extraditable common crimes under all treaties on extradition that have been concluded or may be concluded in the future by the States parties. Should no such treaty exist, the future convention shall be taken as the legal basis for such extradition". {For the purposes of extradition or mutual legal assistance, none of the offenses established in the international instruments listed above shall be regarded as a political offense or an offense connected with a political offense or an offense inspired by political motives. Accordingly, a request for extradition or mutual legal assistance may not be refused on the sole ground that it concerns a political offense or an offense connected with a political offense or an offense inspired by political motives}.

— {*Jurisdiction*: jurisdiction can be established with respect of the offence by: i) the State within whose territory the offence has

under the title "Inter American Cooperation to confront International Terrorism" and from 1995 onwards under the title "Inter American Cooperation to confront Terrorism".

[81] See Doc. OEA/Sec.Gral. DDI/Doc.12/01, 26 September 2001.

* Amendments proposed in January 1996 are within [ ]. Final amendments are in italics. Parts omitted or present in the final text are within {}.

been committed or the effects of the offence have taken place; ii) the State of nationality or permanent residence of the victim; iii) the State of nationality or permanent residence of the alleged offender}.

— {*Definition of alleged offender:* "the party with respect to whom there exists sufficient evidence for a *prima facie* determination that such party has committed or intends to commit the offences specified in Art 2"}.

However, since the beginning the Rapporteur stated that the normative framework already in effect within the Inter-American system provided the necessary basis for the adoption of measures that could prove valid responses to the terrorist threat[82] and that the Treaty of Rio could be applied.[83]

This may explain why the draft did not circulate among OAS Member States, and remained a merely internal document until 28 September–17 October 2001, when it was transmitted to the States during the second special session of CICTE. Shortly after, some of them[84] presented their observations.[85] The Working Group met again

[82] He referred to Arts 2(b) and (d), 3(b), (d), and (g), and Arts 10, 12, 17, 21, 22, 27, 28, 81, 82 and 90 of the OAS Charter.

[83] Doc.CJI/SO/I/doc.5/96, 30 January 1996: "Confronting this new threat would not require the adoption of new juridical instruments, with the cumbersome process that proceeds the signature of a treaty or convention and its later entry into effect".

[84] Namely Argentina (CP/CAJP-1829/01 corr. 1add.3), Antigua and Barbuda (add 7), Canada (add 5), Chile (add 6), Ecuador (add 4), Peru (OEA/Ser.G- CP/CAJP-1844/01 corr 1,) the US (add 1a) and Venezuela (add 2). The US' observations appear to be the most critical: "In light of this massive international framework already in place, we suggest the following criteria: A) the Convention should be focused on achievable objectives. Negotiating a new convention in a compressed time-frame will not be possible if we get swept into innovative drafting matters ... ; C) The Convention should not attempt to define terrorism. Efforts in the UN and elsewhere have indicated clearly that efforts to define the term are likely to result in deadlock. The network of the UN Conventions have been agreed upon only because they avoid the issue and seek to identify acts that are appropriate for international cooperation regardless of their motivation; D) We should be willing to abandon or suspend efforts to create an OAS Convention if it appears from further discussions that such an agreement will not materially add to the framework of treaties and conventions that addresses these issues, or if the negotiations will be divisive in a time when our efforts should be focused on practical efforts to address the problem of terrorism. Moreover, States parties should adopt the appropriate measures, in keeping with applicable rules of domestic and international law, including international human rights standards, before granting asylum or refuge, in order to ensure that it is not granted to a person when there exist reasonable indications that he or she has been involved in any of the offenses specified in Art 2".

[85] Canada's view was that a convention which is merely reiterative of existing law would not advance the cause against terrorism and would be an unproductive diversion of political attention and human and financial resources. The logical first step toward advancing the legal framework to combat terrorism is for OAS Member States to put a clear priority on the implementation of the existing UN Conventions on terrorism, as well as the OAS Mutual Legal Assistance Treaty on Criminal Matters and other related instruments. As evidenced by Doc. OEA/Ser.G-CP/doc.3517/01 dated 18 September 2001, also Brasil implicitly sponsored the idea of prioritising the Rio Treaty, *in lieu* of a new convention.

on 14,[86] 26–28[87] November 2001 and 22–25 January 2002.[88] It was recognized that existing instruments on this matter, both at the inter-American and the global levels, constituted an input that should be taken into account. However, it was agreed that the mandate called for a comprehensive approach to the aspects of the problem, with a view to presenting it to the General Assembly at its next regular session, scheduled to be held in Barbados in June 2002.[89] The final meeting of the Working Group took place from 18 to 21 March 2002[90] and resulted in a text which was subsequently approved by the General Assembly in Bridgetown.[91]

No substantial difference[92] exists between the draft and the final text. Prominent focus is given to the need to enact legislation and the measures to be taken in order to prevent and eradicate the financing of terrorism, mainly through international cooperation in terms of bank control, and the freezing or seizing of any funds or other assets "constituting the proceeds of, used to facilitate, or used or intended to finance, the commission of any of the offences established in the international existing instruments on terrorism, committed both within in and outside the jurisdiction of a State Party" (Article 5).

However, when looked at more closely, Articles 4, 5 and 6 seem to be more technical inclusions rather than reflecting real necessity, since even US Intelligence recognises that Latin American terrorist movements never enjoyed any financial aid or support from abroad, nor do they have any financial link to international terrorist movements as such. Furthermore, the inapplicability of the political exception clause (Article 11),[93] although

[86] OEA/Ser.G-CP/CAJP-1851/01, 21 November 2001.
[87] OEA/Ser.G-CP/CAJP-1848/01, 14 December 2001.
[88] OEA/Ser.G-CP/CAJP-1866/02, 1 February 2002.
[89] "The Working Group decided to interpret the mandate it received as meaning that the draft convention would be based on existing international conventions on the matter, would help to create the regulatory framework for instituting cooperation against terrorism in the Hemisphere, and should be an up-to-date agreement on cooperation, which would consider new topics, such as border-related and financial matters."
[90] OEA/Ser.G-CP/CAJP-1891/02 corr 4.
[91] OEA/Ser.P-AG/doc 4100/02 rev, 3 June 2002. According to Art 22, the Convention was to enter into force on the 30th day following the date of deposit of the sixth instrument of ratification with the General Secretariat of the OAS. It entered into force on 10 July 2003. As at September 2003, Member States are Antigua and Barbuda, Canada, El Salvador, Mexico, Nicaragua and Peru.
[92] Except for Art 16: "Training — 1. The State Parties shall promote technical cooperation and training programs at the national, bilateral, sub regional, and regional levels and in the framework of the OAS to strengthen the national institutions responsible for compliance with the obligations assumed under this Convention; 2. The State Parties shall also promote, where appropriate, technical cooperation and training programs with other regional and international organizations conducting activities related to the purposes of this Convention".
[93] "For the purposes of extradition or mutual legal assistance, none of the offences established in the international instruments listed in Art 2 shall be regarded as a political offence or an offence connected with a political offence or an offence inspired by political motives. Accordingly, a request for extradition or mutual legal assistance may not be refused on the

mitigated by Article 14,[94] seems somehow inadequate in respect of the main features of Latin American terrorism, ie its preponderantly domestic character and its being a reaction to foreign interference with domestic regimens and economics. In this respect, it is worth noting that the only request for extradition known of so far, was addressed by Chile to the Fujimori government of Peru, but it was not insisted upon.[95] As far as Article 12 and the denial of refugee status[96] is concerned, this provision seems to be anticipating possible future claims, since no Latin American terrorists have ever requested refugee status to date.[97]

In light of the above, the Convention seems to be two steps forward and one step backwards in comparison with the initial project of 1996. The positive aspects may be identified with provisions which set concrete measures to prevent, combat and eradicate the financing of terrorism[98] together with Article 13,[99] which is clearly designed to deprive suspected terrorists of any possible safe haven, either to hide their persons or their money or goods. On the other hand, Article 2 represents a regression: no definition of terrorism is attempted, and reference is only made to the twelve existing UN Conventions.

The Convention also states that all actions undertaken to combat terrorism must strictly abide by international law, international human rights law, international humanitarian law, and international law governing the

sole ground that it concerns a political offence or an offence connected with a political offence or an offence inspired by political motives".

[94] Former Art 15: "Nondiscrimination — None of the provisions of this Convention shall be interpreted as imposing an obligation to provide mutual legal assistance if the requested state party has substantial grounds for believing that the request has been made for the purpose of prosecuting or punishing a person on account of that person's race, religion, nationality, ethnic origin, or political opinion, or that compliance with the request would cause prejudice to that person's position for any of these reasons".

[95] See *Castillo Petruzzi et al v Peru*, Preliminary Objections, IACHR C 41, paras 65–66: "According to the application, Peru violated the right to nationality of … by trying and convicting them of the crime of treason against the fatherland, although they are not Peruvians … The State added that the Peruvian Courts exercise jurisdiction over crimes committed within Peruvian national territory as an expression of sovereignty, and that the criminal law of Peru is binding independent of the perpetrator's nationality and domicile … The State asserted that it offered the Chilean consular officials all of the facilities to visit the persons of their nationality who were detained … In the public hearing, the State indicated that the report of the Chilean delegation's visit had not been a topic of debate and discussion at the level of the Inter-American Commission nor had it been a subject of the confidential report".

[96] "Denial of asylum — Each State Party shall take appropriate measures, consistent with the relevant provisions of national and international law, for the purpose of ensuring that asylum is not granted to any person in respect of whom there are reasonable grounds to believe that he or she has committed an offence established in the international instruments listed in Art 2 of this Convention".

[97] Lagos and Rudy, above n 65, 1638–40.

[98] In general, see LE Nagle, "The Challenges of Fighting Global Organized Crime in Latin America", (2003) 26 *Fordham International Law Journal*, 1699–705.

[99] "Denial of asylum — Each state party shall take appropriate measures, consistent with the relevant provisions of national and international law, for the purpose of ensuring that asylum

status of refugees. It also reasserts the right to due process of law and non-discrimination against the accused. In terms of human rights, undoubtedly the main problem relating to Latin American terrorism, it is worth noting that a Special Resolution[100] was passed in Barbados *a latere* of the Convention, which states that "the fight against terrorism must be waged with full respect for the law, human rights, and democratic institutions so as to preserve the rule of law, freedoms, and democratic values in the Hemisphere", and reaffirms the duty of Member States to ensure that all measures taken to combat terrorism are in keeping with obligations under international law. The need for this special resolution, which explicitly recalls the Resolution "Terrorism and Human Rights" of the Inter-American Commission on Human Rights (IACommHR) of 12 December 2001,[101] seems to hide the fear that, despite its wording, Article 15 of the Convention might be understood more as a statement of intent than as a binding provision, and the same fear possibly underlies the Special Resolution adopted at the fourth plenary session of the General Assembly (4 June 2002) on the "Promotion of and Respect for International Humanitarian Law".[102]

This impression seems to be even more founded by the fact that another Special Resolution was simultaneously passed,[103] reaffirming the principles of the Inter-American Democratic Charter, ie that the peoples of the Americas have a right to democracy and their governments have an obligation to promote and defend it; that democracy is essential for the social, political, and economic development of the peoples of the Americas, and that the maintenance and strengthening of the rule of law and strict respect for the democratic system are, at the same

is not granted to any person in respect of whom there are reasonable grounds to believe that he or she has committed an offense established in the international instruments listed in Article 2 of this Convention".

[100] AG/RES 1906 (XXXII-O/02).
[101] "Terrorism must not go unpunished. States have the right and indeed the duty to defend themselves against this international crime within the framework of international instruments that require domestic laws and regulations to conform to international commitments. The terrorist attacks have prompted vigorous debate over the adoption of anti-terrorist initiatives that include, *inter alia*, military commissions and other measures. According to the doctrine of the IACHR, military courts may not try civilians, except when no civilian courts exist or where trial by such courts is materially impossible. Even under such circumstances, the IACHR has pointed out that the trial must respect the minimum guarantees established under international law, which include non-discrimination between citizens and others who find themselves under the jurisdiction of a State, an impartial judge, the right to be assisted by freely-chosen counsel, and access by defendants to evidence brought against them together with the opportunity to contest it".
[102] AG/RES 1904 (XXXII-O/02): "The General Assembly resolves: ... 15. To urge the Member States and all parties to an armed conflict to observe their obligations under the 1949 Geneva Conventions, in particular those that are applicable to the protection of the civilian population ... ".
[103] AG/RES 1907(XXXII-O/02).

time, a goal and a shared commitment. Moreover, at its opening session of 7 October 2002, the IACommHR issued a *communiqué*[104] in which the situation of human rights in Latin America after 11 September 2001 was defined as serious, and which called for compliance of Member States to the Inter-American Convention on Human Rights.[105]

On the other hand, the so-called "Bridgetown Declaration";[106] the Special Resolution on "The Multidimensional Approach to Hemispheric Security";[107] AG/Res 1877 (XXXII-O/02) entitled "Support for the Work of the Inter-American Committee against Terrorism"[108] and AG/Res 1874 (XXXII-O/02) concerning the Inter-American Convention against the Illicit Manufacturing of and Trafficking in Firearms, Ammunitions, Explosives, and Other Related Materials[109] seem to be the other side of the coin, since their only concern is to reaffirm and stress the need to combat terrorism as one of the threats, concerns and other challenges to hemispheric security. However, it is worth noting that these new threats, concerns and other challenges are identified not only in terms of political factors, but also in terms of economic, social, health, and environmental factors, thus encompassing all and every sort of external (international) interference with domestic sovereignty.[110]

[104] C-197/02 : "*La CIDH Advierte sobre Clima de Desconfianza en la Lucha contra el Terrorismo*" (not yet translated into English). Above all, see the Commission's "Report on Terrorism and Human Rights", OEA/Ser.L/V/II.116, Doc. 5 rev. 1 corr., 22 October 2002, where special attention is drawn to, and a thorough analysis is made of, the various aspects of human rights respect in emergency situations as well as in case of internal armed conflict.

[105] "*Los actos terroristas del 11 de septiembre de 2001 en los Estados Unidos han generado un clima de sospecha y desconfianza que, lamentablemente, ha llegado en algunos casos al extremo de la xenofobia. A raíz de los ataques terroristas algunos Estados han respondido de manera inmediata con la sanción de nuevas leyes y la adopción de medidas administrativas. Sin embargo en algunos casos tal respuesta estatal ha incluido la adopción de distintas medidas represivas, restricciones irrazonables a la libertad de expresión, limitaciones arbitrarias en materia migratoria, detención indefinida sin juicio o la propuesta de crear tribunales especiales que apliquen procedimientos sumarios y admitan pruebas secretas* ... ".

[106] AG/DEC. 27 (XXXII-O/02).

[107] *Ibid.*

[108] "The General Assembly ... resolves: 1. To reaffirm its commitment to strengthen hemispheric cooperation and continue to implement specific measures to prevent, combat and eliminate international terrorism ... 5. To underscore the importance of collaboration and coordination on counter-terrorism programs and activities between CICTE, Member States, permanent observers, the UN Counter-Terrorism Committee, other regional organizations, and other bodies of the Inter-American system. 6.To urge Member States to: a. Continue efforts to implement the recommendations on financial and border controls agreed to at the Second Regular Session of CICTE, as well as those set forth in the UN Security Council Resolution S/RES/1373 (2001). b. Report to the third regular session of CICTE on measures taken to implement the said recommendations, and provide a copy of their reports on measures taken to implement the said UN Security Council Resolution ... ".

[109] "The General Assembly ... resolves: 1. To urge all Member States that have not already done so to sign and ratify the Convention, as appropriate ... ".

[110] For example, see T Feinstein and C Youngers, "Shedding Light on the Past: Declassification of US Documents", <http://www.wola.org>: "*Documentos desclasificados confirman violaciones*": "National Security Archive published 41 documents from the US State Department obtained via the FOIA. The releasing documentation was declared definitive proof of many of the abuses that took place during Peru's dirty war. Most of the information in the

In brief, the Resolutions adopted by the General Assembly in Barbados and the Inter-American Convention on Terrorism seem to run with the hare and hunt with the hounds. In any case, since no explicit reference is made texts to the Rio Treaty, it seems reasonable to say that no open will and no means exist in Latin American States to support operatively any military initiative of the US against international terrorists but modest help and moral support.[111]

documents simply provides further evidence of what Peruvian and international human rights groups had documented throughout the course of the conflict. The documents also reveal that the US government was well aware of both the corrupt practices and death squad activities fomented by Montesinos from the time he first emerged at Fujimori's side. The documents reveal that Washington ultimately decided to give priority to maintaining smooth relationships with the Fujimori government over human rights and democracy-related concerns. The Truth and Reconciliation Commission has formally requested assistance from Washington in expediting the release of documents that could be useful in its investigations but, although the initial signals from Washington seem to be positive, the US government's response to the request remains an open question. The requested subjects cover human rights in Peru, US relations with Peru, and issues related to Vladimiro Montesinos. So far, only the State Department has provided information to the Congressional Commission, whereas key government agencies such as the CIA and DEA have not yet responded. Unlike in Central America, the US did not play a central role in the counter-insurgency effort in Peru, and so the request was much less controversial than in the case of either El Salvador or Guatemala. However, the reports covering the period from 1980 to 2000 could provide useful clues for the Truth and Reconciliation Commission investigators. There are both optimistic and pessimistic signs as to whether the expedited process will be adopted and, even if it is, whether agencies outside the State Department will cooperate effectively. The tragic events of 11 September 2001 have created a climate of fear and a sense of vulnerability that is propitious for those opposed to opening the files because the main concerns of US policy makers are national security interests and homeland defence. Civil liberties, access to information and transparency in government are being sacrificed in order to facilitate anti-terrorist operations, including intelligence gathering and operations. As a result, there is a clear move towards a greater restriction of information that has manifested itself in a number of ways. One example is a new policy memorandum on the FOIA issued by Attorney General John Ashcroft on 12 October 2001. Although it states the administration's commitment to comply with the FOIA and notes that "it is only through a well-informed citizenry that the leaders of our nation remain accountable to the governed", it also emphasises the need for safeguarding our national security, enhancing the effectiveness of our law enforcement agencies, protecting sensitive business information and, not least, preserving personal privacy. It advises all federal agencies to carefully consider these interests before making any discretionary disclosures of information. Another example of increasing restrictions on access to information is the executive order issued by President Bush on 1 November 2001, which lays down new procedures that may help to delay or restrict public access to Presidential records. The Presidential Records Act allows for a 12-year restriction period before Presidential records are made available to the public. The new order also provides that access to the records may be delayed for an unlimited time beyond this 12-year period, while both the former and incumbent Presidents review the material proposed for release.

[111] According to <http://fhrg.org/> (*Political Analysis*), November 2001, "Since the terrorist attacks on Washington and New York, the Guatemalan FRG administration has complied with two agreements that arose out of the Conference of the Central American Armed Forces. First, Portillo created the position of Inter-institutional Coordinator of Security (under the new Presidential Anti-Terrorist Commission). With approval from the US

VI. LATIN AMERICAN "TERRORISM" AND THE INTER-AMERICAN COURT OF HUMAN RIGHTS[112]

The reaction of military *juntas* and/or democratically elected governments to international and domestic terrorism[113] in Latin America was mainly to enforce special laws[114] aimed at re-establishing order and responding to, far more than preventing, criminal offences resulting from such acts.

The common aspects of these laws were that they declared a state of emergency in the country concerned,[115] suspended many

Embassy, the administration named retired general Miguel Angel Posadas to the position. Second, the government sent troops to Afghanistan. These actions reveal the extent to which the Guatemalan military continues to play an active role in the political decision-making process".

[112] D Baluarte and E Chlopak, "The Case of Myrna Mack Chang: Overcoming Institutional Impunity in Guatemala", (2003) 10 *Human Rights Brief*, 11 ff ; T Buerghenthal and D Cassel, "The Future of the Inter-American Human Rights System", *"El Futuro del Sistema Interamericano de Protección de los Derechos Humanos"*, JE Méndez and F Cox (eds) (San José, Costa Rica, Instituto Interamericano de Derechos Humanos, 1998) 539–73; AA Cançado Trindade, "The Consolidation of the Procedural Capacity of Individuals in the Evolution of the International Protection of Human Rights: Present State and Perspectives at the Turn of the Century", (1998) 30 *Columbia Human Rights Law Review*, 1 ff ; AA Cançado Trindade, "Current State and Perspectives of the Inter-American System of Human Rights Protection at the Dawn of the New Century", (2000) 8 *Tulane Journal of International and Comparative Law*, 5 ff; AA Cançado Trindade, "Las cláusolas pétreas de la protección internacional del ser humano: El acceso directo de los individuos a la justicia a nivel internacional y la intangibilidad de la jurisdicción obligatoria de los tribunales internacionales de los derechos humanos", *El Sistema Interamericano de Protección de los Derechos Humanos en el Umbral del Siglo XXI*, (San José, Costa Rica, Corte Interamericana de Derechos Humanos, 2001) I, 5–71; AA Cançado Trindade, Reflexiones sobre el Futuro del Sistema Interamericano de Protección de los Derechos Humanos, *"El Futuro del Sistema Interamericano de Protección de los Derechos Humanos"*, JE Méndez and F Cox (eds) (San José, Costa Rica, Corte Interamericana de derechos Humanos, 1998) 573–603; C Medina, "Toward Effectiveness in the Protection of Human Rights in the Americas", (1998) 8 *Transnational Law & Contemporary Problems*, 337 ff; V Rodríguez Rescia and MD Seitles, "The Development of the Inter-American Human Rights System: An Historical Perspective and a Modern-Day Critique", (2000) 16 *New York Law School Journal of Human Rights*, 593 ff ; WM Reisman and W Newcomb, "Practical Matters for Consideration in the Establishment of a regional Human Rights Mechanism: Lessons from the Inter-American Experience", (1995) *Saint Louis-Warsaw Transatlantic Law Journal*, 89 ff; KC Sokol, Vinson and Elkins, "Ivcher Bronstein. Jurisdiction", (2001) 95 *The American Journal of International Law*, 178 ff; RJ Wilson and J Perlin, "The Inter-American Human Rights System: Activities During 1999 through October 2000", (2001) 16 *American University International Law Review*, 315–26; RJ Wilson and J Perlin, "The Inter-American Human Rights System: Activities from Late 2000 Through October 2002", (2003) 18 *American University International Law Review*, 651 ff.

[113] A range of acts have been defined as terrorism (eg belonging to leftist trade-unions; students" associations, charities etc).

[114] Eg the Peruvian *"Legislación sobre Terrorismo y Pacificación"*.

[115] See eg *Loayza Tamayo v Peru*, Merits, IACHR C 33, para 3d: "At the date on which the victim was detained, a state of emergency had been declared in the Department of Lima and the Constitutional Province of Callao under Supreme Decree 006-93-DE-CCFFAA of 19 January 1993, for a period of sixty days starting on 22 January 1993".

of the fundamental rights set forth in Constitutions[116] and in the American Convention on Human Rights (ACHR), established special, political (counter-insurgency)[117] police corps and/or increased the traditional powers of the military.[118] It is notable that, in disregard for the obligations under Articles 27(1)[119] and 3[120] of the ACHR, no previous notification of a state of emergency was ever provided by any Latin American State to the Secretary General of the OAS.[121]

Some of these special laws (eg in Peru)[122] conceived terrorism as two[123] different, albeit somehow overlapping crimes, thus leading to the prosecution of not only those who had participated in attacks, sabotage attempts, etc, but also those who had shown intellectual approval of

[116] "The constitutional guarantees established in paras 7, 9, 10 and 20(g) of Art 2 of the 1979 Constitution of Peru had been suspended ... Decree-Law No 25.659 provided that persons accused of had to be tried in the military courts, thereby submitting civilians to trial by a military court, which is a special jurisdiction": IACHR C 33, para 3(d).

[117] For example, the use of civil patrols. See eg *Blake v Guatemala*, Merits, IACHR C 36, paras 76–77: "on the basis of the evidence examined ..., the Court considers it proven that, at the time the events in this case occurred, the civil patrols enjoyed an institutional relationship with the Army, performed activities in support of the armed forces' functions, and, moreover, received resources, weapons, training and direct orders from the Guatemalan Army and operated under its supervision. A number of human rights violations, including summary and extra-judicial executions and forced disappearances of persons, have been attributed to those patrols .... The function of some civil self-defence patrols, known as Voluntary Civil Defence Committees, had been perverted over the years ... and they fulfilled missions belonging to the regular State organs, provoking repeated human rights violations".

[118] Special laws were often associated with *Leyes de Arrepentimiento* (Repentance Laws), which granted "repentant" terrorists who denounced other persons as terrorists a reduction in the jail sentence. See eg IACHR C 33, para 3(a).

[119] "In time of war, public danger, or other emergency that threatens the independence or security of a State Party, it may take measures derogating from its obligations under the present Convention to the extent and for the period of time strictly required by the exigencies of the situation, provided that such measures are not inconsistent with its other obligations under international law and do not involve discrimination on the ground of race, color, sex, language, religion, or social origin".

[120] "Any State Party availing itself of the right of suspension shall immediately inform the other States Parties, through the Secretary General of the Organization of American States, of the provisions the application of which it has suspended, the reasons that gave rise to the suspension, and the date set for the termination of such suspension."

[121] See eg *Cantoral Benavides vs. Peru*, Merits, IACHR C 69, para 33: "On 27 March 2000, the Court asked the Secretary General of the OAS for information as to whether the State had informed the OAS of a state of emergency or suspension of guarantees decreed between 3 February 1993 and 6 October 1995. On 10 May 2000, the Director of the International Law Department of the General Secretariat of the OAS informed the Court that no notification had been received from the Peruvian State regarding a suspension of guarantees on the dates cited."

[122] J Belaúnde, "Justice, Legality and Judicial Reform", in J Crabtree and J Thomas (eds), *Fujimori's Peru: The Political Economy* (London, Institute of Latin American Studies, 1998) 173–91 and E Obando, "Fujimori and the Military", *ibid*, 192–208.

[123] IACHR C 33, para 38(g): "Decree-Law No 25.659 introduced the crime of treason against the Fatherland, while Decree-Law No 25.475 the crime of terrorism. Treason is not aggravated terrorism, but draws specific criminal actions from the former and incorporates them into the new crime, which could not be interpreted as constituting the same unlawful criminal act".

terrorist ideology and/or movements, be it explicitly or implicitly, consciously or subconsciously.[124]

Forced disappearances,[125] arrests without warrants,[126] *incommunicado* detention,[127] torture,[128] inhumane prison conditions,[129] lack of any control on indictments,[130] denial of fair trial,[131] special military tribunals[132] and

[124] People acquitted for the crime of treason to the Fatherland could therefore be convicted and condemned for the crime of terrorism on the basis of the same evidence, despite *res judicata*. IACHR C 69, para 43(e): "The judgment of acquittal was reviewed and modified, even though the same was *res judicata*". See also J Davis, "A Cautionary Tale: Examining the Use of Military Tribunals by the United States in the Aftermath of the September 11 Attacks in Light of Peru's History of Human Rights Abuses Resulting from Similar Measures", (2003) 31 *The Georgia Journal of International and Comparative Law*, 428–434; PA Morisette, "The Lori Berenson Case: Proper Treatment of a Foreign Terrorist Under the Peruvian Criminal Justice System", (2002) 26 *Suffolk Transnational Law Review*, 88–91 and 93–101. Compare J Gallo, "Human Rights Policy or Hardball Politics? Why the United States Should Press Peru to Extradite Lori Berenson for a Fair Trial", (2001) 25 *Suffolk Transnational Law Review*, 91 ff.

[125] Eg Informe 101/01 dated 10.11.2001 on case 12.047 concerning Peru: "*Ejecuciones extrajudiciales y desapariciones forzadas de personas*"; IACHR sentences in *Velásquez Rodríguez vs Honduras*, Merits, C 4, para 155 and 158; *Godínez Cruz v Honduras*, Merits, C 5, paras 163 and 166; IACHR C 36, paras 52, 62, 63, 65; *Bámaca Velásquez v Guatemala*, Merits, IACHR C 70, paras 18, 121, 124, 125,128 and 153. See also M Gibney, "United States' Responsibility for Gross Levels of Human Rights Violations in Guatemala from 1954 to 1996", (1997) 7 *Journal of Transnational Law & Policy*, 77 ff; TJ Kepner, "Torture 101: The Case Against the United States for Atrocities Committed by School of the Americas Alumni", (2001) 19 *Dickinson Journal of International Law*, 475 ff; EL Lutz, "International Law in the Americas: Rethinking National Sovereignty in an Age of Regional Integration: Strengthening Core Values in the Americas: Regional Commitment to Democracy and the Protection of Human Rights", (1997) 19 *Houston Journal of International Law*, 643 ff; D Weissbrodt and ML Bartolomei "The Effectiveness of International Human Rights Pressures: The Case of Argentina, 1976–1983", (1991) 75 *Minnesota Law Review*, 1009 ff; K Zoglin, "Paraguay's Archive of Terror: International Cooperation and Operation Condor", (2001) 32 *The University of Miami Inter-American Law Review*, 57 ff .

[126] Eg IACHR C 69, para 43(a). See also J Davis, "A Cautionary Tale ... " above n 124, 435–40; M Mofidi and AE Eckert, " 'Unlawful Combatants' ... ", above n 9, 79–82 and R J Wilson and J Perlin, "The Inter-American Human Rights System: Activities from Late 2000 ... ", above n 112, 729–33, reporting the request for precautionary measures issued by the IAcommHR to the US on behalf of the detainees in Guantanamo Bay. At 732, the authors write: "The core of the Commission's ruling lies in its conclusion that the executive branch of the US government is not entitled to unilateral and unreviewable designation of the Guantanamo detainees as unlawful combatants under international humanitarian law. Such designation has the legal effect of leaving the detainees without any legal protection for so long as armed conflict continues, and the definitions of armed conflict and its termination are also left to the executive branch's discretion. The detainees are entitled, the Commission concludes, to access to a competent tribunal to determine their legal status. The Commission's interpretation of international humanitarian law is relatively new, but its interpretation of its own norms by use of other treaties and treaty body decisions is hardly unique in the Commission's history, nor in that of other international tribunals".

[127] Eg IACHR C 33, paras 3(b) and 27.

[128] Eg IACHR C 33, para 3(c); IACHR C 69, para 43(a); *Bámaca Velásquez v Guatemala*, Merits, IACHR C 70, paras 147–58 and reparations, IACHR C 91, para 87 .

[129] See IACHR C 33, paras 24(a) and (b) and 46(k); IACHR C 69, paras 43(a), (c) and (d).

[130] Eg IACHR C 33, paras 24(a), 46(i) and 51.

[131] IACHR C 69, paras 43(d) and (e).

[132] *Ibid*, para 43(d).

unidentified judges (*jueces sin rostro*)[133] were everyday routines, leading to gross and massive violations of human rights.[134]

These were so common and widespread, that the IACommHR and the IACHR defined them as a *práctica violatoria*, ie a systematic practice of human rights infringements.[135] Exacerbating these injustices, general amnesty laws or amnesty laws related to specific crimes (*leyes de amnistía — leyes de amnistía general*) were passed nearly everywhere,[136] ensuring the impunity of the people responsible for the human rights violations.[137] The IACHR[138] has held that these amnesty laws are an inadmissible offence (*una afrenta inadmisible*) against the right to justice and the right to truth.

When the IACHR was first asked to pronounce on problems relating to terrorism, in the mid-1980s, it was not via contentious cases, but via two Advisory Opinions[139] requested by the

[133] See eg IACHR C 33, para 3(d) and IACHR C 69, paras 29, 43(a) and (e) and 53. Unnamed judges were identified by alphabet letters and numbers, since their identity, in accordance with Art 15 of Decree Law No 25.475, was to remain secret to the accused and his/hers attorney. See also LE Nagle, "Colombia's Faceless Justice: a Necessary Evil, Blind Impartiality or Modern Iinquisition?", (2000) 61 *University of Pittsburgh Law Review*, 886–912.

[134] See eg IACHR C 36, paras 32 and 66. On relations between terrorism and human rights violations see S Von Schorlemer, "Human Rights: Substantive and Institutional Implications of the War Against Terrorism", (2003) 14 *European Journal International Law*, 265 ff.

[135] Eg IACHR C 4, paras 71–72 and 76; IACHR C 70, para 130.

[136] Eg in Argentina, Chile and Peru. See eg IACHR C 69, para 43(d). See also SB Abad Yupanqui, "La Justicia Tarda pero Llega, Amnistía vs. Derechos Humanos", <http://www.uc3m.es/uc3m/inst/MGP/JCI/05-13-foro-peruamnistia.htm>; V Abellán Honrubia, "Impunidad de violaciones de los derechos humanos fundamentales en América Latina: Aspectos jurídicos internacionales", in *Jornadas Iberoamericanas de la Asociación Española de Profesores de Derecho Internacional y Relaciones Internacionales — La Escuela de Salamanca y el derecho internacional en América — del pasado al futuro*, Salamanca, 1993, 191–204; K Ambos, "Impunity and International Criminal Law: A Case Study on Colombia, Peru, Bolivia, Chile and Argentina", (1997) 18 *Human Rights Law Journal*, 1 ff; J Kokott, "No Impunity for Human Rights Violations in the Americas", (1993) 14 *Human Rights Law Journal*, 153 ff; R Quinn, "Will the Rule of Law End? Challenging Grants of Amnesty for the Human Rights Violations of a Prior Regime: Chile's New Model", (1994) 62 *Fordham Law Review*, 905 ff; D Robinson, "Serving the Interests of Justice: Amnesties, Truth Commissions and the International Criminal Court", (2003) 14 *European Journal International Law*, 481 ff; L Roninger and M Sznajder, *The Legacy of Human Rights Violations in the Southern Cone, Argentina, Chile, and Uruguay*, (Oxford, Oxford University Press, 1999) 91–108; N Roht-Arriaza and L Gibson, "The Developing Jurisprudence on Amnesty", (1998) 20 *Human Rights Quarterly*, 843–85; PA Schey, DL Shelton and N Roht-Arriaza, "Addressing Human Rights Abuses: Truth Commissions and the Value of Amnesty", (1997) 19 *Whittier Law Review*, 325 ff.

[137] Some of the pardon laws granted freedom to unjustly sentenced innocent people But no compensation was provided whatsoever for moral and/or material damages.

[138] See *Barrios Altos* case (*Chumbipuma Aguirre et al v Peru*), Merits, IACHR C 75, paras 41–44 and the Concurring Opinion of President Cançado Trindade, para 5.

[139] In general, see T Buerghenthal, "The Advisory Practice of the Inter-American Court of Human Rights", (1985) 79 *American Journal International Law*, 1 ff; D Cassel, "The Inter-American Human Rights System: A Functional Analysis", *Liber Amicorum Héctor Fix-Zamudio* (San José, Costa Rica, Instituto Interamericano de Derechos Humanos, 1998) I, 521 ff; C Cerna, "The Structure and Functioning of the Inter-American Court of Human Rights (1979–1992)" (1992) 63 *British Yearbook of International Law*, 135 ff; H Fáundez-Ledesma,

ACommHR[140] and the Government of Uruguay.[141] Much was at stake in both requests, since they not only referred to some of the most important norms of the ACHR[142], but these Advisory Opinion would be the very first occasion in which the Court could pronounce on this matter clearly, although without reference to any specific Parties or domestic laws. The Court seized the opportunity and established the following principles, which were to become the basic pillars of its case-law:

(a) In serious emergency situations it may be lawful to temporarily suspend certain rights and freedoms whose free exercise must, under normal circumstances, be respected and guaranteed by the State. However, since not all the rights and freedoms established by the ACHR may be suspended even temporarily,[143] it is imperative that the judicial guarantees[144] "essential" for their protection remain in force.[145]

"El sistema interamericano de protección de los Derechos Humanos — Aspectos institucionales y Procesales", (San José, Costa Rica, Instituto Interamericano de Derechos Humanos, 1999) 577–610; P Nikken, "La función consultiva de la Corte Interamericana de Derechos Humanos", *El Sistema Interamericano de Derechos Humanos en el Umbrál del Siglo XXI*, (San José, Costa Rica, Corte Interamericana de Derechos Humanos, 2001) I, 161–84; M Pacheco Gómez, "La competencia consultiva de la Corte Interamericana de Derechos Humanos", *ibid*, 71–92; C Ruiz Miguel, "La función consultiva en el sistema Interamericano de Derechos Humanos: crisállida de una jurisdicción supra-constitucional?" *Liber Amicorum Héctor Fix-Zamudio* (San José, Costa Rica, Instituto Interamericano de Derechos Humanos, 1998) II, 1345–63; M Ventura-D Zovatto, "La función consultiva de la Corte Interamericana de Derechos Humanos" (Madrid, Editorial Civitatis, 1989).

140 OC 8/87, "*Habeas Corpus* in Emergency Situations", dated 30 January 1987. The question submitted to the Court was "Is the writ of *habeas corpus*, the legal basis of which is found in Arts 7.6 and 25.1 of the ACHR, one of the judicial guarantees that, pursuant to the last clause of Art 27.2 of that Convention, may not be suspended by a State Party to the American Convention?"

141 OC 9/87 "Judicial Guarantees in states of Emergency", dated 6 October 1987. The request specifically referred to the interpretation of the expression "essential judicial guarantees" found in Art 27.2 of the ACHR, as related to Arts 25 and 8 of the same. "Because even in time of war, public danger, or other emergency that threatens the independence or security of a State Party it is not possible to suspend the judicial guarantees essential for the protection of such rights, the Government of Uruguay requests the Court's opinion, in particular, regarding: (a) which of these judicial guarantees are 'essential' and (b) the relationship between Art 27.2, in that regard, and Arts 25 and 8 of the American Convention": paras 2 and 10(1).

142 Arts 7(6), 8(1), 25(1), 27(2) and 29.

143 *Ibid*, para 27. The rights and freedoms from which no derogation is permitted under any circumstances are the right to juridical personality (Art 3); the right to life (Art 4); the right to humane treatment (Art 5); freedom from slavery (Art 6) and freedom from *ex post facto* laws (Art 9); the right to freedom of conscience and religion (Art 12); the rights of the family (Art 17); the right to a name (Art 18); the rights of the child (Art 19); the right to nationality (Art 20) and the right to participate in government (Art 23).

144 *Ibid*, para 30: "The expression 'judicial' can only refer to those judicial remedies that are truly capable of protecting these rights. Implicit in this conception is the active involvement of an independent and impartial judicial body". See also *Durán y Ugarte v Peru*, Merits, IACHR C 68, para 59 ñ.

145 OC 8/87, paras 28, 36, 38 and OC 9/87, paras 35 and 39: "There exists an inseparable bond between the principle of legality, democratic institutions and the rule of law. When

(b) For such a remedy to exist, it is not sufficient that it be provided for by the Constitution or by law or that it be formally recognized, but rather it must be truly effective in establishing whether there has been a violation of human rights and in providing redress.[146] A remedy which proves illusory because of the general conditions prevailing in the country, or even in the particular circumstances of a given case, cannot be considered effective.[147]

(c) Among the judicial remedies, above all, the writ of *habeas corpus*[148] has to remain in effect even during states of emergency, despite the fact that

guarantees are suspended, some legal restraints applicable to the acts of public authorities may differ from those in effect under normal conditions. These restraints may not be considered to be non-existent, however, nor can the government be deemed thereby to have acquired absolute powers that go beyond the circumstances justifying the grant of such exceptional legal measures ... The determination as to what judicial remedies are 'essential' for the protection of the rights which may not be suspended will differ depending upon the rights concerned. The judicial guarantees essential for the protection of the human rights not subject to derogation, according to Art 27.2 of the Convention, are those to which the Convention expressly refers in Arts 7.6 and 25.1, considered within the framework and the principles of Art 8, and also those necessary to the preservation of the Rule of Law, even during the state of exception that results from the suspension of guarantees".

[146] See IACHR C 68, paras 59(f) and 93(b), (c), and (d). The absence of an effective judicial remedy to violations of all the rights recognized by the Convention is itself a violation of the Convention by the State Party.

[147] OC 9/87, para 24: "That could be the case, for example, when practice has shown its ineffectiveness; when the Judicial Power lacks the necessary independence to render impartial decisions or the means to carry out its judgments; or in any other situation that constitutes a denial of justice, as when there is an unjustified delay in the decision; or when, for any reason, the alleged victim is denied access to a judicial remedy". Compare *inter alia*, IACHR C 68, paras 59(q) and 100 ("Supreme Orders No 012-86-IN of 2 June 1986 and No 006-86 JUS of 19 June 1986 did not suspend the *habeas corpus* recourse explicitly, but it was inefficient") and IACHR C 70, paras 190–91.

[148] "*Amparo*, which is a simple and prompt remedy designed for the protection of all of the rights recognized by the Constitutions and laws of the States Parties and by the ACHR, comprises a whole series of remedies: the writ of *habeas corpus* is one of its components. The purpose of *habeas corpus* is to obtain a judicial determination of the lawfulness of a detention. Therefore, it is necessary that the detained person be brought before a competent judge or tribunal with jurisdiction over him. Here *habeas corpus* performs a vital role in ensuring that a person's life and physical integrity are respected, in preventing his disappearance or the keeping of his whereabouts secret and in protecting him against torture or other cruel, inhumane, or degrading punishment or treatment". On *habeas corpus* and *amparo* in Latin American countries and in the IACHR's case-law, see C Anicama Campos, "Derechos Humanos y estados de Excepción", Comisión Andina de Juristas, Junio 2003; J Detzner, "Tribunales chilenos y Derecho Internacional de Derechos Humanos", Comisión Chilena de Derechos Humanos, Santiago, 1988, 61 ff; H Faúndez Ledesma, "El Sistema ...", above n 139, 94–95; EA Faulkner, "The Right to Habeas Corpus: Only in the Other Americas", (1994) 9 *The American University Journal of International Law & Policy*, 653 ff; H Gross-Espiell, "Algunas cuestiones relativas al derecho interno en la jurisprudencia consultiva de la Corte Interamericana de Derechos Humanos", (1999) 3 *Anuario Iberoamericano de Justicia Constitucional*, 349–71; JL Lazzarini, "El juicio de amparo", (2000) 4 *Anuario Iberoamericano de Justicia Constitucional*, 211–20; M Mejicanos Jiménez, "El amparo como garantía para el acceso a la justicia y protección de los derechos humanos en la jurisdicción constitucional guatemalteca", (1995) 32–33 *Revista Instituto Interamericano de Derechos Humanos*, 175 ff; H Nogueira, "El recurso de protección en Chile", (1999) 3 *Anuario Iberoamericano de Justicia Constitucional*, 175–79; F Orrego Vicuña and F Orrego Bauzá, "The Implementation of the

Article 7 is not listed among the provisions that may not be suspended in exceptional circumstances.[149]

These principles, reaffirmed in all the contentious cases subsequently submitted by the ACommHR,[150] were further elaborated in the *Loayza Tamayo v Peru* case,[151] in which the Court proclaimed that exceptional

International Law of Human Rights by the Judiciary: New Trends in the Light of the Chilean Experience", in Conforti and Francioni (eds), *Enforcing International Human Rights in Domestic Courts,* (The Hague, Martinus Nijhoff, 1997) 135–47 and 145–46; F Tocora, "Control Constitucional y Derechos Humanos", (Santafé de Bogotá, Librería del Profesional, 1992) 79 ff and D Zovatto, *Los Estados de Excepcion y los Derechos Humanos en América Latina* (San José, Costa Rica, Instituto Interamericano de Derechos Humanos, 1990), *passim.*

[149] OC 8/87, para 37 and OC 9/87, paras 30–33: "The principles of due process of law cannot be suspended in states of exception insofar as they are necessary conditions for the procedural institutions regulated by the Convention to be considered judicial guarantees. This result is even more clear with respect to *habeas corpus* and *amparo,* which are indispensable for the protection of the human rights that are not subject to derogation. The suspension of guarantees must not exceed the limits strictly required and any action on the part of the public authorities that goes beyond those limits, which must be specified with precision in the decree promulgating the state of emergency, is unlawful". See also *Velásquez Rodríguez, Fairen Garbi and Solís Corrales and Godínez Cruz v Honduras,* Preliminary Objections, IACHR C 1-2-3, paras 90 and 92 respectively; *Idem,* Merits, IACHR C 4-5-6, paras 65, 68 and 90 respectively; *Caballero Delgado and Santana v Colombia,* Preliminary Objections, IACHR C 17, para 64; *Neira Alegría et al v Peru.,* Merits, IACHR C 20, paras 77–80; *Durán y Ugarte v Peru,* Preliminary Objections, IACHR C 50, paras 34–7; *Castillo Páez v Peru,* Preliminary Objections, IACHR C 24, para 40; *Loayza Tamayo v Peru,* Preliminary Objections, IACHR C 25, para 40 and *Cantoral Benavides v Peru,* Preliminary Objections, IACHR C 40, para 31. See also D García Belaunde, "El *habeas corpus* en América Latina", (1994) 20 *Revista Instituto Interamericano de Derechos Humanos,* 41–62; H Faúndez Ledesma, "La Convención Americana sobre Derechos Humanos y el régimen jurídico de los estados de emergencia", (1996) 101 *Revista de la Facultad de Ciencias Jurídicas y Políticas, Universidad Central de Venezuela, 27–72;* JY Morin, "L'Etat de Droit: Emergence d'un Principe du Droit International", (1995) 254 *Recueil de Cours,* 281–92 and 296–99.

[150] At the sole exception of the *Genie Lacayo vs. Nicaragua* case, Merits, IACHR C 30, paras 83–86, 88–89 and 91–92 ("The military courts do not *per se* violate the Convention and the fact that a procedure concerning a civilian involves a military court does not *per se* signify that the human rights guaranteed the accusing party by the Convention are being violated"). See also *Caballero Delgado y Santana v Colombia,* Merits, IACHR C 22, para 66; C 33, paras 50 and 55 ("Art 27 of the ACHR governs the suspension of guarantees in time of war, public danger, or other emergency that poses a threat to the independence or security of a State Party, in which eventuality the latter must inform the other States Parties, through the Secretary General of the OAS, of the provisions the application of which it has suspended, the reasons that gave rise to the suspension, and the date set for the termination of such suspension. While it is true that personal liberty is not expressly included in those rights, the suspension of which is, in any event, not authorized, it is equally true that the Court has found that writs of *habeas corpus* and of *amparo* are among those judicial remedies that are essential for the protection of various rights whose derogation is prohibited by Art 27.2 and that serve, moreover, to preserve legality in a democratic society [and that] the Constitution and legal systems of the States Parties that authorize, expressly or by implication, the suspension of the legal remedies of *habeas corpus* or of *amparo* in emergency situations cannot be deemed to be compatible with the international obligations imposed o these States by the Convention"). See *Paniagua Morales et al v Guatemala,* Merits, IACHR C 37, paras 96–103.

[151] Paras 59–65, and see in *Castillo Páez v Peru,* IACHR C 34, Merits, paras 30(d), (e), and (f); 43 (a), (b), and (c); 47–61; 80–84.

procedures which greatly restrict the fundamental rights embodied in the concept of due process[152] do not meet the criteria of a fair trial when the person is detained without a warrant;[153] the presumption of innocence is not observed; the defendants are not allowed to challenge or examine the evidence; the defence attorney[154] cannot communicate freely with his or her client and intervene in all stages of the proceeding[155] and the principle of *ne bis in idem* is not respected.[156]

The concurring opinion of Judges Cançado Trindade and Jackman goes further, anticipating future legal battles: "Special military tribunals composed of military personnel appointed by the Executive Power and subject to the dictates of military discipline, assuming a function which belongs to the Judicial Power, endowed with jurisdiction to judge not only the military but civilians as well", they state, "do not meet the standards of independence and impartiality imposed by Art 8.1 of the ACHR, as an essential element of the concept of due process".[157] This decision was a severe blow not only to the Peruvian emergency legislation, but also to many other Latin American legislative acts and decrees.

Shortly thereafter, in the *Castillo Petruzzi et al v Peru* case,[158] the whole Court reaffirmed this assertion,[159] stressing that military tribunals are not

[152] Right to a hearing by an independent and impartial tribunal (Art 8(1)); right to be presumed innocent (Arts 8(1) and 8(2)); right to full equality during the proceedings (Art 8(2)); right to defend oneself (Art 8(2)(d)); right not to be compelled to be a witness against oneself and not to be subject to coercion of any kind (Arts 8(2)(g) and 8(3)); and the judicial guarantee not to be subjected to double jeopardy (Art 8(4)).

[153] See IACHR C 68, para 91.

[154] If the convicted is permitted to appoint one: see IACHR C 68, para 59(c).

[155] See paras 59–66.

[156] See paras 67–68: "In the instant case, the Court observes that Ms. María Elena Loayza-Tamayo was tried in the military criminal courts for the crime of treason, which is closely linked to the crime of terrorism, as may be seen from a comparative reading of Art 2a, b and c of Decree-Law No 25.659 (crime of treason) and Arts 2 and 4 of Decree-Law No 25.475 (crime of terrorism). Both Decree-Laws refer to actions not strictly defined, so that they may be interpreted similarly within both crimes. Consequently, the aforementioned decrees/laws are contrary to Art 8(4) of the American Convention in this regard".

[157] From this moment, the principle became *jurisprudence constante*: see eg *Las Palmeras v Colombia*, Merits, IACHR C 90, paras 51–54 (and 58–66).

[158] See J Bucherer, "Castillo Petruzzi, Merits", (2001) 95 *American Journal of International Law*, 171 ff, and, in general, F Mégret, "Justice in Times of Violence", (2003) 14 *European Journal International Law*, 327 ff.

[159] See paras 109–10, 125, 127–34, 135–36, 138–56, 174–88 and 222: "Transferring jurisdiction from civilian courts to military courts, thus allowing military courts to try civilians accused of treason, means that the competent, independent and impartial tribunal previously established by law is precluded from hearing these cases. In the case under study, the armed forces, fully engaged in the counter-insurgency struggle, are also prosecuting persons associated with insurgency groups. This considerably weakens the impartiality that every judge must have. Moreover, under the Statute of Military Justice, members of the Supreme Court of Military Justice, the highest body in the military judiciary, are appointed by the minister of the pertinent sector. Members of the Supreme Court of Military Justice also decide who among their subordinates will be promoted and what incentives will be offered to whom; they also assign functions. This alone is enough to call the independence of the military judges into serious

the tribunals previously established by law for civilians,[160] and extended its statement to military courts of second instance.[161] The ACommHR assented.[162]

What is more, the *Castillo Petruzzi* judgment goes right into the heart of the domestic emergency laws involved, and a second shot is given to the defendant State:

> "Crimes must be classified and described in precise and unambiguous language that narrowly defines the punishable offense, thus giving full meaning

question. What is more, because judges who preside over the treason trials are 'faceless,' defendants have no way of knowing the identity of their judge and, therefore, of assessing their competence. Compounding the problem is the fact that the law does not allow these judges to excuse themselves". See also IACHR C 68, para 117: "In a democratic Government of Laws the penal military jurisdiction shall have a restrictive and exceptional scope and shall lead to the protection of special juridical interests, related to the functions assigned by law to the military forces. Consequently, civilians must be excluded from the military jurisdiction scope and only the military shall be judged by commission of crime or offenses that by its own nature attempt against legally protected interests of military order".

[160] See para 128: "In effect, military tribunals are not the tribunals previously established by law for civilians. Having no military functions or duties, civilians cannot engage in behaviors that violate military duties. When a military court takes jurisdiction over a matter that regular courts should hear, the individual's right to a hearing by a competent, independent and impartial tribunal previously established by law and, *a fortiori*, his right to due process are violated. That right to due process, in turn, is intimately linked to the very right of access to the courts".

[161] See para 161: "The right to appeal the judgment, also recognized in the Convention, is not satisfied merely because there is a higher court than the one that tried and convicted the accused and to which the latter has or may have recourse. For a true review of the judgment, in the sense required by the ACHR, the higher court must have the jurisdictional authority to take up the particular case in question. It is important to underscore the fact that from first to last instance, a criminal proceeding is a single proceeding in various stages. Therefore, the concept of a tribunal previously established by law and the principle of due process apply throughout all those phases and must be observed in all the various procedural instances. If the court of second instance fails to satisfy the requirements that a court must meet to be a fair, impartial and independent tribunal previously established by law, then the phase of the proceedings conducted by that court cannot be deemed to be either lawful or valid. In the instant case, the superior court was part of the military structure and as such did not have the independence necessary to act as or be a tribunal previously established by law with jurisdiction to try civilians. Therefore, whereas remedies, albeit very restrictive ones, did exist of which the accused could avail themselves, there were no real guarantees that the case would be reconsidered by a higher court that combined the qualities of competence, impartiality and independence that the Convention requires".

[162] See para 89 of the sentence and IACommHR's Resolution "Human Rights and Terrorism", 10 December 2001, <http://www.cidh.oas.org/resterrorism.htm>: "States have the right and indeed the duty to defend themselves against terrorism within the framework of international instruments that require domestic laws and regulations to conform with international commitments. Military courts may not try civilians, except when no civilian courts exist or where trial by such courts is materially impossible. Even under such circumstances, the trial must respect the minimum guarantees established under international law, which include non-discrimination between citizens and others who find themselves under the jurisdiction of a State, an impartial judge, the right to be assisted by freely-chosen counsel, and access by defendants to evidence brought against them together with the opportunity to contest it".

> to the principle of *nullum crimen, nulla poena sine lege praevia* in criminal law. This means a clear definition of the criminalized conduct, establishing its elements and the factors that distinguish it from behaviors that are either not punishable offences or are punishable but not with imprisonment.[163] The criminal offenses of treason and terrorism are similar in certain fundamental respects.[164] The fact that both have certain elements in common and the vague distinction between the two categories of crime is prejudicial to the defendants' legal situation on several counts: the applicable penalty, the court with jurisdiction, and the nature of the proceedings".[165]

The consequences which the Court draws from the above are of great importance: (a) "the domestic judgment is automatically invalid, as it does not meet the requirements for it to stand and have the effects that normally follow from an act of this nature.[166] It is up to the State, then, within a reasonable time period, to order a new trial that *ab initio* satisfies the requirements of due process of law";[167] (b) "the State is to adopt the appropriate measures to amend[168] domestic laws that place civilians under the jurisdiction of the military courts and ensure the enjoyment of the rights recognized in the Convention to all persons within its jurisdiction";[169] (c) "the State must pay the expenses and costs that the victims" relatives incurred by reason of these proceedings".[170]

The echo of sentence C 52 was disruptive and Government's reaction rude and inconsistent: the Supreme Court declared the sentence not executable[171] and the State withdrew from the contentious jurisdiction of

[163] See para 121: "Ambiguity in describing crimes creates doubts and the opportunity for abuse of power, particularly when it comes to ascertaining the criminal responsibility of individuals and punishing their criminal behavior with penalties that exact their toll on the things that are most precious, such as life and liberty. Laws of the kind applied in the instant case, that fail to narrowly define the criminal behaviors, violate the principle of *nullum crimen nulla poena sine lege praevia* recognized in Art 9 of the ACHR".

[164] "The crime called treason is aggravated terrorism, regardless of the label the lawmaker chose to give it": para 120.

[165] Para 119.

[166] See para 221 and Operating Para 13: "Failure to fulfill the requirements of due process renders the proceedings invalid"; "The Court unanimously finds the proceedings conducted ... invalid, as they were incompatible with the ACHR, and so orders that the persons in question be guaranteed a new trial in which the guarantees of due process of law are ensured".

[167] *Ibid.*

[168] On the basis of Articles 1 and 2 of the ACHR.

[169] See para 222 and Operating Paras 11 and 14.

[170] See para 223 and Operating Para 15.

[171] *"La Corte, al haber ordenado adoptar las medidas apropiadas para reformar las normas que han sido declaradas violatorias de la Convención Americana sobre Derechos Humanos, ha incurrido en un exceso de su competencia funcional, pues la compatibilidad o incompatibilidad entre el Derecho Interno de los Estados partes y la Convención sólo puede ser definida por la Corte Interamericana en via de consulta y a modo de opinion, exclusivamente por iniciativa de tales Estados parte. La orden de reformar disposiciones legales emanadas del Poder Legislativo exige una nueva norma legal, lo que implica ordenar que los Congresistas de la República voten en el sentido indicado; los Congresistas*

the Court.[172] Nevertheless, the IACHR reaffirmed its competence for the pending Peruvian cases[173] and continued dealing with them,[174] applying its established principles on judicial guarantees (including *habeas corpus* and *amparo*) and due process.[175] On 23 January 2001, Peru's Embassy in Costa Rica forwarded the Court a copy of Legislative Resolution No 27.401,[176] in which one article established that the contentious jurisdiction of the IACHR was fully restored for the State of Peru.

Then, the *Barrios Altos* case[177] was examined, which referred to the Amnesty Laws passed by the Fujimori Government shortly after a Judge of the Criminal Court of Lima had initiated a formal investigation on the massacre happened in the neighbourhood known as *Barrios Altos*.[178]

representan a la Nación y no están sujetos a mandato imperativo, per lo que la Corte no puede ordenarles la materia ni la forma como deben emitir sus votos; en consecuencia ese mandato de la Corte es inejecutable y excede en forma absoluta a su competencia; al pretender la Corte Inter-Americana importar una sanción económica, ella no solo esta reñido con los más elementares principios de respeto a un pueblo castigado por más de trece años con el flagelo del terrorismo, sino que además prejugza ordenando un nuevo juzgamiento y anticipando el pago de gastos y costas ...En consequencia, la aceptación y ejecución de la sentencia de la Corte en este tema pondria en grave riesgo la seguridad interna de la República, y lo expresado demuestra fehacientemente que el fallo de la Corte Inter-Americana DDHH carece de imparcialidad y vulnera la Constitución Política del Estado, siendo por ende de imposible ejecución".

172 See Legislative Resolution No 27.152, 8 July 1999, deposited with the General Secretariat of the OAS the following day. The withdrawal had to take immediate effect, and applied to all cases in which Peru had not answered the application filed with the Court.

On this topic, see D Cassel, "Peru Withdraws from the Court: Will the Inter-American Rights System Meet the Challenge", (1999) 20 *Human Rights Law Journal*, 169 ff; P Frumer, "Denonciation des traités et remise en cause de la compétence par des organes de contrôle. A propos de quelques entraves étatiques récentes aux mécanismes internationaux de protection des droits de l' homme", (2000) *Annuaire Français Droit International*, 939–64; M Scalabrino, "Vittime e risarcimento del danno : l'esperienza della Corte Interamericana dei Diritti dell'Uomo", (2002) XXII *Comunicazioni e Studi dell'Istituto di Diritto Internazionale della Università di Milano*, 1013–92.

173 The *Ivcher Bronstein* and the *Constitutional Court* cases, sentences IACHR C 54 and C 55 on competence, paras 32, 36, 39, 51–54.

174 The defendant State did not appear before the Court and filed no written plea in the *Constitutional Court* case.

175 See *Constitutional Court v Ivcher Bronstein* cases, Merits, IACHR C 71 and C 74, paras 66–75, 81–95 respectively.

176 Published in the Official Gazette *El Peruano* on 19 January 2001.

177 IACHR C 75 dated 14 March 2001.

178 *Ibid*, para 2 (d), (g), (i), (j), (k) and (m): "Although the events occurred in 1991, the judicial authorities did not commence a serious investigation of the incident until April 1995, when the Criminal Prosecutor of Lima accused five Army officials of being responsible for the events, including several who had already been convicted in the massacre of *La Cantuta* case. On several occasions, the prosecutor tried unsuccessfully to compel the accused men to appear before the court to make a statement. Consequently, she filed charges before the Sixteenth Criminal Court of Lima. As soon as a formal investigation began, the military courts filed a petition before the Supreme Court claiming jurisdiction in the case, alleging that it related to military officers on active service. Before the Supreme Court could take a decision on this matter, the Congress of Peru adopted Amnesty Law No 26.479, which exonerated members of the army, police force and also civilians who had violated human rights

The respondent State recognized its international responsibility in the case and declared itself to be ready to initiate a friendly settlement procedure with both the ACommHR and the petitioners.[179]

In spite of this, the Court did not waste the historical opportunity to pronounce on the merits, and its statements on the case are a landmark in the history of the Latin American jurisprudence. It held that "[a]ll amnesty provisions, provisions on prescription and the establishment of measures designed to eliminate responsibility are inadmissible[180]...the adoption of self-amnesty laws[181] is a violation of the obligation to adapt internal legislation, embodied in Art 2 of the ACHR".[182] "Owing to the manifest

or taken part in such violations from 1980 to 1995 from responsibility. The draft law was not publicly announced or discussed, but was adopted as soon as it was submitted, in the early hours of 14 June 1995. The President promulgated the law immediately and it entered into force on 15 June 1995. The effect of this law was to determine that the judicial investigations were definitively quashed and thus prevent the perpetrators of the massacre from being found criminally responsible. Law No 26.479 granted an amnesty to all members of the security forces and civilians who had been accused, investigated, prosecuted or convicted, or who were carrying out prison sentences, for human rights violations. The few convictions of members of the security forces for human rights violations were immediately annulled. Consequently, the eight men who had been imprisoned for the case known as *'La Cantuta'*, some of whom were being prosecuted in the *Barrios Altos* case, were liberated. The Judge refused to apply Amnesty Law, since the amnesty violated constitutional guarantees and the international obligations that the ACHR imposed on Peru. Judge Saquicuray's refusal to apply Amnesty Law No 26.479 led to another congressional investigation. Before the public hearing could be held, the Congress of Peru adopted a second amnesty law, Law No 26.492, which was directed at interfering with legal actions in the *Barrios Altos* case. This law declared that the amnesty could not be "revised" by a judicial instance and that its application was obligatory. Moreover, it expanded the scope of Law No 26.479, granting a general amnesty to all military, police or civilian officials who might be the subject of indictments for human rights violations committed between 1980 and 1995, even though they had not been charged. The effect of this second law was to prevent the judges from determining the legality or applicability of the first amnesty law, invalidating Judge Saquicuray's decision and preventing similar decision in the future".

[179] See IACHR C 75, para 31.
[180] *Ibid*, para 41, since "they are intended to prevent the investigation and punishment of those responsible for serious human rights violations such as torture, extrajudicial, summary or arbitrary execution and forced disappearance, all of them prohibited because they violate non-derogable rights recognized by international human rights law".
[181] Concurring Opinion of Judge García Ramírez, para 10: "Self-amnesties are promulgated by and for those in power, and differ from amnesties that may be the result of a peace process, have a democratic base and a reasonable scope, that preclude prosecution of acts or behaviors of members of rival factions, but leave open the possibility of punishment for the kind of very egregious acts that no faction either approves or views as appropriate".
[182] See IACHR C 75, paras 42–43: "In the light of the general obligations established in Arts 1.1 and 2 of the ACHR, the States Parties are obliged to take all measures to ensure that no one is deprived of judicial protection and the exercise of the right to a simple and effective recourse, in the terms of Arts 8 and 25 of the Convention. Consequently, States Parties to the Convention which adopt laws that have the opposite effect, such as self-amnesty laws, violate Arts 8 and 25, in relation to Arts 1.1 and 2 of the Convention. Self-amnesty laws lead to the defenselessness of victims and perpetuate impunity; therefore, they are manifestly incompatible with the aims and spirit of the Convention. This type of law precludes the identification of the individuals who are responsible for human rights violations, because it obstructs the

incompatibility of self-amnesty laws and the ACHR", it added, "the said laws lack legal effect,[183] nor can they have the same or a similar impact with regard to other cases that have occurred in Peru, where the rights established in the American Convention have been violated".[184] According to the concurring opinion of President Cançado Trindade, not only do self-amnesty laws have no legal validity in the light of the norms of the international law of human rights,[185] but they are "the source of an international illicit act: as from their own adoption and irrespectively of their subsequent application, they engage the international responsibility of the State. Their being in force creates *per se* a situation which affects in a continuing way non-derogable rights".[186]

Three months after the Court had delivered its judgment, the ACommHR filed a request for the interpretation of the same, based on the fact that in the negotiations between the petitioners' representatives and the Government on the matter of reparations, the former had argued that the State had to nullify the effects of the amnesty laws in all cases of human rights violations where these laws had been or had to be applied, whereas the government delegation insisted that the judgment of the IACHR applied only to the *Barrios Altos* case.[187] With a single statement, the Court concisely decided that "given the nature of the violation that amnesty laws constitute, the decision in the judgment on the merits in the *Barrios Altos* case has generic effects".[188] While it is hard to say whether the judgment on the merits is meant to have *erga omnes* effects, it is worth

investigation and access to justice and prevents the victims and their next of kin from knowing the truth and receiving the corresponding reparation" and F Guariglia, "Los limites de la impunidad : la sentencia de la Corte Interamericana de Derechos Humanos en el caso '*Barrios Altos*' ", (2001) *Nueva Doctrina Penal*, 209–30. See also RJ Wilson and J Perlin, "The Inter-American Human Rights System: Activities from Late 2000 … ", above n 112, 657.

[183] *Ibid*, para 44: "and may not continue to obstruct the investigation of the grounds on which this case is based or the identification and punishment of those responsible".
[184] See para 44 and Operative Para 4.
[185] See also Concurring Opinion of Judge García Ramírez, para 15: "Those laws are null and void, because they are at odds with the State's international commitments. Therefore, they cannot produce the legal effects inherent in laws promulgated normally and which are compatible with the international and constitutional provisions that engage the State [of Peru]. The incompatibility determines the invalidity of the act, which signifies that the said act cannot produce legal effects".
[186] *Ibid*, para 11.
[187] The IACommHR's question was the following: "Is the Judgment in the *Barrios Altos* case, concerning the incompatibility of laws Nos 26.479 and 26.492 with the ACHR, general in scope or confined to that specific case only?" The IACommHR's contention was that "the effects of the Court's judgment are not confined exclusively to the *Barrios Altos* Case, but rather to all those in which those amnesty laws were applied, since para 44 of the Court's judgment could hardly be interpreted any other way" (see IACHR C 83, paras 9 and 14).
[188] Operative para 2 and para 18: "Enactment of a law that is manifestly incompatible with the obligations undertaken by a State Party to the Convention is *per se* a violation of the Convention for which the State incurs international responsibility. The Court therefore considers that given the nature of the violation that amnesty laws No 26.479 and No 26.492

noticing that on 6 March 2001 the Argentinian self-amnesty laws *Ley de Punto Final* (Art 1) and *Ley de Obediencia Debida* (Arts 1, 3 and 4) have been declared as having no legal validity *"por ser incompatibles con la Convención Americana de Derechos Humanos* (*Artículos* 1, 2, 8 *y* 25)".[189]

The IACHR has also been called to pronounce on denial of justice and forced disappearances in situations of guerrilla warfare. Cases have arisen in respect to Colombia[190] and Guatemala.[191] In the former case, the Court noted that the very same individuals in military forces engaged in fighting the insurgent groups were those responsible for prosecuting their colleagues for executing civilians. In order to meet the requirements of Article 8(1) of the ACHR, the Court stated, "the prosecution and punishment of those responsible should have been handled by the ordinary justice system, irrespective of whether the suspected authors were police officers in active service. Nevertheless, the State ordered that the military courts preside over the investigation into the incident".[192] For these reasons, the Court found that Article 8(1) had been violated.

More than seven years after, the case was passed to ordinary criminal courts, but no definitive judgment naming, convicting or punishing those responsible was ever pronounced. The fact is "that these proceedings have failed to convict and punish the responsible parties, also because the

constitute, the effects of the decision in the judgment on the merits of the *Barrios Altos* case are general in nature, and the question put to the Court in the ACommHR's request for interpretation must be so answered".

[189] *"La ley del gobierno militar No 22.924, al declarar extinguidas las acciones penales derivadas de todos los hechos de naturaleza penal realizados en ocasión, o con motivo del desarrollo de acciones dirigidas a prevenir, conjurar o poner fin a las actividades terroristas o subversivas, intentó dejar en la impunidad hechos brutales que desconocieron la dignidad humana y que se hallaban comprendidos en el artículo 29 de la Constitución Nacional. La posibilidad de amnistiarse a sí mismo es algo vedado para el Congreso de la Nación, y con mayor razón para quien por la fuerza usurpe funciones. Al igual que ocurriera con la ley 22.924, las leyes 23.492 y 23.521 tienen como consecuencia que queden impunes hechos que desconocieron la dignidad humana y excluyen del conocimiento del Poder Judicial el juzgamiento de tales ilícitos. Por lo tanto, las consecuencias de estas leyes alcanzan los extremos que el art. 29 de la Constitución Nacional rechaza enfáticamente, por lo que, estas leyes denominadas 'Ley de Punto Final' y 'Ley de Obediencia Debida' carecen de efectos jurídicos: llevan consigo una nulidad insanable"*. See AS Brown, "Adios Amnesty: Prosecutorial Discretion and Military Trials in Argentina", (2002) 37 *Texas International Law Journal*, 203 ff.

[190] See *Las Palmeras* case, Merits, IACHR C 90. See also RJ Wilson and J Perlin, "The Inter-American Human Rights System: Activities from Late 2000 ... ", above n 112, 687–89.

[191] See IACHR C 70, para 121(b), (d) and (h): "At the time when the facts relating to this case took place, Guatemala was convulsed by an internal conflict"; "In 1992, there was a *guerrilla* group called the Organization of the People in Arms (ORPA) in Guatemala, which operated on four fronts, one of which was the Luis Ixmatá Front, commanded by Efraín Bámaca Velásquez, known as Everardo"; "On 12 March 1992, there was an armed encounter between *guerrilla* combatants belonging to the Luis Ixmatá Front and members of the Army on the banks of the Ixcucua River. Efraín Bámaca Velásquez was captured alive during this encounter". See also RJ Wilson and J Perlin, "The Inter-American Human Rights System: Activities from Late 2000 ... ", above n 112, 665–75.

[192] See IACHR C 90, paras 53–4.

National Police officers implicated in the events obstructed or refused to properly cooperate with the investigations undertaken to clarify the case, and either tampered with, concealed or destroyed evidence".[193] All this, the Court concludes, fosters impunity[194] and impunity fosters chronic recidivism of human rights violations, and total defenseless of victims and their relatives.[195] Consequently, the guarantees established in Articles 8(1) and 25 must not be deemed to apply only to the immediate victims: they also apply to their relatives who, because of the events and particular circumstances of a given case, are the parties that exercise the right in the domestic system.[196] Moreover, since twelve years have expired, and the proceedings initiated in the military court and in the regular criminal courts have failed to identify the responsible parties, Articles 8(1) and 25(1) have been violated also inasfar as the obligation to provide judicial remedies within a reasonable time is concerned.

As for forced disappearances, in the *Bámaca Velásquez* case the IACommHR had correctly pointed out that most of the victims of

[193] *Ibid*, paras 55 and 57. See also IACHR C 70, para 200. Some of the obstructionist behaviors are the following: changing the clothing worn by the victims and then destroying the victims' clothes; failing to search the bodies at the scene of the crime; failing to collect evidence; threatening and intimidating relatives and witnesses, and circulating false information concerning the victims' activities.

[194] Ie "the total lack of investigation, prosecution, capture, trial and conviction of those responsible for violations of rights protected by the American Convention, by virtue of the obligation of the State to use all the legal means at its disposal to combat that situation: para 56.

[195] See para 58: "It is the *jurisprudence constante* of this Court that it is not enough that such recourses exist formally; they must be effective; that is, they must give results or responses to the violations of rights established in the Convention. This Court has also held that remedies that, due to the general situation of the country or even the particular circumstances of any given case, prove illusory cannot be considered effective. This may happen when, for example, they prove to be useless in practice because the jurisdictional body does not have the independence necessary to arrive at an impartial decision or because they lack the means to execute their decisions; or any other situation in which justice is being denied, such as cases in which there has been an unwarranted delay in rendering a judgment".

See also *Conclusiones Generales del Informe Final de la Comisión de la Verdad y Reconciliación del Perú*, September 2003, para 168: "*La CVR considera que una parte esencial del proceso de reparación es la justicia. La Comisión advierte que ningún camino hacia la reconciliación será transitable si no va acompañado de un ejercicio efectivo de la justicia, tanto en lo que concierne a la reparación de los daños sufridos por las víctimas cuanto en lo relativo al justo castigo a los perpetradores y el consiguiente fin de la impunidad. No se puede construir un país éticamente sano y políticamente viable sobre los cimientos de la impunidad. A través de los casos que entrega al Ministerio Público, de la identificación de alrededor de 24 mil víctimas del conflicto armado interno y de los hallazgos de sus investigaciones en general, la CV busca sustentar el reclamo de justicia de las víctimas y sus organizaciones, así como de los organismos defensores de los Derechos Humanos y ciudadanos en general*".

[196] See paras 58 and 61–5: "Art 8.1 of the ACHR, in relation to Art 25.1 thereof, gives the victims' relatives the right to have the victims' death effectively investigated by the State authorities; to have the persons responsible for these unlawful acts prosecuted; where appropriate, they have the right to have the proper punishment applied to the responsible parties, and they are entitled to be compensated for the damages and injuries they have suffered".

the dirty wars (*guerras sucias*) had not died in combat or accidentally, in the crossfire between the armed rebel groups and the Army. Rather, the great majority had been confined in clandestine detention centres, where they had been tortured, killed and buried without dignity or respect in unnamed graves or thrown from airplanes into the sea.[197] The Court considered these facts to be proved in respect of the respondent State: in Guatemala, the Army had in fact a practice of capturing guerrillas, detaining them clandestinely, physically and mentally torturing them in order to obtain information about the organization and activities of the rebel group of which they were members and, eventually, killing them.[198] There was sufficient evidence, the Court declared, "to conclude that Efraín Bámaca Velásquez was detained by the Guatemalan army in clandestine detention centers for at least four months, thus violating Art 7 of the ACHR"[199] and that "the facts indicated in relation to him were carried out by persons who acted in their capacity as agents of the State, which involves the international responsibility of Guatemala as State Party to the ACHR".[200] In the light of principles established in the cases against Peru, the Court added that even in case of internal conflict and in case of the detention of a guerrilla, a detainee should be ensured the guarantees that exist under the rule of law, and be submitted to a legal proceeding.[201]

The Court also found that Articles 8 and 25 of the Convention had been violated: by keeping Bámaca Velásquez in clandestine detention,

[197] See IACHR C 70, para 123.

[198] *Ibid*, para 124 . The State actually admitted to these facts: para 125.

[199] *Ibid*, para 143.

[200] *Ibid*, para 133. The Court also recalls (paras 130–31) its previous jurisprudence on forced disappearance, according to which "due to the nature of the phenomenon and its probative difficulties, if it has been proved that the State promotes or tolerates the practice of forced disappearance of persons, and the case of a specific person can be linked to this practice, either by circumstantial or indirect evidence or both, or by pertinent logical inference, then this specific disappearance may be considered to have been proven. Taking this into account, the Court attributes a high probative value to testimonial evidence in proceedings of this type, that is, in the context and circumstances of cases of forced disappearance, with all the attendant difficulties, when, owing to the very nature of the crime, proof essentially takes the form of indirect and circumstantial evidence". Reference is also made (para 153) to the UN Human Rights Committee, according to which, in case of forced disappearances, "the burden of proof cannot fall solely on the author of the communication, considering, in particular, that the author and the State Party do not always have equal access to the evidence and that, frequently, it is only the State Party that has access to the pertinent information ... In cases when the authors have presented charges supported by attesting evidence to the Committee ... and in which subsequent clarification of the case depends on information that is exclusively in the hands of the State Party, the Committee may consider that those charges are justified unless the State Party presents satisfactory evidence and explanations to the contrary".

[201] *Ibid*, para 143: "This Court has already stated that, although the State has the right and obligation to guarantee its security and maintain public order, it must execute its actions within limits and according to procedures that preserve both public safety and the fundamental rights of the human person".

"the State denied his right to file a judicial recourse by his own means; furthermore, by not adequately investigating the petitions for *habeas corpus* filed by his wife Jennifer Harbury, Bámaca Velásquez was deprived of the right to the judicial protection of his life and safety and Jennifer Harbury was deprived of her right to know the fate of her husband and, then, to know the whereabouts of his remains".[202] Consequently, Jennifer Harbury de Bámaca Velásquez is a direct victim in this respect, as the State itself admits.[203]

In the final part of the sentence, the Court deals with the IACommHR's request that Article 3 common to the Geneva Conventions be applied, Guatemala being one of the States Parties thereof.[204] In a previous case,[205] a similar request, in relation to Article 4 of the ACHR,[206] had been concisely responded to by the Court. The Court found that the Convention had only given the Court competence to determine whether the acts of States party to the ACHR are compatible with the Convention itself, and not with the 1949 Geneva onventions.[207] In the *Bámaca Velásquez* case, on the contrary, the Court enlarges the

[202] See paras 182(c), and 190–94. The Court also stresses (para 200) the fact that several judicial remedies were attempted in this case to identify the whereabouts of Bámaca Velásquez and that not only these remedies were ineffective but, furthermore, high-level State agents exercised direct actions against them in order to prevent them from having positive results. Evident obstructions were also conducted with regard to the many exhumation procedures that were attempted and have not permitted the remains of Efraín Bámaca Velásquez to be identified.

[203] See para 186: "Guatemala accepts the facts set out in numeral II of the application, inasmuch as it has still not been possible to identify the persons or person criminally responsible for the unlawful acts against Mr. Bámaca Velásquez and, thus, clarify his disappearance".

[204] See paras 203–4. On whether humanitarian law should be applied to terrorists, see J Klabbers, "Rebel with a Cause? Terrorists and Humanitarian Law?", (2003) 14 *European Journal International Law*, 299 ff.

[205] *Las Palmeras v Colombia*, Preliminary Objections, IACHR C 67, para 33.

[206] *Ibid*, para 31: "The Commission affirms that there is a specific relationship between Art 4 of the ACHR and Art 3 common to all the Geneva Conventions, and that the purpose and goal of the former and the need to apply it effectively uphold the competence of the organs of the system to decide on violations of Art 4 in a way which is coextensive with the norm of general international law embodied in Art 3 common to all the Geneva Conventions".

[207] *Ibid*, para 33: "The ACHR is an international treaty according to which States Parties are obliged to respect the rights and freedoms embodied in it and to guarantee their exercise to all persons subject to their jurisdiction. The Convention provides for the existence of the IACHR to hear all cases concerning the interpretation and application of its provisions (Art 62.3). When a State is a Party to the ACHR and has accepted the contentious jurisdiction of the Court, the Court may examine the conduct of the State to determine whether it conforms to the provisions of the Convention, even when the issue may have been definitively resolved by the domestic legal system. The Court is also competent to determine whether any norm of domestic or international law applied by a State, in times of peace or armed conflict, is compatible or not with the American Convention. In this activity, the Court has no normative limitation: any legal norm may be submitted to this examination of compatibility. In order to carry out this examination, the Court interprets the norm in question and analyzes it in the light of the provisions of the Convention. The result of this operation will always be an opinion in which the Court will say whether or not that norm or that fact is compatible with the ACHR".

scope of its reasoning. It observes first "that certain acts or omissions that violate human rights, pursuant to the treaties that it does have the competence to apply, also violate other international instruments for the protection of the individual, such as the 1949 Geneva Conventions and, in particular, common Art 3"[208] and further notes that "indeed, there is a similarity between the content of Art 3, common to the 1949 Geneva Conventions, and the provisions of the ACHR and other international instruments regarding non-derogable human rights (such as the right to life and the right not to be submitted to torture or cruel, inhuman or degrading treatment)".[209] Although the Court lacks competence to declare that a State is internationally responsible for the violation of international treaties that do not grant it such competence, it then concludes, "the relevant provisions of the Geneva Conventions may be taken into consideration as elements for the interpretation of the ACHR".[210]

VII. CONCLUSION

When considering terrorism, the usual language used in relation to the phenomenon is that of "violence against a State" through violence against its population. Insofar as Latin America is concerned, one should probably speak of "State terrorism against civilians", the harm produced by State responses to terrorist acts and guerrillas (so called "counterterrorism"), having been arguably far more serious and deplorable than the acts being fought against.[211] Moreover, while "international terrorism" generally means violence brought by individuals against a targeted foreign State, one cannot forget that for two decades the US has been heavily conditioning the economic, social and political existence of Latin America political regimes and training the local military for heavy and indiscriminate violence against civilians.

Together with the peculiarities of the Latin American phenomenon described in Part I, this may possibly explain why a number of Latin American countries has not yet ratified the UN *ad hoc* conventions and why the Inter-American Convention to Prevent and Punish Terrorism (Barbados Convention) has been ratified only by six States at the time of writing, out of a total of thirty-five Members of the OAS. For the remaining body of non-binding instruments passed by the OAS General

208 See para 208.
209 See para 209.
210 See paras 208–9.
211 One may make reference to the number of indiscriminate arrests, the detention conditions and the way trials have been carried out by military courts of "terrorist" suspects.

Assembly and the CICTE, they seem to be little more than the "words" to which Hamlet referred.[212]

By contrast, as evidenced in Part VII, the IACHR stands out for its strong decisions on enforcing norms, especially in the contentious cases against Peru and Guatemala. Its assertions are a real challenge to fragile Latin American democracies, and perhaps (see sentence on the interpretation of the *Barrios Altos* case) one of the best guarantees for the prevention of reoccurrences of serious human rights violations ("*nunca más*" never again).

Of course, one can still question *in abstracto* whether the legal (jurisdictional) approach, via international courts, is the most appropriate vehicle to respond to massive and serious violations of human rights, or whether truth and reconciliation Commissions are preferable, which also provide a way for transitional societies to deal with their pasts. Nevertheless, once there is the existence of a mechanism of control such as internationally (or regionally) agreed norms in a legally binding instrument, international courts on human rights have the duty to pronounce of violations thereof, and the value of their decisions should be measured by the consequences and the effects they have on the peoples concerned, as well as on domestic legislation and practice.

Peru is such an example. Shortly after the *Barrios Altos case*, on 21 February 2003, the Constitutional Court nullified some of the norms of both the Fujimori's anti-terrorism Decree Laws,[213] thus forcing Congress to pass five new Decrees,[214] one of them[215] stating in particular that trials concerning treason to the Fatherland were going to be declared void and the convicted detainees retried by civil courts ("*dispone la remisión de los expedientes por delito de traición a la patria de la jurisdicción militar a la ordinaria*").[216] It is worth noting that the Constitutional Court was seized by 5,000 petitioners: this demonstrates that the decisions of the IACHR had created an increased awareness among Peruvian citizens of the need to reestablish the rule of law, as well as a "fair" way to judge their own recent past.

[212] Hamlet, Prince of Denmark — Act II, Scene 2: "What do you read my lord?" "Words, words, words".

[213] Sentence 010-2002-AI/TC. See also SB Abad Yupanqui, "Legilación Antiterrorista, un Modelo a Desarmar", <http://www.uc3m. es/uc3m/.inst/MGP/JCI/05-24-foro-antiterrorista.htm>.

[214] See "*Consejo de Ministros Aprobó Cinco Decretos Legislativos Para la Lucha Antiterrorista*", <http://www2.gestion.com.pe/html/2003/02/20/5/10.htm>.

[215] Decreto Legislativo No 926 published in the Offical Gazette *El Peruano* on 20 February 2003, 239440–41.

[216] See "*Perú: Chilenos MRTA condenados recurrirán a Corte Interamericana*" — Lunes 8 de Septiembre de 2003 — <http://www.emol.com/noticias/internacional/detalle/detalle_noticia.asp?idnoticia = 122481>.

Of course, much still has to be done, in Peru and elsewhere in Latin America hemisphere, and no one can possibly expect from an international court on human rights that it redress alone the heavy heritage of dark decades. A universal conscience is anyway spreading that it is not useful, nor opportune, to fight unlawful acts by unlawful means.

Part III

International Terrorism as an Individual Crime: Jurisdictional Issues, Human Rights Standards and Beyond

10

Terrorism as an International Crime

ANTONIO CASSESE

I. THE PREVAILING VIEW ABOUT TERRORISM AS A CRIME

IN ITS DECISION of 4 April 2003 in *United States v Yousef and Others*,[1] the US Court of Appeals for the Second Circuit, following in the footsteps of the ruling made in *Tel-Oren* by the Court of Appeals of the District of Columbia Circuit eighteen years before,[2] held that "terrorism is a term as loosely deployed as it is powerfully charged". It went on to say that "there continues to be strenuous disagreement between States about what actions do or do not constitute terrorism". The Court drew from such lack of agreement the consequence that, among other things, terrorism "does not provide a basis for universal jurisdiction."[3]

Many scholars share this view about the notion of terrorism.[4] In their opinion, since States have never agreed upon a definition of terrorism, it would be impossible to criminalize this phenomenon as such. At present it would be possible to consider as criminal only single and specific

[1] 327 F.3d 56, at 84; 2003 US App LEXIS 6437, at 64.
[2] 233 US App DC 384, 726 F.2d 774 (DC Cir1984), at 795, 806–7, 823.
[3] *Ibid*, at 86 (or 65).
[4] See in particular R Baxter, "A Skeptical Look at the Concept of Terrorism", (1974) 7 *Akron Law Review*, 380 ff; R Mushkat, "'Technical' Impediments on the Way to a Universal Definition of International Terrorism", (1980) 20 *Indian Journal of International Law*, 448–71; WR Farrell, *The US Government Response to Terrorism: In Search of an Effective Strategy* (Westview Press, Boulder, Col, 1982) at 6; CC Joyner, "Offshore Maritime Terrorism: International Implications and Legal response", 36 *Naval College Law Review* (1983), at 20; G Levitt, "Is 'Terrorism Worth Defining?'" (1986) 13 *Ohio New University Law Review*, at 97; JF Murphy, "Defining International Terrorism: A Way Out of the Quagmire", in (1989) 19 *Israel Yearbook of International Law*, 13–37; O Schachter, "The Extraterritorial Use of Force Against Terrorist Bases", (1989) 11 *Houston Journal of International Law*, at 309; K Skubiszewski, "Definition of Terrorism" (1989) 19 *Israel Yearbook of International Law*, 39–53; G Guillaume, "Terrorisme et droit international", (1989–III) 215 *Hague Recueil*, at 295–307; D Kash, "Abductions of Terrorists in International Airspace and on the High Seas", (1993) 8 *Florida Journal of International Law* at 72; IM Porras, "On Terrorism: Reflections on Violence and the Outlaw", (1994) *Utah Law Review* at 124; R Higgins, "The General International Law of Terrorism", in R Higgins and M Flory (eds), *Terrorism and International Law* (Routledge, London and New York, 1997), 14–19.

instances of terrorism specifically prohibited by some treaties: hijacking of aircraft, terrorist crimes against internationally protected persons including diplomatic agents, the taking of hostages, terrorist acts against the safety of maritime navigation, terrorist bombing, financing of terrorism, etc. This proposition amounts to saying that terrorism *per se* is not a discrete crime under customary international law.

In this paper I would like to dispute this view. To my mind a definition of terrorism does exist, and this phenomenon also amounts to a customary international law crime.

II. EVOLUTION OF THE NOTION OF TERRORISM

One may trace how an accepted definition has gradually evolved in the international community. For more than 30 years after the Second World War, member States of the United Nations (UN) debated the question of the need to punish acts of terrorism. However, they were unable to agree upon a definition of this crime. Developing countries staunchly clung to their view that this notion could not cover acts of violence perpetrated by so-called "freedom fighters", i.e. individuals and groups struggling for their right to self-determination. Furthermore, these countries vociferously insisted on the notion that no treaty could be adopted to ban terrorism unless at the same time the historical, economic, social and political causes underlying the resort to terrorism were studied in depth and thrashed out.[5]

In fact, it is not true that a definition of terrorism was lacking. A definition had evolved since 1937 but developing countries in the UN (with the support of socialist States, whilst they existed) were loath to accept it unless what they considered a *caveat* (and which could probably more accurately be defined as an *exception*) was added: namely to exclude from the definition of terrorism the acts or transactions of national liberation movements or, more generally, "freedom fighters". The refusal of developed countries to accept this exception led to a stalemate, which has erroneously been termed as a "lack of definition" of terrorism. What indeed was lacking was *agreement on the exception*. The general notion of the crime of terrorism was not in question. The contrary view gives rise to two objections, one based on logic, the other on existing legal rules. Logically, to say that because there is no consensus on the exception a general notion has not evolved would be a misconception. It is as if one were to say that,

[5] See, among others, C Greenwood, "Terrorism and Humanitarian Law — The Debate over Additional Protocol I", in (1989) 19 *Israel Yearbook on Human Rights*, 187–207; S Oeter, "Terrorism and 'Wars of National Liberation' from a Law of War Perspective", (1989) 49 *Zeit. aus. Öff. Recht und Völkerrecht* 445–85; A Cassese, *Terrorism, Politics and Law — The* Achille Lauro *Affair* (Cambridge, Polity Press, 1989), at 1–16.

since in international criminal law it is doubtful whether murder may exceptionally be justified by duress, as a result one could not define murder. The second objection is based on the existence of international treaty provisions that explicitly prohibit terrorism, without adding any definition or qualification: for instance, Article 33(1) of the Fourth Geneva Convention of 1949 provides that "collective penalties and likewise all measures of intimidation or of terrorism are prohibited". Similarly, Article 4(2)(d) of the Second Additional Protocol of 1977 to the Geneva Conventions, on internal armed conflicts, prohibits "acts of terrorism" "at any time and in any place whatsoever." One may also mention Article 4 of the Statute of the International Criminal Tribunal for Rwanda (ICTR) which, among other things, adopts the Second Additional Protocol's criminalization of (or rather, grants the Tribunal jurisdiction over) "acts of terrorism" perpetrated in an internal armed conflict. Plainly, if all these treaties speak of "terrorism" or "acts of terrorism" without specifying what is covered by this notion, it means that the draftsmen had a fairly clear idea of what they were prohibiting. It is warranted to believe that they either deliberately or unwittingly were referring to a general notion underlying treaty law and laid down in customary rules. It should be added that in 1999 a treaty was agreed upon in the UN General Assembly that, in addition to prohibiting specific acts of terrorism, also added a definition of this phenomenon: the International Convention for the Suppression of the Financing of Terrorism (GA resolution 54/109 of 9 December 1999). In defining terrorism the Convention takes a twofold approach. First, in Article 2(a) it refers to the acts prohibited by nine treaties listed in the Annex (on hijacking, terrorist bombing etc.); secondly, in Article 2(1)(b) it sets forth a sort of all-inclusive formula, that completes the previous "definition by reference". This provision stipulates that terrorism is:

> Any ... act intended to cause death or serious bodily injury to a civilian, or to any other person not taking an active part in the hostilities in a situation of armed conflict, when the purpose of such act, by its nature or context, is to intimidate a population, or to compel a government or an international organization to do or to abstain from doing an act.

The Supreme Court of Canada, in *Suresh* held that the above definition "catches the essence of what the world understands by "terrorism". Particular cases on the fringes of terrorist activity will inevitably provoke disagreement. Parliament is not prevented from adopting more details or different definitions of terrorism." (paragraph 98).[6] The Court

[6] The Supreme Court stated (§ 93) that it shared the view of the Federal Court of Appeal in the same case that the term "terrorism" is not inherently ambiguous "even if the full meaning ... must be determined on an incremental basis." (§ 69 of the appellate judgment).

nonetheless held the definition sufficiently "certain to be workable, fair and constitutional" and therefore used it for interpreting the Canadian Immigration Act.

Finally, numerous national laws prohibit terrorism as such.[7] Interestingly, they substantially converge in the definition of terrorism they set out.[8] Strikingly, even the 1998 Arab Convention for the Suppression of Terrorism defines in Article 1(2) terrorist acts along the same lines[9] (although it then goes on to except from terrorism acts committed in struggles for the self-determination of peoples).

Having pointed to the fallacious character of the current views about the crime of terrorism, the following should, however, be added: it is a fact that the failure of States to agree upon an exception to the notion of terrorism impelled them to adopt a rather roundabout strategy for facing, and coming to grips with, this odious phenomenon. The majority of UN members preferred to draw up conventions prohibiting individual sets of well-specified acts. In this way, the thorny question of hammering out a broad and generally acceptable definition plus exceptions, if any, was circumvented. The Conventions at issue deal with the hijacking of aircraft, crimes against internationally protected persons including diplomatic

[7] For a careful perusal of some of these laws, see JF Murphy, "Defining International Terrorism: A Way Out of the Quagmire", above n 4, 22–29. In particular, for the text of US legislation, see HS Levie (ed), *Terrorism — Documents of International and Local Control* (Oceana, Dobbs Ferry, New York, 1995), 317–68.

[8] For instance, the United States "Iran and Libya sanctions Act of 1996" (*Public Law* 104–72, 5 August 1996, reproduced in HS Levie (ed), *ibid*, at 487) provides that "an act of international terrorism" means an act "(A) which is violent or dangerous to human life and that is a violation of the criminal laws of the United States or of any State or that would be a criminal violation if committed within the jurisdiction of the United States or any State; and (B) which appears to be intended (i) to intimidate or coerce a civilian population; (ii) to influence the policy of a government by intimidation or coercion; or (iii) to affect the conduct of a government by assassination or kidnapping. See also the US "Antiterrorism and Effective Death Penalty Act of 1996" (*ibid*, vol 10, at 521–23).

In the UK the "Terrorism Act 2000" provides in Article 1 that "terrorism":

(1) "means the use or threat of action where (a) the action falls within subsection (2), (b) the use or threat is designed to influence the government or to intimidate the public or a section of the public, and (c) the use or threat is made for the purpose of advancing a political, religious or ideological cause".

(2) Action falls within this subsection if it (a) involves serious violence against a person; (b) involves serious damage to property; (c) endangers a person's life, other than that of the person committing the action, (d) creates a serious risk to the health or safety of the public or a section of the public, or (e) is designed to interfere with or seriously to disrupt an electronic system" (<http://www.legislation.hmso.gov.uk/acts2000>).

See also Article 100.1 (2) of the Australian Schedule to the Security Legislation Amendment (Terrorism) Bill 2002, as well as the Canadian Bill C–36 ("Anti-terrorism Act"), Article 2(2).

[9] Terrorism includes "Any act or threat of violence, whatever its motives or purposes, that occurs in the advancement of an individual or collective criminal agenda and seeking to sow panic among people, causing fear by harming them, or placing their lives, liberty and security in danger, or seeking to cause damage to the environment or to public or private installations or property or occupying or seizing them, or seeking to jeopardize a national resource."

agents, the taking of hostages, unlawful acts against the safety of maritime navigation, terrorist bombing as well as the financing of terrorism.[10] In addition, at the regional level, in 1971 the US and various Latin American countries plus Sri Lanka agreed upon a convention for the prevention and punishment of acts of terrorism[11], and a European convention on the suppression of terrorism was adopted in 1977.[12]

The condemnation of terrorism did, however, increase over time. In addition, many States probably became convinced that the First Additional Protocol of 1977 to the Geneva Conventions provided an acceptable solution to the question of avoiding labelling "freedom fighters" as terrorists (the Protocol recognises as combatants, and extends the protection of the laws of war to, those who "are fighting against colonial domination and alien occupation and against racist regimes in the exercise of their right of self-determination" and Article 44(3) of the Protocol grants, under certain conditions, legal status as combatants, and prisoner-of-war status in case of capture, to fighters who are not members of the armed forces of a State and normally do not carry their arms openly).[13] Furthermore, the change in the general political climate in the world community following the downfall of socialist regimes, as well as the gradual demise of wars of national liberation, led to a change in attitude towards terrorism. For instance, General Assembly resolutions on terrorism adopted since 1991 have dropped the reference to the underlying causes of the terrorist phenomenon.

As a result, broad agreement gradually evolved on a general definition of terrorism that did not provide for any exception (in spite of the fact that in 1998 the League of Arab States adopted an Arab Convention for the

[10] See the Conventions on the safety of civil aviation (the Tokyo Convention of 14 September 1963 on offences and certain other acts committed on board aircraft, the Hague Convention of 16 December 1970 for the suppression of unlawful seizure of aircraft, the Montreal Convention of 23 September 1971 for the suppression of unlawful acts against the safety of civil aviation), the UN Convention of 14 December 1973 on the prevention and punishment of crimes against internationally protected persons; the New York Convention of 17 December 1979 against the taking of hostages, the Montreal Protocol of 24 February 1988 for the suppression of unlawful acts of violence at airports serving international civil aviation, supplementary to the Montreal Convention of 1971, the Rome Convention of 10 March 1988 for the suppression of unlawful acts against the safety of maritime navigation, with a Protocol on the safety of fixed platforms located on the continental shelf, the UN Convention of 15 December 1997 for the suppression of terrorist bombings, and the UN Convention for the suppressing of the financing of terrorism, of 9 December 1999.

[11] Convention to Prevent and Punish the Acts of Terrorism Taking the Form of Crimes Against Persons and Related Extortion that are of International Significance, of 2 February 1971, in DJ Musch (ed), *Terrorism — Documents of International and Local Control*, vol 14, (Oceana Publications Inc, Dobbs Ferry, New York, 1997), at 523–28. 22 Latin or Central American countries, plus the US and Sri Lanka, signed the Convention.

[12] See text in RA Friedlander (ed), *Terrorism: Documents of International and Local Control* (Oceana, Dobbs Ferry, New York, 1979), vol 2, 565–69.

[13] See the writings cited in note 4.

Suppression of Terrorism that in Article 2(a) envisaged that exception). A resolution passed by consensus in the UN General Assembly (resolution 49/60, adopted on 9 December 1994) reflects this agreement. In the annexed Declaration it contains a provision (paragraph 3) stating that:

> Criminal acts intended or calculated to provoke a state of terror in the general public, a group of persons or particular persons for political purposes are in any circumstance unjustifiable, whatever the considerations of a political, philosophical, ideological, racial, ethnic, religious or any other nature that may be invoked to justify them.[14]

This definition in substance takes up that laid down in Article 1(2) of the unratified 1937 Convention, whereby terrorism encompasses "criminal acts directed against a State and intended or calculated to create a state of terror in the minds of particular persons, or a group of persons or the general public".[15] In addition, the definition is not far from, and indeed to a large extent dovetails with, the notion of terrorism laid down in the aforementioned 1999 Convention on the financing of terrorism.

It is submitted in light of the above that there exists an accepted and sufficiently clear definition of this crime, and in addition the crime is envisaged and banned by customary law, that is, it is no longer simply a treaty law crime.

It may be added that, despite the gradually emerging consensus on an *unqualified* definition of terrorism, in the recent drafting process of the Statute of the International Criminal Court (ICC), States eventually decided not to include terrorism among the crimes under the Court's jurisdiction on a number of grounds. Chief among them was the alleged lack of an agreed definition of terrorism (the other grounds being that (i) the inclusion of the crime would have resulted in politicising the Court, (ii) it was not sufficiently serious an offence to be within the Court's jurisdiction, and (iii) terrorism would have been more effectively prosecuted at the national level, if need be by coordinated action of individual States).

[14] See also other resolutions adopted by the UN General Assembly, for instance resolution 49/60 of 17 February 1995, resolution 51/210, of 16 January 1997, resolution 55/158 of 30 January 2001.

[15] In 1995 the Special Rapporteur of the UN International Law Commission on the Draft Code of Crimes Against the Peace and Security of Mankind, Mr. Doudou Thiam, suggested the following definition for international terrorism imputable to State officials: "Undertaking, organising, ordering, facilitating, financing, encouraging or tolerating acts of violence against another State directed at persons or property and of such nature as to create a state of terror [fear or dread] in the minds of public figures, groups of persons or the general public in order to compel the aforesaid State to grant advantages or to act in a specific way" (UN, Report of the ILC on the Work of its 47th Session (1995), GAOR, Suppl. no 10, A/50/10 at 58, note 45). However, any references to terrorism were subsequently dropped in the final Draft (see UN, Report of the ILC on the Work of its 48th Session (1996), GAOR, 51st Session, Suppl. no.10 (A/51/10), 9–120.

III. THE DEFINITION OF TERRORISM AS AN INTERNATIONAL CRIME

Three main elements seem to be required for the crime of international terrorism: (i) the acts must constitute a criminal offence under most national legal systems (for example, assault, murder, kidnapping, hostage-taking, extortion, bombing, torture, arson, etc); (ii) they must be aimed at spreading terror (that is, fear and intimidation) by means of violent action or the threat thereof directed against a State, the public or particular groups of persons; and (iii) they must be politically, religiously or otherwise ideologically motivated, that is, not motivated by the pursuit of private ends.

IV. MAIN FEATURES OF TERRORISM AS AN INTERNATIONAL CRIME

Terrorism is a phenomenon that may take on diverse forms and manifestations. It has judiciously been said that it has a "chameleon-like" character.[16] Hence it should not be surprising that it may fall under various categories of crime, depending on the circumstances within which acts of terrorism are perpetrated.[17]

Before considering each of these categories separately, the general features that they all share may be outlined. One of the most striking hallmarks of terrorism is the "depersonalization of the victim" (*dépersonnalisation de la victime*), to borrow an expression from the distinguished French criminal lawyer M Delmas-Marty.[18] In the case of terrorism (as well as, albeit in a lesser striking manner, in the case of genocide and of persecution as a crime against humanity) the perpetrator does not attack a specific victim, on account of a personal relationship or animosity, or of the victim possessing certain assets, of his or her gender or age, of his or her nationality, social position, etc. Here the perpetrator is "blind", as it were, to the victim; it does not matter to him whether he or she is young or old, male or female, a fellow-countryman or a foreigner, wealthy or poor, etc. He attacks persons at random. What matters is that the victim be murdered, wounded, threatened or otherwise coerced so that the political, religious or ideological purpose of the perpetrator may be attained. In the eyes of the perpetrator, the victim is simply an anonymous and expendable tool for achieving his aim.

[16] A Roberts, "Can We Define Terrorism?" (2002) 14 *Oxford Today*, at 18.

[17] See among others Y Dinstein, "Terrorism as an International Crime", (1989) 18 *Israel Yearbook on Human Rights*, 55–73.

[18] See M Delmas-Marty, "Les crimes internationaux peuvent-ils contribuer au débat entre universalisme et relativisme des valeurs?" in A Cassese and M Delmas-Marty (eds), *Crimes internationaux et juridictions internationales* (Presses Universitaires de France, Paris, 2002), at 67.

A further distinguishing trait of terrorism is that to amount to an international crime, terrorist acts must show a nexus with an *international* or *internal armed conflict* (that is, a military clash between two States or between armed groups within one State and the government or between such groups), or acquire such a *magnitude* as to exhibit the hallmarks of a crime against humanity, or they must involve State authorities and exhibit a *trans-national dimension,* that is, they do not remain confined to the territory of one State but spill over into and jeopardize the security of other States. This is among other things evidenced by provisions of international treaties that exclude from the treaties' application merely "domestic" terrorism.[19]

Another general feature of terrorism is that it is criminal whether perpetrated by *individuals acting in a private capacity* (normally as members of a terrorist group or organization) or by *State officials.* In the latter case, of course, alongside individual criminal liability there may arise State responsibility: the State on whose behalf the agent engages in terrorist action may incur international responsibility for breaching the international customary and treaty rules that make it unlawful to organize, instigate, assist, finance or participate in terrorist acts in the territory of other States. In the former case States are internationally responsible if they acquiesce in, tolerate or encourage activities within their territory directed towards the commission of such acts abroad.[20]

Depending on the class of crimes to which the terrorist act may belong (war crimes, crimes against humanity, crimes of international terrorism), the victim protected by international law may vary. As we shall see, terrorist acts are prohibited as war crimes when directed against civilians or civilian objects; when they fall under the category of crimes against humanity, they are normally banned if they target civilians (although in my opinion this view, taken in the statutes of various international criminal tribunals, is at variance with customary law); finally, when terrorist acts may be classified as international crimes of terrorism, they are prohibited whatever their target.

V. TERRORISM AS A WAR CRIME

First of all, terrorism may amount to a war crime. As mentioned above, Article 33(1) of the Fourth Geneva Convention of 1949 prohibits acts of

[19] See for instance Article 3 of the UN Convention on terrorist bombing, of 12 January 1998 ("this Convention shall not apply where the offence is committed within a single State, the alleged offender and the victims are nationals of that State, the alleged offender is found in the territory of that State and no other State has a basis under Article 8(1) or Article 6(2) of this Convention to exercise jurisdiction, except that the provisions of Articles 10 to 15 shall, as appropriate, apply in those cases"). For a similar provision see Article 3 of the Convention on financing of terrorism, of 20 January 2000.

[20] See for example the various UN General Assembly resolutions cited in note 14 above.

terrorism committed against civilians eligible for the status of "protected persons", whether they are perpetrated by the armed forces of a belligerent against persons who find themselves in the belligerent's territory as internees, or in an occupied territory. The same acts are of course prohibited if committed by civilians fighting alongside one of the belligerents, or by civilians or organized armed groups fighting against an Occupying Power. As explained in the authoritative *Commentary* published by the International Committee of the Red Cross, this prohibition is motivated by the need to forestall a common practice, that of belligerents resorting to "intimidatory measures to terrorise the population" in the hope of preventing hostile acts.[21]

Similarly, acts of terrorism against civilians or persons that have ceased to take part in the conflict are prohibited in internal armed conflicts (see Article 4(2)(d) of the Second Additional Protocol of 1977), irrespective of the party to the conflict that resorts to terrorist methods.

In addition, under both the First and the Second Additional Protocols "acts or threats of violence the primary purpose of which is to spread terror among the civilian population are prohibited" (Articles 51(2) and 13(2) respectively). These provisions to a large extent take up, extend the scope of, and codify a principle that had already been laid down, albeit exclusively with regard to aerial warfare, in Article 22 of the 1923 Hague Rules on Aerial Warfare. Pursuant to this provision "aerial bombardment for the purpose of terrorizing the civilian population, of destroying or damaging private property not of military character, or of injuring non-combatants is prohibited".[22]

It is thus clear that, under international humanitarian law, terrorism is prohibited and criminalized so long as it is directed *against civilians*. The inference can be drawn that it is allowed against belligerents or, more generally, *combatants*. However, as is underlined in the ICRC *Commentary* to the Additional Protocols to the Geneva Conventions, the fact that some provisions prohibit acts of terrorism without specifying that such acts must be directed against civilians implies that terrorist acts which target objects (such as, for instance, civilian aerial installations) are also prohibited, and therefore criminalized.[23]

The *actus reus* is an attack or a threat of an attack on civilians (or civilian objects), or the adoption of other intimidatory measures designed to spread fear and anguish among civilians. The subjective element must be the intent to carry out unlawful acts or threats or violence against civilians.

[21] See ICRC Commentary, Fourth Geneva Convention (ICRC, Geneva, 1958), at 225–26.
[22] For the text of the Rules and their legal status in international law see A Roberts and R Guelff (eds), *Documents on The Laws of War*, 3rd edn (Oxford University Press, Oxford, 2000), 139–53.
[23] See ICRC, *Commentary on the Additional Protocols to the Geneva Conventions* (M Nijhoff, Geneva, 1986), at 1399, para 4538.

However, this *general intent* must always be accompanied by a *special criminal intent*, that is, to bring about terror (fear, anxiety) among civilians. It is apparent from the relevant provisions that the spreading of threat or fear among civilians must be the "primary purpose" of the unlawful acts or threats of violence.

Interestingly, in a recent case (*Galić*) brought before the International Criminal Tribunal for the former Yugoslavia (ICTY), the Prosecutor raised the issue of the criminal liability of the accused for unlawfully inflicting terror upon civilians as a war crime. The accused was a Bosnian Serb major-general who commanded the troops surrounding and besieging Sarajevo between September 1992 and August 1994. According to the Prosecutor he was responsible under the doctrine of command responsibility for the campaign of sniping and shelling of civilians in Sarajevo by Bosnian Serb troops.[24]

VI. TERRORISM AS A CRIME AGAINST HUMANITY

Acts of terrorism may amount to crimes against humanity when they meet the special requirements of these crimes, that is, when: (i) they are part or a widespread or systematic attack on civilians; and (ii) the perpetrators are aware or cognizant of the fact that their criminal acts are part of a general or systematic pattern of conduct.

It would seem that, when it takes the form of crimes against humanity, terrorism may manifest itself as murder, extermination, torture, rape, persecution or be encompassed by "other inhumane acts".

As under the Statutes of the ICTY, the ICTR and the ICC, the definition of crimes against humanity includes only acts committed against civilians, terrorist acts perpetrated against servicemen or military installations would not fall under the jurisdiction of these tribunals. However, in my opinion customary international law on the matter has a broader scope than those provisions of treaty law (or of binding Security Council resolutions); it also

[24] See the Indictment (Case no IT-98-29-I) and the Prosecutor's Pre-Trial Brief, of 23 October 2001. In this brief the Prosecutor, after briefly referring to the "sniping" and "shelling" incidents (§§15–21), stated as follows: "The principal objective of the campaign of sniping and shelling of civilians was to terrorize the civilian population. The intention to spread terror is evident, *inter alia*, from the widespread nature of civilian activities targeted, the manner in which the unlawful attacks were carried out, and the timing and the duration of the unlawful acts and threats of violence, which consisted of shelling and sniping. The nature of the civilian activities targeted demonstrates that the attacks were designed top strike at the heart, and be maximally disruptive, of civilian life. By attacking when civilians were most vulnerable, such as when seeking the necessities of life, visiting friends or relatives, engaging in burial rites or private prayer, or attending rare recreational events aimed precisely at countering the growing social malaise, the attacks were intended to break the nerve of the population and to achieve the breakdown of the social fabric." (§§ 22–25).

encompasses acts targeting military people or military installations. Consequently, if this view were to be accepted, one could also consider that such terrorist acts as the September 11 crashing of a civilian aircraft into the Pentagon could amount to a crime against humanity (on the assumption that this act was part of a widespread or systematic practice of terrorism against US civilian objects or persons or military personnel or installations).

VII. TERRORISM AS A DISCRETE INTERNATIONAL CRIME

As pointed out above, not all terrorist acts amount to international crimes proper. Terrorist activities carried out within a State (for example, attacks by the terrorist group ETA in Spain or the IRA in the United Kingdom, or by the Red Brigades in Italy) are criminal offences punishable under the law of the relevant State; other States, if bound by treaties with that State, may also be obliged to cooperate in searching for, prosecuting and punishing the perpetrators of terrorist actions.[25]

Terrorist acts amount to *international crimes* when: (i) they are not limited in their effects to one State solely, but *transcend national boundaries* as far as the persons implicated, the means employed and the violence involved are concerned; and (ii) are carried out with the support, the toleration or acquiescence of the State where the terrorist organization is located or of a foreign State. The element of *State-promotion* or *State-toleration*, or even *State acquiescence* due to an inability to eradicate the terrorist organization, seems crucial for elevating the offence to the rank of an international crime. This is so because it is at this stage that terrorism stops being a criminal activity against which States can fight by bilateral or multilateral cooperation, to become (iii) a phenomenon of concern for the *whole international community* and a threat to the peace.

On 12 September 2001 the UN Security Council, in its resolution 1368 (2001) on the terrorist attacks in New York and Washington the previous day, underscored this feature of terrorism, when it stated that it "unequivocally" condemned "in the strongest terms the horrifying terrorist attacks which took place on 11 September 2001 in New York, Washington (D.C.) and Pennsylvania" and regarded such acts, "like any act of international terrorism, as a threat to international peace and security". It would seem that terrorist acts, if they fulfil the above conditions and in addition (iv) are *very serious or large-scale*, may be regarded as international crimes. To quote again that resolution of the Security Council, all States are called upon "to work together urgently to bring to justice the perpetrators, organizers and sponsors of these terrorist attacks; ... those responsible for aiding,

[25] See above, note 10 and the treaty provisions mentioned there.

supporting or harbouring the perpetrators, organizers and sponsors of these acts will be held accountable"; this recommendation was echoed by the General Assembly, in its resolution of 12 September 2001 (Res 56/1).

It would also appear that the general revulsion against this crime, as evinced by increasingly frequent and consistent statements and declarations of many States as well as resolutions of international organizations, coupled with parallel acts and conduct of States fighting terrorism at various levels, indicates that international terrorism, as defined above, has become a crime proscribed by customary international law. Consequently, any State is legally entitled to bring to trial the alleged authors of such acts of terrorism who are found on its territory.

The *actus reus* of the crime of terrorism has been substantially delineated above: (i) terrorist acts must constitute a criminal offence under most national legal systems (for example, assault, murder, kidnapping, hostage-taking, extortion, bombing, torture, arson, etc.); (ii) they must be aimed at spreading terror (that is, fear and intimidation) by means of the threat or use of violent action among the public or particular groups of persons; and (iii) they must be politically, ideologically or religiously motivated, that is not motivated by private ends. It should be noted that the *victims* of terrorist acts may be both civilians and military personnel, or other public officials.

As for *mens rea*, State practice, national legislation as well as the conventions mentioned above all point in the same direction. In addition to the subjective element required for the underlying offence (serious bodily harm, murder, kidnapping, arson, destruction of private or public property, etc), there must be a *special intent*, that is, to spread terror among the population.

VIII. CATEGORIES OF TERRORIST ACTION PROHIBITED BY TREATY

In addition to the categories of crimes considered so far, one should also take into account those terrorist acts that are explicitly banned by the various treaties on terrorism mentioned above.[26] As in my opinion international crimes proper are only those which are provided for in international customary law and which offend universal values recognized and upheld in international legal rules, these specific acts of terrorism should not be characterized as international crimes proper. What matters, however, more than any legal definition or classification of those crimes, is the manner in which they are repressed. What is striking in the treaties at issue is that they aim at coordinating the prosecution and punishment of those

[26] See on these treaties AF Panzera, *Attività terroristiche e diritto internazionale* (Jovene, Napoli, 1978), 35–109; G Guillaume, "Terrorisme et droit international", above n 4, at 330–31, 338–71.

terrorist offences by the contracting States. In other words, the primary purpose of those treaties is to achieve the prompt and effective punishment of terrorism by *national* authorities. Each contracting State is duty bound to cooperate in and lend assistance to the repression of terrorism, that is, the apprehension and prosecution or extradition of alleged perpetrators of terrorist acts. No international body is entrusted with the task of prosecuting and punishing those criminal offences.

IX. FINAL OBSERVATIONS

International *substantive* rules on international crimes of terrorism are fairly satisfactory. In addition to covering most manifestations of terrorism, they regard as criminal all terrorist acts whether they emanate from private individuals or State officials. However, in spite of the apparent trend emerging in the UN towards universal and unqualified condemnation of terrorism, many developing States still cling to the old political doctrine whereby so-called "freedom fighters" are entitled to shirk the stigma of terrorism on account of the political ends they pursue. This political stand has generated much confusion and spawned a tendency to hold the view that there still does not exist a generally accepted definition of terrorism. On the contrary, however, international rules do cover in sufficiently clear terms at least the most conspicuous and odious manifestations of terrorism.

Nonetheless, as usual, where international law fails is at the *enforcement* level. As I have briefly noted above, even international treaties on specific classes of terrorism are relatively disappointing as far as repression is concerned, for they do not impose upon contracting States an explicit obligation to prosecute and bring to justice alleged terrorists on their territory. In addition, neither national nor international courts have made effective use of the existing potential of international legal rules, subject to a few exceptions (such as Israeli or US courts[27] or Scottish courts sitting in the Netherlands, in the *Lockerbie* case[28]). In particular, it is a matter of regret that the ICC has not been granted jurisdiction over terrorist acts and that rather than relying on collective enforcement or international judicial cooperation, many States still tend to tackle the question forcibly, that is by use of military violence, often preferring this response to that of resort to criminal justice.

[27] For US cases, se for example those reported in RA Friedlander (ed), above n 12, 227–317 and 369–429, plus the cases cited above at notes 1 and 2. For Israeli cases see for example (1989) 19 *Israel Yearbook on Human Rights*, 371–97.

[28] See *Her Majesty's Advocate* v. *Al-Megrahi and Lamen Khalifa Fhimah*, High Court of Justice, decision of 31 January 2001, on line: <http://www.scotscourts.gov.uk/html/lockerbie.asp#verdict>.

11

The Exercise of Criminal Jurisdiction over International Terrorists

ROBERT KOLB

I. THE PROBLEM OF DEFINING INTERNATIONAL TERRORISM

IT IS NOT possible to talk about the suppression of a criminal act by the exercise of criminal jurisdiction if the act in question is not properly defined. The problem is rendered even more acute in modern criminal systems predicated on the liberal principle of *nullum crimen sine lege*.[1] The question of a proper definition is particularly delicate in the context of international terrorism. It is not only political divisions on essential points (such as the question of State terrorism, the issue of the means used by movements of national liberation or by secessionist movements, whether the motives of terrorists should be taken into account or only their acts, the question of who is an "innocent" target, etc)[2], which have proved to be insurmountable obstacles up to the present. It is also the

[1] This principle was developed at the time of enlightenment as a protection against arbitrary acts and extraordinary penalties (*poenae extraordinariae*). The formula was coined by JPA von Feuerbach (*Lehrbuch des peinlichen Rechts* (1801), 20). On Feuerbach, see J Bohnert, *P.J.A. Feuerbach und der Bestimmtheitsgrundsatz im Strafrecht* (Minutes of the meeting of the Heidelberger academy of the sciences, philosophical — historical class, Heidelberg, 1982). See Cicero, *In Verrem*, lib II, cap XXXXII; T Hobbes, *De Cive*, cap XIII and *Leviathan*, cap XXVIII; S Pufendorf, *De iure naturae et gentium*, lib VIII, cap III, par VII. See also the foreshadowing of the principle as a maxim of interpretation in *Dig*. 50, 16, 131 (Ulpianus); and *Dig*. 50, 16, 244 (Paulus), both in the title "de verborum significatione". On these historical sources, see HL Schreiber, *Gesetz und Richter – Zur geschichtlichen Entwicklung des Satzes nullum cimen, nulla poena sine lege* (Frankfurt, 1976).

[2] On these questions there is very ample literature. See eg R Mushkat, "Technical Impediments on the Way to A Universal Definition of International Terrorism", (1980) 20 *Indian Journal of International Law*, 20, 448 ff: J Dugard, "International Terrorism: Problems of Definition", (1974) 50 *International Affairs*, 75 ff. For a more recent assessment, see J Dugard, "Terrorism and International Law: Consensus at Last?", *Essays in Honour of M Bedjaoui* (The Hague v Law International, 1999), 159 ff. The differences of opinion persist up to the present work of the United Nations bodies. See the Summary of the exchanges of views in the *Report of the Ad Hoc Committee Established by General Assembly Resolution 51/210 of 17 December 1996*, GAOR, 56th Session, Suppl no 37 (A/56/37), Fifth Session (12–23 February 2001), Annex V,

intrinsic difficulty of grasping the constitutive elements of a crime which is over-loaded with different connotations and of finding any general element, common to its multifaceted expressions.[3] It would seem, at first sight, that "terrorism" is the catch-word for a number of crimes somewhat haphazardly thrown together under this heading.[4] One may add to this the multiplicity of functional definitions valid only in a specific context. "Terrorism" for the purpose of seizing financial assets of doubtful groups may not necessarily correspond to "terrorism" when dealing with individual criminal prosecution.[5] Add to this that there are numerous definitions of terrorism under the domestic laws of States, definitions which differ significantly from one to the other. Each of them reflects a specific focus, due to the particular socio-political history and concerns of the collectivity in question.[6] Some other problems can still be added to those mentioned. For example, international terrorist offences possess only a limited autonomy with respect to those defined in the municipal law of the various States. As there is an interplay between both legal orders, if only for the fact that the enforcement of international law rests largely on municipal law and the organs of the State, conflicts and tensions between these legal orders may appear.[7] Further, there is uncertainty as to the role assigned to elements of subjective qualification of the crime of terrorism, especially intent or motive.[8] To this list of difficulties others could easily be added.

p. 11 ff. See also the *Report of the Working Group, Sixth Committee, Measures to Eliminate International Terrorism*, 29 October 2001, Doc. A/C.6/56/L.9, Annex IV, p. 33 ff. On the ambiguities within the United Nations in that field, see also JM Sorel, "Le système onusien et le terrorisme ou l'histoire d'une ambiguïté volontaire", (1996) 6 *L'observateur des Nations Unies*, 31 ff.

[3]See C Daase, "Terrorismus — Begriffe, Theorien und Gegenstrategien", (2001) 76 *Die Friedenswarte*, 59.
[4]See R Higgins, "The General International Law of Terrorism", in R Higgins and M Flory (eds), *Terrorism and International Law*, (London / New York, Routledge, 1997), 27.
[5]See T Stein, "International Measures Against Terrorism and Sanctions by and Against Third States", (1992) 30 *Archiv des Völkerrechts*, 40; JF Murphy, "Defining International Terrorism: A Way Out of the Quagmire", (1989) 19 *Israel Yearbook on Human Rights*, 32 ff.
[6]Some overview over that state of affairs is offered by the periodic reports prepared by the Secretary-General of the United Nations, eg *Report of 3 July 2001*, Doc. A/56/160, p. 3 ff., and the Addendum, A/56/160/Add. 1. At the level of Europe, see the Report of the Commission of the E.C., *Proposal for a Council Framework Decision on Combating Terrorism*, 19 September 2001, COM(2001)521, p. 6–7. A Resolution by the Organization of American States calls its members to provide similar information on their internal legislation to the Organization: *Plan of Action on Hemispheric Cooperation to Prevent, Combat, and Eliminate Terrorism*, Resolution of 26 April 1996, see <http://www.oas.org/juridico>.
[7]On such problems, see eg B Stern, "A propos de la compétence universelle", *Essays in Honor of M. Bedjaoui*, (The Hague / London / Boston, Kluwer Law International, 1999), 741–6. See also JA Carrillo Sacedo, "Les aspects juridiques du terrorisme international", *Centre d'étude et de recherche de droit international et de relations internationales*, Hague Academy of International Law, *Les aspects juridiques du terrorisme international*, (1988 Session, The Hague / Boston / London, 1989), 20.
[8]See eg Murphy, above n 5, 22 ff; Mushkat, above n 2, 464 ff; TM Franck and BB Lockwood, "Preliminary Thoughts Towards an International Convention on Terrorism", (1974)

Faced with these obstacles due to a high level of conceptual uncertainty and a equally high level of political dissent, international practice has for a long time tried to avoid defining the general concept of terrorism. After an unsuccessful attempt in 1937, with an anti-terrorist Convention signed under the auspices of the League of Nations containing a general definition of terrorism,[9] and a clear deadlock in the United Nations after the events at the Olympic games of 1972,[10] a new approach to the problem was adopted. The international community shied away from any attempt to tackle the problem of terrorism generally. Instead, it was considered more conducive to success to suppress specific acts of terrorism, on which some consensus could be achieved, often after tragic events. This so-called sectoral approach produced a long series of conventions, each one dealing with a specific form of terrorism. While the subject matter of these conventions thus varies, the provisions directed at criminal prosecution are largely similar. We are thus confronted with a network of treaties,

68 *American Journal of International Law*, 78–80; K Skubiszewski, "Definition of Terrorism", (1989) 19 *Israel Yearbook on Human Rights*, 50–1. The modern tendencies are to exclude motive from the definition of terrorism through a clause termed "regardless of motive": see for example the Resolution of the Sixth Committee of the United Nations (19 November 2001), A/C.6/56/L.22, para 2: "Reiterates that criminal acts intended or calculated to provoke a state of terror in the general public, a group of persons or particular persons for political purposes are in any circumstances unjustifiable, whatever the considerations of a political, philosophical, ideological, racial, ethnic, religious or other nature that may be invoked to justify them". It will be nd that there is a distinction between the general political or ideological purposes of the action (as distinguished from purely personal or private ends) and the specific motives, the concrete political, religious or other causes, which are irrelevant.

[9] On the Convention of 1937, see A Sottile, "Le terrorisme international", (1938-III) 65 *Recueil des Cours de l'Académie de Droit International*, 116 ff. P Wurth, *La répression internationale du terrorisme*, thèse, (Lausanne, 1941) 48 ff and 91 ff; H Mosler, "Die Konferenz zur internationalen Bekämpfung des Terrorismus", (1938) 8 *ZaöRV*, 99 ff; H Donnedieu de Vabres, "La répression internationale du terrorisme: Les Conventions de Genève (16 novembre 1937)", (1938) 19 *Revue de droit international et de législation comparée*, 37 ff; V Pella, "Les Conventions de Genève pour la prévention et la répression du terrorisme et pour la création de la Cour pénale internationale", (1938) 18 *Revue de droit pénal et de criminologie et archives internationales de médecine légale*, 402 ff; AF Panzera, *Attività terroristiche e diritto internazionale* (Naples, 1978), 22 ff; T Herzog, *Terrorismus — Versuch einer Definition und Analyse internationaler Uebereinkommen zu seiner Bekämpfung* (Frankfurt/Main, 1991), 170 ff; E Chadwick, *Self-Determination, terrorism and the International Humanitarian Law of Armed Conflict* (The Hague / Boston / London, Kluwer, 1996), 97 ff. On the drafting of the Convention: G von Gretschaninow, "Der Plan eines internationalen Abkommens betreffend die Bekämpfung politischer Verbrechen und die Errichtung eines internationalen Strafgerichtshofes", (1945) 5 *ZaöRV*, 181 ff. For the official documents: League of Nations, *Actes de la Conférence internationale pour la répression du terrorisme*, Doc. C.94. M. 47 1935 V.

[10] See SM Finger, "International Terrorism and the United Nations", in Y Alexander (ed), *International Terrorism—National, Regional and Global Perspectives* (New York, Simon & Schuster, 1976), 323 ff. L Migliorini, "International Terrorism in the United Nations Debates", (1976) 2 *Italian Yearbook of International Law*, 102 ff. JF Murphy, "United Nations Proposals on the Control and Repression of Terrorism", in MC Bassiouni (ed), *International Terrorism and Political Crimes* (Springfield, Thomas, 1975), 493 ff; Panzera, above n 9, 112 ff; R Lagoni, "Die Vereinten Nationen und der internationale Terrorismus", (1977) 32 *Europa Archiv*, 171 ff.

which could easily be unified by listing the several acts they prohibit and by adding the common jurisdictional provisions aimed at criminal repression. These treaties are mainly the following:[11] the three Conventions on the Safety of Civil Aviation of Tokyo (14 September 1963, Convention on Offences and Certain Other Acts Committed on Board Aircraft), The Hague (16 December 1970, Convention for the Suppression of Unlawful Seizure of Aircraft) and Montreal (23 September 1971, Convention for the Suppression of Unlawful Acts against the Safety of Civil Aviation, with its supplementing Protocol on the Suppression of Unlawful Acts of Violence at Airports Serving International Civil Aviation signed at Montreal on 24 February 1988);[12] the United Nations Convention on the Prevention and Punishment of Crimes against Internationally Protected Persons, including Diplomatic Agents, adopted via General Assembly Resolution 3166 (XXVIII) on 14 December 1973;[13] the *New York* Convention against

[11] See the list of treaties presented at: <http://www.untreaty.un.org/English/terrorism.asp>; see also the list in the report by the Secretary General of the United Nations, *Measures to Eliminate International Terrorism*, A/56/160, 3 July 2001, 18 ff or C Bassiouni, "International Terrorism", in C Bassiouni (ed), *International Criminal Law*, vol I, 2nd edn (New York, Transnational, 1999), 767 ff. For a list of these Conventions with a brief comment on each, see B Boutros-Ghali, "The United Nations and Comprehensive Legal Measures for Combating International Terrorism", *Essays in Honor of E Suy* (The Hague / Boston / London, Martinus Nijhoff, 1998), 290 ff.

[12] On these Conventions, see JM Breton, "Piraterie aérienne et droit international public", (1971) 75 *Revue Générale de Droit International Public,* 392 ff; G Guillaume, "La Convention de La Haye du 16 décembre 1970 pour la répression de la capture illicite d'aéronefs", (1970) 16 *Annuaire Français de Droit International,* 35 ff; RH Mankievicz, "La Convention de Montréal (1971) pour la répression d'actes illicites dirigés contre la sécurité de l'aviation civile", (1971) 17 *Annuaire Français de Droit International,* 855 ff; K Hailbronner, *Luftpiraterie in rechtlicher Sicht* (Hannover, 1972); C Emmanuelli, "Etude des moyens de prévention et de sanction en cas d'action illicite contre l'aviation civile internationale", (1973) 77 *Revue Générale de Droit International Public,* 577 ff; E McWhinney, "Illegal Diversion of Aircraft and International Law", (1973-I) 138 *Recueil des Cours de l'Académie de Droit International,* 261 ff. E McWhinney, *Aerial Piracy and International Terrorism,* 2nd edn (Dordrecht, Kluwer, 1987). WD Joyner, *Aerial Hijacking as an International Crime* (Oceana, New York, 1974); *Proceedings of the Conference held in the Hague, Aviation Security,* Leyden, 1987; B Cheng, "Aviation, Criminal Jurisdiction and Terrorism: The Hague Extradition/Prosecution Formula and Attacks at Airports", *Essays in Honor of G Schwarzenberger* (London, 1988), 25 ff. Y Alexander and E Socher (eds), *Aerial Piracy and Aviation Security* (Dordrecht, Martinus Nijhoff, 1990); G Guillaume, "Terrorisme et droit international", (1989-III) 215 *Recueil des Cours de l'Académie de Droit International,* 311 ff; Panzera, above n 9, 45 ff; Herzog, above n 9, 201 ff. See also the *Ekanayake* case (1986), Sri Lanka Court of Appeals, 87 *ILR,* 296 ff. and the *Yunis (no 2)* case (1988), US District Court, 82 *ILR,* 344 ff, 347–49, confirmed by the Court of Appeals (88 *ILR,*176 ff).

[13] On this Convention, see LM Blomfield and GF Fitzgerald, *Crimes Against Internationally protected Persons: Prevention and Punishment. An Analysis of the UN Convention* (New York, Praeger, 1975); M Wood, "The Convention on the Prevention and Punishment of Crimes against Internationally Protected Persons, Including Diplomatic Agents", (1974) 23 *International and Comparative Law Quarterly,* 791 ff; F Przetacznik, "Convention on the Prevention and Punishment of Crimes Against Internationally Protected Persons", (1974) 52 *Revue de droit international, de sciences diplomatiques et politiques,* 208 ff; AF Panzera, "La Convenzione sulla prevenzione e la repressione dei reati contro persone che godono di protezione internazionale", (1975) 58 *Rivista di diritto internazionale,* 80 ff; Panzera,

the taking of Hostages (17 December 1979);[14] the Rome Convention for the Suppression of Unlawful Acts against the Safety of Maritime Navigation with its attending Protocol on the Safety of Fixed Platforms Located on the Continental Shelf, both concluded on 10 March 1988;[15] and the International Convention for the Suppression of Terrorist Bombings adopted via General Assembly Resolution on 25 November 1997.[16] One may also mention the Convention on the Physical Protection of Nuclear Material, adopted at Vienna on 26 October 1979,[17] and the International Convention for the Suppression of the Financing of Terrorism adopted by the United Nations General Assembly on the 9 December 1999.[18] Apart from the very first of these treaties, the Tokyo Convention, all the other

above n 9, 77–87; Herzog, above n 9, 319–42; Finger, above n 10, 337 ff; JJ Lambert, *Terrorism and Hostages in International Law: A Commentary on the Hostages Convention* 1979 (Cambridge, Cambridge University Press, 1990); AC McWillson, *Hostage-Taking Terrorism: Incident-Response Strategy* (Basingstoke, St Martin's Press, 1992).

[14] On this Convention, see R Rosenstock, "The International Convention Against the Taking of Hostages: Another International Community Step Againt Terrorism", (1980) 10 *Denver Journal of International Law and Policy*, 169 ff; S Rosenne, "The International Convention Against the Taking of Hostages", (1980) 10 *Israel Yearbook of International Law*, 109 ff; HG Kausch, "Das internationale Uebereinkommen gegen Geiselnahme", (1980) 28 *Vereinte Nationen*, 77 ff; KW Platz, "Internationale Konvention gegen Geiselnahme", (1980) 40 *Zeitschrift für ausländisches öffentliches Recht und Völkerrecht*, 276 ff; S Shubber, "The International Convention Agaist the Taking of Hostages", (1981) 52 *British Yearbook of International Law*, 205 ff; Herzog, above n 9, 343–74. See also the *Von Dardel v USSR* case, US District Court (1985), 77 *ILR*, 274.

[15] See A Cassese, *Terrorism, Politics and Law: The Achille Lauro Affair* (Cambridge, Cambridge University Press, 1989); D Momtaz, "La Convention sur la répression d'actes illicites contre la sécurité de la navigation maritime", (1988) 34 *Annuaire Français de Droit International*, 589 ff; G Plant, "The Convention for the Suppression of Unlawful Acts Against the Safety of Maritime Navigation", (1990) 39 *International and Comparative Law Quarterly*, 27 ff; C Joyner, "The 1988 IMO Convention on the Safety of Marine Navigation: Towards a Legal Remedy for Terrorism at Sea", (1988) 31 *German Yearbook of International Law*, 230 ff; F Francioni, "Maritime Terrorism and International Law: The Rome Convention of 1988", (1988) 31 *German Yearbook of International Law*, 263 ff; M Halberstam, "Terrorism on the High Seas: The Achille Lauro, Piracy and the IMO Convention on Maritime Safety", (1988) 82 *American Journal of International Law*, 269 ff; N Ronzitti (ed), *Maritime Terrorism and International Law* (Dordrecht, Kluwer, 1990); M Munchau, *Terrorismus auf See aus völkerrechtlicher Sicht*, (Frankfurt, 1994); Herzog, above n 9, 290–309.

[16] Annex to Resolution A/52/653, 7 ff. See (1998) 37 *ILM*, 249 ff. SM Witten, "The International Convention for the Suppression of Terrorist Bombings", (1998) 92 *American Journal of International Law*, 774 ff; SA Williams, "The Terrorist Bombings Convention: Another Step Forward in the Fight against International Terror Violence", in Canadian Council on International Law (ed), *From Territorial Sovereignty to Human Security* (The Hague, Kluwer, 2000), 96 ff.

[17] For its text, see (1979) 18 *ILM*, 1419 ff. On this Convention, see International Atomic Energy Agency (ed), *Convention on the Physical Protection of Nuclear Material* (New York, 1982).

[18] For its text, see (2000) 39 *ILM*, 268 ff. On this Convention, see R Lavalle, "The International Convention for the Suppression of the Financing of Terrorism", (2000) 60 *Zeitschrift für ausländisches öffentliches Recht und Völkerrecht*, 491 ff. A Aust, "Counter-Terrorism, a New Approach: The International Convention for the Suppression of the Financing of Terrorism", (2001) 5 *Max Planck Yearbook on United Nations Law*, 285 ff.

texts contain a clause according to which the State on whose territory the alleged offender is found is obliged in any case whatsoever and without delay to extradite him or to submit him to the competent authorities for prosecution (*aut dedere aut prosequi*, or *aut dedere aut judicare* clause). Currently, for the first time since the deadlock of 1973, the United Nations envisages a general convention on terrorism.[19] These efforts follow the particularly appalling events of 11 September 2001, which have given a new impetus to the search for an international consensus on terrorism.

These efforts have been paralleled by similar action at the regional level, where stronger cultural and political ties seem to allow less burdensome action. The Organization of American States opened the path with the adoption of the Convention to Prevent and Punish Acts of Terrorism Taking the Form of Crimes against Persons and Related Extortion that are of International Significance (Washington DC, 1971).[20] The European Convention on the Suppression of Terrorism (Strasbourg, 1977)[21] followed which focuses on facilitating extradition by limiting the availability of the political-offence exception. However, this aim was imperfectly realised, due to some exceptions to the stated principle and the possibility to enter reservations, a possibility used by some States. The partial closing, at least, of such loopholes was soon considered necessary. Consequently, the European Community drafted the Dublin Convention of 1980.[22] Its official title is: Agreement Concerning the Application of the

[19] See Resolution of the 6th Committee of the GA, A/C.6/56/L.22, 19 November 2001, para 16. See also the *Report of the Working Group*, above n 2.

[20] For the text of the Convention: (1971) 10 *ILM*, 255 ff. On this Convention, see RS Brach, "The Inter-American Convention on the Kidnapping of Diplomats", (1971) 10 *Colombia Journal of Transnational Law*, 392 ff; P Juillard, "Les enlèvements de diplomates", (1971) 17 *Annuaire Français de Droit International*, 223 ff; F Przetacznik, "Convention on the Special Protection of Officials of Foreign States and International Organizations", (1973) 9 *Revue belge de droit international*, 455 ff; PP Camargo, "La protección interamericana de functionarios diplomáticos y consulares contra el terrorismo", (1973/4) 26/7 *REDI*, 111 ff. Panzera, above n 9, 74–77; Herzog, above n 9, 310–328.

[21] See the text of the Convention in (1976) 15 *ILM*, 1272 ff. On the European Convention, see C Vallee, "La Convention européenne pour la répression du terrorisme", (1976) 22 *Annuaire Français de Droit International*, 756 ff; L Migliorino, "Iniziative europee nella lotta al terrorismo: la Convenzione del 27 gennaio 1977", (1977) 13 *Rivista di diritto internazionale privato e processuale*, 469 ff; T Stein, "Die Europäische Konvention zur Bekämpfung des Terrorismus", (1977) 37 *ZaöRV*, 668 ff; G Fraysse- Druesne, "La Convention européenne pour la répression du terrorisme", (1978) 82 *Revue Générale de Droit International Public*, 969 ff; F Mosconi, "La Convenzione europea per la repressione del terrorismo", (1979) 62 *RDI*, 303 ff; AV Lowe and JR Young, "Suppressing Terrorism under the European Convention: A British Perspective", (1978) 25 *Netherlands International Law Review*, 305 ff; I Lacoste, *Die Europaïsche Terrorismus-Konvention* (Zurich, 1982); HJ Bartsch, "Das europäische Übereinkommen zur Bekämpfung des Terrorismus", (1977) 30 *Neue Juristische Woche*, 1985 ff; R Linke, "Das europäische Übereinkommen zur Bekämpfung des Terrorismus vom 27 Jänner 1977", (1977) 32 *Oesterreichische Juristenzeitung*, 232 ff; Panzera, above n 9, 129–136; Herzog, above n 9, 375–431.

[22] Its text can be found in (1980) 19 *ILM*, 325 ff. See eg G Gilbert, "The Law and Transnational Terrorism", (1995) 26 *Netherlands Yearbook of International Law*, 19 ff.

European Convention on the Suppression of Terrorism among the Member States of the European Community. Its purpose, amongst others, is to limit the opposability of reservations to the European Convention as among member States of the Community. Next was the Convention on the Suppression of Terrorism of the South Asian Association for Regional Cooperation (Kathmandu, 1986).[23] This treaty focuses on extradition and contains a *aut dedere aut prosequi* clause.[24] On 22 April 1998, the Arab League opened to signature the Arab Convention on the Suppression of Terrorism (Cairo, 1998).[25] Three more conventions may be mentioned: First, the Convention of the Organization of the Islamic Conference on Combating International Terrorism (Ouagadougou, 1999).[26] It contains a sweeping definition of terrorism (Article 1(2)) and concentrates on cooperation to fight terrorism and on extradition; it does not contain an *aut dedere* clause. Second, the Convention of the Organization of African Unity on the Prevention and the Combating of Terrorism (Algiers, 1999).[27] In contrast to the previous agreement, this convention contains an *aut dedere aut prosequi* clause.[28] Third, the Treaty on Cooperation among States Members of the Commonwealth of Independent States in Combating Terrorism (Minsk, 1999).[29]

Most of these sectoral or regional conventions are concerned only with specific types of terrorist acts and do thus not contain any general definition of terrorism. Their subject matter is defined according to the principle of speciality. However, an adding up of those several definitions leads to a body of law covering a considerable segment of terrorist activities. It may be advantageous for any comprehensive definition of terrorism to operate a *renvoi* (referral) to those texts, while adding a second limb with a more general definition of terrorism, designed to complement those special expressions. In the chain of these sectoral conventions, the first text to express a general definition of terrorism was the Convention for the Suppression of the Financing of Terrorism (1999).[30] We should, however,

[23] See the text with a short introductory commentary in H Levie (ed), *Terrorism — Documents of International and Local Control*, vol. 10, (New York, Oceana Publications, 1996), 313 ff. The text is also printed in (1987) 27 *Indian Journal of International Law*, 308 ff.

[24] The *aut dedere* clause is in Article 4.

[25] See its text at: <http:www.web.amnesty.org/ai.nsf/recent/IOR510012002?Open Document>.

[26] See its text at: <http:www.oic-un.org/26icfm/c.html>; on the role of the Islamic conference in combating terrorism, see E Alehabib, "The role of Islamic Conference in Combating Terrorism", (1999/2000) 11 *The Iranian Journal of International Affairs*, 524 ff.

[27] See H Boukrif, "Quelques commentaires et observations sur la Convention de l'Organisation de l'Unité Africaine sur la prévention et la lutte contre contre le terrorisme", (2001) 11 *African Journal of International and Comparative Law*, 753 ff.

[28] See Art 6(4). Text of the Convention in Boukrif, *ibid*, 765 ff.

[29] It has been deposited with the Secretariat of the Community of Independent States.

[30] See Art 2 ((2000) 39 *ILM*, 271). Art 2 first makes a *renvoi* to the treaties mentioned in its annex (the previous sectoral conventions), and then adds in letter (b): "[A terrorist offence for the purposes of this Convention is] any other act intended to cause death or serious bodily

not conclude too hastily that such a definition, contained in a sectoral convention, really embodies an all-purposive definition of terrorist acts. In fact, such definitions are always expressly limited to the specific convention at stake ("for the purposes of this convention…"). They are more functional than general. Thus, in a convention on combating doubtful financial streams, a field where terrorist groups merge into other organised criminality, one may well expect a broad definition of the activities covered. Only then can proper investigations be guaranteed, there being moreover no reason to limit such investigations by a narrow scope of the activities encompassed. The question will present itself under another angle if a convention deals with individual criminal prosecution. Here the principle of the *nullum crimen* poses more stringent conditions and generally the focus is different.

This being said, it is still possible to analyze the various definitions of terrorism which have been envisaged during the 20th century and after 11 September 2001. From a bird's perspective, it can immediately be said that the crime of terrorism has proven too multifaceted and composite to be expressed in a simple definition. Given the extraordinary variety of the acts under scrutiny, it was deemed preferable to indicate the typical elements, which define the range and provide the measuring tool for the phenomenon to be considered. Consequently, all the attempts at definition more or less split up the phenomenon into several elements whose variable, indeed spectral, interaction is thought to flexibly bundle up the diverse forms of expression of political violence. In that sense, all definitions of terrorism are "elementary" definitions: they combine different elements, either cumulatively or alternatively. In particular, some aspects can be envisioned as central, while others are peripheral, their absence not being fatal to the qualification of certain acts as terrorist.[31]

A. Single Element Definitions

There are only a few definitions which focus on a single element. These definitions are concerned with the specific means used by the offenders in order to achieve their political ends. Thus, for example, some authors and some official texts equate terrorist acts with criminal violence using

injury to a civilian, or to any other person not taking an active part in the hostilities in a situation of armed conflict, when the purpose of such act, by its nature or context, is to intimidate a population, or to compel a government or an international organization to do or to abstain from doing any act".

[31] For such an approach, see in particular C Greenwood, "Terrorism and Humanitarian Law — The debate Over Additional Protocol I", (1989) 19 *Israel Yearbook on Human Rights*, 189.

"indiscriminate means".[32] Other texts add to this element the further alternative of the use of "heinous means" ("*moyens odieux*").[33] For the reasons already pointed out, it does not seem that such one-tier definitions are able to adequately deal with the complex phenomenon of terrorist violence. Non-discrimination may well be a distinctive sign of some terrorist actions, but it by no means exhausts the phenomenon. Consider, for example, the killing of carefully selected persons of symbolic value. Furthermore, not all indiscriminate violence must necessarily be terrorist. Apart from the question of State terrorism (eg indiscriminate bombings), there is also the aspect of individuals using random violence for non-political ends. It may then well be doubtful if such a crime must be termed terrorist, or if there is much to be gained by such a qualification. The classical example is the threat or use of indiscriminate means in order to extort money from a targeted company or group; or the use of a bomb killing many people randomly if the ultimate aim is to kill a specific person in order to gain the proceeds of his life-insurance.

Another form of one-tier definition is to define a series of acts of violence which amount to terrorism if the foreign ministry (in the United States the Secretary of State) designates the organisation from which they emanate as a terrorist group. This is the basis of Sections 1182(a)(3) and 1189(a)(1) of the Antiterrorism and Effective Death Penalty Act (1996) in the United States of America.[34] This simplified definition rests on a political

[32] See eg *T v Secretary of State for the Home Department*, England, Court of Appeal, (1994) 104 *ILR*, 656 ff, 663, 665: "the use of indiscriminate violence which would or might lead to the deaths of innocent people". See also the *SAARC Convention* (above n 23), Art 1(e): which defines a terrorist act as the commission of certain acts plus indiscriminate means: "Murder, manslaughter, assault causing bodily harm, kidnapping, hostage-taking and offences relating to firearms, weapons, explosives and dangerous substances when used as a means to perpetrate indiscriminate violence involving death or serious bodily injury to persons or serious damage to property".

[33] See eg, the Centre d'étude et de recherche de droit international et de relations internationales, Hague Academy of International Law, *Les aspects juridiques du terrorisme international*, 1988 Session (The Hague, Kluwer, 1989), 16: "Les actes terroristes au sens des présents principes sont, entre autres, les agressions ou les menaces contre la vie ou l'intégrité affectant aveuglément des personnes, ou utilisant des méthodes odieuses condamnées par la communauté internationale…".

[34] See 8 USC § 1182(a)(3)(B)(ii): "Terrorist activity is defined as any activity which is: unlawful… where it is committed…, and which involves any of the following: (I) The hijacking or sabotage of any conveyance (including an aircraft, vessel or vehicle). (II) The seizing or detaining, and threatening to kill, injure or continue to detain, another individual in order to compel a third person (including a governmental organization) to do or to abstain from doing any act as an explicit or implicit condition for the release of the individual seized or detained. (III) A violent attack upon an internationally protected person…or upon the liberty of such a person. (IV) An assassination. (V) the use of any — (a) biological agent, chemical agent, or nuclear weapon or device, or (b) explosive or firearm (other than for mere personal monetary gain), with the intent to endanger, directly or indirectly, the safety of one or more individuals or to cause substantial damage to property. (VI) A threat, attempt, or conspiracy to do any of the foregoing". For an application of this section, see the *People's Mojahedin*

qualification process with all its selectivity and unilateralism.[35] It hardly recommends itself for international relations where there is no comparable authority and where any broad consensus as to the groups to be put in that category is lacking. For this reason the Security Council of the United Nations is equally unsuited to perform any function of this type.

B. Two Element Definitions

There are other definitions which rely essentially on two elements, however combined. Some sources stress the elements of terror (intimidation)/purpose;[36] or the elements terror (intimidation)/coercion;[37] or specified acts of violence/political purpose;[38] or such acts of violence/

Organization of Iran v US Department of State (1999), US Court of Appeals, Columbia, (1999) 38 *ILM*, 1287 ff.

[35] Section 1189(a)(1) of the quoted act empowers the Secretary of State to designate a foreign terrorist organization if he finds three things: (1) the organization is a foreign organization; (2) the organization engages in terrorist activity as defined by the applicable provisions; and (3) the terrorist activity of the organization threatens the security of the United States nationals or the national security of the United States.

[36] See for example M Williams and SJ Chatterjee, "Suggesting Remedies for International Terrorism, Use of Available International Means", (1976) 5 *International Relations*, 1071: "... terrorism may be defined as an act directed to create fear, panic and/or alarm by means of violence or the threat thereof with a view or not to achieving certain purposes, political or otherwise". See also Sottile, above n 9, 96: "... *acte criminel perpétré par la terreur, la violence, par une grande intimidation en vue d'atteindre un certain but*". See also *Resolution on Measures to Eliminate International Terrorism*, UNGA, Sixth Committee, A/C.6/56/L.22, 19 November 2001, para 2: "... criminal acts intended or calculated to provoke a state of terror in the general public, a group of persons or particular persons for political purposes ...".

[37] See G Wardlaw, *Political Terrorism: Theory, Tactics and Counter-Measures* (Cambridge, Cambridge University Press, 1982), 16: "... the use, or threat of use, of violence by an individual or a group, whether acting for or in opposition to established authority, when such action is designed to create extreme anxiety and / or fear–inducing effects in a target group larger than the immediate victims with the purpose of coercing that group into acceding to the political demands of the perpetrators". See also the proposal of the Ivory Coast at the United nations Ad Hoc Committee Established by GA Resolution 51/210 of 17 December 1996, *Report of the Fifth Session (12–23 February 2001)*, GAOR, 56th Session, Suppl no 37 (A/56/37), Annex III, p. 6: "Terrorism means any act or omission, whoever the author or authors, that is intended to inflict terror, that is, fear, panic or serious and profound anguish, upon one or more natural or legal persons, with a view to coercing such person or persons, in particular the government authorities of a State or an international organization, to take or to refrain from taking some action".

[38] See ILA, *Report of the Sixty-First Conference*, Paris Session, 1984, p. 314: "... acts of international terrorism include but are not limited to atrocities, wanton killing, hostage taking, hijacking, extortion, or torture committed or threatened to be committed whether in peacetime or in wartime for political purposes ...". At the level of municipal law, see the Immigration Amendment Act of New Zealand, 1978: "(a) any act that involves the taking of human life, or threatening to take human life, or the wilful or reckless endangering of human life, carried out for the purpose of furthering an ideological aim" ((1989) 19 *Israel Yearbook on Human Rights*, 23); the United Kingdom Prevention of Terrorism (Temporary Provisions) Act, 1984: "... the use of violence for political ends, [including] any use of

coercion;[39] or such acts of violence/terror (intimidation);[40] or such acts of violence/creation of a common danger;[41] or the creation of a common

violence for the purpose of putting the public or any section of the public in fear" (*ibid*, 23–4); US Executive Branch definition during the 1980s: "... premeditated use of violence against noncombatant targets for political purposes..." (*ibid*, 26; R Oakley, "International Terrorism", (1987) 65 *Foreign Affairs*, 611); United Kingdom Terrorist Act of 20 July 2000, s 1, where terrorism is defined according to the following parameters: use or threat of action including serious violence against a person or damage to property or risk to the health or safety of the public or a section of the public, for the purpose of advancing a political, religious or ideological cause (by intimidating the public or the government).

[39] See the US Foreign Intelligence Surveillance Act (FISA) of 1978, s 101(c), 50 USC §1801(c): "International terrorism means activities that — (1) involve violent acts or acts that are dangerous to human life...(2) appear to be intended — (A) to intimidate or coerce a civilian population; (B) to influence the policy of a government by intimidation or coercion; or (C) to affect the conduct of a government by assassination or kidnapping ...".

[40] See eg Articles 1(2) and 2 of the League of Nations Convention against Terrorism of 1937 (above n 9): "... criminal acts directed against a State and intended or calculated to create a state of terror in the minds of particular persons, a group of persons or the general public" (Art 2). Art 2 enumerates the *acta rea*, eg "any wilful act causing death or grievous bodily harm or loss of liberty" to some specified persons. Art 1(2) of the Convention of the Organization of the Islamic Conference on Combating International Terrorism (1999): "Terrorism means any act of violence or threat thereof notwithstanding its motives or intentions perpetrated to carry out an individual or collective criminal plan with the aim of terrorizing people or threatening harm to them or imperiling their lives, honour, freedoms, security or rights or exposing the environment or any facility or public or private property to hazards or occupying or seizing them, or endangering a national resource, or international facilities, or threatening the stability, territorial integrity, political unity or sovereignty of independent States". Art 16 of the ILC's *Draft Code on Crimes against the Peace and Security of Mankind*: "...acts against another State directed at persons or property and of such nature as to create a state of terror in the minds of public figures, groups of persons or the general public" (Doc A/45/10, 1990). See also the *Draft Single Convention on the Legal Control of International Terrorism*, International Law Association, 59th Conference, Belgrade, 1980, p 497: "... any serious act of violence or threat thereof by an individual whether acting alone or in association with other persons which is directed against internationally protected persons, organizations, places, transportation or communication systems or against members of the general public for the purpose of intimidating such persons, causing injury to or the death of such persons, disrupting the activities of such international organizations, of causing loss, detriment or damage to such places or property, or of interfering with such transportation and communication systems in order to undermine friendly relations among States or among the nationals of different States or to extort concessions from States". At the level of municipal law, see eg the French Criminal Code, Art 421(1): "... *actes... intentionnellement en relation avec une entreprise individuelle ou collective ayant pour but de troubler gravement l'ordre public par l'intimidation ou la terreur*". At the level of judicial practice, Lord Mustill and Lord Slynn of Hadley endorsed the definition contained in the 1937 League of Nations Convention: see the *T. v Immigration and Secretary of State for the Home Department* case (1996), House of Lords, 107 *ILR*, 575, 576. In doctrine, see eg G Gilbert, "The Law and Transnational Terrorism", (1995) 26 *Netherlands Yearbook of International Law*, 8: "... includes violent crimes committed with the intention of intimidating some government or group within a State".

[41] See eg the *Third Conference for the Unification of Penal Law* held under the auspices of the International Association of Penal Law at Brussels in 1930. Committee V of that Conference defined the act of terrorism as "the deliberate use of means capable of producing a common danger" to commit "an act imperiling life, physical integrity or human health or threatening to destroy substantial property". At the Paris Session of 1931, the following definition was proposed: "*Quiconque aura, en vue de terroriser la population, fait usage, contre les personnes ou*

danger/indiscrimination of the acts at stake;[42] or finally acts of violence /purpose of provoking international tension (or destabilizing the internal situation of a State).[43] As can be seen in the descriptions given, these elements may merge into one another.

C. Three Tier Definitions

In order better to capture the phenomenon of terrorism, a series of three-tier definitions was proposed. Especially in recent times, such descriptions combining three elements gain more and more ground. Such definitions put forward the elements of acts of violence/terror (intimidation)/political purpose;[44] or, in a slight variation, acts of violence/terror

les biens, de bombes, mines, machines ou produits explosifs ou incendiaires, armes à feu ou autres engins meurtriers ou destructeurs, ou aura provoqué ou tenté de provoquer, propagé ou tenté de propager une épidémie, une épizootie ou une autre calamité, interrompu ou tenté d'interrompre un service public ou d'utilité publique, sera puni ...". (cf. *Actes de la Conférence internationale pour l'unification du droit pénal*, Paris, 1938, p 49). See VS Mani, "International Terrorism: Is A Definition Possible?", (1978) 18 *Indian Journal of International Law*, 207. See also Sottile, above n 9, 113–15; Wurth, above n 9, 27 ff; I Lacoste, *Die Europäische Terrorismus-Konvention* (Zurich, 1982), 14–16; JF Prevost, "Les aspects nouveaux du terrorisme international", (1973) 19 *Annuaire Français de Droit International*, 580–81; G Guillaume and G Levasseur, *Terrorisme international* (Paris, 1977), 82–83. See also *Official Documents of the United Nations, Study by the Secretariat of the United Nations*, Doc A/C.6/418, 2 November 1972, p 10 ff.

[42] See the definition proposed by the ILA's Committee on *Legal Problems of Extradition to Terrorist Offences* (Warsaw Session, 1988), draft Art 1: "... acts which create a collective danger to the life, physical integrity or liberty of persons and affect persons foreign to the motives behind them" (ILA, *Report of the 63rd* Conference, p. 1035).

[43] See the legislation of Belarus, *Report of the Secretary-General* ...(above n 6), 4, para 18, Art 126 of the Criminal Code of Belarus, defines international terrorism as: "organizing the carrying out of explosions, arson or other acts in the territory of a foreign State with a view to causing loss of life or physical injury, destroying or damaging buildings, installations, means of transport, means of communication or other property for the purpose of provoking international tension or hostilities or destabilizing the internal situation in a foreign State, or murdering or causing physical injury to a political or public figure of a foreign State or damaging property belonging to such persons for the same purpose ... ".

[44] See eg the *Report of the Secretary-General, Measures to Eliminate International Terrorism, Addendum*, 12 October 2001, A/56/160/Add.1, p 6, para 48, Poland: "... the use of or threat to use violence for political purposes; a method of fighting or reaching specific goals based on intimidation of a society and government by causing human casualties and loss of property, characterized by ruthlessness and violation of moral and legal norms". In legal writings, see Chadwick, above n 9, 2–3: "Terrorist offence includes, but is not limited to, acts of violence or deprivations of freedom which are directed against persons or their property for a political purpose (...). [T]hese acts are intended in the main to spread fear or terror, in order to coerce a change in policy. Thus the instigators of terrorist violence can be an individual, a group, or a government". See also G Guillaume, "Terrorisme et droit international", (1989–III) 215 *Recueil des Cours de l'Académie de Droit International*, 300, who quotes English legislation in the following terms: "*Usage de la violence à des fins politiques, y compris tout usage de la violence dans le but de créer la peur dans le public ou une partie du public*".

(intimidation)/a specific purpose;[45] or acts of violence/terror (intimidation)/attack on the political, economic or social order;[46] sometimes such acts are limited to attacks against civilians.[47] Finally, there is a combination of factors, which is constantly gaining ground, especially within the United Nations. This equation on terrorism reads as follows: acts of violence/terror (intimidation)/coercion.[48]

[45] In doctrine, see Guillaume, *ibid* 306: "*Le terrorisme implique l'usage de la violence dans des conditions de nature à porter atteinte à la vie des personnes ou à leur intégrité physique dans le cadre d'une entreprise ayant pour but de provoquer la terreur en vue de parvenir à certaines fins*". C Bassiouni, "International Terrorism", in C Bassiouni (ed), *International Criminal Law*, 2nd edn, vol I, (New York, Transnational, 1999), 777–78 adds to this only the ideological motives: "... an ideologically-motivated strategy of internationally proscribed violence designed to inspire terror within a particular segment of a given society in order to achieve a power-outcome or to propagandize a claim or grievance, irrespective of whether its perpetrators are acting for and on behalf of themselves, or on behalf of the state".

[46] These elements were already stressed at the beginning of the XXth century under the heading of anarchist violence: see Conférence pour l'unification du droit pénal, Madrid, 1933, Art 1 of the Draft Convention. "*Celui qui, en vue de détruire toute organisation sociale aura employé un moyen quelconque de nature à terroriser la population, sera puni ...*" (*Actes de la Conférence ...* (above n 41), 50). This type of definition has been used equally in more recent legislations of continental European States. They are not any more directed to the aim of destroying "any social order" but more concretely to the attacks upon the specific social and constitutional order of a State. See eg the Portuguese Criminal Code, Art 300, mentioning prejudice to national interests and the fact of altering or disturbing State's institutions ("*visem prejudicar a integridade ou a independência naciolais, impedir, aqlterar ou subverter o funcionamiento das instituçoes do Estado previstas na Constitiçao ...*"); Art 571 of the Spanish Criminal Code, alluding to the aim of subverting the constitutional order and altering seriously public peace ("*...cuya finalidad sea la de subvertir el orden constitutional o alterar gravemente la paz pública ...*"); or Articles 270bis, 280, 289bis of the Italian Criminal Code, speaking of subversion to the democratic order of the State ("*eversione dell'ordine democratico*"). On these pieces of legislation, see the Report of the Commission of the EC, *Proposal for a Council Framework Decision on Combating Terrorism*, 19 September 2001, COM(2001)521, 7. In its Report, the European Commission proposes the following definition of terrorism: "Terrorist offences can be defined as offences intentionally committed by an individual or a group against one or more countries, their institutions or people, with the aim of intimidating them and seriously altering or destroying the political, economic, or social structures of a country"; see also p 7, 17 (Art 3 of the Framework Decision).

[47] See eg the definition given by the United States Congress: "... premeditated, politically motivated violence perpetrated against noncombatant targets by subnational groups or clandestine agents" (quoted by M Reisman, "International Legal Responses to Terrorism", (1999) 22 *Houston Journal of International Law*, 9). See also the definition given in the Convention for the Suppression of the Financing of Terrorism (1999), above n 30.

[48] See eg Art 24(2) of The ILC *Draft on a Code of Offences against the Peace and Security of Mankind*, Report on the Work of its 47th Session, 13th Report of D Thiam, Doc A/50/10, p 56–59, paras 105–11, p 58, above n 40: "The following shall constitute an act of international terrorism: undertaking, organizing, ordering, facilitating, financing, encouraging or tolerating acts of violence against another State directed at persons or property and of such a nature as to create a state of terror [fear or dread] in the minds of public figures, groups of persons or the general public in order to compel the aforesaid State to grant advantages or to act in a specific way". See also the more recent *Report of the Working Group* of the United Nations (supra, above n 2), p. 16, informal Article 2: "[if a person] by any means, unlawfully and intentionally, causes: (a) Death or serious bodily injury to any person; or (b) serious damage to public or private property, including a place of public use, a

D. Multi-Dimensional Definitions

In a last group, we may assemble all efforts to describe the notion of terrorism flexibly, by enumerating a series of criteria, which may be relevant in order to catch a phenomenon not reducible to a linear definition. Thus, for Skubiszewski, the terrorist act is characterized by its effect (creation of a common danger; fear), its means (symbolic violence), its victims (indiscriminate number or singled-out prominent figures), and its authors (only individuals, never States *per se*).[49] Oppermann qualifies the crime according to its philosophy (the end justifies the means), its authors (marginal groups), its victims (common danger, indiscriminate violence), its motives (political, religious, social, or military), and its goals (in depth transformation of existing power attributions).[50] Herzog points to the following chain of elements: (1) the threat or carrying out of grievous acts of violence; (2) by individuals not acting on behalf of a State; (3) in the pursuit of political ends, widely defined; (4) with the intent of inducing a state of terror; (5) within the frame of a long-term strategy.[51]

State or government facility, a public transportation system, an infrastructure facility or the environment; or (c) Damage to property, places, facilities .... resulting or likely to result in major economic loss; when the purpose of the conduct, by its nature or context, is to intimidate a population, or to compel a Government or an international organization to do or to abstain from doing any act". The elements of terror and coercion are presented in a disjunction ("or"). See also the definition advances by Panama, in *Report of the Secretary-General, Measures to Eliminate Intrenational Terrorism*, 3. July 2001, A/56/160, p. 8, §64: "... committing, organizing, ordering, financing, encouraging, instigating or tolerating acts of violence directed against persons or their property, creating a state of terror (dread or fear) in the minds of leaders, a group of persons or the general public with a view to compelling them to concede certain advantages or act in a given way ... ". See also the proposal of South Africa concerning draft Art 2(1) quoted above which largely follows the definition proposed by the Working group: *Report of the Ad Hoc Committee* ... (above n 37), p. 7, no. 5 or Doc. A/AC.252/2001/WP.5. In legal literature, see eg J Paust, "Terrorism and the International Law of War", (1974) 64 *Military Law Review*, 3–4: "... the purposive use of violence or the threat of violence by the perpetrators against an instrumental target in order to communicate to a primary target a threat of future violence so as to coerce the primary target into behavior or attitudes through intense fear or anxiety in connection with a demanded (political) outcome".

[49] K Skubiszewski, "Definition of Terrorism", (1989) 19 *Israel Yearbook on Human Rights*, 42–49.

[50] T Oppermann, "Der Beitrag des internationalen Rechts zur Bekämpfung des internationalen Terrorismus", *Mélanges H.J Schlochauer* (Berlin / New York, 1981), 496–502.

[51] Herzog, above n 9, 106–7. See also Stein, above n 5, 40. For such a "complex" definition, see also A Schmid and AJ Jongman, *Political Terrorism. A New Guide to Actors, Authors, Concepts, Data Bases, Theories and Literature* (New Brunswick, Transaction Books, 1988), 28; Lacoste, above n 21, 10 ff, discussing: (1) the means (eg indiscriminate acts); (2) the effects (eg the production of fear); (3) the aims (eg exception for wars of national liberation?); (4) the motives (eg the furthering of social or political causes); and any combination of such elements.

E. Combining the Sectoral Approach with a Global Approach

The most recent tendencies combine the sectoral (or "piecemeal") approach with the global approach. The definition of terrorism is sought by identifying two limbs, one listing the acts covered by the several specific conventions, the other adding a general definition of terrorist acts by having more often than not recourse to the three elements of violent acts/terror/coercion. To the *leges speciales* of the conventions is thus added a *lex generalis* trying to devise the core elements of the terrorist offence beyond the specific subject matter. At the level of definition this merging of the two streams can easily be achieved. More intricate problems may arise when one is dealing with the respective field of application and potential conflicts between a new general convention on international terrorism and the old multiple conventions concluded since 1963.[52] The two-limb approach just described can be found for example in the European Convention on the Suppression of Terrorism of 1977,[53] the Convention for the Suppression of the Financing of Terrorism (1999),[54] the Convention of the Organization of the Islamic Conference on Combating International Terrorism (1999),[55] and the Draft Comprehensive Convention on International Terrorism of the Working Group of the Sixth Committee of the UN General Assembly.[56] In view of the preceding discussion, it may be said that some progress has been made towards the definition of a "qualified" terrorist act beyond purely piecemeal descriptions. The point reached is all the more commendable if one takes into account the considerable political obstacles to agreement in such a field. It may well be that the events of 11 September[57] will serve to catalyze further progress, once the urgency of the matter is fully understood. However, for the moment one can only take note of the absence of a universally agreed definition of terrorist acts to be criminally prosecuted. The events concerning the

[52] As to this aspect, see the debates at the United Nations: *Report of the Ad Hoc Committee* ... (above n 37), Annex V, para 16 ff.

[53] Art 1.

[54] Art 2. It reads as follows: "Any person commits an offence within the meaning of this Convention if that person by any means, directly or indirectly, unlawfully and wilfully, provides or collects funds with the intention that they should be used or in the knowledge that they are to be used, in full or in part, in order to carry out: (a) an act which constitutes an offence within the scope of and as defined in one of the treaties listed in the annex; or (b) any other act intended to cause death or serious bodily injury to a civilian, or to any other person not taking an active part in the hostilities in a situation of armed conflict, when the purpose of such act, by its nature or context, is to intimidate a population, or to compel a government or an international organization to do or to abstain from doing any act" (see (2000) 39 *ILM*, 271).

[55] Articles 1(2) and 1(4).

[56] Informal Articles 2 and 2bis. See the *Report of the Working Group* ... (above n 2), p. 16.

[57] On these events see the measured and brief analysis of C Tomuschat, "Der 11 September 2001 und seine rechtlichen Konsequenzen", (2001) 28 *EuGRZ*, 535 ff.

International Criminal Court[58] show quite well the obstacles which are still to be overcome on the path of international jurisdiction. At the moment, the matter of arriving at a general definition of terrorism is in full flux, producing many ideas and moving towards a process to crystallize some core definition of a terrorist act in general. But no such definition is yet identifiable in positive law, a state of affairs which cannot be ignored or discussed away. This has considerable impact on the legal means for the prosecution of terrorist crimes available at the time being in international law. A further point deserves brief attention. It is often claimed that any definition of terrorism which contains the element of "terror" is tautological.[59] This is not exactly the case. The element at stake would be tautological only if it had no other meaning than terrorism itself, i.e. if it was indissolubly linked to terrorism. But this is not true. The element of "terror" can be replaced by any other word connoting the same idea, as for example fear, anguish, dread, intimidation, etc, adding to it eventually a qualification such as "extreme", "considerable", etc. That course was in fact chosen by the ILC when drafting the Code of Offences against the Peace and Security of Mankind.[60] If it is thus replaced, the tautology visibly disappears. There remains an element which may be quite open-ended, but this is another problem, if it is one at all.

F. International Element

International law only deals with terrorist acts which affect international relations. In other words, it is concerned in principle only with international terrorism while leaving local terrorist acts to the exclusive control of the territorial State. International terrorism is made up of terrorist acts (however defined) plus an international element.[61] No further proof of any international element is needed in the context of some anti-terrorist conventions, especially those dealing with the safety of civil aviation.

[58] See infra, II. B.
[59] See already Sottile, above n 9, 95.
[60] See above n 48.
[61] On that question, see Sottile, above n 9, 98–99; Murphy, above n 5, 16, 27, 32; Skubiszewski, above n 49, 49–50; Mushkat, above n 2, 467 ff; Lacoste, above n 21, 21 ff; Franck and Lockwood, above n 8, 78; Wurth, above n 9, 57 ff; Guillaume and Levasseur, above n 41, 66–67; Prevost, above n 41, 589; Oppermann, above n 50, 501–3; Gilbert, above n 40, 10; Bassiouni, above n 45, 778; E. David, "Le terrorisme en droit international", in *Colloque de l'Université libre de Bruxelles, Réflexions sur la définition et la répression du terrorisme* (Brussels, 1974), 127 ff. See also the Report of the Ad Hoc Committee ... (above n 37), Discussion Paper prepared by the Bureau as a Basis for Discussion in the Working Group of the Sixth Committee at the fifty-sixth Session of the General Assembly, A/56/37, p. 3, Art 3: "This Convention shall not apply where the offence is committed within a single State, the alleged offender is found in the territory of that State and no other State has a basis ... to exercise jurisdiction".

Their subject matter is *eo ipso* international and pertains to international law. It is therefore only for the acts not covered by these conventions (and possibly for States not parties to the conventions) that the question of the international character of the acts involved may arise. This may occur, for instance, when national law provides for prosecution or control of acts of "international terrorism" as does the US Foreign Intelligence Surveillance Act (FISA) of 1978.[62] The question may also arise at the international level, in three contexts. First, in those conventions the subject matter of which is not *eo ipso* international, the question is regulated by a specific clause, defining the acts considered to be attacks on international interests.[63] Second, the question may arise in the case of prosecution of terrorist acts by a State outside the framework of a specific convention. If a State claims a form of universal jurisdiction over a terrorist act, be it in the form of customary universality or of *aut dedere aut judicare* derived by analogy from treaty law,[64] it may well be that such a jurisdiction can be exercised only if the acts at stake are to be considered acts of international terrorism, as opposed to purely internal terrorism.[65] Third, the question puts itself in any case to the legislator, since he has to decide which acts constitute a sufficient attack on international interests such as to warrant international control or jurisdiction.

Having thus determined the relevance of the international element we must now turn to its content. Roughly speaking, there is internationality if an act has international consequences in the sense that it affects the duties or rights of more than one State or foreign interests. Hence, there is an international terrorist act when, either: (1) the act or the acts take place in more than one State; (2) the act or the acts take place in a space where no State has exclusive national jurisdiction, eg on the high seas; (3) the perpetrator and victim are citizens of different States; (4) the act or acts affect citizens of more than one State; (5) the acts affect targets having an international status (independently from a specific anti-terrorist convention), eg personnel of international organisations, international communications, transport, postal or other, etc; (6) the effects of the terrorist act are

[62] Sect. 101(c), 50 U.S.C. § 1801 (c): "(3) [activities that] occur totally outside the United States, or transcend national boundaries in terms of the means by which they are accomplished, the persons they appear intended to coerce or intimidate, or the locale in which their perpetrators operate or seek asylum". See also Murphy, above n 5, 27.

[63] See eg Art 3 of the Convention for the Suppression of the Financing of Terrorism (1999): "This Convention shall not apply where the offence is committed within a single State, the alleged offender is a national of that State and is present in the territory of that State and no other State has a basis ... to exercise jurisdiction ..." ((2000) 39 *ILM*, 272). See equally Art 3 of the Convention for the Suppression of Terrorist Bombings (1998), (1998) 37 *ILM*, 254.

[64] On this question, see below, II.

[65] Apart from the fact that in case of purely internal terrorism further problems may arise under the doctrines of double criminality (at the place of the offence and at the place of the forum) and of the political offence exception.

felt in a third State.[66] Conversely, the fact that a perpetrator flees in a third State after the act does not entail that the act itself transforms itself into an act of international terrorism. Rather, the extradition process may be set in motion, but this inter-State procedure concerns only the question of physical control of the culprit, not the quality of the act itself.[67]

The elements internationalising a terrorist act just discussed are quite sweeping and pose many questions of delimitation. Thus, for example, the effects-doctrine permits a considerable extension of coverage,[68] since in the modern interdependent world some effects will easily be felt collaterally to a terrorist offence. There is no means to assign a limited and precise scope to such "effects" which are by their very nature vaguely defined. May one say that simply on account of its gravity an act becomes one of international concern, even if all the victims and other immediate connections of it are exclusively from and in one State?[69] Does its gravity alone make the act a sort of crime *erga omnes*, since it could be seen as attacking the fundamental values of the international community,[70] especially because the protection of human rights has become since 1945 increasingly one of the core elements of the international legal order?[71] It could equally be said that such acts by very definition (or legal fiction) have "effects" felt in other States, to the extent that fundamental common interests are infringed. On the other hand, one could limit that statement to terrorist acts committed by indiscriminate means. If a bomb is placed in a public place, it may well be that by chance no foreign national is injured or killed. But the mere fact of the randomness of the attack created a danger that such foreign nationals could have been killed or injured.

[66] One may also mention the recent efforts under the aegis of the United Nations to prepare a comprehensive convention against terrorism. In that context, some definition of terrorism of international concern was felt necessary. Art 3 of the Discussion Paper prepared by the Bureau as a Basis for Discussion in the Working Group of the Sixth Committee at the fifty-sixth Session of the General Assembly, A/56/37, *Report of the Ad Hoc Committee ...* (above n 37), 3, reads as follows: "The Convention shall not apply where the offence is committed within a single State, the alleged offender and the victims are nationals of that State, the alleged offender is found in the territory of that State and no other State has a basis ... to exercise jurisdiction [under this Convention] ... ".

[67] Compare Gilbert, above n 40, 10. As the present author, Skubiszewski, above n 8, 50. Art 3 of the Discussion Paper quoted in the above note seems to imply that the flight into a third State could trigger the application of norms relative to international terrorism, but as explained this position does not seem legally correct (see in Art 3 the limb "the alleged is found in the territory of that State").

[68] See for instance the *United States v Noriega* case (1990), United States District Court for the Southern District of Florida, 99 *ILR*, 145 ff.

[69] Compare Mushkat, above n 2, 468, *de lege lata*.

[70] For such statements, see R Kolb, "Universal Criminal Jurisdiction in Matters of International Terrorism: Some reflections on Status and Trends in Contemporary International Law", (1997) 50 *Hellenic Review of International Law*, 70 ff.

[71] See eg the decided statement of C Tomaschat, "International Law: Ensuring the Survival of Mankind on the Eve of A New Century, General Course on Public International Law", (1999) 281 *Recueil des Cours de l'Académie de Droit International*, 220 ff.

That potential damage or that risk may be enough to create an international link, eg under the effects-doctrine (constructive effects or effect through risk). The recent events prompting an upsurge in combating international terrorism and an increase of international solidarity in that enterprise may well be taken as having expanded the circle of "internationality" of terrorist acts while narrowing the correspondent circle of purely domestic terrorism. But what gravity of the act is necessary in order to trigger internationalisation is a delicate question which cannot yet be answered with any degree of certainty.

Another question which may be asked is that concerning secessionist violence. To the extent that such violence is directed solely against the interests of the former unitary State, can it be said that these are acts of international terrorism? Quite apart from the highly controversial question of whether movements of national liberation should be covered by the definition of terrorism[72] (and whether secessionist movements are entitled to such status), it seems that the answer will depend on the internationalisation of the conflict itself, mainly through recognition by foreign States. The applicable law would then be the law of internal (or, if there is foreign involvement, of international) armed conflicts.[73]

Many other questions could be raised, but we stop here, since the essential elements giving rise to the internationalisation of the terrorist act are fairly clear. It may be simply recalled, in conclusion, that an effect of the growing inter-penetration of the modern world has been the increasing internationalisation of terrorist acts. Today, most terrorist

[72] See above n 2.

[73] See, among others, Chadwick, above n 9, 65 ff, 129 ff, 179 ff. As to the question of terrorism in armed conflicts there is ample literature. See eg K Hailbronner, "International Terrorism and the Laws of War", (1982) 25 *CYIL*, 169 ff; C Greenwood, "Terrorism and Humanitarian Law: The Debate Over Additional Protocol I", (1989) 19 *Israel Yearbook on Human Rights*, 187 ff; H-P Gasser, "Interdiction des actes de terrorisme dans le droit international humanitaire", (1986) 68 *Revue internationale de la Croix Rouge*, 207 ff; JJ Paust, "Terrorism and the International Law of War", (1974) 64 *Military Law Review*, 1 ff; AP Rubin, "Terrorism and the Laws of War", (1983) 13 *Denver Journal of International Law and Policy*, 219 ff; Guillaume, above n 44, 375 ff; JA Frowein, in Hague Academy of International Law, 1988, *Les aspects juridiques du terrorisme international* (The Hague/Boston/London, 1989), 75–8; J Paust in AE Evans and JF Murphy (eds), *Legal Aspects of International Terrorism* (Toronto, Lexington Books, 1978), 352–53; WT Mallison and SV Mallison, "The Control of State Terrorism Through the Application of the International Humanitarian Law of Armed Conflict", in MH Livingston, LB Kress and MG Wanek (eds), *International Terrorism in the Contemporary World* (London, Greenwood Press, 1978), 325 ff; M Sassoli, "International Humanitarian Law and Terrorism", in P Wilkinson and AM Stewart, *Contemporary Research on Terrorism* (Aberdeen, Aberdeen University Press, 1987), 466 ff; LC Green, "Terrorism and Armed Conflict", (1989) 19 *Israel Yearbook on Human Rights*, 131 ff; WA Solf, "International Terrorism in Armed Conflict", in HH Han (ed), *Terrorism and Political Violence* (New York, University Press of America, 1993), 317 ff; G Stuby, "Humanitarian International Law and International Terrorism", in H Köckler (ed), *Terrorism and National Liberation* (Frankfurt, 1988), 237 ff. For a critique, see Panzera, above n 9, 180–82. See also Chadwick, above n 9.

strategies are aimed at provoking international concern for their causes, thus wilfully attacking or affecting international interests.

II. THE EXERCISE OF CRIMINAL JURISDICTION OVER INTERNATIONAL TERRORISTS

A. Jurisdiction Exercised by States

Terrorist offences may be prosecuted before domestic courts or at the level of an international criminal tribunal. The latter situation is highly exceptional, since from the Nuremberg Trial up to the *ad hoc* tribunals created by the Security Council in the 1990s in order to deal with the crimes perpetrated in the former Yugoslavia and in Rwanda, there was no international criminal tribunal. In July 2002, the Statute of the International Criminal Court entered into force, and therefore there is now a permanent international court dealing with criminal prosecution at the international level. However, the great mass of crimes will continue to be prosecuted by national courts, since only the State possesses the infrastructure able to deal with the great number of cases arising in situations of armed conflict such as those in former Yugoslavia or in Rwanda. It is thus justified to consider first the jurisdictional bases States possess under international law in the context of the criminal prosecution of terrorist crimes, before reverting to the possibilities in this context of the International Criminal Court.

We will not go into the matter of prosecution of terrorist acts as defined by the numerous pieces of internal legislation of States. This is a matter of internal law only, to the extent that it does not correspond to terrorism as envisaged by international law norms. Conversely, to the extent internal law is necessary for or conflicting with international norms on the suppression of terrorism, either because it implements the latter, or because it claims national jurisdiction for acts of (international) terrorism beyond the provisions of the latter, or because it does not allow implementation of the latter, the problem touches on international law and must thus be addressed.

B. The National Suppression of Terrorist Acts under the Conventional Systems

1. *The Rules Contained in the Conventions*

The several anti-terrorist Conventions concluded on the global level after 1963 are all based on a similar jurisdictional system, with only slight variations due to experience of shortcomings and emergent political consensus. These conventions provide a series of jurisdictional titles for all the States parties. These titles fall in two categories: (1) a series of specific titles, eg territoriality, personality, State of registration of an air carrier, etc., for which the State is either obliged or allowed to establish jurisdiction; (2) a general clause providing that in all cases where the offender is found in the territory of one State party, it shall in any case exercise jurisdiction if it does not extradite the offender to a more convenient forum (*aut dedere, aut iudicare* or more accurately, *aut dedere, aut prosequi*).[74] Articles 6 and 8 of the recent International Convention for the Suppression of Terrorist Bombings (1998) may serve as an illustration:[75]

"Article 6.

1. Each State party shall take such measures as may be necessary to establish its jurisdiction over the offences set forth in article 2 when:
   (a) The offence is committed in the territory of that State; or
   (b) The offence is committed on board a vessel flying the flag of that State or an aircraft which is registered under the laws of that State at the time the offence is committed; or
   (c) The offence is committed by a national of that State.
2. A State Party may also establish its jurisdiction over any such offence when:
   (a) The offence is committed against a national of that State; or
   (b) The offence is committed against a State or government facility of that State abroad, including an embassy or other diplomatic or consular premises of that State; or
   (c) The offence is committed by a stateless person who has his or her habitual residence in the territory of that State; or
   (d) The offence is committed in an attempt to compel that State to do or abstain from doing any act, or
   (e) The offence is committed on board an aircraft which is operated by the Government of that State.

[74] For a precise analysis of these conventional systems, see M Henzelin, *Le principe de l'universalité en droit pénal international*, (Geneva, Helbing & Lichtenhahn/Bruylant , 2000), 294 ff. These conventions suffer from a number of problems, such as: (1) the insufficiency of the numbers of ratification or accession for the conventions to fulfill their purpose to close down any save havens; (2) the insufficient application of the treaties; (3) the existence of too many loopholes, eg with the political offence exception or with a too loose duty to search for and to arrest the suspects (on these points see below, § 15 and § 16). See eg A Cassese, "The International Community's Legal response to Terrorism", (1989) 38 *International and Comparative Law Quarterly*, 593–5.

[75] See (1998) 37 *ILM*, 254–6.

4. Each State Party shall likewise take such measures as may be necessary to establish its jurisdiction over the offences set forth in article 2 in cases where the alleged offender is present in its territory and it does not extradite that person to any of the States Parties which have established their jurisdiction in accordance with paragraph 1 or 2 of the present article."

"Article 8

1. The State Party in the territory of which the alleged offender is present shall, in cases to which article 6 applies, if it does not extradite that person, be obliged, without exception whatsoever and whether or not the offence was committed in its territory, to submit the case without undue delay to its competent authorities for the purpose of prosecution, through proceedings in accordance with the laws of that State...."

Under the heading of special jurisdictional titles are thus listed the principles of territoriality, registration, active personality; then passive personality, State security and some other minor bases. The whole scheme is supplemented by the residual clause of *aut dedere aut prosequi*. The special titles slightly vary in the different conventions, according to their subject matters. A convention on terrorist bombings, by its very subject matter, is likely to have a large jurisdictional reach. Conversely, a convention against acts of violence directed at certain defined persons has a narrower jurisdictional ambit. One must note, moreover, that all these conventions contain a clause whereby they do not purport to exclude any criminal jurisdiction exercised in accordance with national law.[76] Thus, to the extent that there are further jurisdictional titles provided for in the national criminal codes, and that these titles are not contrary to international law, a prosecution may be based on them quite independently of the specific provisions of the convention at stake. In legal terms, the titles provided for in the conventions are not exclusive, but complementary to those of national law. There is a difference to the extent that the convention obliges a State to exercise jurisdiction under some titles. Then jurisdiction becomes mandatory, whereas the jurisdiction based on municipal law is optional. The municipal titles correspond to those listed in Article 6(2) of the Convention on Terrorist Bombings, which are expressly termed as being optional ("may also establish jurisdiction"). One may add that the two-tier approach distinguishing at the level of the conventions between mandatory and optional titles is a new technique. In the older conventions, such as the Montreal Convention for the

[76] See eg Art 6(5) of the Convention against Terrorist Bombings.

Suppression of Unlawful Acts against the Safety of Civil Aviation (1971), there were only mandatory titles.[77]

It does not seem warranted at this stage to discuss the specific titles of jurisdiction. Territoriality, personality, active and passive[78], State security or other special links are well-known principles of criminal jurisdiction which do not prompt any particular problems in the context of terrorism.[79] Conversely, the principle *aut dedere aut prosequi* requires more detailed discussion. It is a title specific to international crimes, which has been popularised precisely through the anti-terrorist conventions.

2. *Aut Dedere Aut Prosequi = Conventional Universal Jurisdiction?*

The first question to be raised as to the character of the *aut dedere* principle is whether we can envision it as a type of conventional universal jurisdiction. Universal jurisdiction[80] allows every State to exercise its

[77] See Art 5 of the Convention.

[78] This title has been traditionally somewhat controversial, in particular since the anglo-saxon legal orders did not endorse it. However, the criminal codes of many States contain that principle, allowing them to prosecute persons having committed crimes against their nationals abroad. See generally L Oppenheim in R Jennings and A Watts, *International Law*, 9th edn (London, 1992), 471–72. As for a State applying the principle, see Art 5(1) of the Swiss Criminal Code: "*Le présent code est applicable à quiconque aura commis à l'étranger un crime ou un délit contre un Suisse, pourvu que l'acte soit réprimé aussi dans l'Etat où il a été commis, si l'auteur se trouve en Suisse et n'est pas extradé à l'étranger, ou s'il est extradé à la Confédération à raison de cette infraction*". For judicial practice on this principle in Switzerland, see eg Arrêts du Tribunal Fédéral (ATF), 108 *Recueil officiel*, part IV, 147 ff; ATF 119 IV, 117 ff; ATF 121 IV, 148 ff. For jurisprudence in general, see the cases quoted in Oppenheim, *ibid*.

[79] See generally Oppenheim, *ibid*, 456 ff, with numerous references.

[80] Universal jurisdiction thus touches closely on the categories of an international public order, of rights *erga omnes* and of *ius cogens* understood as a series of fundamental norms embodying the essential values of the contemporary international community. On the international public order, see H Mosler, "The International Society as a Legal Community, General Course of Public International Law", (1974–IV) 140 *R.CADI*, 33–36; H Mosler, "Der Gemeinschaftliche ordre public in den europäischen Staatengruppen", (1968) 21 *Revista española de derecho internacional*, 523 ff; G Jaenicke, "International Public Order", 7 *EPIL*, 314–18; G Jaenicke, "Zur Frage des internationalen ordre public", (1967) 7 *Berichte der deutschen Gesellschaft für Völkerrecht*, Karlsruhe, 85–96; G Schwarzenberger, "The Problem of International Public Policy", (1965) 18 *Current Legal Problems*, 191 ff (the author rejects the notion); H Rolin, "Vers un ordre public réellement international", *Mélanges J. Basdevant* (Paris, 1960), 441 ff, 451 ff; W Levi, "The International Ordre Public", (1994) 72 *Revue de droit international, de sciences diplomatiques et politiques*, 55 ff. On obligations *erga omnes*, see amongst others M Ragazzi, *The Concept of International Obligations Erga Omnes* (Oxford, Oxford University Press, 1997); A De Hoogh, *Obligations Erga Omnes and International Crimes* (The Hague, Kluwer, 1996). See also the synthesis in R Kolb, *Théorie du ius cogens international* (Paris, 2001). Thus, under universal jurisdiction certain crimes are deemed to affect the interests of the international community as a whole in so serious a manner as to warrant an exception to the requirement of a specific link in order to be allowed to prosecute them. Crimes like piracy, the slave trade, war crimes and crimes against humanity constitute offences against the international public order (*delicta iuris gentium*). They infringe upon interests which are common to all members of a given society: this common interest and the seriousness of the crimes legitimize the right of any State that manages to apprehend an alleged culprit to prosecute them. (Note continues overleaf.)

criminal jurisdiction over a number of offences which constitute, in the main, international crimes of concern to the entire international community. This prosecution shall take place regardless of any specific link to the crime or the offender, provided the alleged author is in the custody of that State. Thus, universal jurisdiction is normally based on the idea of a *iudex deprehensionis*: the State who puts its hands on the criminal should be able to try him. This holds particularly true in the context of terrorist offences as defined by the conventions. The legal aim of this title is to ensure that for certain acts there be no safe havens and that the probability of prosecution is raised to a maximum. This in turn rests on the nature of the crimes, namely their particular gravity and the common concern they arouse.

Ordinary universal jurisdiction is rooted in customary international law. It is under that law that the principle evolved, when it began to be applied to pirates.[81] Consequently, at its beginnings, universal jurisdiction was universal also as to its spatial scope of application, it being devised for crimes addressed by general custom, binding all States. On the other hand universal jurisdiction under customary law was only permissive: it allowed any State to start prosecution if it so wished, but it did not compel it to do so. Classical universal jurisdiction under customary

On universal jurisdiction, see M Henzelin, *Le principe de l'universalité en droit pénal international* (Basel/Brussels, 2000); KC Randall, "Universal Jurisdiction under International Law", (1988) 66 *Texas Law Review*, 785 ff; L Benavides, "The Universal Jurisdiction Principle: Nature and Scope", (2001) 1 *Anuario Mexicano de derecho internacional*, 19 ff (with many references); B Stern, "A propos de la compétence universelle... ", *Essays in Honor of M. Bedjaoui* (The Hague, 1999), 735 ff; C Bassiouni, "Universal Jurisdiction for International Crimes: Historical Perspectives and Contemporary Practice", (2001) 42 *Virginia Journal of International Law*, 81 ff. See equally R Higgins, "General Course on Public International Law: International Law and the Avoidance, Containment and Resolution of Disputes", (1991–V) 230 *Recueil des Cours de l'Académie de Droit International*, 90–100; O Schachter, "International Law in Theory and Practice", (1982-V) 178 *Recueil des Cours de l'Académie de Droit International*, 262–65; M Akehurst, "Jurisdiction in International Law", (1972/3) 46 *British Yearbook of International Law*, 160–166; G Guillaume, "La compétence universelle, formes anciennes et nouvelles", *Essays in Honor of G Levasseur* (Paris, 1992), p 23 ff. D Oehler, *Internationales Strafrecht*, 2nd edn (Cologne, 1983), 519–45; DW Bowett, "Jurisdiction: Changing Patterns of Authority over Activities and Resources", (1982) 53 *British Yearbook of International Law*, 11–14; FA Mann, The Doctrine of Jurisdiction in International Law", vol 111, 1964–I, 95; L Oppenheim in RY Jennings and A Watts (eds), *International Law*, 9th edn (London, Longman, 1992), 469–70; BH Oxman, "Jurisdiction of States", (1984) 10 *EPIL*, 281; B Graefrath, "Universal Criminal Jurisdiction and an International Criminal Court", (1990) 1 *JEDI*, 67 ff; *Conseil de l'Europe, Comité européen pour les problèmes criminels, Compétence extraterritoriale en matière pénale* (Strasbourg, 1990), 15–16; The American Law Institute (ed), *The Foreign Relations Law of the United States, Restatement of the Law Third*, vol I (St Paul, 1987), 254–58, para 404; Harvard Draft, "Jurisdiction with Respect to Crime", (1935) 29 *American Journal of International Law*, Supp, 573–92. See also the detailed analysis by the Australian High Court in *Polyukhovich v Commonwealth of Australia and Another*, (1990) 91 *ILR*, 40 ff, 117 ff.

[81] See Oppenheim, above n 78, 746. Henzelin, above n 80, 269 ff; Benavides, above n 80, 42 ff.

international law was thus both general *ratione personae* and optional *ratione materiae*.

Some authors limit the ambit of universal jurisdiction to the traditional customary principle.[82] They would at maximum concede that a mandatory jurisdiction under customary law (eg for grave breaches to the Geneva Conventions of 1949) could also be covered. They refuse, however, to consider that a convention could create a true universal jurisdiction, and in particular, they do not consider that the principle *aut dedere aut prosequi* could be considered as a form of universal jurisdiction.[83] At most, some of them view the pricciple of *aut dedere* as a quasi-universal jurisdiction,[84] but keep it neatly distinct from it. Conversely, other authors hold that *aut dedere* is a conventional universal jurisdiction principle.[85]

[82]See eg Higgins, above n 80, 98. Benavides, above n 80, 32 ff, 40.

[83]Higgins, *ibid*: "In so far as this provides for the jurisdiction of all parties to the Convention ... it is perhaps understandable that it is spoken of as universal jurisdiction. But it is still not really universal jurisdiction *stricto sensu*, because in any given case only a small number of contracting parties would be able to exercise jurisdiction ...". See also MN Shaw, *International Law*, 3rd ed. (Cambridge, Cambridge University Press, 1991), 414.

[84]Oxman, above n 80, 281; Henzelin, above n 80, 302, 317 ("*système d'obligation répressive quasi-universelle*"); SA Williams, "International Law and Terrorism: Age-Old Problems, Different Targets", (1988) 26 *CYIL*, 91, for example, hold that this system bears a close resemblance to that of universal jurisdiction, without quite attaining it. See also A Cassese, "The International Community's Legal Response to Terrorism", (1989) 38 *International and Comparative Law Quarterly*, 593. A distinction is also introduced by Oehler, above n 80, 532–33, 497 ff.

[85]Guillaume, above n 44, 350 ff; Guillaume, above n 80, 33–34; D Freestone, "International Cooperation Against Terrorism and the Development of International Law Principles of Jurisdiction", in R Higgins and M Flory (eds), *Terrorism and International Law* (Routeledge, London, 1997), 50; G De La Pradelle, "La compétence universelle", in H Ascensio, E Decaux and A Pellet (eds), *Droit international pénal* (Paris, 2000), 908; LS Sunga, *Individual Responsibility in International Law for Serious Human Rights Violations* (The Hague, 1992), 102; Stern, above n 80, 739; Bassiouni, above n 80, 82, 125 ff; Kolb, above n 70, 58 ff; Panzera, above n 9, 160; A Cassese, "The International Community's 'Legal' Response to Terrorism", (1989) 38 *International and Comparative Law Quarterly*, 593; *Final Document of the Conference of Syracuse* (1973), in MC Bassiouni (ed), *International Terrorism and Political Crimes* (Springfield, 1975), XIX; O Schachter, "General Course on Public International Law", (1982-V) 178 *Recueil des Cours de l'Académie de Droit International*, 262–63; B de Schutter, "Problems of Jurisdiction in the International Control and Repression of Terrorism", in Bassiouni (ed), above, 388; S Sucharitkul, "International Terrorism and the Problem of Jurisdiction", (1987) 14 *Syracuse Journal of International Law and Commerce*, 171; Y Dinstein, "Terrorism As An International Crime", (1989) 19 *Israel Yearbook on Human Rights*, 69–70; T Treves, *La giurisdizione nel diritto penale internazionale* (Padova, 1973), 287 ff; H Labayle, "Droit international et lutte contre le terrorisme", (1986) 32 *Annuaire Français de Droit International*, 117; H Labayle, "Sécurité dans les aéroports et progrès de la collaboration internationale contre le terrorisme", (1988) 35 *Annuaire Français de Droit International*, 719–21; Herzog, above n 9, 235–36; Oppenheim, above n 78, 470; G Dahm and J Delbrück and R Wolfrum, *Völkerrecht*, 2nd edn, t. I/1 (Berlin, 1989), 321–22; A Verdross and B Simma, *Universelles Völkerrecht*, 3rd edn (Berlin, 1984), 779; Graefrath, above n 80, 87; Akehurst, above n 80, 161; Randall, above n 80, 819; *Conseil de l'Europe ...* (above n 80), 16; *Restatement Third of the Foreign Relations Law of the United States* (above n 80) 255–57. In its recent work on a *Draft Code of Crimes against the Peace and Security of Mankind*, the ILC clearly assimilated the rule *aut dedere aut iudicare* to universal jurisdiction: Art 4 of the Draft, see *Yb.ILC* 1987–II, part 1, 3–4; *Yb.ILC* 1993–II, part 2, 107; *Report of*

Thus, Guillaume writes that the conventions embodying the principle create a system of mandatory but subsidiary universal jurisdiction.[86] In contrast to the customary principle this jurisdiction must be exercised by the State; on the other hand, it is softened by the alternative of extraditing.

The core of the matter is, as often, a problem of definition. Nobody contests that there are differences between the *aut dedere* principle and the classical universal jurisdiction principle. The differences stressed are: (1) *aut dedere* is not universal but limited to the parties to the Convention;[87] (2) universal jurisdiction is a right, an entitlement, whereas *aut dedere* is a duty; (3) universal jurisdiction is a title to try, *aut dedere* is an alternative of either trying or extraditing; (4) universal jurisdiction applies only to a limited number of international crimes on account of their particular gravity, whereas *aut dedere* is contemplated in a number of conventions for a larger category of crimes.[88] All these differences may be acknowledged. They may justify putting the *aut dedere* principle in a separate category, as they can construe it as a special category of conventional universal jurisdiction, a sort of modified, albeit closely related principle (special universal jurisdiction). All depends on the essential criterion which is used to distinguish universal jurisdiction from other types of prosecution titles. If that criterion is seen in its generality *ratione personae*, ie that it applies to all States by virtue of a general custom (on account of the nature of the

the ILC on the Work of its 46th Session, Official Records of the General Assembly of the United Nations, Suppl No 10 (A/49/10), p 78. (For a criticism of this equation, see Benavides, above n 80, 35). The decision of the Bavarian Supreme Court in the *Antonin L c Federal Republic of Germany* case (1979) 80 *ILR*, 679 establishes a linkage with domestic law (universal jurisdiction under Art 316(c) of the German Criminal Code implementing the Hague Convention of 1970 on hijacking of aircraft and its relation to the laws on asylum). On the equivalence between universal jurisdiction and the *aut dedere aut iudicare* rule, see, in the *Aylor* case (1994), the legal opinion of the *Commissaire du gouvernement français*, Commission européenne des droits de l'homme, 100 *ILR*, 670–1, or the *Yunis (no 2)* case (1988), United States District Court, 82 *ILR*, 348–49 [confirmed by the Court of Appeals, 88 *ILR*, 176 ff, 181)]. See also the Statement of the Delegate of Sri Lanka, Mr Perera, at the Sixth Commission of the United Nations, 27th session, 2 December 1997, Doc. A/C.6/52/SR. 27, § 54, in the context of the recent international convention on terrorist bombings. See also the statement of Switzerland in the Report of the Secretary-General of the United Nations, Measures to Eliminate International Terrorism, 3 July 2001, Doc. A/56/160, p. 13, § 100.

[86] See Guillaume, above n 44, 350 ff.
[87] See eg Higgins, above n 80.
[88] For the most decided criticism of any confusion, see Benavides, above n 80, 32 ff. As to this last element, namely that universal jurisdiction applies only to some international crimes, one may mention that even under classical international law it was not always accepted. Rather, there were some authors equating the existence of an international crime with the existence of universal jurisdiction. See eg P Fiore, *Il diritto internazionale codificato*, 2nd edn (Turin, 1898), 143, Art 240: "*Apparterrà alla sovranità di ciascuno Stato la giurisdizione penale rispetto ad uno, che sia imputato di avere commesso un fatto qualificato reato secondo il diritto internazionale*". Art 241 shows that he had in mind not only the most egregious crimes, since he mentions, *inter alia*, the damaging of submarine telegraphic cables.

crime which must be an offence against the most fundamental values of the international community), then *aut dedere* is indeed no universal jurisdiction. However, nothing forces us to limit the scope of universality in that way. We may see its essential criterion not in universality *ratione personae* or any other specificities in conventional law, but the *absence of any requirement that there be a specific link in order to be allowed to prosecute.*[89] Then, there is no reason to deny that universal jurisdiction could operate only between the parties to a given agreement. The jurisdiction indeed remains universal, in that it casts away the usual requirement of a specific link between State and individual before allowing the former to prosecute the latter for the commission of acts defined in the agreement. Hence, the difference between a customary universal jurisdiction and a conventional one is merely one of range of application: one is valid *erga omnes*, the other (possibly)[90] only *inter partes*, but in both cases the essential mechanism of universality remains the same. This last interpretation, which makes all due allowance for the differences between *aut dedere* and classical customary universality seems to be preferable in that it goes much more to the core of the matter than to factual aspects such as the number of States involved.

It may be said in sum that *aut dedere aut prosequi* is a universal jurisdiction which is *relative, compulsory* and *subsidiary*. As to relativity, it can be seen that the universal jurisdiction established by anti-terrorist conventions has a double relative effect: one in terms of the parties to the agreements (*ratione personae*), and one in terms of the object and purposes thereof (*ratione materiae*).[91] As to compulsoriness, the conventions against terrorism invariably transform this mere faculty into an obligation for the State that holds a suspect. Criminal proceedings must be initiated and carried out against the individual by judicial authorities competent to deal with the case.[92] Finally, as to subsidiarity, the rigidity of the obligation

[89] As is correctly said by De La Pradelle, above n 85, 905: "*La compétence pénale d'une juridiction nationale est dite 'universelle' quand elle s'étend, en principe, à des faits commis n'importe où dans le monde et par n'importe qui; lorsque, par conséquent, un tribunal que ne désigne aucun des critères ordinairement retenus — ni la nationalité d'une victime ou d'un auteur présumé, ni la localisation d'un élément constitutif d'infraction, ni l'atteinte portée aux intérêts fondamentaux de l'Etat – peut, cependant, connaître d'actes accomplis par des étrangers, à l'étranger ou dans un espace échappant à toute souveraineté*".

[90] See below, III.

[91] Cassese, above n 84, 593.

[92] See the several treaty provisions, eg Art 4(2) of the Hague Convention for the Suppression of Unlawful Seizure of Aircraft (1970), Art 5(2) of the Montreal Convention for the Suppression of Unlawful Acts against the Safety of Civil Aviation (1971), Art 3(2) of the United Nations Convention on Internationally Protected Persons (1973), Art 6 of the European Convention on the Suppression of Terrorism (1977), Art 5(2) of the Convention against the Taking of Hostages (1979), Art 6(4) of the Rome Convention on the Safety of Maritime Navigation (1988), and Articles 6(4) and 8(1) of the International Convention for the Suppression of Terrorist Bombings (1997). See also Guillaume, above n 44, 350–353, 367–71; Randall, above n 80, 821.

to try is softened by the alternative option, namely to extradite the alleged culprit to a State able to claim a jurisdictional link. The conventions concerned often favour this option under the *forum conveniens* doctrine.[93] Having thus qualified the "conventional universality" of *aut dedere*, all the similarities and also all the differences with traditional universality under customary international law are put in a clear perspective.

3. *Relationship of the* Aut Dedere *Principle to the Specific Titles of Jurisdiction Contained in the Conventions*

A further question refers to the precise link of the *aut dedere* principle with the several special titles of jurisdiction mentioned in the conventions, eg territoriality or personality. It has been said by authoritative authors[94] that the provision that imposes a duty to prosecute or extradite is not normative in itself, but merely constitutes a *renvoi* to the specific grounds of jurisdiction be they territorial, personal (nationality or flag) or otherwise based, invariably listed in the conventions. Hence, such agreements would merely coordinate repression on those specific grounds, without creating a separate basis of universal jurisdiction.

This restrictive interpretation is not convincing. If such an interpretation were accepted, the separate articles dealing with the obligation to exercise jurisdiction in any case where there is no extradition[95] would be without any *effet utile*. It would have been sufficient to say that a State must exercise its jurisdiction under the specific titles unless it extradites. However, the relevant articles invariably dispose that a contracting State shall be obliged, *without exception whatsoever*, to prosecute if it does not extradite. This is not the same thing as saying that jurisdiction under the specific titles must compulsorily be exercised. A teleological perspective

[93] Guillaume, above n 44, 350, 353, 355 ff. For the European Convention (1977), see eg, G Fraysse-Druesne, "La Convention européenne pour la répression du terrorisme", (1978) 82 *Revue Générale de Droit International Public*, 993 ff.

[94] Higgins, above n 80, 98; Oehler, above n 80, 539.

[95] See eg Art 7 of the Montreal Convention (1971): "The Contracting State in the territory of which the alleged offender is found shall, if it does not extradite him, be obliged, without exception whatsoever and whether or not the offence was committed in its territory, to submit the case to its competent authorities for the purpose of prosecution . . .". In the Convention of Terrorist Bombings (1998), this clear clause was somewhat complicated by the insertion of a sentence which could lend arguments to the opposers: "in cases to which article 6 applies" (see the relevant text above, para 8). However, on closer inspection, no substantive difference can be found. This sentence operates a *renvoi* to Art 6(1) but also to 6(4), ie to the specific ground of jurisdiction and also to the *aut dedere*-ground. Art 6(4) asks any State party to take all necessary measures to establish its jurisdiction over the offences set forth in Art 2 in cases where the alleged offender is present in its territory and it does not extradite him. Consequently, the new *renvoi* in Art 8 must be taken to mean that *as already stated* in Art 6, the States parties must establish jurisdiction over the crimes envisioned by the convention for any case where the offender is found on their territory and is not extradited.

confirms this reading. If the specific grounds listed in the agreements were exclusive, the purpose of these instruments, which is to fill any *lacuna* or safe haven that would result in impunity for a guilty individual, would be defeated.[96] The contribution of these treaties would be limited to rendering prosecution on the basis of specific grounds of jurisdiction compulsory rather than facultative. Unfortunately, the traditional, specific mechanisms do not suffice to ensure punishment. This is precisely the problem that the conclusion of the agreements was intended to correct.

Moreover, an article common to the various conventions provides for the establishment in domestic systems of grounds of jurisdiction allowing in any case the prosecution of a suspect held in custody.[97] Were the strict interpretation to be retained, the systematic and practical use of this article would also become virtually insignificant: since one finds in almost all domestic legal systems the principles of territoriality, personality, and security of the State, requiring the compulsory introduction of such grounds of jurisdiction in national legislation would be meaningless, except in very marginal cases.[98] While such a narrow reading of the agreements would deprive the text of much of its pertinence, an interpretation that admits the existence of universal jurisdiction explains why the addition of new grounds of jurisdiction is necessary.

This conclusion is also warranted by the examination of the various *travaux préparatoires*, which show the larger interpretation to be most in accordance with the will of the contracting parties. The drafters frequently made explicit as well as implicit references to the principle of universality.[99] Thus, it is not surprising to find that the vast majority of authors and official committees alike consider the rule *aut dedere aut prosequi* to be in itself a ground of jurisdiction, and not a mere cross-reference to the specific links traditionally used in such cases.[100]

In sum, it may be said that the conventions establish a true two-tier system of jurisdiction. One limb is erected on a series of specific titles of jurisdiction, either mandatory or optional, which the States must ensure (or may retain) for prosecuting the persons suspected of having committed a crime within the scope of the convention. Another limb is the jurisdiction based on the *aut dedere* principle, which obliges States to establish in their internal law a right to prosecute also in cases without any specific link to the forum any person charged with such acts, to the extent that no extradition takes place. Thus, the States are obliged, by virtue of the

[96] This object and purpose is underlined by F Francioni, "Maritime Terrorism and International Law: The Rome Convention of 1988", (1988) 31 *GYIL*, 276.

[97] See the provisions cited in above n 92.

[98] See for instance in cases relating to the passive personality principle. On this principle, see Oehler, above n 80, 413–29; Oppenheim, above n 80, 471–72.

[99] Randall, above n 80, 826, with numerous references at above n 238.

[100] See the authors referred to above n 80.

conventions, to amend their internal law so that they may prosecute under universal jurisdiction the crimes defined in those conventions. The ultimate basis of jurisdiction in such cases is the presence of the alleged culprit on the territory of the prosecuting State.

4. *Nature of the Duty to Establish the Necessary Criminal Jurisdiction in Municipal Law: Absolute Duty or Duty to Use Best Endeavours?*

The next aspect to be discussed relates to the question if there is a strict duty of the States parties to provide the necessary criminal jurisdictional titles in their internal law or if there is only an obligation to use best endeavours. The answer to this question is two-fold. At the universal level of the conventions concluded under the aegis of the United Nations, there is a strict obligation to extend the national criminal jurisdiction to the contemplated crimes. The relevant clauses read: "Each State shall take such measures as may be necessary to establish its jurisdiction over the offences mentioned ...".[101] The terms of that provision are mandatory as the use of the word "shall" shows. The term "as may be necessary" related to the means by which the obligation is fulfilled. On this point, the conventions respect the constitutional autonomy of the various States. Thus, in some of them a piece of legislation may be necessary in order to make punishable the contemplated acts, whereas in others a decree or an enactment of administrative rules possibly suffices. One can say that the conventions through the words "as may be necessary" insist on the fact that the obligation posed is one of result rather than of means. However, it is clearly a mandatory obligation, as to the result to be achieved.

The same cannot be said of some regional conventions, which, strangely enough if one thinks of the potentially greater solidarities at the regional level, contain only an obligation to use "(best) endeavours" to extend their national criminal jurisdiction to the acts at stake. Thus, Article 8 of the OAS Convention to Prevent and Punish Acts of Terrorism Taking the Form of Crimes against Persons and related Extortion that are of International Significance (1971) reads as follows: "[Contracting States have the obligation] to endeavour to have the criminal acts contemplated in this Convention included in their penal laws, if not already so included". This clause seems to be unique. It is not repeated elsewhere, notably not in the European Convention on the Suppression of Terrorism of 1977, which is aligned with the universal conventions.[102] It seems that

[101] See eg Art 5 of the Montreal Convention for the Suppression of Unlawful Acts against the Safety of Civil Aviation (1971); Art 6 of the Convention on the Suppression of Terrorist Bombings (1998), etc.

[102] See Art 6: "Each Contracting State shall take such measures as may be necessary to establish its jurisdiction over an offence mentioned in article 1 ...". No such clause at all is found in other treaties, eg the SAARC Convention on the Suppression of Terrorism of 1987.

the specific tradition of the American States, particularly attentive as to the protection of their internal affairs, has prompted this deviation from the mainstream. In the context of the best endeavours clause, the yardstick for its interpretation can be only the principle of good faith.[103] Its concrete reach is to be determined according to the socio-political environment, as it evolves. To the extent that events, declarations and perceptions bear witness as to an evolution towards a more strongly felt solidarity in matters of terrorism, the result can only be that the best endeavours clause will be strengthened and the interpretation of what it demands will become more exacting. The legal standard[104] of "(best) endeavours" requires an understanding in the light of social background; only therefrom can its concrete and specific content be identified.

5. *The Obligation to Try or to Extradite: True Alternative or Priority of One Element over the Other?*

At the universal level, and more generally speaking at the only exception of the European Convention and its follow-up texts, the obligation seems at first sight to be a true alternative: either the State tries or extradites, at its choice. As to the result considered in synthesis, this reading is certainly correct. However, from one point of view, one may find that the whole system leans toward the "*prosequi*" limb more than to the "*dedere*" limb, in other words that there is some imbalance. The reason for this is that there is in any case a subsidiary obligation to prosecute, whereas there is no obligation at all to extradite.[105] That means that prosecution must in any case take place, subject only to the possibility of setting it aside if extradition happens to take place. Practically speaking, prosecution must start immediately, or within a reasonable time period it then being able to be stopped if there is extradition (or eventually not to start if extradition is granted immediately). In order to determine if extradition may take place, it will, however, often be necessary that some prosecutorial acts have been performed. This interpretation seems to be confirmed by the aim of these conventions, which is to make sure that the chances to see the alleged culprits prosecuted and tried are raised to a maximum. Extradition is only a device for trial, it has no value in itself except to guarantee the most convenient forum.

On a slightly different reading, one might say that the extradition limb is theoretically and practically dominant. The theoretical reason is precisely to ensure the prosecution at the most convenient place, notably

[103] On this principle, see R Kolb, *La bonne foi en droit international public* (Paris, 2000).
[104] On the concept of legal standards, see the explanations in Kolb, *ibid*, 134 ff., with many references.
[105] This is the system of the conventions, independently from other bilateral or multilateral extradition treaties.

where the crime was committed (*forum conveniens*). The practical reason is that a State not otherwise linked with the offence will have some difficulty in prosecuting without the legal aid of other States concerned. Thus, from a practical perspective, it will seek first for extradition to a more convenient forum. Both ways of looking at the relationship of the two limbs are correct. They grasp the phenomenon under different but complementary perspectives.

Furthermore one understands that in regard to the aims only extradition for trial (i.e. extradition proper) suffices to satisfy the conventional requirement. An expulsion is not covered, since it would defeat the object and purpose of the convention, which is to assure that prosecution takes place.

As the preceding explanations have shown, the conventions establish an original obligation to prosecute, unless extradition takes place. In particular, this means that prosecution is not dependent on the existence of a request to extradite that was not acted upon (*primo dedere secundo prosequi*). However, a State may on its own initiative take up contacts with other interested States in order to see if an extradition is possible, desired or otherwise recommended. Its primary obligation to prosecute does not mean that it is precluded to actively seek extradition.[106]

At the European level, the priorities are reversed. In fact, the European Convention on the Suppression of Terrorism (1977) is in the first place an extradition treaty. Thus, it privileges extradition over prosecution. The obligation to prosecute is here limited to cases where an extradition is requested but not granted.[107] The situation is further complicated by a rule of double jurisdiction: the request for extradition must emanate from a State party whose jurisdiction is based on a rule of jurisdiction existing equally in the law of the requested State. Put simply: if the request for extradition is based on the principle of passive personality, that title must exist at the level of both municipal laws, that of the requesting State and that of the requested State. The European Convention thus establishes a system of *primo dedere secundo prosequi*. And extradition can be refused if it is not based on the stringent conditions laid down in Article 6 of the Convention. If such refusal takes place, there is a subsidiary obligation to prosecute. This obligation is formulated in Article 7. The whole system, contrary to the other conventions, is not, however, watertight. Its

[106] See Henzelin, above n 80, 298 ff.

[107] See Art 6 of the Convention: "1. Each Contracting State shall take such measures as may be necessary to establish its jurisdiction over an offence mentioned article 1 in the case where the suspected offender is present in its territory and it does not extradite him after receiving a request for extradition from a Contracting State whose jurisdiction is based on a rule of jurisdiction existing equally in the law of the requested State". See also Henzelin, above n 80, 318 ff. As to the European system, see also Freestone, above n 85, 55 ff.

purpose cannot be said to guarantee prosecution in any case where the offender is apprehended on the territory of a State party, since in the absence of a request of extradition, there is no obligation whatsoever to prosecute. It is true that optional prosecution according to the existing jurisdictional titles of municipal law is still possible in such cases. But there is no precise obligation. Such a system, which remains behind the achievements of the global community, is more than strange within a regional community, which misses no occasion to stress its bonds of solidarity.

Extradition in the sense of the conventions is the delivery of a person to another State in order that this State exercises criminal jurisdiction. The terminology used to describe this procedure is not material. The surrender of an alleged culprit to an international tribunal, to the extent that it has jurisdiction over the acts, is also such a procedure, even if there is technically no "extradition". This is to be understood in the sense that the handing over must be for the purpose of prosecution and trial elsewhere. A more delicate question, which could arise in the future, is if the obligation under the convention is satisfied in the following case. A person is delivered to an international tribunal, eg the International Criminal Court, which has no jurisdiction over terrorist crimes as such, but which could try the culprit for other crimes, even more grave in nature (eg crimes against humanity). If the terrorist acts in question, because of their magnitude, fall into such a category, there is no legal difficulty in establishing jurisdiction. In view of the gravity of the crimes, it may well be that the delivery of a terrorist suspect to the Court fulfils the conventional requirement to prosecute suspects, at least as to their spirit: i.e. the alleged culprit will be tried. But he will not be tried for the terrorist acts envisaged in the convention.

Another question arises. The conventions envisage extradition without specifying if this means only extradition to another State party or extradition to any State whatsoever. The fact that the aim of the conventions is to ensure prosecution and that the aim of extradition is to ensure prosecution at the most convenient forum, warrants the interpretation that extradition to any relevant State is allowed.[108] The conventions do not establish a closed system of extradition, aiming only at extraditions *inter partes*. They envisage extradition *tout court*, as an effective means of suppression; that is not linked to the status of a State as a party to the convention. Moreover, by the rules of treaty construction it would have to be expected that the parties, had they intended such a restriction on the scope of extradition, should have expressed it so in the text. Not having qualified the mechanism of extradition in any manner, it is hard to read into the text such a limitation. In a word, such important limitations cannot be presumed in

[108] In the same sense Henzelin, above n 80, 304.

the absence of clear language, or at least intent made explicit in the phase of preparatory work.

Finally it may be noted that the conventions also seek to promote extradition by providing new bases for its performance. Thus, the conventions provide that the offences they list shall be deemed to be included as extraditable offences in already existing extradition treaties.[109] By this technique, the conventions modify older extradition treaties within their scope of application, by way of the *lex posterior* rule. Moreover, the conventions stipulate that they may in themselves be taken as an extradition title if an extradition treaty is absent between the concerned States and this absence would otherwise preclude extradition: "If a Contracting State which makes extradition conditional on the existence of a treaty receives a request for extradition from another Contracting State with which it has no extradition treaty, it may at its option consider this Convention as the legal basis for extradition in respect of the offences".[110] Note that this provision is only optional, not obligatory.

6. *Conventional Universal Jurisdiction as Mandatory Jurisdiction*

Under customary international law, there is hardly any case in which the principle of universality *must* be exercised by the State holding the offender. An exception may exist for grave breaches of the Geneva Conventions, since under the Conventions jurisdiction is mandatory and it could be argued that by the practically universal ratification of (or accession to) these conventions, the mandatory jurisdiction over grave breaches has become part of customary international law. Apart from this peculiar case, customary universal jurisdiction is optional: international law allows prosecution by any State for the crimes defined under customary law. It does not, however, oblige those States to prosecute. In legal terms, customary universality is predicated on a faculty, not an obligation.[111] Conventional universality may also be optional. One may mention Article 5 of the Convention on the Suppression and Punishment of the Crime of Apartheid (1973).[112] In the other conventions, universality, in the form of the *aut dedere* principle, is mandatory. It is an obligation not a faculty. This holds true for all universal and most regional anti-terrorist conventions. The precise extent of that obligation still has to be analysed.

[109] See eg Art 8(1) of the Montreal Convention (1971) or Art 11(1) of the Convention on Terrorist Financing. In the United Nations Draft Convention on Terrorism (2001), see Art 17(1) (see *Report of the Working Group* ... (above n 2), 13).

[110] See eg Art 8(2) of the Montreal Convention (1971) or Art 11(2) of the Convention on Terrorist Financing. In the United Nations Draft Convention on Terrorism (2001), see Art 17(2) (see *Report of the Working Group* ... (above n 2), 13).

[111] See on this point Stern, above n 80, 737 ff; De La Pradelle, above n 85, 912 ff.

[112] See 1015 UNTS 246.

More precisely, is there simply a formal duty to prosecute or also an obligation to carry out that duty effectively? Can prosecution be prevented or stopped according to rules of internal law, eg by virtue of the opportunity principle?

It should be stressed again that the obligation to prosecute is subsidiary in the sense that it is subject to the absence of extradition. The legal fact of extradition extinguishes that duty.

7. *Duty to Prosecute "in the same Manner as in the Case of any Ordinary Offence of a Serious Nature under Municipal Law"*

The several universal and regional conventions contain a clause whereby the prosecution, if extradition is refused or does not take place, shall be conducted according to the standards of municipal law. This clause reads more or less invariably as follows: "The authorities shall take their decision in the same manner as in the case of any ordinary offence of a serious nature under the law of that State".[113] The clause amounts to a species of "national treatment" standard as opposed to an international minimum standard, if the analogy may be taken that far.[114]

This aspect of the law may hamper the effective application of the conventions and especially the fulfilment of their primary aim, which is to ensure that prosecution should take place. It is beyond doubt that the clause is a major drawback in the system, since a frequent problem in the field of anti-terrorist action is that even when there are bases of jurisdiction, States often display great reluctance to exercise their right of prosecution. The reasons for this state of affairs are political. In particular, many States fear the political implications of such proceedings or shy away from them because they expect to become the target of terrorist "reprisals". The clause at hand gives them the legal tool in order to comply with the conventional obligation to prosecute. It is obvious that the clause greatly weakens the incisiveness of the obligations. It may be going too far to say that the obligation thus transforms itself into a soft-law duty. However, if one considers the links between the executive branch and the prosecuting organs in many States, the result may not be too far from such a soft duty. Even abuse of the clause may be difficult to claim if the internal practice usually follows such patterns, whereby the executive intervenes in matters of the judiciary.

[113] See eg Art 7 of the Montreal Convention for the Suppression of Unlawful Acts against the Safety of Civil Aviation (1971); Art 8(1) of the Convention on the Suppression of Terrorist Bombings (1998), the term "serious nature" being here replaced by the term "grave nature" which does not entail any substantive difference. At the regional level, see eg Art 7 of the European Convention on the Suppression of Terrorism (1977).

[114] As to this question of the law of State responsibility for damages suffered by foreigners on its territory, see eg the synthesis in DF Vagts, "Minimum Standard", (1985) 8 *EPIL*, 382–5.

Conversely, it could be argued that with the ratification of, or accession to, the conventions, and the undertakings thus assumed towards the other States parties, the reach of the "national treatment clause" has been somewhat modified. In other words, it could be said that there is a prevailing duty to investigate the case in good faith according to a minimum standard of diligence. If a prosecution is interfered with or stopped by the political organs for reasons unconnected to the file of the accused, the object and purpose of the conventions would may been circumvented,[115] amounting to a breach of the State's obligations under international law.

Sometimes the problem is that no reasonable prosecution can be expected by the State holding the alleged culprit since it holds a protective hand over him. That was the problem encountered (or at least denounced) by the Western States in the *Lockerbie* case, in which Libya insisted on its right to prosecute the alleged perpetrators of the Panam flight bombed when flying over the locality of Lockerbie.[116] In such cases, the problem is to determine which are the most appropriate remedies. It may be asked, for instance, if it is possible to presume *a priori* that no serious prosecution will take place and hence to take preventive action to secure extradition or surrender of the persons involved. Alternatively — and there are some good arguments for it — the State of custody must first be given a chance to show that it will seriously prosecute, according to the general presumption in international law of the good faith of a State until the contrary is proven.[117] Moreover, what action could be taken, either preventively or after failure to adequately prosecute? In the *Lockerbie* case the Western States were sure to have the backing of the Security Council, which could impose on Libya an obligation to extradite under Chapter VII of the Charter of the United Nations; in fact the Council did so.[118] It may be questioned whether this is an adequate or even practicable way to solve future cases of the same type. Finally, it may be asked who or which body appraises if the prosecution was carried out by the State of custody seriously. A lenient penalty or even the dismissal

[115] Violation of the object and purpose of a treaty may be a ground of breach of the treaty. See R Kolb, *La bonne foi en droit international public* (Paris, 2000), 283 ff. In judicial practice, see notably the *Military and paramilitary activities in and against Nicaragua* (Merits), ICJ Rep 1986, 135 ff.

[116] As to this case in our context, see eg Gilbert, above n 40, 24–25. See also J Chappez, "Questions d'interprétation et d'application de la Convention de Montréal de 1971 résultant de l'incident de Lockerbie. Mesures conservatoires, Ordonnance du 14 avril 1992", (1992) 38 *Annuaire Français de Droit International*, 468 ff. See also A Aust, "Lockerbie: The Other Case", (2000) 49 *International and Comparative Law Quarterly*, 278 ff. On the action of the Security Council in relation to the *aut dedere* principle, see M Plachta, "The Lockerbie case: The Role of the Security Council in Enforcing the Principle Aut Dedere Aut Judicare", (2001) 12 *European Journal of International Law*, 125 ff.

[117] See eg the *Certain German Interests in Polish Upper Silesia* case (1926), PCIJ, ser A, no 7, p 30. See generally Kolb, above n 115, 124–27.

[118] See Resolution 748 of 1992.

of the proceedings cannot necessarily be seen as proof of lack of good faith. At most, such events may be the cause for further investigation. But who can or should be in a position to judge such facts objectively?

The precise scope of the mentioned "national treatment clause" must be clarified in three ways.

First, it is not automatically incompatible with the conventions to handle a case arising under their regimes according to the principle of opportunity of prosecution. Some degree of discretion may be left to the prosecutor to decide if the case should be pursued or not if the criteria he uses in this regard also apply to comparable municipal crimes. The point would be to know how the discretion has been exercised, i.e. if there are cogent or at least understandable reasons for abandoning prosecution. It needs not be stressed that the appraisal of such discretion by third States is a most difficult undertaking. Probably only cases of the most egregious abuses could give rise to international claims.

Second, proceedings may *a fortiori* be dismissed if it appears that the alleged culprit is innocent or otherwise not punishable. The obligation of the State is not to try, but to submit the case to the competent authorities in view of prosecution. That is the reason why it is preferable to speak of *aut dedere aut prosequi* rather than using the more frequently encountered version of *aut dedere aut iudicare*. If on the face of the proceedings it proves impossible to continue the prosecution of the alleged culprit because of some obstacle of municipal law (eg an amnesty law), is there a newly emerging duty under customary law to extradite the person concerned? It seems that the point has not been raised up to now. It can be argued that such an obligation, dormant pending prosecution, arises once prosecution is barred for reasons other than proof of innocence. This would be consistent with the aim of the conventions, which is to assure widest possible prosecution. More delicate still is the question if such a duty arises also if a prescription or time bar prevents prosecution in a particular State. An affirmative answer is possible, but it could also be argued that in such a case there is no punishable crime any more in the prosecuting State, this being a bar to extradition. And finally it could be asked if a duty of extradition may arise anew if a tribunal dismissed the claim of the accused on some formal grounds. True, the principle *ne bis in idem* does not apply directly to proceedings in two different States.[119] But it seems difficult to impose a duty of extraditing after such a judicial procedure, in the absence of any clear wording in the conventional texts.

[119] See the jurisprudence of the United Nations Committee on Human Rights, *AP v Italy* (1988), *Communication no 204/1986*, para 7.3: "[A]rticle 14(7)… does not guarantee *ne bis in idem* with regard to the national jurisdictions of two or more States. The Committee observes that this provision prohibits double jeopardy only with regard to an offence adjudicated in a given State". See also M Nowak, *UN Covenant on Civil and Political Rights, CCPR Commentary* (Kehl/Strasbourg, 1993), 272–73.

Third, it may be asked to what extent pardon or any type of amnesty after conviction is compatible with the conventions. The letter of the conventions, which reserves the whole prosecution phase to internal law, covers such pardons or amnesties. This is so because internal law continues to be applicable after conviction. On the other hand, it is apparent that the device of pardon can be used to play havoc with the conventional obligations: a State seems to respect the relevant convention by convicting, but soon after doing so, it empties the obligation to prosecute of all content by exercising its right to grant amnesty. The granting of amnesties for international crimes has been denounced in legal doctrine as being incompatible with the conventions.[120] It could be argued that such acts would be contrary to good faith. If, however, the pardon or amnesty is granted after a long period of time (or even after a shorter period but because of good reasons), it may still be compatible with the conventions. There is no clause in the conventions which expressly takes away from States their sovereign right to grant pardon or amnesty. However, when prosecution of a terrorist suspect takes place by (indirect) application of an international convention, the prosecuting State acts not only for itself but also on behalf of the other States parties. It thus loses the right to grant pardon or amnesty as a means of circumventing the convention, since by that conduct it affects the legal interests of the other States parties. The line between a legitimate and an illegitimate use of pardon or amnesty may be thin in some cases. It may be added that the Rome Statute of the International Criminal Court (1998) provides in Article 110(1) that "the State of enforcement shall not release the person before expiry of the sentence pronounced by the Court". Paragraph 2 adds that "the Court alone shall have the right to decide any reduction of sentence ...". The reasons for such regulation is precisely to forestall actions taken by States parties in bad faith and more generally to prevent inequalities in the length sentences as a result of political influences in the States of enforcement.

Finally, it may be asked to what extent the States having become parties to the conventions assumed a duty to guarantee the effective application of their obligations thereof.[121] It is clearly not sufficient for States to formally submit a case for prosecution to the competent authorities if there is no real intent to carry out that prosecution. Following this line of thinking, it has been argued that the obligation is to handle the case in good faith without seeking to circumvent the obligations under the conventions; no specific guarantee as to effectiveness is spelled out in the conventions or is otherwise incumbent on the States parties.[122] It seems that a somewhat more far-reaching interpretation can be given. As it was

[120] See JA Frowein in *Centre d'étude*, above n 33, 84.
[121] See generally Henzelin, above n 80, 304–6.
[122] *Ibid.*

explained, States undertake to act in good faith, ie in a manner not frustrating the object and purpose of the conventions. Moreover, they undertake the obligation to prosecute (or to extradite) to the maximum possible extent. This duty may provoke international claims that States parties are acting contrary to the object and purpose of the conventions or are failing to fulfil the criterion of effectiveness where municipal law hampers a prosecution. In other words, the *renvoi* to internal law could be construed as a *renvoi* to the ordinary and reasonable rules governing prosecution. Therefore extraordinary and excessive limitations to prosecution under domestic law would be deemed incompatible with the State's treaty obligations. Consequently, effectiveness would be measured according to: (1) the general prohibition of defeating the object and purpose of the convention under the principle of good faith; and (2) the prohibition of excessive municipal law impediments. In the latter case, if a State wants to become a party to the convention, it would have to modify its internal law or enter a valid reservation.

8. *The Faculty of Qualifying a Terrorist Act as a Political Offence*

Most States reserve to their courts or to the executive the right to decide whether a person requested for extradition is a political offender and, if they so find, to refuse extradition. This is part of a long-standing tradition, in particular in anglo-saxon States, but also elsewhere. The idea that terrorist acts should not be covered by the privilege of the political offence exception has since the XIXth century led to the inclusion of so-called Belgian clauses[123] into a series of treaties of extradition. Their aim was to exclude certain terrorist acts from the the political offence exception. A person whose act threatens not only the political system of a State but also the interests of the entire international community should *a fortiori* not qualify for an exemption from extradition. Thus, in principle, the acts listed in the terrorist conventions should not be regarded as political offences. However, the long-standing tradition in several States of allowing the State authorities to decide whether to grant perpetrators the status of a political offender remained. Consequently, since the 1937 League of Nations Convention, when such a clause was debated but not adopted,[124]

[123] This clause owes its name to a modification of the Belgian law on extradition operated in 1856. Its purpose was to deny the status of political offence to acts of violence perpetrated against the person of a foreign head of government or of State or against members of his their family. It had been a consequence of a request for extradition submitted by France against two French anarchists having fled to Belgium after having attempted at the life of Napoléon III. On this clause, see G Wailliez, *L'infraction politique en droit positif belge* (Brussels, 1970), 225.

[124] See J Dugard, "International Terrorism: Problems of Definition", (1974) 50 *International Affairs*, 77–78.

the several anti-terrorist conventions make allowance for political offence qualification. The relevant articles operate a *renvoi* to municipal law, thereby implicitly recognising the availability of the political offence doctrine. Thus, for instance, Article 8 of the Montreal Convention for the Suppression of Unlawful Acts against the Safety of Civil Aviation (1971) provides that any extradition is subject to the extradition treaties among the States concerned (these treaties including normally the political offence reservation) or, if extradition takes place outside such a treaty, that it is subject to the "conditions provided by the law of the requested State" (which again contains that limitation).

One might have thought that at the regional level, where solidarities are more strongly felt, the political offence exception would have become less prevalent. The European Convention on the Suppression of Terrorism of 1977 shows that this is not necessarily the case. Although Article 1 provides that "for the purposes of extradition between contracting States, none of the following offences shall be regarded as a political offence ...", Article 13 allows reservations, and it explicitly allows States to "declare that [a State] reserves the right to refuse extradition in respect of any offence mentioned in article 1 which it considers a political offence".[125] Consequently, the restrictions to the political offence exception listed in Article 1 can be effectively nullified by Article 13. To some extent, this avenue has been narrowed by the Dublin Agreement of the member States of the EC concerning the application of the European Convention of 1977 (1980).[126] Further progress will be made when extradition procedures will be abolished within the EC and replaced by a form of simplified delivery. Developments in that sense are under way.[127]

On the universal level signs of a tightening of the political offence exception have also become apparent. This may reflect the increased perception that terrorism constitutes a common scourge. In parallel, it means that its highly political character is diminishing in favour of a more technical conception which considers only the need to suppress such acts of violence and not the whole context of causes and justifications for terrorist activity. It was the Convention for the Suppression of Terrorist Bombings (1998) which first included the following clause: "None of the offences set forth in article 2 shall be regarded, for the purposes of extradition or mutual legal assistance, as a political offence ...".[128] Moreover, in order to close any loophole, the Convention adds in Article 9(5) that the provisions of all extradition treaties (or other arrangements) incompatible

[125] On the whole question within European Law, see Gilbert, above n 40, 14 ff.
[126] *Ibid*, 19.
[127] See the Commission's Proposal for a *Council Framework Decision on the European Arrest Warrant and the Surrender Procedures between the Member States*, Doc. COM(2001) 522 final/2, 25 September 2001.
[128] Art 11. See (1988) 37 *ILM*, 257.

with regard to offences set forth in Article 2 shall be deemed to be modified as between the States parties to the extent that they are incompatible with the Convention. Thus the Convention with its exclusion of the political offence exception takes precedence over any political offence exception clause contained in previous extradition treaties. Finally, Article 9(1) obliges States parties to include such offences as extraditable offences in any extradition treaty subsequently concluded. Similar clauses are to be found in the later Convention on the Suppression of the Financing of Terrorism (1999)[129] and in more recent regional Conventions, eg the Convention of the Organization of the Islamic Conference on Combating International Terrorism (1999).[130] A similar provision is included in the Draft Convention of the United Nations on International Terrorism (2001). Article 14 of that Draft[131] provides that none of the listed offences may be considered as political offences for the purpose of extradition.

To this it may be added that State practice is equally moving towards such a restriction, at least in the practice of Western States.[132] In particular, domestic courts have followed suit. In the United States, the courts in the cases of *Eain v Wilkes* (1981)[133] and *Quinn v Robinson* (1989)[134] opened the way for this evolution. The political offence clause was interpreted to exclude acts of terrorism, particularly where they involved indiscriminate bombings of civilian targets. In *T v Immigration Officer and Secretary of State for the Home Department* (1996),[135] the English House of Lords interpreted the terms of Article 1(F) of the Convention Relating to the Status of Refugees (1951), ie "serious non-political crime", as excluding acts of terrorism, namely acts of indiscriminate killing. In the Netherlands, the State Secretary of Justice sent a letter to the Parliament on the application of the Refugees Convention. In this letter dated 28 November 1997, he explained that hijacking, assaults upon diplomats, kidnapping, hostage-taking, bomb attacks and letter bombs will not be considered political crimes in the context of Article 1F. He added that, furthermore: "[I]n interpreting the concept serious non-political crime, I will take into account the recent developments in the field of suppression of terrorism in the various international fora ...".[136]

It is too early to see in this evolution a growing obsolescence of the political offence exception in the context of terrorist acts. It is difficult to

[129] See Articles 14 and 11: (2000) 39 *ILM*, 275–6.
[130] See Art 1(4)(c). See the text in: <http//www.oic_un.org/26icfm/c.html>;.
[131] See *Report of the Working Group*, above n 2, 12.
[132] See eg J Dugard, "Terrorism and International Law: Consensus at Last?" in *Essays in Honor of M Bedjaoui* (The Hague, 1999), 168–70.
[133] 641 F 2d 504 (7th Cir 1981), 520.
[134] 783 F 2d 776 (9th Cir 1989), 805–6.
[135] 107 *ILR*, 552 ff.
[136] (1999) 30 *Netherlands Yearbook of International Law*, 178 ff, 185.

retroactively read into the earlier conventions an abrogation of the political offence exception in the light of the new tendencies. But a slight change of perspective may shed a different light on the matter. Such an interpretation could be adopted in the more recent conventions which list the acts contained in the previous ones as not falling into the category of political offences.[137] A modification of the old conventions by the *lex poterior* rule could then be assumed, particulary because the older conventions do not contain any explicit clause reserving the political offence qualification. However, this modification would be *inter partes* and could not be automatically taken as extending to all the States parties. As for third States, a general *opinio iuris* would have to be shown. The new tendencies could, however, be considered as exerting a general pressure to interpret those acts listed in older conventions as being exempt from the political offence exception.

To the foregoing it may be added that a State may always refuse extradition on the grounds that it appears that the person whose extradition is requested would face torture or other inhumane treatment in the State seeking his extradition, or if it appears that extradition is sought only to persecute him on account of his race, religion, nationality or political opinion.[138]

9. *The Presence of the Alleged Offender in the Territory of the State*

In order that a State party be subject to the obligation of *aut dedere aut prosequi*, all the conventions invariably require that the alleged offender must be present in its territory. This requirement shows that the *aut dedere* principle is based on the idea of a *iudex deprehensionis*. *In absentia* proceedings are ruled out. To the extent that municipal law is unchanged by the conventions and to the extent that such a requirement is not reflective of customary law, it can still be argued that under other bases of jurisdiction the prosecution of such acts may be also undertaken in cases where the offender is absent from a territory. But under the convention regime this is not possible, and to the best of this author's knowledge, no State yet has passed legislation empowering it

[137] See eg Art 2(1)(a) of the Convention for the Suppression of the Financing of Terrorism (2000), (2000) 39 *ILM*, 271. That provision operates a *renvoi* to all the main anti-terrorist treaties.

[138] See generally DJ Harris, M O'Boyle and C Warbrick, *Law of the European Convention on Human Rights* (London/Dublin/Edinburgh, Butterworths, 1995), 73 ff; Nowak, above n 119, 136–7. See also the article by the present author "La jurisprudence internationale en matière de torture et de traitements inhumains ou dégradants", (2003) *Revue universelle des droits de l'homme* (forthcoming). As for conventional clauses, see eg Art 8(2) of the European Convention on the Suppression of Terrorism (1977).

to institute *in absentia* proceedings for a person suspected of terrorist acts prohibited by the conventions.[139]

A further problem is to define the precise scope of the obligations of the States parties in regards to this requirement. If the authorities happen to stumble upon an alleged offender, it stands to reason that they must arrest him and initiate prosecution. But such situations form only part of the matter. It has been argued by many commentators that in order to fulfil the conventional requirement, a State party is obliged to make investigations into the whereabouts of alleged offenders, eg if private persons make a report to the police, or otherwise institute proceedings.[140] It is argued that it is only by such a duty that the obligation to suppress terrorist acts could be fulfilled. No other actor but the State has the means of carrying out such investigations. The duty to investigate would thus be thus incumbent on States party to anti-terrorist conventions. This argument produces the further question as to the scope of that duty on the part of the State. If a duty to actively search for terrorist suspects can be inferred, it would seem excessively onerous to assume that States must take all necessary (and presumably legal) measures in order to secure the presence of the alleged culprits in their territory. States may take such measures,[141] but they are not obliged to do so under the conventions. This interpretation is affirmed by the more recent anti-terrorist conventions. Thus, the Convention on the Suppression of Terrorist Bombings (1998),[142] the Convention for the Suppression of Terrorist Financing (1999),[143] and the United Nations Draft Convention on International Terrorism (2001)[144] all contain a clause which reads as follows: "Upon receiving information that a person who has committed or is alleged to have committed an offence as set forth in article [x] may be present in its territory, the State Party concerned shall take such measures as may be necessary under its domestic law to investigate the facts contained in the information". This clause may be interpreted as providing an obligation to search for alleged offenders, since otherwise the said investigation would lose much of its value. No further positive duties seem to arise under the conventions. The question can be asked if this more extensive duty may have become

[139] The Belgian Legislation of 1993 does not contain any condition of presence in the territory for prosecuting war crimes, crimes against humanity and genocide; terrorism is however not covered. On the Belgian Legislation, see A Andries, C Van Den Wijngaert, E David and J Verhaegen, "Commentaire de la loi du 16 juin 1993 relative à la répression des infractions graves au droit international humanitaire", (1994) 11 *Revue de droit pénal et de criminologie,* 1114 ff.

[140] On this question, see eg B Stern, "A propos de la compétence universelle ...", *Essays in Honor of M. Bedjaoui* (The Hague/London/Boston, 1999), 747 ff.

[141] See Stern, *ibid*, 748.

[142] Art 7(1).

[143] Art 9(1).

[144] Art 10(1).

incorporated into the older conventions by reason of recent practice and agreements. If so, this would constitute an informal modification of the former conventions. The answer to this question is uncertain, but it does seem possible to argue that such an implied treaty modification has taken place.

A further point relates to the question of what happens if the alleged offender is not any more on the territory of the prosecuting State. Consider the situation where the suspect is in the territory at the moment the prosecution is launched, but later, because of some reason, eg flight, does not any more find himself in that territory. Must the prosecution be stopped? It has been suggested[145] that the answer depends on municipal law: if such discontinuance is necessary for comparable common crimes under domestic law, then the State may stop the prosecution without violating the convention by applying its internal law to which the conventions refer. This means that a State may also continue the prosecution without violating the convention, to the extent its internal law allows it to do so (which is normally the case). If this interpretation is correct, the rule as to the required presence of the alleged offender in the territory of the prosecuting State must be read to mean that the offender must definitely be present in the territory at the beginning of the proceedings, but that later default of this requirement does not vitiate proceedings already started. This is comparable to the judicial rule of the *forum perpetuum*.[146]

10. *The Problem of Incongruent Offences under the Conventions and Municipal Law*

There is a further problem which will be dealt with only briefly. The conventions oblige States parties to adopt in their internal law legislation

[145] See Henzelin, above n 80, 306.

[146] A rule recently reaffirmed by the International Court of Justice in the *Lockerbie (Preliminary Objections)* case, Judgment of 27 February 1998, ICJ Reports 1998, 9 ff, paras 37–38: "37. In the present case, the United Kingdom has contended, however, that even if the Montreal Convention did confer on Libya the rights it claims, they could not be exercised in this case because they were superseded by Security Council resolutions 748 (1992) and 883 (1993) which, by virtue of Articles 25 and 103 of the United Nations Charter, have priority over all rights and obligations arising out of the Montreal Convention. The Respondent has also argued that, because of the adoption of those resolutions, the only dispute which existed from that point on was between Libya and the Security Council; this, clearly, would not be a dispute falling within the terms of Article 14, paragraph 1, of the Montreal Convention and thus not one which the Court could entertain.

38. The Court cannot uphold this line of argument. Security Council resolutions 748 (1992) and 883 (1993) were in fact adopted after the filing of the Application on 3 March 1992. In accordance with its established jurisprudence, if the Court had jurisdiction on that date, it continues to do so; the subsequent coming into existence of the above-mentioned resolutions cannot affect its jurisdiction once established (See *Nottebohm*, Preliminary Objection, Judgment, ICJ Reports 1953, p 122; *Right of Passage over Indian Territory*, Preliminary Objections, Judgment, ICJ Reports 1957, p 142)."

necessary to suppress the acts listed in the conventions. If the States incorporate into their internal law the list of acts under the conventions as such, there would be a perfect congruence between the conventions and internal law. Obviously the interpretations given to the same terms contained in the conventions may differ from State to State, but this is another problem. Sometimes, however, States do not incorporate the crimes in the conventions precisely as they figure in the conventions. While States parties may not fail to suppress all the acts listed in the conventions, they may add to the list of acts in the conventions, either by broadening their definitions, or by providing for the possibility to prosecute further acts not listed in the conventions. To the extent that the conventions do not "exclude any criminal jurisdiction exercised in accordance with national law",[147] there may be no legal difficulty with such a course. It should nonetheless be stressed that for the acts listed in the conventions, there exists *ipso facto* an international title for prosecution at the national level, at least *inter partes*. For acts other than those listed in the conventions, the State must show that national prosecution is allowed under international law, more precisely, under general international law or under some specific title as against the other State(s) involved.

In some cases there may be delicate problems when acts are to be prosecuted by national authorities pursuant to a piece of domestic legislation which goes beyond what is customarily the recognised scope of the universality principle. For example, the Belgian legislation of 1993 provides for prosecution of grave breaches of the Geneva Conventions of 1949 in the context of non-international armed conflicts. It is commonly understood that international law does not go that far. Universality is recognised only for grave breaches committed in the course of an international armed conflict. The problems that may arise in such cases are numerous and cannot be addressed here.[148]

C. The National Suppression of Terrorist Acts under Customary International Law

At the level of customary international law, we must immediately distinguish two sets of situations: (1) the definitions of terrorist acts under the conventions whose status in general international law may be the object of enquiry; (2) the crime of terrorism as such (however defined), which may

[147] See eg Art 5(3) of the Montreal Convention on the Suppression of Unlawful Acts against the Safety of Civil Aviation (1971), or Art 6(5) of the Convention on the Suppression of Terrorist Bombings (1998).
[148] See the reflections of Stern, above n 140, 741 ff.

give rise to national prosecutions, especially under universal jurisdiction. Both aspects have to be analysed separately.

1. *Universal Jurisdiction under General International Law for Terrorist Offences as Defined in the Conventions*

What is the status of the various universal anti-terrorist conventions under customary international law? Can they have some normative effects on States not party to them even outside the realm of customary law? In other words: can States initiate the prosecution of suspects on the basis of the universality principle without being party to the instruments that provide for and organise such prosecution? Can their own nationals be prosecuted under universal jurisdiction by a State party to such a convention? Legal commentators answer these questions in three different ways.

The first possible answer is that the anti-terrorist conventions set rules and principles which are strictly conventional and thus only valid *inter partes*. Consequently, the principle *aut dedere aut prosequi* binds only States party to the conventions.[149] It has not yet become customary.[150] There is thus no *erga omnes* universality (*aut dedere*) for terrorist offences as defined by the conventions.[151] This view entails two consequences: (1) the *aut dedere aut prosequi* obligation *must* be exercised only by States parties, third States having no obligation to apply it; but also, (2) the *aut dedere aut prosequi* rule *may* be exercised only by States parties, third States having no title to do so under general international law (but they may have a particular title if there is a delegation of jurisdiction by a State holding jurisdiction). As can be seen, proposition (2) goes very much beyond proposition (1) and is not self-evident. According to both scenarios, a third State has neither the duty, nor the faculty to exercise universality over the offences listed in the conventions. Some authors of this group have recently somewhat softened their position, albeit maintaining that the *aut dedere* principle remains for the time being only conventional. Higgins,[152] for example, is of the view that for the moment the principle is only treaty-based, but that it will soon be possible to ask, as ratification of the anti-terrorist treaties augments, if it does not also apply customarily.

149 See eg Oehler, above n 80, 520; Cassese, above n 85, 593–4; De Schutter, above n 85, 388; Dinstein, above n 85, 70; Higgins, above n 80, 98; L Migliorino, "La Dichiarazione delle Nazioni Unite sulle misure per eliminare il terrorismo internazionale", (1995) 78 *Rivista di diritto internazionale*, 970.

150 See LFE Goldie, "Profile of a Terrorist: Distinguishing Freedom Fighters from Terrorists", (1987) 14 *Syracuse Journal of International Law and Commerce*, 141 ff, p. 131; Dinstein, above n 85, 70; *Centre d'étude et de recherche*,above n 33, 39; Migliorino, above n 149, 970; Henzlin, above n 80, 306, according to whom it is specifically the *opinio iuris* that is lacking.

151 See eg Benavides, above n 80, 59–61.

152 See Higgins, above n 4, 26.

A second view holds that the principle *aut dedere aut iudicare* already belongs to general international law. This may be argued in several ways. One school of thought[153] is that one needs only to look at State practice and *opinio iuris*. There is the series of treaties which invariably reproduce the same principles, thus showing that there is a general conviction in their suitability or even necessity. There may also be sufficient practice in the form of statements and recommendations at the international level as well as judicial decisions by national courts affirming the principle. Proponents of another school of thought examine the matter on a more axiomatic level. They anchor the customary status of the *aut dedere* principle to a vision of the international community as *civitas maxima* whose role is to safeguard vital interests common to all its members. The prevention and suppression of international crimes is unquestionably a vital need of the international community.[154] A slightly different version of this axiomatic reasoning suggests that the duty to try or extradite is inherent in the concept of an international criminal act (*delictum iuris gentium*). Given that acts that violate the international public order are contrary to an essential aspect of the international rule of law, and that they cannot be punished by non-existent international organs dedicated to this purpose, international law would make their repression (through trial or extradition) incumbent upon each State, through some form of compulsory *dédoublement fonctionnel.*[155] Identifying the source defining the offence, be it custom or a multilateral treaty, would be irrelevant in such a case.[156]

[153] See eg Freestone, above n 85, 60, at least for the conventions having secured a substantial degree of ratifications or accessions: "Indeed, in relation to the core of offences which are covered by those multilateral conventions which have achieved wide adherence – such as hijacking and hostage-taking — it might be argued that this general pattern of treaty practice ... suggests that ... a wider core of terrorist offences are subject to jurisdiction according to this principle [*aut dedere aut prosequi*] under customary international law."

[154] MC Bassiouni and EM Wise, *Aut dedere aut judicare: The Duty to Extradite or Prosecute in International Law* (Dordrecht, Martinus Nijhoff Publishers, 1995), 22–24, 26 ff; EM Wise, "Extradition, the Hypothesis of a Civitas Maxima and the Maxim Aut Dedere Aut Judicare", (1991) 62 *Revue internationale de droit pénal*, 109 ff. For I Detter, *The International Legal Order* (Aldershot, Dartmouth, 1994), 175, the application of universal jurisdiction to the repression of terrorism is inherent to the prohibitive rule, given the norm's *ius cogens* character.

[155] The term *"dédoublement fonctionnel"* was coined by Scelle. It means that, absent centralized, regular and compulsory organs exercising legislative, executive and judiciary functions on the global plane, State organs that act according to powers they hold through their domestic constitutional regime are also acting on behalf of the international community, filling in a decentralized manner such functions at the international level. See G Scelle, *Précis de droit des gens*, t. I (Paris, 1932), 55–57.

[156] See to that effect MC Bassiouni, *Crimes Against Humanity in International Criminal Law* (Dordrecht/Boston, 1992), 499–508; MC Bassiouni, *International Extradition: United States Law and Practice*, 2nd edn (London, 1987), 22–24; MC Bassiouni, "The Penal Characteristics of Conventional International Criminal Law", (1983) 15 *Case Western Reserve Journal of International Law*, 34–36; Bassiouni and Wise, above n 154, 21, 24.

A third position is[157] that the conclusion of a series of substantially similar treaties to respond to the diverse expressions of international terrorism is evidence of the recognition by a large part of the international community that it is urgent and legitimate to facilitate repression of a particular crime on the basis of universal jurisdiction. The conventions are construed as the expression of the general interest in sanctioning a category of offences deemed especially serious by the international community. While this does not suffice *per se* to raise their content to a customary status, other legal effects may nevertheless be attached to the conventional provisions. For instance, one could deduce therefrom a type of permissive value, akin to that of certain resolutions of international organisations. Hence, a third-party State could justify its use of criminal jurisdiction by relying on the growing *opinio* evidenced by the multitude of conventions. The difference between parties to the conventions and non-party States would reside in the fact that the latter, although arguably possessing the *faculty* to proceed according to the universality principle given the increasing acceptance of this exercise, would be under no *obligation* to do so.

A variation on this theme would be the view that the treaties institute universal jurisdiction as declaratory instruments, through which the international community acknowledges the existence of universal jurisdiction for a given crime. The agreement serves here as a catalyst, instantly crystallising the rule into custom. However, this new customary rule is not identical with the conventional rule: it is again only permissive, ie it entitles the third States to prosecute but does not require them to do so. Recent trends seem to reinforce this argument, although States continue to waver between the concept of strict privity of contract inherent in treaty-making and broad acceptance of the duty to prosecute or extradite as an established rule of customary law. There is a number of recommendations, declarations of international political organs (General Assembly or Security Council) and of States (political summits), judicial precedents (especially as to hijacking of air carriers), ILC texts, doctrinal opinion, and

[157] On this third approach, see Randall, above n 80, 821–832. An excellent synthesis can be found in Schachter, above n 80, 263: "May States confer jurisdiction on themselves by agreement? Two possible answers may be given. The first explanation is that a necessary implication (or assumption) is that the community of States recognize that universal jurisdiction exists for the crime in question and consequently States may oblige themselves to exercise it. It follows from this that while non-parties have no such obligation they have the same right (or options) as a party to exercise jurisdiction. It should be nd that this is an inference from the adoption of a general multilateral treaty through the processes of international organization. … It is not based on State practice as such. … If a non-party asserts the right to try and punish an offender under one of the treaties in question as an 'international criminal' without any jurisdictional link other than the universality principle, and no protests are made by other States (for example, the offender's national State or the State where the crime occurred) the exercise of jurisdiction would constitute significant precedent for the universality principle".

so forth, which stress the importance of the effective fight against terrorism or which link the principle of universality to the suppression of terrorist acts, without any significant dissent.[158] It can thus be concluded that the practice of States, evidenced by the large number of conventions — now reinforced by the efforts of the United Nations to draft a comprehensive convention against terrorism, based upon a sweeping *aut dedere* principle for all terrorist acts — together with the diffuse non-treaty related practice previously mentioned, has the effect of potentially legitimising a claim of universality by a non-party State to suppress a terrorist offence defined in an anti-terrorist convention. Such a claim of universal jurisdiction might even be seen today as an exercise of an international public order function. It unlikely that any protest to such State action would ensue (except in highly politicised contexts), and if it did occur, it probably would have little force. Consequently, it seems that at least under international law the barriers for the exercise of such jurisdiction have largely been removed, whereas a positive customary title allowing prosecution for terrorist crimes has not yet been firmly established. What was written by the present author some years ago may thus apply *a fortiori* today, when the events of the 11 September 2001 have considerably reinforced the collective conscience and willingness to fight international terrorism:

> [T]here is no heresy in affirming that current international law acknowledges the unilateral *faculty* to claim the privilege of exercising universal jurisdiction for qualified terrorist acts as defined by ... the several anti-terrorist treaties. The strength of the new trends that have emerged in international society can be construed at least as having removed the justification (or the *opinio iuris*) of the alleged prohibitive rule, if it even existed at all. Whether the potential customary rule granting universal jurisdiction for the prosecution of terrorists has positively crystallised or merely remains *in statu nascendi* might not affect the heart of our problem. Suffice it to say that, in all probability, a State's claim to exercise universal jurisdiction in a case related to our topic *would not arouse any protest* in principle on the part of other interested States. Instead of granting a jurisdictional title through custom, the growth of a sufficiently general legal conviction may have reoriented the law towards the recognition of the power (*faculté*) to engage in a repressive endeavour based on titles of municipal law. This would be an intermediary stage between a mere freedom, based on an abstract, negative presumption [that of the *Lotus* case], and an established custom based upon a series of concrete, positive acts. The difference between this stage and a general presumption of freedom lies in its justification, which in the former case is buttressed by additional considerations provided by circumstantial factors. The freedom is not here negatively presumed, but positively conferred.

[158] On this trends, see R Kolb, "Universal Criminal Jurisdiction in Matters of International Terrorism: Some Reflections on Status and Trends in Contemporary International Law", (1997) 50 *Hellenic Review of International Law*, 70 ff.

A relatively uniform and prolonged use of this faculty may, in accordance with recognised rules, result in the emergence of a real customary rule.[159]

2. *Universal Jurisdiction under Customary International Law for Terrorist Offences in General*

The greatest obstacle in the way of recognising universal jurisdiction (or the *aut dedere* principle) over terrorist acts in general is the lack of any universally accepted definition of terrorism. The multiplicity of definitions makes it extremely difficult to identify a sufficiently accepted core definition of the terrorist crime as such. One of the minimum conditions for recognising the capacity of States to prosecute international crimes under the title of universal jurisdiction is that the crime is properly defined: *Nullum crimen sine lege*, but also *nulla iurisdictio sine crimine*. Moreover, that definition must be accepted at the international level, since the crime envisaged should be international in nature and not merely criminalised at the national level. This absence of an agreed definition is the principal reason that many authors simply refute the suggestion that there is any universal jurisdiction over terrorism in customary international law as it stands today.[160] Others acknowledge a growing tendency towards universality for the crime of terrorism in general, but maintain that such a tendency probably falls short of a customary rule,[161] presumably once more because of absence of any commonly agreed definition of terrorism. Another view is that universality is desirable *de lege ferenda* and States are and should be working towards the establishment and acceptance of such a principle.[162] Conversely, certain commentators hold that international terrorism as such is already subject to universality, since the offences involved are directed against the whole international community.[163] In this respect, the recent efforts of the United Nations Working Group to draft a comprehensive convention on international terrorism which is precisely based on the *aut dedere* universality principle, may be seen as a

[159] *Ibid*, 87–8.

[160] See eg Chadwick, above n 9, 106; Freestone, above n 85, 60. See as to the result also Higgins, above n 4, 24, 28.

[161] See eg Randall, above n 80, 789–90, 815 ff. *Restatement Third*, above n 80, 255–7; Schachter, above n 80, 264 (a good case can be made for the customary status); Oppenheim, above n 78, 470.

[162] See eg the Principles adopted in the final Report of the *Centre d'étude*, above n 33, 16: "*Les Etats devraient accepter le principe aut dedere aut prosequi comme règle générale lorsque des personnes présumées coupables d'actes terroristes contre des Etats ou des ressortissants étrangers sont découverts sur leur territoire*". For Reisman, above n 47, 56, the universality principle is "desirable".

[163] See eg Sucharitkul, above n 85, 171; Bassiouni and Wise, above n 154, 31 ff. See also the Draft Single Convention on the Legal Control of International Terrorism of the ILA (1980), Art 2(3), ILA, Proceedings of the 59th Conference, Belgrade, 1980, 498 (*aut dedere aut prosequi*).

further step in the direction of establishing that principle under customary international law.[164] However, this position has still to be widely accepted. Moreover, the UN comprehensive convention itself will have only the scope of a treaty. It will be instructive to note the degree of consensus on such issues during the process of elaboration of the draft convention in order to gain some measure of the customary status of such rules. At the time of writing, it is too early to judge.

As to the definition of terrorism, which remains the major stumbling block in the way of universality, it will be possible to use the definition adopted in the United Nations draft comprehensive convention to the extent that it secures widespread ratification. Nothwithstanding this convention, it could be argued that there is already some convergence in modern international law on a two-tier definition of terrorism, one limb covering the acts listed in the several anti-terror conventions, the other being centered on three elements: certain violent acts/terror (intimidation)/coercion.[165] However, there are still too many uncertainties in these definitions to make any assured statement. Perhaps the most one can say is that a State exercising universality for an egregious act of international terrorism, falling squarely under a recognised form of terrorism in the conventions, might not face today a significant protest for its unilateral assertion of jurisdiction. Thus, the positions outlined above on the recognition of the customary status of the conventional crimes under general international law may be argued, but not *a fortiori*, only tentatively and *a minori*, and, to put it bluntly, with some optimism which might not prove well-founded.

Some authors, faced with the absence of any clearly defined and accepted international crime of terrorism, hold that only some specific terrorist crimes give rise to universality under customary international law. For Freestone,[166] it is only the crime of aerial hijacking which unquestionably possesses that status, this being the result of the very large number of ratifications and accessions to the relevant conventions. Other authors argue that there is universality for hostage-taking[167] or for terrorist bombings,[168] presumably within the scope of the definitions of the crimes in the conventions. If a single terrorist offence has achieved the status of universality under general international law, it would be

[164] See Article 11 of the Draft Convention: *Report of the Working Group*, above n 2, 11.
[165] On the question of definition of terrorism, see above, I.
[166] Freestone, above n 85, 60. See also JN Douglas, *Aerial Hijacking as an International Crime* (New York, Oceana Publishers, 1974), 182 ff.
[167] F Malekian, *International Criminal Law*, vol II (Uppsala, Almqvist & Wiksell 1991), 1 ff.
[168] G Dahm, J Delbrück and R Wolfrum, *Völkerrecht*, vol I/1, 2nd edn (Berlin/New York, 1989), 321–22, presumably also under customary international law.

aerial hijacking. This crime has given rise to the clearest judicial practice[169] and to the most widely ratified international conventions.

There is another way by which customary universal jurisdiction can be exercised in regard to terrorist offences. If a terrorist offence fulfils all the elements of another international crime which is subject to universality under customary international law, then the terrorist acts will be subject to universality under that parallel heading.[170] Thus, for instance, if a terrorist attack, by reason of its magnitude, amounts to a crime against humanity,[171] then it will be subject to universality, since crimes against humanity may be covered by universal jurisdiction. This could provide a way for the International Criminal Court to judge some terrorist offences, since the Statute of the Court does not grant any specific jurisdiction for acts of terrorism.

It may be useful, at the end of this section, to briefly point out the major drawbacks of universality in international law. The most conspicuous problem is that universality potentially gives rise to conflicting claims of jurisdiction and that the standards of prosecution and length of sentences vary from State to State. This puts in danger the fair trial to which the accused is entitled.[172] Moreover, the objectivity of municipal courts is not always guaranteed. Universal jurisdiction may also augment tensions between States, which may substantially disagree over a specific prosecution. This issue leads us directly to the question of prosecution of crimes of international terrorism by international tribunals, in particular the International Criminal Court.

3. *Jurisdiction Exercised by the International Criminal Court*[173]

On 1 July 2002, the Rome Statute on the International Criminal Court[174] (ICC) entered into force. The ICC does not have jurisdiction to try persons

[169] See Kolb, above n 158, 74. See also the *US v Yunis* case (1988), United States District Court of Columbia Circuit, 82 *ILR*, 344 ff, particularly 348–49, and the judgment of the Court of Appeals (1991) 30 *ILM*, 403.
[170] See Higgins, above n 4, 28.
[171] It has for example been said that the attacks of the 11 September 2001 in the United States constituted because of their magnitude crimes against humanity. See N Schrijver, "Responding to International Terrorism: Moving the Frontiers of International Law for Enduring Freedom", (2001) 48 *NILR*, 287 ff.
[172] See eg Oxman, above n 80, 281; Graefrath, above n 80, 85; Bassiouni, above n 80, 82.
[173] On the jurisdiction of the ICC in matter of terrorist crimes, see the unpublished paper of J Sulzer, "Réflexion sur la compétence de la Cour pénale internationale pour juger certains actes constitutifs du crime de terrorisme", (on file with author). On the question of advantages and disadvantages to have the crime of terrorism subjected to the jurisdicion of the Court, see S Oeter, "Terrorismus — Ein völkerrechtliches Verbrechen? Zur Frage der Unterstellung terroristischer Akte unter die internationale Strafgerichtsbarkeit", (2001) 76 *Die Friedenswarte*, 12 ff, 27 ff.
[174] See Doc A/CONF.183/9, 17 July 1998.

suspected of terrorist crimes as such. Several proposals to add terrorism to the list of punishable offences were defeated at the 1998 Rome Conference. At the beginning of the Conference, the draft convention contained the offence of terrorism[175] along the lines of the definition proffered by the ILC in its 1995 Draft Code on Offences against the Peace and Security of Mankind.[176] The Netherlands backed this proposal.[177] In the face of the resistance of many States to such an inclusion, mainly because of fears of opening a Pandora's Box on the definition of the crime, the status of movements of national liberation, or the question of State terrorism, some States attempted to indirectly include the crime of terrorism by listing it under acts amounting to crimes against humanity.[178] Terrorism would be punishable if it fulfilled the constitutive elements of that crime. This proposal was equally dismissed. On 14 July, the same States who had sponsored that proposal[179] deployed a last effort to salvage the inclusion of terrorism. They proposed that the same approach be taken for terrorism as for the crime of aggression. A reference to terrorism could then have been included in Article 5 of the Statute, leaving the elaboration of

[175] See Doc. A /CONF.183/2/Add.1, 14 April 1998. The French version reads:

"Aux fins du présent Statut, on entend par 'crime de terrorisme':

1) *Le fait d'entreprendre, d'organiser, de commanditer, d'ordonner, de faciliter, de financer, d'encourager ou de tolérer des actes de violence dirigés contre des ressortissants ou des biens d'un autre État et de nature à provoquer la terreur, la peur ou l'insécurité parmi les dirigeants, des groupes de personnes, le public ou des populations, quels que soient les considérations et les objectifs d'ordre politique, philosophique, idéologique, racial, ethnique, religieux ou autre qui pourraient être invoqués pour les justifier;*
2) *Toute infraction définie dans les conventions ci-après:*
    a) *Convention pour la répression d'actes illicites dirigés contre la sécurité de l'aviation civile;*
    b) *Convention pour la répression de la capture illicite d'aéronefs;*
    c) *Convention sur la prévention et la répression des infractions contre les personnes jouissant d'une protection internationale, y compris les agents diplomatiques;*
    d) *Convention internationale contre la prise d'otages;*
    e) *Convention pour la répression d'actes illicites contre la sécurité de la navigation maritime;*
    f) *Protocole pour la répression d'actes illicites contre la sécurité des plates-formes fixes situées sur le plateau continental.*
3) *Le fait d'utiliser des armes à feu ou d'autres armes, des explosifs ou des substances dangereuses pour commettre des actes de violence aveugle qui font des morts ou des blessés graves, soit isolément soit dans des groupes de personnes ou des populations, ou qui causent des dommages matériels importants.]"*

[176] See Articles 20 and 24(2) of the Draft Code, *Report of the ILC to the General Assembly of the United Nations*, A/49/10, para 91 and A/50/10, 58, above n 40.

[177] On the Dutch proposals, see MC Bassiouni, *The Statute of the International Criminal Court, A Documentary History* (New York, Transnational, 1998), 234–5.

[178] See the proposal of India, Sri Lanka, Algeria and Turkey in A/CONF.183/C.1/L.27/Corr.1.

[179] See above n 177.

its precise definition to later stages, i.e. to a revision conference. However, even that proposal was defeated. Thus, the only result reached at the Rome Conference was that in Resolution E, sponsored by Turkey and integrated into the Final Act of the Statute, a later inclusion of the crime in the list of punishable offences is recommended.[180]

After the events of 11 September 2001, Turkey immediately seized the opportunity to insist again upon such an inclusion.[181] Moreover, the Parliamentary Assembly of the Council of Europe adopted two resolutions by which it requests that the Statute of the ICC be revised in order to insert in the list of the punishable offences the crime of terrorism.[182] For

[180] The text of this Resolution is the following (it can be consulted on <http://www.un.org/law/icc/statute/finalfra.htm>): "The United Nations Diplomatic Conference of Plenipotentiaries on the Establishment of an International Criminal Court,

Having adopted the Statute of the International Criminal Court,

Recognizing that terrorist acts, by whomever and wherever perpetrated and whatever their forms, methods or motives, are serious crimes of concern to the international community,

Recognizing that the international trafficking of illicit drugs is a very serious crime, sometimes destabilizing the political and social and economic order in States,

Deeply alarmed at the persistence of these scourges, which pose serious threats to international peace and security,

Regretting that no generally acceptable definition of the crimes of terrorism and drug crimes could be agreed upon for the inclusion, within the jurisdiction of the Court,

Affirming that the Statute of the International Criminal Court provides for a review mechanism, which allows for an expansion in future of the jurisdiction of the Court,

Recommends that a Review Conference pursuant to article 123 of the Statute of the International Criminal Court consider the crimes of terrorism and drug crimes with a view to arriving at an acceptable definition and their inclusion in the list of crimes within the jurisdiction of the Court".

[181] See Sulzer, above n 173, 2–3: "*Suite aux événements du 11 septembre à New York, la Turquie a été la seule délégation à recommander l'insertion du crime de terrorisme dans la compétence de la CPI en proposant une: «approche pragmatique [en vue] d'examiner la question dans le cadre des délibérations en cours de la Commission préparatoire» ou «organiser une conférence internationale ayant précisément pour mandat de revoir la question de la juridiction de la Cour afin que les crimes de terrorisme constituent une catégorie distincte de crimes, à côté de ceux qui sont déjà énumérés dans le Statut». Ces propositions n'ont été reprises par aucune délégation*".

[182] See Sulzer, above n 173, 3: "*Plus préoccupant, lors de la dernière Assemblée parlementaire du Conseil de l'Europe, une recommandation et une résolution intitulées' «Les démocraties face au terrorisme» ont été adoptées allant dans le sens d'une révision du Statut de la CPI pour inclure les actes de terrorisme.*

Selon la Recommandation 1534 (2001)[1]

«[...]4. L'Assemblée estime que la nouvelle Cour pénale internationale est l'institution propre à juger les actes relevant du terrorisme international.[...]

[...]5. L'Assemblée prie instamment le Comité des Ministres: [...]

[...]xi. d'étudier d'urgence la possibilité d'amender et d'élargir le Statut de Rome, pour que figure, parmi les attributions de la Cour pénale internationale, l'aptitude à juger les actes relevant du terrorisme international [...]»

Selon la Résolution 1258 (2001)[1]

«[...]5. L'Assemblée estime que la nouvelle Cour pénale internationale est l'institution propre à juger les actes terroristes.[...]

[...]17. L'Assemblée appelle les Etats membres du Conseil de l'Europe à:

[...]ix. étudier d'urgence la possibilité d'amender et d'élargir le Statut de Rome, pour que figure, parmi les attributions de la Cour pénale internationale, l'aptitude à juger les actes relevant du terrorisme international ; [...]".

the time being, things have not progressed, and are not likely to do so in the near future. This course, preserving for the moment the integrity of the Statute, is to be welcomed. The Court must now be able to work on a secured Statute, not opened up for a possibly indeterminate number of modifications. The revision conference, which will take place in 2009, will be able to appraise the situation and possibly add a new crime of terrorism to the punishable offences. If a comprehensive United Nations Convention on Terrorism is by that time adopted, States will also be able to take advantage of the legitimacy which it will carry and any agreed definition of the crime of terrorism within the text.

In conclusion, it may be said that the law in relation to the criminal prosecution of international terrorists is at once richly articulated and in ongoing evolution. The anti-terrorist conventions (with their complex blend of customary international law together with treaty rules) provide for a great variety of jurisdictional titles, the most salient and multifaceted of which is the *aut dedere aut prosequi* principle, constituting a form of universality. The relationship between international and internal law is particularly close in this matter, creating a multitude of legal problems. On the other hand, the law is quickly developing in this field. The events of 11 September 2001 bolstered the already felt need to better combat terrorism. It is not difficult to foresee that a further broadening of the law is forthcoming, possibly with a general convention on the suppression of terrorism. If that happens, a milestone will indeed have been reached, the piecemeal approach of specific conventions, which up to now so conspicuously characterised this branch of law, being finally overcome. One may thus follow the events of the next months and years with studious attention. But too much should not be expected.

12

Terrorism, National Measures and International Supervision

ANDREW CLAPHAM

THIS CHAPTER LOOKS at national measures, adopted as part of recent counter-terrorism policies, and the conformity of such measures, with international law. In particular, it looks at some very specific examples from the United Kingdom and the United States and uses these situations to re-examine the scope and importance of international mechanisms that monitor national compliance with international law.

In the 1980s and 1990s the emphasis within the international human rights movement, and in the official discourse of the human rights bureaucracy in organizations such as the United Nations, was placed on *implementation* at the national level. Great efforts were made to ensure that States incorporated international standards in their domestic legislation and created national remedies to ensure the protection of those same rights. National judges were trained in international standards, *Ombudsman* procedures were encouraged, national human rights institutions were spawned, and the emphasis was on bringing the protection of international human rights closer to the people. Today we might even find this emphasis on national measures, rather than international initiatives, described as enhancing "complementarity" or "subsidiarity".

In this chapter it is suggested that, while ensuring greater access to justice at the local level remains essential, we should not lose sight of the special complementary function of international monitoring. In the context of counter-terrorism, where personal and national security are presented as essential priorities of governments, it is the international supervision of human rights which is coming under particular strain. National protection mechanisms, while obviously the most appropriate in normal circumstances, may not be in a position to take the necessary distance from the Executive or the Legislature and offer human rights protection to those specially affected by legislation which risks undermining human rights protection. Even where this legislation has been hastily adopted it is inevitably defended as absolutely essential for security and may even be backed by popular (national) sentiment. Although national mechanisms may in some jurisdictions be fully competent to apply international human rights standards, this chapter highlights the continuing importance of international control over national counter-terrorism measures.

I. THE UNITED KINGDOM DEROGATIONS

At the time of writing the United Kingdom is the only State which has taken concrete measures to derogate both from the European Convention on Human Rights (ECHR) and the International Covenant on Civil and Political Rights (ICCPR). The UK's new legislation is being questioned and examined in multiple fora. There have been challenges in the national courts, there are detailed examinations through national processes which examine different aspects of the measures,[1] through an Opinion of the Council of Europe's Commissioner for Human Rights, and in the end it is likely that some aspects of the legislation will be challenged through an application to the European Court of Human Rights. In addition, various measures have already been discussed in the context of the examination of the UK report submitted to the UN Human Rights Committee with regard to the UK's compliance with its obligations under the ICCPR. In order to highlight the importance of international control we shall concentrate on one aspect of the counter-terrorism legislation: the derogations to the two human rights treaties referred to above.

The UK derogations have been the subject of considerable scrutiny and this process has provided new jurisprudence on the whole question of derogations to human rights treaties in times of emergency. The derogations are aimed at allowing the Government, in some cases of foreigners (aliens) suspected of terrorism, to detain these aliens for months, or even years, where deportation to their country of origin is not an option due to a fear of torture or ill-treatment in the receiving country.

[1] Space does not permit a detailed examination of the various processes organized by the Government. Suffice it to briefly mention the Joint Committee on Human Rights Report, discussed below, the Review conducted by Lord Carlisle of Berriew whose review covers: the process of certification in each case, the procedure surrounding appeals and reviews by the Special Immigration Appeals Committee, as well as the role of the Special Advocates and the form of detention; and the statutory Review Committee inquiring in to the Anti-Terrorism, Crime and Security Act 2001, Chaired by Rt Hon Lord Newton of Braintree.

Before examining the derogations in detail, it is worth recalling the facts and importance of the 1996 *Chahal* judgement of the European Court of Human Rights. Mr Chahal was about to be deported to India on the grounds that his presence in the UK threatened national security. He complained that his deportation to India would put him at a real risk of torture or inhuman or degrading treatment. He complained that a decision to deport him by the UK authorities would be a violation of his human rights, including Article 3 of the ECHR. Although the UK Government argued that there was an implied limitation to Article 3 ECHR, and alternatively that there was a need to balance the risk of ill-treatment against the perceived threat to national security, the European Court of Human Rights held that "the national interest of the State could not be invoked to override the interests of the individual where substantial grounds had been shown for believing that he would be subject to ill-treatment if expelled."[2] The Court was careful to state explicitly that it "is well aware of the immense difficulties faced by States in modern times in protecting their communities from terrorist violence."[3] But the Court continued:

> The prohibition provided by Article 3 against ill-treatment is equally absolute in expulsion cases. Thus, whenever substantial grounds have been shown for believing that an individual would face a real risk of being subjected to treatment contrary to Article 3 if removed to another State, the responsibility of the Contracting State to safeguard him or her against such treatment is engaged in the event of expulsion ... In these circumstances, the activities of the individual in question, however undesirable or dangerous, cannot be a material consideration.[4]

Accordingly, the Court did not consider it necessary to enter into a consideration of the Government's allegations about the applicant's terrorist activities and the threat posed by him to national security.

The result of the *Chahal* case is that no State party to the Convention can deport or extradite to a country a person where there are substantial grounds for believing that he or she faces a real risk of treatment contrary to Article 3 ECHR. May a Convention State then simply detain the individual in its own facilities until such time as it is safe to deport? Could a Convention State simply hold such a detainee until the individual no longer poses a threat to national security? In the *Chahal* case the Court did not find that Mr Chahal had been detained illegally because there had

[2] *Chahal v United Kingdom* (1996-V) ECHR Rep. Judgements & Decisions 1831 (1996) at para 78.
[3] *Ibid* at para. 79.
[4] *Ibid* at para. 80.

been proceedings to deport him, and so he had been lawfully detained within the meaning of Article 5(1)(f) ECHR.[5] However, following the *Chahal* judgement it became clear that it would not be possible under the ECHR to detain someone with a view to deportation where that deportation gives rise to the sort of risk which would violate Article 3 ECHR. We could call this the *Chahal* rule.

In the wake of the 11 September 2001 attacks the UK government found itself in the position of wanting to deport certain suspected terrorists who could not be deported without breaching the *Chahal* rule; if there was no possibility of deportation then the grounds for detention would be invalid under the Convention. The Government decided to derogate under the terms of the relevant human rights treaties. In derogating from their European Convention obligations the UK referred to paragraph 113 of the Court's *Chahal* judgement. The relevant part of the paragraph reads:

> The Court recalls, however, that any deprivation of liberty under Article 5 para. 1(f) will be justified only for as long as deportation proceedings are in progress. If such proceedings are not prosecuted with due diligence, the detention will cease to be permissible under Article 5 para. 1(f).

In order to avoid a future finding of a violation under the Convention with regard to a detention, where deportation would not be possible due to a substantial risk of ill-treatment, the United Kingdom derogated from its obligations with regard to Article 5(1)(f). On 18 December 2001, the Council of Europe registered a Note Verbale from the Permanent Representation of the United Kingdom, conveying the UK's intention to derogate from its obligation under Article 5(1) ECHR. According to the Note Verbale, since 11 September 2001 there exists a terrorist threat to the United Kingdom and, as a result, a public emergency, within the meaning of Article 15(1) ECHR, has arisen. To deal with this situation, the Anti-Terrorism, Crime and Security Act 2001 provides for an extended power to arrest and detain a foreign national suspected of being an international terrorist and a threat to national security, where it is intended to remove or deport the person from the UK, but where removal or deportation is not for the time being possible, with the consequence that the detention would normally be unlawful under domestic law powers. The Note Verbale recalls the rule established by *Chahal* that Article 5(1)(f) permits the deportation of a person with a view to deportation only

[5] 5(1) ECHR provides: "Everyone has the right to liberty and security of person. No one shall be deprived of his liberty save in the following cases and in accordance with a procedure prescribed by law: ... (f) the lawful arrest or detention of a person to prevent his effecting an unauthorised entry into the country or of a person against whom action is being taken with a view to deportation or extradition."

in circumstances where "action is being taken with a view to deportation" (*Chahal* at paragraph 112). The Note Verbale States that this extended power of arrest and detention in the Act is of a temporary nature and is "strictly required by the exigencies of the situation".

A. Conditions for Derogation under ECHR and the Parliamentary Process

The first issue to be considered is whether there actually exists a situation that represents a "time of war or other public emergency threatening the life of the nation." (Article 15 ECHR). The European Court of Human Rights has in the past given governments a wide margin of appreciation with regard to this question. In all the cases where derogations have been challenged the Court has considered that national authorities are, in principle, better placed to decide on the presence of such an emergency. These situations involved Ireland in 1957, Northern Ireland in 1971, Northern Ireland in 1988 and 1999, and South-East Turkey in 1990.[6]

Although, at the time of writing, the current situation facing the UK could be considered different from those outlined above, as there has been no actual attack on the UK or a specific UK target abroad, it is possible, as suggested, in the opinion prepared for the non-governmental organization Justice, by David Anderson QC and Jemima Stratford,[7] that the UK Courts, and ultimately the Strasbourg-based European Court of Human Rights, could accept the Government's assessment that, since 11 September 2001, there is such a public emergency threatening the life of the UK. In particular, this opinion points to the UK's support for the US and Israel and the ongoing threat to the UK and UK nationals. Since the time that Justice opinion was written there have been additional explicit threats to the UK and its nationals, made via various tapes apparently linked to Al-Qaeda. Even more recently the UK's involvement in Iraq has further increased the likelihood of attacks on UK nationals at home and abroad. The 2003 attacks in Istanbul on the British

[6] For a review of some of the cases see: K Reid, *A Practitioner's Guide to the European Convention of Human Rights* (London, Sweet and Maxwell, 1998) 187–90; D Harris, M O'Boyle and C Warbrick, *Law of the European Convention on Human Rights* (London, Butterworths, 1995) ch 16. The cases are: *Lawless case*, ECHR (1961) Series A, No 3; *Ireland v United Kingdom*, ECHR (1978) Series A, No 25, 90; *Brannigan and McBride v United Kingdom*, ECHR (1993) Series A, No 258–B; and *Aksoy* v *Turkey* ECHR (1996) 23 EHRR 553.

[7] Opinion dated 16 November 2001, available from Justice, on file with the author. See also the opinion of D Pannick for Liberty, dated 16 November 2001, (on file with the author) which simply concludes that the "Government has not established (even with the wide margin of appreciation enjoyed by it) that there is a 'public emergency threatening the life of the nation.'" He quotes the Home Secretary addressing the House of Commons on 15 October 2001 stating: "There is no immediate intelligence pointing to a specific threat to the United Kingdom."

Consulate and the HSBC Bank have reinforced the sense that the UK and its nationals are under threat of violent attacks. Given the magnitude of the 11 September 2001 attacks, and the continuing threats of spectacular incidents targeted at the UK, it is likely that the UK would be given a certain degree of latitude, or a margin of appreciation, with regard to the assessment of the seriousness of the threat. This is especially so in the present context due to the secrecy which may attach to key parts of the evidence concerning the imminence of the threat.

The second issue to be considered concerns the extent to which the derogating measures go beyond what is necessary. The derogation measures reach beyond terrorists connected to Al-Qaeda, and those that pose a direct threat to the UK and its nationals, and include all those who pose a threat to foreign States. British judges have developed the notion of national security so that a threat to a foreign nation by a Pakistani national staying in the UK could lead to the conclusion by the Secretary of State that this threatens national security for the purposes of refusing indefinite leave to remain in the UK. This reasoning, based on the grounds that reciprocal co-operation between the UK and other States in combating international terrorism was capable of promoting the UK's national security[8], would, however, be a strained understanding of the explicit conditions necessary for derogations to the ECHR. The conditions necessary to justify *limiting rights on grounds of national security* are not the same as those that allow for *derogation from certain rights in the context of an emergency* threatening the life of the nation. As we shall see, these issues have been addressed by the British Courts.

An interesting aspect of this derogation is that, due to the incorporation of the Convention into national law through the Human Rights Act 1998, national law was changed almost immediately following the derogation. The fact that human rights obligations now take effect in the national legal order of the UK has led to greater internal scrutiny of changes to those obligations. This scrutiny has taken place not only through the courts but also through Parliamentary processes. Parliament's Joint Committee on Human Rights has conducted an inquiry into the UK derogation.[9] What is interesting is that there is the concern, expressed by the Joint Committee, as well as the Council of Europe's Human Rights Commissioner, that there should be parliamentary scrutiny of measures contained in international derogations before they take effect in international law and national law.[10] For a State where there is normally no requirement of parliamentary

[8] *Home Secretary* v *Rehman* [2001] 3 WLR 877.

[9] Joint Committee Report "Continuance in Force of Sections 21 to 23 of the Anti-Terrorism, Crime and Security Act of 2001," available from: <http://www.publications.parliament.uk/pa/jtrights.htm>.

[10] See para. 24 of the report and the conclusions.

scrutiny of international treaties before ratification this represents an interesting change of attitude with regard to parliamentary involvement in the international law obligations of the UK. Moreover, when the Joint Committee examined the question of whether the derogation from Article 5 ECHR properly ensured the protection of human rights, they concluded that:

> Although the wording of sections 21 to 23 of the ATCS Act is wider than is required by the exigencies of the public emergency, the availability of appeals to, and reviews by SIAC provides a sufficient safeguard to ensure that the powers are exercised only when, and for as long as, there is a public emergency threatening the life of the nation, and that each individual detention is lawful only so long as that public emergency continues and the detention itself is strictly required by the exigencies of the situation.

This poses an interesting conundrum. If this Committee after months of deliberation and evidence determines that the international conditions are indeed met how would the European Court deal with such a determination? Presumably it will be even harder for the European Court to "overrule" this careful appreciation of the situation through a parliamentary process than it would be for the Court to overrule the Executive or even the Judiciary (which will have essentially heard the same arguments as the European Court). Should the issue come before the European Court of Human Rights it will be interesting to see whether the Court differentiates between the margin of appreciation that it affords to national decision makers, such as the Executive and the Judiciary, and what sort of appreciation will be offered to a Legislature's delegates evaluating legislative conformity with the Convention.

B. Challenges to the Derogation in the Courts of the United Kingdom

The derogation has, in a parallel set of developments, been challenged in the Courts. Under the relevant legislation the first challenge came before the Special Immigration Appeal Commission (SIAC). The judgement of the Commission draws a careful distinction between the imminence of the terrorist threat and the actuality of the emergency, stating "it is not the imminence of a [terrorist] threat which is required: it is the actuality or imminence of an emergency." The Commission finds that the measures which involve the need to derogate (the detention of suspected terrorists) are required to try to prevent an actual terrorist threat. Thus "it would be absurd to require the authorities to wait until they were aware of an imminent attack before taking the necessary steps to avoid such an attack".

On appeal the Court of Appeal did not interfere with this approach but the Court's approach to its role is revealed in the Summary: "the Court must also recognise that the Executive is in a better position than a Court to assess both the situation and the action which is necessary to address it. The Court, therefore, accords a degree of deference to the view of the Executive."[11] Few analysts will be surprised by this deference to the Executive in the context of a terrorist threat, however, the judgements warrant careful reading for what they say about the parameters of legitimate derogations from human rights obligations in the face of the present terrorist threat.

The SIAC and the Court of Appeal did not agree on whether the discrimination against non-British nationals was justifiable and thus legal. The SIAC found that, in the absence of a derogation from Article 14 ECHR (on non-discrimination) the application of the legislation only to aliens represented discrimination and therefore a violation of human rights. While the SIAC felt that detention was a measure which struck a fair balance between the interests of the state to protect its population from harmful aliens and the human right of such aliens not to be expelled to face torture[12], "a person who is irremovable cannot be detained or kept in detention simply because he lacks British nationality".[13] Instead, the SIAC considered that a derogation from the right to liberty enshrined in Article 5 in respect of suspected terrorists ought to extend to all irremovable suspected international terrorists. Finding that the threat to the UK was not confined to the alien section of the population, the SIAC did not see how the derogation could be regarded as other than discriminatory on the grounds of national origin.[14] Therefore, as there was no scheduled derogation under Article 14, the SIAC found that the detention of the appellants breached the ECHR.

The Court of Appeal unanimously allowed the Secretary of State's Appeal against this judgement. The reasoning emerges from the judgement of the Lord Chief Justice, Lord Wolfe CJ who found that "there are objectively justifiable and relevant grounds which do not involve impermissible discrimination. The grounds are the fact that the aliens who can not be deported have, unlike nationals, no more right to remain, only a right not to be removed, which means legally that they come into a different class from those who have a right of abode."[15] The Chief Justice

[11] Summary for the Press (not part of the judgement).
[12] *A and Others v Secretary of State for the Home Department*, 30 July 2002, Special Immigration Appeals Commission, Appeal No. SC/1-7/2002, para. 88.
[13] *Ibid* at para. 94.
[14] *Ibid* at para. 95.
[15] *A, X and Y, and others v Secretary of State for the Home Department* EWCA [2002] Civ 1502, case No. C/2002/1710, judgement approved by the Court for handing down, para. 47.

took into account the fact that because of the requirement not to discriminate, the Secretary of State would presumably have to decide on more extensive action which would apply to both nationals and non-nationals. Far from promoting human rights, such an extensive action, he contended, would be "an additional intrusion into the rights of the nationals so that their position would be same as non-nationals".[16] Wolfe CJ saw the detentions as necessary and the least intrusive measure available to the Government. The issue becomes one of deportation rather than discrimination. Because deportation does not apply to British nationals discrimination is said not to arise. According to Wolfe CJ, there has to be a pragmatic solution. He continued his judgement "It is suggested that the action is not proportionate. However I disagree. By limiting the number of those who are subject to the special measures, the Secretary of State is ensuring that his actions are proportionate to what is necessary. There is no alternative which the respondents can point to which is remotely practical".[17]

The Parliamentary Joint Committee, some of whose conclusions we discussed above, deferred on this point to the Court of Appeal:

> The Government is entitled to rely at present on the decision of the Court of Appeal in *A, X and Y and Others v. Secretary of State for the Home Department* that the difference between the treatment of nationals and non-nationals under the Act is justified so as to be compatible with ECHR Article 14 coupled with Article 5, although the matter would need to be reviewed if the House of Lords or the European Court of Human Rights were to take a different view.[18]

The Committee recalled that "the Court accorded a degree of deference to the views of the executive."[19]

In the detailed interpretation of the legitimacy of the discrimination, deferences and derogations under the European Convention, a legal case can indeed be made that aliens can not be compared to nationals. The empowering legislation can probably be ring-fenced from a human rights legal challenge. National security interests can be framed so that they override principles of non-discrimination and personal liberty. This is being done through a careful application of the human rights treaties and international law. The Court of Appeal judgements stress at length how international law preserves the right of the state to discriminate against aliens with regards to entry and stay on the territory of the state.

[16] *Ibid* at para. 49.
[17] *Ibid* at para. 53.
[18] Joint Committee Report above n. 9, HL Paper 59, HC 462 at p. 20.
[19] *Ibid* at para. 31.

In terms of human rights, the arguments about the protection of individual freedoms often seem overtaken by the sophisticated interpretations of the meaning of discrimination, the scope of the margin of appreciation, and the possibilities of implied derogations from treaty obligations. But human rights activists are entitled to ask: if international human rights law is really said to sanction such detention without trial— has human rights law now been stripped of its protective value?

Of course we should not forget that the detainees are free to leave the UK for another destination, and, at the time of writing, two of the sixteen detainees had done this. But the others are simply detained without any concrete prospect of trial. It seems likely that these or similar cases could eventually come before the European Court of Human Rights in one form or another. As stated above, the margin of appreciation will be invoked by the UK Government in this case and the Court will be asked to show particular deference to the decisions of the Judiciary (who have already considered the action's conformity with the Convention) and further deference to the views of the elected representatives in the Legislature (who have already considered the Judiciary's consideration of conformity with the Convention). As these branches have already shown some deference to the Executive and the Judiciary respectively one has to wonder where the checks and balances now lie.

Perhaps we should step back a little and take a less formalistic approach. Let us consider the issue from the perspective of the Council of Europe's Human Rights Commissioner.

C. The Council of Europe's Commissioner for Human Rights

On the invitation of the Joint Committee, the Council of Europe's Human Rights Commissioner, Mr Alvaro Gil-Robles issued an opinion on certain aspects of the UK derogation.[20] The Opinion is a useful contribution to the framework which governs the procedures for derogations and it has important suggestions for improved parliamentary scrutiny of derogations to human rights treaties. But for present purposes we should note the arguments made about encroachments on human rights by the application of the anti-terrorism legislation. First, according to the Commissioner, "[e]ven assuming the existence of a public emergency, it is questionable whether the measures enacted by the United Kingdom are strictly required by the exigencies of the situation".[21] He noted that in

[20] Opinion 1/2002, Of The Commissioner For Human Rights, Mr Alvaro Gil-Robles On Certain Aspects Of The United Kingdom 2001 Derogation From Article 5 Par. 1 Of The European Convention On Human Rights.

[21] *Ibid* at para. 33.

interpreting the strict necessity requirement, the UK Court did not examine the relative effectiveness of competing measures. While demonstrating the availability of equally effective non-derogating alternatives may not necessarily cast doubt on the necessity of the derogating measures, "[i]t is, at any rate, not clear that the indefinite detention of certain persons suspected of involvement with international terrorism would be more effective than the monitoring of their activity in accordance with standard surveillance procedures".[22] Second, the proportionality of the derogating measures is further brought into question by the definition of international terrorist organisations provided by section 21(3) of the Act: "The section would appear to permit the indefinite detention of an individual suspected of having links with an international terrorist organisation irrespective of its presenting a direct threat to public security in the United Kingdom and perhaps, therefore, of no relation to the emergency originally requiring the legislation under which his Convention rights may be prejudiced."[23]

Third, Mr Gil-Robles finds that an anomaly arises in regard to the fact that an individual detained on suspicion of links with international terrorist organisations must be released and deported to a safe receiving country should one become available. This is anomalous because, subject to any controls instigated by the receiving State, such individuals will still be able to plan and carry out acts potentially harmful to the security of the United Kingdom.[24] Thus it appears that "the derogating measures of the Anti-Terrorism, Crime and Security Act allow both for the detention of those presenting no direct threat to the United Kingdom and for the release of those of whom it is alleged that they do. Such a paradoxical conclusion is hard to reconcile with the strict exigencies of the situation".[25] The detention under the derogating powers of the Anti-Terrorism, Crime and Security Act depends ultimately only on the Home Secretary's suspicion of a person's involvement with an international terrorist organisation. The detention is effected without any formal accusation and subject only to a review in which important procedural guarantees are absent. He concludes that: "The indefinite detention under such circumstances represents a severe limitation to the enjoyment of the right to liberty and security and gravely prejudices both the presumption of innocence and the right to a fair trial in the determination of ones rights and obligations or of any criminal charge brought against one. It should be recalled that an ill-founded deprivation of liberty is difficult, indeed impossible, to repair adequately."[26]

[22] *Ibid* at para. 35.
[23] *Ibid* at para. 36.
[24] *Ibid* at para. 37.
[25] *Ibid* at para. 38.
[26] *Ibid* at para. 39.

This opinion is not required to interpret the applicable treaty law, yet it sets out the human rights arguments. The Commissioner's Europe-wide perspective informs the question of necessity; there may be evidence to suggest that the UK is in a different position from other countries in Europe, but the Commissioner's opinion shifts the argument from the textual possibilities allowed under the Convention to one about the values central to the Council of Europe: democracy, human rights and the rule of law. Whether or not the measures taken under the derogation are actually in violation of the Convention rights of the detainees, such an input seems a crucial element in the discourse concerning human rights and the anti-terrorism legislation. Of course there will be some who claim that human rights are simply what the European Court of Human Rights judge to be human rights — but from another perspective human rights are seen as an evolving set of demands purposefully posed as a challenge to fundamental encroachments on individual liberty and well-being. Human rights are part of the argument when the collective interest seems to override individual interests in an unjust way. In the rush to implement through law human rights at the national level we should not lose sight of the basic idea that human rights protection should cover those who are vulnerable to mistreatment at the hands of the authorities and the collective will. The Commissioner's Opinion reminds us that, even if a legal argument can be made that the Treaty allows for certain restrictions against foreigners, a commitment to human rights may actually demand more than referral to a court. The protection of human rights need not be seen as the exclusive domain of those entitled to deliver legally binding decisions.

D. The ICCPR Derogation and the Role of the Security Council

The derogation with regard to the ICCPR is in similar terms to the derogation under the ECHR. The legality of the measures could eventually be raised by the UN Human Rights Committee in connection with the regular examination of the UK's reports under the treaty. The UK's last report was in 2001, a couple of months before the UK derogation was sent to the United Nations, and the Government's responses with regard to the counter-terrorism legislation are interesting because they introduce a further legal argument as to justify the national counter-terrorism measures. When asked to consider the protection of basic rights in connection with Article 4 of the ICCPR on derogations during times of emergency and the prospect of legislation to respond to Security Council Resolution 1373, the UK Delegate responded, according to the summary records, in the following way:

> With regard to the relationship between Security Council resolution 1373 (2001) and the Covenant, he was unable to say whether the action against terrorism called for in the resolution would involve a derogation from Covenant rights, but if it did the provision of Article 103 of the Charter of the United Nations to the effect that obligations under the Charter prevailed over those under any other international agreement would apply.[27]

This response came as a shock to some in the human rights community. At present there is little or no institutionalized international human rights check on the national legislation being promulgated as a result of Security Council Resolution 1373. If all national counter-terrorism measures, challenged for non-compliance with human rights treaties, could be justified and legitimated through a simple reference to Article 103 of the UN Charter, human rights would be officially downgraded to norms which are simply overridden by the need to respond to the security concerns expressed by the Security Council. It is probably unnecessary to develop further the rules for resolving this apparent clash of norms as the Security Council has subsequently adopted a Resolution which makes it clear that counter-terrorism measures taken in order to implement Resolution 1373 must comply with international human rights law. Resolution 1456, of 20 January 2003, includes the following key paragraph:

> 6. States must ensure that any measure taken to combat terrorism comply with all their obligations under international law, and should adopt such measures in accordance with international law, in particular international human rights, refugee, and humanitarian law.

So the issue is less one of a hierarchy of norms and more one of the importance of international supervision of national counter-terrorism measures. The UN High Commissioner for Human Rights has promulgated guidelines for the Security Council's Counter-Terrorism Committee, and for the preparation of reports pursuant to paragraph 6 of Resolution 1373,[28] but an attempt to have an independent expert appointed by the UN Commission on Human Rights has come to nothing. There have been presentations by representatives of the Human Rights Committee and the Security Council to the Council and Committee respectively, but the Council has been wary of any institutionalized follow-up to the suggestion of expert human rights scrutiny of national legislation adopted in the context of counter-terrorism. The only other attempt to address the compatibility of national legislation adopted in the light of Resolution 1373 involves a set of Council of Europe Guidelines on "Human Rights

[27] UN Doc. CCPR/C/SR.1963, 23 October 2001, para. 25.
[28] E/CN.4/2002/18 of 27 February 2002.

and the Fight against Terrorism". These guidelines were adopted by the Committee of Ministers on 15 July 2002, and having been drafted by a Group of Specialists, represent authoritative guidelines with regard to issues such as detention and fair trial.[29] Although they simply synthesise the human rights guarantees that governments need to bear in mind when adopting national measures, the principles are stated in clear terms and are a potentially helpful tool for international supervision of national measures by more political bodies. So far few political bodies have had the inclination to properly scrutinize national measures against this check list; perhaps we should again blame the assumption that human rights are legal questions to be exclusively protected by the courts in the context of actual complaints.

Whether or not the UN Human Rights Committee finds the derogation, or the measures associated with it, in conformity with the Covenant, the hint of the subservience of human rights norms to the Security Council's demands for anti-terrorism laws warrants a response. As we saw above, the subsequent Resolution 1456 demands compliance by States with human rights law thus removing any doubt as to the hierarchy of values to be protected. Second, we should be aware that we are not really faced with a clash of norms but rather with a context where human rights law is accepted as important, but may be unincorporated into the processes which legitimize counter-terrorism measures at the national level. Having sounded this warning, it is perhaps too early to say whether much legislation introduced as a result of the Security Council Resolution 1373 process has actually resulted in violations of international law. Even where new legislation has been introduced, this often represents legislation which was already drafted and waiting in the wings.

In fact most of the concern in this context actually focuses on the overly flexible definitions of "terrorism" and "terrorist groups" being adopted at the national level. In the absence of a position in the Security Council on what constitutes terrorism, for the purposes of the 1373 process, it seems probable that anti-terrorism laws may be applied in ways which hinder the legitimate exercise of human rights to freedom of expression and association of opposition groups and dissidents around the world. The former Chair of the Security Council's Counter Terrorism Committee, Ambassador Greenstock, explained the approach of this political body to

[29] For example Guideline VII reads: "Arrest and police custody — 1. A person suspected of terrorist activities may only be arrested if there are reasonable suspicions. He/she must be informed of the reasons for the arrest. 2. A person arrested or detained for terrorist activities shall be brought promptly before a judge. Police custody shall be of a reasonable period of time, the length of which must be provided for by law. 3. A person arrested or detained for terrorist activities must be able to challenge the lawfulness of his/her arrest and of his/her police custody before a court."

the definition of terrorism: "Our job is to help raise the capability of every Member State to deal with terrorism on its territory. For the Committee, terrorism is what the members of the Committee decide unanimously is terrorism."[30] Such an approach reveals the subjective approach of the Security Council to terrorism and terrorists. Such subjectivity opens the Council up to accusations of double standards and duplicity, it also reinforces the fear that the UN, and the Security Council in particular, are unlikely to take a principled approach to threats to human rights in the context of counter-terrorism. A more transparent approach by the Security Council to both their working definition of terrorism and the conformity of national counter-terrorist measures with human rights law would do much to reinforce the UN's credibility and would mark an important step for the protection of human rights more generally. In a recent review of the use and abuse of the terrorist label Conor Gearty recently concluded:

> The spuriously deployed notion of the 'terrorist' is the cornerstone of the counter-terrorist enterprise; if it can be dislodged, then it will be a small victory for many of the things that we hold valuable and which collectively help to civilise us: integrity in the use of the language; honesty in our moral judgment; consistency in our approach to international affairs; respect for the human rights of all and not just those we know.[31]

II. GUANTANAMO BAY: HUMAN RIGHTS AND INTERNATIONAL HUMANITARIAN LAW

The situation of the prisoners captured in Afghanistan in 2001 by the United States and detained in Guantanamo Bay, Cuba, raises two issues central to the contemporary application of international human rights law. First, does human rights law continue to apply in situations of armed conflict that are regulated by international humanitarian law? And second, does human rights law apply outside the territory of the state concerned?

In the concluding observations with regard to Israel by the UN Economic Social and Cultural Rights Committee both questions have already been addressed. In terms of the first question, the Committee rejected Israel's assertion that the Committee's mandate "cannot relate to events in the Gaza Strip and West Bank", stating that:

> even during armed conflict, fundamental human rights must be respected and that basic economic, social and cultural rights as part of the minimum

[30] *The Counter-terrorism Committee,* pamphlet produced by the Permanent Mission of the United Kingdom to the United Nations.
[31] C Gearty, "Terrorism and Morality", (2003) *European Human Rights Law Review* 377–83 at 383.

> standards of human rights are guaranteed under customary international law and are also prescribed by international humanitarian law.[32]

As regards the second question, the Committee criticized Israel's refusal to report on the occupied territories and its position that the Covenant does not apply to "areas that are not subject to its sovereign territory and jurisdiction". The Committee noted the statement of Israel "that powers and responsibilities 'continue to be exercised by Israel in the West Bank and Gaza Strip' according to agreements reached with the Palestinians."[33]

Similar statements concerning extraterritorial jurisdiction have been made in the context of the work of the UN Committee Against Torture and the UN Human Rights Committee. At least according to the UN treaty bodies the legal framework is clear. Most recently with regards to Guantanamo the General Counsel of the US Department of Defense, in response to growing concern about the mistreatment of detainees in Guantanamo and Afghanistan wrote a letter which explicitly refers to the specific obligations of the US under the Convention against Torture and Other Cruel, Inhuman and Degrading Treatment and States a policy to "treat all detainees and conduct all interrogations, wherever they may occur, in manner consistent with this commitment".[34]

The second question, relationship between human rights law and humanitarian law, is at the heart of the Guantanamo Bay controversy. It is generally accepted that, in situations of armed conflict, in order to tell whether there has been a violation of a human rights provision, recourse may be needed to international humanitarian law. We might recall the paragraph in the Advisory Opinion on the *Legality of the Threat or Use of Nuclear Weapons* of the International Court of Justice (ICJ) which suggests that whether the deprivation of life is arbitrary under international human rights law may have to be determined by the *lex specialis* found in the relevant provisions of the international law of armed conflict, but the Court was clear that human rights norms can continue to apply alongside international humanitarian law.[35] The Opinion addressed the issue of simultaneous application in the following terms:

> It was suggested that the Covenant was directed to the protection of human rights in peacetime, but that questions relating to unlawful loss of life in

[32] E/C.12/1/Add.69, 31 August 2001, at para 12.
[33] *Ibid* at para. 12.
[34] Letter to Senator Leahy, 25 June 2003, available on the website of Human Rights Watch and referred to by Ruth Wedgwood "Let military rules apply while the war goes on" *International Herald Tribune* 2 December 2003 in connection with the US commitments under the Convention against Torture.
[35] ICJ Reports, 8 July 1996.

hostilities were governed by the law applicable in armed conflict. The Court observes that the protection of the International Covenant on Civil and Political Rights does not cease in times of war, except by operation of Article 4 of the Covenant whereby certain provisions may be derogated from in a time of national emergency. Respect for the right to life is not, however such a provision. In principle, the right not arbitrarily to be deprived of one's life applies also in hostilities.[36]

After a detailed examination of the observations by the ICJ, the case-law of the European Court of Human Rights, and the approach of the various UN mechanisms, Vera Gowlland has concluded "that a view of the law of armed conflict as *leges specialis* totally pre-empting the *leges generalis* of the rest of international law, including human rights law, and which originated at a time when strict compartmentalism between conditions of peace and war were possible, is no longer tenable today."[37]

The Court, in addition to this affirmation of the parallel application of human rights and international humanitarian law, explained how recourse to international humanitarian law may be necessary to explain a human rights notion such as "arbitrary":

The test of what is an arbitrary deprivation of life, however, then falls to be determined by the applicable *lex specialis*, namely the law applicable in armed conflict which is designed to regulate the conduct of hostilities. Thus whether a particular loss of life, through the use of a certain weapon in warfare, is to be considered an arbitrary deprivation of life contrary to Article 6 of the Covenant, can only be decided by reference to the law applicable in armed conflict and not deduced from the terms of the Covenant itself.[38]

This statement should perhaps properly be seen as restricted to the legality of weapons as threats to the right to life.[39] In other contexts, such as arbitrary detention, international humanitarian law may simply inform and complement rather than contain the human rights obligations themselves.

To summarize, human rights law and international humanitarian law apply alongside each other in times of armed conflict. With regards to certain human rights it may be necessary to refer to international humanitarian law to interpret or determine the exact scope of the human rights

[36] *Ibid* at paras 24–25.

[37] V Gowlland-Debbas, "The Right to Life and Genocide: The Court and an International Public Policy", in L Boisson de Chazournes and P Sands (eds), *International Law, The International Court of Justice and Nuclear Weapons* (Cambridge, Cambridge University Press, 1999), 315–337.

[38] *Legality of the Threat or Use of Nuclear Weapons*, above n 35, para. 25.

[39] See Gowlland above n 37, at 326.

in question. Let us now see how these principles have been applied in the complaints brought by detainees in Guantanamo Bay.

A. Different Views of the International Legality of the Detention of Prisoners in Guantanamo

A first set of complaints were brought against the United States for a violation of the American Declaration of the Rights and Duties of Man 1948 before the Inter-American Commission on Human Rights. This was not the first time the United States had responded to human rights complaints before this international Commission in the context of an armed conflict, and the question of the relationship between human rights and international humanitarian law had already been addressed by the Commission in situations such as the decision in *Coard* which stressed the complementary nature of human rights law and international humanitarian law in the context of the US action in Grenada.[40] In response to the complaint concerning the Guantanamo prisoners the Commission reaffirmed its interpretation of this question:

> It is well recognized that international human rights applies at all times, in peacetime and in situations of armed conflict. In contrast, international humanitarian law does not apply in peacetime and its principal purpose is to place restraints on the conduct of warfare in order to limit or contain the damaging effects of hostilities and to protect the victims of armed conflict, including civilians and combatants who have laid down their arms or have been placed hors de combat. Further, in situations of armed conflict, the protections under international human rights and humanitarian law may complement and reinforce one another, sharing as they do a common purpose of promoting human life and dignity.[41]

The Commission stated that where there are circumstances connected to an armed conflict individuals' "fundamental rights may be determined

[40] *Coard v United States of America,* Case 10,951, Report 109/99 (1999) esp paras 36–44. See for example regarding detention para 42: "In the present case, the standards of humanitarian law help to define whether the detention of the petitioners was 'arbitrary' or not under the terms of Articles I and XXV of the American Declaration. As a general matter, while the Commission may find it necessary to look to the applicable rules of international humanitarian law when interpreting and applying the norms of the inter-American human rights system, where those bodies of law provide levels of protection which are distinct, the Commission is bound by its Charter-based mandate to give effect to the normative standard which best safeguards the rights of the individual." See also D Weissbrodt, and B Andrus "The Right to Life During Armed Conflict: *Disabled Peoples' International v United States*" (1988) 29 *Harvard International Law Journal*, 59–83.

[41] Decision of 12 March 2002, precautionary measures, reproduced in (2002) 23 *Human Rights Law Journal* at 15–16.

in part by reference to international humanitarian law as well as international human rights law".[42] Where international humanitarian law does not apply, such persons remain protected by at least the non-derogable rights under international human rights law. The Commission underlined that "no person under the authority and control of a state, regardless of his or her circumstances, is devoid of legal protection for his or her fundamental and non-derogable rights".

The US has responded that: "Under international humanitarian law, States engaged in armed conflict have the right to capture and detain enemy combatants, whether or not the combatants are POWs."[43] The US claims that the applicable *lex specialis* comprises "international humanitarian laws on detention" and that these are "explicit". According to the US, humanitarian law "affords the detainees, as captured unlawful enemy combatants, no right of access to the detaining power's courts."[44] The US suggests that humanitarian law supplants human rights law in these circumstances and that, as the Commission has no jurisdiction over the humanitarian law questions, the complaints must be dismissed. The US takes the position that the Commission is precluded from hearing such complaints due to the *lex specialis* of international humanitarian law. In the words of the US Government's communication: "It is humanitarian law, not human rights law, that governs the capture and detention of enemy combatants in armed conflict."[45] The US have gone further and rely on the ICJ Advisory Opinion discussed above to claim that "international human rights law is not applicable to the conduct of hostilities or the capture and detention of enemy combatants, which are governed by the more specific laws of armed conflict".[46] To support this position, the United States notes that the ICJ explained, in its Advisory Opinion on the *Legality of the Threat or Use of Nuclear Weapons*, "that human rights law, to the extent it is applicable during

[42] *Ibid*. See also the *Coard* above n 40 at para 59: "While the need to protect the rights of others may provide a basis for the limitation of certain rights under the Declaration, any such restriction must flow from and be governed by law. Even under extreme circumstances, the Commission has consistently found that resort to restrictive measures under the American Declaration may not be such as to leave 'the rights of the individual without legal protection ... [C]ertain fundamental rights may never be suspended, as is the case, among others, of the right to life, the right to personal safety, or the right to due process .... under no circumstances may governments employ ... the denial of certain minimum conditions of justice as the means to restore public order. While international human rights and humanitarian law allow for some balancing between public security and individual liberty interests, this equilibrium does not permit that control over a detention rests exclusively with the agents charged with carrying it out." Footnotes omitted.

[43] At p. 24 of the Reply by the US to the Inter American Commission on Human Rights.

[44] *Ibid* at 27.

[45] *Ibid* at 15.

[46] *Ibid* at 21.

armed conflict, must be interpreted in the light of relevant *lex specialis* as set forth in the body of humanitarian law".[47]

In the petition for precautionary measures brought on 25 February 2002 the petitioners demanded among other things that the prisoners in Guantanamo Bay be treated as prisoners of war (POWs) and that they be free from arbitrary, incommunicado and prolonged detention as well as unlawful interrogations and trials by military commissions, citing Articles I, XVII, XXV, XXVI of the Declaration. On 12 March 2002 the Commission decided to adopt precautionary measures whereby they asked the US government to "take the urgent measures necessary to have the legal status of the detainees at Guantanamo Bay determined by a competent tribunal". This evokes the language of the Third Geneva Convention on Prisoners of War and in particular Article 5. The Commission also refers to the Martens clause to remind the US that everyone benefits from minimum standards of international law whether or not they fall under the specific treaties concerned.[48] In the adoption of the precautionary measure the Commission concludes that the refusal by the United States to clarify the legal status of the detainees means that the state is failing to offer effective legal protection in denial of their rights under international law. At the time of writing the Commission has not issued a final decision on the merits.

The UN Working Group on Arbitrary Detention and the UN Special Rapporteur on the Independence of Judges and Lawyers have both raised concerns about the status of the detainees. They consider that the detainees should be accorded international guarantees which are currently being denied them.[49] The Working Group stated the matter plainly: either the detainees are entitled to prisoner-of-war status and all the guarantees related to fair trial in Articles 105 and 106 of the Third Geneva Convention, or they fall under the protection of the International Covenant on Civil and Political Rights and Articles 9 and 14 in particular.

At the national level, the US Court of Appeals has rejected petitions for *habeus corpus* and other claims on the grounds that the detainees are outside the jurisdiction of the United States',[50] this issue is now due to be settled by the Supreme Court in the middle of 2004.[51] Across the Atlantic

[47] *Ibid.*

[48] A revised version of the Martens clause is provided in Art 1(2) of the Protocol Additional to the Geneva Conventions of 12 August 1949, and Relating to the Protection of Victims of International Armed Conflicts (Protocol I), of 8 June 1977: "In cases not covered by this Protocol or by any other international agreements, civilians and combatants remain under the protection and authority of the principles of international law derived from established custom, from the principles of humanity and from the dictates of public conscience."

[49] For the Working Group's Report see UN Doc. E/CN.4/2003/8, 16 December 2002 paras 61–64. For the expression of concern by the Special Rapporteur see UN Press Release of 12 May 2003.

[50] AL ODAH *et al v United States of America*, judgement of 11 March 2003, US Court of Appeals for the District of Columbia Circuit.

[51] *Shafiq Rasul et al v George W Bush, President of the United States, et al.* The petition was granted on 10 November 2003 and limited to the following question: "Whether United States

the UK Court of Appeal, in a case requesting diplomatic protection for a British detainee in Guantanamo Bay, Mr Abbasi, refrained from ordering the Foreign Office to intervene with the US authorities. However, the English Court of Appeal did voice some concern about the absence of judicial determination of the status of these detainees: "What appears to us to be objectionable is that Mr Abbasi should be subject to indefinite detention in territory over which the United States has exclusive control with no opportunity to challenge the legitimacy of his detention before any court or tribunal."[52]

What emerges from this cursory overview is that the main national implementation mechanism (the US Federal Judiciary) has so far stated that it has no jurisdiction over detainees held by the US military in Guantanamo Bay, and that the international mechanisms that have addressed the issue have so far been powerless to protect the rights of those detained even though they are unsatisfied with the respect for human rights actually offered to the Guantanamo detainees. The priority which is supposed to be given to human rights over other considerations has again been downplayed with priority being given to technical debates about the relationship between the law of war and human rights, and arguments over the jurisdictional competence of the relevant tribunals. These "preliminary" distractions have prevented proper engagement with the central issue: what is the actual scope of the human rights protection? Argument about the scope of the rights in question remains obscured because the dispute remains arcane and jurisdictional. The argument has been that: these people have no legally enforceable human rights to start with — first, because they are covered by humanitarian law and not human rights law, and second they have no right of access to the courts because they fall outside the jurisdiction of the courts. This obfuscation of the real issues again warns against the rush to equate human rights with what a judicial body is able to enforce.

III. CONCLUSIONS

Both case-studies involve governmental justifications for detention without trial. Both situations illustrate draconian decisions taken with a

courts lack jurisdiction to consider challenges to the legality of the detention of foreign nationals captured abroad in connection with hostilities and incarcerated at the Guantanamo Bay Naval Base, Cuba." For some of the issues regarding judicial review of detainees in the US see: JJ Paust "Judicial Power to Determine the Status and Rights of Persons Detained Without Trial", (2003) 44 *Harvard Int'l LJ*, 503–33.

52 *Abbasi and another v Secretary of State for the Foreign and Commonwealth Affairs and Secretary of State for the Home Department*, Court of Appeal, 6 November 2002, Case No: C/2002/0617A; 0617B at para 66.

degree of popular approval. In some ways we are entering a new era when measures which clearly challenge human rights expectations are adopted without necessarily being seen as a technical violation of the constitution or any internal laws. International law is similarly seen as either inapplicable or something which can be derogated from under the terms of the treaty.

But there is concern from certain international bodies that the contexts discussed above represent situations where basic human rights principles are under threat.[53] The relative weakness of the international machinery, compared to the comprehensive nature of protections promulgated, needs to be readdressed. The credibility of the human rights normative framework is under threat. Norms such as freedom of arbitrary detention and the right to be brought before a judge to challenge the legality of one's detention suddenly seem surrounded by legal exceptions which empty the rights of their meaning at a time when they seem to be most needed. One can argue that exceptions apply in exceptional circumstances, but the damage being done to the human rights project goes much wider than the cases of the detainees themselves. Already the obstacles placed in the way of the detainees in their attempt to get access to the courts have undermined the case that human rights standards are universal. Human rights risk being seen as norms for another era, for peacetime, for a time when the war on terrorism has been won.

The cases from the UK and the US illustrate the limits of human rights protection by the national judiciary. One might not be too surprised to find the judiciary deferring to the executive on matters of national security. The conclusion of this chapter is that this deference should not be seen as the last word concerning the rights of suspected terrorists. The international concern may reveal more about the treatment of detainees

[53] In addition to the Opinion of the Council of Europe Commissioner above n 16 we could mention with regards to the Guantanamo detainees, the UN Working Group on Arbitrary Detention and the Special Rapporteur on Judges and Lawyers, discussed above, as well as the numerous statements from the UN High Commissioners for Human Rights Mary Robinson (16 January 2002) and Sergio Vieira de Mello (various press interviews). More recently the International Committee of the Red Cross has expressed its concern in the following terms: "For the ICRC, the question of the legal status of the persons held at Guantanamo Bay and the legal framework applicable to them remains unresolved. The ICRC's main concern today is that the US authorities have placed the internees in Guantanamo beyond the law. This means that, after more than eighteen months of captivity, the internees still have no idea about their fate, and no means of recourse through any legal mechanism. Through its visits, the ICRC has been uniquely placed to witness the impact this uncertainty has had on the internees. It has observed a worrying deterioration in the psychological health of a large number of them. This has prompted the ICRC to ask the US authorities to institute a due legal process in accordance with the judicial guarantees stipulated by international humanitarian law. This process should formalize and clarify the fate of each and every individual in Guantanamo and put an end to the seemingly open-ended system of internment that currently exists." Operational update, Guantanamo Bay: Overview of the ICRC's work for internees, 25 August 2003.

in extreme circumstances than the national decisions on the legitimacy of derogations and the scope of the court's jurisdiction. The limits of the judicial role should be acknowledged. The fight for the rights of suspected terrorists will take place not only in the law courts but also in the court of public opinion. Although the legal issues are complex, and relate to completely different contexts, the two sets of detainees are now becoming linked in the public eye. The *Economist* writes of "Guantanamo-on-Thames" with regards to the detainees in the UK,[54] and a commentator in the *Times* writes that "in Britain, anti-terrorism laws have built a miniature Guantanamo of our own".[55] Both situations present national measures that have been questioned by international bodies for their conformity with international norms; but the relative weakness of the international enforcement machinery is apparent to everyone. At the national level, up till now, national courts have been, in their own terms, deferential to the executive. Remarkably, it is an acting British Law Lord, Lord Steyn who, in the context of an extra-judicial speech about Guantanamo, has highlighted the historical precedents and sounded the alarm bells:

> One tool at hand is detention without charge or trial, that is, executive detention. Ill conceived rushed legislation is passed granting excessive powers to executive governments which compromise the rights and liberties of individuals beyond the exigencies of the situation. Often the loss of liberty is permanent. Executive branches of government, faced with a perceived emergency, often resort to excessive measures. The litany of grave abuses of power by liberal democratic governments is too long to recount, but in order to understand and to hold governments to account we do well to take into account the circles of history.
>
> Judicial branches of government, although charged with the duty of standing between the government and individuals, are often too deferential to the executive in time of peace. How then would the same judges act in a time of crisis? The role of the courts in time of crisis is less than glorious.[56]

[54] "Guantánamo on Thames?" 6 December 2003 at 6.

[55] Libby Purves "Saddam's trial will test our ideas of civilisation" *The Times*, 16 December 2003 at 18.

[56] Twenty-Seventh FA Mann Lecture, British Institute of International and Comparative Law and Herbert Smith, Lincoln's Inn Old Hall, 25 November 2003, "Guantanamo Bay: The Legal Black Hole", Johan Steyn.

13

National Courts and the 'War on Terrorism'[*]

EYAL BENVENISTI

I. INTRODUCTION

THE "War on Terror" declared after 11 September 2001 by the government of the United States and others will not end soon. It may continue indefinitely. Determined individuals are likely to continue to pose threats to democratically elected governments, making use of available technologies and taking advantage of open societies. These threats may not be merely existential; they are palpable risks that from now on will be taken very seriously. And while limiting the technology flow to potential terrorists is almost impossible — simple recipes for bombs, poisons and chemical weapons are readily available on the Internet — limiting civil liberties and curtailing human rights of terrorist suspects seem, on the other hand, effective, necessary, and almost costless. This is particularly so when the threatened societies are able to single out "others" — foreigners, non-citizens or members of suspect minority groups — as the primary targets of liberties-depriving policies. Racial profiling of people of Middle-Eastern descent for purposes of interrogations and searches, expulsion without judicial review of non-citizen residents and indefinite administrative detention of suspected terrorists, are only some examples of government actions taken in the wake of September 11 under the guise of the new war.[1]

* I thank Renana Kedar for superb research assistance.

[1] See the US President's Declaration of National Emergency by Reason of Certain Terrorist Attacks, Proc. 7463, 13 November 2001 (available at <http://www.whitehouse.gov/news/releases/2001/11/20011113-27.html>); The Canadian Anti-Terrorism Act entered into force December 24, 2001, available at <http://www.parl.gc.ca/37/1/parlbus/chambus/house/bills/government/C-36/C-36_3/C-36TOCE.html>; the British Anti-Terrorism, Crime and Security Act, 2001, available at http://www.legislation.hmso.gov.uk/acts/acts2001/20010024.htm, supersedes the already tough Terrorism Act 2000 that entered into force on February 19, 2001.

International human rights law provides mechanisms for derogating from certain rights and liberties in a "time of public emergency which threatens the life of the nation."[2] Under certain conditions, this body of law allows for limitations "of an exceptional and temporary nature [that] may only last as long as the life of the nation concerned is threatened."[3] National constitutions offer similar arrangements for balancing individual rights against public interests, usually a variation of what is known in Europe as the proportionality principle, or "strict scrutiny" in American constitutional law. These mechanisms put tremendous strain on domestic decision-makers, who must ascertain the existence of a threat to national security, or "the life of the nation", determine the likely duration of that threat, and assess the extent to which specific rights should and ought to be restricted. National courts, called upon to review the government's decisions in this regard, face a dual challenge: they have no institutional qualifications to gauge independently the severity of threats to national security, and they often operate within a society that is unsympathetic to the plight of the ethnic, religious or national group to which the suspected terrorists may belong. In situations of public emergency, it often happens that the group as such becomes the enemy in public eye, or at least as the group whose members' rights should be collectively responsible for the acts of individuals.[4] Judges who refuse to accept such group-based discrimination and who uphold the human rights of the individual members of those targeted groups often find themselves without widespread support due to limited popular demand for governmental accountability in situations of high security such as that being prevalent in the war on terror, and must confront criticism for exposing the population to excessive risks.

This contribution documents the tendency of national courts to defer to the executive's assessment of security threats in times of war, and analyses the consequences of such deference. I distinguish between two types of wars. In Part II I discuss the attitude of courts during full-scale military conflicts, such as the two World Wars. In Part III I deal with

[2] Article 4(1) of the International Covenant on Civil and Political Rights, and also Article 15 of the European Convention on Human Rights and Article 27 of the American Convention on Human Rights. On judicial review in this context see O Gross and F Ni Aolain, "From Discretion to Scrutiny: Revisiting the Application of the Margin of Appreciation Doctrine in the Context of Article 15 of the European Convention on Human Rights" (2001) 23 *Human Rights Quarterly* 625; F Ni Aolain, "The Emergence of Diversity: Differences in Human Rights Jurisprudence" (1995) 19 *Fordham International Law Journal* 101.

[3] Human Rights Committee, General Comment 5, Article 4 (Thirteenth session, 1981). Compilation of General Comments and General Recommendations Adopted by Human Rights Treaty Bodies, UN Doc. HRI\GEN\1\Rev.1 at 5 (1994).

[4] On collective responsibility and collective guilt see G P Fletcher, "The Storrs Lectures: Liberals and Romantics at War: The Problem of Collective Guilt" (2002) 111 *Yale Law Journal* 1499.

prolonged struggles against terrorist threats, exploring the British and Israeli experiences. This inquiry aims at assessing the prospects of judicial assertiveness or deference in deciding on the legality of limitations on individual liberties in cases dealing with suspected terrorists.

II. THE LEGACY OF WARTIME DECISIONS

When we study law we learn that "hard cases make bad law". Hard cases are the ones in which judicial creativity needs to be exercised in order to adjust existing doctrines to fit new situations or policies. Often it is the executive branch that defines new societal goals, and the judiciary is traditionally hesitant to demur. As Roger Cotterrell observed, "Judges (…) as state functionaries, *cannot* neglect considerations of state interests and these may, on occasions, demand that doctrinal niceties be given short shrift in order to meet particular governmental emergencies."[5] Considerations of State interests carry particular weight during wars. Decisions that must balance individual rights with public interests are hard cases, or at least they are presented as such, and they too often make bad law. The wars of the twentieth century have provided us with quite a clear legacy of wartime jurisprudence. Section A of this section examines Anglo-American wartime judicial opinions discussing the balancing of human rights of individuals, whether citizens or residents, against security interests. Section B looks at the readiness of these courts to exercise judicial scrutiny over the executive's decisions in regards to military actions.

A. Balancing Human Rights Against Threats to National Security

In the United States, a restrictive attitude towards civil liberties is closely associated with the two World Wars, and the early stages of the Cold War when the threat of communism loomed large. The clear constitutional commitment of the First Amendment to the right of freedom of speech failed to protect non-conformist views during these periods, just when such protection was most needed.[6] Writing in 1919, and referring to a case during the World War I, Justice Oliver Wendell Holmes observed the

[5] R Cotterrell, *The Sociology of Law*, 2nd edn, (Butterworth Publishing, London, 1992) at 235 (emphasis in original).
[6] *Schenck v United States* 249 US 47 (1919); *Frohwerk v United States*, 249 US 204 (1919); *Debs v United States*, 249 US 211 (1919); *Abrams v United States*, 250 US 616 (1919). *Dennis v United States*, 341 US 494 (1951). M Horwitz, *The Transformation of American Law 1870–1960* (Cambridge, Harvard University Press, 1977) at 260; PL Murphy, *World War I and the Origin of Civil Liberties in the United States*, at 71 (WW Norton, New York, 1979).

outcome of the tension: "When a nation is at war many things that might be said in time of peace are such a hindrance to its effort that their utterance will not be endured so long as men fight and that no Court could regard them as protected by any constitutional right."[7]

During World War II, the United States Supreme Court sanctioned the curfew and internment of American citizens of Japanese descent,[8] and the imposition of martial law in Hawaii.[9] The constitutional guarantees were superceded by "the judgment of the military authorities and of Congress that there were disloyal members of that population [of citizens of Japanese ancestry], whose number and strength could not be precisely and quickly ascertained".[10] The Court did not perceive itself capable of exercising judicial review over the decisions of the military authorities, asserting "that the war-making branches of the Government did not have grounds for believing that in a critical hour such persons could not readily be isolated and separately dealt with, and constituted a menace to the national defense and safety, which demanded that prompt and adequate measures be taken to guard against it".[11] In the Japanese internment case, Justice Jackson offered a more general observation as to the limited authority of the judiciary during wars:

> In the nature of things, military decisions are not susceptible of intelligent judicial appraisal. They do not pretend to rest on evidence, but are made on information that often would not be admissible and on assumptions that could not be proved (...) Hence courts can never have real alternative to accepting the mere declaration of the authorities that issued the order that it was reasonably necessary from a military viewpoint.[12]

Justice Black, in his dissent in the *Dennis* case, lamented the dilution of First Amendment guarantees by a majority bowing to the executive's anti-Communist drive, and expressed hope that "in calmer times, when present pressures, passions and fears subside, this or some later Court will restore the First Amendment liberties to the high preferred place where

[7] Schenck, above n 6, at 52.
[8] *Hirabayashi v US* 63 S Ct 1375 (1943); *Korematsu v US* 65 S Ct 193 (1944).
[9] *Duncan v. Kahanamoku* 66 S.Ct. 606 (1946).
[10] *Hirabayashi*, above n 8, at 99
[11] *Ibid.*
[12] *Korematsu*, above n 8 at 245. Cf. the conclusion of Currie: "The war produced a number of governmental actions difficult to reconcile with our libertarian traditions — military trials, deportation and internment of citizens accused of no offenses, and draconian limitations on judicial review of administrative action. In each of these areas the Supreme Court interfered only when the inconsistency with fundamental principles became patent, and even then without invoking the rather hazy limits of the Constitution. By and large, however, it was not the Court but the other branches of government that were less than zealous in protecting our basic liberties." DP Currie "The Constitution in the Supreme Court: The Second World War, 1941–1946" (1987) 37 *Catholic University Law Review* 1.

they belong in a free society."[13] In a book published in 1998 Chief Justice William H Rehnquist approves Justice Jackson's approach. In his view,

> Judicial inquiry, with its restrictive rules of evidence, orientation towards resolution of factual disputes in individual cases, and long delays, is ill-suited to determine an issue such as "military necessity."[14]

Chief Justice Rehnquist's observations apply with equal force to the experience in the United Kingdom. The decision that epitomizes the British wartime deference to the government's security concerns is the House of Lords decision in *Liversidge v Anderson*.[15] This decision follows the similar World War I case of *Rex v Halliday*,[16] but has captured public attention perhaps because of the strong dissent of Lord Atkin. Mr Liversidge was born in London as Jacob Perlsweig to a Jewish family of Russian immigrants. He was detained by an order signed by Sir John Anderson, the Home Secretary, on 26 May 1940, ostensibly because in his application form to the Royal Air Force he stated misleading information to improve his chances.[17] The order was based on Defence (General) Regulations, 1939, reg 18B, para (1) which provided as follows:

> If the Secretary of State has reasonable cause to believe any person to be of hostile origin or associations or to have been recently concerned in acts prejudicial to the public safety or the defence of the realm or in the preparation or instigation of such acts and that by reason thereof it is necessary to exercise control over him, he may make an order against that person directing that he be detained.

Mr Liversidge sought to have the court declare his detention unlawful as constituting false imprisonment. The lower courts determined that the detainee carried the burden to prove that the detention order was illegal. The detainee then requested the court to order the Home Secretary to present evidence on which he had based his claim that Mr Liversidge had ties with the enemy.[18]

[13] *Dennis* above n 6, at 581; and see PL Murphy, *The Shaping of the First Amendment* (Oxford University Press, New York, 1992) at 108–12.
[14] WH Rehnquist, *All the Laws but One: Civil Liberties in Wartime* (Knopf Publishing, New York, 1998) at 205.
[15] *Liversidge v Anderson* [1942] AC 206 (HL 1941).
[16] [1917] AC 260, 270.
[17] See AW Brian Simpson, *In the Highest Degree Odious* 333–37 (1992); AW Brian Simpson, "Rhetoric, Reality, and Regulation 18B" (1988) 123 *Denning Law Journal* at 123. In the application form Mr Liversidge stated that he was born in Canada to Canadian parents.
[18] As Brian Simpson's inquiry suggests, there was no evidence linking Liversidge with the enemy; the reasons for his long detention (20 months) remain obscure (Simpson, *Rhetoric*, above n 17 at 142).

The lower courts denied Liversidge's request, and the House of Lords approved their denial. As a rule of interpretation of the relevant statute, the court rejects the detainee's "emphatic" reliance on the Magna Carta and the Bill of Rights, and his contention "that legislation dealing with the liberty of the subject must be construed, if possible, in favour of the subject and against the Crown". Adopting the language of Lord Finlay in the World War I case of *Rex v Halliday*[19] Lord Maugham held "that the suggested rule has 'no relevance in dealing with an executive measure by way of preventing a public danger' when the safety of the state is involved."[20] Instead, relying on the "plain meaning" rule of construction, Lord Maugham asserts:

> It seems to me reasonably clear that, if the thing to be believed is something which is essentially one within the knowledge of A.B. or one for the exercise of his exclusive discretion, the words might well mean if A.B. acting on what he thinks is reasonable cause (and, of course, acting in good faith) believes the thing in question.[21]

To bolster this conclusion, the court refers to the nature of the evidence concerned in such cases, evidence that tends to be confidential, as well as to the high character of the decision-maker, the Home Secretary, who is "one of the principal Secretaries of State, and a member of the government answerable to Parliament for a proper discharge of his duties."[22] In other words, the Minister's subjective belief in a person's ties with the enemy excludes judicial oversight,[23] and hence there is no basis to require him to provide reasons for the detention to the detainee or the court. In Lord Maugham's words,

> The result is that there is no preliminary question of fact which can be submitted to the courts and that in effect there is no appeal from the decision of the Secretary of State in these matters provided only that he acts in good faith.[24]

The opinion of the sole dissenter, Lord Atkin, explores Parliament's wish to qualify the Secretary's discretion by insisting on a "reasonable cause to believe" in the authorizing statute. He argues that this requirement must be read as legislative authority for the court to exercise judicial review.

[19] *Ibid*.
[20] *Liversidge v Anderson*, above n 15 at 218–19.
[21] *Ibid*, at 220.
[22] *Ibid*, at 222.
[23] As Lord MacMillan notes (*ibid*, at 254): "It will naturally be in the most dangerous cases, where detention is most essential to the public safety, that the information before the Secretary of State is most likely to be of a confidential character, precluding its disclosure."
[24] *Ibid*, at 224.

Indeed, the legislative history indicates that the House of Commons wanted to ensure at least a limited system of accountability by substituting the government's earlier bid that the Minister would be able to decide if he "was satisfied that ..." with a reasonableness test.[25] Subsequent to this interpretation of the particular statute, Lord Atkin added a memorable, but ultimately unsubstantiated[26] call:

> I view with apprehension the attitude of judges who on a mere question of construction when face to face with claims involving the liberty of the subject show themselves more executive minded than the executive ... In this country, amid the clash of arms, the laws are not silent. They may be changed, but they speak the same language in war as in peace. It has always been one of the pillars of freedom, one of the principles of liberty for which on recent authority we are now fighting, that the judges are no respecters of persons and stand between the subject and any attempted encroachments on his liberty by the executive, alert to see that any coercive action is justified in law. In this case I have listened to arguments which might have been addressed acceptably to the Court of King's Bench in the time of Charles I.[27]

Lord MacMillan's concluding remarks seem to offer a response, which captures more realistically the attitude of national courts in times of war:

> I yield to no one in my recognition of the value of the jealous scrutiny which our courts have always rightly exercised in considering any invasion of the liberty of the subject. But I remind myself, in Lord Atkinson's words, that "however precious the personal liberty of the subject may be there is something for which it may well be, to some extent, sacrificed by legal enactment, namely, national success in the war or escape from national plunder or enslavement".[28] The liberty which we so justly extol is itself the gift of the law and as Magna Carta recognizes may by the law be forfeited or abridged. At a time when it is the undoubted law of the land that a citizen may by conscription or requisition be compelled to give up his life and all that he possesses for his country's cause it may well be no matter for surprise that there should be confided to the Secretary of State a discretionary power of enforcing the relatively mild precaution of detention.[29]

25 Simpson, *Rhetoric,* above n 17. Lord MacMillan refers to this history as follows (*Liversidge v Anderson,* above n 15, at 256: "I do not know, and it would not be proper for me to inquire why a change was made, but it may well be that in view of the gravity of this matter of detention it was thought right to adopt more emphatic words by way of admonition to the Secretary of State to make sure of his grounds before he took action."

26 Brian Simpson calls it "the rhetoric of fiction". Simpson, *Rhetoric,* above n 17, at 152.

27 *Liversidge v Anderson,* above n 15, at 244. For an insightful discussion of this case and its influence on both English and South African law see D Dyzenhaus, *Hard Cases in Wicked Legal Systems* (Clarendon Press, Oxford, 1991) Chapters 4 and 8.

28 Citing *Rex v Halliday,* above n 16, at 271.

29 *Liversidge v Anderson,* above n 15, at p. 257.

The *Liversidge v Anderson* decision has had a lasting effect on English law, as described below. It has also influenced a series of peacetime cases in which security interests were implicated.

B. Refusal to Review Measures Beyond the State's Borders

Judicial reluctance to constrain executive power is even more prevalent in cases dealing with the activities of the executive or the army beyond national borders. Thus, the British Act of State doctrine provides that English courts shall not entertain a claim of an alien regarding the activities on foreign soil done on behalf of the Crown or ratified by it.[30] Other courts reach the same outcome through different doctrines that put up barriers to claims against national executives. US law contains several such obstacles, ranging from standing requirements, the political question and non-justiciability doctrines, and the doctrine of sovereign immunity, to lack of cause of action against governmental violations of international law. Several courts have held that individuals have no standing to challenge alleged violations of international law as long as the involved foreign sovereign did not register a formal complaint regarding the violation.[31] This rule was invoked by the District Court for the Southern District of Florida to reject the claim of General Noriega, the abducted Panamanian strongman, that the illegality of the invasion of Panama deprived the court of jurisdiction over him.[32] The US Supreme Court later qualified this rule so as to limit criticism of the abduction of a Mexican national by US agents.[33]

Claims of aliens harmed during the US night bombing of Libya in 1986 and during the invasion of Panama in 1989 were also unsuccessful. In the former case, the D.C. Circuit Court upheld the personal immunity of the defendants, President Reagan and Prime Minister Thatcher,[34] while in the latter case the court relied on the Alien Tort Claims Act in determining that the actions engaged in during Operation Just-Cause were within the

[30] See F A Mann, *Foreign Affairs in English Courts* (Clarendon Press, Oxford, 1986) 184–90, at 187; T Hartley & J Griffith, *Government and Law* (Weidenfield and Nicolson, London, 1981) 312–16.

[31] *United States v Hensel* 699 F.2d 18, 30 (1st Cir, 1983), Cert denied, 461 US 958, 103 S.Ct. 2431, 77 L.Ed.2d 1317 (1983); *United States v Verdugo-Urquidez* 939 F.2d 1341, 1357 (9th Cir, 1991).

[32] *United States v Noriega* 746 F.Supp. 1506, 1532–33 (1990).

[33] *United States v Alvarez-Machain* 504 US 655 (1992) (this requirement does not apply to claims made under self-executing treaties).

[34] *Saltany v Reagan*, 886 F.2d 438 (DC Cir, 1989). For criticism of this decision, and the unusual imposition of costs on the plaintiffs' lawyers see A D'Amato, "The Imposition of Attorney Sanctions for Claims Arising from the U.S. Air Raid on Libya" (1990) 84 *American Journal of International Law* 705.

"discretionary functions" of the US Executive, and thus immune from judicial review.[35]

Claims against the executive for violation of international norms can ultimately fail, since according to one interpretation of the US Constitution, the President is not bound to comply with international law,[36] and may also terminate international agreements unilaterally.[37]

The US Supreme Court's opinion in the *Verdugo-Urquidez* case discusses the Justices' concerns with the application of constitutional guarantees towards non-citizens abroad:

> The United States frequently employs armed forces outside this country — over 200 times in our history — for the protection of American citizens or national security. Application of the Fourth Amendment to those circumstances could significantly disrupt the ability of the political branches to respond to foreign situations involving our national interest. [...] If there are to be restrictions on searches and seizures which occur incident to an American action, they must be imposed by the political branches through diplomatic understanding, treaty, or legislation.[38]

The choice is therefore to uphold national interests as viewed by the executive. This approach fits with the generally deferent attitude applied to judicial review of activities of the executive abroad under the international obligations of the State. Judicial interference with treaty obligations is deemed an intervention in international affairs, regardless of the domestic implications. The basic attitude has been that in international affairs "[o]ur State cannot speak with two voices on such a matter, the judiciary saying one thing, the executive another,"[39] and the executive's voice is preferred because of an inherent "advantage of the diplomatic approach to the resolution of difficulties between two sovereign nations, as opposed to the unilateral action by the courts of one nation."[40] Therefore, not only do courts tend to abstain from reviewing international treaties for compatibility with domestic laws, but when interpreting them they also defer to the executive's interpretation.[41]

[35] *Industria Panificadora SA, et al v United States*, 763 F Supp 1154 (DDC, 1991).
[36] *Garcia-Mir v Meese*, 788 F.2d 1446 (11th Cir, 1986).
[37] Restatement (Third) of the Foreign Relations Law of the United States, 1987, Sec 339(b): "Under the law of the United States, the President has the power ... to make the determination that would justify the United States in terminating or suspending an agreement because of its violation by another party or because of supervening events, and to proceed to terminate or suspend the agreement on behalf of the United States."
[38] *United States v Verdugo-Urquidez* 110 S Ct 1056, 29 ILM 441, 449–50 (1990).
[39] *The Arantzazu Mendi* 1939 App Cas 256, 264 (HL) (granting of immunity to the nationalist government of Spain by the British House of Lords following recognition by the Foreign Office as a de-facto government).
[40] *United States v Alvarez-Machain* above n 34, at n 16.
[41] See E Benvenisti, "Judicial Misgivings regarding the Application of International Law: An Analysis of Attitudes of National Courts" (1993) 4 *European Journal of International Law* 159, 166–68.

III. WILL THE COURTS BE SILENT DURING AN INDEFINITE WAR ON TERRORISM?

Acknowledging the maxim *inter armas silent leges,* Justice Rehnquist suggested in 1998 that courts should simply defer judgment till after the war: "If, in fact, courts are more prone to uphold wartime claims of civil liberties after the war is over, may it not actually be desirable to avoid decision on such claims during the war?"[42] This suggestion may perhaps suit short-term wars that have definite start and end points. It does not fit the current "war against terror" which has no identifiable or foreseeable finish. What then can we expect from our national courts in the coming years? Will we see a backlash against human rights condoned by the courts in the name of national security, or will the courts assert their capacity to evaluate the proper balance between civil liberties and threats to national security? I will try to explore these questions by reflecting on the legal experience of United Kingdom and Israel, two countries that faced and still face an indefinite struggle against terrorist threats. I begin with a description of the evolving jurisprudence of the British courts, which basically follows the *Liversidge v Anderson* rationale. The Israeli jurisprudence is then overviewed which demonstrates a more mixed response by courts.

A. The UK Experience

The wartime cases of *Halliday*[43] (WWI) and *Liversidge*[44] (WWII) have resonated through the post war jurisprudence dealing with a variety of issues concerning the balancing of individual rights against national security imperatives. The case law shows a clear deference of courts to the executive in these matters. In certain cases, one can discern the expression of judicial concern in this regard. In a decision involving the deportation of Mr. Hosenball, an American journalist (apparently due to his gathering of information in the course of his work) in 1977, Lord Denning said:

> It is a case in which national security is involved; and our history shows that, when the state itself is endangered, our cherished freedoms may have to take second place. Even natural justice itself may suffer a set-back. Time after time Parliament has enacted and the courts have loyally followed … [Halliday and Liversidge were] in time of war. But times of peace hold their dangers too. Spies, subverters and saboteurs may be mingling among us,

[42] Rehnquist, above n 14, at 222.
[43] Above n 16.
[44] Above n 20.

putting on a most innocent exterior. They may be endangering the lives of the men in the secret service, as Mr. Hosenball is said to do.[45]

There was little surprise when during the 1991 Gulf War, the English court declined to review the Home Secretary's orders to detain and deport hundreds of residents of Iraqi and Palestinian descent. An application filed by one such resident, a Lebanese man who had lawfully resided in United Kingdom with his family since 1975, against the detention and the intended deportation was rejected.[46] The court reasoned that national security was exclusively the responsibility of the executive, and that under the Immigration Act the court had no jurisdiction to inquire into the facts on which the Home Secretary had relied, particularly where there was evidence that further details could not be divulged without an unacceptable risk to security. In so holding the court endorsed the reasoning set forth in well-known and widely criticized House of Lords decision in *Council of Civil Service Unions v Minister for the Civil Service*,[47] wherein Lord Diplock observed that national security "is par excellence a non-justifiable question".

As one British commentator noted:

Time and again, the [British] judges have shown their true colors by upholding war-time emergency powers, extending police powers of arrest, extending powers of search and seizure, and legitimizing executive attacks on freedom of political association. Crises such as the industrial disputes that racked the 1980s and the ongoing conflict in Northern Ireland have shown the English senior judiciary at least to be invariably on the side of the executive ... The protection of civil liberties in Britain's non-rights based, unwritten constitution has been based on two false premises. The first is that Parliament would be careful about restricting civil liberties, and the second is that the judiciary would be vigilant in their support. Neither being the case, those seeking to assert their civil liberties in controversial circumstances have had next to nothing with which to defend themselves from executive aggression.[48]

And another added: "the judicial trend in England has been to fudge security issues. While English judges have since the Second World War roared by grandly asserting jurisdiction in security matters, they have mice-like refrained from doing anything with that jurisdiction ... English

[45] *R v Secretary of State for Home Affairs ex. Parte Hosenball* [1977] 1 WLR 766, 778.
[46] *R v Secretary of State for the Home Department, ex parte Cheblak* [1991] 2 All ER 319 (CA).
[47] [1984] 3 All ER 935.
[48] C Gearty, "Reflections on Human Rights and Civil Liberties in Light of the United Kingdom's Human Rights Act 1998" (2001) 35 *University of Richmond Law Review* 1, 17.

judges ... have used their jurisdiction only in matters where state security was not the issue."[49]

It may be fair to conclude that the British experience does not lend itself to a clear distinction between war-related jurisprudence and jurisprudence related to an ongoing need to counter terrorist threats; the judiciary generally opts for what Lord Denning calls "loyalty" to the political branches.[50]

B. The Israeli Experience

An overview of the Israeli jurisprudence presents a different model of judicial response to terrorist threats and reactions thereto. It provides one example of how the prolongation of a low-intensity war maintains the institutional necessity of an administration to rely on the courts as a legitimizing agent. At the same time, it demonstrates the courts' resolve to remain independent from government. These two factors may take a back seat during short and clearly identified emergency situations, but where a state of emergency becomes a way of life, the public's — and hence also the government's — interest in and reliance on an independently minded court resumes.

The Israeli High Court of Justice ("Court"), acting as first and final instance for reviewing governmental action, never identified special rules for war-related cases. The Court did not admit, for example, that it would not review the military authorities' discretion in military matters. It did not assert bluntly that during national emergency civil liberties may be compromised. It rejected "avoidance doctrine" such as lack of standing or non-justiciability as grounds to refuse adjudication. To the contrary, it virtually eliminated the requirement of standing and volunteered to review the policies of the military authorities beyond Israel's boundaries despite the lack of an explicit mandate for exercising such an authority. After some internal debates, it agreed to examine to the choice of targets for attack (the question referred to as targeted killings of terrorists).[51] The Court addressed the military authorities as any other administrative agency, in the sense that its actions must be based on statutory authority, follow the decision-making procedures prescribed by the authorizing law, and be based on a proper exercise of discretion.

The Court's deference to the government's security claims showed itself mainly in three ways. First, in the interpretation of the law — domestic

[49] Dyzenhaus, above n 27, at 178.
[50] Above n 46.
[51] Despite early announcement that this question is not justiciable (HCJ (High Court of Justice) 5872/01 *Barake v The Prime Minister* (unpublished opinion, 29 January 2002)) the court is seized with this matter at the time of writing.

and international law — that enabled the military to resort to most, but — quite significantly — not all, of the measures they sought. Second, in deferring, in the majority of cases, to the discretion of the military administration to decide how individual rights may be balanced against security interests. Third, in delaying the scheduling of court hearings and postponing the announcement of decisions. The general attitude of the Court has been aptly documented and elaborated elsewhere.[52] I will focus on cases showing notable exceptions to the generally deferent attitude. In the light of the Anglo-American practice described above, it seems worthwhile to demonstrate the more assertive role assumed by the Israeli High Court and to examine the factors that led the Israeli Court to adopt this attitude.

The Court's often widely criticized interpretation of the 1907 Hague Regulations and the 1949 Fourth Geneva Convention[53] on questions such as house demolition and deportations signaled a general attitude of playing down the role of international law. At the same time, however, the Court did emphasize the constraining power of Israeli constitutional and administrative law. In 1999 the Court determined that the use of physical pressure during interrogations was not authorized under Israeli law and hence outside the competence of the various Israeli agencies.[54] In 2001 it ruled that the indefinite detainment of so-called "illegal combatants" was also outside the authority of the Israeli authorities and hence necessitated an authorizing statute.[55] The Court's reliance on Israeli law as the basis of its constraining decisions apparently was motivated by the greater domestic legitimacy to domestic law (the Court made special efforts to refer to Jewish heritage[56]), but also enabled the court to share responsibility

[52] On the first policy of favorable interpretation of the law see D Kretzmer, *The Occupation of Justice* (Albany, State University of New York Press, 2002); Y Dotan, "Judicial Rhetoric, Government Lawyers, and Human Rights: The Case of the Israeli High Court of Justice during the Intifada' (1999) 33 *Law & Sociology Review* 319, D Simon; 'The Demolition of Houses in the Israeli Occupied Territories" (1994) 19 *Yale Journal of International Law* 1; E Benvenisti, *The International Law of Occupation*, (Princeton, Princeton University Press, 1993) Chapter 5, R Shamir, "'Landmark Cases' and the Reproduction of Legitimacy: The Case of Israel's High Court of Justice", (1990) 24 *Law & Sociology Review* 781. On the balancing of civil liberties and security interests within Israel see E Benvenisti, "Freedom of Speech in a Divided Society: Reflections after the Assassination of Prime-Minister Rabin" (1997) 57 *Zeitschrift fuer auslaendisches oeffentliches Recht und Voelkerrecht* (Heidelberg J. of Int'l L.) 806.

[53] See Benvenisti, Kretzmer, Simon, above n 52.

[54] HCJ 5100/94 *Public Committee Against Torture in Israel v The Government of Israel*, P.D. (Piskey Din, *lit.* Judgments) 53(4) 817 (1999).

[55] CrimFH (Appeals Court in Criminal Matters, Further Hearing) 7048/97 *Anonymous v The Government of Israel*, P.D. 53(1), 721 (2000).

[56] See for example, the following passage from the most recent decision on deportation from the West Bank to Gaza [(HCJ 7015/02 *Ajuri v IDF Commander in the West Bank* (not yet reported; decision of 3 September 2002) translation by the court]: "this conclusion is required by our Jewish and democratic values. From our Jewish heritage we have learned that 'Fathers shall not be put to death because of their sons, and sons shall not be put to death

with the legislature that was thus given the discretion to overturn its decisions by enacting new laws.

Most recently, however, the Court departed from the prevailing emphasis on the primacy of Israeli legislation. In the *Ajuri* case, the Court rejected the government attempt to deport en-bloc the families of "suicide bombers" from the West Bank to Gaza (what the government euphemistically called "confinement of residence" to conform with the language of Article 78 of Geneva Convention IV relative to the protection of civilian persons in time of war).[57] In this case international law plays a significant role in constraining governmental powers, and the Court does not leave legal loopholes for the Israeli legislature or the military commanders to modify the law. Although finding that Article 78 provided for the possibility of a deportation (or "confinement of residence") from the West Bank into Gaza, the Court insisted that Article 78 required that the authorities show that each individual deportee poses a substantial risk to public security. As Judge Barak noted:

> [A]n essential condition for being able to assign the place of residence of a person ... is that the person himself constitutes a danger, and that assigning his place of residence will aid in averting that danger. It follows that the basis for exercising the discretion for assigning residence is the consideration of preventing a danger presented by a person whose place of residence is being assigned. The place of residence of an innocent person who does not himself present a danger may not be assigned, merely because assigning his place of residence will deter others ... This conclusion is required by the outlook of the Fourth Geneva Convention that regards the measures of internment and assigned residence as the most severe and serious measures that an occupying power may adopt against protected residents (see Pictet, *id.*, at p. 257). Therefore these measures may be adopted only in extreme and exceptional cases.[58]

Israeli administrative law also provided rules constraining the decision-making process, in particular in the context of prior hearing.[59] In 1988,

because of their fathers; a person shall be put to death for his own wrongdoing' (Deuteronomy 24, 16) ... The character of the State of Israel as a democratic, freedom-seeking and liberty-seeking State implies that one may not assign the place of residence of a person unless that person himself, by his own deeds, constitutes a danger to the security of the State (cf. *A v Minister of Defence*, above n 55)."

[57] *Ajuri v IDF Commander in the West Bank*, above n 57.

[58] Para. 24 of the judgement.

[59] The Court was particularly keen to keep to the procedure as provided by statute, in particular the right to prior hearing. Thus, in 1948, at the height of the struggle for independence for the Jewish State, the Court accepted a petition of a Palestinian who had been detained on the basis of the Defense (Emergency Provisions) Regulations. The Court found that no detention was possible until an Appeals Committee, prescribed by the Regulations has been constituted. HCJ 7/48 *El Karbutli v The Minister of Defense* 2, P.D. 5 (1948).

one year into the first Palestinian *intifada*, the Court held that the military commanders must give the right of prior hearing before they decide to demolish homes of Palestinian terrorists.[60] The decision documents a powerful dialogue between the president of the Court and the Minister of Defense at the time, Itzhak Rabin. The Minister insisted that granting the right of hearing would delay demolitions as individuals would try to have the demolition orders annulled in the court. This, the Minister argued, would compromise the expected retaliatory effect of the demolition, and as a result the fight against terror would be less effective. The Court was not convinced by these arguments.

Subsequently, however, the Court succumbed to intense pressure coming from the army. Apparently unsatisfied with the judicially imposed limitations on its house demolition authority, the army sought new grounds for justifying demolitions. In 1990, in the wake of a lynching of an IDF soldier, an army general briefed the court in person explaining that the demolition of several buildings was necessary to protect the lives of IDF soldiers patrolling the street below. With the lives of soldiers potentially on the balance, and without asking why they needed to patrol in the midst of a populated neighborhood, the Court relented, recognizing an exception to the prior hearing rule in "a serious and uncontrollable situation of endangerment of human life which obligates immediate action".[61] The rule of prior hearing was again circumvented two years later, this time in the context of the deportation without prior hearing of 415 suspected members of the terrorist group Hamas from the West Bank and Gaza into Lebanon. The Court apparently was influenced by an unparalleled combination of circumstances: the previous acts of terror that spread fear and anger in the civilian population, the drama involving hundreds of deportees waiting for hours on buses near the border for the Court to decide their fate, the Chief of Staff addressing the judges in military uniform, describing the damage to security that would be caused if the judges were to undermine what to his best judgement were measures ensuring national security, and the wide international attention and condemnation sparked by Lebanon's unwillingness to grant the deportees passage into its territory.[62]

Nevertheless, during the intense fighting in the summer of 2002, the Court maintained the rule that procedures with respect to demolitions of homes of suspected terrorists must be fully complied with before demolition could go ahead. With the intensification of terrorist threats and the

[60] HCJ 358/88 *The Association for Civil Rights in Israel v The Commander of the Central Command*, P.D. 43(2) 529 (1988).
[61] HCJ 4112/90 *The Association for Civil Rights in Israel v The Commander of the Southern Command*, P.D. 44(1) 626 (1990) at 640.
[62] HCJ 5973/92 *The Association for Civil Rights in Israel v The Minister of Defense*, P.D. 47(1) 267 (1992).

prevalence of suicide bombings, the army refused to allow prior hearing before the demolition of homes of suspected terrorists, citing the concern that such a warning could threaten the lives of soldiers. The Court paid respect to the army's concerns, yet at the same time it underlined the army's obligation to provide the opportunity for prior hearing when circumstances allow. It also elaborated on the conditions that render such a hearing possible and on the necessity to justify the lack of hearing with concrete evidence as a basis for deciding whether or not to hold such a hearing.[63]

Judicial inquiry into the decision-making of the military authorities, while generally being deferent to their assessment of what constituted military necessity, nevertheless resulted in the upholding of a few basic principles. One constant concern of the Court was to prevent as far as possible damage to individuals who were not associated with terrorist activity. Consonant with its insistence on the military complying with relevant procedures, the Court began to examine in some detail the effect each house demolition would have on third parties. Whereas the suspected terrorist's home was considered a legitimate object of demolition (even after his death), the homes of other parts of his family and of neighbors were not, and as a result demolitions were approved only after a detailed examination proved that the damage would be adequately confined.[64] In a few cases, the Court rejected the State's claim for security grounds as unconvincing[65] or as insufficient reason to limit individual rights.[66]

The 2002 *Ajuri* decision discussed above[67] is significant also for its judicial review of the Military Commander's assessment of the danger posed by a certain individual. The Court found that, "[I]n view of the special nature of this measure, it may usually only be exercised if there exists administrative evidence that — even if inadmissible in a court of law — shows clearly and convincingly that if the measure of assigned residence is not adopted, there is a reasonable possibility that [the individual in question] will present a real danger of harm to the security of the territory." Moreover, "just as with any other measure, the measure of assigned residence must be exercised 'proportionately.' An appropriate relationship must exist between the purpose of preventing danger from the person whose place of residence is being assigned and the danger that he would present if this measure were not exercised against him." In this context, "each case must be examined to see whether filing a criminal

[63] HCJ 6696/02 *Amer v. The IDF Commander in the West Bank* (not yet reported, decision of 5 August 2002).
[64] HCJ 5510/91 *Turkeman v The Minister of Defense*, P.D. 48(1) 217 (1993).
[65] HCJ 390/79 *Doikat v The Minister of Defense*, P.D. 34(1) 1 (1979).
[66] *Ajuri*, above n 57.
[67] *Ibid.*

indictment will not prevent the danger that the assigned residence is designed to prevent."[68]

Finally, to fully appreciate the Court's impact on safeguarding civil liberties one must also consider the numerous applications to the Court that have been resolved in out of court settlements, by direct negotiations between government representatives and Palestinian petitioners. The number of successful out of court settlements for Palestinian applicants is a lot higher than those of litigation. Yoav Dotan has studied this evolving and quite effective dispute-settlement process.[69] He observes that with or without the intervention of the judges during the hearings, the judges put pressure on the government's legal representative to find relief in specific cases. The Court's decision in a case concerning a particularly fierce battle in Jenin in April 2002 demonstrates the mediating role of the Court. President Barak's submission documents the agreement reached between the petitioners and the government, with the assistance of the Court during the hearings, on the involvement of the Red Cross and Red Crescent in the identification and burial of Palestinian casualties.[70] Another example of the interplay between the Court and the army is reflected in the August 2002 case dealing with the procedure of house demolition.[71] The decision may be read as a negotiated arrangement between the Court and the army. While the Court accepts the army's agreement to provide a prior hearing when circumstances allow, it spells out in considerable detail the conditions that would render a hearing possible and stipulates the need for higher evidentiary requirements when a hearing is not possible.

The mixed picture of the evolving jurisprudence of the Israeli Court that this brief overview offers suggests that the Court walked on a judicial tight rope in an attempt to juggle what seem to be at least five main concerns (described here not necessarily in their order of importance). First, the court exercises a legitimating function: judicial review legitimates the decisions emanating from the administration.[72] This is why the Israeli government welcomed and in fact invited the Court to pass judgment over its activities in the occupied territories. This legitimating effect was sought in response to criticisms in Israel, in the occupied territories and abroad, against Israeli measures.[73] At the same time the Court made it clear that it would not provide this legitimating function without it

[68] *Ibid*, at para. 26.
[69] Dotan, above n 53.
[70] HCJ 3114/02 *Barak v The Minister of Defense*, (not yet reported, decision of 14 April 2002).
[71] Discussed above n 64 and accompanying text.
[72] Cotterrell, above n 5; Shamir, above n 53.
[73] In the case dealing with the burial of Palestinian corpses after the battle in Jenin (above n 67), rendered at a time of (ultimately unsubstantiated) accusations of a massacre in the Jenin refugee camp, the Court added the following observation: "It was alleged in the petitions that a massacre was committed in the refugee camp in Jenin. The respondents vehemently dispute this claim. There was a battle in Jenin — a battle in which many of our

being able to maintain its own independent status. Excessive deference to the government threatened its independence and stature. Therefore the Court resisted quite resolutely the few attempts of the government to circumvent judicial review. It was strict in its holdings that the military authorities abide by the procedures provided by law, procedures that ultimately opened the possibility of petitions to the Court. In two cases, involving deportations, when the military tried to avoid judicial intervention by acting swiftly and clandestinely, the Court intervened and insisted on *ex-post factum* hearings. In both cases the measures were not rescinded (in one case because the hearing endorsed the earlier act and in the other because the deportees refused to cooperate with the IDF), but in both cases the very intervention of the Court by temporarily withholding the military measure received worldwide attention and taught the government a painful lesson.[74] The third concern was the inherent institutional weaknesses of the Court in its ability to exercise judicial review over military decisions concerning national security. The Court tried to avoid interference with military discretion, preferring to focus on statutory authority and on procedural requirements. The fourth concern was the impact of public opinion. On the one hand, the Court lacked public support within the Israeli society for displaying an assertive judicial role by "liberal judges",[75] but on the other hand, it was criticized by foreign public opinion, and particularly by peers in foreign courts and academic institutions. Finally, the plight of the individual Palestinians who came before the Court was an important concern. The mix of landmark cases, some of them translated into English and published on the Court's website, together with a few unreported ones, and numerous applications that have been resolved through settlements negotiated directly or indirectly by the judges, enabled the Court over the years to respond to those pressures in a way the judges thought was reasonable under the circumstances.

In the final analysis we may therefore conclude that the High Court in Israel with respect to its war on terror has not been completely influenced by

soldiers fell. The army fought from house to house and did not use air bombardment, in order to avoid civilian casualties as much as possible. Twenty three IDF soldiers lost their lives. Dozens of soldiers were injured. The petitioners did not lift the burden of proof. A massacre is one thing. A fierce battle is another thing. The respondents reiterate that they have nothing to hide and that they wish to hide nothing. The practical arrangement that we arrived at reflects this position." (section 11 of the opinion; my translation).

[74] The deportation of three Palestinians in 1980 (HCJ 320/80 *Kawwassme v The Minister of Defense*, PD 35(3) 113 (1980)), and the deportation of 415 Hamas activists in 1992 (above n 62).

[75] The lack of public support in Israel for the court's assertiveness in protecting the liberties of Palestinians is well documented: See G Barzilai, E Yaar & Z Segal, *The Supreme Court in the Eye of Israeli Society* (1994, in Hebrew).

security concerns. It has not upheld the absolute protection of individuals either, as such courts have done in other contexts. In a few celebrated "landmark cases" it refused to be swayed by military pressure or offered redress to individuals without reaching the public eye. These may have been too little or too late compared to what was desired. But the court certainly offers a model that is significantly more interventionist than the Anglo-American model of the twentieth century.

C. The United States?

Will the US courts in the post September 11 era revert to the attitude that characterized their wartime decisions, or will they attempt to restrain the executive during this indefinite, perhaps endless "war on terrorism"? Initially at least, it seemed that the US administration had no particular desire to profit from the legitimizing function of judicial review. In fact, this administration tried to block judicial monitoring as effectively as it could. This policy was particularly noteworthy in the context of indefinite administrative detention of suspected terrorists or so-called "enemy combatants." The administration explained to the courts that the suspects' detention was part of the effort to elicit information from the detainees and prevent communications. Whereas other states such as Canada and Britain continued to refer to the regular court system to supervise the implementation of their post September 11 anti-terror laws (or, in the UK case, resort to judicially-monitored administrative detention of non-national suspects of international terrorism),[76] the US President opted for insulation from the regular court review. The Presidential Order entitled the "Detention, Treatment, and Trial of Certain Non-Citizens in the War Against Terrorism" issued on November 13, 2001[77] set up a special forum for both detention and trial.[78] Individuals who are not US citizens with respect to whom the President determines in writing that there is reason

[76] On the legality of the UK measure authorizing the administrative detention of non-nationals see *A, X and Y, v Secretary of State for The Home Department* [2002] EWCA Civ 1502 (UK, Court of Appeals).

[77] Proc. 7463, Declaration of National Emergency by Reason of Certain Terrorist Attacks. Available at <http://www.whitehouse.gov/news/releases/2001/11/20011113-27.html>. This proclamation, draws on the President's previous proclamation of a national emergency on 14 September 2001.

[78] In the order, the President declares, *inter alia*, that "(e) To protect the United States and its citizens, and for the effective conduct of military operations and prevention of terrorist attacks, it is necessary for individuals subject to this order ... to be detained, and, when tried, to be tried for violations of the laws of war and other applicable laws by military tribunals. (f) Given the danger to the safety of the United States and the nature of international terrorism ... that it is not practicable to apply in military commissions under this order the principles of law and the rules of evidence generally recognized in the trial of criminal cases in the United States district courts."

to believe that they are or were members of Al-Qaeda, or have engaged in "international terrorism",[79] would be detained in "an appropriate location designated by the Secretary of Defense outside or within the United States" (Section 3(a)); and "in accordance with such other conditions as the Secretary of Defense may prescribe" (Section 3(e)). The order further delegates authority to the Secretary of Defense to set up military commissions to try and punish those individuals with no judicial review in federal courts.[80] US nationals suspected of international terrorism are also detained indefinitely, so far without access to judicial review through habeas corpus proceedings.[81] Finally, detention and deportation proceedings against non-US citizens found inside the US are kept behind closed doors,[82] and information regarding the identities of these detainees is suppressed.[83]

[79] Section 2.

[80] Section 4: Authority of the Secretary of Defense Regarding Trials of Individuals Subject to this Order.

> (a) Any individual subject to this order shall, when tried, be tried by military commission for any and all offenses triable by military commission that such individual is alleged to have committed, and may be punished in accordance with the penalties provided under applicable law, including life imprisonment or death.
> (b) As a military function and in light of the findings in section 1, including subsection (f) thereof, the Secretary of Defense shall issue such orders and regulations, including orders for the appointment of one or more military commissions, as may be necessary to carry out subsection (a) of this section.
> (c) Orders and regulations issued under subsection (b) of this section shall include, but not be limited to, rules for the conduct of the proceedings of military commissions, including pretrial, trial, and post-trial procedures, modes of proof, issuance of process, and qualifications of attorneys, which shall at a minimum provide for —
>
> (1) military commissions to sit at any time and any place, consistent with such guidance regarding time and place as the Secretary of Defense may provide;
> (2) a full and fair trial, with the military commission sitting as the triers of both fact and law;
> (3) admission of such evidence as would, in the opinion of the presiding officer of the military commission (or instead, if any other member of the commission so requests at the time the presiding officer renders that opinion, the opinion of the commission rendered at that time by a majority of the commission), have probative value to a reasonable person; . . . ."

This military order attracted wide criticism, addressing the constitutional authority of the President to issue such order, the possible infringement of the internationally guaranteed Prisoner-of-War status to some of the detainees, and the impact on the detainees' liberties. See eg "Agora: Military Commissions" in (2002) 96 *American Journal of International Law* 320–58; NK Atyal & LH Tribe "Waging War, Deciding Guilt: Trying the Military Tribunals" (2002) 111 *Yale Law Journal* 1259.

[81] *Hamdi v Rumsfeld*, 316 F.3d 450 (4th Cir 2003) (US citizen captured in Afghanistan, thought to be a Taliban fighter); *Padilla v Rumsfeld*, 243 F Supp 2nd 42 (SDNY 2003) (US citizen captured in the US, thought to be Al-Qaeda operative).

[82] *North Jersey Media Group, Inc v Ashcroft*, 308 F.3d 198 (3d Cir 2002), cert denied, 155 L Ed 2d 1106, 123 S Ct 2215 (2003). For the opposite decision see *Detroit Free Press v Ashcroft*, 303 F.3d 681(6th cir 2002).

[83] *Center for National Security Studies v US Department Of Justice* 331 F.3d 918 (DC CA, 2003).

At the time of writing, there are mixed signals from US courts, although a trend is beginning to show itself. The US Court of Appeals for the Sixth Circuit affirmed a decision of a lower federal court that had declared that the blanket closure of deportation hearings in so-called "special interest" cases was an unconstitutional violation of the First Amendment.[84] Using very strong language,[85] the court found that the closing off to the public of hearings in certain classes of cases of deportations was not narrowly tailored to meet the compelling State interest in fighting terrorism. Instead, the court recommended that the government give reasons for such closure on a case-by-case basis. In rejecting the administration's argument that such a case-by-case closure would obstruct the war on terror, the court put a clear limit to governmental secrecy:

> The Government could use its "mosaic intelligence" argument as a justification to close any public hearing completely and categorically, including criminal proceedings. The Government could operate in virtual secrecy in all matters dealing, even remotely, with "national security," resulting in a wholesale suspension of First Amendment rights. By the simple assertion of "national security," the Government seeks a process where it may, without review, designate certain classes of cases as "special interest cases" and, behind closed doors, adjudicate the merits of these cases to deprive non-citizens of their fundamental liberty interests. This, we simply may not countenance. A government operating in the shadow of secrecy stands in complete opposition to the society envisioned by the Framers of our Constitution.[86]

However, two months later, in a similar case, the Court of Appeals for the Third Circuit disagreed.[87] After examining the historical right of access to governmental proceedings and reaching the conclusion that there was a tradition of closing off of sensitive proceedings before administrative agencies in general, and in deportation hearings in particular, the court ruled that the press and public possessed no First Amendment right of access. It accepted the government's contention concerning the potential danger that open proceedings may pose, arguments that had not proved convincing before the Sixth Circuit.

[84] *Detroit Free Press*, above n 82.
[85] *Ibid*, at 683: "Today, the Executive Branch seeks to take this safeguard away from the public by placing its actions beyond public scrutiny. Against non-citizens, it seeks the power to secretly deport a class if it unilaterally calls them 'special interest' cases. The Executive Branch seeks to uproot people's lives, outside the public eye, and behind a closed door. Democracies die behind closed doors. The First Amendment, through a free press, protects the people's right to know that their government acts fairly, lawfully, and accurately in deportation proceedings. When government begins closing doors, it selectively controls information rightfully belonging to the people. Selective information is misinformation."
[86] *Ibid*, at 709–10.
[87] *North Jersey Media Group*, above n 82.

With language replete of deference to the executive conducting military action abroad, the Court of Appeals of the 4th Circuit,[88] of the 7th Circuit,[89] the 9th,[90] and the Ditrict of Columbia,[91] joined forces with the 3rd Circuit, rendering the 6th Circuit a lone voice in favor of some role to the judiciary in monitoring executive's detention powers.

It remains to be seen whether and what will emerge as the consistent pattern of US judicial responses to the variety of measures to fight terrorism. At least one foreign court expressed hopes that ultimately the US courts would provide protection to foreign nationals detained by the US.[92] In a measured tone, the UK Court of Appeals said:

> The position of detainees at Guantanamo Bay is to be considered further by the appellate courts in the United States. It may be that the anxiety that we have expressed will be drawn to their attention. We wish to make it clear that we are only expressing an anxiety that we believe was felt by the court in *Rasul*. As is clear from our judgment, we believe that the United States courts have the same respect for human rights as our own.[93]

IV. CONCLUSION

We live in an era that poses new challenges to national security and to human rights. Balancing rights versus security threats is a constant exercise in risk-management. It involves the appraisal of uncertainties that may affect fundamental rights. This process is prone to partial attitudes by decision-makers whether in the bureaucracy or in the judiciary, as they may be influenced by public opinion that is not particularly sensitive to minority rights and concerns. Such deliberations cannot be based on exact scientific findings, but rather on vague assessments, tainted by conscious and

[88] *Hamdi v Rumsfeld*, above n 81.
[89] *Global Relief Foundation v O'Neill*, 315 F.3d 748 (7th Cir 2002). (upholding against constitutional challenge a portion of the USA PATRIOT Act, which authorizes the *ex parte* use of classified evidence in proceedings to freeze the assets of terrorist organizations).
[90] *Coalition of Clergy, Lawyers and Professors v Bush et al*, 310 F 3d 1153 (9th cir 2002) (see footnote 4) (dismissing a *habeas corpus* petition for all Guantanamo detainees on the ground that those bringing the action — clergy, lawyers, and law professors — were not proper "next friends" and therefore had no standing to sue).
[91] *Al Odah v USA*, 321 F.3d 1134 (DC Cir, 2003) (Kuwaiti, Australian and British citizens captured abroad during hostilities in Afghanistan and held under US military custody at the Guantanamo Bay Naval Base in Cuba were not entitled to resort to US courts to contest the lawfulness and conditions of their confinement); *Center for National Security Studies*, above n 83.
[92] *Abbasi v Secretary of State for Foreign and Commonwealth Affairs* [2002] EWCA Civ 1598. (judicial review of the diplomatic protection offered by UK authorities to UK nationals detained in Guantanamo).
[93] *Ibid*, para 107(iii). The *Rasul* decision to which reference is made was decided in the meantime in *Al Odah*, above n 91, by the DC Cir.

subconscious prejudices, existing social constraints, and past experience.[94] This last factor may prove significant in future US terror-related jurisprudence, as previous wartime experience indicates. To the extent that public pressure would insist on governmental accountability, it is possible to expect judicial responses to ensure at least some form of effective supervision of security measures.

While this contribution focused on national courts, it is important to note that supranational adjudicators are also called upon to decide such issues. The European Court on Human Rights is an example of a judicial body that has reviewed national policies affecting the rights of persons suspected of posing security threats. Such international judicial bodies seem to be less subjected to public pressure of a threatened society, and thus may adopt a more even-handed attitude. Thus, for example, the European Court on Human Rights found on two occasions that anti-IRA measures of the British government violated rights under the European Convention on Human Rights.[95] It is fair to expect, however, that tribunals such as the European Court on Human Rights will feel awkward to exercise judicial scrutiny over national assessments of threats in the face of international terrorism.[96] As that court already declared,

> It falls in the first place to each Contracting State, with its responsibility for "the life of [its] nation", to determine whether that life is threatened by a "public emergency" and, if so, how far it is necessary to go in attempting to overcome the emergency. By reason of their direct and continuous contact with the pressing needs of the moment, the national authorities are in principle in a better position than the international judge to decide both on the presence of such an emergency and on the nature and scope of derogations necessary to avert it.[97]

[94] See Benvenisti, *Free Speech*, above n 52 (suggesting that Germany and the United States provide two examples of societies which during the twentieth century altered their attitudes towards free speech on the basis of what they perceived to be the bad or even dangerous consequences of past policies; Germany adopted a restrictive view on free speech, whereas the US preferred to relax its control of political speech).

[95] *Ireland vs UK* (1978) (interrogation measures an inhuman and degrading treatment); *McCann v UK*, 21 EHHR 97 (1996) (Killing of IRA members in Gibraltar a violation of the right to life).

[96] See Gross & Aolain, above note 2; Aolain, above note 2.

[97] *Ireland v the United Kingdom* above n 95, at para 207.

14

The Rendition of Terrorist Suspects to the United States: Human Rights and the Limits of International Cooperation

SILVIA BORELLI

I. INTRODUCTION

FROM THE MOMENT the first plane hit the World Trade Center in New York, killing thousands of innocent people, the fight against terrorism has been an absolute priority for the international community. The episodes of terrorist violence that, with an unprecedented and alarming frequency, have taken place since then in many countries around the world dramatically demonstrate that the fight is still far from over.

In relation to the terrorist phenomenon, the importance of bringing to justice the individuals responsible for terrorist acts cannot be overestimated; and there can be no doubt that the common goal of the United States and of every other democratic State in the world is to hold accountable those responsible for the carnage of 11 September 2001 and subsequent attacks.

However, even in pursuing such a legitimate and sacrosanct objective, certain limits on State action cannot and should not be passed. Values such as the rule of law and respect for the dignity of each individual cannot be permitted to be trampled underfoot, even in grave situations such as that in the aftermath of September 11.

The aim of the present paper is to analyse the limits international human rights norms impose both on the exercise of criminal jurisdiction over terrorist suspects (including where the suspect has been forcibly abducted from another State), and on the capability of third States to extradite or otherwise surrender terrorist suspects to a State which wishes to try them, even where the threat to the prosecuting State and its citizens is as grave as that which seems to exist following the events of September 11. In this context, particular attention is devoted to the modalities of prosecution of terrorist suspects put in place by the United States following the events of September 11.

II. EXTRADITION AND EXPULSION

A. Relevant Aspects of the Law of Extradition

The crucial legal questions concerning trials of alleged terrorists are *where* and *how* they should be prosecuted. As to *where*, the International Criminal Court has no jurisdiction over such acts[1] and no step towards the establishment of an *ad hoc* tribunal for the prosecution of international terrorists has been taken.[2] The prosecution of terrorist acts[3] is thus left to municipal legal systems in accordance with the international treaty-based co-operation schemes against terrorism, which favour domestic prosecution of terrorist suspects.[4] These anti-terrorism conventions impose obligations on national systems to either prosecute terrorists in their national courts, or to extradite them to States Parties that are willing to prosecute them.[5]

A necessary precondition in order to ensure the effective punishment of crimes of transnational character is that domestic courts must be able

[1] See Art 11(1), Statute of the International Criminal Court (Rome, 17 July 1998, UN Doc. A/CONF.183/9 (1998), entered into force 1 July 2002). See RJ Goldstone and J Simpson, "Evaluating the Role of the International Criminal Court as a Legal Response to Terrorism", (2003) 16 *Harvard Human Rights Journal* 13.

[2] On this topic, see DF Vagts, "Which Courts Should Try Persons Accused of Terrorism?", (2003) 14 *European Journal of International Law* 313; F Mégret, "Justice in Times of Violence", (2003) 14 *European Journal of International Law* 327.

[3] It is beyond the scope of this paper to attempt to provide a comprehensive definition of "terrorism" or of "terrorist acts". After decades of negotiations at the international and regional level, and the adoption of numerous anti-terrorism conventions, the international community has yet to find a generally-accepted comprehensive definition of terrorism. However, for the purpose of this paper, "terrorism" may be defined as "premeditated, politically motivated violence perpetrated against noncombatant targets by subnational groups or clandestine agents, usually intended to influence an audience", while "international terrorism" can be defined as "terrorism involving citizens or the territory of more than one country." See Title 22 of the United States Code, Section 265f(d). On the issue of the definition of terrorism, see, *inter alia*, CM Pilgrim, "Terrorism in National and International Law", (1990) 8 *Dickinson Journal of International Law* 147, at 157; MP Scharf, "Defining Terrorism As The Peace Time Equivalent Of War Crimes: A Case Of Too Much Convergence Between International Humanitarian Law And International Criminal Law?," (2001) 7 *ILSA Journal of International and Comparative Law* 391.

[4] For a detailed analysis of internationally recognized criteria of jurisdiction for terrorist offences, see R Kolb, "Universal Criminal Jurisdiction in Matters of International Terrorism: Some Reflections on Status and Trends in Contemporary International Law", (1997) 50 *Revue Hellenique de Droit International* 42.

[5] On the obligation to extradite or prosecute terrorist suspects, see *infra* section IV.

to establish jurisdiction over alleged criminals.[6] The rendition of a fugitive, ie the process of transferring an individual from one State to another for the purpose of prosecution, can take place by a number of different methods: extradition, expulsion, deportation or forcible abduction.

States usually provide assistance to each other in criminal matters by entering into extradition treaties.[7] Even if the fight against crime is the primary aim of extradition agreements, extradition proceedings are also of cardinal importance in order to protect the fundamental rights of the fugitive. Extradition proceedings should strike a balance between the need for international co-operation in criminal matters on the one hand, and the necessity of safeguarding the basic human rights of individuals on the other.

From the perspective of protection of the individual, the first and foremost concern in extradition proceedings has always been to safeguard the fugitive from persecution in the requesting State on account of his or her personal characteristics, beliefs or political opinion. Extradition agreements commonly contain a *non-discrimination clause*, providing for the possibility of refusing extradition where there are substantial grounds to believe that the extraditee will be prosecuted or punished on account of his race, religion, nationality or political opinion, or would be discriminated against for any of these reasons in the territory of the requesting State.[8]

The *political offence exception* is another recurrent safeguard clause contained in extradition agreements, according to which extradition shall not be granted if the crime for which it is sought is a political offence.[9] A political offence may be defined as "an act that although it is in itself a

[6] This article deals with terrorist actions perpetrated by persons or groups who act independently from any State, albeit that they may have, in a varying degree, the support of one or more States. It therefore focuses on the prosecution of the "authentic" private actor responsible for a terrorist act, ie the individual or group of individuals that, although they may share the ideology of a State or of other religious or political groups, are not affiliated with any State and which design and conduct their operations on their own behalf. Al-Qaeda ostensibly represents such an autonomous private actor.

[7] See, in general, IA Shearer, *Extradition in International Law* (Manchester University Press, Manchester, 1971); G Gilbert, *Aspects of Extradition Law* (Kluwer, Dordrecht, 1991); G Gilbert, *Transnational Fugitive Offenders in International Law: Extradition and Other Mechanisms* (Kluwer, Dordrecht, 1998); MC Bassiouni, *International Extradition and World Public Order* (Oceana, Sijthoff, 1974).

[8] See, for instance, Art 3, UN Model Treaty on Extradition, UN Doc. A/45/49 (1990), 30 *ILM* 1407; Art 3(2), European Convention on Extradition (Paris, 13 December 1957, *ETS* No. 24, in force 18 April 1960); Art 4(5), Inter-American Convention on Extradition (Caracas, 25 February 1981, *OAS Treaty Series* No. 60, in force 28 March 1992); Art 5, European Convention on the Suppression of Terrorism (Strasbourg, 27 January 1977, *ETS* No. 90, in force 4 August 1978). An express non-discrimination clause is also contained in Art 9, International Convention against the Taking of Hostages (New York, 18 December 1979, 1316 *UNTS* 21931, in force 3 June 1983).

[9] For a detailed analysis of the historical development of the rule, see G Gilbert, *Aspects of Extradition Law*, above n 7, at 115.

common crime, acquires a predominantly political character because of the circumstances and motivations under and for which it was committed."[10] The political offence exemption has been raised many times in relation to terrorist activities. The problem here — as in many other areas — is that of defining "terrorism" and distinguishing between "terrorist acts" and other politically motivated actions which can include violent crimes. Obviously, terrorist acts properly so-called should not be regarded as political offences for the purposes of extradition. On the other hand, the political offence exception can also be an important tool to provide protection to opposition leaders accused of political crimes by their non-democratic governments. Judicial attempts to draw a distinction between terrorist acts and political violence have been made; however, while national courts judging on the basis of domestic interpretations of the concept of political offence, enjoy more latitude in qualifying an act or an omission as a political crime,[11] international monitoring bodies usually refrain from making qualifications of this kind.[12]

State practice shows that the political offence exception rarely represents an obstacle to extradition in cases of international terrorism.[13] Within the Council of Europe, the political offence exception has been expressly excluded for persons carrying out specified and precisely defined violent "terrorist" offences by the Council of Europe Terrorism Convention of 1977.[14] A similar approach has been taken by the South Asian

[10] G von Glahn, *Law Among Nations*, 7th edn (Allyn and Bacon, Boston, 1996), at 249.

[11] For instance, in the case of *In re Doherty*, 599 F Supp 270 (1984), at 275, the Court, refusing a request for extradition of a British Army officer on a charge of murder on the ground that the act charged was a political offence, tried to provide some criteria by which to determine whether a violent, politically-oriented crime falls within the exemption: "[t]he court must asses the nature of the act, the context in which it is committed, the status of the party committing the act, the nature of the organization on whose behalf it is committed, and the particularized circumstances of the place where the act takes place."

[12] See, eg, the decision of the European Commission of Human Rights in *X and Y v Ireland* (Application No 8299/78), in 22 *DR* (1981) 51, at 73, para. 20: "... the Irish interpretation of the term 'political offence' differs ... from that in the United Kingdom, and [the commission] finds no basis in the Convention for an authoritative interpretation of this widely disputed notion."

[13] See RS Phillips, "The political offence exception and terrorism: its place in the current extradition scheme and proposal for its future", (1997) 15 *Dickinson Journal of International Law* 337.

[14] Art 1, 1977 European Convention on the Suppression of Terrorism (above n 8) excludes from the concept of political offence a number of crimes of the type committed by terrorists, thus excluding from the protection of the political offence exemption anyone accused of those acts. Under Art 2, other serious offences of the same nature may, at the discretion of the Parties, be treated as not constituting a political offence. See also Art 1, Protocol amending the European Convention on the Suppression of Terrorism (Strasbourg, 15 May 2003, *ETS* No 190, not yet in force), which extends the list of offences. On the practice of European States relating to the political offence exception to extradition, see E Muller-Rappard, "The European Response to International Terrorism", in MC Bassiouni, *Legal Responses to International Terrorism: US Procedural Aspects* (Kluwer, Dordrecht, 1988), at 385.

Association for Regional Cooperation (SAARC),[15] and by the Organisation of American States.[16]

However, apart from the theoretical and sometimes subtle distinction between terrorist acts and other politically motivated crimes covered by the political offence exception, it is well established that — no matter how noble or legitimate the ultimate aim of the action is — there must be limits to the action of any group.[17] In the light of this consideration, the characterisation of the attacks against the United States as terrorist acts (and not as political offences) does not seem to pose any particular problem.

The principle of *specialty* represents a rule of extradition law aiming to protect both the rights of the extraditee and the sovereignty of the asylum State.[18] According to this principle, a fugitive may only be prosecuted in the requesting State for those offences for which extradition was sought; he or she cannot be put on trial for any offence not disclosed in the extradition request. The rule of specialty, accepted by most States as a customary rule of extradition law, has undergone some developments: several regional extradition agreements provide for the possibility that

[15] Art 1, SAARC Regional Convention on Suppression of Terrorism (Kathmandu, 4 November 1987, in force 2 August 1988).

[16] Art 11, Inter-American Convention against Terrorism (Bridgetown, 3 June 2002) (not yet in force). See also the Art 4(1), Treaty on Cooperation among the States Members of the CIS in Combating Terrorism (Minsk, 4 June 1999) (not yet in force): "In cooperating in combating acts of terrorism, including in relation to the extradition of persons committing them, the Parties shall not regard the acts involved as other than criminal." See Art 2, Arab Convention on Suppression of Terrorism (Cairo, 22 April 1998) (not yet in force), which although providing that a variety of terrorist offences shall not be regarded as political offences (para. 2), states that "All cases of struggle by whatever means, including armed struggle, against foreign occupation and aggression for liberation and self-determination, in accordance with the principles of international law, shall not be regarded as an offence (para. 1)." See also International Convention for the Suppression of Terrorist Bombing (New York, 15 December 1997, UN Doc. A/Res/52/164 (1997), in force 23 May 2001), Art 11: "[n]one of the offences set forth in the Convention shall be regarded for the purpose of extradition or mutual legal assistance as a political offence or as an offence connected with a political offence or as an offence inspired by political motives ..."

[17] See "Measures to prevent international terrorism which endangers or takes innocent human lives or jeopardizes fundamental freedoms and study of the underlying causes of those forms of terrorism and acts of violence which lie in misery, frustration, grievance and despair and which cause some people to sacrifice human lives, including their own, in an attempt to effect radical changes: Study prepared by the Secretariat in accordance with the decision taken by the Sixth Committee at its 1314th Meeting on 27 September 1972", UN Doc. A/C.6/418, 2 May 1973: "even when the use of force is legally and morally justified, there are some means, as in every form of human conflict, which must not be used". See also Resolution on "New Problems of Extradition", Institut de Droit International (Session of Cambridge, 1 September 1983), 68-II Ann. IDI 304, Art II (3): "Acts of a particularly heinous character, such as acts of terrorism, should not be considered political crimes."

[18] The term "asylum State" is used here simply to indicate the State upon whose territory the fugitive is currently present, without any implication that the State has granted either asylum or refugee status to the fugitive.

the requesting State may charge the individual with further extraditable offences after extradition, provided that the asylum State consents.[19] These developments, while improving international co-operation in criminal matters, represent a serious threat to the rights of the extraditee, as the consent to additional charges will usually be granted by the executive authorities of the asylum State without the judicial scrutiny which characterises extradition proceedings.

Another widely accepted standard of extradition which provides a valuable protection of the rights of the fugitive is the *double criminality* requirement. Under this rule, a State cannot obtain the custody of an individual for conduct that is not recognised as criminal in the asylum State. Thus, for an individual to be extradited, his conduct should be criminalized both by the law of the requesting and that of the asylum State. In particular, such a rule requires that, if the same case were to be presented before the courts of the requested State, *mutatis mutandis*, it could be prosecuted on the same facts. The rule of double criminality can be considered a customary rule of international extradition law;[20] as such, it can be expressly derogated from by extradition treaties,[21] but — in the absence of such a specific and express derogation — double criminality has to be considered a tacit precondition for extradition.

It has been suggested, that, at least from a theoretical perspective:

> there are two methods of interpreting the double criminality requirement: … *in concreto* (objective) and *in abstracto* (subjective). The first approach relies on the label of the offence and a strict interpretation of its legal elements. The second approach relies on the criminal character of the activity, regardless of its specific label and full concordance of its elements in the respective laws of the two states.[22]

Recent trends in international practice show that domestic courts are more inclined towards the application of the subjective approach.[23] Nevertheless, the rule of double criminality can still pose some problems even when the conduct of the fugitive is undoubtedly criminal.

[19] See, eg, Art 14, European Convention on Extradition (above n 8).
[20] RY Jennings and A Watts (eds), *Oppenheim's International Law*, 9th ed (Longman, London, 1992), at 107. Some domestic courts recognise the customary nature of the double criminality requirement: see eg, the decisions of the Swiss Federal Court in *M v Federal Department of Justice and Police* (21 September 1997), 75 ILR 107, at 113 and the Irish case of *The State (Furlong) v Kelly*, [1971] IR 132, at 141. See also the Harvard Research in International Law: Draft Convention on Jurisdiction with Respect to Crime (1935) 29 AJIL 443 (Supp. 1935): "… no person shall be extradited whose deed is not a crime according to the Criminal Law of the State which is asked to extradite, as well as of the State which demands extradition".
[21] See, eg, *Riley v The Commonwealth of Australia*, 159 CLR [1985] 1, at 12, where the court held that treaty provisions could expressly exclude the double criminality requirement.
[22] Bassiouni, above n 7, at 322.
[23] See *Oppenheim's International Law*, above n 20, at 958.

In particular the rule can represent an obstacle to extradition when applied by domestic courts of States that follow the territorial principle of jurisdiction. Domestic courts in such States may not limit their inquiry to the evaluation of the *prima facie* criminal character of the conduct of the extraditee and to the determination whether the alleged facts would be an extradition crime if committed in the asylum State, but sometimes will also look at jurisdictional issues. In particular, they may evaluate if — in a similar case — their domestic laws on criminal jurisdiction would allow them to exercise jurisdiction. Obviously, such an approach can represent an obstacle to the extradition of individuals if the requesting States seeks to prosecute on the basis of extraterritorial principles of jurisdiction.

In relation to requests for extradition for terrorist acts, however, the rule of double criminality should not represent an obstacle to the rendition of suspected terrorists to the US. The conduct of which those individuals will be accused is undoubtedly a serious criminal offence under the law both of the United States and, presumably, of every other country as well as under international law. Nor are the jurisdictional aspects of the rule likely to raise any problems, as the offences took place in the territory of the United States, and in any case they are crimes for which States are generally recognised as having (or even being required to exercise) extra-territorial jurisdiction.

One of the most important issues concerning the guarantees provided by international extradition law is whether individuals should have standing to claim violations of an extradition treaty — or its circumvention — as a defence before the municipal courts of the requesting State. Traditionally, extradition treaties were conceived as a method to create effective co-operation in criminal matters among States, in full respect of each other's sovereignty. The obligations laid down by extradition treaties are owed "horizontally" to the other party (or parties) to the agreement; the procedural and substantive guarantees set forth in extradition treaties were therefore mainly envisaged as protective of States' sovereignty, and not of the rights of individuals.[24] Although in principle extradition treaties were not conceived as creating rights or duties for individuals, in this as in many other fields, individuals can be the indirect beneficiaries of obligations entered into by States.[25] As a consequence of this traditional

[24] For an example of this approach, see G Schwarzenberger, "The Problem of International Criminal Law", (1950) 3 *Current Legal Problems* 263, at 272.

[25] It seems that individuals can also be the *direct* beneficiaries of State obligations outside the special field of human rights: see for instance *LaGrand Case (Germany v United States)*, judgment of 27 June 2001, para. 77, where the International Court of Justice held that the Vienna Convention on Consular Relations 1971, Art 36 (1)(b), confers *individual rights* that may be invoked before the Court by the national State of the individuals involved. For an earlier example, see the judgment of the Permanent Court of International Justice in *Jurisdiction of the Courts of Danzig*, PCIJ, *Series B*, No. 15 (1928), at pp. 17 ff. See also *Treatment of Polish Nationals and Other Persons of Polish Origin or Speech in the Danzig Territory*, PCIJ, *Series A/B*, No. 44 (1932), at 20.

view, if an individual is extradited pursuant to an extradition treaty, and the provisions of the treaty are violated by the receiving State (for instance by violating the principle of specialty), in the absence of the express waiver by the requested State he is able to claim the violation of such treaty as a defence before the courts of the requesting State.[26]

In some cases the requesting and the asylum State tacitly agree to utilise means different from extradition. Occasionally, extradition proceedings may be felt to be too slow or too complicated, or may be doomed to failure or even impossible. For instance, the length of the extradition proceedings may give the fugitive time to flee again, the requirement of double criminality may not be met, there may be no extradition treaty between the requesting and the asylum States or the crime may not be extraditable under such a treaty. In such cases, the State to which the fugitive has fled can nevertheless choose to return the fugitive by means of deportation or expulsion.[27] In these circumstances, the procedures and protections of extradition law in the asylum State do not apply. Further, in cases where the rendition of a fugitive takes place by means other than extradition proceedings, the asylum State has not only no interest in, but above all no grounds for making a formal complaint for the violation of an existing extradition agreement, and therefore on the traditional view the fugitive cannot invoke the guarantees provided by extradition law before the courts of the requesting State. The circumvention of extradition proceedings and consequentially of the protection given by extradition treaties in these cases cannot therefore be invoked directly by individuals as a defence to prosecution before the courts of the requesting State.[28]

B. Human Rights Provisions Applicable to Extradition or Expulsion Cases

To offset the apparent lack of protection of fundamental rights under the traditional approach, recourse has been made to international human rights law.[29] Quite apart from the guarantees of extradition law, many human

[26] See, for instance, *United States v Noriega*, 746 F Supp 1506, 1533 (S D Fla 1990): "as a general principle of international law, individuals have no standing to challenge violations of international treaties in the absence of protest by the sovereign involved."

[27] Given that the purpose of deportation and expulsion is to remove unwanted aliens from the territory of the State, in theory at least, the deporting/expelling State should not be interested in the destination of the expelled immigrant. Deportation/expulsion may therefore be considered a form of "disguised" extradition where the territorial State deports the alien to a specific State, which is seeking his return for prosecution.

[28] See the parallel question of the inability of individuals to invoke the provisions of an extradition treaty following an illegal forcible abduction, *infra*, section III B.

[29] On the relevance of international human rights law to extradition proceedings and, in general, to rendition cases, see C Van den Wyngaert, "Applying the European Convention of Human Rights to Extradition: Opening Pandora's Box?", (1990) 39 *International and Comparative*

rights provisions are relevant to extradition and expulsion/deportation;[30] in some domestic systems the violation of these provisions may be directly invoked by individuals before municipal courts either to prevent extradition, or in order to challenge the exercise of jurisdiction and prosecution. Where the State in question has consented to a right of individual petition, claims may be brought before international judicial or supervisory bodies. From the point of view of the fugitive, international human rights law offers at least one fundamental advantage when compared to the more traditional international mechanisms. While under traditional institutions such as the law of extradition or diplomatic protection, individuals are mere indirect beneficiaries of rights vested in States,[31] under international human rights law individuals are the right-holders of obligations incumbent on States. Moreover, international human rights law is equally applicable to cases of expulsion/deportation as it is to regular extradition; it is arguably even more important in protecting individual rights in cases of irregular rendition.

Law Quarterly 757; JG Kester, "Some Myths of United States Extradition Law", (1988) 76 *Georgetown Law Journal* 1441, at 1465–68; P Michell, "English-Speaking Justice: Evolving Responses to Transnational Forcible Abduction After Alvarez-Machain", (1996) 29 *Cornell International Law Journal* 383, at 436 ff; J Dugard and C Van den Wyngaert, "Reconciling Extradition with Human Rights", (1998) 92 *American Journal of International Law* 187.

[30] In addition to the limitations discussed *infra*, international refugee law sets forth some additional limits to the liberty of a State to deport or expel an individual from its territory: the Convention Relating to the Status of Refugees (Geneva, 28 July 1951, 189 *UNTS* 150, in force 2 April 1954) provides for an obligation of *non-refoulement* of refugees, whether lawfully or unlawfully present [in the territory of a State Party] stating that "a refugee ... must not be returned to the frontiers of territories where his life or freedom would be threatened on account of his race, religion, nationality, membership of a particular social group or political opinion (Art 33(1)). Both State practice and international legal scholarship support the view that this clause of the Convention states a rule of customary law. It has to be noted, however, that the same Convention sets forth an exception to this rule, providing that: "[the benefit of the present provision may not ... be claimed by a refugee whom there are reasonable grounds for regarding as a danger to the security of the country in which he is, or who, having been convicted by a final judgment of a particularly serious crime, constitutes a danger for the community of that country" (Art 33 (2)).

[31] That diplomatic protection is a right pertaining to States and not to individuals and that it can be exercised at the discretion of the "injured State" is uncontroversial. This basic principle was elaborated by the Permanent Court of International Justice in the *Mavrommatis Palestine Concession Case*, PCIJ, *Series A*, No 2 (1924), at 12, where the Court held that "by taking up the case of one of its subjects and by resorting to diplomatic action or international judicial proceedings on his behalf, a state is in reality asserting its own rights, its rights to ensure, in the person of its subjects, respect for the rules of international law ... "; see also *Panevezys-Saldutiskis Railway*, PCIJ, *Series A/B*, No 76 (1939), at 4; *Barcelona Traction, Light and Power Company Limited*, ICJ Reports 1970, p 3, at p 45–46, paras. 85–86. See further, C de Visscher, "Cours Général de Principes de Droit International Public", 86 *RdC* (1954, II), at 507. Note also the challenge mounted to this traditional approach by Professor Dugard in his Reports to the International Law Commission on Diplomatic Protection, and the subsequent rejection of his proposals. See J Dugard, *First Report on Diplomatic Protection*, UN Doc A/CN.4/506 and Add 1 (2000), paras 24–25 and 29; and *Report of the International Law Commission on the work of its fifty-second session (1 May-9 June and 10 July-18 August 2000)*, UN Doc A/55/10 (2000), at para 416.

While irregular rendition does not necessarily represent a violation of the internationally protected human rights of the deported individual *per se*,[32] this does not mean that, in particular circumstances, the use of deportation or expulsion in lieu of extradition cannot constitute a violation of the international human rights obligations of the deporting State. As the European Commission has noted:

> There is nothing in the Convention to prevent a State from expelling a person to his home country even if criminal proceedings are already pending in that country or if he has already been convicted in that country. Nor does the Convention prevent coopexration between the States concerned in matters of expulsion, *provided that this does not interfere with any specific right recognised in the Convention.*[33]

Therefore, while the traditional institutions of international law do not grant any protection to individuals deported to face criminal prosecution in other States, under human rights law the deported individual can rely upon the same human rights which he could have claimed if he had been surrendered by means of a regular extradition procedure.[34]

Turning to the human rights provisions relevant to the rendition (regular or irregular) of a fugitive, the impact of human rights obligations on extradition and expulsion proceedings derives from the widely recognised principle that when a State extradites, or otherwise surrenders, an individual subject to its jurisdiction to another State, the former is directly responsible for every foreseeable violation of any human right and fundamental freedom the extraditee may suffer in the latter.[35] While not dealing directly with extradition matters, all the major international instruments on human rights extend their protection to all persons *within the jurisdiction* of the States Parties,[36] and thus impose obligations that

[32] See European Commission of Human Rights, *Altmann v France* (Application No 10689/83), 37 *DR* (1994) 225, at 233: "the Convention contains no provision under which extradition may be granted or on the procedure to be applied before extradition may be granted. It follows that, even if the applicant's expulsion could be described as disguised extradition, this would not, as such, constitute a breach of the Convention." See also the opinion of the Commission in *Stocké v Germany*, judgment of 19 March 1991, ECHR, *Series A*, No 199, p 21, at 24, para 168.

[33] European Commission of Human Rights, *C v Germany* (Application No 10893/84), 45 *DR* (1986) 198, at 203 (emphasis added).

[34] Moreover, the deportation or the expulsion may take place in such a way as to infringe the right to freedom and security of the person: *Bozano v France*, judgment of 18 December 1986, ECHR, *Series A*, No 111; 9 *Eur H R Rep* 297 (1987).

[35] European Commission of Human Rights, *X v Sweden* (Application No 434/58), 2 *Ybk ECHR* 354. See also *Soering v United Kingdom*, judgment of 7 July 1989, ECHR, *Series A*, No 161, paras 88, 91; *Cruz Varas et al v Sweden*, judgment of 20 March 1991, ECHR, *Series A*, No 201, para 70; *Vilvarajah et al v United Kingdom*, judgment of 30 October 1991, ECHR, *Series A*, No 215, para 103.

[36] See Art 2, International Covenant on Civil and Political Rights (New York, 16 December 1966, 999 UNTS 171, entered into force 23 March 1976) (hereinafter "ICCPR"); Art 1,

apply in the context of extradition or other means of rendition. Thus, while States are potentially free to enter into and to give execution to extradition agreements, their rights under international law, including the right to expel foreigners, are limited by the obligations that they have accepted under international human rights instruments and by customary principles of international human rights law.[37] Consequently, the decision to extradite or deport an individual may involve a breach of international law "where substantial grounds have been shown for believing that the person concerned ... faces a real risk" of violation of one of his fundamental human rights in the territory of the requesting State.[38] Apart from the requirement of showing "a real risk"[39] and the fundamental character of the endangered right,[40] in order for the requested State to breach its obligation under any human rights instrument, another condition must be met. The violation of the rights of the

European Convention for the Protection of Human Rights and Fundamental Freedoms (Rome, 4 November 1950, *ETS* No. 5, in force 3 September 1953) (hereinafter "ECHR" or "European Convention on Human Rights"); Art 1, American Convention on Human Rights (San José, 22 November 1969, *OAS Treaty Series* No. 36, in force 18 July 1978) (hereinafter "ACHR"). See T Vogler, "The Scope of Extradition within the European Convention of Human Rights", in F Matscher and H Petzold (eds), *Protecting Human Rights: the European Dimension. Studies in honour of Gérard J. Wiarda* (Heymanns Verlag KG, Köln, 1988).

[37] *Soering*, above n 35, para. 88. See also the European Court in *Vilvarajah and Others v the United Kingdom*, above n 35, para. 102: "the Contracting States have the right, as a matter of well-established international law and subject to their treaty obligations, including the Convention, to control the entry, residence and expulsion of aliens. Moreover, the right to political asylum is not contained in either the Convention or its Protocols."

[38] *Soering*, above n 35, para. 88 (extradition); *Cruz Varas v Sweden*, above n 35, para. 69 and 70 (expulsion). See also *Chahal v United Kingdom*, judgment of 15 November 1996, *Reports* 1996-V, paras. 73–74, and, more recently, *Hilal v United Kingdom*, judgment of 6 March 2001, *Reports* 2001-II, para. 59; *Mamatkulov and Abdurasulovic v Turkey*, judgment of 6 February 2003, available at: <http://hudoc.echr.coe.int/Hudoc1doc2/HEJUD/200303/mamatkulov%20-%2046827jv.chb1%2006022003.trade.doc> para. 66. See Art IV, IDI Resolution on "New Problems of Extradition", above n 17: "In cases where there is a well-founded fear of the violation of the fundamental human rights of an accused in the territory of the requesting State, extradition may be refused, whosoever the individual whose extradition is requested, and whatever the nature of the offence of which he is accused." See also the UN Model Treaty on Extradition (above n 8) which excludes extradition if there are "substantial grounds for believing" that the person will be prosecuted or punished on discriminatory grounds (Art 3(b)), or if he would be subjected to torture or denied the enjoyment of the right to a fair trial (Art 3(e)).

[39] In certain cases, the monitoring body is willing to infer a real risk from the "co-existence of sufficiently strong, clear and concordant inferences or unrebutted presumptions": see European court of Human Rights, *Aydin v Turkey*, judgment of 25 September 1997, *Reports* 1997-VI, para. 73.

[40] The European Court has so far recognised the right to be free from torture and inhuman treatment contained in Art 3 of the European Convention as forming part of this group (see the cases cited in the previous footnote); the Court has also indicated that where the individual has suffered or risks a "flagrant denial of justice" in the requesting country, the obligation to respect the right to a fair trial contained in Art 6 may also preclude extradition (see *Soering*, above n 35, para. 113 (quoted *infra* fn. 81), and *Mamatkulov and Abdurasulovic v Turkey*, above n 38, para. 85.

extraditee in the territory of the requesting State must be a direct and foreseeable consequence of the decision to extradite.[41]

While this approach may seem to imply that States — at least in where certain rights are at issue — have to accord priority to their human rights obligations over their obligations deriving from treaties on co-operation in criminal matters, the issue of what to do if the two sets of obligations conflict needs to be carefully assessed.

For at least some of the rights protected by universal and regional agreements on human rights, there can be little doubt as to their fundamental character. The right to life and to physical integrity and the right to be protected from torture or inhuman treatment are widely accepted as fundamental rights and the fear that those rights may be violated in the requesting State may prevent the extradition of an individual, "whosoever the individual whose extradition is requested and whatever the nature of the offence of which he is accused".[42] For those norms which are widely-recognised as falling into the category of *ius cogens*, there is little difficulty in postulating that they must prevail over the obligations contained in an extradition treaty. The relevance to extradition proceedings of other rights laid down in human rights instruments, in particular the right to fair trial, is much more controversial; not only are these norms not widely-accepted as *ius cogens*, but, further, the exact content of the norms is nowhere near as neatly defined as the concepts of torture or capital punishment, and thus the discretion of the competent authorities of the requested State is wider.[43]

[41] See *Soering*, above n 35, para 91: "[i]n so far as any liability under the Convention is or may be incurred, it is the liability incurred by the extraditing Contracting State by reason of its having taken action which has as *a direct consequence* the exposure of an individual to proscribed ill-treatment" [emphasis added].

[42] See Resolution on "New Problems of Extradition", above n 17, at 304.

[43] It is noteworthy that past US practice in extradition cases seems to reflect concern over the respect for the fundamental rights of the extraditee in the requesting country. Even if the practice of the US executive and judiciary has not always been consistent, mainly depending on the relationship with the government of the requesting country, in principle, the US position is one of not granting the extradition of individuals "if the requested state has reason to believe that ... there is substantial ground for believing that the person sought will not receive a fair trial in the requesting state": see *Restatement Third of the Law of Foreign Relations of the United States*, at 711, § 476 Reporters Comments (g), (h). See also MC Bassiouni, *International Extradition: United States Law and Practice*, 4th edn (Oceana Publications, 2002). Similar principles are embodied in relation to other norms in several international agreements to which the US is a party: see Art 3 (1), UN Convention against Torture and Other Cruel, Inhuman or Degrading Treatment and Punishment (New York, 10 December 1984, UN Doc A/39/51 (1984), entered into force 26 June 1987); Art 9, 1979 Hostages Convention, above n 8; arts 1(a)(2) and 33(1), 1951 Convention on the Status of Refugees, above n 30. See RJ Wilson, "Representing Defendants in International Criminal Cases. Asserting Human Rights and Other Defenses: Toward the Enforcement of Universal Human Rights through the Abrogation of the Rule of Non-inquiry in Extradition", (1997) 3 *ILSA Journal of International and Comparative Law* 751.

1. *Torture and Inhuman Treatment*

There can be little doubt as to the customary nature of the international norm prohibiting torture. Torture is universally condemned and, whatever its actual practice, no State publicly supports torture or opposes its eradication. The *ius cogens* nature of the international norm prohibiting torture has been recognised both by domestic and international judicial and quasi-judicial bodies.[44] The ban on torture and other ill-treatment has been incorporated in many human rights instruments, both at the universal and at the regional level,[45] and in three *ad hoc* conventions, widely ratified by States, specifically designed to outlaw such conduct.[46] The prohibition against torture is absolute and applies even during times of armed conflict or when national security is threatened. In the aftermath of the terrorist attacks against the United States, the Committee against Torture, in condemning the attacks of 11 September and expressing condolences for the victims, reminded States Parties to the Convention against Torture of the non-derogable nature of many of the obligations undertaken by them in ratifying the Convention.[47]

As a consequence of the absolute prohibition of torture, the risk that the fugitive, if extradited or otherwise surrendered, may be subjected to torture justifies — and, arguably, in many cases compels — the refusal of extradition by the requested State. This obligation of the requested State is explicitly set forth by the Convention against Torture, which provides that "[n]o State Party shall expel, return ('refouler') or extradite a person to another State where there are substantial grounds for believing that he would be in danger of being subjected to torture."[48] In the Council of

[44] See the decision of the Trial Chamber of the ICTY in *Prosecutor v Furundzija,* Case No. IT-95-17/1-T (10 December 1998), (1999) 38 *ILM* 317, para. 153. See also *Al-Adsani v United Kingdom,* ECHR, *Reports* 2001-XI, para. 61; Human Rights Committee, General Comment 24 (52), UN Doc. CCPR/C/21/Rev.1/Add.6, para. 8; *Filartiga v Peña-Irala,* 630 F.2d 876, 77 *ILR* (1980) 169, at 177–179 (Court of Appeals, 2nd Circuit); *R. v Bow Street Metropolitan Magistrate, ex p. Pinochet Ugarte (No. 3)* [1999] 2 WLR 827, at 841, 881.

[45] Art 7, ICCPR; Art 3, ECHR; Art 5, ACHR. See also Art 5, Universal Declaration of Human Rights, GA res. 217A (III), (UN Doc A/810 (1948), at 71) (hereinafter "UDHR").

[46] UN Convention against Torture, above n 43; Inter-American Convention to Prevent and Punish Torture (Cartagena de Indias, 9 December 1985, OAS Treaty Series No. 67, in force 28 February 1987), European Convention for the Prevention of Torture and Inhuman and Degrading Treatment and Punishment (Strasbourg, 26 November 1987, *ETS* No. 126, in force 1 February 1989).

[47] Statement of the Committee against Torture, 22 November 2001, UN Doc. CAT/C/XXV11/Mis.7 (2001). The Committee cited in particular Art 2 (whereby no exceptional circumstances whatsoever may be invoked as a justification of torture), Art 15 (prohibiting confessions extorted by torture being admitted in evidence, except against the torturer) and Art 16 (prohibiting cruel, inhuman or degrading treatment or punishment) as three such provisions which must be observed in all circumstances.

[48] Art 3(1), UN Convention against Torture, above n 43. See also the opinion of the Committee Against Torture in *Alan v Switzerland* (Communication No. 21/1995) (UN Doc.

Europe human rights system, the case law of the European Court and, previously, the practice of the European Commission of Human Rights, demonstrate that the fact that there are substantial grounds to believe that the surrendered person will be subjected to torture once returned to the requesting State represents an absolute obstacle to extradition or expulsion.[49]

Apart from the prohibition of torture, the prohibition of inhuman, cruel or degrading treatment or punishment set forth by many human rights instruments can also prove extremely relevant in cases of extradition. The concept of inhuman or degrading treatment or punishment is broad and covers many diverse forms of abusive conduct. The prohibition has thus been invoked as a circumstance precluding extradition in many different cases.

The prohibition of degrading treatment could possibly be invoked to prevent extradition to countries in which the extraditee may be subjected to interrogation techniques that violate internationally recognised human rights standards. The use of force or the infliction of pain to overcome an individual's desire to remain silent during an interrogation constitutes a violation of his or her right not to speak during an interrogation, and of the privilege against self-incrimination. Quite apart from these aspects relating to the right to a fair trial,[50] the use of harsh interrogation

CAT/C/16/D/41/1996 (1997), reprinted in 4 *IHRR* 66). The petitioner was a Turkish citizen, and a member of an outlawed Kurdish organisation in Turkey. He was detained in Turkish prisons and allegedly tortured. In 1990, he sought asylum in Switzerland, where the Swiss authorities rejected his asylum request. The Committee, with which the petitioner lodged a complaint relating to the alleged breach of Art 3 of the Convention, found that the return of the petitioner to Turkey would amount to a violation of Switzerland's obligation under Art 3(1) of the Convention. The Committee noted that "the main aim and purpose of the Convention is to *prevent torture,* and not to redress torture once it has occurred" (para. 11.5).

[49] In *Cruz Varas*, above n 35, paras. 69–70, the European Court held that the expulsion by a Contracting State of an asylum seeker may give rise to an issue under Art 3, and hence engage the responsibility of that State under the Convention, where substantial grounds have been shown for believing that the person concerned faced a real risk of being subjected to torture or to inhuman or degrading treatment or punishment in the country to which he was returned. See also *Tomasi v France*, judgment of 27 August 1992, ECHR, *Series A,* No. 241-A, para. 115 and *Vilvarajah and Others v the United Kingdom,* above n 35, para. 102. In *Vilvarajah,* the Court also observed, that in cases of expulsion "[t]he examination of the existence of a risk of ill-treatment in breach of Article 3 at the relevant time must necessarily be a rigorous one in view of the absolute character of this provision and the fact that it enshrines one of the fundamental values of the democratic societies making up the Council of Europe" (*ibid.,* para. 108; see also *Chahal v United Kingdom,* above n 38, para. 96). From a survey of the domestic legislation of members of the European Union on expulsions and deportation matters it can be seen that, while the asylum policy of those States is based on rather heterogeneous criteria, it is possible to identify in every country a principle prohibiting the expulsion of an alien threatened with torture or other ill-treatments. See B Nascimbene and A Di Pascale, in B Nascimbene (ed), *Expulsion and Detention of Aliens in the European Union Countries* (Giuffré, Milan, 2001), 550 ff.

[50] *Infra* section II B (2).

techniques can also constitute a violation of the victim's right to be free from torture or inhuman treatment.

While, under particular circumstances, the procedural right of a defendant in criminal proceedings against self-incrimination and his or her right to remain silent is not absolute,[51] the separate right to be free from torture or cruel and degrading treatment can never be derogated from to overcome a prisoner's desire to remain silent.[52] Domestic and international judicial bodies have recognized that particularly harsh methods of pre-trial interrogation can constitute a violation of the prohibition of cruel and inhuman treatment.[53] In 1978, the European Court of Human Rights found that intimidatory interrogation techniques could constitute inhuman and degrading treatment.[54] The prohibition of cruel, degrading and inhuman treatment applied to interrogation techniques militates in favour of the conclusion that the use of the so-called "truth serums" is contrary to international human rights standards. Whereas the forcible administration of these drugs does not involve the infliction of severe pain which would qualify it as an act of torture, their use to secure information is nevertheless prohibited by international law, in that it would — as a minimum — violate an individual's right to be free from degrading treatment.

2. *The Death Penalty*[55]

The possibility that a fugitive, once extradited or otherwise surrendered, may be sentenced to death and executed represents may be the major obstacle to the rendition of terrorist suspects to the US, at least from European States. In the light of the developments both in the domestic

[51] See eg, *Murray (John) v United Kingdom*, judgment of 8 February 1996, ECHR, *Reports* 1996-I, para. 47.

[52] From a procedural perspective, Art 15 of the UN Convention against Torture, above n 43, provides that any statement that has been made as a result of torture shall not be invoked as evidence in any proceedings, except against a person accused of torture as evidence that the statement was made. See also Art IV, *Guidelines on Human Rights and the Fight against Terrorism, infra* n 177.

[53] The Committee against Torture has ruled that certain methods of interrogation may not be used in any circumstance as they violate the prohibition of torture or ill treatment. Such methods include "restraining in very painful conditions, playing of loud music, prolonged sleep deprivation, threats, including death threats, violent shaking and using of cold air to chill the detainee", UN Doc. CAT/C/SR.297/Add. 1 (1997), para. 5 reporting on Israel's compliance with the Convention Against Torture: the Committee recommended that interrogation by Israeli security officers applying these methods, including hooding, cease immediately.

[54] *Ireland v United Kingdom*, judgment of 18 January 1978, ECHR, *Series* A, No. 25, para. 90.

[55] On the death penalty in general, see WA Schabas, *The Abolition of the Death Penalty in International Law*, 3rd edition (Cambridge University Press, Cambridge, 2002).

practice of European States[56] and of regional organisations, one may feel confident in saying that a regional customary rule prohibiting capital punishment has developed in Europe and that the necessary corollary of such rule is the prohibition of extradition of individuals that may be subjected to capital punishment in the requesting country. The European Court of Human Rights has addressed the issue of the death penalty in *Soering*, a case concerning a request for extradition of an individual charged with a capital offence in the requesting country.[57] The Court recognised that, under Article 2 of the European Convention, capital punishment was an admissible exception to the right to life, but underlined how some factors related to the imposition of the death penalty may be regarded as a violation of the right to be free from cruel and inhuman treatment.[58] Therefore, the court recognized that the decision to extradite an individual facing the death penalty might amount, depending on the circumstances of the case, to a violation of Article 3 of the Convention.[59]

Indeed, even though Article 2 of the European Convention expressly recognises capital punishment as an admissible exception to the right to life, the death penalty in time of peace has been abolished *de jure* in all the Member States of the Council of Europe, with the sole exception of Russia, which, however, declared a moratorium on capital execution in 1996. Moreover, Protocol No 6 to the European Convention,[60] on the abolition of the death penalty, has been signed by all the States Parties to the Convention and ratified by forty-one of the forty-four States Parties to the European Convention[61] and Protocol No 13, on the abolition of capital punishment in all circumstances has been signed by a large number of States.[62]

[56] See, eg, the decisions of the Netherlands Supreme Court in *Short v The Netherlands* (3 March 1990, translated in (1990) 29 *ILM* 1375) and of the Italian Constitutional Court in *Venezia v Ministero di Grazia e Giustizia* (27 June 1996), reprinted in (1996) 79 *RDI* 815. See the case-note by A Bianchi, in (1997) 91 *American Journal of International Law* 727.

[57] *Soering,* above n 35, paras. 88, 91.

[58] In particular, the Court addressed the issue concerning the compatibility of the practice of protracted detention prior to execution with the prohibition of cruel and inhuman treatment laid down by Art 3 of the Convention. The Court recognized that the so-called "death row phenomenon" can amount, in particular circumstances, to a violation of the prohibition of cruel and inhuman treatment. *Ibid*, paras. 104, 111.

[59] *Ibid*, para. 111.

[60] Protocol No 6 to the European Convention for the Protection of Human Rights and Fundamental Freedoms, Concerning the Abolition of the Death Penalty, Strasbourg, 28 April 1983, *ETS* No. 114 (in force 1 March 1985).

[61] Source: Council of Europe Treaty Office at <http://conventions.coe.int (last visited 20 July 2003>.

[62] Protocol No 13 to the European Convention for the Protection of Human Rights and Fundamental Freedoms, Concerning the Abolition of the Death Penalty, (Vilnius, 3 May 2002, *ETS* No. 187, in force 1 July 2003). As of 20 July 2003, Protocol No. 13 had been ratified by 16 States and signed by another 25 States (source: Council of Europe Treaty Office at <http://conventions.coe.int>).

The virtually unanimous condemnation of capital punishment by all European States has recently led the European Court of Human Rights to modify its position on the issue of the admissibility of the death penalty under the European Convention of Human Rights. In the *Öcalan* judgement,[63] the Court recognised in an *obiter dictum* that the developments in the practice of the States Parties to the European Convention "may be taken as signalling the agreement of the Contracting States to abrogate, or at the very least to modify, the second sentence of Article 2 § 1" and that "it cannot now be excluded ... that the States have agreed through their practice to modify the second sentence in Article 2 § 1 in so far as it permits capital punishment in peacetime."[64] Accordingly, the Court continued, "capital punishment in peacetime has come to be regarded as an unacceptable, if not inhuman, form of punishment which is no longer permissible under Article 2"[65] and it constitutes *per se* inhuman and degrading treatment contrary to Article 3 of the Convention.[66]

The impact on extradition cases of the decision of the Court in *Öcalan* is, however, limited to those States which are not yet parties to Protocol No 6, as the extradition of individuals charged with capital offences was in any case already precluded for all States Parties to that instrument. According to Article 1 "no one shall be condemned [to the death penalty] or executed." Even if the Protocol does not expressly deal with extradition matters, in the light of the practice of the monitoring bodies of the European Convention, and in particular of the judgement of the Court in the *Soering* case, the extradition of an individual subject to the jurisdiction of a State Party in cases where a substantial risk that he might have been subjected to capital punishment existed would have undoubtedly amounted to a breach of the obligations set forth in the Protocol.

For those States party to the Convention, but not party to the Protocol, however, it follows from the statement of the Court in *Öcalan* that the extradition of individuals facing capital punishment in the requesting country can now be considered *per se* a violation of the Convention, and in particular of Article 3, regardless of the circumstances of each single case.

[63] European Court of Human Rights, *Öcalan v Turkey* (Merits), Application No. 46221/99, judgment of 12 March 2003, available at: <http://hudoc.echr.coe.int/Hudoc1doc2/HEJUD/200307/ocalan%20-%2046221jv.chb1%2011032003e.doc>.
[64] *Ibid*, para. 198.
[65] *Ibid*.
[66] *Ibid*. A similar position had been expressed by Judge De Meyer in its concurring opinion in the *Soering* case: "[t]he second sentence of Article 2 para. 1 of the Convention was adopted, nearly forty years ago, in particular circumstances, shortly after the Second World War. In so far as it still may seem to permit, under certain conditions, capital punishment in time of peace, it does not reflect the contemporary situation, and it is now overridden by the development of legal conscience and practice", *Soering*, above n 35. Concurring opinion of Judge De Meyer, p. 51.

Within the European Union, one may also note in this context the recent Charter of Fundamental Rights, adopted by the European Union at Nice in December 2000, which prohibits extradition where the death penalty may be imposed, regardless of the circumstances of the case. According to Article 19 of the Charter, "[n]o one may be removed, expelled or extradited to a State where there is a serious risk that he or she would be subjected to the death penalty."[67]

In relation to non-European States, the decision by the United States to seek capital punishment for individuals convicted of terrorist crimes may also represent an obstacle to the rendition of terrorist suspects. While it is true that the major human rights treaties expressly recognise the permissibility of the death penalty — when imposed according to the limits set forth in those instruments — as a lawful exception to the right to life,[68] the monitoring organs of those treaties have held that, depending on the circumstances of the single case, and in particular the personal characteristics of the extraditee, the length of his detention prior to execution, the modalities through which the capital sentence will be carried out and the fairness of the trial, the extradition of individuals facing capital punishment in the requesting State may amount to a violation of the prohibition of cruel and inhuman treatment or of the right to life itself.[69]

Moreover, within the United Nations and Inter-American human rights systems, the provisions allowing the imposition of capital punishment have been superseded by protocols that in effect repeal the capital punishment exception.[70] Thus, States parties to those instruments have undertaken to abolish the death penalty in their legal system and not to impose it on individuals under their jurisdiction and are under an obligation to refuse the extradition of people who may face capital punishment in the requesting country. In recent times, several abolitionist States outside Europe, including Canada[71] and South Africa[72], have started to

[67] Art 19(2), Charter of Fundamental Rights of the European Union, *OJEC*, C 364/1, 18 December 2000.

[68] Art 3, UDHR; Art 5, ICCPR; Art 6, ACHR.

[69] Human Rights Committee, *Ng v Canada*, UN Doc. CCPR/C/48/D/470/1991 (1993), para. 16.

[70] Second Optional Protocol to the International Covenant on Civil and Political Rights, aiming at the Abolition of the Death Penalty (GA res. 44/128, UN Doc. A/44/49 (1989), entered into force 11 July 1991); Protocol to the American Convention on Human Rights to Abolish the Death Penalty, (Asuncion, 8 June 1990, OAS Treaty Series No. 73, in force). As of 20 July 2003, the aforementioned instruments have been ratified, respectively, by 49 and by 8 States (sources: Office of the UN High Commissioner for Human Rights, at <http://www.unhchr.ch>; OAS Secretariat for Legal Affairs, at <http://www.oas.org>).

[71] *United States v Burns*, 2001 SCC 7; [2001] 1 SCR 283 (Supreme Court of Canada). See S Borelli, "Estradizione e pena di morte: considerazioni in margine alla recente sentenza della Corte Suprema del Canada nel caso Burns", (2001) *Rivista Internazionale dei Diritti dell'Uomo* 807.

[72] *Mohammed and Dalvie v The President of the Republic of South Africa and others*, CCT 17/01; [2001] 3 SA 893 (Constitutional Court of South Africa).

subordinate extradition of individuals charged with capital crimes in the requesting State to the submission of guarantees that the extraditee will not be condemned to death, or, if condemned, will not be executed.

3. *Fair Trial*

The right to a fair trial, recognized, albeit in different terminology, by many human rights treaties[73] and by the constitutional law of most States, may be considered one of the most important civil rights.[74] The International Covenant on Civil and Political Rights provides for one of the most widely accepted conventional definitions of fair trial,[75] providing, *inter alia*, that "all persons shall be equal before the courts and the tribunals", that "everyone charged with a criminal offence shall have the right to be presumed innocent until proved guilty according to law" and that, in criminal matters, "everyone shall be entitled to a fair and public hearing by a competent, independent and impartial tribunal established by law."[76] On several occasions the main human rights bodies have stressed the fundamental importance of the right to be tried by a proper court and to be granted a fair trial and the fact that such rights must be guaranteed to every individual even in situations of national emergency, and regardless of the gravity of the crime of which the defendant is accused.[77]

[73] Art 14, ICCPR; Art 6, ECHR, Art 8, ACHR.

[74] See the European Court in *Soering*, above n. 35, at para. 113: the right to fair trial holds "a prominent place in a democratic society". See also the US Supreme Court in *Estes v Texas*, 381 U.S. 532 (1965), at 540 holding that the right to a fair trial is "the most fundamental of all freedoms".

[75] As of 20 July 2003, 149 States have ratified the ICCPR (source: Office of the United Nations High Commissioner for Human Rights, at <http://www.unhchr.ch>).

[76] Art 14 paras. 1 and 2. ICCPR

[77] See Human Rights Committee, General Comment 24(52), UN Doc. CCPR/C/21/Rev.1/Add.6 (1994), para. 8: "while reservations to particular clauses of Article 14 may be acceptable, a general reservation to the right to fair trial would not be"; and General Comment 29, States of Emergency, UN Doc. CCPR/C/21/Rev.1/Add.11 (2001), para. 11: "States parties may in no circumstances invoke article 4 of the Covenant as justification for acting in violation of ... peremptory norms of international law, for instance ... by deviating from fundamental principles of fair trial, including the presumption of innocence." See also *Judicial Guarantees in States of Emergency (Arts. 27(2), 25 and 8 of the American Convention on Human Rights)*, Advisory Opinion OC-9/87 of 6 October 1987, IACtHR, *Series A*, No. 9 (1987); Art IX, *Guidelines on Human Rights and the Fight Against Terrorism, infra* n 177: "1. A person accused of terrorist activities has the right to a fair hearing, within a reasonable time, by an independent, impartial tribunal established by law. 2. A person accused of terrorist activities benefits from the presumption of innocence. 3. The imperatives of the fight against terrorism may nevertheless justify certain restrictions to the right of defence, ... 4. Such restrictions to the right of defence must be strictly proportionate to their purpose, and compensatory measures to protect the interests of the accused must be taken so as to maintain the fairness of the proceedings and to ensure that procedural rights are not drained of their substance."

The violation of the right to fair trial in extradition cases can be difficult to assess. For a violation to be attributed to a State, as already noted, it must be a direct and foreseeable consequence of the decision to extradite. This implies that, before granting extradition, the organs of the requesting State should evaluate, if not the general compatibility of the judicial system of the requesting State with internationally accepted standards, at least the compatibility of the trial that will be granted to the fugitive in the specific case with international standards on fair trial. Such an inquiry can prove both difficult and politically embarrassing for the organs, whether judicial or executive, of the requested country.[78] This probably accounts for why the monitoring organs established by human rights instruments adopt a less strict definition of fair trial when they are called upon to judge an alleged violation of such right in cases of extradition, than in cases of alleged violation perpetrated by States in their own territory. For example, the European Court of Human Rights seems reluctant to accept the claim that the right to fair trial has been violated in cases concerning extradition proceedings.[79]

However, the protection offered to the extraditee by the application of the international human rights standards on fair trial to extradition cases should not be underestimated. The prohibition of extraditing a fugitive where there is a real risk that he will not be given a fair trial or where his conviction results from a trial which did not satisfy the requirements of a fair trial[80] can represent a valuable protection of such a right at least in cases where the foreseeable violation of the right to fair trial in the receiving country would amount to a *flagrant denial* of justice.[81]

[78] See, eg, *R v Secretary of State for the Home Department, ex p Launder* [1997] 1 WLR 839 (HL), a case concerning a judicial review of the British Home Secretary's decision to extradite the applicant to Hong Kong, where he alleged that, *inter alia*, he would not receive a fair trial. The House of Lords refused to interfere with the Home Secretary's finding under the relevant legislation that extradition would not be "unjust or oppressive".

[79] See, eg, *Drodz and Janousek v France and Spain*, judgment of 26 June 1992, ECHR, *Series A*, No 240, para 110: "the Convention does not require the Contracting Parties to impose its standards on third States. ... To require a review of the manner in which a court not bound by the Convention has applied the principles enshrined in Art 6 would also thwart the current trend towards strengthening international co-operation in the administration of justice, which is in principle in the interest of the persons concerned." See the apparently more intrusive approach in *Soering*, above n 35, at para 91 in relation to Art 3: "the establishment of such responsibility inevitably involves an assessment of conditions in the requesting country against the standards of Article 3 of the Convention. Nonetheless, there is no question of adjudicating on or establishing the responsibility of the receiving country, whether under general international law, under the Convention or otherwise."

[80] See Art 3(g), UN Model Treaty on Extradition, above n 8, which provides that extradition shall be refused if there are serious grounds for believing that the fugitive "has not received or would not receive the minimum guarantees in criminal proceedings as contained in the International Covenant on Civil and Political Rights, Article 14."

[81] *Soering*, above n 35, para. 113: "The right to a fair trial in criminal proceedings, as embodied in Article 6 holds a prominent place in a democratic society. The court does not exclude

III. FORCIBLE ABDUCTION AND THE INTERNATIONAL LAW OF JURISDICTION

A. Forcible Abduction Defined

Extradition treaties and other conventional methods of international co-operation have often proven ineffective in the fight against international terrorism. Thus in cases where the asylum State refuses to extradite or otherwise surrender the fugitive, or in cases where the authorities of the requesting State have reasons to believe that extradition will be refused, States sometimes avail themselves of unorthodox methods to gain custody of fugitives.

The US in the past has resorted to forcible abduction abroad in order to gain custody of criminals, including terrorists.[82] In June 1995, President Clinton signed a Presidential Decision Directive on the subject of "US Policy on Counterterrorism",[83] which provided: "We shall vigorously apply extraterritorial statutes to counter acts of terrorism and apprehend terrorists outside of the United States."[84] After providing that the initial approach would be *via* use of extradition procedures or diplomacy, it continued: "If we do not receive adequate cooperation from a state that harbors a terrorist whose extradition we are seeking, we shall take appropriate measures to induce cooperation. Return of suspects by force may be effected without the cooperation of the host government, consistent with the procedures outlined in NSD-77."[85] In the light of the past practice of the US in matters of forcible abduction and considering the recent cases of abduction of terrorist suspects from foreign countries by US agents,[86]

that an issue may be raised under Article 6 in circumstances where a fugitive has suffered or risks suffering a *flagrant denial of a fair trial* in the requesting country" [emphasis added]; *Drodz and Janousek v France and Spain*, above n 79, para 110: "[t]he Contracting States are … obliged to refuse their co-operation if it emerges that the conviction is the result of a *flagrant denial of justice*" [emphasis added]. See also Art XIII (4), *Guidelines on Human Rights and the Fight Against Terrorism, infra* n 177: "[w]hen the person whose extradition has been requested makes out an arguable case that he/she has suffered or risks suffering a flagrant denial of justice in the requesting State, the requested State must consider the well-foundedness of that argument before deciding whether to grant extradition."

82 See RJ Beck and AC Arend, " 'Don't Tread on Us': International Law and Forcible State Responses to Terrorism", (1994) 12 *Wisconsin International Law Journal* 153, at 174–79.

83 Presidential Decision Directive 39, "US Policy on Counterterrorism", 21 June 1995, available at <http://www.fas.org/irp/offdocs/pdd39.htm>. For an argument in favour of the legality, see Kash, "Abducting Terrorists Under PDD-39: Much Ado About Nothing New", (1997) 13 *American University International Law Review* 139.

84 Presidential Decision Directive 39, above n 83, Section 2(3).

85 *Ibid*. National Security Directive 77, passed by President Bush in January 1993, remains classified.

86 See Amnesty International, "United States of America: No return to execution. The US death penalty as a barrier to extradition", 29 November 2001, available at <http://www.amnesty.org>, reporting, *inter alia*, the case of Mir Aimal Kasi, a Pakistani

it cannot be excluded that, in the context of the present "war against terrorism" the US will resort to unorthodox measures in order to gain control over suspected terrorists.

For the purpose of this chapter, the practice of forcible abduction may be defined as the abduction by force of a suspected terrorist from the territory of one State, carried out by agents of the abducting State, or by persons acting for those agents, without the consent of the territorial State.[87]

From the perspective of inter-State relations, the practice of transnational abduction represents a clear violation of the customary principle of territorial sovereignty. As the Permanent Court of International Justice said in 1917, "the first and foremost restriction imposed by international law on a State [is] that — failing the existence of a permissive rule to the contrary — it may not exercise its power in any form in the territory of another State" at least without the consent of the latter.[88] Classical interna-

national wanted in the US for the murder of two CIA agents in Virginia in 1993. In 1997, Kasi was forcibly abducted by FBI agents from Pakistan, brought in the United States, where he was sentenced to death in 1998. In relation to the issue of the forcible abduction of the defendant, the Supreme Court of Virginia, relying on the decision of the Supreme Court in *United States v Alvarez-Machain* (*infra* n 90), held that "Contrary to defendant's contention, nothing in [the extradition treaty] can be construed to affirmatively prohibit the forcible abduction of defendant in this case so as to divest the trial court of jurisdiction or to require that "sanctions" be imposed for an alleged violation of the treaty"; *Kasi v Commonwealth of Virginia*, 508 S.E.2d 57, at 63.

[87] According to Michell, above n 29, at 389–90, the practice of transnational forcible abduction in order to gain control of a suspected criminal consists of three elements: "the first element of a transnational forcible abduction requires there to be a fugitive, ie an individual suspected or convicted for a criminal offence in one State, who has fled to another State. The second element is the use of coercion in order to abduct the fugitive. Third, the abduction must have been carried out by State agents or by private individuals acting under State direction." On State-sponsored forcible abduction see EE Dickinson; "Jurisdiction Following Seizure or Arrest in Violation of International Law", (1934) 28 *American Journal of International Law* 231; F Morgenstern, "Jurisdiction in Seizures Effected in Violation of International Law", (1952) 29 *British Yearbook of International Law* 265; P O'Higgins, "Unlawful Seizure and Irregular Extradition", (1960) 36 *British Yearbook of International Law* 279; FA Mann, "Reflections on the Prosecution of Persons Abducted in Breach of International Law", in Y Dinstein (ed), *International Law at a Time of Perplexity* (Martinus Nijhoff, Dordrecht, 1988), at 407; M Garcia Mora, "Criminal Jurisdiction of a State Over Fugitives Brought From a Foreign Country by Force or Fraud: a Comparative Study", (1958) 32 *Indiana Law Journal* 427; D Kash, "Abduction of Terrorists in International Airspace and on the High Seas", (1993) 8 *Florida Journal of International Law* 65.

[88] *SS "Lotus" Case (France v Turkey)*, PCIJ, *Series A*, No 10 (1927), at 18. Such a principle, apart from being a fundamental rule of customary international law, is incorporated in numerous treaties to which the United States is a party, among them the United Nations Charter (San Francisco, 26 June 1945, in force 24 October 1945, Art 2(4)) and the Charter of the Organization of the American States (Bogotá, 30 April 1948, 119 UNTS 3, entered into force 13 December 1951, amended 721 UNTS 324, entered into force 27 February 1990, Art 17). Commentators generally agree that the forcible abduction of a suspected criminal represents an extraterritorial use of force that infringes the principle of territorial sovereignty. See, eg, L Henkin, "A Decent Respect to the Opinions of Mankind", (1992) 25 *Marshall Law Review* 215,

tional law dealt with the issue of forcible abduction only as a question of the violation of State rights, and ignored the interests of the individual.[89] Therefore, the attitude of the injured State was a central consideration: the asylum State could complain of the violation of its territorial sovereignty or, if an extradition treaty existed in relation to the State which performed the abduction, of the breach of such a treaty.

Individuals were not able to invoke the violation of international rules on territorial sovereignty and, in the absence of protest by the asylum State, they could not even invoke the breach of the provisions of extradition treaties in order to challenge the jurisdiction of the courts of the abducting State, on the basis of the *male captus bene detentus* principle.

B. The Doctrine of *Male Captus Bene Detentus* in International Practice

Traditionally, the doctrine of *male captus bene detentus* has been held to be applicable to cases of forcible abduction by national courts. According to this doctrine, *in the absence of protest from another State*, once an individual is brought within the jurisdiction, even if he was apprehended by irregular means (including forcible abduction), he may be tried in the apprehending State.[90]

at 231: "when done without consent of the foreign government, abducting a person from a foreign country is a gross violation of international law and gross disrespect for a norm high in the opinion of mankind. It is a blatant violation of the territorial integrity of another state; it eviscerates the extradition system established by a comprehensive network of treaties involving virtually all states"; see also L Henkin, "International Law: Politics, Values and Functions", (1989-IV) 216 *RdC* 310, Mann, above n 37, at 412, *Oppenheim's International Law*, above n 20, at 388–89.

[89] This approach results clearly from the Harvard Research Draft Convention on Jurisdiction with Respect to Crimes, above n 20. Art 16, concerning "Apprehension in Violation of International Law" provides that "[i]n exercising jurisdiction under this Convention, no State shall prosecute or punish any person who has been brought within its territory or a place subject to its authority by recourse to measures in violation of international or international conventions *without first obtaining the consent of the State or States whose rights have been violated by such measures*" [emphasis added].

[90] In *Attorney General of the Government of Israel v Eichmann* (District Court of Jerusalem (1961), 36 *ILR* 5, aff'd, Supreme Court of Israel (1962) 36 *ILR* 277, hereinafter *Eichmann*), the District Court of Jerusalem, after a very detailed analysis of State practice, held that "it is an established rule of law that a person being tried for an offence against the laws of a State may not oppose his trial by reason of the illegality of his arrest or of the means whereby he was brought within the jurisdiction of the State" (para. 41). See also *Ker v Illinois* 119 US 436 (1886) (cited in *Eichmann*, para. 42): "where a fugitive is brought back by kidnapping, or by other irregular means, and not under an extradition treaty, he cannot, although an extradition treaty exists between the two countries, set up in answer to the indictment the unlawful manner in which he was brought within the jurisdiction of the court. It belongs exclusively to the government from whose territory he was wrongfully taken to complain of the violation of its rights." The rule that a court has jurisdiction to try the accused for any offence he may have committed, irrespective of the circumstances in which he was brought within the

Until recently, the practice of domestic courts was fully consistent with the principle, in that they refused to inquire into the way in which a defendant was brought before them (the so-called "doctrine of non-inquiry")[91] and tended to assert jurisdiction over defendants regardless of the circumstances of the arrest. As to the question of the status of such a principle in international law, given the absence of references by domestic courts to any international law norm providing for the application of the *male captus* doctrine and the consequent lack of *opinio iuris*,[92] it would have been improper to qualify the principle as an international customary norm.[93] Nevertheless, given the consistency of national case law on the matter, one could arguably have framed it as a "general principle of law recognized by civilised nations."[94] A relevant obstacle to such a qualification

jurisdiction, has been applied by US courts since 1886. See: *Ker v Illinois, supra; Frisbie v Collins* (1952) 342 US 510; *US ex rel Lujan v Gengler* 510 F.2d 62 (1975); and *United States v Alvarez-Machain*, 504 US 655 (1992), 31 *ILM* 902. On US practice in cases of forcible abduction, see Mann, above n 37, at 412 ff. The *male captus* doctrine has been applied also by civil law courts: see, eg, the decision of the French *Cour de Cassation* in the *Argoud* case, *Crim* 4 June 1964; 45 *ILR* 90.

[91] According to such an approach, the courts of the requested State shall not look behind the request for extradition to the judicial system of the requesting State before granting the extradition of a fugitive. Such inquiry would be an infringement of the requesting country's sovereignty and a violation of the principle of international comity. The assumption behind this doctrine is that consideration of this kind should be left to the executive and that if the executive decides to enter into an extradition treaty with another State it has already evaluated the compatibility of its legal system with the international and domestic standards on human rights protection. See J Quigley, "The Rule of Non-Inquiry and the Impact of Human Rights in Extradition Law", (1990) 15 *North Carolina Journal of International Law and Commercial Regulation* 401; J Quigley, "The Rule of Non-Inquiry and Human Rights Treaties", (1996) 45 *Catholic University Law Review* 1213; J Semmelman, "Federal Courts, the Constitution, and the Rule of Non-Inquiry in International Extradition Proceedings", (1991) 76 *Cornell Law Review* 1198; Wilson, above n 43.

[92] Domestic courts have never claimed that the application of the *male captus* doctrine was required by international law. The doctrine was almost invariably applied on the basis of domestic law norms, in particular those regulating the relationship between the judiciary and the executive.

[93] Both the PCIJ and the ICJ have recognized that *opinio juris*, ie the belief that a specific conduct is legally obligatory, is a constituent element of international custom. See, eg, SS *"Lotus" Case* (above n 88), in particular at 28, and *North Sea Continental Shelf Cases*, ICJ Reports 1969, 3. On the relevance of the subjective element for the coming into existence of customary norms, see, *inter alia*, M Akehurst, "Custom as a Source of International Law", (1974–75) 47 *British Yearbook of International Law* 1, at 31–44; P Haggenmacher, "Des deux elements du droit cotumier dans la pratique de la Cour Internationale", (1985) 89 *RGDIP* 5; I Brownlie, *Principles of Public International Law*, 5th edn (Clarendon Press, Oxford, 1998), at 4–12; O Elias, "The Nature of the Subjective Element in Customary International Law", (1995) 44 *International and Comparative Law Quarterly* 501; M Mendelson, "The Formation of Customary International Law", (1998) 272 *RdC* 155.

[94] See Art 38(1)(c) of the Statute of the International Court of Justice. On the different contents that international scholars have attributed to such a provision, see B Vitanyi, "Les positions doctrinales concernant le sens de la notion de 'principes généraux de droit reconnus par les nations civilisées'", (1992) 86 *RGDIP* 48; B Cheng, *General Principles of Law as Applied by International Courts and Tribunals* (Stevens and Sons, Ltd, London, 1953).

could derive from the theories that claim that, for a principle applied by municipal jurisprudence to be considered a general principle of the kind mentioned in the ICJ Statute, it has to be "applicable to relations of States".[95] In fact, such a restrictive view of the category of "general principles" is no longer justified, especially when one considers the plethora of international norms addressing situations other than "relations of States". If such principles as those relating to the right to fair trial or the principle of *ne bis in idem* — which, apart from being embodied in several international agreements, are undoubtedly a principle recognized in the legal systems of most countries — are unanimously recognized as general principles of law, one can apply the same qualification to the *male captus bene detentus* principle. The international relevance of such principles is reinforced by the way in which the whole body of criminal procedure relating to individual international criminal responsibility draws heavily on municipal legal principles.[96]

Recent developments in State practice seem to show a different attitude of national courts in cases involving the forcible abduction of the defendant. In particular, since the beginning of the last decade, in several cases the domestic courts of different States have started to consider the way in which the defendant had been brought within their jurisdiction as a circumstance that could preclude the exercise of criminal jurisdiction, thus rejecting the doctrine of *male captus bene detentus*.

The doctrine has been challenged for two different but inter-related reasons. First, domestic courts are abandoning their attitude of deference towards the actions of the executive in cases where such actions imply a violation of the international obligations of their State.[97] In several cases domestic courts have held that they not only have a discretionary power to inquire into the international legitimacy of executive conduct, but also that in certain circumstances they have a duty to do so.[98] Thus, if a State violates its international obligations, for instance that of respecting the territorial sovereignty of other States by forcibly abducting a suspected

[95] See *Oppenheim's International Law*, above n 20, at 36–37.
[96] The ICTY has already dealt with questions arising from the circumstances surrounding the apprehension of defendants. See *Prosecutor v Nicolić* ("Decision on Interlocutory Appeal Concerning Legality of Arrest") (case IT-94-2-AR73) handed down by the Appeals Chamber of the ICTY on 5 June 2003, applying a "balancing" version of *male captus* whereby the fundamental rights of the defendant must be weighed against "the essential interests of the international community in the prosecution of persons charged with serious violations of international humanitarian law" (para. 30). See also the decision of the Trial Chamber of the ICTY of 25 March 1999, in the case of *Prosecutor v Simić et al* (case IT-95-9-PT), dismissing a defence motion for evidentiary hearing on the allegedly illegal arrest of one of the defendants, available at <http://www.un.org/icty/simic/trialc3/decision-e/90325MS56368.htm> and the decision on the motion for release issued by the Trial Chamber on 22 October 1997, in the case *Prosecutor v Mrksić et al* (case IT-95-13a-PT), reprinted in 111 *ILM* 458.
[97] See the articles cited above n 86.
[98] See *Ebrahim, infra* n 110.

criminal for trial, it is incumbent upon domestic courts to ensure that the violation ceases. Secondly, with the development of international human rights law, the issue of forcible abduction can be framed in ways other than the traditional issue of inter-State responsibility.[99]

Forcible abduction is not expressly prohibited by any human rights treaty or customary rule. Nevertheless, the kidnapping of an individual implies *per se* the violation of several fundamental rights protected by international law.[100] For instance, concerns like the preservation of the security of the individual, the condemnation of arbitrary arrest and detention, the respect of the right to fair trial may be interpreted to preclude State-sponsored kidnapping. Thus, forcible abduction may constitute a human rights violation subject to vindication by the victims before the domestic courts of the abducting State, independently from any protest of the territorial State.

Many international human rights bodies have underlined how the State-sponsored kidnapping of an individual for trial can represent a violation of his fundamental rights. In particular, the Human Rights Committee has held in several decisions that forcible abduction for the purpose of criminal prosecution represents a violation of the individual rights protected by the International Covenant on Civil and Political Rights.[101] The Committee has constructed an international prohibition of

[99] See RJ Stark, "The Ker-Frisbie-Alvarez Doctrine: International Law, Due Process, and United States Sponsored Kidnapping of Foreign Nationals Abroad", (1993) 9 *Connecticut Journal of International Law* 125.

[100] The forcible abduction of a suspected criminal implies, *per se*, the violation of his "liberty rights" such as the right to liberty and security of the person, the rights related to the prohibition of arbitrary arrest and detention and the right to fair trial. For the purposes of this article, we will not take into consideration cases that imply other serious breaches of fundamental rights, such as torture and cruel or inhuman or degrading treatment, which can be related to episodes of State-sponsored kidnapping. It is understood that the considerations on the fundamental role of the judiciary in sanctioning such conducts are *a fortiori* applicable to such situations. It has to be noted, however, that part of the doctrine holds that not all abductions fall into the category of human rights violations: see J Paust, "After Alvarez-Machain: Abduction, Standing, Denials of Justice, and Unaddressed Human Rights Claims", (1993) 67 *St John's Law Review* 551, at 553. See also M Halberstam, "In Defense of the Supreme Court Decision in Alvarez-Machain", (1992) 86 *American Journal of International Law* 736.

[101] For instance, the Committee has held in several decisions that the forcible abduction of an individual for the purpose of criminal prosecution represents a violation of Art 9 (1) of the Covenant, which provides that "[e]veryone has the right to liberty and security of the person. No one shall be subjected to arbitrary arrest or detention. No one shall be deprived of his liberty except on such grounds and in accordance with such procedures as are established by law"; see, eg, *Lopez Burgos v Uruguay*, Comm No R.12/52, UN Doc A/36/40 (1981), at 176; 68 *ILR* 29 (abduction from Argentina by Uruguayan agents of an Uruguayan refugee). In *Lopez Burgos*, the Committee also ruled that Uruguay was obligated to free the arrested and allow him to leave the country (para 14). See also *Celiberti de Casariego v Uruguay*, Comm No R.13/56, UN Doc A/36/40, 185 (1981); 68 *ILR* 41; *Almeida de Quinteros v Uruguay*, Comm No 107/1981 (1981), at 11; reprinted in 2 *Selected Decisions of the Human Rights Committee under the Optional Protocol* (UN Doc. CCPR/C/OP/2 (1990)), at 138; *Cañón García v Ecuador*, Comm No 319/1988 UN Doc CCPR/C/43/D/319/1988 (1991), para 41.

forcible abduction into the context of human rights protection, framing the issue as one concerning the violation of individual rights and not of inter-State obligations, to the extent that the collusion or consent of the State from whose territory the person is abducted is irrelevant.[102]

Similar evidence of the emergence of an international human rights norm prohibiting forcible abduction can also be found in the case law of the European Court of Human Rights and in the earlier practice of the Commission. The organs of the European Convention have held that the arrest of an individual by the agents of one State in the territory of another State without the consent of the latter does not only involve the international responsibility of the abducting State *vis-à-vis* the territorial State, but it may also affect the person's individual rights under the Convention.[103]

However, in contradistinction to the Human Rights Committee, the European Court of Human Rights seems still inclined to consider that the attitude of the State where the abduction has taken place is relevant, and that forcible abduction of a fugitive constitutes *per se* a violation of the rights protected by the Convention only in the case where the authorities of the territorial State do not consent to the abduction, and where the procedures put in place by any existent extradition treaty have not been followed. In the *Öcalan* case, the accused, without having previously been arrested by the Kenyan authorities, was brought to Nairobi airport where members of the Turkish security forces were waiting. The Court held that for there to be an actionable violation of Article 5 of the Convention,

> it must be established to the Court "beyond all reasonable doubt" that the authorities of the State to which the applicant has been transferred have acted extra-territorially in a manner that is *inconsistent with the sovereignty of the host State and therefore contrary to international law.*[104]

On the facts of the case, the Court held that the handover of Öcalan by Kenyan officials constituted cooperation between the Turkish and Kenyan authorities, and that the acts of the Turkish officials on Kenyan soil had been carried out with consent and had accordingly not violated Kenyan sovereignty or international law;[105] therefore, no violation of the Convention was found.[106]

[102] See, eg, *Lopez Burgos, Celiberti de Casariego* and *Cañón García*, above n 101.

[103] In particular, the Court has considered forcible abduction to be a violation of Art 5(1) of the Convention: see *Bozano v France*, above n 34. See also the European Commission in *Stocké v Germany*, above n 32, p. 24, para. 167; *Öcalan*, above n 53, para. 89.

[104] *Öcalan*, above n 53, para. 92, citing the decision of the European Court in *Stocké v Germany*, ECHR, *Series A*, No. 199, p. 19, para. 54 (emphasis added).

[105] *Öcalan*, above n 53, para. 95. The Court seems to have been particularly impressed by the fact that there were no diplomatic repercussions of the incident.

[106] It seems that the situation might have been different if there was an extradition treaty in place: see *Öcalan*, above n 53, para. 101.

As a consequence of these developments, domestic courts appear more inclined to take into account the way in which the defendant has been brought before them and to challenge the legitimacy of the exercise of criminal jurisdiction over abducted individuals. [107] Even the courts in some common law systems, after a long history of adherence to the *male captus bene detentus* rule, have started inquiring whether a particular forcible abduction from the territory of another State has violated international law and – if the answer is in the affirmative — will decline to exercise of jurisdiction over the defendant.[108] The decision not to allow criminal proceedings against a fugitive to proceed has been justified in different ways. In some cases the court acknowledged jurisdiction but exercised a discretion not to allow proceedings to continue in respect of individuals abducted in violation of international law.[109] In other cases the court declared that it had no jurisdiction as a matter of national law to try an abducted individual.[110] From a pragmatic perspective, the difference in reasoning is not particularly relevant: however from a theoretical perspective, arguably the better approach is to recognise that in principle courts have jurisdiction to try fugitives brought before them, but that they may decline to exercise it, taking into consideration the circumstances surrounding the apprehension of the defendant, and evaluating their correspondence with both domestic standards on criminal prosecution and the international obligations of the State.

In 1993, the British House of Lords rejected the *male captus bene detentus* rule,[111] holding that "[e]xtradition procedures are designed not only to ensure that criminals are returned from one country to another but also to protect the rights of those who are accused of crimes in the requesting country .... If a practice developed in which the police or prosecuting

[107] Quite apart from the more active approach of domestic courts to extradition cases, it should be noted that, at the legislative level, many States have implemented legislation aimed at guaranteeing the respect of fundamental rights in cases of extradition. For a survey of these initiatives, see C Van den Wyngaert, "The Political Offence Exception to Extradition: How to Plug the Terrorist Loophole Without Departing from Fundamental Human Rights", 62 *International Review of Penal Law* 291, at 307–8.

[108] For a detailed discussion of the relevant case-law, see Michell, above n 29, in particular at 427–35.

[109] *Regina v Horseferry Road Magistrates' Court (Ex Parte Bennett)*, [1994] 1 AC 42 (Eng HL 1993) (hereafter *Bennett*).

[110] *State v Ebrahim*, 1991 2 SA 553; 95 *ILR* 417, at 445 "the Trial Court, in accordance with our common law, did not have jurisdiction to try the Appellant", citing *United States v Toscanino*, 500 F. 2d 267 (1974).

[111] In *Bennett* (above n 109) a New Zealand national who was wanted for fraud offences committed in England was located in South Africa. After consulting with the Crown Prosecution Service, the English police decided not to seek his extradition under the Extradition Act 1989. The defendant was deported from South Africa with the connivance of South African authorities and irregularly returned to England, where he was arrested.

authorities of this country ignored extradition procedures ... they would be ... depriving the accused of the safeguards built into the extradition process for his benefit."[112] Thus, in order to prevent the police or the prosecuting authorities from taking advantage of their own irregular conduct, the courts could exercise their inherent jurisdiction to stay proceedings relating to an accused when he has been forcibly brought within such jurisdiction in disregard of extradition procedures.[113]

British courts are not alone in questioning the applicability of the *male captus* rule to cases of forcible abduction. In the *ex parte Bennett* case, the House of Lords had before it decisions from New Zealand[114] and South Africa[115] in which the courts had equally ruled against the exercise of jurisdiction in cases of forcible abduction.

Notwithstanding these developments in international practice, courts in the United States still hold that they may properly exercise jurisdiction over a defendant even though his or her presence was procured by forcible abduction. US courts favour the application of the *male captus bene detentus* doctrine, holding that the fact that the custody of a defendant has been secured in violation of international law cannot be directly invoked by the defendant as a circumstance precluding the exercise of criminal jurisdiction by domestic courts.[116] US courts have gone beyond

[112] *Bennett*, above n 109, at 62.

[113] *Ibid*.

[114] In *Regina v Hartley*, 2 NZLR 199 (1978), the appellant was removed from Australia by force, with the co-operation of New Zealand police, and brought to New Zealand to face prosecution on a manslaughter charge. The Court of Appeal gave emphasis to the requirements of the extradition process, holding that "[t]here can be no possible question of the Court turning a blind eye to action of the New Zealand police which had deliberately ignored those imperative requirements of the statute [on extradition cases]", *ibid*, at 216.

[115] In *Ebrahim*, above n 110, the Supreme Court of South Africa reversed a conviction and ordered the release of a defendant kidnapped from Swaziland. The Court held (at 95 ILR 441–42) that domestic law contained "several fundamental legal principles ... namely the protection and promotion of human rights, good inter-state relations and a healthy administration of justice. The individual must be protected against illegal detention and abduction, the bounds of jurisdiction must not be exceeded, sovereignty must be respected, the legal process must be fair to those affected and abuse of law must be avoided in order to protect and promote the integrity of the administration of justice. This applies equally to the State. When the State is a party to a dispute, as for example in criminal cases, it must come to court 'with clean hands' as it were. When the State itself is involved in an abduction across international borders, as in the present case, its hands are not clean". See the case report by J Semmelmann, in (1993) 87 *American Journal of International Law* 133.

[116] *Frisbie v Collins*, above n 90; *United States v Winter*, 509 F 2d 975 (5th Cir 1975), at 985–86; *United States v Alvarez-Machain*, above n 90; *Noriega v United States*, 808 F Supp 791 (SD Fla 1992), aff'd, 117 F 3d 1206 (11th Cir 1997);*United States v Yunis*, 681 F Supp 909 (DC, DC 1988), rev'd, (59 F 2d 953) (DC Cir 1988); See also recently, in a terrorism case: *United States v Yousef et al*, (2nd Cir) judgment of 4 April 2003. See MJ Glennon, "State-Sponsored Abduction: A Comment on United States v Alvarez-Machain", (1992) 86 *American Journal of International Law* 746; Michell, above n 29, at 440 ff. For a narrow line of decisions in the opposite direction, see *United States v Toscanino*, 500 F 2d 267 (1974), holding that a court must "divest itself

the traditional application of the rule, asserting its applicability even to cases where the abducting State and the State in whose territory the fugitive has sought asylum are bound by an extradition treaty and the asylum State did not consent to the abduction. The Supreme Court of the United States held that — provided the treaty did not explicitly prohibit the abduction[117] — the forcible abduction did not represent a violation of an extradition treaty between the abducting State and the asylum State, and that the protest of the asylum State did not represent an obstacle to the exercise of criminal jurisdiction.[118]

Apart from the notable exception of United States courts which still adhere to the *male captus* doctrine,[119] contemporary international practice shows that the doctrine is no longer the only answer to the issue of the exercise of criminal jurisdiction over individuals abducted in violation of international law. In particular, domestic case law on forcible abduction reveals certain elements that must be taken into consideration in order to evaluate the permissibility of the exercise of jurisdiction over an abducted defendant. First, the court should consider whether there has been a violation of territorial sovereignty, or of an extradition treaty. Second, domestic courts should consider the compatibility of the abduction with the international human rights obligations binding on the State. International human rights law limitations to forcible abduction become

of jurisdiction over the person of a defendant where it has been acquired as the result of the Government's deliberate, unnecessary and unreasonable invasion of the accused's constitutional rights" (at 275). The decision has subsequently been narrowly interpreted, so that the exercise of jurisdiction may be refused only where there is implicated shocking governmental conduct prior to trial: see, eg, *United States ex rel Lujan v Gengler*, 510 F 2d 62 (2nd Cir 1975); cert denied 421 US 1001 (1975): threshold of "torture, brutality, and similar outrageous conduct" (at 65).

[117] The courts will not exercise jurisdiction where the abduction is in violation of an extradition treaty (*United States v Rauscher* (119 US 407 (1886)); however, given the holding in *Alvarez-Machain*, it seems that forcible abduction must be expressly prohibited by the treaty before the exception will come into play (*United States v Alvarez-Machain*, above n 90, at 666).

[118] *United States v Alvarez-Machain* (above n 90, at 670). For a detailed analysis of US practice see AF Lowenfeld, "US Law Enforcement Abroad: The Constitution and International Law, Continued", (1990) 84 *American Journal of International Law* 444.

[119] It should be noted, however, that a recent decision of the United States Court of Appeals for the 9th Circuit recognises the human rights implications of forcible abductions (*Alvarez-Machain v United States et al* (No. 99–56762); *Alvarez-Machain v Sosa et al* (No. 99–56880), (9th Cir (*en banc*)), 3 June 2003). The case is a sequel to the *Alvarez-Machain* litigation in the Supreme Court, and involves a claim brought under the Alien Tort Claims Act following the acquittal of Alvarez-Machain of the criminal charges levelled against him. The Court, although denying the existence of a clear and universally recognized norm of customary international law prohibiting transborder abduction, acknowledged that "there exists a clear and universally recognized norm prohibiting arbitrary arrest and detention," (para 5) and that this provided a valid basis for a claim under the Act, at least for the period of detention before he was brought to the United States (para 17).

relevant either *via* the direct application of the relevant international norms (in cases where such direct application is possible in domestic law) or by an interpretation of domestic legal doctrines such as due process or abuse of process of the court in the light of international standards. While challenging the applicability of the *male captus bene detentus* doctrine, domestic courts have not relied upon the existence of an international law norm requiring them to decline the exercise of jurisdiction over abducted defendants. While mentioning principles such as the respect of State sovereignty and of human rights, the courts have based their decisions almost exclusively on the interpretation of domestic law, in particular relying on the provisions relating to the domestic guarantees of due process of law or analysing the problem by reference to the abuse of process doctrine.

This brief survey of domestic case law related to cases of forcible abduction brings into question the qualification of the *male captus* doctrine as a "principle of law recognized by civilised nations". The divergent approaches taken by courts of very similar judicial systems demonstrate that, if on the one hand it may still be premature to affirm the existence of a customary rule, or even of a "general principle of law", compelling the courts to divest themselves from jurisdiction over abducted defendants,[120] it would on the other hand be extremely inaccurate to maintain, as some authors did until relatively recently, that "the violation of [international] law does not affect the validity of the subsequent exercise of jurisdiction over [illegally seized] offenders",[121] or that "with rare unanimity and undeniable justification the courts of the world have held that the manner in which an accused has been brought before the court does not and, indeed, cannot deprive it of its jurisdiction."[122]

Laying aside the question of whether the application of the *male captus* principle was ever accepted as part of international law, or whether it was merely a rule of national practice, it is clear that the development of human rights requires a new evaluation of the question of exercise of jurisdiction over persons who are forcibly abducted. Merely clinging to the argument that the application of the doctrine of *male captus* was not prohibited by international law in the past is no answer to arguments based on human rights norms (some of which may be considered peremptory) which have come into existence in the meantime. Further, if courts continue to apply national rules which rely on the doctrine of *male*

[120] For a different position, see S Wilske, *Die völkerrechtswidrige Entführung und ihre Rechtsfolgen* (Duncker and Humblot, Berlin, 2000), concluding that customary international law prevents courts from exercising criminal jurisdiction over abducted defendants. See also the criticisms of this thesis made by D Pulkowski, (2001) 12 *European Journal of International Law* 1035.

[121] Brownlie, *Principles of Public International Law*, above n 93, at 320.

[122] Mann, above n 37, at 414.

captus, they may well engage the responsibility of their State by violating the human rights of the accused (quite apart from the responsibility that the State may already have incurred by the abduction itself). The judges in some countries seem to have realised this; unfortunately the prospects of US courts doing so in the near future seem slight.

IV. INTERNATIONAL CO-OPERATION AS A VIABLE ALTERNATIVE TO ABDUCTION. THE EXTRADITION OF TERRORIST SUSPECTS TO THE US: PROSPECTIVE SCENARIOS

In any case, the need for forcible abduction is not as strong as it was in the past; States are increasingly working together to solve the problems of international crime and of terrorism in particular. A multiplicity of bilateral agreements and regional or universal conventions on police and judicial co-operation increasingly govern international law enforcement. Apart from State-sponsored kidnapping, there are many alternative ways to ensure that suspected criminals are prosecuted and punished.[123]

In particular, with reference to terrorist activities, a large number of States are parties to international conventions requiring mutual co-operation for the suppression of international terrorism. The focus should be on the identification, apprehension and prosecution of international terrorists and not on the place in which the prosecution will take place. As regards terrorist suspects, although mechanisms for effective co-operation among States are already present, they could undoubtedly still be improved. As has already been noted, many treaties ensure that terrorist acts are extraditable offences,[124] whilst others provide that they are in no circumstances to be treated as political offences. Moreover, *ad hoc* conventions on terrorism, while broadening the range of jurisdictional criteria, almost invariably set forth a mechanism based on the *aut dedere aut iudicare* rule, which, at least in theory, guarantees comprehensive and effective enforcement.

[123] MM Laflin, "Kidnapped Terrorists: Bringing International Criminals to Justice Through Irregular Rendition and Others Quasi-legal Options", (2000) 26 *Journal of Legislation* 315.

[124] Art 8(1), Convention for the Suppression of Unlawful Seizure of Aircraft (The Hague, 16 December 1970, 860 UNTS 12325, in force 14 October 1971). See also Art 8(1), Convention for the Suppression of Unlawful Acts Against the Safety of Civil Aviation (Montreal, 23 September 1971, 974 UNTS 14118, in force 26 January 1973); Art 8(1), Convention on the Prevention and Punishment of Crimes against Internationally Protected Persons, Including Diplomatic Agents (New York, 14 December 1973, 1035 UNTS 15410, in force 20 February 1977); Art 10(1), International Convention Against the Taking of Hostages 1979, above n 8; Art 11(1), Convention on the Physical Protection of Nuclear Material (Vienna, 26 October 1979, 1456 UNTS 24631, in force 8 February 1987); Art 11(1), Convention for the Suppression of Unlawful Acts against the Safety of Maritime Navigation (Rome, 10 March 1988, IMO Doc. SUA/CONF/15/Rev.1, in force 1 March 1992); Art 9(1), International Convention for the Suppression of Terrorist Bombing, above n 16; Art 11(1), International Convention for the Suppression of the Financing of Terrorism (New York, 9 December 1999, UN Doc. A/Res/54/109 (1999), in force 10 April 2002).

The conventions on international terrorism, with the sole exception of the 1963 Tokyo Convention,[125] provide for the twofold obligation either to investigate and prosecute or to extradite individuals suspected of terrorist offences. The Hague Convention, for instance, provides that

> [t]he Contracting State in the territory of which the alleged offender is found shall, *if it does not extradite him*, be obliged without exception whatsoever and whether or not the offence was committed in its territory, to *submit the case to its competent authorities, for the purpose of prosecution.*[126]

This does not mean that there could not be cases where the requested State is unwilling to extradite or to prosecute suspected terrorists. Yet, even in cases where a State in whose territory a terrorist is found does not extradite and is not genuinely willing to prosecute the individual, the forcible abduction of an individual represents a violation of his fundamental rights. This approach precludes any attempt to characterise forcible abduction as a legitimate measure of self-help against a failure by the asylum State to comply with a treaty based obligation either to extradite or to prosecute a suspected criminal.[127]

International co-operation is therefore — especially in relation to the repression of crimes stigmatised by a large number of States — a viable alternative to abduction. Whether or not such an alternative proves effective depends largely on the attitude of the authorities of the requesting

[125] Convention on Offences and Certain other Acts Committed on Board Aircraft (Tokyo, 14 September 1963, in force 4 December 1969).

[126] Art 7, Convention for the Suppression of Unlawful Seizure of Aircraft, above n 124 (emphasis added). See also Art 5(2), Convention for the Suppression of Unlawful Acts Against the Safety of Civil Aviation, above n 124; Art 7, Convention on the Prevention and Punishment of Crimes against Internationally Protected Persons, above n 124; Art 8(1), International Convention Against the Taking of Hostages, above n 8; Art 10, Convention on the Physical Protection of Nuclear Material, above n 124; Art 10, Convention for the Suppression of Unlawful Acts against the Safety of Maritime Navigation, above n 124; Art 8(1), International Convention for the Suppression of Terrorist Bombing, above n 16; Art 10 (1) International Convention for the Suppression of the Financing of Terrorism, above n 124; Art 7, European Convention against Terrorism, above n 8. On the obligation either to extradite or to prosecute terrorist suspects, see Kolb, above n 4.

[127] For this argument see MJ Matorin, "Unchaining the Law: the Legality of Extraterritorial Abduction In Lieu of Extradition", (1992) 42 *Duke Law Journal* 907, arguing that "[t]he exigencies of international law enforcement justify the availability of irregular means of gaining custody over fugitives in certain limited cases. The use of such methods is limited to extraordinary cases by the inevitable political and diplomatic repercussions, but in those cases where the executive concludes that the benefits outweigh the disadvantages, the courts have no cause to intervene". See also B Izes, "Drawing Lines in the Sand: When State-Sanctioned Abduction of War Criminals Should be Permitted", (1997) 31 *Columbia Journal of Law and Social Problems* 1. Note in this regard Art 50(1)(a) and (b) of the International Law Commission's Articles on State Responsibility 2001, which prohibits countermeasures which affect the "obligation to refrain from the threat or use of force" or "obligations for the protection of fundamental human rights".

State concerning the way in which prosecution and punishment of suspected terrorists will be carried out.

In the aftermath of the events of September 11, most States were ready to extradite suspected terrorists to the US *provided that their fundamental rights be respected*, and in cases where extradition would have been impossible, to prosecute them before their domestic courts.

Evaluating the stance taken by US authorities on prosecution of terrorist suspects, many obstacles seem to prevent fruitful cooperation, if such co-operation has to take place in compliance with international law. If the limits set by extradition law do not seem to represent an obstacle to the extradition of suspected terrorists, the obligations deriving from human rights law norms can pose serious problems.

Firstly, the issue of the death penalty — which has seen, for many years, the United States opposed to all other Western States — will certainly represent an obstacle to the extradition of terrorist suspects from abolitionist countries, including Latin American and the European States, but also Canada and other States. Many European States have already expressed their dissent over the imposition of capital punishment on their own nationals accused of terrorism in the United States. A first sign of potential friction between the United States and Europe in dealing with terrorists was represented by a declaration of the Minister of Justice of France, stating that "[France] is not going to accept the death penalty" and demanding that the US not execute a French national charged with plotting the September 11 attacks should a US federal court convict him of terrorist acts.[128] Spanish authorities have also already made clear that extradition would not be granted if suspects faced the death penalty.[129] The opposition of European countries towards the death penalty in all circumstances has been clearly restated, after the events of September 2001, by the Council of Europe. In May 2002, the Committee of Ministers of the Council of Europe adopted Protocol No. 13 to the European Convention of Human Rights, banning the death penalty in all circumstances, including for crimes committed in times of war and imminent threat of war.[130] The adoption of this instrument, which might seem redundant as none of the members of the Council of Europe retains the death penalty, and its prompt signature by a large number of European States,[131] is a strong political signal to the United States

[128] See "USA Death Penalty Bar to Extradition of Criminal Suspects", Amnesty International, *Death Penalty News*, December 2001, p. 1.

[129] See "Spain Sets Hurdle for Extradition", *New York Times*, 24 November 2001. Germany has agreed to cooperate with regard to the trial of a terrorist in the US on the basis that evidence provided would not be used to obtain the death penalty; in order to obtain the extradition of two terrorist suspects, the US has made assurances that prosecutors will not seek the death penalty ("German Court Backs Extradition of Yemeni Suspects", Reuters, 21 July 2003).

[130] Above n 62.

[131] As of 20 July 2003, Protocol No. 13 has been signed by 41 States and ratified by 16 (source: Council of Europe Treaty Office at <http://conventions.coe.int>).

that the imposition of the death penalty will be considered unacceptable in all circumstances. The clear intention of the Member States of the Council of Europe to prevent the extradition of terrorist suspects facing capital punishment in the requesting country and "to strengthen the fight against terrorism *while respecting human rights*"[132] is also reflected by the adoption of the Protocol amending the European Convention on the Suppression of Terrorism.[133] According to article 4 of the Protocol,

> Nothing in [the] Convention shall be interpreted ... as imposing on the requested State an obligation to extradite if the person subject of the extradition request risks being exposed to the death penalty ... unless under applicable extradition treaties the requested State is under the obligation to extradite if the requesting State gives such assurance as the requested State considers sufficient that the death penalty will not be imposed or, where imposed, will not be carried out.

Again, while this provision may seem somewhat redundant, given that no State within the Council of Europe retains the death penalty,[134] the political message is clear.

Secondly, the announcement by the US executive that the United States will use military commissions to try terrorism cases has stirred strong criticism not only among US public opinion, but also among US allies in Europe and around the world. On 13 November 2001, the President of the United States issued a controversial Military Order.[135] The order states that

> [t]o protect the United States and its citizens, and for the effective conduct of military operations and prevention of terrorist attacks, it is necessary for individuals subject to this order[136] ... to be detained, and, when tried, to be

[132] Preamble, Protocol amending the European Convention on the Suppression of Terrorism, above n 4.

[133] Above n 4.

[134] It should be noted that the Convention on Terrorism (and therefore also the Protocol) applies only between States parties, and accordingly does not impose an obligation on the States parties not to extradite to a retentionist State outside the Council of Europe.

[135] Presidential Military Order on Detention, Treatment, and Trial of Certain Non-Citizens in the War Against Terrorism, issued by President Bush, 13 November 2001 (66 FED. REG. 57833 (2001)) (hereafter "Presidential Order").

[136] Presidential Order, Section 2(a): "The term 'individual subject to this order' shall mean any individual who is not a United States citizen with respect to whom [the President] determine[s] from time to time in writing that: (1) there is reason to believe that such individual, at the relevant times, (i) is or was a member of the organization known as al Qaeda; (ii) has engaged in, aided or abetted, or conspired to commit, acts of international terrorism, or acts in preparation therefore, that have caused, threaten to cause, or have as their aim to cause injury to, or adverse effects on, the United States, its citizens, national security, foreign policy, or economy; or (iii) has knowingly harboured one or more individuals described in subparagraphs (i) or (ii) of subsection 2(a)(1) of this order; and (2) it is in the interest of the United States that such individual be subject to this order."

> tried for violations of the laws of war and other applicable laws by *military tribunals.*[137]

The use of "military courts" is not a problem *per se*[138] and does not of itself represent an obstacle to the surrender of terrorist suspects to the United States. Rather, the issue is the composition, functioning and guarantees for individuals provided by these tribunals.

The Presidential Order states that "[g]iven the danger to the safety of the United States and the nature of international terrorism, and to the extent provided by and under this order, ...it is not practicable to apply in military commissions under this order the principles of law and the rules of evidence generally recognised in the trial of criminal cases in the United States district courts."[139] On 21 March 2002, the Department of Defense issued, according to Section 4(b) of the Presidential Order,[140] a Regulation that will govern the conduct of the Military Commissions.[141] The Regulation has been further elaborated by the Military Commission Instructions issued by the General Counsel of the Department of Defense on 30 April 2003.[142] According to US officials, "[these] military commissions will ensure a fair trial, but also deal with very special conditions under which some of these trials may have to take place."[143]

According to the regulations, the commissions will have jurisdiction to try non-US citizens who are allegedly connected to Al-Qaeda or other terrorist movements.[144] The decision to try these individuals before the military commissions rests with the US President. On 3 July 2003, President

[137] Presidential Order, Section 1(e).

[138] See European Commission of Human Rights, *Sutter v Switzerland* (Application No. 8209/78), 16 *DR* (1979) 166, at 174.

[139] Presidential Order, Section 1(f).

[140] Presidential Order, Section 4(b): "As a military function ... the Secretary of Defense shall issue such orders and regulations, including orders for the appointment of one or more military commissions, as may be necessary to carry out [prosecution of individuals subjected to the Order]. Section 4(c) provides that '[o]rders and regulations issued under subsection (b) of this section shall include, but not be limited to, rules for the conduct of the proceedings of military commissions, including pretrial, trial, and post-trial procedures, modes of proof, issuance of process, and qualifications of attorneys, which shall at a minimum provide for (1) military commissions to sit at any time and any place, consistent with such guidance regarding time and place as the Secretary of Defense may provide; (2) a full and fair trial, with the military commission sitting as the triers of both fact and law; (3) admission of such evidence as would, in the opinion of the presiding officer of the military commission ... have probative value to a reasonable person".

[141] Department of Defense, Military Commission Order No. 1, 21 March 2002 (hereinafter "Military Commission Order").

[142] Department of Defense, Military Commission Instructions No. 1–8, 30 April 2003 (hereinafter "Military Commission Instructions"), available at <http://www.defenselink.mil>.

[143] Press release of Deputy Secretary of Defense Paul Wolfowitz, 21 March 2002, available at <http://www.pbs.org/newshour/bb/military/jan-june02/wolfowitz_3-21.html>.

[144] Military Commission Order, Sec. 3(1)(2).

Bush designated six "enemy combatants" under the Presidential Order as being subject to the jurisdiction of the Military Commissions.[145]

In detail the Regulations provide that:

- — the members of the Commissions will be directly appointed by the Secretary of Defense, and they will be chosen among officers of the United States Armed Forces;
- — the Presiding Officer, chosen among the Commission member by the Secretary of Defense, will have the authority to exclude or admit evidence and to close proceedings to protect classified information, judges, witnesses, or for other reasons of national security;
- — the verdict and the sentencing require a two-thirds majority. Commission members will deliberate in closed conference by secret ballot;
- — the verdicts will be submitted to automatic review: a three-member Review Panel appointed by the Secretary of Defense will review trial findings and either provide a recommendation to the Secretary of Defense or return the case for further proceedings;
- — findings and sentences are not final until approved by the President or by the Secretary of Defense, but findings of "Not Guilty" cannot be changed.

As a preliminary matter, the mode of appointment of the Commissions is problematic. The very concept of a fair trial implies a "competent, independent and impartial tribunal established by law."[146] In this respect, the Presidential Order provides that the members of the Commissions will be directly appointed by the Secretary of Defense,[147] and they will be chosen among officers of the United States Armed Forces.[148] It is, at the very least, debatable that a judicial body established by an act of the executive and whose composition is entirely determined by the executive in circumstances such as these meets the criteria of independence, of the judiciary. The independence of the judges is compromised by the power of the Secretary of Defense to remove any member of the Commission "for good cause."[149] Further doubts regarding the impartiality of the tribunals are

[145] Press Release, "President Determines Enemy Combatants Subject to his Military Order", 3 July 2003, available at <http://www.defenselink.mil>. The Press Release continued "The Department of Defense is prepared to conduct full and fair trials if and when the Appointing Authority approves charges on an individual subject to the President's military order." The names of the individuals were not released.

[146] Art 14(1), ICCPR. See Art 6(1) ECHR: "a fair and impartial tribunal established by law"; and Art 8(1), ACHR "a competent, independent and impartial tribunal, previously established by law".

[147] Section 4(b), Presidential Order.

[148] Section 4.A(3), Military Commission Order.

[149] See Section 4.A(3), Military Commission Order. See *Sutter v Switzerland*, above n 138, at 174: "a judge's independence does not necessarily imply that he should be appointed for

raised by the fact that all members will be serving or retired members of the armed forces. Further, the very fact that *ad hoc* tribunals have been created to prosecute non-US citizens allegedly responsible of terrorist acts represents a violation of internationally recognized principles of criminal prosecution.[150]

As for the fundamental guarantees of a fair trial, the regulation at least in appearance provides for guarantees of such rights, in that it establishes the right to defence counsel,[151] the presumption of innocence,[152] the requirement of proof beyond reasonable doubt,[153] as well as automatic review of the verdict.[154] However, upon closer examination it becomes apparent that these protections are qualified, to the point where they cannot be regarded as sufficient

With regard to the right to defence counsel, although such a right is formally recognized by both the Military Commission Order and the Instructions, it seems that individuals tried before the Commission will not be entitled to a free choice of legal defence fully in accordance with international standards. The Order and Instructions, provide that every accused shall be assigned Defense Counsel, chosen by the Chief Defense Officer among the Judges Advocate of the United States Armed Forces, who have the duty to "defend the accused zealously within the bounds of the law without regard to personal opinion as to the guilt of the accused [sic]."[155] In this respect, the proceedings before the Commissions seem to comply with the internationally recognized right of accused in criminal proceedings to have "legal assistance assigned to him, in any case where the interests of justice so require, and without payment by him in any such case if he does not have sufficient means to pay for it."[156] When it comes to the possibility of the accused to defend themselves fully "... through legal assistance of [their] own choosing" the Regulations provide for the possibility of replacing the assigned attorney with another of

life ... or that he should be irremovable in law ... But it is essential that he should enjoy a certain stability, if only for a specific period, and that he should not be subject to any authority in the performance of his duties as a judge."

150 See, eg, the *Basic Principles on the Independence of the Judiciary*, UN Doc. A/CONF 121/22/Rev 1, at 59, adopted at the 1985 Milan conference and approved by the UN General Assembly (GA Res. 40/32 (29 November 1985) and GA Res. 40/146 (13 December 1985)). Art 5 provides: "Everyone shall have the right to be tried by ordinary courts or tribunals using established legal procedures. Tribunals that do not use the duly established procedures of the legal process shall not be established to displace the jurisdiction belonging to the ordinary courts or judicial tribunals".

151 Military Commission Order, Section 5 (D), Section 6 (B) (1)(2). Cf also Military Commission Instruction No 4, Section 3 and Military Commission Instruction No 5.

152 Military Commission Order, Section 5 (B).

153 Military Commission Order, Section 6 (F).

154 Military Commission Order, Section 6 (H).

155 Section 4.C(2), Military Commission Order.

156 Art 14(3)(d) ICCPR.

his choosing at no personal cost, although the replacement must also be a Judge Advocate of the US Armed Forces.[157] The accused may also choose a Civilian Defense Counsel at his own expense; however the Civilian Defense Counsel, does not replace, but only works alongside the assigned (military) attorney. Civilian Defense Counsel must be US citizens and must have been determined to be eligible for access to classified information.[158] However, the Civilian Defense Counsel enjoys more limited procedural powers than the military counsel, in particular with regard to access to certain documents, and participation in closed proceedings.[159]

With regard to what may be considered one of the most important characteristics of a fair trial, the presumption of innocence, the instructions improperly shift the burden of proof on the wrongfulness of the conduct to the accused by stating, "Conduct satisfying the elements found herein shall be *inferred to be wrongful in the absence of evidence to the contrary* ... The burden of going forward with evidence of lawful justification or excuse or any applicable defense shall be upon the Accused".[160] Such a provision clearly contradicts the requirement that the prosecution has the burden to prove each element beyond a reasonable doubt.

The right to an appeal in criminal proceedings[161] is also implemented in a flawed manner. Under the Military Commission Order, the verdicts of the Commissions will be submitted to automatic review: a three-member Review Panel appointed by the Secretary of Defense will review trial findings and either provide a recommendation to the Secretary of Defense or return the case for further proceedings.[162] Indisputably, such a procedure delegated to the Review Panel, whose composition is inherently flawed by its composition, and the way in which its members are to be appointed, cannot be considered an independent and impartial second degree of jurisdiction.

It should also be noted that the Presidential Order seems to seek to expressly exclude the possibility of the defendant resorting to ordinary justice or to international bodies.[163] There is also provision for a "final

[157] Section 4.C(3)(a), Military Commission Order; Section 3.D, Military Commission Instruction No. 4.

[158] Section 4.C(3)(b), Military Commission Order; Section 3.E, Military Commission Instruction No. 4. See also Military Commission Instruction No. 5 providing details of the necessary qualifications of Civilian Defence Counsel.

[159] Section 4.C(3)(b) *in fine*, Military Commission Order; Section 3.E(4), Military Commission Instruction No. 4.

[160] Section 4.B, Military Commission Instruction No. 2.

[161] Art 14(5) ICCPR: "Everyone convicted of a crime shall have the right to his conviction and sentence being reviewed by a higher tribunal according to law".

[162] Section 6.H(4), Military Commission Order.

[163] Presidential Order, Section 7(b): "With respect to any individual subject to this order (1) military tribunals shall have exclusive jurisdiction with respect to offences by the individual; and (2) the individual shall not be privileged to seek any remedy or maintain any proceeding, directly or indirectly, or to have any such remedy or proceeding sought on the

review" conducted by either the President or the Secretary of Defense.[164] The participation of a member of the executive in determining the final findings of fact and choice of sentence seems completely antithetical to any concept of independent and impartial justice.

In addition, some of the procedural rules that will be applied by the commission are in striking contrast with internationally accepted standards on fair trial; for instance, the fact that the trial may be closed for a number of indefinite reasons — such as vague reasons of "national security"- at the sole discretion of the Presiding Officer and that such decision is not subject to any form of judicial review in itself arguably represents a violation of the principle that any defendant shall be afforded a trial open to the public.[165] Furthermore, the regulations issued by the Secretary of Defense provide for "conviction only upon the concurrence of two-thirds of the members of the commission present at the time of the vote, a majority being present", except in cases where capital punishment can be imposed or carried out.[166] The allowance of a two-thirds majority decision instead of a unanimous verdict, even in cases involving the possibility of life prison sentences represents a significant difference in respect to the procedural rules applying under ordinary criminal procedure law. Moreover, the proceedings before the military commissions are in sharp contrast with the internationally recognized right to have an appeal in criminal proceedings. The Presidential Order seems expressly to ban the possibility for the defendant to resort to ordinary justice or to international adjudicating bodies;[167] the procedure of automatic review delegated to the Review Panel cannot be considered an independent and impartial second degree of jurisdiction, for the same reasons concerning appointment as for the Commissions themselves.

In response to the many criticisms coming from NGOs and from governments of several allied countries, US authorities have argued in favour of the legality of the institution of military commissions on the basis of

individual's behalf, in (i) any court of the United States, or any State thereof, (ii) any court of any foreign nation, or (iii) any international tribunal". See also Section 6, Military Commission Instruction No. 1.

[164] Section 4.C(8), Presidential Order; Section 6.H(5) and (6), Military Commission Order.

[165] See Art 14(1), ICCPR "the Press and the public may be excluded from all or part of a trial for reasons of morals, public order (*ordre public*) or national security in a democratic society". See Art 6(1), ECHR (in similar terms) and Art 8(5), ACHR: "Criminal proceedings shall be public, except insofar as may be necessary to protect the interests of justice".

[166] Military Commission Order, Section 6 (F).

[167] Presidential Order, Section 7(b): "With respect to any individual subject to this order (1) military tribunals shall have exclusive jurisdiction with respect to offences by the individual; and (2) the individual shall not be privileged to seek any remedy or maintain any proceeding, directly or indirectly, or to have any such remedy or proceeding sought on the individual's behalf, in (i) any court of the United States, or any State thereof, (ii) any court of any foreign nation, or (iii) any international tribunal".

the practice of prosecuting enemy combatants seized in war, namely the war on terrorism.[168] To corroborate their position US spokesmen have made references to various precedents in which the Supreme Court of the US has upheld the legitimacy of military commissions.[169] It should to be noted, however, that until very recently, the United States has strongly condemned the establishment of military commissions and of domestic *ad hoc* tribunals. In particular, the US State Department has repeatedly criticised the use of military tribunals to try civilians and other similar limitations on due process around the world. Indeed, its annual Country Reports on Human Rights Practices evaluate each country on the extent to which it guarantees the right to a "fair public trial", which it defines to include many of the same due process rights omitted by the Presidential Order of November 2001.[170]

Overall, the present position of US authorities with respect to the prosecution of non-US suspected terrorists leaves little room for positive conclusions about the respect of fundamental rights of individuals extradited or otherwise surrendered from third countries once they reach US territory. Further, it seems likely that the US will face difficulties in obtaining the extradition of terrorist suspects from other countries, in particular those in Europe, no matter how heinous the crimes of which they are accused.[171] As noted above, the strengthening of universal and regional human rights obligations compelling States to protect the fundamental

[168] See "News Briefing on Military Commissions", Department of Defense, Secretary Rumsfeld, 21 March 2002: "Let there be no doubt that these commissions will conduct trials that are honest, fair and impartial . . . While ensuring just outcomes, they will also give us the flexibility we need to ensure the safety and security of the American people in the midst of a difficult and dangerous war", available at <http://www.defenselink.mil/news/Mar2002/t03212002_t0321sd.html>.

[169] In particular, US authorities have made reference to cases that took place during the Second World War, in which the Supreme Court upheld the legitimacy of the institution of military commissions. In 1942 (*ex parte Quirin* 317 US 1 (1942)) the Supreme Court denied habeas relief to eight Germans detained during trial by a military commission. They were held on charges that they violated the law of war and that they had committed acts of sabotage and spying. The Supreme Court upheld the jurisdiction of the commission. Most notably, the Court refused to be drawn into a discussion of the jurisdictional boundaries of military commissions when it stated, "we have no occasion now to define with meticulous care the ultimate boundaries of the jurisdiction of military tribunals to try persons according to the law of war"; in *Application of Yamashita* (327 US 1 (1946)) the Supreme Court upheld the jurisdiction of an American military commission, established pursuant to the laws of war to try Japanese General Yamashita in the fall of 1945 for alleged war crimes in the Philippines.

[170] Annual Country Reports on Human Rights Practices Released by the Bureau of Democracy, Human Rights, and Labor of the Department of State. The most recent reports (1999/2000/2001) are available on the official website of the Department of State at <http://www.state.gov>.

[171] In this context, see the observations of the European Court in *Chahal v the United Kingdom*, above n 38, paras. 79–80: "The Court is well aware of the immense difficulties faced by States in modern times in protecting their communities from terrorist violence. However, even in these circumstances, the Convention prohibits in absolute terms torture or inhuman or

rights of all individuals subject to their jurisdiction has brought about substantial changes in the approach of domestic courts in relation to their attitude towards conditions in the requesting country in extradition cases. Domestic courts in many jurisdictions seem to be increasingly aware both of their role in the international legal system and of the fact that, as State organs, they are called upon, as much as the executive, to ensure compliance with the international obligations of their State.

The US seems ready to counter European concerns over extraditing terrorist suspects to face the death penalty, and has already declared that the individuals found guilty on terrorism charges would not inevitably risk capital punishment.[172] Thus, the obstacle represented by the possible imposition of the death penalty can, in some cases, be circumvented, in particular for those States that are able to grant extradition dependant on guarantees presented by the requesting country that capital punishment will not be inflicted or that the sentence will not be executed. In the case of States where the refusal of extradition is absolute where the extraditee could face the death penalty in the requesting State,[173] the only option would probably be that the suspected terrorist be tried in the requested State.

With respect to the establishment of the Military Commissions, it is doubtful whether the courts of any European State,[174] or any other country bound by international human rights obligations, would agree to the

degrading treatment or punishment, irrespective of the victim's conduct. Unlike most of the substantive clauses of the Convention and of Protocols Nos. 1 and 4, Art 3 makes no provision for exceptions and no derogation from it is permissible under Art 15 even in the event of a public emergency threatening the life of the nation ... whenever substantial grounds have been shown for believing that an individual would face a real risk of being subjected to treatment contrary to Art 3 if removed to another State, the responsibility of the Contracting State to safeguard him or her against such treatment is engaged in the event of expulsion. In these circumstances, the activities of the individual in question, however undesirable or dangerous, cannot be a material consideration."

172 US Attorney-General John Ashcroft has declared that each extradition case would be considered separately, implying that the US government would consider making guarantees that the death penalty would not be imposed or that, if imposed, it would not be carried out; see "Ashcroft says death penalty- extradition issue to be handled case-by-case", Associated Press, 12 December 2001. In relation to the two British and one Australian nationals captured in Afghanistan, the US has given assurances that the death penalty will not be sought: see Press Releases "DoD Statement on British Detainee Meetings"; "DoD Statement on Australian Detainee Meetings", 23 July 2003, available at <http://www.defenselink.mil>.

173 As is the case in Italy: see *Venezia v Ministero di Grazia e Giustizia*, above n 56.

174 The European Court of Human Rights has recently restated that the trial of civilians by military or mixed tribunals may constitute a violation of the right to fair trial protected by Art 6 of the Convention, on the basis that the presence of a military judge — even if undoubtedly considered necessary because of his competence and experience in military matters — can raise legitimate doubts on the independence and impartiality of the court (*Öcalan*, above n 53, para. 120–121). See also *Incal v. Turkey*, judgment of 9 June 1998, ECHR, *Reports* 1998–IV, at 1547; and *Ciraklar v Turkey*, judgment of 28 October 1998, ECHR, *Reports* 1998-VII at 3073–3074, para. 40.

extradition of a person that would involve the possibility of military trials like the ones envisaged in the regulations.[175] In theory, there could have been one option under the Presidential Order, which would have met the needs of security and flexibility required by the circumstances, while, at the same time, guaranteeing fair trials: suspected terrorists could have been tried by military commissions under the Uniform Code of Military Justice of the United States.[176] Under this option due process guarantees analogous to the ones already used for military courts-martial would have been applicable. While not being particularly wide in scope, such guarantees would have been at least in conformity with the minimum standards of fair trial recognised by international law. However, such an option has been clearly disregarded or at least too quickly dismissed, favouring the adoption of *ad hoc* regulations with inadequate fair trial provisions. As for now, military trials before *ad hoc* military commissions like the ones envisaged in the Presidential Order and subsequently developed by the regulations of the Department of Defence, together with the possibility of the imposition of capital sentences, are the worst of all possible options if the United States hopes to obtain the rendition of terrorist suspects from Europe or from any other State bound by human rights obligations and willing to respect them.[177]

[175] The use of military tribunals whose procedures do not meet the basic requirements of a fair trial has been strongly condemned also by the Inter-American Court and Commission of Human Rights. See *Castillo Petruzzi v Peru* (Merits), judgment of 30 May 1999, IACtHR, *Series C*, No 52 (1999), paras 221–22, 226, where the Court found that the military trials of four Chilean citizens violated several rights guaranteed under the American Convention. See also *Cesti Hurtado v Peru* (Merits), judgment of 29 September 1999, IACtHR, *Series C*, No 56 (1999), paras 65 and 77–80 and the *Loayza Tamayo v Peru* (Merits), judgment of 17 September 1997, IACtHR, *Series C*, No 33 (1997), para 62–63. Note also that in its General Comment No 13 on the right to fair trial, the Human Rights Committed declared that the trial of civilians by military special courts has to be justified by exceptional circumstances and that, in any event, it must "genuinely afford the full guarantees stipulated in Art 14" of the ICCPR: General Comment No 13, UN Doc HRI/GEN/1/REV.1 (1984), para 4.

[176] USC, Title 10, Subtitle A, Part II, Chapter 47.

[177] The first signals of this attitude have already materialised. On 15 July 2002, the Committee of Ministers of the Council of Europe adopted the *Guidelines on Human Rights and the Fight Against Terrorism*. In the *Guidelines* the Committee of Ministers, while reaffirming the need for co-operation among States in the fight against terrorism, underlined that "it is not only possible, but also absolutely necessary, to fight terrorism while respecting human rights, the rule of law and, where applicable, international humanitarian law", (Preamble) and reaffirmed "states" obligation to respect, in their fight against terrorism, the international instruments for the protection of human rights and, for the member states in particular, the Convention for the Protection of Human Rights and Fundamental Freedoms and the case-law of the European Court of Human Rights' (Preamble). With regard to extradition and expulsion in particular, see arts. XII and XIII. Similar signals come from the Organization of American States: the Inter-American Convention Against Terrorism, adopted on 3 June 2002 (above n 16), which clearly aims at strengthening international co-operation "to prevent, punish and eliminate terrorism" (Art 1), expressly states that "[t]he measures carried out by the States Parties under this Convention shall take place with the full respect for the rule of law, human rights and fundamental freedoms" (Art 16).

Part IV

International Terrorism and Economic Activities: Old and New Challenges for International Law Enforcement Mechanisms

15

Freezing the Assets of International Terrorist Organisations

LUCA G RADICATI DI BROZOLO AND MAURO MEGLIANI

I. INTRODUCTION

THE RECOURSE TO measures freezing or otherwise blocking assets belonging to foreign States or to foreigners is a traditional instrument of foreign policy and international relations. As is well known, foreign asset freezes have been very extensively resorted to by the United States. This country has a long tradition, going back at least to the Fifties, of resorting to such measures, and has developed a sophisticated legislation to deal with the matter. Actually, the freezing of foreign assets tends to be an immediate, almost automatic, reaction by the United States in the event of international crises. In many cases the measures were adopted primarily in retaliation against the expropriation or confiscation of US assets abroad, with a view to permitting some form of compensation for the US victims of such actions. Over time, however, the measures came to be used for a broader array of purposes, such as those against Iraq and against Libya.[1]

This type of measure has now come to be used also on a multilateral level with broader aims than simply that of serving as a tool for retaliations against violations of the international rules on the expropriation of foreign property.

It is in this broader perspective that the freezing of assets has been resorted to in the context of the Afghanistan/Taliban crisis.

The recourse to the freezing of assets in the context of the Afghan terrorist crisis is based on the obvious premise that, like everyone else, terrorists need money and financial services, and that the financing of

[1] The US experience has heavily contributed to the application of blocking measures in situations of international crises or national emergency; see G Burdeau, "Le gel d'avoirs étrangers", (1997) *Journal du Droit International*, 7–10.

terrorist activities is usually based on a variety of mechanisms, some quite complex, which may rely on the financial systems of many different countries.

Consistent with this, several of pieces of legislation, both international and domestic, have been adopted with a view to drying up the finances and sources of financing of terrorist organisations.

II. THE LEGAL BASES OF THE FREEZES

A. The Action of the UN

The natural starting point of this analysis is the work of the United Nations, which in the past decade, in a Convention and in several Declarations and Resolutions, has identified actions aimed at stopping the financing of terrorism as a critical aspect of their fight against terrorism.[2]

1. *The Convention for the Suppression of the Financing of Terrorism*

The most far-reaching instrument relating to the financing of terrorism is the International Convention for the Suppression of the Financing of Terrorism adopted by the General Assembly on 9 December 1999[3] which entered into force on 10 April 2002, probably partly as a result of the adoption by the Security Council, in the wake of the September 11 events, of Resolutions No 1368 (2001) and No 1373 (2001)[4] specifically calling upon States to sign and ratify the Convention.

The Convention is based on the assumption that "the financing of terrorism is a matter of grave concern to the international community" and that "the number and seriousness of acts of international terrorism depend on the financing that terrorists may obtain".[5] Although referred to in earlier General Assembly Resolutions, the financing of terrorism had not been defined as an international offence.[6] The novelty of the

[2] See generally, T Marauhn, "Terrorism: Addendum 1999", in R Bernhardt (ed), *Encyclopaedia of Public International Law*, IV (Elsevier, Amsterdam, 2000), 849.
[3] In (2000) 39 *ILM*, 270, with an introductory note by CM Johnson.
[4] See below, para II.A.4.
[5] A terrorist offence under the Convention is an offence as defined in the treaties listed in the annex (Article 2.1.a) or an act of killing or injuring a civilian not taking direct part in hostilities in a situation of armed conflict, when the purpose of such an act is to intimidate a population or to compel a government or an international organisation to do or to abstain from doing any act (Article 2.1.b).
[6] In a Declaration on the measures to eliminate international terrorism, attached to Resolution A/RES/49/60 of 9 December 1994, terrorism financing was referred to only implicitly. The matter was approached more directly by the General Assembly in Resolution

Convention lies in the fact that it specifically makes an offence of "by any means, directly or indirectly, unlawfully and willfully, provid[ing] or collect[ing] funds with the intention that they should be used, or in the knowledge that they are to be used, in full or in part, in order to carry out" a terrorist offence (Article 2.1). It is not required that the funds actually be used for a terrorist act. It is sufficient that the provider be aware of their potential destination (Article 2.3). To guarantee the Convention's effectiveness, contracting States are required to consider the financing of terrorists as a criminal offence in their legal systems and to make it punishable by suitable sanctions, in accordance with the character of the offence (Article 4).[7]

The Convention purports to apply only to "international" situations and is thus not applicable when the financing of terrorism occurs within a single State and the offender is one of its nationals and is present in its territory (Article 3). In such purely domestic situations other States are not entitled to exercise jurisdiction under the Convention.

As regards the bases of jurisdiction over these offences, the Convention relies on the principles of territoriality and nationality. States are required to exercise their jurisdiction when acts of financing terrorists are committed on their territory (including aircraft and vessels having their nationality) or by their nationals (Article 7.1). States may also have recourse to broader bases of jurisdiction to cover acts of financing committed abroad by non-nationals when these acts are directed towards, or resulted in, a criminal act within, their territory or against their nationals or against facilities or premises of the State abroad (Article 7.2).

As regards specifically the freezing of assets (which is governed by Article 8), States are required to take appropriate measures, in accordance with their respective legal systems, to identify and freeze or seize any funds, and proceeds therefrom, used or allocated to finance terrorism. Measures adopted in this respect must be "without prejudice to the rights of third parties acting in good faith", but no further clarification is provided on this point which is thus probably left to the domestic law of each State. States are permitted to give consideration to concluding agreements with other States aimed at sharing the forfeited funds on a regular or case by case basis, and to use such funds to compensate the victims of terrorist acts or their families. Article 8 does not lay down any jurisdictional criteria for the blocking of funds, and thus does not address

A/RES/51/210 of 17 December 1996 where all States were called upon to prevent every kind of terrorism financing and in the Declaration attached thereto where it was proclaimed that knowingly funding terrorists is contrary to the purposes and the principles of the UN Charter.

[7] Quite significantly, Article 5 provides for criminal, civil or administrative liability even for legal persons, whenever this is provided by domestic legal systems.

the issue of the potential extraterritorial reach of measures purporting to freeze terrorist assets.[8]

Recognizing the essential role of banks and other financial institutions in the context of terrorist financing and drawing on the FATF framework on money laundering,[9] the Convention imposes on States the obligation to require these institutions to identify their customers and to pay attention to suspicious transactions and to report suspicious dealings (Article 18).

2. *The Resolutions on the Financing of Terrorism*

Although it does not address all the problems related to the financing of terrorism, the Convention lays a very important groundwork, and its entry into force is therefore a fundamental development. The issue is addressed more specifically in several Security Council Resolutions adopted both before and after the September 11 events.

The Security Council had adopted measures relating to the availability of funds and the carrying out of transactions in the context of Resolutions under Chapter VII of the UN Charter (Article 41), notably on the occasion of the invasion of Kuwait by Iraq,[10] as well as in other crises such as the ones in Serbia,[11] Haiti,[12] Libya,[13] Angola,[14] and the post Iraq crisis.[15] Although these Resolutions did not deal with the financing of terrorism,[16] they provided a sound basis for a new Security Council Resolution addressing the matter.

[8] No provision is made for the solution of the conflicts of jurisdiction which may arise from the concurrent exercise of jurisdiction by different States over the same offences. The States concerned are simply required "to strive to coordinate their actions appropriately" (Article 7.5).

[9] FATF (Financial Action Task Force) is an intergovernmental body whose Secretariat in housed at the OECD. It is currently composed by some thirty States, basically western countries, plus two international organisations, the European Commission and the Gulf Co-operation Council. It was established by the G-7 summit in Paris in 1989 as a "policy-making body" to bring about national law and regulation to combat money laundering. In 1990, immediately after its establishment, FATF issued the Forty Recommendations on money laundering, then revised in 1996 (see below, para. II B). Now, this soft international organisation is enlarging its area of intervention focusing on terrorist financing. For more information see <www.fatf-gafi.org>. On FATF see J Fischer, "Recent International Developments in the Fight Against Money Laundering", in (2000) *Journal of International Banking Law*, 68–71.

[10] S/RES/661 (1990) of 9 August 1990 (para. 4).

[11] S/RES/757 (1992) of 30 May 1992 (para. 5).

[12] S/RES/841 (1993) of 16 June 1993 (para. 8).

[13] S/RES/883 (1993) of 11 November 1993 (para. 3).

[14] S/RES/1173 (1998) of 12 June 1998 (para. 11).

[15] S/RES/1483 (2003) of 22 May 2003 (para. 23).

[16] The first clear mention of terrorism financing can be found at para. 4 of Security Council Resolution S/RES/1269 (1999) of 19 October 1999.

3. *The Resolutions on Afghanistan and the Taliban*

With specific regard to Afghanistan, in 1999 the Security Council adopted Resolution 1267 (1999) imposing economic sanctions on the Taliban regime for failing to surrender Osama bin Laden.[17] The sanctions included the freezing of all funds directly or indirectly referable to the Taliban for their role in harboring and training terrorists on their territory, as indicated by the Sanctions Committee. The Resolution called upon all States to prohibit their respective nationals and residents from making available the blocked funds or any other funds to the Taliban (para 4.b) and to bring proceedings for the violation of the blocking measures (para 8).

The scope of these measures was broadened by Security Council Resolution 1333 (2000)[18] which extended the freeze and other prohibitions to the funds directly or indirectly attributable to Osama bin Laden, to Al-Qaeda and to related individuals and entities (para 8.c).[19] Resolution 1452 (2002) subsequently introduced an exemption from the total freeze for ordinary expenses and, under specific circumstances, for extraordinary expenses.[20]

This Resolution was followed by Resolution 1363 (2001) which established a Monitoring Group of five experts to control, *inter alia*, financial transactions and money laundering,[21] and by Resolution 1390 (2002) which — following the change in the Afghan government after the invasion by the Anti-terrorism alliance — restricted the scope of the sanctions, previously directed at Afghanistan, to the Taliban, Osama bin Laden and Al-Qaeda.[22] A recent Resolution — 1455

[17] S/RES/1267 (1999) of 15 October 1999. A previous Resolution regarding the Taliban regime, S/RES/1214 (1998), did not address the blocking of assets.

[18] S/RES/1333 (2000) of 19 December 2000.

[19] With this perspective, under Resolution 1333 the Committee was requested, *inter alia*, to maintain and update a list of persons associated to Osama bin Laden, (para 16.b), where in Resolution 1267 it was simply charged to list locations of funds (para 6.e).

[20] S/RES/1452 (2002) of 20 December 2002. The proceeding for exemptions follows a quite different path in accordance with the typology of expense: for ordinary expenses the interested State notifies the Committee of its intention to authorize an access to frozen assets and absent a negative decision by the Committee within two days of the notification, the authorization can have effect; for extraordinary expenses the request for an authorization must be approved by the Committee (para 1).

[21] S/RES/1363 (2001) of 30 July 2001. The monitoring of financial transactions is aimed at permitting the discovery of the connection between the financing of terrorism and arms purchases (para 4.a).

[22] S/RES/1390 (2002) of 16 January 2002. This Resolution decided to terminate the measures of para 4.a of Resolution 1267 regarding the prohibition of flight ban and export restrictions with Afghanistan. At the same time, the Security Council requested the Committee established under Resolution 1267 to maintain the freezing of funds of Al-Qaeda, the Taliban and related entities, and to update regularly the list of members of those groups on the basis of information provided by member States and regional organisations, to make periodic reports to the Security Council on the implementation of this Resolution, to draft guidelines

(2003)[23] — enhanced the effect of the freezes by imposing on Member States the obligation to transmit to the Sanctions Committee at least every three months the list of persons whose assets are to be blocked and to submit the names of persons belonging to the Taliban and Al-Qaeda and of persons related to them (para 4).

The central role in the implementation of the sanctions system imposed by these Resolutions is played by a Sanctions Committee[24] — the Al-Qaida and Taliban Sanctions Committee (the "Taliban Committee" or the "Committee")[25] — established by Resolution 1267 which has the power to designate persons whose assets are to be blocked (para 6.e).[26]

The procedure of the Taliban Committee is governed by guidelines adopted on 7 November 2002 and amended on 10 April 2003.[27] The most significant rules concern the insertion in, and removal from, the list of persons whose assets are to be frozen maintained by the Committee. The insertion of persons on the list is decided by the Taliban Committee at the request of any government or international organisation setting out the reasons for the request and the information allowing the identification of the persons in question (para 5). The Committee updates regularly the list on the basis of the information received, but cannot appraise the merit of the information.[28]

Removal from the list is subject to a request submitted to the Committee by the government of citizenship or residence of the person concerned, possibly jointly with the government having requested the inclusion on the list which must have been contacted in advance with a view to persuading it to submit a joint request (para 7).

4. *The Resolutions on International Terrorism*

Although the fight against terrorism provided the backdrop for them, the Resolutions discussed in the previous section concerned only the actions

and criteria to facilitate the freezing of terrorist assets, and to cooperate with the Terrorism Committee (para 5).

[23] S/RES/1455 (2003) of 17 January 2003. Under this Resolution Member States are required to submit the Committee with a report on the steps taken, *inter alia*, to implement freezing measures and a summary of the frozen assets (para 6).
[24] For an overview of the working system of the UN Sanctions Committees see F Alabrune, "La pratique des comités des sanctions du Conseil de sécurité depuis" 1990, (1999) *Annuaire Français de Droit International*, 226.
[25] On 2 September 2003 the Security Council Committee established in accordance with Resolution 1267 adopted the name of "Security Council Committee concerning Al-Qaida and the Taliban and Associated Individuals and Entities", in short, "Al-Qaida and Taliban Sanctions Committee" (Press Release SC/7865).
[26] The Committee, established under rule 28 of Security Council provisional rules, is composed by all the members of the Council (para. 6 of Resolution 1267).
[27] In <www.un.org/Docs/sc/committees>.
[28] See below, para III A 2.

of the Taliban and related entities and persons, and could therefore be applied exclusively in respect of persons or funds directly connected to the Taliban, and more specifically to the persons identified by the Taliban Committee. As their scope was defined by relation to specific terrorist persons and entities, they were inapplicable to other terrorist threats.

The framework changed completely after the events of 11 September 2001. In a sweeping Resolution adopted a few weeks after the attack on the Twin Towers, 1373 (2001),[29] the Security Council decided that States "shall prevent and suppress the financing of terrorist acts ... and criminalize the willful provision or collection ... of funds by their nationals or on their territories with the intention that the funds should be used, or in the knowledge that they are to be used, in order to carry out terrorist acts" (para 1, a and b).

The financing of terrorism was thus explicitly made a general offence, with no reference to specific countries or situations, thereby eliminating the need to adopt a new resolution upon the occurrence of each new terrorist event or threat.[30] This is, of course, in line with the obligations descending from the 1999 Convention, which had not yet entered into force at the time of the adoption of Resolution 1373.

Consistent with this obligation and with the approach of the 1999 Convention, Resolution 1373 adopts a broad obligation for States to freeze all financial assets and economic resources belonging to persons in any way involved in the commission, or in the attempt to commit, terrorist acts (para 1.a). The freeze extends to assets of entities directly or indirectly controlled by those persons. It applies also to persons and entities acting on behalf of, or under the direction of, persons involved in terrorist acts or entities controlled by them. The freeze further applies to funds generated by properties controlled directly or indirectly by such persons, associated persons and entities (para 1.c). States are required to prohibit anyone within their personal or territorial jurisdiction from making any funds, resources or financial services available to persons who commit terrorist acts or to entities controlled by them or to persons or entities acting on behalf or under the direction of those persons (para 1.d).

Furthermore, States must deny safe haven to persons financing terrorist acts (para 2.c), prevent them from using their territories as a base for financing terrorism (para 2.d), bring to justice anyone taking part in

[29] S/RES/1373 (2001) of 28 September 2001; it was preceded by S/RES/1368 (2001) of 12 September 2001.

[30] Recalling GA Declaration of 1996 (above n 6), para 5 of Resolution 1373 underlies that knowingly financing terrorist acts is contrary to the purposes and principles of the Charter. The Declaration on the global effort to combat terrorism, attached to Resolution S/RES/1377 (2001) of 12 November 2001 goes farther in this direction and, omitting any reference to intention, clarifies that terrorism financing as such is "contrary to the purposes and the principles of the Charter of the United Nations".

terrorist financing, and consider such activity a serious criminal offence and punish it adequately (para 2.e).

Not surprisingly the obligations descending from this Resolution mirror fairly closely, although in less detail, those of the 1999 Convention. Even after the entry into force of the latter these obligations remain important considering the relatively small number of States having ratified it.

However, Resolution 1373 (2001) goes further than the Convention in one aspect, in that it establishes the Counter-terrorism Committee aimed at increasing the capability of States to fight terrorism and to which all States are required to report the measures adopted by them to implement the Resolution (para 6).[31] This Committee, which is called upon to work in cooperation with the Taliban Committee,[32] may make confidential comments on each government's report and may request further information or clarification.

The most significant difference with the Taliban Committee is that this Committee is not a Sanctions Committee and therefore does not maintain a list of persons whose assets are to be frozen. Each State is thus directly responsible for discovering the persons whose assets must be frozen and for enforcing blocking orders enacted by other States, in accordance with the cooperative spirit of Resolution 1373.

B. Other International Responses

In reviewing the actions undertaken at international level mention must be made of those of the group of the most industrialised countries. On 16–17 November 2001 the G-20 Finance Ministers and Central Bank Governors adopted a comprehensive Action Plan of multilateral cooperation on terrorism financing. The Action Plan rests on the following pillars: freezing terrorist assets, implementing international instruments, enhancing international co-operation, providing technical assistance and

[31] The Committee, established pursuant to Rule 28 of the provisional rules of procedure of the Security Council, is composed of all the members of the Council with the assistance of experts. The Committee adopted Guidelines for the submission of the reports: see *Guidance for the Submission of Reports pursuant to paragraph 6 of Security Council Resolution 1373 (2001) of 28 September 2001*, in <www.un.org/Docs/committes/1373/guide/htm>. In their reports States are required to inform the Committee on four fundamental points: relevant legislation, administrative measures, other actions and international co-operation. Moreover, para. 4 of the Declaration attached to Security Council Resolution S/RES/1456 (2003) of 20 January 2003 emphasized the obligation of every State to report to the Counter-Terrorism Committee.

[32] Para. 3 of Security Council Resolution 1455 (above n 23) stresses the need to enhance coordination and intensify exchange of information between the two Committees.

promoting compliance and reporting.[33] A crucial element of this program is the implementation of Eight Special Recommendations on Terrorist Financing adopted by FATF in Washington on 30 October 2001.[34]

Coupled with FATF's Forty Recommendations on money laundering, these Eight Special Recommendations constitute the framework around which FATF member States are called upon to build a common program against terrorism financing.[35] The first five recommendations concern the implementation of UN instruments (n I), the criminalization of financing terrorism (n II), the freeze and forfeiture of terrorist assets (n III),[36] the reporting of suspicious transactions (n IV) and the improvement of co-operation in criminal, civil enforcement and administrative investigations, inquiry and proceedings on terrorism financing (n V). The remaining Recommendations deal with more technical issues, such as the regulation of alternative remittances, pursuant to which persons involved in informal money or value transfer systems must be licensed or registered and made subject to FATF Recommendations, in the same way as any other financial institution (n VI).[37] Moreover, each State must require financial institutions — including money remitters — to attach originator information on fund transfers and to maintain such information on the entire chain of payments;[38] close monitoring of suspicious transactions lacking

[33] This plan represents a comprehensive program of multinational co-operation to deny terrorists access to financial systems and to stop abuse of informal banking networks; see <www.g20.org>.

[34] Above n 9.

[35] Following their adoption, FATF undertook to monitor the implementation of the Recommendations by providing a self-assessment questionnaire and guidance for financial institutions in detecting financing activities.

[36] Under the Eight Recommendations the terms of "property" and "funds" have a broader meaning with respect to the corresponding definitions under the Forty Recommendations: JJ Norton and H Shmas, "Money Laundering Law and Terrorism Financing: Post-September 11 Responses — Let Us Step Back and Take a Deep Breath?", (2002) 36 *The International Lawyer*, 112–14.

[37] A parallel banking system is *Hawala*, literally "providing a code", developed in the Middle East and South Asia well before the western banking system to transfer money swiftly and securely. Under this system a person wishing to transfer funds to another country deposits the money with a dealer. The depositor provides the dealer with a code by means of which the intended recipient of the money can withdraw the funds from the dealer's agents. Thanks to a network of accounts, the dealer can move the funds to his agents in other countries, essentially without paper. This underground system, initially used in western countries by Eastern immigrants as a means to remit money without paying banking fees for wire transfers, was then misused both for money laundering and for terrorist financing: K Natarajan, "Combating India's Heroin Trade through Anti-money Laundering Legislation", (1998) 21 *Fordham International Law Journal*, 2021. A similar informal financial system — mainly used in the Chinese region — is *Fei Ch'ien*; see J Trehan, "Underground and Parallel Banking Systems", (2002) 10 *Journal of Financial Crime*, 76.

[38] This specific Recommendation is intended to block operations performed over the internet from WAP mobile phones: S Thye Tan, "Money Laundering and E-Commerce", in (2002) 9 *Journal of Financial Crime*, 279.

complete originator data is also required (n VII). Each State must review or enact laws and regulations on non-profit organisations aimed at preventing that these bodies be used as conduits for terrorist financing and as a cover for the clandestine diversion of lawful funds towards terrorists (n VIII).

In its fight against terrorism financing FATF can rely on financial intelligence units (FIUs), a network of national specialized agencies created in 1995 to deal with financial crimes. This informal organisation — known as the Egmont Group — intends to develop an effective co-operation in exchanging information and sharing expertise. In October 2001 the Egmont Group agreed to improve exchange of information regarding terrorism financing and to make this a specific offence distinct from money laundering.[39]

The FATF Recommendations are explicitly recalled in the Inter-American Convention against Terrorism of 3 June 2002[40] which requires that contracting States take them into account in implementing the regulatory and supervisory regime to prevent and eradicate terrorism financing (Article 4).[41] To combat terrorism financing the Convention calls upon all States party to it to identify, freeze, seize and confiscate the funds derived from, used for or aimed at, committing one of the offences contemplated by the international instruments on terrorist activities (Article 5).

Other relevant regional instruments are the Arab Convention for the Suppression of Terrorism of 22 April 1998[42] and the Islamic Convention on Combating International Terrorism of 1 July 1999.[43] However, these address the subject only superficially: contracting States are simply called upon to avoid financing terrorism and to prevent the use of their territories to channel resources to terrorists, but are under no precise obligation to block assets connected to terrorists[44] (Article 3 of the Arab Convention and Article 3 of the Islamic Convention).[45] The African Convention on the Prevention and Combating of Terrorism of 14 July 1999,[46] instead, lays

[39] See K Alexander, "United States Financial Sanctions and International Terrorism: Part 2", (2002) *Butterworths Journal of International Banking and Financial Law*, 220–21.
[40] Convention of the American States, see the text in <www.oas.org>.
[41] Other guidelines to take into consideration as appropriate are referred to the Inter-American Drug Abuse Control Commission, the Caribbean Financial Action Task Force, and the South American Financial Action Force.
[42] Convention of the League of the Arab States, see the text in <www.leagueofarabstates.org>.
[43] Convention of the Organisation of the Islamic Conference, see the text in <www.oic.org>.
[44] This absence is particularly regrettable for the Islamic Convention which was adopted after the UN Convention on terrorism financing (above para II A 1).
[45] However, what is significant, and ends up impairing the effectiveness of these regional instruments, is constituted by the defence of the struggle against foreign occupation and aggression, which excluding freedom movements from the Conventions will restrict their range of application (Article 2.a of the Arab Convention and Article 2.a of the Islamic Convention).
[46] Convention of the Organization of African Unity, see the text in <www.oua.org>.

down a precise obligation to seize and confiscate funds used, or intended, for terrorist acts (Article 5.b).[47]

C. The United States Legislation

Predictably, the United States of America was the first country to adopt legislation blocking terrorist assets following the events of September 11. On 23 September 2001, a few days before the adoption of Security Council Resolution 1373 (2001) but when this was already in preparation, President GW Bush signed Executive Order 13224 "Blocking property and prohibiting transactions with persons who commit, threaten to commit, or support terrorism" (the "Order").[48]

The Order, which entered into force on the following day, was enacted under the authority vested in the President by the Constitution and by the specific and detailed statutes (often resorted to also in the past) which empower the President to adopt this type of measure.[49] The Order is considerably more far-reaching than the UN Resolutions and, as will be discussed, gives rise to considerable controversy with other States.

1. *The Scope of Executive Order 13224*

Although directly targeted against the terrorist organisations linked to the September 11 events, the Order is worded quite broadly, thus making it applicable to other terrorist activities (the Order refers expressly to "grave acts of terrorism ... including the terrorist attacks in New York"). This is a significant expansion with respect to earlier Executive Orders which were focused on specific terrorist organisations, such as the Taliban.[50]

[47] Nevertheless, even here there is incorporated a defence for struggle for liberation and self-determination against colonialism, occupation, aggression and domination by foreign forces (Article 3.1).

[48] In 50 USC 1791.

[49] Mainly, the International Emergency Economic Powers Act (50 USC 1701 *et seq*), the National Emergencies Act (50 USC 1601 *et seq*) and sec 301, title 3 of the USC. Under those Acts the President is allowed to use specific powers only with respect to a particular threat upon the declaration of a national emergency (see MP Malloy, "Embargo Programs of the United States Treasury Department", (1981) 20 *Columbia Journal of Transnational Law*, 495). The September 11 attack was considered a new threat with respect to the previous terrorist assaults and justified the enactment of a new order (see SD Murphy, "Contemporary Practice of the United States Relating to International Law", (2002) 96 *American Journal of International Law*, 241–42).

[50] Executive Order 13099 enacted in 1998 by President Clinton provided for the freeze of the US assets connected to Osama bin Laden and to persons related to him. However, this Order achieved no substantial effect since these had no assets in the US. The following year President Clinton issued Executive Order 13129 imposing the freeze of all Taliban property in the US. The last measure led to the freeze of several assets in the US (see Center for Defense Information, *The Financial War against Terrorism* (Washington, 2001) 2).

Pursuant to the Order, a terrorist offence is an activity involving "a violent act or an act dangerous to human life, property or infrastructure" and appearing to be intended "to intimidate or coerce civilian population, to influence the policy of a government by intimidation or coercion, or to affect the conduct of a government by mass destruction, assassination, kidnapping or hostage-taking" (sec. 3).[51]

The Order is aimed at blocking all property and interests in property located in the United States or which subsequently comes to that country or into the possession or control of United States persons (sec. 1). These persons belong to different categories. The first one includes foreign persons directly connected with the acts of September 11 and listed in the annex to the Order (sec. 1.a). The second category embraces foreign persons to be identified by the Secretary of State (in consultation with the Secretary of the Treasury and the Attorney General) who have committed or are likely to commit acts of terrorism threatening US citizens, national security or economy and foreign policy (sec. 1.b). The third category includes persons — not necessarily foreigners — identified by the Secretary of the Treasury (in consultation with the Secretary of State and the Attorney General) that are owned or controlled by, or act on behalf of, persons subject to the Order (sec. 1.c).[52] The final category includes persons — nationals and foreigners — identified by the Secretary of the Treasury (in consultation with the Secretary of State and the Attorney General and, if appropriate, with foreign authorities) who assist, sponsor or provide financial, material or technological support or financial services for terrorist acts or for persons identified under the Order or associated with such persons (sec. 1.d).

In addition to freezing their assets, the Order forbids any additional funding to such persons. Sec. 2 prohibits any transaction or dealing in property or in interests in blocked property, including the making or receiving of funds to, or for the benefit of, the persons determined in sec. 1.[53] The prohibition goes so far as to include any transaction that avoids or evades, or seeks to avoid or to evade or attempts to violate, the prohibitions.

[51] Sec. 3. See HE Sheppard, "U.S. Actions to Freeze Assets of Terrorism: Manifest and Latent Implications for Latin America", (2002) 17 *American University International Law Review*, 625. The definition of terrorism is broader than that embodied in Article 2 of the UN Convention on terrorism financing and this difference may give rise to controversy with other countries.

[52] More precisely, pursuant to the wording of the sec. 1.c, those are persons (individual or entities) owned or controlled by, or acting on the behalf of, persons listed in the annex, persons committing or being likely to commit terrorist acts, persons assisting or providing financial or material support to persons determined in the Order, or persons owned or controlled by, or acting on the behalf of such persons.

[53] The term "making or receiving fund" is to be construed in a broad manner, so as to include even donations of articles, such as food, clothes and medicines. See sec. 2 of the Order and sec. 1702.b.2 of 50 USC.

The obligation to freeze the assets applies if the prohibited acts are carried out by any person in the US or by US persons anywhere. This would seem to exclude acts carried out abroad by foreigners. However, having regard to the wording of sec. 2.c even foreign persons abroad could be caught to the extent that they appear to be associated with persons listed subject to the Order or to be involved in a conspiracy to violate the prohibitions laid down in sec. 2.[54] This is particularly significant for foreign financial institutions not cooperating in freezing terrorist assets, as their resources and their transactions in the US can be blocked.[55]

2. *The Enforcement of the Executive Order*

The implementation of the Order depends on rules and regulations to be adopted by the Secretary of the Treasury in consultation with the Secretary of State and the Attorney General (sec. 7), as well as on pre-existing rules and regulations set forth in the Code of Federal Regulations (sec. 8). The inclusion in the list of persons whose assets are to be frozen occurs at the initiative of the Office of Foreign Assets Control (OFAC) of the Department of the Treasury,[56] as well as of the Department of State under the Antiterrorism and Effective Death Penalty Act of 1996 (ADEPA).[57] However, the latter piece of legislation is unlikely to be much resorted to as it is not broad enough to permit the freezing of assets of persons other than terrorists.[58]

[54] The Federal Conspiracy Statute has extraterritorial effect. See 18 USC 371.

[55] Unless they cooperate by sharing information and freezing funds, foreign banks are denied of doing business in the US; see JM Myers, "Disrupting Terrorist Networks: The New U.S. and International Regime for Halting Terrorist Funding", (2002) 34 *Law & Policy in International Business*, 18. See below, para. III.B.3.

[56] So far, OFAC has not issued any regulation specifically implementing the Order. As a result, pre-existing regulations are used, ie those embodied in chapter V "Office of Foreign Assets Control, Department of the Treasury" of title 31 "Money and Finance: Treasury" of the Code of Federal Regulation (CFR). The most relevant pieces of that Chapter are part 595 "Terrorism Sanctions Regulations" and part 597 "Foreign Terrorists Organisations Sanctions Regulations". Both the parts are to be considered, since the Order targets both individuals and entities.

[57] In 8 USC 1189.

[58] An act of designation made under the ADEPA is more likely to be challenged than an act made under the Order. The evidence is given by the conclusions drawn by the 5th Circuit Court in *Paradiossitis v Rubin* (171 F. 3d 983 (1999)) where the claim of the appellant was dismissed on the assumption that a bill of attainder is only applicable to legislative acts and not to administrative measures. More generally, lower courts tend to refrain from reviewing OFAC decisions arguing that they are expression of the foreign policy and national security of the country. On the contrary, ADEPA classifications result legally and constitutionally more questionable as they imply heavier sanctions than the mere blocking measures envisaged by the Order. See R Leher, 'Unbalancing the Terrorists, Checkbook: Analysis of U.S. Policy in Its Economic War on International Terrorism', in (2002) 10 *Tulane Journal of International and Comparative Law*, 342–352.

The Order is addressed to any holder of the relevant assets. Financial institutions are required to freeze immediately any account in their possession or control connected to any listed person or entity as well as any additional asset coming into their possession, and immediately thereafter must file a report with the OFAC Compliance Programs Division.[59] The reporting requirement extends to any transfers received and blocked by the financial institutions[60] and even to the transfer of funds that are not frozen, but the processing of which would nevertheless undermine a prohibition set forth in the Order.[61]

Once an account or an asset is blocked, payments, transfers, withdrawals or any other dealings — including set-off — may no longer be made unless authorized by OFAC.[62] Therefore, any transfer in violation of the prohibitions set forth in the Order or in the CFR or in other acts is null and void and cannot constitute the basis for the assertion of any right concerning the frozen funds or assets. Nevertheless, payments of funds or transfers of credits into a blocked account in a US bank are generally authorised, provided that those payments come from another frozen account of the same persons within the same US financial institution.[63] Likewise, entries in a blocked account for ordinary service charges are normally authorized. The authorizations can be in the form of a general licence or a specific licence. General licences are usually provided in regulations issued pursuant to the relevant executive orders, while specific licences are granted on a case-by-case basis by OFAC.[64]

[59] Banks are required to appoint officers responsible for compliance with the prohibitions and for managing the frozen funds. See Department of Treasury, *Foreign Assets Control Regulations for the Financial Community* (Washington, 2002), 3.

[60] Initial report on blocked property shall describe the account party, any existing or new account number, the name of the holder, along with the number of a contact person of the institution involved. If the report points out the receipt of a payment or transfer of blocked funds, it shall also include a photocopy of the payment or transfer instructions and the details of the new or existing account where the payment has been deposited. The account where the sums are placed shall be set up in the name of the individual or the entity whose assets are blocked (31 CFR 501.603).

[61] In this case the financial institution shall reject the transfer and the report must contain the bases of the rejection. See 31 CFR 501.604.

[62] See 31 CFR 595.201 and 31 CFR 597.201. The banking industry has developed software to intercept prohibited transfers of funds. When the system identifies a name appearing in an OFAC list the transfer is rejected and the operation is reported to a reviewer. Although the use of these systems is supported by OFAC, it does not constitute a defence in civil penalty proceedings in the event of breach of the prohibitions on the transfers. See Department of Treasury, *Foreign Assets Control Regulations for the Financial Community*, above n 59, 3.

[63] See 31 CFR 595.503 and 31 CFR 597.503. The transfers can occur only within the US. That excludes any transfer in a blocked account held in a foreign branch of a US financial institution.

[64] For a comparison with the measures adopted in connection with the Gulf crisis, see DL Bethlehem (ed), *The Kuwait Crisis: Sanctions and their Economic Consequences. Part I*, (Grotius Publications, Cambridge, 1991), 426.

It is not always easy to refer a financial transaction to persons identified in sec. 2 of the Order. It is true that pursuant to US banking regulations specific circumstances financial institutions can be required to report to the Government any transfer of money.[65] Terrorist organisations often resort to complex systems of multiple transfer, such as *hawala* to circumvent the prohibitions and to avoid identification.[66] For this reason in 1990 the Department of the Treasury established the Financial Crimes Enforcement Network (FinCEN)[67] to create a link between law enforcement and financial institutions to share information on suspicious transactions.[68] As a result, financial institutions are required to report dubious transactions on a Suspicious Activity Report (SAR).[69] FinCEN has identified certain elements and types of transactions that can be associated with terrorism funding.[70]

Non-compliance with the Order — ie failing to retain control over funds related to terrorists or to report the existence of such funds — is sanctioned by OFAC by civil penalties or criminal sanctions.[71]

Since the freeze is only a temporary measure, frozen assets cannot be disposed of prior to a proper forfeiture which allows their utilisation in the interest of and for the benefit of the United States.[72]

[65] See 31 USC 5313, 5315, 5316 and 5331.
[66] See above n 37.
[67] The FinCEC must, *inter alia*, advise and make recommendations on financial criminal activities, manage a data access service on the basis of information collected by it, identify criminal activities and trends in financial crimes, constitute a financial crimes information center; see 31 USC 310 and B Zagaris and S Castilla, "Construing an International Financial Subregime: The Implementation of Anti-Laundering Policy", (1993) 19 *Brooklyn Journal of International Law*, 871.
[68] The USA Patriot Act 2001 provides for an exchange of information both between financial institutions and the government and among financial institutions themselves (sec. 314). The link between FinCEN and OFAC is now assured by the recently established Foreign Terrorist Asset Tracking Center (FTATC), whose tasks are, *inter alia*, to enhance inter-agency cooperation and to identify terrorist financial networks. See *Treasury News*, October, 2001. The operational and investigative arm of OFAC, FinCEN and FTATC, is the Operation Green Quest, a multi-agency initiative concocted to target current and future terrorism funding.
[69] Banks and other financial institutions are required to report any suspicious transaction involving at least US $ 5,000. The report shall be filed directly with the Treasury Department or indirectly with the FinCEN, through the SAR (31 CFR 103.18). Since 1 January 2003 those rules apply even to transactions made by brokers and dealers.
[70] To assist the financial community in identifying dubious transactions, the FinCEN issues a bulletin (SAR Bulletin) providing some indicators likely to connect those transactions to terrorist financial activities.
[71] 31 CFR 595.701 and 31 CFR 597.701 (see also 50 USC 1705.a and b). See Department of Treasury, *Foreign Assets Control Regulations for the Financial Community*, above n 59, 2.
[72] Forfeiture, in this case, may be ordered by the President under 50 USC 1702.a.1.C. Frozen terrorist assets could be used to compensate the victims of terrorism or their relatives. See S Foster, "An American Inquiry into Contemporary Terrorist Accountability", (2002) 6 *Texas Review of Law and Politics*, 527–31.

D. The European Union

The UN Resolutions dealing with terrorism financing have been implemented in the European legal order within the framework of both the Treaty on the European Union (TEU) and the Treaty establishing the European Community (TEC).[73] The EU and EC actions, which address different aspects of terrorism and closely mirror the Resolutions, give particular importance to the freezing of terrorists' assets.[74]

1. *The Afghanistan-Taliban Regulations*

The first EU action following UN Resolution 1267 (1999) was Council Common Position 1999/727 adopted pursuant to Article 15 TEU which blocked Taliban financial resources.[75] Since these measures were considered to fall within the scope of the EC Treaty, the terms of the Common Position were translated into a piece of Community legislation based on Articles 60 and 301 TEC, ie Council Regulation 337/2000 on the freeze of funds and other financial resources of persons designated by the UN Taliban Committee.[76] Further to UN Resolution 1333 (2000) a new Common Position (2001/154) was adopted to freeze the funds of, and to prohibit financials transactions with, Osama bin Laden and persons associated with him.[77] At EC level Regulation 337/2000 was replaced by Regulation 467/2001[78] prohibiting nationals and legal persons of Member States (Article 15) from channeling any additional resources to persons included in the list maintained by the Taliban Committee (Article 2.2) as

[73] Implementation of the UN Resolutions at EU level occurs by means of a Common position (Second Pillar), defining the common approach of the EU on a particular issue, which Member States are required to respect. When the subject matter falls within the purview of the EC a regulation can be adopted to guarantee a uniform implementation within the Member States, although Member States remain responsible for any complementary actions which may be required. See S Bohr, "Sanctions by United Nations Security Council and the European Community", (1993) 4 *European Journal of International Law*, 256 and L Benoit, "La lutte contre le terrorisme dans le cadre du deuxième pilier: un nouveau volet des relations extérieures de l'Union européenne", (2002) *Revue du droit de l'Union européenne*, n. 2, 283.

[74] The legal basis for Community legislation in this field is Article 301 EC (formerly Article 228 A). This provision has been used as a legal basis for asset freezes for Council Regulation (EC) n. 2471/94 of 10 October 1994 (*OJEC* L 266/1 of 30 October 1994) relating to Bosnia-Herzegovina; Council Regulation (EC) n. 2488/2000 of 10 November 2000 (*OJEC* L 287/19 of 14 November 2000), in relation to the funds of Mr Milosevic and persons associated with him; Council Regulation (EC) n. 1081/2000 of 22 May 2000 (*OJEC* L 122/29 of 24 May 2000) in relation to Burma/Myanmar; Council Regulation (EC) n. 310/2002 of 18 February 2002 (*OJEC* L 50/4 of 21 February 2002) concerning Zimbabwe; and Council Regulation (EC) n. 1210/2003 of 7 July 2003 (*OJEC* L 169/6 of 8 July 2003) concerning Iraq.

[75] *OJEC* L 294/1 of 16 November 1999.

[76] *OJEC* L 43/1 of 16 February 2000.

[77] *OJEC* L 57/1 of 27 February 2001.

[78] *OJEC* L 67/1 of 9 March 2001.

well as from taking part in any ancillary activities directly or indirectly intended to finance them (Article 8).

These Common Position and Regulation were in turn replaced respectively by Common Position 2001/402[79] and by Regulation 881/2002,[80] implementing UN Resolution 1390 (2002). Regulation 881/2002 significantly expanded the category of assets subject to the freeze, to include any economic resource (Article 1), and of persons subject to the prohibition, to include legal persons, groups and entities doing business within the Community (Article 11).

To permit the monitoring of compliance with Regulation 881/2002 all natural or legal persons, namely banks and other financial institutions, are required to report any information on blocked funds to the competent national authorities and to the European Commission (Article 5).[81] The Commission plays an important role in the enforcement of the freezing system since it is responsible for updating by means of regulations the list of persons, attached to Regulation 881, whose assets are to be frozen and with whom transactions are prohibited, drawing on the indications of the UN Security Council or of the Taliban Committee, with which it maintains regular contacts (Article 7).

The EC is not competent to set the nature and the amount of the sanctions for the infringement of the Regulation, as these fall within the competence of Member States. However, under the general principles of Community law the sanctions must be effective, proportionate and dissuasive to ensure a level playing field for the enforcement of the Regulation.[82] Member States are responsible for bringing proceedings against any person or entity under their jurisdiction who infringes the Regulation (Article 13).[83]

2. *The Regulations on International Terrorism Financing*

The EU's second line of action against terrorism financing is the implementation of UN Resolution 1373 (2001) which, as mentioned above, does not provide for a mechanism for the designation of persons whose assets

[79] *OJEC* L 139/4 of 29 May 2002.
[80] *OJEC* L 139/9 of 29 May 2002.
[81] The reports to the Commission may be filed directly or through national authorities (Article 3.1.a). The information collected by the Commission is turned to the relevant national authorities and to the EU Council (Article 3.3).
[82] See *Commission v Greece*, case 68/88, [1989] *ECR*, 2979. In the case at hand national authorities do not enjoy much discretion as to the type of sanction since Article 4 of the UN Convention for the suppression of the financing of terrorism and para. 2.e of UN Resolution 1373 require States to make the financing of terrorism a criminal offence.
[83] The differences in the criteria for personal and territorial jurisdiction could lead to conflicts of jurisdiction between Member States. See Article 31.d TEU.

are to be blocked such as the one of Resolutions 1267 (1999) and 1333 (2000).[84]

The first step is constituted by Common Position 2001/930,[85] a faithful transposition of Resolution 1373 (2001),[86] followed by Common Position 2001/931[87] calling upon the EC to freeze terrorist funds and to forbid Member States nationals and residents from making funds available to terrorists and to related persons or entities (Articles 2 and 3), and upon Member States to develop police and judicial cooperation within the Third Pillar (Article 4). With this perspective Common Position 931 establishes a list of persons whose assets are to be frozen (Article 1.4).[88]

To implement Articles 2 and 3 of Common Position 2001/931[89] and to ensure a homogeneous application of UN Resolution 1373 within the Member States[90] the Council adopted Regulation 2580/2001.[91] This Regulation, which applies within the territory of the Community to nationals of Member States and to any entity established under the law of a Member State and to anyone doing business in the Community (Article 10), restates the obligation of Common Position 2001/931 to freeze the funds, financial assets or resources belonging to, owned or otherwise held by, the persons designed by the Council (Article 2.1) and to prohibit the making in any way available to such those persons of funds,

[84] See above para. II.A.3.

[85] *OJEC* L 344/90 of 28 December 2001. This Common Position is based both on the Second Pillar (Article 15 TEU) and on the Third Pillar (Article 34 TEU).

[86] Accordingly the Common Position requires the criminalization of the willful collection of funds to terrorists (Article 1), freezing of terrorists assets (Article 2); the prohibition of making funds available to terrorists (Article 3), the denying of safe harbor to terrorists (Article 6); the bringing to justice of persons involved in financing terrorism (Article 8); the adhesion to the UN Convention on financing terrorism (Article 14).

[87] *OJEC* L 344/93 of 28 November 2001.

[88] The list specifies which persons fall in both EC and JHA domains and which ones are subject to Article 4 only.

[89] Article 4 of the Common Position was implemented by Council Framework Decision n. 2003/577/JHA of 22 July 2003 on the execution in the European Union of orders freezing property or evidence (*OJEC* L 196/45 of 8 August 2003).

[90] National legislation implementing UN Resolutions was complementary to Regulation 2580/2001 and in some cases even preceded it. The adoption of national freezing measures before the enactment of the regulation is permitted under Article 60.2 TEC (unilateral urgent measures on movement of capitals for political reasons) and under Article 297 TEC (obligations concerning the maintenance of peace and international security). In Italy Decree-Law n. 369/2001 providing for urgent measures to combat terrorism was enacted on 12 October 2001 and subsequently converted on 14 December 2001 in the Law n. 431/2001 (in *Gazzetta Ufficiale* n. 290 of 14 December 2001).

[91] Council Regulation (EC) n. 2580/2001 of 27 December 2001 on specific restrictive measures directed against certain persons and entities with a view to combating terrorism, *OJEC* L 344/70 of 28 December 2001. The Regulation explicitly excludes form its domain persons and groups covered by UN Resolutions 1267 (1999) and 1333 (2000), already falling in the domain of Regulation 467/2001.

financial assets and economic resources.[92] Increments on accounts are allowed but must be frozen (Article 5.1).

The list of persons caught by the prohibition is decided by the Council which can review and amend it acting by unanimity.[93] The list must include natural and legal persons or other groups or entities committing or attempting to commit, or simply participating in or facilitating the commission of, any act of terrorism; legal persons, groups or entities owned or controlled by these persons; and natural or legal persons, groups or entities acting on behalf of or under the direction of natural, legal persons, groups or entities committing or attempting to commit, participating or facilitating terrorist acts (Article 2.3).[94]

Once frozen, the funds cannot be transferred. Nonetheless, the competent authorities of Member States may grant specific authorizations on the conditions they deem appropriate to satisfy the basic human needs of the persons concerned or their families, and for the payment of taxes, fees for public utilities, charges for the maintenance of the account, and payments under obligations arisen before the entry into force of the Regulation, but only into a blocked account in the Community (Article 5.2–3).

Likewise, Member State authorities are allowed to terminate the freeze of funds, to make funds available to the persons designated by the Council and to provide financial services to such persons when this is justified by a balancing of the interests of the Community (including those of residents and citizens) against the interest of the fight against international terrorism (Article 6).[95] A national authority receiving a request for such an authorization must inform the national authorities of other Member States, the Commission and the Council of the grounds for the

[92] Member States are called upon to ban any activity intended to avoid the prescription embodied in Article 2 (Article 3.1). The infringement of those prohibitions will be punished by sanctions effective proportionate and dissuasive (Article 9).

[93] With this perspective, it is important to stress that the list drawn up by the EU Council is formed not only on the basis of a UN Security Council identification, but also on the grounds of decisions taken by any other competent authority (not necessarily a Member State authority). Acting under this provision, the EU Council enjoys a certain amount of discretion in identifying persons to enlist (see Article 1.4 of Common Position 2001/931). See below, para. III.C.2.

[94] The list of the persons envisaged in the provision in issue is definitely less inclusive than that laid down the US Executive Order (see below, para. III.B.3). It may contain even persons or entities linked or related to third countries as well as persons representing the focus of Common Position 2001/931 (14th Recital of Regulation 2580). In practice Council decisions substantially reproduce the list established and further amended by relevant Common Positions, with the exception of persons merely interested by JHA measures (above n 88). To draw a comparison see the list attached to CFSP 931 and the initial list embodied in Council Decision n. 2001/927 of 27 December 2001 (*OJEC* L 344/83 of 28 December 2001).

[95] This approach differs from the one of Regulation 881/2002 under which exemptions are granted by the Taliban Committee.

rejection or for the granting of the authorization and of any conditions appended thereto (Article 6.2).[96]

The European legislation sets considerable store on co-operation between Member States and between these and the European institutions. Article 4 of Regulation 2580/2001 (like Article 5 of Regulation 881/2002) requires financial institutions to communicate all relevant information regarding frozen accounts and exemptions to the competent authorities of the State where they are located, which must then pass it on to the Commission; the latter, in turn, must deliver any information to the authorities of the Member States concerned and to the Council.[97] All the information concerning the circumvention of the Regulation is to be transmitted to the competent national authorities and to the Commission (Article 3.2).[98]

III. SOME ISSUES RAISED BY INTERNATIONAL AND NATIONAL INSTRUMENTS

The national and international instruments providing for the freeze of terrorist assets discussed in the foregoing section raised several thorny issues some of which deserve to be addressed here.

A. The UN System

1. *The Two Approaches to the Identification of the Persons whose Assets can be Frozen*

A first issue relates to the methods for the identification of the persons whose assets are to be frozen. On this point the UN Resolutions provide for two different systems.

The first one, which is specific to the Taliban threat, imposes upon States an obligation to freeze the assets of individually identified persons included in a list maintained and updated by the UN itself through the Taliban Committee. The second one, which addresses international

[96] A national authority intending to grant an authorization must take into account the remarks of the Commission, the Council and other Member States (Article 6.2).

[97] Under Regulation 881/2002 the Council is not informed since it is not the designating body.

[98] In the 10th recital of Regulation 2580 it is clearly stated that the establishing of an adequate system of information is aimed at preventing phenomena of circumvention of the Regulation. A general duty to inform is then laid down at Article 8, pursuant to which both the Member States and the Commission and the Council are to share each other all the relevant information, including violation and enforcement matters or judgments.

terrorism in general, is more limited in scope in that it requires States to cooperate on a bilateral basis in enforcing their respective freezing orders.

This difference is due to the lack of a clear notion of international terrorism in international law. Although there are conventions which criminalize specific terrorist activities[99] and a fairly broad definition is contained in the Convention for the suppression of the financing of terrorism (Article 2.1)[100] and in Resolution 1373,[101] there is still no consensus on a proper definition of the term, mostly because of the difficulty in drawing a distinction between international terrorism and freedom movements.[102]

In the case of the Taliban, Al-Qaeda and Osama bin Laden, there was a broad agreement as to the terrorist qualification of the persons and activities involved. Since it was these which were specifically targeted by the UN Resolutions, it was not difficult to reach a general agreement also on the persons whose assets had to be frozen, and it was thus possible to establish the mechanism of the Taliban Committee to identify such persons.

This option was not available when the principle of freezing terrorist assets was extended generally by Resolution 1373.[103] Absent a clear

[99] Convention on Offences and Certain Other Acts Committed on Board Aircraft (1963); Convention for Suppression of Unlawful Seizure of Aircraft (1970); Convention for the Suppression of Unlawful Acts Against the Safety of Civil Aviation (1971); Convention on the Prevention and Punishment of Crimes Against Internationally Protected Persons (1973); International Convention Against the Taking of Hostages (1979); Convention on the Physical Protection of Nuclear Material (1980); Convention for the Suppression of Unlawful Acts Against the Safety of Maritime Navigation (1988); Convention on the Making of Plastic Explosives for the Purposes of Identification (1991); International Convention for the Suppression of Terrorist Bombing (1998). In <http://untreaty.un.org>.

[100] See above, para. II.A.1.

[101] Resolution 1373 potentially covers all forms of terrorism, including those not addressed by specific Conventions, and imposes precise obligations. However, absent a definition of the term some States can restrict the application of the Resolution thereby frustrating the system of co-operation: see J Trehan, "Terrorism Conventions: Existing Gaps and Different Approaches", (2002) 8 *New England International and Comparative Law Annual*, 240–42.

[102] This is one of the most debated questions within the Ad Hoc Committee which elaborated and adopted on 28 January 2002 the Draft Comprehensive Convention on Terrorism and within the Working Group of the Sixth Committee of the UN General Assembly which is considering the Draft Convention (A/57/37). The members of the Islamic Conference (OIC) raised an exception to exclude from the scope of the Draft Convention the activities of parties to armed conflicts, consistently with the provisions of the Islamic Convention (above para. II.B). Since few terrorist acts are unconnected to armed conflicts this exception could undermine the concrete applicability of the future UN Convention. See M Halberstam, "The Evolution of United Nations Position on Terrorism: From Exempting National Liberation Movements to Criminalizing Terrorism Whenever and by Whomever Committed", in (2003) 41 *Columbia Journal of Transnational Law*, 577–584. However, if an agreement were reached on the definition of terrorism and this were incorporated in a convention, it would be binding only on the ratifying States, unless it became a matter of customary law.

[103] Resolution 1373 does not define the term, as its main object is to promote capacity-building among member States to fight terrorism: see N Rostow, "Before and After: The Changed UN Response to Terrorism Since September 11th", (2002) 35 *Cornell International Law Journal*, 484.

definition of terrorism and of terrorists, which is thus left essentially to national or regional legislation, it proved impossible to set up a body with powers similar to those of the Taliban Committee.[104] The Counter-Terrorism Committee thus decided to maintain a low profile and to deal simply with the technical aspects of the problem, prompting States to adopt severe legislative measures against terrorism without defining it.[105]

2. *The Working Method of the Taliban Committee*

The identification of the persons whose assets are to be frozen poses problems even with respect to the Taliban despite the existence of the Taliban Committee created *ad hoc* for this purpose. Notwithstanding the general understanding that the Taliban and related entities are terrorist organisations, problems arise in the identification of individual members of these organisations. This is because the most recent version of the Guidelines of the Committee does not contain common substantive rules regarding the insertion or removal of persons on the list.[106]

As mentioned above,[107] the designation of individuals, groups and organisations occurs at the request of a State or a regional organisation on the basis of information provided by the latter which the Committee is called upon to appraise. However, the Committee's powers in this regard are limited because it is under an obligation to deal with requests to update the list expeditiously and on the basis of the information received. The Committee could not thus require further information and must take a decision on a *prima facie* evaluation of the information received.

Owing to the lack at UN level of substantive rules for identifying terrorist and related persons and of procedural rules on the freezing assets each State is essentially free as to how to identify the persons it wishes to have included in the list and as to how to freeze their assets once they have been included, and the Committee has little say as to the criteria underlying the request. This can lead to considerable controversy

[104] Due to the less stringent obligations under Resolution 1373, more country reports were submitted to the Counter-Terrorism Committee than to the Taliban Committee: see E Rosand, "Security Council Resolution 1373, the Counter-Terrorism Committee, and the Fight Against Terrorism", (2003) 97 *American Journal of International Law*, 337.

[105] The down-side of this neutral and pragmatic approach is that is taken by some States as a justification for the repression of oppositions. To avoid this States are required to respect human rights in the fight against terrorism in accordance with the recommendations of the Declaration attached to Security Council Resolution 1456 (2003); see M Lippman, "The New Terrorism and International Law", (2003) 10 *Tulsa Journal of Comparative & International Law*, 365.

[106] The new Guidelines were adopted in November 2002 at the request of the French and Swedish Governments following the case of the Somali born Swedish citizens (see the following paragraph).

[107] See above, para. II.A.3 *in fine*.

within the Committee, or the Security Council if the decision is referred to it for lack of consensus within the Committee, because of diverging views between the States on the criteria for the designation of terrorists and on the procedural guarantees for the freeze. Controversy can arise also with respect to the removal from the list when the decision is referred to the Security Council failing the consensus within the Committee.

The effect of the voting system is that at the first stage a decision of insertion or removal can be blocked by any member of the Committee, while upon referral to the Security Council the decision can be blocked by the veto of permanent members.[108]

3. *The Problems of Extraterritorial Enforcement of Freezes*

Absent a shared definition of terrorism in international law, the United States attempt to enforce their freezing orders globally relying on a broad definition under their domestic law, but this strategy encounters resistance by other States.

An example is the US attempt to enforce in Lebanon a freezing order against the Hezbollah invoking the spirit of cooperation underlying Resolution 1373. The request was rejected by the Lebanese authorities on the grounds that the Hezbollah could not be considered a terrorist group, a position shared by other States.[109] This position is theoretically admissible because many organisations have a borderline character, with a charitable and political wing and a more radical one without the two being easily distinguishable.[110] Nevertheless, it underscores the need for a clear distinction between national freedom movements and terrorist organisations in the context of the fight against the financing of terrorism.[111]

The difficulty in identifying terrorists and persons associated with them in connection with the Taliban is evidenced by a US attempt to

[108] Since the matter falls under Chapter VII of the Charter, the duty of States party to the dispute to abstain from voting on Security Council resolutions does not apply. This confers a veto right on any decision on all permanent members, particularly the US which are particularly prone to enforce their freezing orders abroad.

[109] The Lebanese authorities objected that the Hezbollah had been designated by the US and not by the UN, that the request was not based on criminal evidence and that there were no bilateral agreements with the US. However, the main argument was that UN has not dealt with the difference between terrorism and the freedom movements. See AD Hardister, "Can We Buy Peace on Earth? The Price of Freezing Terrorist Assets in a Post-September 11 World", (2003) 28 *North Carolina Journal of International Law and Commercial Regulation*, 642–48.

[110] In support of the applicability of Resolution 1373 to the non-armed ramifications of these organisations it can be argued that, while not participating in terrorist activities, they are nevertheless involved in collecting and channeling funds to the more operative wings: M Levitt, "Iraq, U.S., and the War on Terror: Stemming the Flow of Terrorist Financing: Practical and Conceptual Challenges", (2003) 27 *Fletcher Forum of World Affairs*, 64–65.

[111] Above n 102.

enforce multilaterally, via the Taliban Committee,[112] a freeze against Somali born Swedish citizens whose names had been inserted in the list maintained by OFAC and which the US agreed to remove from the list only after considerable criticism from other States.[113] This dispute contributed to reveal the defects of the US system for the identification of terrorists which may lead to serious debate with States which place greater emphasis on the rule of law in fighting terrorism funding.[114]

4. *The Sanctions for Failure to Co-operate*

One further issue relates to the consequences of the failure by a State to comply with the freezing orders of other States. The answer varies depending on the UN Resolutions on which the orders are based.

With regard to the Taliban, as mentioned above States are required to freeze the assets of the persons on the list maintained by the Committee. In the event of failure by a State to comply, the Security Council could adopt measures not implying the use of force pursuant to Article 41 of the Charter. What is less clear is to what extent this failure would justify the recourse to self-defence under Article 51 of the Charter.[115] To date this right has been invoked by the United States for the armed campaign against the Taliban regime in Afghanistan following the events of September 11.[116] Should States other than the former Taliban Afghanistan

[112] Zagaris and Castilla, above n 67, 80–82.

[113] The US Government transmitted to the Taliban Committee the names of three Somali-born Swedish citizens it had placed on the OFAC list requesting that the freeze be enforced in Sweden. The affected persons contested the measure, alleging the absence of contacts with terrorists. The Swedish Government requested information from the US to determine whether those persons had engaged in terrorist funding. The US Government dismissed the request claiming that the disclosure of such information would endanger national security. Eventually, Sweden froze the assets, as it was required to do under the Security Council Resolutions concerning the Taliban but this decision was challenged before the Swedish courts. See Alexander, above n 39, 218–19. The persons in question submitted a complaint to the European Court of Human Rights (see below, para. III.C.2).

[114] See below, para. III.B.1.

[115] The right of self-defence operates even with respect of categories of persons other than those indicated in the UN Resolutions: see below para. III.B.3. According to Article 21 of the *Draft Articles on Responsibility of States for internationally wrongful acts* (A/CN.4/L.602.1), the "the wrongfulness of an act of a State is precluded if the act constitutes a lawful measure of self-defence taken in conformity with the Charter of the United Nations" (J Crawford, *The International Law Commission's Articles on State Responsibility* (Cambridge University Press, Cambridge, 2002), 166–67).

[116] The military expedition to Aghanistan was regarded as lawful under Security Council Resolutions 1373 and 1368 in consideration of the strict relationship between the Taliban and Al-Qaeda: J Delbrück, "The Fight Against Global Terrorism: Self-Defense or Collective Security as International Police Action? Some Comments on the International Legal Implications of the 'War Against Terrorism'", (2001) 44 *German Yearbook of International Law*, 13–14. So far, this is the only case in which the assimilation of an aiding State to a terrorist organisation was accepted: see I Bantekas, "The International Law of Terrorist Financing", (2003) 97 *American Journal of International Law*, 317.

refuse to freeze assets connected to the Al-Quaeda, absent a more organic connection, the United States could act in self-defence — proportionally — resorting to measures not implying the use of force.[117] As the right of self-defence has been recognised only in favour of the United States, other States can react against those non-freezing States by adopting counter-measures, but only if the Security Council were unable to sanction such non-cooperative behavior because of the exercise of the veto rights.[118]

The matter is more complex with regard to a failure to comply with the Resolutions on the financing of international terrorism in general. The refusal by a State to cooperate with other States in the fight against the financing of terrorism could justify the adoption by the Security Council of measures under Article 41 of the Charter.[119] However, although under para 8 of Resolution 1373 the Security Council is entitled to adopt all steps for the implementation of the Resolution, the absence of a definition of terrorism in international law could lead to a stalemate within the Security Council.

Consequently some States, foremost amongst which the United States, could rely on a broad definition of terrorism to push for a worldwide enforcement of their domestic freezing orders, whilst others which adopt a more restrictive definition could refuse to give effect to these.[120] In the event of such a disagreement, and failing any action by the UN, the States requiring enforcement could adopt retaliatory measures against non-complying States.[121] The point is whether these could take the form of counter-measures or simply of acts of retorsion. On the assumption that terrorism financing is contrary to the principles and purposes of the Charter, as would seem to be indicated by the Resolution, and that consequently States are obliged to freeze terrorist assets, even

[117] In this case such a measure could be regarded as a kind of anticipatory self-defense; see I Brownlie, *Principles of Public International Law*, 6th edn, (Oxford University Press, Oxford, 2003), 713–14.

[118] From a substantive point of view the characterization of an act of reprisal as self-defence or as a counter-measure is not always clear. Nevertheless, the distinction becomes more understandable on considering that in the case of self-defence third States can act under collective self-defence together with the injured State; while in case of a counter-measure, third States can support the injured State just by means of an act of retorsion. On the differences between counter-measures and self-defence, see P Malanczuk, "Countermeasures and self-defense as circumstances precluding wrongfulness in the International Law Commission's draft Articles on State responsibility", in M Spinedi and B Simma (eds), *United Nations Codification on State Responsibility* (Oceana Publications, New York, 1987), 213, 270–72.

[119] Such a resolution should require the explicit or implied consent of all the permanent members of the Security Council: Bantekas, above n 116, 328.

[120] Hardister, above n 109, 629–31.

[121] The US reaction to a refusal to enforce a freeze is to be regarded as a counter-measure and not as an act of self-defence, as the latter is deemed inapplicable to situations other than the Taliban threat (see above in the text).

counter-measures would be lawful.[122] However, the lack of consensus on the definition of terrorism and the difficulty in identifying the persons associated with terrorists could cast in doubt the lawfulness of such measures.[123] Thus a prudent approach is that States intending to retaliate against a refusal by other States to enforce their freezing orders should confine themselves to an act of retorsion in order to preserve the harmony of the international relations.

B. The US Legislation

1. *The Due Process Clause*

A first problem of the measures providing for the freezes under US law relates to the Due Process Clause of the Fifth Amendment to the Constitution, according to which property rights cannot be taken away without constitutionally adequate procedures.[124]

Following the September 11 events this right has been considerably limited. This is not so much a problem with regard to persons with a weak constitutional presence in the US, ie having contacts with the US but not being within the US territory, because with respect to these the President's competence in matters of foreign policy can override the Fifth Amendment.[125] More problems arise with regard to US citizens and to foreign citizens having a constitutional presence in the US, ie persons who enter the US and develop therein a substantial connection.[126] With regard to these the Due Process Clause can be suspended for reasons of national emergency, which include the events of September 11. Since funds or assets can be transferred immediately, sec. 10 of the Order suspends the obligation to give prior notice to persons to be inserted in the

[122] According to Article 22 of the *Draft Articles on Responsibility of States for internationally wrongful acts*, above n 115, the wrongfulness of an act in violation of an international obligation is precluded if the act is a counter-measure: Crawford, above n 115, 168–69.

[123] An unlawful counter-measure can justify — on the same ground of Article 22 of the above mentioned *Draft Articles on Responsibility of States* — a lawful reaction by the target State.

[124] The Due Process Clause (*USCA, Amendment V.*) includes the right to receive notice, the right to a formal hearing, the confrontation of evidence and the right to a just compensation for the taking of property: see PL Fitzgerald, "If Property Rights Were Treated Like Human Rights, They Could Never Get Away With This. Blacklisting and Due Process in US Economic Sanctions Programs", (1999) 51 *Hastings Law Journal*, 105–6.

[125] The Administration can deny due process in a confiscation to persons having little constitutional presence: see *US v Pink*, 315 US 203 (1942).

[126] Foreign persons without property in the US or in a US financial institution enjoy no constitutional rights. See *People Mojahedin Org. of Iran v US Department of State*, in 182 F.3d 17 (1999); however, Congress can grant protection even in these cases. See R Colgate Selden, "The Executive Protection: Freezing the Financial Assets of Alleged Terrorists, the Constitution, and Foreign Participation in US Financial Markets", (2003) 8 *Fordham Journal of Corporate and Financial Law*, 525.

OFAC list;[127] and, designated persons have no right of access to the evidence underlying their inclusion in the list. Moreover, this evidence is often constituted by soft intelligence and not by verifiable sources and the freeze orders are adopted by an administrative authority and subject only to limited judicial review.[128] With this perspective, the lawfulness of individual freeze orders should be assessed case-by-case based on a balance between the intensity of the national emergency and the constitutional rights at stake.[129]

2. *The Personal Scope of the Order*

As regards the personal scope of the Order, this affects both US and foreign individuals and entities (sec. 3, a and b). The term "US person" is defined broadly. Under sec. 3.c it encompasses US citizens, permanent resident aliens, entities organized under US law (including foreign branches of US persons) and any other person in the US. Moreover, it applies to persons simply doing business in the US.

Foreign subsidiaries of US persons are not considered US persons, and may fall under the purview of the Order only to the extent that foreign persons may do so. This exclusion is consistent with the more recent US practice[130] and with the *Restatement (Third) of Foreign Relations*[131] according to which a State may exercise limited prescriptive jurisdiction on foreign branches of corporations organized under its laws and only in exceptional cases on subsidiaries of these persons incorporated under the laws of other countries.[132]

3. *Persons Outside the Scope of the UN Resolutions*

The personal reach of the Order is broader than that of the UN Resolutions. Whilst the latter target persons having close direct or indirect link with terrorists, the Order applies not only to terrorists and persons associated

[127] The respect of procedural guarantees of subsec. 3 of sec. 431 of the *Restatement (Third) on the Foreign Relations of the United States* (The American Law Institute, St. Paul (Minn), 1987) — ie the right to be noticed and the right to be heard — can be put aside as circumstances of exigency occur, such as the continuing and immediate threat of further attacks on US and US nationals (see *Comment sub e.(iv)*).

[128] See *People's Mojahedin Organization of Iran v US Department of State*, above n 126, and *Parassidiotis v Rubin*, above n 58.

[129] Colgate Selden, above n 126, 528.

[130] In the Eighties the Iranian Assets Control Regulation covered even US subsidiaries. The difficulties in enforcing those Regulations abroad led the US Administration to draft the Libyan and Iraqi Orders more narrowly, thus limiting their reach to US foreign branches: RR Gerstenhaber, "Freezer Burn: Unites States Extraterritorial Freeze Orders and the Case for Efficient Risk Allocation", (1992) 140 *University of Pennsylvania Law Review*, 2344–46.

[131] Above n 127.

[132] Sec. 414.2.b of the *Restatement* stresses the exceptional character of the extraterritorial regulation of the activities of foreign subsidiaries for which all the relevant factors must be

with them, but also to persons having only a weak or occasional link with terrorists. Although this is intended to apply mainly to foreign financial institutions which happen to have a course of dealing with persons affected by the Order or which simply do not comply with the reporting obligations, other persons could be affected as well.[133]

Here too a distinction must be drawn between the Taliban and other terrorist groups. With regard to the former, Resolution 1373 adopted after Executive Order 13224 recognized to the United States the right to act in self-defence against the Taliban threat. It could consequently be held that this right of self-defence includes also the right to freeze the assets of categories of persons not mentioned in the Taliban Resolutions.[134] On the other hand, for persons linked to other terrorist organisations the Resolution probably does not provide a sufficient umbrella for a unilateral and extraterritorial enforcement of national measures, with the consequence that such an enforcement would have to be assessed on the score of the general principles on extraterritorial exercise of jurisdiction.[135]

The United States can assert prescriptive jurisdiction on the matter pursuant to the criteria laid down in secs. 402 and 403 of the *Restatement (Third) of Foreign Relations*:[136] when persons transfer money or other resources to terrorists in the US from abroad (objective territoriality, ie conduct originating abroad and completed within the territory); when an act of terrorist financing occurs entirely abroad but is likely to entail a harmful terrorist event in the US (effects doctrine);[137] and when terrorism financing abroad is instrumental to offences against the national security

balanced, such as the national interests of the State of the parent company and the effectiveness of the sanctions program.

133 Foreign banks are generally not required to disclose any information to US authorities on their foreign activities. Nevertheless, under the Patriot Act financial institutions belonging to jurisdictions not complying with international money laundering standards are asked to submit to US regulatory control (see sec. 311.b of the Patriot Act, Pub. Law No. 107–56). If these institutions do not consent to this type of control, they are obliged to terminate all their accounts with US banks. The exclusion from US markets represents a sufficient threat to induce foreign banks to consent to reporting. K Alexander, "United States Financial sanctions and International Terrorism. Part 1", (2002) *Butterworths Journal of International Banking and Financial Law*, 83.

134 Since the right of self-defence has not been recognized with reference to other terrorist menaces further to the Taliban, it cannot be extended to categories of persons linked to other terrorist groups (above para. III.A.4).

135 This difference also has the consequence that in case of non-compliance by the requested State the US can act in self-defence as regards the Taliban but as regards international terrorism they could adopt a counter-measure or an act of retorsion.

136 In sec. 402 are set forth the bases for the jurisdiction to prescribe, while sec. 403 contains the limits to this jurisdiction.

137 It is not required that such an event actually takes place. To assert jurisdiction it is sufficient to appraise that an act of terrorism financing has direct, substantial and foreseeable effects in the US. Since the US are likely to be the primary target of international terrorism, it could be argued that every terrorist act is potentially addressed against the US.

and the integrity of the governmental functions, as the events of September 11 testify (protective principle) or aimed at injuring US citizens abroad (passive personality principle).[138]

Furthermore, even absent any territorial link with the financing of terrorism, the Order could still be applied extraterritorially on the score of the principle of universality,[139] considering that this activity is a universally condemned offense recognized in international agreements and in acts of international organisations and in view of the interest of States in cooperating to suppress it.[140]

Even where these criteria could lead to the inclusion of foreign persons in the lists, a subjective element must be taken into account since these persons could be unaware of the identity of the beneficiaries of their support. Thus, blocking their assets in the US or preventing them from doing business there could lead to conflicts with their respective countries of citizenship or residence. To avert such conflicts the Order empowers the Secretary of the Treasury, after consulting the Secretary of State and the Attorney General, to confer with the competent foreign authorities before entering the name of foreigners on a list and to adopt measures consistent with national interests[141] other than the complete freeze of property proportionate to the degree of involvement or to the awareness of the persons in question.[142]

C. The Action of the European Union

1. *The Balance of Interests*

In Europe the need to balance the individual right to the enjoyment of property against the collective interest in the prevention of terrorism is

[138] It is not necessary to appraise the Order in the light of any single criterion embodied at sec. 403. According to the Supreme Court the effects principle (sec. 403.2.a) is sufficient to establish the jurisdiction of the US over a foreign conduct without the need to resort to a further balance of interests (*Hartford Fire Insurance Co v California*, 509 US 764 (1993)): AF Lowenfeld, "Conflict, Balancing of Interests, and the Exercise of the Jurisdiction to Prescribe: Reflections on the Insurance Antitrust Case", (1995) 89 *American Journal of International Law*, 42.

[139] According to sec. 404 of the *Restatement* "a State has jurisdiction to define and prescribe punishment for certain offenses recognized by the community of nations as of universal concern".

[140] See *Comment* to sec. 404 of the *Restatement*. The point is that in establishing terrorism financing as an international offence it is necessary to define the elements of the offence: the material element as such is not enough to make an offence. It is still essential the presence of a psychological element. That means that funding directly or indirectly terrorists becomes a universal offence only if it is put into being with some degree of awareness.

[141] The Secretary of State enjoys an ample discretion in this field. First of all, he is free to determine what are the actions other than the full blocking of property. Then, he makes an appraisal of such actions against national interests, considering any "such factors he deems appropriate", as the necessity to avoid controversy with other States.

[142] Those actions may range from a partial freeze to a substantially different type of measure: Sheppard, above n 51, 629, footnote 9.

one of the most delicate aspects of the recourse to asset freezes in the struggle against the financing of terrorism. Article 6.2 TEU which requires the EU to respect the fundamental rights recognized by the European Convention on Human Rights (ECHR) and by the constitutional traditions of the Member States is particularly relevant.

The problem has been addressed in several judgments of the European Court of Human Rights which set the basic criteria for the limitation of the right of property.[143] In the *Agosi* case[144] the Court held that there must exist a reasonable and proportional relationship between the means employed and the aims pursued, in other words a fair balance between general and individual interest. The Court recognized that States enjoy ample discretion in the choice of the means of enforcement and in the appreciation as to whether the consequences of a freeze are justified with respect to its purported object. Nevertheless, such a measure is justified only in the presence of a proper link between the behavior of the owner of the assets and the breach of law, taking into account the degree of fault or care.

The position of the ECJ is significantly different. In the *Bosphorus* case[145] concerning the freeze of Serbian assets during the Balkan crisis it held that the right to the peaceful enjoyment of property is not absolute but is subject to restrictions justified by Community objectives of general interest, such as the need to prevent terrorist attacks.[146] Being the scope of the action against terrorism of the EU and of the EC so exceptional, negative consequences for some persons, including third parties not linked with the matter, can be justified.[147] Accordingly, the freezing of all

[143] The legal basis is Article 1 of Protocol 1 to the ECHR, pursuant to which every person is entitled to the peaceful enjoyment of his property. See JL Charrier (ed), *Code de la Convention européenne des droits de l'homme*, (Litec, Paris, 2000), 311.

[144] Judgment of 24 October 1986, *Allgemeine Gold und Silberscheideanstalt v The United Kingdom*, in 9 *European Human Rights Reports*, 1987, 1, paras. 48–61. According to the Court a blocking measure should be justified if the requirements of para. 2 of Article 1 of the Protocol are satisfied and if a State has struck a fair balance between the interests at stake. This rule contains no explicit requirement as to the procedural aspects of the freeze. Nevertheless, the owner of the frozen assets must be given "a reasonable opportunity of putting its case to the responsible authorities" (para. 55).

[145] Case C–84/95, *Bosphorus Hava Yollari Turzim ve Ticaret v Minister for Transport, Energy and Communications*, [1996] *ECR*, p. I–3953.

[146] The Court found proportionate and appropriate a measure impounding an aircraft owned by an undertaking operating from the Federal Republic of Yugoslavia, but leased to another undertaking not operating from that country. The Court admitted that any measure imposing sanctions can cause harm to persons not responsible for the situation, but this argument was overcome by the importance of those measures for the international community. Here the Court stressed that the UN measures had been adopted by the Security Council under Chapter VII of the Charter (*Bosphorus*, paras. 21–27).

[147] *Bosphorus*, above n 145, paras. 21–23. This positions was restated in case C–317/00 P(R) *Invest Import und Export Gmbh and Invest Commerce v Commission*, [2000] *ECR*, I–9541, where the Court held that the potentially negative consequences of the freeze cannot be regarded as manifestly disproportionate in the light of Community interests.

the assets of such persons may be reasonable when assessed against the vital interests of the international community. In this case the ECJ did not give particular weight to the respect of the fundamental rights and to the subjective test laid down in *Agosi* by the European Court of Human Rights, first of all because the measure was mandatory under Community legislation[148] and secondly because of the high stake for the international community.

The Court of First Instance of the European Communities now has the opportunity to review this position in the light of the terrorism legislation. A first claim concerning freezing measures was made by the above mentioned Somali-born Swedish citizens, following the inclusion of their names in a Commission Regulation implementing Council Regulation 467/2001,[149] and the case is still pending notwithstanding the deletion of their names from the list of the Taliban Committee on the basis of an agreement between the US and Sweden.[150] A second claim by a Philippine refugee concerns the consistency of the designating system under Regulation 2580/2001 with the fundamental principles of EU Law.[151] On a similar basis two Basque associations brought an action against the insertion of their names in the Annex to CFSP 2001/931.[152] Although this last claim is limited in its application to JHA measures, the arguments adduced are very similar to those advanced in the claims against the EC measures.[153]

[148] See Article 8 of Council Regulation (EEC) n. 990/93 of 26 April 1996, *OJEC* L 102/14 of 18 April 1993.

[149] Above para II.D.1.

[150] See <www.ud.se>. See *A Aden and Others v EU Council and European Commission*, case T–306/01, *pending*, *OJEC* C 44/27 of 16 February 2002, where the applicant alleged a breach of the right to a fair and equitable hearing and a lack of the competence by the Council to impose sanctions against individuals and entities. The CFI on 7 May 2002 by a presidential order rejected the request for provisional measures stating that the condition of urgency was not fulfilled, *A Aden and Others v EU Council and European Commission*, case T–306/01 R, [2002] *ECR*, II–2387.

[151] See *JM Sison v EU Council*, case T–47/03, *pending*, *OJEC* C101/41 of 26 April 2003, *JM Sison v EU Council*, case T–110/03, *pending*, *OJEC* C 146/39 of 21 June 2003, *JM Sison v EU Council and European Commission*, case T–150/03, *pending*, *OJEC* C 213/36 of 6 September 2003. These actions were brought by the same applicant invoking a violation of fundamental rights and general principles (principle of sound administration, right of access to documents, general principles of Community law enshrined in the ECHR) and a lack of competence by the Council to adopt the measures. Even in this case the CFI rejected a request for provisional measures arguing that the condition of urgency was not fulfilled as the applicant had failed to demonstrate that there was no possibility to obtain an authorisation by national authorities under Articles 5 and 6 of Regulation 2580 (above para. II.D.2), order of 15 May 2003, *JM Sison v EU Council*, case T–47/03 R (not yet published).

[152] *Gestoras Pro Amnistia and Others v Council*, case T–333/02, *pending*, *OJEC* C 19/36 of 25 January 2003 and *SEGI and Others v Council*, case T–338/02, *pending*, *OJEC* C 7/24 of 11 January 2003.

[153] The insertions of the names of those entities in the Annex to CFSP 931/2001 occurred at the request of Spain, as they were alleged to have close ties to the terrorist group ETA.

The ECJ's position might have to be reconsidered also depending on the decision of the European Court of Human Rights in a case brought by the defeated parties in the above mentioned *Bosphorus* case.[154] Although this case does not deal specifically with the compatibility with human rights of the EC Regulations on terrorism financing,[155] the principles at stake are basically the same. As a result, were the Court to confirm its reasoning in *Agosi* this approach could not be ignored by the ECJ even with regard to measures relating to terrorism financing.

2. *Problems Arising from Co-operation*

In the context of the European Union the legality of a freeze of all the assets and resources of a person is probably beyond doubt if this is adopted following a conviction for financing of terrorism, while it would seem more dubious if it is adopted merely on the basis of soft intelligence and without the interested parties being permitted to make their position known.[156]

The issue is particularly relevant with regard to attempts by the US to enforce their blocking orders. The different emphasis on the respect of procedural guaranties in the identification of terrorists by the US could be held to violate the fundamental principles embodied in the constitutions of the Member States and in the European Convention of Human Rights

Although their inclusion was confined to the application of measures of police and judicial cooperation (Article 4), potentially it could be extended to a proper freezing. From the one hand, Member States can unilaterally block the assets belonging to these persons, from the other, can be required to do under the framework decision on the execution of freezing orders within the EU (above n. 89). See EU Network of Independent Experts in Fundamental Rights, *The balance between freedom and security in the response by the European Union and its member States to the terrorists threats* (41–43), thematic comment submitted to the European Commission on 31 March 2003.

[154] The claim was declared admissible on 13 September 2001 ((2002) 23 *Human Rights Law Journal*, 279) on the score of the principle (stated by the Court in *Matthews v The United Kingdom*, Judgment of 18 February 1999, (1999) 28 *European Human Rights Reports*, 361, para. 32) that "acts of the EC as such cannot be challenged before the Court because the EC is not a Contracting Party. The Convention does not exclude the transfer of competence to international organisations provided that the Convention rights continue to be secured. Member States responsibility therefore continues even after such a transfer": I Canor, "Primus Inter Pares, Who is the Ultimate Guardian of the Fundamental Rights in Europe?", (2000) 25 *European Law Review*, 3.

[155] In May 2003 the European Court of Human Rights significantly declared the inadmissibility of the application by the above mentioned Basque persons whose names had been inserted in a list attached to CFSP 2001/931, on the grounds that the complainants could not technically be considered as victims of the measure, since a CFSP is not directly applicable in Member States (Decisions of 23 May 2002, *Segi and others* (pl. 6422/02) and *Gestoras pro Amnistia and others* (pl. 9916/02), in <www.coe.int>).

[156] S Peers, "EU Responses to Terrorism", (2003) 41 *International and Comparative Law Quarterly*, 239.

which must be respected also under European Union law.[157] The question is whether a request for enforcement in the European Union of a US freezing order could be denied on the grounds of a contrast with such fundamental principles.[158]

Problems could arise were the EU to refuse to enforce foreign, especially US, freezing orders in the event of a reversal of *Bosphorus* by the ECJ. Any attempt to refer the question to the Security Council for the adoption of sanctions could well encounter the opposition of at least one of the two European permanent members of the UN Security Council. In such a case the US could be tempted to enforce their freezing orders on private persons, mostly financial institutions, by preventing them from doing business in the US. In such an event the EU could retaliate[159] by resorting to a blocking statute, namely Regulation 2271/96,[160] to protect persons, citizens and residents in EC countries from the extraterritorial effects of the legislation of third countries.

If, on the other hand, the ECJ were to confirm its position in *Bosphorus*, the decision to block the enforcement of foreign orders purportedly adopted in violation of fundamental rights could be adopted under the constitutional law of some Member States. In such a case these States could theoretically face a double layer of responsibility, at UN and at EC level. An attempt to sanction this behavior at the UN level could be paralyzed again by the opposition of (at least) one of the two permanent members of the Security Council which are also members of the EU, provided that its view is consistent with that of the non-complying State. The infringement of EU law consisting in the failure to implement a piece of Community legislation could instead be brought before the ECJ under Articles 226 or 227 TEC. This could lead to a clash with domestic constitutional courts which could be

[157] The Executive Order permits the freeze of assets connected to persons even having very weak links with terrorism while the EC Regulations require a more consistent link between the persons whose assets are to be blocked and terrorists.

[158] As to the Taliban affair, the case of the Somali-born Swedish citizens (above n 113) demonstrated that in the case of persons on the list maintained by the Taliban Committee the obligation to block their assets is absolute. The situation may be less clear with regard to the obligations stemming from the UN Resolutions on international terrorism financing because of the potential disputes regarding the identification of terrorists and of the persons associated with them.

[159] See above para. III.A.4. A possible retaliation consisting of a counter-measure should be unlawful unless is directed against a measure adopted by the US for failure to enforce a freezing order concerning categories of persons not covered by UN Resolutions on international terrorism for whose involvement with terrorists there is not a sufficient piece of evidence (see above para. III.B.1).

[160] Council Regulation (EC) 2271/96 of 22 November 1996 (*OJEC* L 309/1 of 29 November 1996) on the effects of the extraterritorial application of legislation of third countries. This Regulation was adopted following the enactment by the United States of the *Helms-Burton Act* (22 USC 6021–91): see A Bianchi, "Le recenti sanzioni unilaterali adottate dagli Stati Uniti nei confronti di Cuba e la loro liceità internazionale", (1998) *Rivista di diritto internazionale*, 369–74.

the occasion to define further the relationship between EU and national legal systems as to the protection of human rights.[161]

IV. THE EFFECTS OF ASSET FREEZES ON PRIVATE LAW RELATIONS

The foregoing discussion has dealt with the enforcement of national or international measures providing for the freeze of assets related to the financing of terrorism by government, or administrative, bodies. A different set of issues arises when the issue of the application or effects of such measures comes into play in the context of the relations between private parties. Typical cases are those where the owner or the beneficiary of frozen assets claims the restitution of these from the holder (eg a depositor whose assets have been frozen claims the return of the deposit from a bank) or contests the effect of the measures on a private law claim (eg set off, excuse the performance of a contract, etc.).

These problems have emerged in the litigation before domestic courts which has often accompanied asset freezes in the past, in particular with regard to the freeze of Iranian assets in the wake of the hostage crisis which — largely because of the volume of the assets affected by the measures — resulted in an extremely abundant case law.[162] Save perhaps for issues of constitutional law (such as the ones referred to in the preceding section) and possibly of sovereign immunity (where the measures directly affect assets belonging to a State), the problems do not arise so much where the litigation takes place before the courts of the State which has adopted the measures. In these cases there is little doubt that the measures must always be applied or taken into account by the courts since the legislation upon which they are based is unquestionably mandatory (*lois de police*, or *lois d'application immediate*) and is therefore applicable even if the law applicable to the relationships at issue is a foreign law.

The situation is more complex when a court is confronted with the application of a foreign measure, particularly if this purports to have extraterritorial effects (such as a blocking order addressed to a bank or other financial institution with regards to assets held by it in a State other than the one having enacted the measures invoked before the court). States are traditionally wary of the extraterritorial application of foreign

[161] See P Craig and G De Burca, *EU Law: Text, Cases and Materials, 3rd* edn, (Oxford University Press, Oxford, 2003), 291–93.

[162] See LG Radicati di Brozolo, "La prima fase del contenzioso relativo agli averi iraniani bloccati dagli Stati Uniti", (1981) *Rivista di diritto internazionale*, 328–57; W Blair, "Interference of Public Law in the Performance of International Monetary Obligations" in M Giovanoli (ed), *International Monetary Law: Issues for the New Millenium* (Oxford University Press, Oxford, 2000), 395.

public law, and in normal circumstances would not cooperate in its enforcement through the action of their courts.[163] However, even when the freezes purport to apply in conformity with more generally accepted principles on the exercise of the jurisdiction to prescribe foreign courts will not necessarily apply them or take them into account. Without going into all the complexities of the matter, it suffices here to recall that the solution may vary depending on whether the rules form part of the proper law of the contract. If they do not, they can generally be applied or taken into account only on the basis of rules such as Article 7, para. 1, of the Rome Convention of 19 June 1980 on the Law Applicable to Contractual Obligations or of Article 19 of the Swiss Statute on Private International Law which permit the taking into account of mandatory rules even of a law different from the *lex causae* and the *lex fori* where this has a sufficient relevance for the transaction.[164]

In principle the same types of problems arise with regard to the freezes of assets aimed at fighting terrorist financing. In practice, however, the difficulties might be less severe than in previous situations where the measures were enacted unilaterally, as was the case in particular of the US measures adopted in retaliation against specific acts against the interests of the United States, such as those relating to Iran, to Cuba and to other States. This is due largely to the broad consensus within the international community as to the illegality of terrorist financing, despite the uncertainties referred to above regarding the identification of terrorists, and more specifically the fact that for the most part these measures are mandated by, or at least are within the spirit of, international instruments, foremost amongst which the UN Resolutions and the Convention for the Suppression of the Financing of Terrorism. This recognition by the international community of the importance of the freezing of assets of terrorist organisations in the fight against terrorism underscores the importance of a rigorous and consistent application of these rules which can hardly be overlooked by courts and is certain to play a significant role in the approach of the latter to the application of these rules in the context of private litigation. Because of this it may be somewhat easier to overcome the obstacles which arise when it comes to putting the freezes in effect also in transnational situations, although the problems will doubtless not disappear entirely.

In many cases it is likely that the foreign measure invoked before a court will be mirrored by a national measure or by national legislation incorporating or enacting the international instruments. Thus — at least from a practical viewpoint — the court will not even have to inquire into

[163] See for instance the reactions of the EC to the sanctions against Cuba enacted by the United States, above n 160.

[164] Blair, above n 162.

the applicability before it of the foreign measure since it will have the possibility to rely on the corresponding domestic measure, unless the foreign measures are clearly beyond the scope of the international instruments, as could be argued to be the case for instance with the US measures insofar as they seek to permit the blocking not only of funds belonging to terrorists themselves, but even to persons with very tenuous links to these. Even in such cases, however, the fact that the foreign measures can probably at least be said to pursue an aim in line with that of the international instruments eliminates the possibility of calling into question the violation of international law which is sometimes invoked to exclude the applicability of foreign law with extraterritorial scope.

The international law backing of measures aimed at fighting the financing of terrorism is relevant also with regard to the recognition of foreign judgments and of arbitral awards which apply such measures or which deal with transactions allegedly falling within their scope of application. There are reasons to hold — and the practice of courts seems to bear out this conclusion — that, in an increasingly global world which depends very heavily on the smooth functioning of international transactions, foreign judgments and arbitral awards should be recognized to the greatest extent possible, and that the purported violation or non-application of domestic mandatory rules should not as a rule be considered a bar to such recognition.[165] In this perspective the public policy exception, which is increasingly the only means to prevent the recognition or enforcement of foreign judgments and awards on grounds having to do with substantive law, tends to be interpreted in an more restrictive sense, and in particular so as not to include all the mandatory rules of the forum.[166] The fact that the rules mandating the freeze of terrorist assets are derived from international law certainly provides a strong reason to hold that, despite this restrictive view of public policy, these rules do form part of the public policy against which foreign judgments and arbitral awards must be measured if they are to be granted recognition and enforcement. Accordingly, any decision or arbitral award which has the effect of thwarting these rules should be considered unenforceable. However, as has been argued elsewhere,[167] this does not necessarily justify an in-depth analysis and

[165] See LG Radicati di Brozolo, "Mondialisation, juridiction, arbitrage: vers des lois d'application semi-nécessaire ?" (2003) *Revue critique de droit international privé*, 1; H Muir Watt, "La mondialisation entre illusion et utopie", (2003) *Archives de philosophie du droit*, 243; LG Radicati di Brozolo, "Antitrust: A Paradigm of the Relations Between Arbitration and Mandatory Rules: a Fresh Look at the 'Second Look'", (2004) *International Arbitration Law Review* (17).

[166] This is particularly evident within the EU where under the Framework Decision on the execution of orders freezing property or evidence (above n 88) the grounds for non-recognition or non-execution of freezing orders are strictly concocted (Article 7).

[167] See the references in n 165 above.

possibly review of the judgment or award, but it requires at least that the forum court verify that the foreign court or arbitrator has duly taken into account the rules in question and has not unreasonably failed to apply them or applied them in an unreasonable manner.

16

The Fight Against the Financing of Terrorism between Judicial and Regulatory Cooperation

ANNA GARDELLA

I. INTRODUCTION

THE FINANCING OF terrorist groups has recently attracted the attention of the international legal community, as one aspect of the multifaceted fight against international terrorism. The increased focus on the prevention, in addition to the repression, of terrorist acts has necessarily involved the conclusion of legal instruments aimed at the suppression of the financing of terrorism, given its strategic role in depriving terrorist organisations of the necessary funds to carry out their activities.

Combating the financing of terrorism, however, is not an easy task. The different patterns of funding put in place by terrorist groups, principally characterised by the cross-border abuse of the financial system, require a multi-disciplinary approach concentrated on criminal and financial law and regulation, as well as coordinated multi-jurisdictional efforts. Whereas international cooperation plays a fundamental role in identifying criminal conduct and in ensuring that the offenders are brought to justice, effective and reciprocal financial regulation is essential to prevent abuses of the financial system for illicit purposes. These latter features are not distinctive traits of the struggle against the financing of terrorism, since they are common to ordinary financial crimes and to money laundering in particular. For this reason, the fight against the funding of terrorism is largely inspired by, and is currently conducted within the legal framework against money laundering, as will be illustrated in the following paragraphs.

The lack of regulation of the financial system, or its unsatisfactory implementation, offer attractive opportunities to terrorists to achieve their criminal goals, enabling a profitable management of financial resources as well as their transfer through banking channels (without material shipment) to the jurisdiction where the preparation of terrorist actions must be supported. All of this occurs without leaving a trace of the criminals' identity, or of the origin and destination of the money. Regardless of the stringent rules in force in the most advanced financial centres, the financing of terrorism takes advantage of the vast opportunities offered by unregulated or insufficiently regulated jurisdictions. For this reason, a multi-jurisdictional approach, characterised by reciprocity and a high degree of international cooperation, is critical to the struggle against financial crime in general. International fora are therefore the most appropriate ones to elaborate a comprehensive legal framework which duly takes into account both the inter-disciplinary and cross-border elements of the puzzle. In addition to the existing legal machinery to fight money laundering, mandatory provisions in UN Security Council Resolutions, as implemented by regional organisations (such as the European Union), together with international conventions and *ad hoc* recommendations adopted by specialised international bodies (such as the Financial Action Task Force), are the most relevant instruments available to national authorities in fighting against the financing of terrorism.[1]

Combating the financing of terrorism may turn out to be more troublesome than ordinary financial crime. Additional hurdles which challenge the current legal framework set up against financial criminality, are represented by the involvement, in the financing of terrorism, of legitimate entities and legitimate financial resources, by the use of small amounts of money which can be easily concealed, being below the existing alert thresholds, and by resort to underground banking networks which escape the existing monitoring and controlling schemes. In this context, the countering of terrorism financing is made more complex by the need to weigh up the public interest to defeat terrorism and the conflicting, but equally important societal needs, of preserving individual civil liberties and privacy.

In the light of the above considerations, the goal of the present paper is to provide an overview of the many issues involved in the fight against the financing of terrorism as well as to envisage effective remedies. Part II describes the financial resources which fuel terrorist groups, in particular the coexistence of illegitimate and legitimate sources of income and the fund-raising role played by charities and legitimate business. To combat these forms of assistance, the need to make the financing of terrorist groups a criminal offence in domestic legislation will be underlined. Part III starts with a survey of the legal instruments already available in

[1] For an overview of the several international institutions actively involved in the fight against the financing of terrorism, see J Fisher, "Recent International Developments in the Fight Against Money Laundering", (2002) 17 *Journal of International Banking Law* 67; see also the Special Issue entirely dedicated to "The Funding of Terror: The Legal Implications of the Financial War on Terror" (2003) 6 *Journal of Money Laundering Control*; I Bantekas, "The International law of Terrorist Financing" (2003) 97 *American Journal* of *International Law* 315.

criminal law within the existing anti-money laundering schemes, and then focuses on actions taken internationally in the aftermath of the September 11th attacks to adapt the existing legal tools to the fight against international terrorism. For this purpose, particular emphasis will be placed on the UN Security Council's Resolution 1373 and on the 1999 UN Convention on the Suppression of the Financing of Terrorism. Part IV analyses the financing of terrorism from the perspective of regulation. In doing so, attention will primarily be directed at the legislative shortcomings vis-a-vis the peculiarities of terrorist funding, which have called into question the adequacy of the current regulation of the financial system and have drawn global attention to the need to enact harmonised regulatory and supervisory standards and to enhance international cooperation also in the form of information-sharing. In the concluding remarks (Part V), it will be emphasised that effective enforcement and implementation at the national level of the international legal norms is necessary, rather than further legislative initiatives.

II. THE FINANCIAL RESOURCES OF TERRORIST GROUPS

A. The Financial Resources of Terrorist Groups

An extensive analysis of the funding methods of terrorist groups and of the financial resources supporting terrorist activities has been carried out by the Financial Action Task Force (FATF). Therefore, the following illustration to a large extent relies on the outcomes of its survey. The FAFT is an inter-governmental organisation established in 1989 by the G7 States, working as a policy-making group entrusted with the task of suggesting legislative and regulatory action to counter money laundering.[2] The FATF is internationally recognised as the leading institution in the combat of money laundering; the "*summa*" of its work is represented by the "Forty Recommendations",[3] originally issued in 1990, and subsequently subject to a review process in 1996 in order to update their content consistent with evolving patterns of money laundering. A further round of consultation for review of the Forty Recommendations was launched in 2002, and the current version was approved in June 2003.[4] The Forty Recommendations are a body of international standards which, despite not being formally

[2] At the time of writing, the FAFT's membership consists of 31 countries and two regional organisations (EC and Gulf Co-operation Council).

[3] The Forty Recommendations are a comprehensive legal framework designed to be of universal application, encompassing measures concerning the criminal justice system and law enforcement, the financial system and its regulation, and international cooperation. The text of the Forty Recommendations is available at <http:www.fatf-gafi.org>.

[4] See respectively, Review of the FATF Forty Recommendations, Consultation Paper, of 30 May 2002; and The Forty Recommendations of 20 June 2003.

binding on the member States of the FATF, hold great authority and are highly considered by national legislators.[5] Indeed, their nature as "soft law" does not prevent them being recognised as the international anti-money laundering framework. "Soft law" is usually defined as consisting of international standards, declarations of principles, and statements generally adopted by international organizations in matters related to the protection of human rights, economic relations and the environment, which embody a common core of principles, approaches or concerns of the international community. Although it might be considered as a "second best" in respect of formal and binding international treaties,[6] it is not tantamount to "weak law"; on the contrary, "soft law" responds to the logic that sometimes "less is more". In matters where the views of States may not yet be sufficiently mature to form the basis of formal agreements, soft law lays down informal commitments with which States can spontaneously comply, or which may be a starting point towards further international efforts to be later translated into "hard law" such as a treaty.[7] The FATF Recommendations fit this scheme and go even further, constituting the general and primary reference for international and domestic legislation. For this reason the efforts undertaken by the FAFT are a chief reference also in the present paper.

Starting from its *Report on Money Laundering Typologies 1999–2000*,[8] analysis by the FATF has included issues concerned with the financing of terrorism, due to the connections with money laundering typologies. After the September 11th attacks, at an extraordinary session held on 29–30 October 2001 in Washington DC, in the light of its expertise in the

[5] Suffice it to recall that the Forty Recommendations have so far been endorsed by 130 States, and that references to the activity of FATF is contained in supranational and national legislation; for instance see recital 14 of Directive 2001/97/EC of 14 December 2001 amending Directive 91/308, on prevention of the use of the financial system for the purpose of money laundering in OJ Eur Comm L 344 of 28 December 2001 at 76; see also Italian law decree n 369, of 12 October 2001, introducing urgent measures to counter the financing of terrorism, converted into law by Law n 431 of 14 December 2001, in OJ n 290 of 14 December 2001. The decree specifies that special attention in updating national law will be paid to the outcomes of the FATF work.

[6] The debate on whether "soft law" is a good or a bad thing has been extensively developed; against the resort to "soft law", perceived as a threat to the prescriptive nature of international law, see P Weil, "Towards Relative Normativity in International Law?" (1983) 77 *American Journal of International Law* 413.

[7] See, G Abi-Saab, "Éloge du 'droit assourdi'. Quelques réflexions sur le rôle de la *soft law* en droit international contemporain", in *Nouveaux itinéraires en droit. Hommage à François Rigaux* (Bruylant, Bruxelles, 1993) 59; RJ Dupuy, "Droit déclaratoire et droit programmatoire: de la coutume sauvage à la soft law" in RJ Dupuy, *Dialectique du droit international* (Pedone, Paris, 1999) 107; A Cassese, *International Law* (Oxford University Press, Oxford, 2002) 160; A Bianchi, "Globalization of Human Rights: the Role of Non-State Actors" in G Teubner (ed), *Global Law without a State* (Dartmouth, Aldershot, 1997) 405 R Luzzatto, "Il diritto internazionale generale e le sue fanti" in SM Carbone, R Luzzatto, A Santa Maria (eds), *Istituzioni di diritto internazionale* (Giappichelli, Turin, 2003) 73.

[8] See FATF-XI, *Report on Money Laundering Typologies 1999–2000*, 3rd February 2000.

field of money laundering control and prevention, the FATF undertook to extend its mandate to the financing of terrorism, and immediately issued the "Eight Special Recommendations" which specifically address terrorist financing.[9] This has been the first specific contribution of the FATF to the fight against the financing of terrorism, to which it is still actively committed. In order to ensure the swift and effective implementation of the Eight Special Recommendations, the FATF has adopted a Plan of Action providing for, *inter alia*, a self-assessment exercise addressed both to member and non-member States directed at evaluating the degree of compliance with the Special Recommendations.[10]

According to the *Reports on Money Laundering Typologies* adopted by the FATF for the years 2001–2 and 2002–3,[11] terrorist organisations rely both on illegal and legal sources of income. With respect to illegal sources of income, the Reports point out the link with transnational criminality, since they derive from criminal "revenue-generating" activities, such as narcotics trafficking,[12] large-scale smuggling, various frauds (such as credit card duplication), kidnapping, extortions and so on. The 2001–2 Report underlines that there is little difference between terrorists and other criminals in the use of the proceeds of crime, since both aim at laundering the dirty money generated by such offences, in order either to make profits or to invest such money in other criminal plans. According to the FATF findings, laundering typologies used by terrorists do not differ from those followed by ordinary criminals. Therefore, to the extent that terrorists are funded by criminal "revenue-generating" activities, the fight against the financing of terrorism can be conducted within the existing framework against money laundering.

Terrorist funding, however, also largely relies on legal financial resources, solicited and collected by associations having a charitable or non-profit status. These funds, which derive from membership

[9] Available at <http:www.fatf-gafi.org>.

[10] The other steps envisaged by the Action Plan agreed upon at the Washington meeting include (i) the development of additional guidance for financial institutions to detect the mechanisms used in the financing of terrorism; (ii) the identification of jurisdictions that lack appropriate measures to combat terrorist financing and discussion of the available remedies to impose compliance; (iii) regular publication by the member States of the amount of suspected terrorist assets frozen; (iv) the provision by FATF members of technical assistance to non-members, as necessary to assist them in complying with the Eight Recommendations. For a review of the FATF's counter-terrorism activity, see FATF Annual Report 2001–2002 of 21 June 2002, and FATF Annual Report 2002–2003 of 20 June 2003.

[11] Respectively FATF–XIII, *Report on Money Laundering Typologies 2001–2002* of 1st February 2002, and FATF–XIII, *Report on Money Laundering Typologies 2002–2003* of 14 February 2003.

[12] Explicit mention to this modality of self-financing is made in UN Security Resolution 1333 of 19 December 2000, where it is acknowledged that "the Taliban benefits directly from the cultivation of illicit opium by imposing a tax on its production and indirectly benefits from the processing and trafficking of such opium and… that these substantial resources strengthen the Taliban's capacity to harbour terrorists".

subscriptions, donations, sales of publications, cultural and social events and appeals to wealthy members of the community, are then diverted to the terrorist cause by the charitable or non-profit association. Therefore, fundraising campaigns promoted for charitable purposes often become willingly or unwittingly a privileged vehicle to collect and transfer money to terrorists: the lawful origin of the funds makes it difficult to detect the sums destined to terrorists. Besides charities, front-stores exercising cross-border business are employed by terrorists as a conduit for the funding of terrorism through legitimate resources: the under-invoicing and over-invoicing of the traded goods allow the allocation of hidden balances to terrorist groups through underground banking channels.[13]

Paradoxically the legal origin of these economic resources hinders the detection, and prevention of such funds from reaching terrorist organisations, since anti-money laundering control and reporting schemes are not triggered without any criminal activity being at their source. Before the legal money reaches terrorist groups, and even at that time, no crime has yet been committed, and this prevents financial institutions from identifying suspicious transactions in accordance with money laundering provisions.[14] Such an undisturbed freedom to move sums of money within the financial system has undoubtedly increased the funding of terrorist groups through legal channels, making financing through "clean" resources a convenient tool for supporting terrorism. The lack of provisions proscribing terrorism financing has also had the adverse effect of formally allowing terrorist groups to carry on fundraising "safe and sound" campaigns in the territory of the State against which the terror plans were eventually directed, exposing governments to adverse political criticism. As will be further illustrated,[15] to redress such an intolerable situation the envisaged remedy has been to make the financing of terrorism as an independent crime, a solution which builds on the existing legal framework against money laundering by introducing the specific crime of terrorist financing within its predicate offences.[16]

[13] For a description of these techniques see J Trehan, "Terrorism and the Funding of Terrorism in Kashmir" (2002) 5 *Journal of Money Laundering Control* 201; K Alexander, "United States Financial Sanctions and International Terrorism, Part 2" (2002) 17 *Butterworths Journal of International Banking and Financial Law* 213, as well as FATF — XIII *Report on Money Laundering Typologies 2001–2002* cit. and FATF — XIV *Report on Money Laundering Typologies 2002–2003*, above n 11.

[14] See also J Jackson, "11th September 2001: Will it Make a Difference to the Global Anti-Money Laundering Movement?", (2002) 5 *Journal of Money Laundering Control* 9, at 11.

[15] See below, Part III B and C.

[16] On the need to include terrorist financing as a predicate offence of money laundering, see FATF –XIII, *Report on Money Laundering Typologies 2001–2002*, above n 11, at 6; as well as S/RES/ 1373.

B. Specific Problems Raised by Charitable Associations in the Enforcement of Measures Against the Financing of Terrorism

The misuse of non-profit and charitable associations is the most distinctive feature of the financing of terrorism and undisputedly the aspect which creates the most serious challenges from a law enforcement and crime prevention perspective. Notwithstanding the normative progress made by the criminalisation of the financing of terrorism, which is primarily targeted at stopping the funding of terrorist organisations through legitimate resources, the reality of enforcement does not correspond to the written law. The ideological and religious elements supporting terrorist acts make these private entities, willingly or unwittingly, a crucial link between civil society and terrorist organisations. Under the cover of the legitimate goal of their front activities, non-profit and religious entities may act freely and above suspicion to support terrorist groups. The protection granted by the constitutional and internationally recognized rights of freedom of association and of freedom of religion, normally shield these entities from administrative control of their activities. These circumstances make charities and non-profit organisations easily exposed to misuse by terrorist financiers, thus representing a crucial weak point in the struggle against the funding of terrorist groups.

That non-profit associations are particularly vulnerable to be misused for purposes of the financing of terrorism is commonly acknowledged and is reflected in the recitals of the UN Convention on the Suppression of the Financing of Terrorism, signed in New York on 9 December 1999 (the "New York Convention")[17] as well as in FATF Special Recommendation VIII, whereby countries are urged to review the adequacy of their laws and regulations governing such entities.[18] With a view to helping member and non-member States to comply and to ensure its swift implementation, the FATF issued an "International Best Practices" guideline, in October 2002.[19]

[17] See recital n 6, recalling that financing of terrorism may be direct or "indirect through organizations which also have or claim to have charitable, social or cultural goals or which are also engaged in unlawful activities ...".

[18] See Special Recommendation VIII which reads "Countries should review the adequacy of laws and regulations that relate to entities that be abused for the financing of terrorism. Non-profit organisations are particularly vulnerable, and countries should ensure that they cannot be misused: (*i*) by terrorist organisations posing as legitimate entities; (*ii*) to exploit legitimate entities as conduits for terrorist financing, including for the purpose of escaping asset freezing measures; and (*iii*) to conceal or obscure the clandestine diversion of funds intended for legitimate purposes to terrorist organisations".

[19] See FATF, *Combating the abuse of non-profit organisations. International Best Practices*, of 11 October 2002. Responses submitted by FATF members States to the self-assessment exercise evidenced difficulties encountered by domestic legal systems in implementing Special Recommendation VIII specifically focused on the misuse of non-profit organisations; see FATF *Annual Report 2001–2002*, at 5.

Consistent with domestic constitutional constraints, the FATF urges the establishment of measures setting up transparency and accountability mechanisms for oversight of the activities carried out by such entities. These measures should enable authorities to verify the actual use of the funds collected by or donated to non-profit associations and specifically verify that they are actually employed in the accomplishment of the promoted charitable programmes and are not diverted to support terrorist acts. In this respect, special efforts are required to monitor those non-profit associations directing their activities to beneficiaries established in foreign countries to whom the funds are transferred. In this regard, the FATF recommends that international cooperation be reinforced, especially in the form of information sharing between the administrative agencies of different jurisdictions.

Despite the valuable efforts undertaken by the FATF in the identification of remedies to the major shortcomings of the current legislation which expose non-profit associations to misuse by terrorist financiers, the envisaged monitoring task may turn out to be ineffective, either because of constitutional constraints — ie prohibition of interference on the free exercise of civil liberties — or because of the practical hurdles of identifying and overseeing such entities. Notwithstanding the normative solution to the prevention of terrorist financing, the trade-off between the expenses jurisdictions would incur in pursuing this goal and the ascertained number of cases of actual misuse of non-profit associations may call into question the proportionate character of the envisaged remedies also in the light of their intrusive nature on the activities of legitimate associations.

III. THE CRIMINAL LAW APPROACH TO COUNTER THE FINANCING OF TERRORISM

A. The Existing Anti-money Laundering Regime and the Limits of its Application Against the Financing of Terrorism

To the extent terrorist organisations do rely on illegal sources of income, the similarities with the operating and financing modalities of international criminality[20] have made resort to the existing legal framework

[20] The connection between international terrorism and transnational organised crime has been stressed in several UN declarations, see A/RES/46/51, 9 December 1991 (UN Doc A/46/654); A/RES/49/60, 9 December 1994, *Measures to eliminate international terrorism;* A/RES/55/25 of 8 January 2001, adopting the UN Convention against Transnational Organised Crime of 15 November 2000, whose ratification is urged by FATF Recommendation n 35; A/RES/55/59 of 17 January 2001, *Vienna Declaration on Crime Prevention and Justice: Meeting the Challenges of the Twenty-first Century;* see also A/RES/45/117 adopting the Model Treaty on Mutual Assistance in Criminal Matters, recalling the need to strengthen cooperation in mutual legal assistance against criminal acts of

against money laundering a natural remedy to counter the funding of terrorism. Although experts have rightly questioned its adequacy to combat all forms of terrorism financing, notably those depending on resources of legitimate origin,[21] it has the unquestionable merit of being a valuable and already available international legal framework, encompassing both the criminal and financial aspect of this complex offence.[22]

Money laundering may be defined as a process aiming at concealing the existence, illegal sources or illegal application of income, in order to disguise that income, make it appear legitimate and inject it into the legal economy. The first international instrument to proscribe money laundering was the UN Convention Against Illicit Traffic in Narcotic Drugs and Psychotropic Substances signed in Vienna on 19 December 1988 (hereinafter the "Vienna Convention"), which in addition to the prohibition of cultivation and export of psychotropic substances, had the merit, having regard to the amounts of money generated by such commerce, of specifically addressing the economic aspects of drug trafficking. In order to prevent the legitimate use of the proceeds of crime, the Vienna Convention adopted a scheme essentially based on three main concepts, notably (i) the obligation to establish money laundering as a separate crime by the national legal systems; (ii) the freezing and seizing of the assets deriving from or constituting the proceeds of crime; and (iii) the enhancement of inter-State cooperation and mutual legal assistance in penal matters.

This basic scheme has been adopted by subsequent international instruments combating money laundering and in particular by the Council of Europe Convention on Laundering, Search, Seizure and Confiscation of the Proceeds of Crime of 8 November 1990 (hereinafter the "Strasbourg Convention").[23] This convention is of paramount

terrorist character. At the domestic level — with specific reference to US law — similarities between international terrorism and transnational organised crime had suggested the application of the Racketeer Influenced and Corrupt Organization Act (RICO), see Z Joseph, "The Application of RICO to International Terrorism" (1990) 58 *Fordham Law Review* 1071; SC Warneck, "A Preemptive Strike: Using RICO and the AEDPA to Attack the Financial Strength of International Terrorist Organizations" (1998) 78 *Boston University Law Review* 177.

[21] See FATF–XII, *Report on Money Laundering Typologies 2000–2001* of 1st February 2001, at 19 and 20.

[22] On the national and international aspects of anti-money laundering regimes see the extensive and in-depth study of G Stessens, *Money Laundering: A New International Law Enforcement Model* (Cambridge, Cambridge University Press, 1999); K Hinterseer, *Criminal Finance: The Political Economy of Money Laundering in a Comparative Legal Context* (Kluwer Law International, The Hague, 2002) J L Di Brina, M Picchio Forlati (eds), *Normativa antiriciclaggio e contrasto alla criminaliã economica*, (CEDAM, Padova, 2002).

[23] ETS, n 141; for commentary see V Delicato, "Reato di Riciclaggio e Cooperazione Internazionale: l'Applicazione in Italia della Convenzione del Consiglio d'Europa del 1990" (1995) 31 *Rivista di diritto internazionale, privato e processuale* 341; E Müller-Rappard, "Inter-State Cooperation in Penal Matters Within the Council of Europe Framework" in M Cherif Bassiouni (ed), *International Criminal Law*, 2nd edn, vol II, *Procedural and Enforcement Mechanisms* (Transnational Publishers, Ardsley, New York, 1999) 331, spec at 349 ff.

importance in that it intends to be a broad and general instrument to prevent the use of proceeds of crime beyond the specific focus on drug-related crimes. To this end, the Strasbourg Convention expands the scope of application of the Vienna Convention, subjecting to the money laundering regime additional predicate offences which are not associated with narcotic trafficking, but which are also capable of generating large profits. This step was taken in the belief that the fight against serious crimes has become an increasingly international problem, which calls for the use of modern and effective methods on an international scale, and in particular of the deprivation of criminals of the proceeds of crime.[24]

The treaty framework is completed by a set of rules on international cooperation covering all procedural stages including investigative assistance as well as the search, seizure and confiscation of the proceeds of crime, accompanied by provisions governing extradition, assistance in evidence gathering and execution of penal sanctions. It is worth noting that the picture of international cooperation in criminal matters is completed by provisions encouraging contracting States to enter Mutual Legal Assistance Treaties (MLATs), establishing more detailed provisions to be of aid to law enforcement authorities.[25]

Indisputably, effective inter-State cooperation is necessary to track money and other assets originating from crimes in order to enable their seizure and confiscation as envisaged by the Conventions. In this regard, one of the most powerful provisions contained in both Conventions is the express waiver of banking secrecy, which removes one of the major obstacles to tracing the proceeds of crime, thus preventing a State Party from declining assistance on this basis.[26] This is a remarkable step in the struggle against criminality and a demonstration that the international community

[24] See preamble of the Strasbourg Convention.

[25] For a review of the principal forms of cooperation contemplated in both the Vienna and Strasbourg Conventions and in bilateral Mutual Legal Assistance Treaties (MLATs), see M Cherif Bassiouni and DS Gualtieri, "International and National Responses to the Globalization of Money Laundering" in M Cherif Bassiouni (ed), *International Criminal Law*, 2nd ed., vol. II, *Procedural and Enforcement Mechanisms* (Transnational Publishers, Ardsley, 1999) 675.

[26] See Art 7(5) of the Vienna Convention stating that "A Party shall not decline to act under the provision of this paragraph on the ground of bank secrecy"; see also Art 5(3) compelling States Parties to the Convention to empower courts or other competent authorities "to order that bank, financial institution or commercial records be made available or be seized". See also Art 18(7) of the Strasbourg Convention excluding banking secrecy as a legitimate ground for refusal of inter-state cooperation; the provision reads "A Party shall not invoke bank secrecy as a ground to refuse any co-operation under this chapter. Where its domestic law so requires, a Party may require that a request for co-operation which would involve the lifting of bank secrecy be authorised by either a judge or another judicial authority, including public prosecutors, any of these authorities acting in relation to criminal offences". For a review of the issues connected to bank secrecy in the context of the fight against money laundering see G Stessens, *Money Laundering. A New International Law Enforcement Model* (Cambridge University Press, Cambridge, 1999) 311.

is increasingly aware of the seriousness of the phenomenon of money laundering, which compels the adoption of extraordinary measures. Unilateral efforts to pierce banking secrecy, through extraterritorial discovery orders adopted by various jurisdictions, and in particular by US authorities, have raised issues of compatibility with international law as well as causing diplomatic tension with jurisdictions providing banking secrecy as a means of protecting financial privacy and fostering economic policy.[27] Therefore, international cooperation has been the only available solution to accommodate these conflicting interests. Various jurisdictions which protect banking secrecy, in particular Switzerland, due to concern with the seriousness of the threats posed by transnational criminality to the soundness and reputation of the financial system, notably when financial institutions are used for sheltering illegally-derived proceeds, have ratified the Vienna Convention, the Strasbourg Convention and have concluded bilateral MLATs explicitly providing for the lifting of banking secrecy in relation to such criminal matters.[28] Piercing of banking secrecy is provided also by the 1990 UN Model Treaty on Mutual Assistance in Criminal Matters.[29] It is worth noting that such international law-making processes have also resulted in amendments to domestic laws on banking secrecy in order to comply with the normative contents of these international instruments.[30]

However valuable the regime provided by the Vienna and Strasbourg Conventions, it can only be of partial aid in the struggle against the funding of terrorism, given that it does not cover the financing of terrorism through legitimate resources absent the establishment of a specific crime of terrorist financing.

Adoption of specific measures at the international level to combat the financing of terrorism is therefore a necessary step to complete and to adjust the anti-money laundering regime to the peculiarities of the funding

[27] For a review of the relevant US case-law and for a comment of the underlining issues, see CT Jones, "Compulsion over Comity: The United States' Assault on Foreign Bank Secrecy", (1992) 12 *Journal of International Law and Business* 454; C McLachlan, "The Jurisdictional Limits of Disclosure Orders in Transnational Fraud Litigation" (1998) 47 *International and Comparative Law Quarterly* 3.

[28] The bilateral MLAT between US and Switzerland has proved to be particularly effective, see KM Singh, "Nowhere to Hide: Judicial Assistance in Piercing the Veil of Swiss Banking Secrecy" (1991) 71 *Boston University Law Review* 847.

[29] See A/RES/45/117 of 14 December 1990. Art 4(f) expressly excludes that assistance be refused "solely on the ground of secrecy of banks and similar financial institutions".

[30] For an overview of the content and of the amendments to the Swiss Criminal Code with regard to banking secrecy, see F Beck and M Jagmetti, "Il segreto bancario in Svizzera" (1993) 7 *Diritto del Commercio Internazionale* 279; P Bernasconi, "Il Segreto Bancario Svizzero nella Collaborazione Giudiziaria Internazinale in Materia Penale e Fiscale" (1995) 66 *Diritto e Pratica Tributaria*, I, 1934; D Poncet, C Lombardini, "Segreto bancario e modifiche recenti nel diritto di cooperazione penale nella Confederazione elvetica" (1998) 51 *Banca Borsa e titoli di credito*, I, 488.

of terrorism.[31] UN Security Council Resolution 1373 and the FATF have envisaged the criminalisation of terrorism financing as the first step to be taken to fight the financing of terrorism, given that it would enable domestic jurisdictions to apply the mechanisms provided by the anti-money laundering regimes which cannot otherwise be applied without the specific proscription of such an offence.

From a criminal law standpoint, contrary to the classic money laundering scenario where the laundering process is undertaken *after* and as a consequence of economic crimes which have been already committed, in the case of terrorist financing, the acts of financial assistance — where the laundering activity may take place — occur *before* an act of terrorism (if any) is actually committed. Therefore, the argument has been made that the crime of financial assistance to terrorists does not fall, strictly speaking, into the category of predicate offences,[32] it being quite obvious that the crime of financing of terrorism has to do with disguising the *destination* of the funds rather than their illicit *origin*. Hence, the criminalisation of terrorist financing has arguably the effect of ultimately expanding the scope of application of the anti-money laundering regime, in order to apply the existing monitoring and law enforcement schemes to a new criminal hypothesis.[33]

From another perspective, it should be stressed that in order to be effective, the criminalisation of the financing of terrorism must be established at the international level, since sporadic prohibitions of financing of terrorism by single jurisdictions risk being inadequate vis-à-vis the global ramifications of terrorism and the dual criminality requirement for the exercise of jurisdiction in criminal matters.[34] Therefore, a multilateral approach, requiring a high degree of consensus on the introduction of this crime is crucial to effective enforcement of the measures enacted against the financing of terrorism, and against terrorism more generally.[35]

[31] The need of specific measures to complement anti-money laundering scheme had been raised by FATF experts who consider the financing of terrorism as a of money laundering, as such requiring *ad hoc* measures; see FATF–XII, *Report on Money Laundering Typologies 2000–2001*, at 20.

[32] JJ Norton and H Shams, "Money Laundering Law and Terrorist Financing: Post-September 11 Responses — Let Us Step Back and Take a Deep Breath?" (2002) 36 *International Lawyer* 103.

[33] See also, J Jackson, "11th September 2001: Will it Make a Difference to the Global Anti-Money Laundering Movement?" (2002) 5 *Journal of Money Laundering Control* 10.

[34] On dual criminality see C van den Wyngaert, "Double Criminality as a Requirement to Jurisdiction", in N Jareborg (ed), *Double criminality. Studies in International Criminal Law* (Iustus Forlag, Uppsala, 1989) 43; reprinted in J Dugard, C van den Wyngaert (eds), *International Criminal Law and Procedure* (Aldershot, Brookfield, 1996) 131.

[35] See JA Carberry, "Terrorism: A Global Phenomenon Mandating a Unified International Response" (1999) 6 *Indiana Journal of Global Legal Studies* 685, arguing in favour of a unified and integrated response to terrorism, demanding a high degree of cooperation.

B. The Criminalisation of the Financing of Terrorism under US Law and the Limits of Unilateral Action

Even before the law-making developments following the events of September 11, steps against the funding of terrorist groups had been taken at the domestic level in the context of the struggle against international terrorism. Special rules proscribing support to terrorists under any form, as well as transactions with such organisations or State sponsors of terrorism had been enacted in US law. Federal law had criminalised financial assistance to terrorism since 1994 in 18 USC 2339A, subsequently amended by the comprehensive Anti-Terrorism and Effective Death Penalty Act of 1996 (AEDPA),[36] which was passed one year after the bombing of the federal building in Oklahoma City. This statute, targeting foreign terrorist organisations on the assumption that these groups "raise significant funds within the United States, or use the United States as a conduit for the receipt of funds raised in other nations" and "are so tainted by their criminal conduct that any contribution to such an organization facilitates that conduct", sets forth rules aiming at preventing such material support. Thus, proscribed conduct includes the supply of material support or resources to terrorists (18 USC 2339A), the provision of material support or resources to designated terrorist organisations (18 USC 2339B); the provision or collection of funds (18 USC 2339C) and the engagement in financial transactions with terrorists (18 USC 2332d).[37] Whereas paragraph 2339A, as amended by the USA PATRIOT Act of 2001,[38] sanctions by up to fifteen years of imprisonment whoever provides material support or resources or conceals or disguises the nature, location, source or ownership of material support or resources, knowing or intending that they are to be used in preparation for, or in carrying out specific mentioned crimes related to terrorism; paragraph 2339B is directed against whoever in the United States or subject to its jurisdiction provides material support or resources to a *foreign* terrorist organisation, or attempts or conspires to do so. With respect to the financial aspects of both offences, "material support or resources" means "currency or monetary instruments or financial securities, financial services …".[39] The

[36] Public Law n 104–32 [S.735], of April 24, 1996.

[37] Similar provisions were already proscribed by the Prevention of Terrorism Act 1989 adopted by the United Kingdom; for a review, see D Schiff, "Managing Terrorism the British Way", in R Higgins and M Flory, *Terrorism and International Law* (Routledge, London, 1997) 129.

[38] Uniting and Strengthening America by Providing Appropriate Tools Required to Intercept and Obstruct Terrorism (USA PATRIOT ACT) Act of 2001, Public Law 107–56, 26 October 2001, see below para 9.1.

[39] See 18 USC 2339A, letter (b), the list also includes "lodging, training, expert advice or assistance, safehouse, false documentation or identification, communications equipment, facilities, weapons, lethal substances, explosives, personnel, transportation and other physical assets, except medicine or religious materials".

offence codified by paragraph 2339A appears broad and generic, whereas the offence proscribed by paragraph 2339B expressly targets foreign terrorist organisations.[40] These are specifically designated by the Secretary of State in accordance with the administrative procedure laid down in the AEDPA, in the light of the threat posed by such organisations to the security of United States nationals and the national security of the United States. Despite the delicate issues that such a designation process is likely to raise in terms of respect for civil liberties and due process,[41] the designation of an entity as a foreign terrorist organisation may be immediately sanctioned: financial institutions may be ordered to freeze assets which are connected to such criminal entities.[42] The conduct proscribed by paragraph 2339C is even broader and is closer to the notion of terrorism financing set forth by the New York Convention. It targets "whoever ... by any means, directly or indirectly, unlawfully and wilfully provides or collects funds with the intention that such funds be used, or with the knowledge that such funds are to be used, in full or in part, in order to carry out" terrorist acts, regardless of the circumstance that the funds are actually used to carry out a particular act.

The offence provided at 18 USC paragraph 2332d operates at a different level in that it prevents any United States person from engaging in financial transactions with the governments of those countries designated by the competent US agencies as a State sponsor of international terrorism. The same effort of isolating State sponsors of terrorism is pursued by the obligation imposed on United States representatives within international financial institutions, such as the IMF and the World Bank, to oppose any loan or other use of the funds of the respective institution to or for a country which has been designated as sponsor of terrorism.[43]

[40] For a commentary see J Benson, "Send Me Money: Controlling International Terrorism by Restricting Fundraising in the United States" (1999) 21 *Houston Journal of International Law* 321, at 327. The author illustrates also, that in the wake of the federal legislation single states, such as Illinois, Maryland, Wisconsin enacted anti-terrorism statutes proscribing terrorist fundraising; W Patton, "Preventing Terrorist Fundraising in the United States" (1996) 30 *George Washington Journal of International Law & Economics* 127, with references also to the British legislation.

[41] See 8 USC 1189. The analysis of the relationship of the AEDPA procedure with human rights standards, however exceeds the scope of the present paper. Lack of review procedures and absence of a common set of rules in accordance to which individuals and groups are designated to be terrorists, have raised criticism also outside the US, in Sweden and France and created diplomatic tension. These countries have challenged the accuracy of the modalities of designation and claimed the disregard of human rights in such a process, see Alexander, above n 13, 219.

[42] See 8 USC 1189, which, in respect of the freezing of assets reads "Upon notification ... , the Secretary of the Treasury may require United States financial institutions possessing or controlling any assets of any foreign organization included in the notification to block all financial transaction involving those assets until further directive from either the Secretary of the Treasury, Act of Congress, or order of the Court".

[43] See 22 USC 262p–4q.

A third provision relates to the issue of State-sponsored financing of terrorism from a reparatory standpoint, by allowing the lifting of sovereign immunity of those States supporting terrorist activities.[44] Although this provision is significant from the perspective of general international law, its effectiveness in the fight against international terrorism is disputable. Suffice it to note here the political nature of such a provision, intended to offer relief to the victims (US nationals) of terrorist acts, rather than actually combating State sponsorship of terrorism. In this regard it should be underlined that even the collection of damages by the victims of terrorism, contemplated by the provision, has long remained ineffective because of the disputes which have arisen within the US itself, in respect of the actual enforcement of the judgments awarding damages against foreign States.[45]

Normative endeavours to fight the financing of terrorist groups, therefore, rather than focusing on State sponsorship of terrorism, concentrate on the non-State actors and their financing patterns, by providing *ex ante*

[44] The AEDPA added section 1605(a)(7) to the Foreign Sovereign Immunities Act which states that the District Courts of the United States may exercise jurisdiction over all claims "in which money damages are sought against a foreign state for personal injury or death that was caused by an act of torture, extrajudicial killing, aircraft sabotage, hostage taking, *or the provision of material support or resources* (as defined in section 2339A of title 18) for such an act if such act or provision of material support is engaged in by an official, employee, or agent of such foreign state while acting within the scope of his or her office, employment or agency, except that the court shall decline to hear a claim under this paragraph…(A) if the foreign state was not designated as a state sponsor of terrorism… at the time the act occurred, unless later designated as a result of such act…" (emphasis added).

[45] The major difficulties have come from the executive branch which on several occasions has opposed the actual collection of the large awards made by the judiciary as a result of suits filed by victims of terrorist attacks; see *Alejandre v Republic of Cuba*, 996 F.Supp 1239 (SDFla 1997); *Flatow v Islamic Republic of Iran*, 999 F.Supp 1 (DDC 1998); *Cicippio v Islamic Republic of Iran*, 18 F.Supp 2d 62 (DDC 1998). For further references see, "State Jurisdiction and Jurisdiction Immunities" (2000) 94 *American Journal of International Law* 117; "Lawsuit by U.S. Hostage Against Iran" (2002) 96 *American Journal of International Law* 463, discussing *Roeder v Iran*, Complaint No 1:00CV03110 (EGS) (DDC 29 Dec 2000), and "Terrorist-Exception Cases in 2002", *ibid* 964, on *Price v Socialist People's Lybian Arab Jamahiriya*, 110 F.Supp 2d 10 (DDC 2000); "2002 Victims of Terrorism Law" (2003) 97 *American Journal of International Law* 187, on *Hegna v Iran*, N 00–00716, slip op (DDC Jan 22, 2002); McKay, "A New Take on Antiterrorism: Smith v Socialist People's Libyan Arab Jamahiriya" (1997) 13 *American University International Law Review* 439; WP Hoye, "Fighting Fire with… Mire? Civil Remedies and the New War on State-Sponsored Terrorism" (2002) 12 *Duke Journal of Comparative & International Law* 105; SP Vitrano, "Hell-Bent on Awarding Recovery to Terrorism Victims: the Evolution and Application of the Anti-terrorism Amendments to the Foreign Sovereign Immunity Act" (2000) 19 *Dickinson Journal of International Law* 213, also for references to the relevant case-law; L Fisler Damrosch, "Sanctions Against Perpetrators of Terrorism" (1999) 22 *Houston Journal of International Law* 63 for an examination of this provision from the perspective of the strengthening of economic pressure against state sponsors of terrorism; for a critique of this exception to sovereign immunity see, D Gartenstein-Ross, "A Critique of the Terrorism Exception to the Foreign Sovereign Immunity Act" (2002) 34 *New York University Journal of International Law & Policy* 887.

and more effective responses in the tools available within criminal law.[46] In this regard, although US domestic law has the merit of addressing terrorist financing as a separate and complementary issue in the fight against international terrorism, its unilateral approach may undermine its effectiveness. In the absence of reciprocal engagements and cooperation schemes with foreign States, the inherent territorial scope of criminal jurisdiction may impair the strength of such internal proscriptions. Even the extraterritorial reach attached to these provisions[47] may prove ineffective against the financing of terrorism. Not surprisingly, considering the transnational ramifications of terrorist groups, the need for inter-State cooperation for an effective response to terrorism financing is acknowledged by US law itself.[48]

The limits of unilateral action, regardless of the extraterritorial reach of the enacted provisions, are expressly admitted also by Presidential Executive Order 13224 of 24 September 2001, issued by President Bush in the immediate aftermath of the events of September 11.[49] The Executive Order, adopted in accordance with the International Emergency Economic Power Act, promptly reacts to the attacks of September 11 from the perspective of the financing of terrorists, by imposing the freezing of assets belonging to designated terrorists or terrorist organisations that "are in the United States or that hereafter come within the United States, or that hereafter come within the possession or control of United States persons" and by prohibiting any transaction or dealing with the blocked assets.[50] Section 4 of the Executive Order prohibits donations to designated terrorist organisations, thus directly intervening in the misuse of charities for terrorist funding purposes. Lastly, it is worth mentioning Section 6 of the Executive Order which calls for cooperation and coordination among the agencies involved as well as for a reinforced and flexible

[46] See also A Einisman, "Ineffectiveness at Its Best: Fighting Terrorism with Economic Sanctions" (2000) 9 *Minnesota Journal of Global Trade* 299, arguing against the resort to economic sanctions in the fight of international terrorism, also in the light of the declining role of State-sponsored terrorism replaced by independent groups.

[47] See for instance Section 303(d) which establishes "extraterritorial Federal jurisdiction over an offence under this section". An extraterritorial character may also be attributed to the prohibition of financial transactions with terrorists, addressed to "whoever, being a United States person", broadly defined as to include "(a) United States citizens or nationals; (b) permanent resident aliens; (c) juridical persons organized under the laws of the United States; or (d) any person in the United States" (AEDPA, Section 321).

[48] See AEDPA, Section 18 USC 2339B (a)(5) note.

[49] 50 USC 1791.

[50] See Executive Order 13224, section 1. The order as well as the freezing of funds and assets is extensively commented upon by LG Radicati di Brozolo and M Megliani in this book, therefore it will not be dealt with in the present chapter. On the US financial sanctions, see also Alexander, above n 13, 80–81; JJ Savage, "Executive Use of the International Emergency Economic Powers Act: Evolution through the Terrorist and Taliban Sanctions" (2001) 10 *Currents: International Trade Law Journal* 28, 36.

international cooperation focused on the sharing of information on the funding activities in support of terrorism.

C. The International Criminalisation of the Financing of Terrorism

Terrorist financing is today proscribed as a separate and autonomous crime by most jurisdictions around the world, due to the joint pressure exercised by the United Nations, the FATF and regional organisations, such as the European Union, in the aftermath of the September 11th attacks.

The cornerstone of the recent normative developments is UN Security Council Resolution 1373 of 28 September 2001,[51] adopted a few days after the terrorist acts against the United States. The Security Council, acting on the basis of Chapter VII of the Charter, having acknowledged that acts "of international terrorism constitute a threat to the international peace and security", addressed the issue of the financing of terrorist organisations, putting on an equal footing the funding and the planning of terrorist acts. This is explicitly stated in paragraph 5 of the Resolution where it is declared that "acts, methods and practices of terrorism are contrary to the purposes and principles of the United Nations and that knowingly financing, planning and inciting terrorist acts are also contrary to the purposes and principles of the United Nations".

Resolution 1373 envisages specific measures against the financing of terrorism to be adopted by *all* States. Such measures are directly targeted to prevent any kind of financial assets from reaching and fuelling terrorist organisations, resorting to substantive criminal and conservatory measures. The strategy envisioned by the Security Council, is basically threefold and consists of (a) the criminalisation of the wilful provision or collection, by any means, directly or indirectly, of funds with the intention that the funds should be used in order to carry out terrorist acts; (b) the freezing of funds and other financial assets or economic resources of persons who commit, or attempt to commit, terrorist acts;[52] and (c) the prohibition that their nationals and entities within their territories make any fund, financial assets or economic resources or financial or other services available, directly or indirectly, for the benefit of persons involved in the commission of terrorist acts. Ancillary to these provisions is the requirement that *all* states (i) deny safe haven to those who finance terrorist acts in addition to those who plan, support and commit such acts, and (ii) extend repressive judicial

[51] See S/RES/1373 of 28 September 2001; reaffirmed by S/RES/1390/2002 of 16 January 2002.
[52] The freezing of terrorists' assets had already been ordered by the Security Council directly addressed to the Taliban government (S/RES/1267 of 15 October 1999) and to "Usama Bin Laden and individuals and entities associated with him ... including those in the Al-Qaida organization" (S/RES/1333 of 19 December 2000).

measures to those who finance the organisations, so that they are actually brought to justice and are subjected to a punishment adequate to the seriousness of the crime committed. In order to achieve these goals, the Resolution urges the ratification of the New York Convention on the Suppression of the Financing of Terrorism, the principal obligations of which are duplicated by the Resolution.[53]

This approach has subsequently been implemented by regional international organisations. The European Union promptly reacted to the UN Security Council Resolution, by enacting specific measures; notably Common Position 2001/931/CFSP,[54] Regulation 2580/2001/EC on the freezing of assets belonging to terrorist entities and individuals,[55] and Directive 2001/97/EC on money laundering.[56] A mechanism for evaluating the legal systems and their implementation at national level in the fight against terrorism has been recently adopted.[57]

The contribution of the FATF to counter the financing of terrorism is particularly valuable both from a policy-making perspective and from a compliance monitoring standpoint. The Special Recommendations include (a) the criminalisation of the financing of terrorism and associated money laundering[58]; (b) the freezing of all funds belonging to terrorist organisations[59]; (c) the ratification of the New York Convention on the suppression of terrorism financing[60] and (d) the intensification of inter-State cooperation.[61]

In addition the FATF has launched a self-assessment questionnaire in order to verify the level of compliance with the Special ecommendations

[53] See Part IV B.

[54] Council Common Position on the application of specific measures to combat terrorism, in O.J. Eur. Comm. L 344 of 27 December 2001, at 93.

[55] Regulation of 27 December 2001, in O.J. Eur. Comm. L 344 of 28 December 2001 at 70, on which see the comments by LG Radicati di Brozolo and M Megliani in this book.

[56] On the initiatives undertaken at Community level, see the contribution by A Reinisch in this book.

[57] Council Decision 2002/996/JHA of 28 November 2002 in O.J. Eur. Comm. L 349 of 24 December 2002.

[58] Recommendation II reads: "Each country should criminalise the financing of terrorism, terrorist acts and terrorist organisations. Countries should ensure that such offences are designated as money laundering predicate offences".

[59] Recommendation III reads "Each country should implement measures to freeze without delay funds or other money assets of terrorists who finance terrorism and terrorist organisations in accordance with the United Nations resolutions relating to the prevention and the suppression of the financing of terrorist acts. Each country should also adopt and implement measures, including legislative ones, which would enable the competent authorities to seize and confiscate property that is the proceeds of, or used in, or intended or allocated for use in, the financing of terrorism, terrorist acts or terrorist organisations".

[60] Recommendation I reads: "Each country should take immediate steps to ratify and implement fully the 1999 United Nations International Convention for the Suppression of the Financing of Terrorism. Countries should also immediately implement the United Nations resolutions relating to the prevention and suppression of the financing of terrorist acts, particularly United Nations Security Council Resolution 1373".

[61] Recommendation V reads: "Each country should afford another country, on the basis of a treaty, arrangements or mechanism for mutual legal assistance or information exchange, the greatest possible measure of assistance in connection with criminal, civil enforcement, and

which reports positive results. Responses submitted by both FATF member States and States who are members of FATF-like organisations show an encouraging level of implementation of the Special Recommendations in domestic legal systems.[62] Similarly encouraging responses come from the reports submitted by UN Member States to the *ad hoc* Counter-Terrorism Committee entrusted with the task of monitoring the implementation of UN Security Council Resolution 1373. Both sources show that many jurisdictions have established in their domestic law the financing of terrorism as an independent and autonomous crime[63] and have ratified the UN 1999 Convention (which was more or less ignored by the international community before the events of September 11), thus speeding up its entry into force on 10 April 2002.[64]

These encouraging data, however, do not actually correspond to the reality of the situation. An accurate analysis shows that in many cases the domestic implementation of the UN Resolution n. 1373 equates only to formal compliance and has not attained the intended degree of uniformity across jurisdictions. This is largely attributable to the different degrees of development of the domestic legal systems, resulting in disparities in technical and administrative skills and in infrastructural support. Such environmental hurdles may lead to transnational divergence between

administrative investigations, inquiries and proceedings relating to the financing of terrorism, terrorist acts and terrorist organisations. Countries should also take all possible measures to ensure that they do not provide safe havens for individuals charged with the financing of terrorism, terrorist acts or terrorist organisations, and should have procedures in place to extradite, where possible, such individuals".

[62] See FATF Annual Report 2001–2002 at 5. The highest levels of compliance have been achieved by the FATF special Recommendations concerning freezing of terrorist assets, followed by the recommendation regarding international cooperation and that urging the criminalisation of the financing of terrorism.

[63] For instance see Article 1 of Italian Law of 15 December 2001, n. 438, which by introducing new Article 270-*bis* in the Criminal Code, proscribes the crime of international terrorism sanctioning whoever promotes, establishes, manages, directs or funds organisations pursuing international terrorism; see also § 2339C of 18 US Code. For a commentary on the new provisions introduced in Luxembourg see A Schmitt and F Sudret, "Cutting the Financial Roots of Terrorism: Introduction of a New Bill in Luxembourg" (2002) 17 *Journal of International Banking Law* 382; for Canadian law see E Machado, "A Note on the Terrorism Financing Offences in Bill C–36" (2002) 60 *University of Toronto Faculty Law Review* 103; BP Bedard and AJ Kilgour, "Tracking Funds: Canada's Recent Initiatives to Combat Money Laundering and the Financing of Terrorism" (2002) 17 *Journal of International Banking Law* 117; and on the recent initiatives in Switzerland refer to EHG. Hüpke, "Keeping Dirty Money and Terrorist Funds Away: the Proposed Money Laundering Regulation of the Swiss Federal Banking Commission" (2002) 10 *Journal of Financial Regulation and Compliance* 317. On the work of the Counter-Terrorism Committee, See E Rosand, "Security Council Resolution 1373, the Counter-Terrorism Committee, and the Fight Against Terrorism" (2003) *American Journal of International Law* 333.

[64] It is worth mentioning, however, that many States particularly exposed to terrorist financing activities, such as Switzerland, Saudi Arabia, Jordan, Bahamnas, China, Luxembourg, the Philippines, and Tunisia, as well as Belgium, Germany, and Greece, have not yet ratified the Convention, thus threatening its overall effectiveness. For further details see <http:www.untreaty.un.org/ENGLISH/Status/Chapter_xviii/treaty11.asp>.

implementing measures, which in light of the cross-border nature of the financing of terrorism and of the requirement of double criminality to promote international criminal proceedings, may impair the effectiveness of the international legal framework.[65]

Lack of consensus has been reported, for instance, on the definition of financing of terrorism, that many States assumed to be already covered by anti-money laundering or by other criminal provisions. Taking into account the recommendation to ratify the New York Convention, a possible solution to enhance the uniform implementation of the Resolution might be to take the definition of the crime provided for in the New York Convention as guidance for national legislators.

Under Article 2 of the New York Convention, the crime of financing of terrorism is committed by any person who "by any means, directly or indirectly, unlawfully and wilfully, provides or collects funds with the intention that they should be used or in the knowledge that they are to be used, in full or in part, in order to carry out" terrorist activities. It is worth noting that while the Convention requires the criminal intent in the supply of funds, it does not require their actual employment for terrorist acts.[66] Some national legislators, however, have adopted more stringent provisions. While the New York Convention prohibits the use of funds for "terrorist activities", UK, Canadian and US laws have codified a broader notion of this crime, proscribing the financing of "terrorist groups", besides that of "terrorist activities". The "organisational approach" endorsed by the proscription of the financing of the group of terrorists in addition to the terrorist acts, may prove more efficient against terrorism since it does not require any particular link with subsequent terrorist activities.[67]

IV. THE ROLE OF FINANCIAL INSTITUTIONS IN FIGHTING THE FINANCING OF TERRORISM

A. The International Framework

The economic feature of the crime of money laundering, ultimately aimed at disguising the revenue's illicit origin with a view to injecting it into the

[65] See W Gehr, "Recurrent Issues (Briefing for Member States) 4 April 2002", available at <http:www.un.org>. See also the realistic criticism expressed by Alexander, above n 13, 218; M Kantor, "Effective Enforcement of International Obligations to Suppress the Financing of Terror — Prepared in conjunction with the ASIL Presidential Task Force on Terrorism — (2002)", available at <http:www.asil.org> , visited on 15 October 2002. Both authors warn against the risk that efforts undertaken internationally are confined solely to the law-making level without sufficient concern as to the implementation of those norms.

[66] Article 2(3) of the New York Convention.

[67] An analysis of Canadian, UK and US law, compared with the New York Convention, has been carried out by KE Davis, "Legislating against the Financing of Terrorism: Pitfalls and Prospects" (2003) 10 *Journal of Financial Crime* 269, at 271.

legitimate economy, makes it a complex offence which calls for an interdisciplinary approach. The criminal law aspects examined so far cannot be successfully enforced unless they are complemented by efficient regulatory provisions tackling the abuse of financial institutions involved in the commission of these crimes. It is a common understanding that banks may be "unwittingly used as intermediaries for the transfer of funds derived from criminal activity"[68] and that in order to preserve financial stability, soundness and the reputation of banks, supervisors have to take steps to avoid the abuse of the financial system for criminal purposes. The achievement of this goal necessarily relies on the cooperation of the private sector, i.e. on financial institutions themselves. In line with this, the comprehensive framework against money laundering, condensed in the FATF's Forty Recommendations,[69] is a prominent contribution to this interdisciplinary approach, since it takes into due account both the criminal and the financial profiles of the struggle to this crime. Section B of the FATF standards specifically addresses the role of the financial system in combating money laundering, by imposing on financial institutions reporting obligations in relation to suspicious transactions and the adoption of transparency requirements in the management of banking relationships.[70]

These deal in particular with the control of the client's identity, the so called "know-your-customer" principle (or "KYC"), which, in the case of accounts opened on behalf of juridical persons, imposes the identification of the beneficial owner, as well as the actual existence of the legal entity. The implementation of the KYC principle has been conducive to the elimination of anonymous bank accounts and to the lifting of bank secrecy in investigations on money laundering offences,[71] thus removing traditional major obstacles to the tracking of funds and the reconstruction of suspicious transactions. In this context, financial institutions are also required to retain for at least five years the necessary transaction records, in order to be able to expeditiously comply with the authorities' requests. The risks of misuse of banking institutions for money laundering purposes have required further reporting duties to the competent authorities regarding all "complex, unusual large transactions, and all unusual patterns of transactions, which have no apparent economic or visible lawful purposes".[72]

[68] Bank of International Settlements, "Prevention of Criminal Use of the Banking System for the Purpose of Money-Laundering", 12 December 1988, available at <http:www.bis.org> .
[69] See above at Part II A.
[70] On the role of financial institutions in the prevention of money laundering see extensively G Stessens, *Money Laundering. A New International Law Enforcement Model* (Cambridge University Press, Cambridge, 1999) 143 ff.
[71] The lifting of banking secrecy is provided for by both the Vienna and the Strasbourg Convention as well as by several MLATs specifically dealing with money laundering offence, see Part III A.
[72] See FATF Forty Recommendations, Recommendation n. 14. For an in-depth analysis of the Italian framework of banking supervision with concern to money laundering, accounting for

Lastly, due to their particular suitability for concealing tracks, the Forty Recommendations also draw attention to the misuse of corporate vehicles such as shell corporations and the use of bearer shares and other negotiable instruments.

These standards have had a critical impact at the domestic and regional level where they have received widespread implementation by legislators. Particularly telling is Directive 91/308/EEC on money laundering,[73] adopted in light of the Community liberalisation of financial services and of the ensuing increased circulation of capital. To prevent criminal activities benefiting from such cross-border liberalisation, the Directive provides for transparency requirements, due diligence provisions and reporting duties inspired by the FATF Forty Recommendations, to be complied with by the financial institutions admitted to operate on the common market.

To complete the picture of the initiatives to protect the financial system from abuses, special consideration must be given to the activity of the FATF in controlling the actual implementation of the Forty Recommendations, in order to assess effective progress in the fight against money laundering. Even though, as observed before,[74] the standards laid down by this inter-governmental body are "soft law" and are not legally binding, they nonetheless hold special authority with national legislators and enjoy a general international consensus. As a result of the country by country review, FATF singles out a list of "non-cooperative countries", which are encouraged to comply with the recommendations. It is hardly questionable that those jurisdictions which disregard internationally agreed standards on financial supervision, transparency requirements and suspicious transactions reporting duties largely impair the effectiveness of the supranational framework to combat money laundering, thus allowing criminals to structure their transactions in such a way as to take advantage of the loopholes in the global financial system.[75] Coordinated international pressure to isolate these countries is therefore a powerful tool to obtain their cooperation.

B. The 1999 UN Convention on the Suppression of the Financing of Terrorism

The legislative experiences against money laundering and the funding of terrorism, accounted for in the previous paragraphs, were important

the different authorities involved and the tasks respectively entrusted to them see A Urbani, "Supervisione Bancaria e Lotta al Riciclaggio" (2002) 55 *Banca, Borsa e Titoli di Credito*, I, 480.

[73] Council Directive 91/308/CEE of 10 June 1991 on prevention of the use of the financial system for purpose of money laundering, in OJ Eur Comm L 166 of 28 June 1991, 77, as recently amended by Directive 2001/97/EC, in OJ Eur Comm L 344 of 28 December 2001, 76.
[74] See Part II A.
[75] See FATF, Report on Non-Cooperative Countries and Territories, 14 February 2000.

terms of reference in the drafting of the UN Convention on the Suppression of the Financing of Terrorism. This international treaty is the last part of the normative piecemeal approach to international terrorism consisting in several "sectoral" conventions, each of which deals with specific aspects of terrorist acts.

The New York Convention specifically addresses the issue of terrorist financing, thus filling an important gap of the international legal framework against international terrorism. It is a comprehensive and valuable tool for combating terrorist financing since it concentrates in one legal instrument the criminal approach endorsed by the anti-money laundering conventions and the obligations imposed on financial institutions to prevent the sheltering of the proceeds of crime.

With regard to the first aspect, besides the cornerstone provision of Article 2, which establishes terrorism financing as an autonomous offence[76], the New York Convention contains a definition of terrorism which delimits the substantive scope of application of the treaty. "Terrorism" is defined as "any act intended to cause death or serious bodily injury to a civilian, or to any other person not taking an active part in the hostilities in a situation of armed conflict, when the purpose of such an act, by its nature or context, is to intimidate a population, or to compel a government or an international organization to do or to abstain from doing any act".[77] Although the effort to set out a definition must be praised as an attempt to reduce the ambiguities which characterise the notion of terrorism and to clarify when the treaty applies, the notion of terrorism is still inevitably loose and prone to divergences of interpretation.

Having defined its ambit of application, the Convention sets provisions reinforcing inter-State cooperation in the tracing, freezing and confiscation of assets and funds of terrorist groups. In addition, States Parties to the Convention are required to afford one another the greatest measure of assistance in connection with investigations or criminal or extradition proceedings, including assistance in obtaining evidence. In this respect, it is worth mentioning that like anti-money laundering treaties, the New York Convention explicitly provides for the waiver of banking secrecy.[78] Consistently with existing international legal instruments against terrorism — but unlike ordinary treaties on criminal matters — the New York Convention prohibits the refusal of extradition or other

[76] See Part III C.

[77] Art 2(b) of the New York Convention; the Convention also makes reference to the offences contained in international treaties against terrorism listed in the Annex to the Convention. It should be noted, however, that many States made reservations on the application of the Convention in relation to some of the international treaties listed in the Annex.

[78] See Art 12(2) which reads "States may not refuse a request of mutual legal assistance on the ground of bank secrecy".

forms of mutual legal assistance on the ground of the political offence exception.[79]

Coming to the financial aspects of the offence of the funding of terrorism, the New York Convention reflects the previously examined endeavours undertaken at the international level by specialised institutions such as the FATF's Forty Recommendations, the Basel Committee's Principles against money laundering, the European Community Directive and national legislation. In this respect, the innovative feature of the New York Convention is to reproduce such international standards in a legally binding treaty.

Accordingly, Article 18 of the Convention singles out a minimum core of principles and practices to combat the financing of terrorism, consisting of requirements of transparency and due diligence in respect of the identity of customers, as well as obligations to detect and report suspicious transactions. For these purposes, the New York Convention provides that States Parties "shall consider" adopting regulations to prevent the opening of anonymous bank accounts and to ensure the full implementation of the KYC principle with regard to individuals and legal entities. The enactment of regulations imposing "on financial institutions the obligation to report promptly to the competent authorities all complex, unusual, large transactions and unusual patterns of transactions" and to "maintain, for at least five years, all necessary records on transactions" (Article 18.1(b)(iii) and (iv)) is also envisaged. An enhanced supervision of financial institutions and the licensing of all money transmission agencies, should also be "considered" by the States Parties (Article 18.2(a)).

Despite the merit of codifying a minimum core of regulatory anti-money laundering measures in a formal treaty, the New York Convention does not go beyond that. Both the style of wording and the content of the envisioned measures are closer to soft law standards than to formal obligations. Requirements to adopt "all practicable measures" or "utilize the most efficient measures *available*" (Article 18.1) call into question the prescriptive nature of the provisions. Also their content

[79] This is explicitly provided at Art 14 of the New York Convention which reads that "[n]one of the offences set forth in article 2 shall be regarded for the purposes of extradition or mutual legal assistance as a political offence inspired by political motives. Accordingly, a request for extradition or for mutual legal assistance based on such an offence may not be refused on the sole ground that it concerns a political offence or an offence connected with a political offence or an offence inspired by political motives". On the political offence exception in relation to acts of terrorism see C van den Wyngaert, "The Political Offence Exception to Extradition: How to Plug the 'Terrorist's Loophole' Without Departing from Fundamental Human Rights" (1989) 19 *Israel Yearbook on Human Rights* 297, reprinted in J Dougard and C van den Wyngaert (eds), *International Criminal Law and Procedure* (Dartmouth, Aldershot, 1996) 191; and F Mosconi, "La Convenzione europea per la repressione del terrorismo" (1979) 62 *Rivista di diritto internazionale* 303.

appears vague and ambiguous, thus leaving the States Parties a significant discretion in the implementation. The need for the FATF guidance is therefore inevitable, to ensure uniformity of national laws. Far from replacing the FATF regulatory standards by an autonomous body of rules, the New York Convention is still dependent on the work of this specialised institution in order to adapt the legal system of the States Parties to the minimum core of practices mentioned in the treaty. The reliance of the Convention on the work of FATF should not necessarily be seen as a weakness so long as its prescriptive character and unformity of application are not impaired. Rather it could be argued that in an evolving and technical field such as criminal finance, rigid (non-amendable) rules are not efficient provisions and that an adjustable set of is more desirable. Put differently, it is legitimate to maintain that in this branch of the law, a strict observance of the hierarchy of the sources of international law is not the best way to achieve with the pragmatic goal that is pursued. In the light of this, failure to acknowledge the role of the FATF or other similar institutions by the convention leaves somewhat unsatisfied. As a matter of fact, reliance upon external assistance is compelled by the evolutionary patterns of criminal finance requiring an on-going normative update. Suffice it here to remark that the provisions of the New York Convention are to some extent already unsatisfactory confronted with the last version of the FATF Forty Recommendations adopted in June 2003. Should the New York Convention be considered an autonomous and self-contained body of rules, the leeway left to the States Parties in its implementation and the degree of obsolescence of its provisions would inevitably lead to divergences of domestic laws, which terrorist financiers would certainly take advantage of.

C. The Need for an On-going Update of the Regulation to Track Transfer of Funds: Alternative Remittance, Underground Banking Systems, Wire Transfers

In the light of the above considerations, the entry into force of the New York Convention is not sufficient alone to combat the financing of terrorism, since it needs a constant and coordinated updating of due diligence requirements, reporting duties and regulation of the financial system to be implemented by the contracting States. For this purpose, the standards issued by specialised bodies such as the FATF are an essential guidance to the States engaged in the war on the financing of terrorism.

It is acknowledged that anti-money laundering schemes have been successful in fighting the criminal patterns covered by the enacted provisions; this has however shifted criminal transactions to unregulated financial channels which are particularly suitable for money laundering purposes.

To stop this migration, the solution consists in bringing unregulated activities within the scope of the existing legislation, by widening the range of subjects affected by anti-money laundering control obligations. Alternative remittance services have therefore become the principal target of regulatory endeavours with a view to ensuring that they be licensed, registered and subject to anti-money laundering obligations.[80] This is the object of FATF Special Recommendation VI, aimed at "persons and legal entities ... that provide a service for the transmission of money for value", which recommends that they should be subject to "all FATF Recommendations that apply to banks and non-bank financial institutions". At the EU level this has required amendments to Directive 91/308 on money laundering so as to update the notion of credit institution in accordance with the definition contained in Article 1 of Directive 2000/12/EC[81] and to expand the notion of "financial institution", which now covers currency exchange offices and money transmittance/remittance offices.[82]

Underground or parallel banking systems, employed by terrorists financiers and other criminals for cross-border money transfers, have also been affected by the post September 11 normative endeavours. In consideration of the poor legal and economic environment in which they operate, however, one can legitimately manifest some scepticism as to the actual implementation and enforcement of the envisioned measures, admittedly a very difficult task.

The underground banking system, known as hawala, hindu, chop shop and chitti banking, is common in some Asian and South Asian countries such as India, Pakistan, Hong Kong and China. Here it has socio-cultural roots which rely on trust and on strong family ties. While it may pursue legitimate business aims, providing good service (it is for instance commonly used by overseas workers for remittances to their families), especially in those jurisdictions where the regulated financial sector is insufficient, costly or not present in the whole territory, its informal nature and its

[80] See FATF Special Recommendation VI which reads "[e]ach country should take measures to ensure that persons or legal entities, including agents, that provide a service for the transmission of money or value, including transmission through an informal money or value transfer system or network, should be licensed or registered and subject to all the FATF Recommendations that apply to banks and non-bank financial institutions. Each country should ensure that persons or legal entities that carry out this service illegally are subject to administrative, civil or criminal sanctions".

[81] Directive 2000/12/EC of the Council of 20 March 2000 on the taking up and pursuit of the business of credit institutions, in OJ Eur Comm L 125 of 26 May 2000 at 1.

[82] For a general overview of the new EU instruments to combat money laundering, see S Mohamed, "Legal Instruments to Combat Money Laundering in the EU Financial Market" (2002) 10 *Journal of Money Laundering Control* 66; J Fisher, "Recent International Developments in the Fight Against Money Laundering" (2002) 17 *Journal of International Banking Law* 67.

international structure make it a suitable channel for money laundering purposes. Expedited (often "real time") cross-border transfer of funds and complete anonymity are attractive features to terrorist financiers, who are thus enabled to move money across jurisdictions without any paper trail.[83] Underground bankers are established in many different countries and are linked with each other; they debit and credit funds on their accounts for movements of money in connection with their legitimate trade or illicit trafficking. Communication of the accomplishment of the transfer of money is given by secret codes.

So far, to counter resort to these underground networks, attempts have been made in developing countries to strengthen exchange control regulations and to make formal banking channels more attractive; in some countries they have also been outlawed. In developed countries, the freezing and confiscation of assets in pursuance of anti-money laundering statutes are considered viable remedies.[84]

The war on terrorism has brought about new efforts aimed at the uncovering and regulation of underground banking networks. To begin with, it is worth noting that as clarified by the Interpretative Note to Special Recommendation VI,[85] the definition of "alternative remittance", by referring to "informal money or value transfer system or network", intends to include also underground or parallel banking systems. To this end, the International Best Practices released by the FATF in June 2003, to combat the abuse of alternative remittance systems, is largely dedicated to the ways of dealing with these informal networks. When the informal systems operate openly, registration with the competent authority is the recommended minimum requirement. In addition, on the assumption that rigid and disproportionate regulatory obligations push money transfer mechanisms underground, flexible oversight and avoidance of excessively burdensome compliance are envisaged remedies. With regard to banking networks operating underground, the task is more difficult, the first issue being their identification. For this purpose, critical is the sharing of information between the investigative units and the regulatory agencies involved. Regulatory efforts, if any, will come later, once the network has been tracked by the competent authorities.

[83] For an overview of the functioning mechanisms of underground banking systems, see J Trehan, "Underground and Parallel Banking System" (2002) 10 *Journal of Money Laundering Control* 76; FATF, Report on Money Laundering Typologies 1999–2000, 3 February 2001, at 4-8; Alexander, above n 13, 215; F El Sheikh, "The Underground Banking Systems and their Impact on Control of Money Laundering: With Special Reference to Islamic Banking" (2002) 5 *Journal of Money Laundering Control* 42.

[84] For further references, see Trehan, *ibid*, 81–82. See also Alexander, above n 13 at 215 warning that the war on financing of terrorism could be lost absent international coordinated efforts tackling informal money networks.

[85] Interpretative Note to FATF Special Recommendation VI: Alternative Remittance.

A further measure envisioned by the FATF to avoid terrorist financiers taking advantage of the loopholes in the system to freely transfer funds across frontiers, is enhanced scrutiny of wire transfers. In the effort to track the complex cross-border movements of funds, credit institutions, including money remitters, are urged to acquire accurate information on the originator and on the transaction and to include them on fund transfers and related messages that are sent through the whole payment chain. The Interpretative Note to Special Recommendation VII has provided practical guidance to its effective implementation.[86]

The need to keep pace with evolving money laundering patterns has directed attention not just to financial entities but also to professionals, such as lawyers, accountants, tax advisors and public notaries, who are particularly vulnerable to being involved in money laundering transactions in connection with their services. The solution adopted has been to expand the anti-money laundering regime to these professionals.[87]

D. Measures Adopted by States to Promote Compliance with International Legal Standards

The lack or paucity of financial regulation is a major threat to the fight against the financing of terrorism. In the previous paragraph, measures to be taken at the domestic level in order to bring unregulated financial services within the control of regulators have been discussed. This level of action, however, is unlikely to be sufficient in respect of off-shore centres and of poorly regulated jurisdictions, which offer a set of "legal facilities" — such as bank secrecy, shell corporations, absence of customer due diligence — which attract terrorist financiers, attempting to hide wealth and to eliminate traces of fund movements.[88] Isolation of such centres, in the form of prevention of their financial institutions from accessing regulated financial systems, is therefore envisaged as an efficient disincentive to

[86] Interpretative Note to FATF Special Recommendation VII: wire transfers.

[87] See Article 2a of Directive 91/308/EC introduced by Directive 2001/97/EC. It is worth noting, however, that notaries and other independent legal professionals are subject to anti-money laundering obligations in as much as they participate "in financial or corporate transactions, including providing tax advice, where there is the greatest risk of the services of those legal professional being misused for the purpose of laundering the proceeds of criminal activity", see recital 16 and Article 2(a)5, although such duties do not apply to lawyers "ascertaining the legal position of a client or representing a client in legal proceedings", unless legal advice is provided for money laundering purposes (see recital 17).

[88] See E Ceriana, "Profili Internazionali del Segreto Bancario nell'Ottica della Lotta all'Evasione e al Riciclaggio del Denaro di Provenienza Illecita" (1994) 65 *Diritto e Pratica Tributaria*, II, at 82, on banking secrecy in off-shore centres and its interplay with tax evasion and money laundering; recently on the interaction of off-shore centres and terrorist financing, see also J Johnson, "11th September and Revelations from the Enron Collapse Add to the Mounting pressure on the offshore financial centres" (2002) 10 *Journal of Financial Regulation and Compliance* 341.

non-compliance with internationally agreed standards.[89] This is the approach endorsed by the USA PATRIOT Act, a comprehensive anti-terrorism act which also strengthens the countering of international money laundering,[90] by far-reaching provisions which subject to in-depth scrutiny banks established in off-shore and non-cooperative countries attempting to open correspondent or payable-through accounts with US financial institutions.

A correspondent account enables a correspondent bank to provide banking services — receipt of deposits, payments and other transactions — on behalf of a respondent bank established abroad; a payable-through account opened at a depository institution by a foreign financial institution, enables customers of the latter to engage directly or through sub-accounts in banking activities, usually in connection with business activities carried on in the foreign country. Although these inter-bank accounts are generally set up for legitimate business purposes, they may turn into money laundering gateways.[91] To avoid this risk of abuse, the USA PATRIOT Act imposes on domestic financial institutions acting as correspondent banks of foreign financial institutions based in targeted jurisdictions (off-shore non-cooperative countries), enhanced due diligence policies, procedures and controls. In particular US credit institutions should take reasonable steps to ascertain the identity of each of the owners of the foreign bank, exercise enhanced scrutiny of such accounts to guard against money laundering and to make sure that the foreign bank does not provide correspondent accounts to other foreign banks and, if so, to identify those foreign banks. With respect to the establishment of a payable-through account relationship, US banks are required to ascertain the ultimate identity of the customer, the source of the funds deposited in the account by their customers, and to exercise reinforced anti-money laundering scrutiny.[92] Additional provisions of the USA PATRIOT Act are concerned with foreign

[89] Compare JJ Norton and H Shams, "Money Laundering Law and Terrorist Financing: Post-September 11 Responses: Let Us Step Back and Take a Deep Breath?" (2002) 36 *International Lawyer* 103 arguing that this approach runs counter to the policy of liberalisation pursued since the end of World War II, originating in the consideration that the post-World War I isolation of Germany had been one of the causes leading to the Second World War.

[90] For comments on the anti-money laundering provisions see Alexander, above n 13, 83 ff; A Rueda, "International Money Laundering Law Enforcement & the USA PATRIOT Act of 2001` (2001) 10 *MSU-DCL International Law* 141; FN Baldwin, Jr, "Money Laundering Countermeasures with Primary Focus upon Terrorism and the USA Patriot Act 2001" (2002) 6 *Journal Money Laundering Control* 105.

[91] See FATF — XIII Report on Money Laundering Typologies 2001–2002, at 8; on correspondent accounts and their misuse for terrorist purposes, see R Cranston, *Principles of Banking Law*, 2nd edn, (Clarendon Press, Oxford, 2002) 44.

[92] See USA PATRIOT Act, section 312. For an in-depth analysis of the anti-money laundering measures provided by the USA PATRIOT Act, see Alexander, above n 13, 83 ff.; Rueda, above n 90, 141; see also J Jackson, 'In Pursuit of Dirty Money: Identifying Weaknesses in the Global Financial System` (2001) 4 *Journal of Money Laundering Control* 122, spec 124; J Abrahamson, "Capitol Outlook" (2002) 17 *Butterworths Journal of International Banking and Financial Law* 102.

shell banks — banks without a physical presence in any country — and prohibit them from holding accounts with US financial institutions; subject to the same prohibition are also foreign banks servicing shell banks.[93]

Under Section 317 of the USA PATRIOT Act, these regulatory obligations are assisted by an aggressive extra-territorial approach enabling the exercise of jurisdiction over matters presenting only tenuous links with the US, for instance which might consist of the simple existence of a bank account in the US.[94]

The ultimate goal pursued by the outlined measures of the USA PATRIOT Act is indirectly to impose compliance with international agreed standards on foreign banks based in non-cooperative jurisdictions, perceived as the only protection against transnational abuse of the financial system. Besides the long-arm provisions set forth in the Statute, the enforcement of the American legal framework, and its overall effectiveness is dependent on the current need of off-shore centres to have access to the US financial market.

The same objective is being pursued at the international level where the FATF and the Basel Committee have expressed concerns about the intermediary role played by correspondent banks in international payments, given the high risks for credit institutions of being involved in money laundering and terrorist financing transactions, especially if the respondent bank itself acts as correspondent bank of other credit institutions.[95] Consistently with this, the revised version of the Forty Recommendations of June 2003 fills the gap of the previous edition by imposing special obligations with regard to correspondent accounts. In accordance with the analysis and suggestions formulated by the Basel Committee in the report on Customer Due Diligence for Banks, the new text of Recommendation 7 requires enhanced due diligence scrutiny by correspondent banks in respect of the respondent bank's ownership, business, supervision, customer due diligence procedures and the legal environment in which the foreign bank operates, with specific attention to the anti-money laundering framework.

E. Further Recent Initiatives to Protect the Financial System

Anti-money laundering regimes and obligations have so far primarily affected credit institutions, given that they are the natural gateway to inject

[93] See USA PATRIOT Act, Section 313.

[94] See 18 US Code, Section 1956 (Section 317 of the USA PATRIOT Act, *Long - arm jurisdiction over foreign money launderers*. Criticism against this aggressive extraterritoriality has been expressed by Norton and H Shams, "Money Laundering Law and Terrorist Financing: Post-September 11 Responses: Let Us Step Back and Take a Deep Breath?" (2002) 36 *International Lawyer* 103.

[95] See FATF, Review of the FATF Forty Recommendations. Consultation Paper, 30 May 2002, at 13 and Basel Committee on Banking Supervision, Customer Due Diligence for Banks, October 2001, at 12, available at <http:www.bis.org/bcbs/publ.htm> .

dirty money into the legitimate economy. Practice has shown however that in addition to credit institutions, financial entities such as securities dealers are also vulnerable and can be exploited for laundering the proceeds of crime. Although the placement stage of the proceeds of crime — the first and most delicate phase of the laundering process — is unlikely to be carried out through securities dealers, given that they are usually prevented from accepting cash, there are signs of an increasing misuse of financial intermediaries for money laundering purposes. Cases have been reported of the purchase of securities with proceeds of crime, where dealers either have accepted cash or have disregarded customer due diligence procedures, relying on the scrutiny already undertaken by credit institutions or other professionals which channel the funds to be invested.

To ensure a more effective enforcement of the anti-money laundering framework, the second EC Directive on money laundering has clarified that the definition of financial institutions includes insurance companies, investment firms and collective investment undertakings.[96] This implies the fulfilment of customer due diligence obligations consisting in the implementation of the "KYC" principle requiring the identification of the individual customer or of the beneficial owner, "in the event of doubt as to whether the customers are acting on their own behalf or whether it is certain that they are not acting on their own behalf".[97]

Besides the hypothesis of laundering of proceeds of crime generated *outside* the capital market, the case of laundering of proceeds of crime generated *within* the securities market (through insider trading, market manipulation and other practices) should also be taken into account, in the light of the findings of connections between abusive market practices and the financing of terrorism.

It is worth noting that the recently adopted EC Directive on market abuse addresses this typology, confirming the heightened awareness of the dangers criminal finance (and its links to terrorism) may create to the integrity of the financial system. By explicitly referring to the events of September 11, it expands the traditional understanding of "inside information" beyond the existence of a fiduciary relationship between the insider and issuer whose financial instruments are traded, to include information acquired by virtue of criminal activities.[98] In doing so, insider dealing committed on the basis of criminal information may become a predicate offence for the purposes of application of the anti-money laundering legislation.

[96] See Art 1(A) and (B) of Directive 91/308/EEC as replaced by Directive 2001/97/EC.
[97] See Art 3(7) of 91/308/EEC Directive as replace by Directive 2001/97/EC.
[98] See Art 2(1)(d) as well as recital n 14 of the Directive/2003/6/EC of the European Parliament and of the Council on insider dealing and market manipulation (market abuse) of 28 January 2003, in OJ Eur Comm L 96 of 12 April 2003, at 16.

The attractiveness of bringing securities dealers and other non-financial institutions within the scope of application of anti-money laundering schemes, besides pursuing the general interest of curbing financial crime, responds to the special need of preserving the integrity of capital markets. On the assumption that the use of funds of illegal origin in capital markets is a threat to the efficient course of transactions and to the soundness of the financial system, several international institutions have taken steps to avoid any contamination with proceeds of crime. It is acknowledged that money laundering affects the efficient allocation of resources, impacts on exchange rates and impinges on the quality of the assets managed by financial institutions.[99] A financial institution's excessive exposure against subjects involved in criminal activities heightens the risks usually managed by banks, such as reputational, concentration and legal risks. This may pose a threat to the stability of the institution and, by contagion, to the whole system. The awareness of the negative consequences to the integrity of the financial system of the contamination of the legitimate economy with the criminal finance, has induced the IMF to include in the assessment of a country's economy, conducted within the Financial Sector Assessment Program (FSAP) jointly carried out with the World Bank, a section dealing with the anti-money laundering framework, considered one of the relevant parameters in the assessment of the condition of a nation's economy.[100] It is worth noting that after the events of September 11, this part comprises an assessment of measures to combat the financing of terrorism.[101]

Concerns relating to the "contamination" of the financial system are not confined to the realm of legislation, but are shared by actors in the financial arena. The "Anti-money laundering guidance notes for insurance supervisors & insurance entities" issued by the International Association of Insurance Supervisors (IAIS) in January 2002,[102] the "Customer due diligence for banks" published by the Basel Committee on Banking Supervision on October 2001,[103] the Wolfsberg Statement on

[99] Adverse effects of money laundering on national economies at the national level have been identified in: "changes in demand for money, exchange and interest rate volatility; heightened risk of asset quality for financial institutions; adverse effects on tax collections and fiscal policy projections; contamination effects on particular transactions or sectors and behavioural expectations of market actors; asset price bubbles etc ...", see D Jayasuriya, "Money Laundering and Terrorism Financing: The Role of Capital Markets Regulator" (2002) 5 *Journal of Money Laundering Control* 30, at 32; see also A Buzelay, "Secret Bancaire, Évasion Fiscale et Blanchiment de l'Argent en Europe" (2001) *Revue Marché Commun et de l'Union européenne* 664.

[100] Details on the initiative are available at <http:www.imf.org/external/np/fsap/fsap.asp> .

[101] See IMF, "Intensified Work on Anti-Money Laundering and Combating Financing of Terrorism. Joint Progress Report on the Work of the IMF and World Bank", of 17 April 2002, available at <http:www.imf.org/external/np/fsap/fsap.asp> .

[102] Available at <http:www.iaisweb.org/1/pasc.html> .

[103] Available at <http:www.bis.org/bcbs/publ.htm> .

the "Suppression of the Financing of Terrorism"[104] as well as the International Organisation of Securities Commissions' (IOSCO) Resolution on Money laundering of 1992[105] are evidence of the rising concern for the preservation of the integrity of the financial system. These documents, wrapped-up in a soft law format, testify a sort of self-consciousness by the relevant actors of the gravity of the issue and provide a spontaneous and transnational response to avert the threat. In this regard, the KYC principle is unanimously recognised as having a pivotal role, whose importance has been further underscored in the aftermath of September 11.[106] Indeed the apparent lawful nature of the transactions carried out to finance terrorist activities make it difficult to identify by financial institutions. It may happen that a cross-check of the customer's identity with that of criminals does not reveal any connection with terrorist activities. This fact, however, should not discourage the assumption of obligations by financial institutions, since the full implementation of the KYC principle, by providing pieces of information, is helpful to uncover links with terrorism. The possession of a high number of pieces of information has been repetitively stressed by the FATF as a critical element to the fight against the financing of terrorism; once collected and matched by the competent authorities, the data may be useful to reconstruct suspicious transactions and to establish relations with terrorism.[107]

F. Prevention of Terrorist Acts and the Critical Role of International Administrative Cooperation

Obviously this task can be best performed if the relevant information is not kept isolated but is shared among the competent authorities involved, who are thus provided with a large number of pieces in order to solve the puzzle. In the light of the transnational character of terrorist financing, it is crucial that information-sharing mechanisms be set up

[104] Available at <http:www.wolfsberg-principles.com/wolfberg_statement.html> . The Wolfsberg Group consists of 11 leading international banks and became known when they agreed to a set of global anti-money laundering guidelines for international private banks in October 2000; see M Pieth and G Aiolfi, "The Private Sector Becomes Active: The Wolfsberg Process" (2003) 10 *Journal of Financial Crime* 359.

[105] Available at <http:www.iosco.org/resolutions/index.html> .

[106] Initiatives for an enhanced due diligence are also being undertaken at the national level in highly exposed countries such as Switzerland, see EHG Hüpke, "Keeping Dirty Money and Terrorist Funds Away: the Proposed Money Laundering Regulation of the Swiss Federal Banking Commission" (2002) 10 *Journal of Financial Regulation and Compliance* 317; see also D Mulligan, "Know Your Customer Regulations and the International Banking System: Towards a General Self-Regulatory Regime" (1999) 22 *Fordham International Law Journal* 2324.

[107] In this regard see remarks laid down by the FATF in its "Guidance for Financial Institutions in Detecting Terrorist Financing", of 24 April 2002.

both at the national (intra-agency) and international level. Indisputably, the need for reinforced international cooperation is the dominant theme of the war on terrorism.

Calls for coordinated efforts and enhanced international cooperation are contained in UN Security Resolution 1373, and have been subsequently reiterated by FATF Special Recommendation V that urges each country "to afford another country ... the greatest possible measure of assistance in connection with criminal, civil enforcement and administrative investigations, inquiries and proceedings".

The policy of prevention rather than exclusively of repression of acts of terrorism has emphasised the need of modern forms of cooperation better suited to identify and to curb typologies of financing of terrorism. Therefore, apart from and alternatively to traditional modalities of international cooperation in criminal matters, consisting of judicial assistance in the course of pending criminal proceedings, the reinforcement of administrative cooperation is a more appropriate manner in which to deal with the financing of terrorism, in particular at the *ex ante*, intelligence stage. This form of cooperation, traditionally developed in the field of international taxation,[108] is executed between administrative authorities[109] and is usually characterised by the goal of preventing administrative violations as well as by the urgency of the request. Whereas international judicial cooperation is directed at the gathering of evidence and is carried out through formalised and lengthy procedures, often letters rogatory, regulated by domestic law or bilateral MLATs, international administrative assistance is usually conducted within informal practices established in Memoranda of Understanding (MOUs). These are non-legally binding arrangements designed to facilitate the cooperation and exchange of information between administrative/regulatory agencies. Rather than purporting to override other channels of international collaboration, such as international judicial assistance, they aim at complementing these formalised manners of cooperation and, by revealing a mutual understanding,

[108] Traditional lack of extraterritorial enforcement of tax laws has made resort to exchange of information between competent tax authorities a valuable tool for filling gaps in their respective data records, see M Udina, *Il diritto internazionale tributario* (Padova, Cedam, 1949) 248; and recently, P Schlosser, "Jurisdiction and International Judicial and Administrative Co-operation" (2000) 284 *Collected Courses* 333 ff.

[109] On the different forms that international administrative cooperation may take, see G Biscottini, *Diritto Amministrativo Internazionale, t. I, La rilevanza degli atti amministrativi stranieri* (Cedam, Padova, 1964) 153, spec. 155, where the author underlines the fact that direct active cooperation between foreign administrative authorities is typical of cases of intense relationships, and of the need arising in special cases to take immediate action; more recently, see T Amy, *L'entraide administrative en matière bancaire, boursière et financière* (Lausanne, 1998) 203 ff, spec. 566.

they seek to foster relations between correspondent administrative authorities.

Undoubtedly, the reliance on informal and flexible procedures which ensure an expedited exchange of information, makes administrative cooperation better fitted for reconstructing patterns of money laundering and for this reason has received significant support by UN Security Council Resolution 1373, as well as by the FATF in Special Recommendation V, where express reference is made to the enhancement of sharing of information mechanisms. Intensification of information-sharing mechanisms, as a strategic tool for the prevention of terrorist financing, was already forcefully stated in the New York Convention. For this purpose, States Parties are called upon to set up appropriate measures to establish channels of communication between agencies and services and to cooperate with one another in conducting inquiries.

Arrangements for the sharing of information are not a novelty but are already in place within the money laundering context and are carried out by the respective national Financial Intelligence Units (FIUs).[110] These are central national agencies with expertise in both criminal and financial law, receiving information such as data on suspicious transactions or customers directly from financial institutions, in order "to collect, analyse and disseminate to the competent authorities such disclosures of financial information".[111] Where instituted under the form of administrative — rather than judicial — agencies, FIUs are also the "centre of gravity" of international information sharing with the reciprocal foreign FIUs; to this end since 1995, FIUs have begun to coordinate their work in an informal organisation known as the Egmont Group, with a view to improving mechanisms for the sharing of information. Mindful of the critical importance that exchange of data has in the fight against financial criminality and thus of a need for developed cooperation, the Egmont Group agreed in June 2001 on a set of principles to be taken as a reference point in the sharing of information. The document stresses the importance of overcoming national obstacles in order to allow FIUs to freely exchange information on the basis of reciprocity and mutual trust, with the limitation that the information so acquired may not, be transferred to a third party or be used in an administrative, investigative prosecutorial

[110] The text of both Directive 91/308/EEC (Art 6) and of the New York Convention may be ambiguous in this respect in that they make a general reference to the obligation to report to the "competent authorities" without any additional specification.

[111] According to the definition adopted by the Egmont Group at the plenary meeting held in Rome on 21–22 November 1996. References are available at <http:www.fatf-gafi.org/pdf/Egstat-200106_en.pdf>; on FIUs see, extensively G Steessens, *Money Laundering: A New International Law Enforcement Model* (Cambridge University Press, Cambridge, 1999) 183–99.

or judicial purpose without the prior consent of the FIU that disclosed the information.[112]

The pivotal role of reinforced international cooperation, especially in the form of information sharing, has been addressed also by international financial bodies. Despite the fact that these kinds of issues do not fall within their ordinary fields of competence, the magnitude of the phenomenon of international terrorism and the threat it poses to financial stability,[113] strengthened the resolve of such institutions to react, thus speeding up the adoption of cooperative measures. Particularly relevant is the Multilateral Memorandum of Understanding concerning Consultation and Cooperation and the Exchange of Information adopted by IOSCO on May 2002, where explicit reference is made to the need for enhanced coordination following the September 11 attacks.[114] This is not an isolated voice, however. The Basel Committee, in its "Sharing of financial records between jurisdictions in connection with the fight against terrorist financing" adopted in April 2002, observed that an increased cross-border sharing of information, in particular between home and host supervisors, is helpful to control the reputational and legal risks to which banks may be exposed.[115] Provisions for an enhanced cooperation among regulatory agencies in the form of information-sharing and investigation activities are contained also in the EC Directive on market abuse, taking into account the increase in cross-border trading.[116]

Mechanisms of exchange of information for supervisory purposes are not a direct consequence of the events of September 11, being already in place before. The initiatives undertaken in the aftermath of September 11 do not purport to engage in a front-line fight against the financing of terrorism; they are however worth mentioning in that they constitute evidence of the pervasiveness of the threats of financial criminality and the need of multiple coordinated efforts to overcome the magnitude and the ramifications of such a phenomenon.[117]

[112] See Egmont Group, "Principles for Information Exchange Between Financial Intelligence Units for Money Laundering Cases, adopted at The Hague, 13 June 2001"; available at <http:www.fatf-gafi.org/pdf/Egstat-200106_en.pdf>. On the actual operation of FIUs and on the advantages of such administrative cooperation within the anti-money laundering framework, see G Steessens, *Money Laundering. A New International Law Enforcement Model* (Cambridge University Press, Cambridge, 1999) 269 ff.

[113] For a review of the regulators' activity in the days immediately following September 11, see MI Steinberg, "The SEC and the Securities Industry Respond to September 11" (2002) 36 *International Lawyer* 131.

[114] Available at <http:www.iosco.org>.

[115] Available at <http:www.bis.org/bcbs/publ.htm>.

[116] See preamble 40, and Art 16 of the EC Directive n. 2003/6.

[117] For an *excursus* see FF Friedman, E Jacobs and SC Macel IV, "Taking Stock of Information Sharing in Securities Enforcement Matters" (2002) 10 *Journal of Financial Crime* 37; CA Greene, "International Securities Law Enforcement: Recent Advances in Assistance and Cooperation" (1994) 27 *Vanderbilt Journal of Transnational Law* 635.

V. CONCLUSION

The several initiatives undertaken to counter the financing of terrorism which have been outlined in this paper have touched upon some of the distinctive traits of today's international law, and provide an interesting portrait of the international legal system.[118]

From a normative standpoint, a significant feature is the proliferation of norms which have been passed after the events of September 11. The multiplicity of sources analysed in the paper — ie UN Security Council Resolutions, European Union Directives and Regulations, ratification of the New York Convention, standards, statements and principles, to cite a few — are evidence of such an approach. This varied normative production induces reflection regarding the dynamic dimension of the international legal system. These reflections concern both the multiplicity of actors involved in the rule-making process as well as the rule-making process itself. Indeed, numerous actors with a different legal nature have taken part in this development, ranging from the UN Security Council, regional inter-governmental organizations such as the European Union, States (either by ratifying international treaties such as the New York Convention, or by implementing supranational measures) as well as other actors with a particular expertise, such as the FATF, an intergovernmental body, and other informal fora like the Basel Committee on Banking Supervision, the IOSCO, the IAIS, the Wolfsberg Group and the Egmont Group. The variety of the legal nature of the actors is also reflected in the different typologies of sources adopted: formally enacted provisions coexist with informal rules/standards, statements, principles, MOUs; regardless of any deference to the classical hierarchy of international law sources, soft law is a reference as much as hard law.

This apparently confused and asystematic way of proceeding actually reveals a pragmatic approach to the common goal of countering the financing of terrorism; in working towards this goal, the purpose of the disparate actors and rules is unified. Such community of intents is reflected in the intensification of international cooperation, which constitutes one of the most distinctive facets of the reaction to the attack on the Twin Towers. The variety of actors involved in the collaborative efforts, and the search for informal and flexible schemes, better suited to the

[118] The literature on the transformation recently undergone by the international legal system is extensive; without pretension of being exhaustive see G Abi-Saab, "Cours général de droit international" (1997) collected courses, vol. 207; R Higgins, *Problems & Process. International Law and How We Use It* (Clarendon Press, Oxford, 1994); B Conforti, *International Law and the Role of Domestic Legal Systems* (Martinus Nijhoff Publishers, Dordrecht, 1993); A Cassese, *International law* (Oxford University Press, Oxford, 2001).

prevention of terror crimes, testify to the solidarity of the international community to thwart this new challenge.[119]

Having said this, it is legitimate to wonder to what extent this pragmatic approach can be effectively realised. It can correctly be objected that the adoption of rules is not a good thing *per se*, and that the emphasis should rather be shifted to their actual enforcement, rightly the central issue of this Symposium.

The focus on the intensification of international cooperation including information-sharing, is an encouraging sign of the increased international community's sensitivity for the effectiveness of international law norms; however, there are gaps that have still to be filled. Divergences in implementation and application which may stem from the ambiguous content of the relevant norms — for example, the definition of "financing of terrorism" or of "terrorism" itself — and the differing levels of sophistication of domestic legal systems challenge the effectiveness of the fight against the financing of terrorism. The international initiatives risk being a suitable remedy only for countries with high quality financial systems and may seem unrealistic when addressed to developing countries with unsatisfactory law enforcement structures, poor in technology and financial culture. The existence of an appropriate legal framework is just one piece of the puzzle and in the absence of a consistent support in technological development, financial training and infrastructures the provisions may appear to be wishful thinking.

[119] Inter-State cooperation has since long envisaged as the sole instrument against transnational criminality and the threats it poses to the international community in the light of the magnitude of its structure, its means and the volume of money controlled world-wide; particularly telling in this regard are the considerations expressed by R Quadri who observed that "[l]e organizzazioni internazionali di malfattori necessariamente dispongono di mezzi superiori per l'attuazione dei loro propositi criminosi e colpiscono indifferentemente, a seconda delle occasioni, la sfera particolare di qualunque Stato; esse costituiscono pertanto un pericolo o male internazionale di fronte al quale solo la solidarietà degli Stati può apportare un rimedio adeguato", R Quadri, *Diritto penale internazionale* (Cedam, Padova, 1944) 41.

17

The Internet and Terrorist Activities

UGO DRAETTA

I. INTRODUCTION

THE FIRST OBSERVATION, which becomes apparent when examining the issue of terrorism and the internet, is the absence of an international legal instrument dealing specifically with such issue. There are a number of international legal instruments concerning terrorism. Some of them, particularly the less recent ones, do not contain any reference to the internet. This is true, for example, for the 1977 European Convention on the Suppression of Terrorism.[1] More recently, some United Nations conventions against terrorism, such as the 1999 International Convention for the Suppression of the Financing of Terrorism,[2] do mention, almost in passing, that terrorist activities can also be carried out using the internet. None of these international legal instruments, however, specifically address the use of the the internet for terrorism in the various forms which it make take.

Conversely, a number of international legal instruments increasingly deal with cyber crimes, namely offences carried on through the internet, but, in general, they do not specifically consider terrorism as one of the possible cyber crimes, nor contemplate for it special legal consequences. A partial exception is the 2001 Council of Europe Convention on Cyber Crime,[3] which contemplates certain offences against the integrity of computer data that may indirectly include terrorist acts.

The lack of provisions dealing with cyber terrorism is somewhat surprising, as the internet is becoming the single most widely used system for communications of any kind among individuals, thus also among criminals and terrorists. It appears therefore appropriate, at the very outset, to consider all the possible interrelations between the internet and terrorism,

[1] Dated 27 January 1977, promoted by the Council of Europe.
[2] Dated 9 December 1999, entered into force on 10 April 2002.
[3] Dated 23 November 2001.

in order to assess the extent to which these interrelations are covered by existing international law norms and, at the same time, to identify any remaining gaps which ought to be filled on a *de jure condendo* basis.

To this purpose, we will consider three separate, but related aspects. First of all we will address those terrorist acts, which have the internet itself as their target. Secondly, we will examine those cases where the Net is used as a tool to carry out specific terrorist acts within a broader terrorist design that, however, does not have the internet as its specific target. In these cases the internet is used in order to maximize the chances of achievement of criminal objectives, with financing as a special category of such internet usage. Finally, we will consider how the internet can be used by the enforcing authorities to fight terrorism, together with the related issue of the need to strike a balance between combating terrorism and protecting fundamental individual rights.

II. THE NET AS TARGET FOR TERRORIST ACTIVITIES: CYBER TERRORISM

It is now generally recognized that terrorism can take the form of an attack on the Net itself, carried out by criminal hackers through the use of viruses or other forms of manipulation of the Net, aimed at causing, for example, the release of contaminating substances, the paralysis or the malfunctioning of vital services, such as the supply of electric powers, water, air navigation systems or electronic financial services. This crime will be referred to as "cyber terrorism". It is also evident that the result of these actions, if successful, can imply the loss of lives and/or other consequences that are well within the scope of the various definitions of terrorist acts contained in the international legal instruments concerning terrorism. The potential disastrous effects of a paralysis or malfunctioning of the Net, due to an unintentional event, such as the so-called Millennium Bug, were dramatically brought to the attention of the media during 1999, until it became clear that, fortunately, the turn of century was not likely to cause these consequences.

Neither the various UN conventions on terrorism, nor the 1977 European Convention on the Suppression of Terrorism expressly contemplate cyber terrorism, leaving those interpreting these conventions, which lack a definition of cyber terrorism, with the difficult task of assessing, on a case-by-case basis, whether the language of these international instruments is adequate to cover a terrorist attack on the Net.

Articles 2 to 6 of the 2001 Council of Europe Convention on Cyber Crime, which contemplate certain offences against the confidentiality, integrity and availability of computer data and systems, represent a partial step ahead. These offences include the following unauthorised acts: (a) the illegal access to the whole or any part of a computer system, (b) the interception of non-public transmission of computer data, (c) the damaging, deletion, deterioration, alteration or suppression of computer data, (d) the serious hindering of the functioning of a computer system by inputting, transmitting, damaging, deleting, deteriorating, altering or suppressing computer data, and (e) the misuse of electronic devices.

It is very likely that these provisions would cover an act of cyber terrorism, except that they are too general in nature and too narrow in their formulation to specifically and effectively fight cyber terrorism. They cover any kind of intentional use of the net "without right" and do not address the special nature of an act of cyber terrorism or contemplate a definite set of consequences for this type of act. It must be noted, in this connection, that the lengthy Explanatory Report to the Convention, adopted on 8 November 2001, never mentions the word "terrorism" in its commentary to Articles 2 to 7 of the Convention. It was clearly not the intent of the drafters to specifically cover cyber terrorism.

Other international legal instruments contain vague allusions to possible acts of cyber terrorism. For instance, UN General Assembly Resolution 51/210, of 16 January 1997, calls upon all member States to "note the risk of terrorists using electronic or wire communications systems and networks to carry out criminal acts and the need to find means ... to prevent such criminality and to promote cooperation where appropriate". In addition, UN Security Council Resolution 1373 (2001), adopted on 28 September 2001, calls upon States to find ways of intensifying the exchange of operational information regarding "use of communications technology by terrorist groups". These provisions, however, seem more addressed to the use of the Net by terrorist groups to foster their criminal activities rather than to cyber terrorism as such, as previously identified.

A more progressive step has been taken in this field at the EU level. First of all, the 19 September 2001 Commission's Explanatory Memorandum of the proposal for a Council Framework Decision on combating terrorism[4] recognizes that "new forms of terrorism are emerging. There have been several recent occasions where tensions in international relations have led to a spate of attacks against information systems. More serious attacks could lead not only to serious damage but even, in some cases, to loss of lives". Article 3 of this proposal, while providing for a definition of terrorist offences,[5] includes within such offences,

[4] COM (2001) 521, in *OJEC* no. C 332 of 27 November 2001. This Framework Decision would be issued in accordance with Art 34 (2)(b) of the Treaty on European Union.

[5] These are offences specifically identified, which become terrorist in nature when "intentionally committed by an individual or a group against one or more countries, their institutions or people with the aim of intimidating them and seriously altering or destroying the political, economic, or social structures of a country".

in paragraphs 1 (h), (i) and (j) respectively, "releasing contaminating substances or causing fires, explosions or floods, endangering people, property, animals or the environment", "interfering with or disrupting the supply of water, power, or other fundamental resources", as well as "attacks through interference with an information system".[6] The latter offence (interference with an information system) is considered as a possible way to commit the other two offences (release of contaminating substances and interference or disruption of the supply of fundamental resources). This is clarified by the aforementioned Explanatory Memorandum, which, in its commentary to Article 3 of the proposal for a Framework Decision, underlines that:

> although terrorist offences committed by computer or electronic devices are apparently less violent, they can be as threatening as the offences previously mentioned, endangering not only life, health or safety of people, but the environment as well. The main characteristic is that their effect is intentionally produced at a distance from the perpetrators, but their consequences may also be much more far reaching. Therefore terrorist offences covering the release of contaminating substances or causing fires, floods or explosions, interfering with or disrupting the supply of water, power or other fundamental resource, and interference with an information system are included under paragraphs I (h), (i) and (j).

It seems, therefore, that cyber terrorism is conceptually analyzed and correctly identified as such, for the purposes of the approximation of the laws of the Member States regarding terrorist offences, which is the objective of the above mentioned proposal for a Council Framework Decision.[7]

Another relevant EU legal instrument is the Council Common Position of 27 December 2001, on the application of specific measures to combat terrorism.[8] This Common Position was issued with the purpose of taking additional measures in order to implement UN Security Council Resolution 137 (2001), freezing certain terrorist assets. In calling upon the Member States to freeze funds and other financial assets of terrorist persons and groups identified in the Annex, the Council Common Position

[6] The abovementioned Commission's Explanatory Memorandum defines as "information systems" computers and electronic communication networks, as well as computer data stored, processed, retrieved or transmitted by them for the purposes of their operation, use protection and maintenance.

[7] It is worthwhile recalling that the proposal contains, in addition to the definition of terrorist offences, provisions regarding its scope of application, the punishment of instigating, aiding, abetting and attempting, norms on penalties and sanctions, as well as on aggrarating and mitigating circumstances, liability and sanctions for legal persons, rules on extraditions, prosecution, cooperation between Member States, exchange of information, protection and assistance to victims, implementation and reports.

[8] *OJEC* no. L 344/93, of 28 December 2001. This Common Position was issued in accordance with Art 34(2)(a) of the Treaty on European Union.

contains a somewhat more refined definition of "terrorist act" with respect to the abovementioned proposal for a Council Framework Decision on combating terrorism,[9] and comprises in such definition the extensive destruction of an infrastructure facility, "including an information system",[10] as well as "release of dangerous substances, or causing fires, explosions or floods, the effect of which is to endanger human life", or "interfering with or disrupting the supply of water, power or any other fundamental natural resource, the effect of which is to "endanger human life", effects which can be well achieved through the manipulation of an information system.[11]

Even if domestic laws are outside the scope of our analysis, it should be mentioned that the USA PATRIOT Act specifically addresses cyber terrorism, particularly in its Section 814.[12]

III. THE INTERNET AS A TOOL FOR CARRYING OUT TERRORIST ACTIVITIES

A second dimension of the problem under investigation is the use by terrorists of the internet as a tool to better achieve their criminal objectives, even when the Net is not itself a target. Such use can vary from simple propaganda aimed at recruiting terrorists, to encoded orders or other communications between individual or terrorist groups, to the use of the internet to procure, preserve, or invest funds aimed at financing terrorist activities.

A number of international legal instruments deal very generally with this issue. We have already mentioned, in this connection, UN General Assembly Resolution 51/210, of 16 January 1997, which calls upon States to "note the risk of terrorists using electronic or wire communications systems and networks to carry out criminal acts". In addition, UN Security Council Resolution 1373 (2001), adopted on 28 September 2001, calls upon States to find ways of intensifying the exchange of operational information regarding the "use of communications technology by terrorist groups".

[9] A "terrorist act" is defined (Art 1, paragraph 3, of the Common Position) as an intentional act "which, given its nature or its context, may seriously damage a country or an international organization", when committed with a number of aims spelled out in such Art 1, paragraph 3. Among them, there is the aim of "seriously destabilizing or destroying the fundamental political, constitutional, economic or social structures of a country or an international organization".

[10] Art 1, paragraph 3 (d), of the Council Common Position.

[11] Art 1, paragraph 3 (g) and (h) of the Council Common Position.

[12] The Uniting and Strengthening America by Providing Appropriate Tools Required to Intercept and Obstruct Terrorism (USA PATRIOT) Act, Public Law 107-56 of 26 October 2001.

More specifically, with respect to the use of the internet for the financing of terrorist activities, we may recall the above-mentioned UN 1999 International Convention for the Suppression of the Financing of Terrorism, Article 1 of which specifically includes "electronic or digital" documents evidencing title in assets, among the "funds" which are the subject of the regulation prescribed by the Convention.[13]

Apart from this convention, many international legal instruments either deal with the issue of the financing of terrorism, or with the issue of cyber crimes of a financial nature, such as market manipulation or money laundering. Very few expressly contemplate the use of the internet to finance terrorism.[14]

Examples of the first type of such international legal instruments include the above-mentioned UN Security Council Resolution 1373 (2001) and the EU Council Common Position of 27 December 2001, on the application of specific measures to combat terrorism,[15] as well as the EU Council Recommendation of 9 December 1999 on cooperation in combating the financing of terrorism[16] and the Conclusions adopted by the Council (Justice and Home Affairs) of 20 September 2001,[17] requesting a more coordinated approach with regard to the global fight against the financing of terrorism.

Examples of the second type of international legal instruments are the more recent texts addressing insider trading, market manipulation and money laundering, which, by their general formulation, cover such acts even when committed through the internet, but which do not specifically address the possible terrorist aim.[18]

[13] This Convention states that it is an offence to provide or collect funds, directly or indirectly, unlawfully and intentionally, with the intent of using them or knowing that they will be used to commit any act included within the scope of the other UN conventions against terrorism.

[14] For example, Recommendation 13 of the Forty Recommendations from the Financial Action Task Force on Money Laundering (FATF-GAF1) states that countries should pay special attention to money laundering threats inherent in new or developing technologies that may favor anonymity; Recommendation VII of the Eight FAFT-GAFI Special Recommendations on Terrorist Financing cover wire transfers.

[15] *OJEC* no L 344/93, of 28 December 2001.

[16] *OJEC* no C 373, of 23 December 1999, p 1.

[17] 40 ILM 1257 (2001). The provision quoted in the text is contained in Part III, no 4, of the Conclusions.

[18] With no intention of being exhaustive, one may mention Directive 2001/97/EC, of 4 December 2001, on the prevention of the use of the financial system for the purpose of money laundering (*OJEC* no L 344/76 of 28 December 2001); the proposal for an EC Directive on insider dealing and market manipulation of 30 May 2001 (COM(2001) 281 final). On the subject, see BAK Rider, "Cyber-Organized Crime — The Impact of Information Technology on Organized Crime", (2001) 4 *Journal of Financial Crime*, No 4, 332–46; E Lomnicka, "Preventing and Controlling the Manipulation of Financial Markets: Towards a Definition of 'Market Manipulation'", (2001) 8 *Journal of Financial Crime*, No 4, 297–304; N Munro, "The internet-based Financial Services: A New Laundry?", (2001) 9 *Journal of*

When we come to examine the international legal instruments on cyber crimes in general, with no specific reference to the financing aspects, it is surprising that terrorist acts carried out through the internet are not singled out as a special type of cyber crime. For example, Section 1 of the 2001 Council of Europe Convention on Cyber Crime which deals with substantive criminal law, expressly contemplates two computer-related offences (forgery and fraud[19]) and two content-related offences (child pornography and infringement of copyright[20]), while a separate Protocol covering the offences of racism and xenophobia committed through the internet is also being discussed. Terrorism is not dealt with as a content-related offence committed through the internet, though it would be hard to maintain that terrorism is a less serious offence than child pornography, infringement of copyright, racism or xenophobia. Terrorism as a cyber crime, because of its particularly odious nature, would deserve, indeed, a specific set of provisions, with related sanctions and measures.

A similar approach is followed at the EU level. First of all, the Conclusions adopted by the Council (Justice and Home Affairs) of 20 September 2001,[21] request the Commission, in paragraph 4, to submit proposals for ensuring that law enforcement authorities are able to investigate terrorist acts involving the use of electronic communication systems, and to take legal measures against perpetrators. More important is the Communication from the Commission to the Council, the European Parliament, the Economic and Social Committee and the Committee of the Regions entitled "Creating a Safer Information Society by Improving the Security of Information Infrastructures and Combating Computer-related Crime" of 26 January 2001.[22] This Communication suggests, among other things, the amendment of the substantive laws of the Member States in the area of high tech crime as a way of ensuring a minimum level of protection for victims of cyber crime, in accordance with the requirement that an activity must be an offence in both countries before

Financial Crime, No 2, 134–52; RG Smith and PN Grabosky, "Online Security Fraud", (2001) 9 *Journal of Financial Crime*, No 1, 54–70; J Veogaert, "Fighting Economic Crime-Action Taken in the European Union", (2001) 9 *Journal of Financial Crime*, No 1, 22–25; TR Hurst, "Security Fraud and the The internet: Adapting Existing Regulatory Schemes to Regulation in Cyberspace", (2001) 8 *Journal of Financial Crime*, No 3, 226–33.

[19] Articles 7 and 8 of the Convention.

[20] Articles 9 and 10 of the Convention.

[21] 40ILM1257 (2001).

[22] COM (2000) 890 final. Another important document on the subject is the Communication from the Commission to the Council, the European Parliament, the European Economic and Social Council and the Committee of the Regions, of 6 June 2001 (COM (2001) 298 final, of June 6, 2001), entitled "Network and Information Security: Proposal for a European Policy Approach", which specifically addresses the need to reinforce the security of the Net against criminality, from a rather technical viewpoint.

mutual legal assistance can be provided and providing greater clarity for the industry. Among the legislative proposals contained in the Communication, however, child pornography offences take the absolute priority. Secondly, the Communication contemplates the high tech offences related to computer hacking and denial of service attacks, and thirdly, racism and xenophobia. Terrorist acts committed through the internet could be indirectly covered by the second category, but it is astonishing that there is no specific mention of terrorism.

IV. PROCEDURAL AND MUTUAL ASSISTANCE INTERNATIONAL LAW NORMS REGARDING THE INTERNET AND TERRORISM

In both cases previously examined under paragraphs 2 and 3 respectively, all the international norms regarding judicial and police mutual assistance and cooperation in criminal matters are, of course, expressly or implicitly applicable to terrorist activities. Since these norms do not specifically refer to the internet, we do not have to deal with them for the purposes of our analysis.[23]

As to international conventions specifically dealing with crime committed through the internet, such as the 2001 Council of Europe Convention on Cyber Crime, we have seen that its substantive criminal law provisions (Articles 2–13) do not specifically address cyber terrorism, nor contemplate terrorist acts as content-related offences. However, the procedural type of provisions of such a convention (Section 2, Articles 14 ff), as well as the provisions for international co-operation (Articles 23 ff) have a broader scope, thus potentially covering terrorism.

Article 14 of the Convention imposes upon the Parties to adopt such legislative measures as may be necessary to establish a number of investigating powers and procedures contemplated by the other provisions of

[23] We may confine ourselves to recalling: (a) general types of conventions on judicial and police mutual assistance, such as the Council of Europe Convention on Mutual Assistance in Criminal Matters, of 20 April 1959 with its two additional Protocols of 17 March 1978 and 8 November 2001 (ETS no 30, 99 and 182), the EU Convention on the same matter dated 29 May 2000 (*OJEC* no C 197, of 12 July 2000, p 1), the 10 March 1995 Convention on simplified extradition procedures between the member States of the EU (*OJEC* no C 78 of March 30, 1995, p 1) and the 27 September 1996 Convention relating to extradition Member States of the EU (*OJEC* no C 373 of 23 October 1996, p 11), the Joint Action of 21 December 1998 (*OJEC* no L 351 of 29 December 1998, p 1), which, in making it a criminal offence to participate in a criminal organisation in the Member States, refers to terrorist offences in Art 2(2); and (b) international legal instruments concerning terrorism, such as, at the EU level, Art 2(1) of the Convention on the establishment of a European Police Office (*OJCE* no C 316 of 27 November 1995, p 1), the Council decision of 3 December 1998 (*OJCE* no C 26 of 30 January 1999, p 22), instructing Europol to deal with crimes committed in the course of terrorist activities, the Council Joint Action of 15 October 1996 (*OJCE* no L 273 of 25 October 1996, p 1), decided to create and maintain a Directory of specialized counter-terrorism competences to facilitate cooperation between Member States of the EU.

Section 2 of the Convention, which include preservation of stored computer data, production orders, search and seizure of stored computer data, real-time collection of traffic data, interception of content data. This obligation of the parties exists not only in connection with the criminal offences identified by the Convention, but also with respect to "other criminal offences committed by means of a computer system", thus including terrorist acts.[24]

In addition, Article 23 of the Convention, containing general principles relating to international co-operation, is expressly applicable to all criminal offences related to computer systems and data, and thus not only to the offences identified in the substantive criminal law section of the Convention. As a consequence, the international co-operation provisions of the Convention, which range from extradition to mutual assistance and many other very detailed clauses, also apply to terrorist acts.

Even if the wording of the Convention with respect to the investigation powers and procedures and international co-operation is broad enough to cover terrorism, it is regrettable that terrorism is not specifically addressed. This because the procedural rules of the Convention are subject to a number of exceptions. For example, Article 21 states that the power to intercept content data shall be limited to a range of serious offences to be determined by domestic law. In addition, Article 20 provides that a Party may apply the measure of real-time collection of traffic data only to certain offences. Of course, the express inclusion of terrorism among the offences not subject to any exception would have been commendable.

Much more important, however, is the fact that the implementation and application by each Party of the powers and procedures defined in the Convention is subject, according to Article 15, to "conditions and safeguards provided for under its domestic law, which shall provide for the adequate protection of human rights and liberties, including rights arising pursuant to obligations it has undertaken under the 1950 Council of Europe Convention for the Protection of Human Rights and Fundamental Freedoms, the 1966 United Nations Covenant on Civil and Political Rights, and other applicable international human rights instruments, and which shall incorporate the principle of proportionality".[25]

[24] See G De Vel (Director General of Legal Affairs of the Council of Europe), "The cyber crime convention: a pioneering effort of wide legal scope", Opening Address on the occasion of the Conference on Cyber crime — First Session — Budapest, 22–23 November 2001 — <http://wpop2.libero.io1.it/cgi-bin/webmail.cgi/>. See on page 6, one of the rare mentions of "terrorism" in connection with these "other criminal offences".

[25] Without limiting the types of conditions and safeguards that could be applicable, the Convention requires specifically that such conditions and safeguards include, as appropriate in view of the nature of the power or procedure, judicial and other independent supervision, grounds justifying the application of the power or procedure and the limitation on the scope or the duration thereof. These conditions and safeguards should clearly be applied with

This is not a new issue. The need to protect human rights, and in particular data privacy and freedom of expression on the internet, is widely acknowledged[26] and Article 15 of the Convention tries to address the issue. The underlying problem, however, is that of striking a balance between two public interests, both deserving protection: combating cyber crimes and protecting human rights, particularly data privacy. This implies some discretionary judgment in evaluating the weight to be given to each one of the two opposing requirements.

At the EU level, the Data Protection Working Party established by Article 29 of the Directive 95/46/EC of 24 October 1995,[27] has systematically commented on a number of legal instruments concerning cyber crimes, consistently proposing improvements aimed at strengthening the clauses concerning the protection of the fundamental rights to privacy and personal data protection of individuals. It did so, very vocally, with its Opinion 4/2001[28] on the Council of Europe's first Draft Convention on Cyber Crime, which was found by the Working Group as "lacking balance" in this respect. Opinion 9/2001[29] addressed the same type of concerns to the above mentioned Communication from the Commission to the Council, the European Parliament, the Economic and Social Committee and the Committee of the Regions entitled "Creating a Safer Information Society by Improving the Security of Information Infrastructures and Combating Computer-related Crime" of 26 January 2001. However, these two opinions addressed the need for protecting human rights with respect to the fight against all type of cyber crimes, with no intention to address terrorism in particular.

There is no question that a balance must be struck between the protection of personal data and the law enforcement authorities" need to gain access to data for the purposes of criminal investigations on terrorist activities. This has recently been reaffirmed by paragraph 4 of the aforementioned Conclusions adopted by the Council (Justice and Home Affairs) of 20 September 2001.[30] The question may arise, instead, as to whether terrorism justifies striking the balance between the two conflicting interests in such a way as to favor somewhat the fight against terrorism with respect to the protection of the fundamental rights to data privacy. It is an open question, as the debate on this point is only starting now.

respect to interception, given its intrusiveness. Other safeguards that should be addressed under domestic law include the right against self-incrimination, and legal privileges and specificity of individuals or places, which are the object of the application of the measure.

[26] On the protection of privacy in the internet, see U Draetta, *Internet e commercio elettronico nel diritto internazionale dei privati* (Giuffre, Milan, 2001), 148 ff.
[27] *OJEC* no L 281 of 23 November 1995, p 31.
[28] 5001/01/EN/Final — WP 41, adopted on 22 March 2001.
[29] 5074/01/EN/Final — WP 51, adopted on 5 November 2001.
[30] 40 ILM 1257 (2001).

Nevertheless, some elements to address this issue can be drawn from the recent Opinion 10/2001[31] of the Article 29 Data Protection Working Party, on the need for a balanced approach in the fight against terrorism. This Opinion does not comment on any specific document but is aimed, in the aftermath of the September 11 events, at recalling the two opinions previously rendered, even in the context of a democratic society now engaged in the fight against terrorism. However, the wording is somewhat ambiguous, and leaves room for interpretation.

Opinion 10/2001 starts from the premise that terrorism is not a new nor a temporary phenomenon and that, consequently, it is necessary "to take into account the long term impact of urgent policies rapidly implemented or envisaged at this moment". It then emphasizes the need to respect the principle of proportionality, which implies the obligation to demonstrate that any measure taken with respect to the use of the Net corresponds to an "imperative social need". Measures, which are simply "useful" or "desirable", may not restrict the fundamental rights and freedoms. This wording is rather circular, as the issue remains the need to identify the "imperative social needs".

Fast conclusions on this issue cannot be made at this juncture: the debate has just started and the developments of international law practice will have to be observed in this respect. A recent decision by the European Court of Human Rights, in the case *Zaoui v Switzerland*, rendered on 18 January 2001,[32] may, however, cast some light on possible future trends. The Swiss police confiscated the computer of Mr Zaoui, a member of the Algerian Islamic Front (FIS), who had used the internet for its political propaganda activity, and blocked his connection to the internet. Mr Zaoui claimed that, in this way, his rights to the freedom of expression and freedom of religion were violated. The Strasbourg Court unanimously found that Switzerland acted legitimately to protect its national security interests and declared the recourse non-receivable.

Finally, it is also worth recalling that, at the domestic law level, the investigation powers of the public authorities with respect to terrorist activities carried out through the internet begin to be clearly spelled out, not only in the US, where they are covered by Title II of the USA PATRIOT Act,[33] but also in Italy, where the new Decree 374 of 18 October 2001 on combating terrorism, deals with such powers in Articles 4 and 5 with respect to interceptions and activities under cover.[34]

[31] 0901/02/EN/Final — WP 53, adopted on 14 December 2001.

[32] Request no 41615/98; Hudoc reference: REF00008448.

[33] The USA PATRIOT Act, above n 12. The text may be found at <http://juTist.law.pitt.edu/terrprism/hr3l62.htm>.

[34] *Official Journal of the Republic of Italy* no 244 of 19 October 2001.

V. CONCLUSION

One general conclusion is that international law norms are not yet updated to specifically address terrorist acts carried out through the internet, though, at the European level, such norms seem to be at a more advanced stage.

In particular, it seems that the notion of cyber terrorism is insufficiently defined and addressed in the international conventional law, with the exception of the regional integration at the EU level, where such a notion seems to be emerging with sufficiently precise contours.

As to terrorist acts carried out through the internet, international legal instruments dealing with cyber crimes do not yet contain specific provisions for terrorism, as they do for child pornography, infringement of intellectual rights, racism and xenophobia. There is here a definite need for improvement.

Finally, when we come to the procedural and mutual assistance international law norms regarding the internet and terrorism, we observe that it is not yet clear if and to what extent terrorism can justify the weakening of the protection of the fundamental rights to data privacy of the individuals, as the debate in this area is very much in an embryonic stage.

18

Cyberterrorism: A New Challenge for International Law

RICHARD GARNETT AND PAUL CLARKE

I. INTRODUCTION

IT IS APPARENT that many activities in contemporary life are controlled by information technology. Important infrastructure like transport, energy supplies, hospitals, national defence and financial institutions are all operated by use of computer networks which has created a dependency in society that may be easily exploited by persons with technological expertise who wish to inflict harm. States, therefore, have been increasingly confronted with offences of sophistication and complexity which defy application of traditional criminal laws. While the problems of computer crime have so far been largely confined to the domestic sphere and States' regulatory responses directed at this situation, more recently there has been a concern that terrorists may use or target information technology to further their objectives. The possible emergence of "cyberterrorism" is now recognized as posing a risk to all States and requiring the attention of international law.

The object of this chapter is to examine the current status of cyberterrorism in international law both in terms of the rights and obligations of States to prosecute such offences and the rules that may apply where a State launches a computer attack against another State.

II. TERRORISM—IN SEARCH OF A DEFINITION

While there is no internationally accepted definition of terrorism, three points can be gleaned from most international instruments and scholarly analyses of the concept. The first point is that terrorism targets noncombatants, a characteristic that differentiates it from war, the second is that terrorism uses violence or the threat of violence for a purpose usually designed to instill terror and the third is that terrorism is motivated by an underlying contextual aggravating factor such as political, religious or ideological grounds.[1] Terrorism has been condemned in UN General Assembly Resolutions,[2] provisions of the UN Charter which prohibit the use of means that are contrary to the purposes of the UN in the settlement of international disputes,[3] and in State practice.[4] For example, in a 1994 resolution, the Declaration on Measures to Eliminate International Terrorism, the General Assembly stated that:

> Criminal acts intended or calculated to provoke a State of terror in the general public, a group of persons or particular persons for political purposes are in any circumstance unjustifiable, whatever the considerations of a political, philosophical, ideological, racial, ethnic, religious or any other nature that may be invoked to justify them.[5]

One reason why it has been difficult to secure a universally accepted definition of terrorism has been that some States, primarily from the developing world, have sought to resist condemnation of practices and activities which they may have resorted to in their acquiring of independence, particularly during decolonization. Moreover, terrorism has been described as having uniquely "political" and "socio-psychological" aspects which make it difficult to regulate with universal and coherent laws.[6] Consequently, the major trend in regulating terrorism at the international level has been to target manifestations of the practice rather than treat it as a generic whole. So, for example, international treaties have been concluded dealing with particular aspects of terrorism such as aircraft hijacking,[7] hostage taking[8] and offences against internationally protected persons[9] each with varying degrees of nation State support.

In this way, the regulatory approach taken with regard to terrorism has been a reductionist one. Reductionism is the idea that regulation is

[1] J Stern, *The Ultimate Terrorists* (Boston, Harvard University Press, 1999) 11.
[2] UN Doc A/Res/39/159 (1984); A/Res/53/108 (1999), A/Res/54/164 (2000) available at <http://www.un.org/documents/resga.htm>.
[3] United Nations Charter Art 2(3) and (4).
[4] See eg, International Convention for the Suppression and Financing of Terrorism 1999, European Convention on the Suppression of Terrorism 1977, OAU Convention on the Preventing and Combating of Terrorism 1999 available at <http://untreaty.un.org/English/Terrorism.asp>.
[5] UN Doc. A/Res/49/60 available at Internet web site listed at n 2 above.
[6] Kleff, "Terrorism: The Trinity Perspective" in H Han (ed), *Terrorism and Political Violence: Limits and Possibilities of Legal Control* (New York, Oceana Press, 1993) 13, 25; CL Blakesly, *Terrorism, Drugs, International Law and the Protection of Human Liberty* (New York, Transnational, 1992) 43.
[7] Convention for the Suppression of Acts against the Safety of Civil Aviation (1971) 974 UNTS 177 available at Internet web site listed at n4 above.
[8] International Convention Against the Taking of Hostages (1979) A/Res/34/146 reprinted in 18 ILM 1456
[9] Convention on the Protection and Punishment of Crimes against Internationally Protected Persons (1973) 1035 UNTS 167 available at Internet web site listed at n 4 above.

reducible to a set of legal instruments that in effect provide the tools necessary to combat terrorism. This approach necessarily rejects the notion that terrorism, in and of itself, can be regulated from the standpoint of a centralized definition.

Despite the difficulties in establishing a precise definition of terrorism, it has been suggested that its particular manifestations may amount themselves to individual crimes in customary international law, particularly, for example, where they can be classified as crimes against humanity.[10] A key issue to be explored in this chapter is whether the offence of cyberterrorism may also amount to a crime in customary international law. This matter will require consideration of both national State practice and measures taken at the transnational level in the area of computer network attacks. Before addressing this question it is first necessary to analyse the phenomenon of cyberterrorism more closely.

III. CYBERTERRORISM: NATURE AND REGULATION

A. The Concept of Cyberterrorism

There is evidence that the internet is increasingly being used as a means by terrorists to access information, raise funds, spread propaganda and plan operations. It also has the clear potential to be used as a medium to attack both government and commercial computer networks in order to inflict terror upon a target population.[11] It is interesting to note that while cybercrime, in the sense of attacks on computer networks, has increased enormously in recent years, cyberterrorism as a distinct phenomenon has not yet been employed to a great extent. Computer attacks may be less popular for terrorists presumably because conventional means of attack are still seen as the most direct and effective way of causing harm to persons and property.[12] However, given the potentially grave consequences that could flow from a cyberterrorist attack, particularly on State infrastructure, the greater use of cyberterrorism in the future seems inevitable.

For the purposes of this chapter, cyberterrorism will be regarded as the performance of ordinary computer crimes but with the added intention to instill fear among a target audience. In examining the status of

[10] I Brownlie, *Principles of Public International Law*, 5th edn (Oxford, Oxford University Press, 1998) 308.

[11] Canadian Security Intelligence Service, *Trends in Terrorism* Report 2000/01 <www.iwar.org.uk/cyberterror/resources/csis/terror-trends.htm> see p 4 of hardcopy printout.

[12] SW Brenner and MD Goodman, "In Defense of Cyberterrorism: An Argument for Anticipating Cyberattacks" (2002) *University of Illinois Journal of Law Technology and Policy* 1, 50.

cyberterrorism in international law, a consideration of domestic State regulatory practice in the field of computer and digital crime generally will first be made followed by an observation of practice in the specific field of cyberterrorism.

Cybercrime is a broad term for the set of criminal activities performed through the use of information and communications technologies. Cybercrimes have traditionally involved two types of offences, the first being where a computer system is the target of the offence, such as attacks on network confidentiality, integrity and availability and the second category consists of conventional offences such as theft and fraud executed with the assistance of computers or information technology.[13]

It is important to note that most computer offences have arisen out of the "architectural vulnerability" of the technology, a problem which has only worsened with the advent of the internet.[14] While the internet has provided a highly efficient distributed mode of communication, its decentralised nature based on the technology of "packet switching",[15] has created a fundamentally insecure environment. While packet switching ensures a continuous and unimpeded flow of information throughout the network, persons may access internet traffic and launch attacks with relative ease from unidentifiable locations. The global scope of the internet also makes apprehension of offenders difficult.[16]

Furthermore, the interconnectedness of the network means that attacks can be made on several geographical targets at once[17] with quick and drastic effects which cannot be easily localised. The integration of important elements of State infrastructure such as telecommunications, transport and energy resources into computer networks[18] gives terrorists a strong incentive to launch computer network attacks. Strikes on public infrastructure have obvious potential to cause chaos and instill fear and loss of confidence in a State's citizenry.[19] Communications technology,

[13] SW Goodman and MD Brenner, "The Emerging Consensus on Criminal Conduct in Cyberspace" (2002) *UCLA Journal of Law and Technology* 3 (no pagination in original).

[14] M Schmitt, "Computer Network Attack and the Use of Force in International Law: Thoughts on a Normative Framework" (1999) 37 *Columbia Journal of Transnational Law* 885, 886.

[15] Packet switching is a method of sending disaggregated data through the network in a manner defined by a protocol. Packets are the result of a larger body of data being deconstructed and arranged into smaller, more manageable pieces that can be reconstructed subsequent to data transfer. The important thing to note is that each packet is sent independently to a "node" on the Internet and then depending on the weight of traffic, the path of least resistance will be chosen.

[16] JF Murphy, "Computer Network Attacks by Terrorists: Some Legal Dimensions" in M Schmitt and B O'Donnell (eds), *Computer Network Attacks and International Law* (Naval War College, 2002) 323, 327.

[17] Brenner and Goodman, n 12 above, 23.

[18] Tubbs, Luzwick and Sharp, "Technology and Law: The Evolution of Digital Warfare" in Schmitt and O'Donnell (eds), above n 16, 7, 9.

[19] Brenner and Goodman, n 12 above, 15.

especially the Internet, has also given individuals and groups enormous control over the flow of information. Such control has largely overcome the physical disparity in power between such groups and their targets, for example governments and large corporations, making these entities more vulnerable to attack. Technology has also provided would be attackers with the ability to inflict harm of a much greater scale than they could cause in the physical world[20] with Internet web sites now available which advertise tools for "disruption and destruction".[21]

B. State Regulatory Responses

The early response of States to computer crime within their societies was to apply existing criminal law, developed for acts in the physical world, to computer-based offences. Such an approach proved to be largely unsatisfactory as many computer attacks did not fall within the scope of such laws. For example, the offences of trespass and theft proved to be difficult to apply to digital subject matter as opposed to physical property.[22] Consequently, States were forced to enact new laws designed to protect the structure and architecture of the technology out of recognition that such an approach would more effectively trap the types of attacks committed. As a result, offences such as unauthorised access, compromising of data integrity and interference with computer systems were typically created.[23] Such digital conduct may have effects within the physical world, such as where infrastructure targets are attacked or the consequences may be contained almost entirely within the digital sphere, for example where data is corrupted or a denial of service occurs.

It is possible to trace the adoption of computer-specific crime laws by States and the relatively high degree of harmonisation of such laws to initiatives of international organisations such as the OECD. In 1992 the Council of the OECD issued a Recommendation Concerning Guidelines for the Security of Computer Systems.[24] The primary objective of the Guidelines was to protect the interests of those relying on information systems from harm resulting from failures of availability, confidentiality and integrity. One of the means suggested for achieving this objective was that member States adopt relevant criminal laws, preferably on a

[20] *Ibid*, 25.
[21] Alexander, "Terrorism in the 21st Century: Threats and Responses" (1999–2000) 12 *De Paul Business Law Journal* 59, 86.
[22] See eg, the English cases of *R v Lloyd* [1985] 1 QB 829 and *Oxford v Moss* [1979] Crim LR 119.
[23] See generally, D Sieber, *Legal Aspects of Computer Related Crime in the Information Society: Comcrime Study*, Study prepared for the European Commission, 1998.
[24] The Guidelines are available at the web site of the OECD at <http://www.oecd.org/>.

harmonised basis. Examples were given of conduct that should desirably be the subject of domestic laws including damaging or disrupting of information systems by insertion of viruses and worms, alteration of data, illegal access to data and computer fraud.

It is likely that the Council of Europe was influenced by the OECD guidelines in its plan to develop and harmonise computer crime laws within Europe, a project which culminated in the 2001 Convention on Cybercrime.[25] This Convention, which is not yet in force, sets out five "norms" which signatory States must adopt in their domestic criminal laws. The relevant categories of conduct include: (1) illegal access to the whole or any part of a computer system, (2) the interception of non-public transmission of computer data (3) the damaging, deletion, deterioration, alteration or suppression of computer data (4) the serious hindering of the functioning of a computer system by imputing, transmitting, damaging, deleting, deteriorating, altering or suppressing of computer data and (5) the misuse of electronic devices.[26] The thread running through each of these norms is again the need to prohibit attacks on the structure or architecture of computer systems.

Another draft treaty which may prove to be influential on the topic is that proposed in 2000 by the US Center for International Security and Co-operation (CISAC), entitled "A Proposal for an International Convention on Cyber Crime and Terrorism".[27] Similar to the Council of Europe Convention, the CISAC Convention does not specifically define offences but requests State parties to criminalize certain categories of conduct. The matters listed include manipulating or interfering with data to disrupt the functioning of a computer system,[28] manipulating or interfering with data for the purpose and with the effect of causing substantial damage to persons or property,[29] illegal entry into a computer system[30] and interfering with computer security mechanisms.[31]

Once again, the emphasis is on "architectural" offences but what may be even more significant in the present context is that the CISAC Convention also includes a separate provision covering cyberterrorism. In this regard, State parties are requested to criminalize conduct where one of the above listed offenses is used "with a purpose of targeting the critical infrastructure of any State Party".[32] The explanatory commentary makes it clear that this provision was directed at combating cyberterrorism.[33]

[25] ETS no. 185 (2001) at <http://conventions.coe.int/Treaty/EN/cadreprincipal.htm>.
[26] *Ibid*, Articles 2–6.
[27] <http://www.iwar.org.uk/law/resources/cybercrime/stanford/cisac-draft.htm>.
[28] *Ibid*, Art 3(1)(a).
[29] *Ibid*, Art 3(1)(b).
[30] *Ibid*, Art 3(1)(c).
[31] *Ibid*, Art 3(1)(d).
[32] *Ibid*, Art 3(1)(g).
[33] See above n 27, 7 (hardcopy printout).

The domestic legislative practice of States on computer crime reflects the above tendency toward the creation of structural offences and is surprisingly uniform in content. A major reason for this convergence in State practice is that information and communication technologies are increasingly ubiquitous in nature and largely render territorial boundaries irrelevant. Consequently, States are encountering the same problems in terms of computer attacks and not surprisingly are adopting similar measures to resolve them. Two surveys can be cited to demonstrate the convergence in State regulation of computer crime: the first by the United Nations Asia and Far East (UNAFE) Institute for the Prevention of Crime[34] and the second by the scholars Goodman and Brenner.[35]

The UNAFE survey of 37 States found that in respect of crimes against confidentiality, integrity and availability of computer systems and data over 60% of nation States surveyed had the offence of unauthorised destruction or alteration of data, 56% penalised unauthorised interference with or access to a computer system and 51% criminalised unauthorised acquisition of data.[36] In the Goodman-Brenner survey of 50 countries, unauthorised access was criminalised by 54% and was the subject of draft laws in 14%, while illegal manipulation or damage to files and data was criminalised by 48% and the subject of draft laws in 12% of nation States. Computer sabotage was criminalised by 44% of States and the subject of draft laws in 8% and unlawful use of information systems was criminalised by 48% and subject to draft laws in 8%.Finally, damage or theft of software or hardware was criminalised by 48% of States and the subject of draft laws in 8%.

A last point to note about the domestic legislative practice of States is that in the United States, in the recent USA Patriot Act, amendments to the US Code[37] were made under the heading "Deterrence and Prevention of Cyberterrorism". In broad terms, the offences provided are (1) knowingly accessing a computer without authorization to access material of the US Government or a financial institution[38] and (2) knowingly causing the transmission of a program or virus to cause damage to a computer system of the US Government or a financial institution.[39]

It can therefore be clearly seen with respect to the crimes of unauthorised access, data corruption, computer sabotage, unlawful use of information systems and damage to hardware or software that a clear

[34] H Kaspersen and A Lodder, *UNAFEI Questionnaire on Computer-Related Crime for the Workshop of the Tenth United Nations Congress on the Prevention of Crime and the Treatment of Offenders* (2000).
[35] Goodman and Brenner, n 13 above.
[36] Kaspersen and Lodder, above n 34, 9–12.
[37] 18 USCS 1030.
[38] Section 1030(1), (2) and (3).
[39] Section 1030(5).

majority of States surveyed either prohibited or intended to prohibit such conduct. These statistics, particularly when coupled with the Council of Europe Convention, lend support to the view that the above computer crimes form the basis of an emerging norm of customary international law. However, it is significant that this practice, apart from the CISAC Convention and the USA Patriot Act, makes no reference to *cyberterrorism* as distinct from cybercrime. While the types of computer offences committed by cyberterrorists will almost certainly fall within the scope of the abovementioned crimes, to find that cyberterrorism exists as a distinct crime in international law, requires further support in State practice. The fact that cyberterrorism requires, in contrast with ordinary computer crime, the use of conduct to instill fear among non-combatants, also suggests that practice addressing it specifically is needed.

It is suggested that such practice can be found in resolutions of the UN General Assembly and, to a lesser extent, instruments of the European Union. In the case of the Assembly resolutions, the central themes are a concern for "cybersecurity" in the global context, recognition of the danger posed by terrorists to electronic and digital systems of States and a call to States to install adequate regulatory measures to combat the problem.

For example, General Assembly Resolution 53/70[40] draws attention to the "risk of terrorists using electronic communications systems and networks to carry out criminal acts" and the need to develop basic laws to protect information security, including "unauthorised interference with or misuse of information and telecommunications systems". Many other resolutions[41] have been adopted to the same effect, emphasising the risk to information security and State infrastructure by terrorist acts and the need for States to enact domestic computer crime laws, for example to protect the confidentiality and integrity of data,[42] and to co-operate on a regional level to combat such activities. Resolution 57/239[43] reiterated the concerns expressed in earlier resolutions and called upon States to create a global "culture of cybersecurity" to be supported not only by the enactment of relevant domestic laws but also by other preventative measures within societies.

It therefore seems clear that the UN General Assembly recognises the threat to global security posed by cyberterrorism and the need for States

[40] UN Doc. A/Res/53/70 (1999) available at Internet web site listed at n 2 above.

[41] See eg, UN Doc.s A/Res/54/49 (1999), A/Res/55/28 (2000), A/Res/55/63 (2001), A/Res/56/19 (2002), A/Res/56/121 (2002), A/Res/57/53 (2002) and A/Res/57/239 (2003) available at Ibid

[42] UN Doc. A/Res/55/63, *ibid.*

[43] UN Doc. A/Res/57/239, *ibid.*

to take regulatory measures to respond to such a challenge. An important element in these resolutions also is the call to member States to apply the legal standards developed to combat computer crime in the domestic context to the problem of cyberterrorism in the transnational sphere. A further supporting piece of practice is the Agreement on 25 Measures from the 1996 Ministerial Conference on Terrorism in Paris.[44] The Agreement called upon States to be aware of the risk of terrorists using electronic communications systems and networks to execute criminal acts and to adopt means to prevent such conduct. Hence, clear steps have been taken on the path to making the prohibition of cyberterrorism a norm of customary international law.

Further support for this view comes from developments in the European Union. The Commission, in its Explanatory Memorandum of the Proposal for a Council Framework Decision on Combating Terrorism,[45] recognised the need specifically to target cyberterrorist activities. The Commission noted that "new forms of terrorism are emerging [and that] there have been several recent occasions where tensions in international relations have led to a spate of attacks against information systems."[46] While such offences are "apparently less violent they can be as threatening as [other] offences ... endangering not only life, health or safety of people but the environment as well. Their main characteristic is that their effect is intentionally produced at a distance from the perpetrators, but their consequences may also be much more far reaching."[47] Consequently, the Commission expressly included the offence of "interference with an information system" within the definition of "terrorist offence" in the Framework Decision.[48] Importantly, it also acknowledged that cyberterrorism may be the cause of other acts which are themselves defined as terrorist offences under the instrument.[49]

The proposed offence of "interference with an information system" is likely to cast a wide net over terrorist activities since "information system" is broadly defined to include "computers and electronic communication networks, as well as computer data stored, processed, retrieved or transmitted by them for the purposes of their operation, use, protection, and maintenance".[50]

[44] <http://www.State.gov/www/global/terrorism/measures.html>.
[45] <http://europa.eu.int/comm/external_relations/cfsp/doc/com_01_521.pdf>.
[46] *Ibid*, p 3 of pdf document.
[47] *Ibid*, p 9 of pdf document.
[48] *Ibid*, Art 3(1)(j).
[49] Such offences included "releasing contaminating substances, causing fires, explosions or floods, endangering people, property, animals or the environment Art 3(1)(h) or 'interfering with or disrupting the supply of water, power or other fundamental resources," Art 3(1)(i).
[50] See above n 45, pp 9–10 of pdf document.

IV. STATE JURISDICTION AND CYBERTERRORISM

Another important issue to consider in the prosecution of individuals for cyberterrorism is the rules of State jurisdiction that apply to this offence. State jurisdiction refers to the capacity of a nation State to adjudicate or apply its domestic laws to a particular offence with customary international law recognizing certain situations in which jurisdiction may be exercised. Domestic jurisdiction is not unlimited in international law or else certain, more powerful States would effectively exercise jurisdiction on a global basis, at the expense of the jurisdictional competence of other States. It is also important to note that, with one possible exception, the customary law bases of State jurisdiction are voluntary, in the sense that they grant power to a State to prosecute a person but do not *require* a State to try or to surrender a person to a State who wishes to do so. As discussed further below, this may seriously weaken the practical utility of the rules as mechanisms for pursuing cyberterrorists.

The first generally accepted basis of State jurisdiction in customary international law is territoriality.[51] Under this principle, a State may exercise jurisdiction over an offence where the crime was committed within its territory. However, the entire offence does not have to take place there; it is enough if a constituent element occurred within the State's territory. Consequently, a State may exercise jurisdiction under the territorial principle where the offence was commenced in the forum and completed elsewhere or initiated elsewhere and consummated in the forum.[52]

The broad scope of this principle may have particular utility in the case of cyberterrorism where conduct may often be initiated from one place but have impact in several States. Two recent decisions involving Internet content may be cited in support of this view. In *R v Waddon*,[53] an English court allowed the prosecution of an English resident for publishing obscene materials in the UK where he set up a pornographic website on a US-based server but the contents of which could be accessed and downloaded in the UK. Similarly, in the *Toeben* case,[54] an Australian resident who established a "Holocaust Denial" site on an Australian server was successfully prosecuted in Germany under the German Anti-Nazi legislation for inciting racial hatred in that country. The basis of jurisdiction, according to the court, was that the Australian site could be accessed in Germany by local residents and so could cause harm there.

[51] Harvard Research in International Law, Draft Convention on Jurisdiction With Respect to Crime (Supp 1935) 29 *American Journal of International Law* 435, 484–87 (Draft Art 3).
[52] *SS Lotus (France v Turkey)* PCIJ (Ser A) No 10 (1927) 23; Harvard Research in International Law, *ibid*, 484, 487–88, 494.
[53] 2000 WL 491456 (English Court of Appeal 6 April 2000).
[54] German Federal Court decision of 12 December 2000 available at <http://normative.zusammenhaenge.at/faelle_de-entsch.html>.

While the context of these cases is distinct from cyberterrorism in that they involved prosecutions for display of harmful content, the underlying principle of territoriality is likely to apply in the same way. In both the *Waddon* and *Toeben* cases the courts were concerned to protect the public in the forum from the *effects* of such material being accessible even though the content was physically located on a computer server outside the forum. A court confronted with a cyberterrorism case is likely to take a similarly broad view of harmful effects in the forum so as to capture a wide variety of offences under the territorial principle. For example, where a person in State A targets a computer system in State B which is linked to important infrastructure in States B, C and D then it is possible that the effects of the attack may be felt in all three States and so each should have a right to prosecute under the territorial principle.

An alternative jurisdictional basis available under customary international law to prosecute cyberterrorists is nationality which grants to the national State of the offender the right to try.[55] Such a ground also has great breadth because it invests, in effect, a State with worldwide jurisdiction over offences committed by its nationals. However, if a State gains custody of one of its citizens but refuses to try them, this ground will be of little value.

Another well recognized basis of jurisdiction in customary international law is universality. Under this principle a court is vested with jurisdiction over certain offences where the circumstances justify prosecution as a matter of international public policy, regardless of whether the forum has any connection with the offence or the offender. Crimes such as drug trafficking, hijacking and piracy all likely fall within this group.[56] In light of the discussion above in section III.B., it is arguable that cyberterrorism is an "emerging" universal offence.[57] According to the General Assembly practice noted above, not only is cyberterrorism considered a threat to international security, but nation States have been requested to enact laws for the prosecution of such offenders.

A final category of State jurisdiction under customary international law is controversial but may be highly relevant to cyberterrorism. Some writers have argued that there exists a distinct basis of State jurisdiction for "crimes under international law".[58] According to this basis, certain offences amount to breaches of international law itself such as war crimes, crimes against humanity and crimes against peace and may be prosecuted

[55] *Restatement (Third) of the Foreign Relations Law of the US* (1987) section 404.
[56] D Harris, *Cases and Materials on International Law*, 5th edn, (London, Sweet & Maxwell, 1998) 290.
[57] In support of this view, see W Dauterman, "Internet Regulation: Foreign Actors and Local Harms: At the Crossroads of Pornography, Hate Speech and Freedom of Expression" (2002) 28 *North Carolina Journal of International Law and Commercial Regulation* 177, 203.
[58] Brownlie, above n 10, 307.

by all States. At first glance, such a category may appear to overlap with universality but an important and unique distinction is said to exist. Under the international crimes ground of jurisdiction, not only are States granted a right to prosecute such offences, but also there is imposed on States an obligation either to try offenders or to extradite them to a State willing to prosecute.[59] This view is highly contentious as international law obligations in the area of State jurisdiction normally only arise where States have entered into a treaty on the subject and freely and consensually accepted such obligations. However, assuming that such an argument is valid could cyberterrorism be classified as a crime in international law?

Given the earlier mentioned controversy about terrorism itself being an international crime[60] a more profitable line of inquiry may be to examine whether cyberterrorism could be classified as a "crime against humanity". In the Rome Statute of the International Criminal Court the term is defined in Article 7 to include "any of the following acts when committed as part of a widespread or systematic attack directed against a civilian population".[61] The acts mentioned include egregious human rights violations such as murder, extermination, torture and rape as well as "other inhumane acts of similar character intentionally causing great suffering, or serious injury to body or to physical and mental health".[62] Assuming that such a definition accurately reflects international practice on the subject, it may be argued that an act of cyberterrorism, at least where it causes and is intended to cause serious personal injury, such as in the case of an infrastructure attack, would amount to a crime against humanity. However, such a conclusion may be premature until further State practice appears.

In the event, though, that the view that an international law crime imports an obligation on States to try or extradite is not accepted, another mechanism for imposing jurisdictional obligations on States needs to be considered, namely, treaties. There is no current treaty in force that specifically applies to cyberterrorism or computer crimes. However, if the view expressed above that cyberterrorism may, under certain circumstances, constitute a crime against humanity is accepted then such an offence may fall within the jurisdiction of the International Criminal Court under Articles 5 and 7 of the Rome Statute.[63] Yet, as noted above, the Statute would only pick up the most extreme forms of cyberterrorism where human life was targeted and harmed. A convention regime needs to be established which encompasses a wider range of manifestations of cyberterrorism.

Fortunately a model for such a treaty exists in the form of the Council of Europe Convention on Cybercrime and the CISAC Convention, which

59 *Ibid*, 318.
60 See section II above.
61 <http://www.un.org/law/icc/statute/romefra.htm>.
62 *Ibid*.
63 *Ibid*.

are in similar terms. Under the Council of Europe Convention a State party must adopt legislation establishing jurisdiction over an offence committed on its territory, on board a ship flying the State's flag, on board an aircraft registered under the laws of the State or by one of its nationals if punishable by the criminal law of the place where the offence was committed.[64] The Explanatory Report to the Convention makes it clear that this provision would apply both to an offence wholly committed within a State and to an offence originated outside the forum State but targeting a system inside. According to the Report, a party "would assert jurisdiction if both the person attacking a computer system and the victim system are located within its territory and where the computer system is attacked within its territory, even if the attacker is not".[65] Such a position therefore represents a partial adoption of the customary international law definition of territoriality discussed above. A second key article on jurisdiction in the Convention provides that if a State party has custody of one of its nationals and another State party wishes to prosecute the person then the custodial State must either prosecute the offender itself or extradite him or her to the other State.[66] In this way, a type of obligatory universal jurisdiction is created, although only triggered where a State party refuses to extradite one of its nationals to another State party.

The provisions of the CISAC Convention[67] are in similar terms, providing for both territoriality and nationality as bases for compulsory jurisdiction.[68] In addition, a form of mandatory universal jurisdiction is created, similar to the Council of Europe Convention, where an offender is present in the territory of a member State but that State refuses to extradite him or her to a member State willing to prosecute.[69]

The jurisdiction provisions in both conventions therefore go a long way to strengthening the emerging customary law condemnation of cyberterrorism by requiring member States in a relatively wide range or circumstances to try or extradite offenders. However, being treaties, States' consent is required before any obligations can be imposed and this will remain a practical hurdle to overcome.

V. STATE ACTORS AND CYBERTERRORISM

"When natural resources were the dominant factor of production, the conquest and control of territory seemed a reliable way to enhance

[64] Above n 25, Art 22(1).
[65] Explanatory Report to the Convention on Cybercrime in *ibid*, para 233.
[66] *Ibid*, Art 22(3).
[67] See above n 27.
[68] *Ibid*, Art 5(1)(a) and (b).
[69] *Ibid*, Art 5(1)(d).

national power. Today, conquest of territory is rarely worth the cost to the nation. It is both much easier and more profitable to conduct information warfare against an adversary's knowledge resources than to conduct a conventional war against its armed forces."[70]

A. Cyberterrorism and State Responsibility

The focus in this section of the chapter shifts to the issue of whether an attack on a computer system launched from the territory of one State against another State's system may give rise to a breach of international law by the State from which the offensive act originated. Since computer network attacks are performed by individuals or groups with differing degrees of connection to the State in which they operate, an important question to consider is when the acts of such individuals or groups will engage the responsibility of the State. This issue is likely to arise commonly in the context of cyberterrorism given the wide proliferation of the tools of computer attack and their easy accessibility.[71]

The matter is also significant because if the acts of individuals or groups cannot be tied to a particular State and so create an international law obligation, then the victim State will likely have no means of redress,[72] unless the territorial State agrees to try or extradite the offenders. Hence, for example, where a State has been the victim of a breach of international law by another State it may be entitled to compensation from that State or even to resort to acts of self-help such as countermeasures and self defence. By contrast, where a State is the victim of an attack by entities for which no State responsibility attaches, international law grants no remedy to the injured State, even though the consequences may have been just as severe as with a State-sanctioned attack.

Principles of State responsibility generally require that for an act of an individual or group to be attributable to a State it must be performed either by a State organ[73] or a person acting with the authority of the State.[74] Additionally, responsibility may arise in the case of an act by a

[70] S Kanuck, "Information Warfare: New Challenges for Public International Law" (1996) 37 *Harvard International Law Journal* 272, 289–290 quoting AJ Edmonds, Address at the Seminar on Intelligence, Command, and Control, John F Kennedy School of Government, Harvard University (20 April 1995).

[71] J Barkham, "Information Warfare and International Law on the Use of Force" (2001) 34 *New York University School of Law Journal of International Law and Politics* 57, 58.

[72] *Ibid*, 103–104.

[73] International Law Commission, *Draft Articles on Responsibility of States for Internationally Wrongful Acts* Arts 1, 4 reprinted in J Crawford, *The International Law Commission's Articles on State Responsibility: Introduction, Text and Commentaries* (Cambridge, Cambridge University Press, 2002) 77, 94.

[74] *Ibid*, Art 5, 100.

private individual or group in circumstances where the State has "effective control" over the act,[75] a matter which would require proof that the State has directed and participated in the specific operations being planned or performed on its territory against other States. A more liberal test for attribution has been recently proposed in the case of acts by organised armed forces and militias. In such a situation a State will be held responsible where it is found to have had "overall control" of such acts,[76] a conclusion which requires evidence that a State has been involved in the general planning and supervision of operations.[77] Hence, it seems that in the context of a computer network attack, State responsibility may only arise where a State has knowledge of and involvement in attacks by an individual hacker or terrorist group against another State.

However it should be noted that establishing the requisite link between actor and State can be much more complicated in the computer context by the difficulty of identifying the attacker. Modern technology has increased the scope for aggressors to conceal both their identity and geographical location.[78] Consequently, in a situation where there have been repeated instances of hostile computer activity emanating from a State's territory directed against another State, it seems reasonable to presume that the host State had knowledge of such attacks and so should incur responsibility.

B. State-Sanctioned Computer Network Attack: An Unlawful Use of Force?

The next question to consider is what infringement of international law may be committed by a State-sanctioned computer network attack. One possible breach suggested by scholars is that such conduct may amount to a prohibited use of force under Article 2(4) of the UN Charter, which has been found by the International Court of Justice to represent customary international law.[79]

Article 2(4) is in the following form:

> All Members shall refrain in their international relations from the threat or use of force against the territorial integrity or political independence of any State, or in any other manner inconsistent with the Purposes of the United Nations.

[75] Y Dinstein, "Computer Network Attacks and Self Defence" in Schmitt and O'Donnell (eds), above n 16, 99, 104 citing *Case Concerning Military and Paramilitary Activities (Nicaragua v United States)* 1986 ICJ Reports 14, 62, 64–65. See also Crawford, above n 73, 111.
[76] Case IT–94–1 *Prosecutor v Tadic* (1999) 38 *International Legal Materials* 1518, 1541.
[77] *Ibid*, 1546.
[78] Dinstein, above n 75, 111; Barkham, above n 71, 99.
[79] *Case Concerning Military and Paramilitary Activities (Nicaragua v United States)* 1986 ICJ Reports 14.

The generally accepted position among courts and scholars is that the prohibition in Article 2(4) is limited to the use of military force and does not extend to economic or other forms of coercion.[80] If this view were applied to an attack on a computer system, it seems hard to argue that such conduct could ever be a use of force given that the required "instrument" is military materiel. If all computer network attacks were considered to fall outside the prohibition on the use of force in Article 2(4), then a serious regulatory gap would exist in customary international law.[81] However, some writers[82] have argued that the effects of political and economic coercion may themselves be as serious as those resulting from a use of military force and hence equally worthy of prohibition. For example, where destruction of life or property has occurred, then there should be less focus on the precise type of weapon used and more on the gravity of the results.[83] Significantly, in the context of computer network attacks, it has been argued that the political and economic sanctions that frequently accompany such conduct will often threaten the territorial integrity and political independence of a State.[84] Similarly, it has been noted that the purpose of Article 2(4) is to promote international peace and stability, and computer network attacks, although not "precisely coincid[ing] with armed force" in terms of appearance, may nevertheless have similar adverse consequences.[85]

Assuming that such an "effects" model could be applied to determine whether a network attack amounted to force within Article 2(4), the question then to consider is what types of attack will fall within the prohibition. A first point to note is that the definition of "computer network attack" has been widely drawn in the scholarly literature and would include activities with both lethal and more trivial consequences. For example, an attack has been described as an "operation to disrupt, deny, degrade or destroy information resident in computers and computer networks".[86] Computer attacks can also serve a variety of purposes, for example: "(1) extracting the information held in the target computer (espionage); (2) disseminating information through the adversary's information network in order to deceive the adversary or stimulate political instability; (3) preparing the battlespace by incapacitating the adversary's

[80] See, eg, O Schachter, "International Law: the Right of States to Use Armed Force" (1984) 82 *Michigan Law Review* 1620, 1624.
[81] Barkham, above n 71, 58.
[82] See, eg, I Brownlie, *International Law and the Use of Force by States* (Oxford, Clarendon Press, 1963) 362–363.
[83] *Ibid.*
[84] W Sharp, *Cyberspace and the Use of Force* (Falls Church, Aegis Research Corporation 1999) 88–91.
[85] Schmitt, above n 14, 908.
[86] *Ibid*, 888 adopted by Murphy, above n 16, 326.

command, control, and communications capabilities; or (4) causing property damage, physical injury, or death by manipulating infrastructure or operational systems controlled by the target computer."[87] While each of the above operations may involve "disrupt[ing], deny[ing], degrad[ing] or destroy[ing] of information resident in a computer" there is a vast difference in consequences with each type of action. Given this disparity in effects, it would seem excessive to include all such conduct within the prohibition on the use of force.

As a result, it is important when determining whether an attack amounts to an unlawful use of force, to examine the consequences and effects in each case. It is accepted among scholars that where an attack causes serious harm in the physical world such as damage to property or human life which may be highly similar in nature to that occurring as a result of military action, then such conduct should also be considered force.[88] The problem with this view, however, is that computer network attacks often do not cause such tangible injuries in the physical world but rather confine their harm to the online environment. Consequently, if the "physical harm" approach were adopted as the sole test to determine whether a computer network attack amounted to force it is likely to be too narrow and under inclusive. An alternative approach would be to argue that a broader notion of effects should be considered when applying Article 2(4) to computer attacks. In support of this view, it may be noted that the terms of Article 2(4) are explicitly technologically neutral — there is no suggestion that a particular type of weapon or military instrument has to be used to fall within the provision.[89] It would seem possible therefore to apply the Article to new forms of technology which embrace harm that would not result from military activity.

The question then becomes: what forms of computer network attack, beyond those causing serious injury in the physical world, may be considered uses of force? It is tentatively suggested in this chapter that the following three types of acts may come within the prohibition, given the severity of their online consequences.[90] A first situation would be where an attack results in the "takedown" of a computer system, with the flow of information disrupted, leading to a suspension of communication within the network. A second case may be where data corruption occurs, through the introduction of a virus, which can have a range of effects from the display of offensive material on a web site to the destruction of computer files and a third example may be where an individual "hacks" into

[87] Silver, "Computer Network Attack as a Use of Force under Article 2(4) of the United Nations Charter" in Schmitt and O'Donnell (eds), above n 16, 73, 76–77.
[88] *Ibid*, 83, 85; Barkham, above n 71, 88.
[89] Silver, n 87 above, 84.
[90] See generally DE Denning, *Information Warfare and Security* (Reading, MA, Addison-Wesley Pub Co, 1999) 230–34, 269–70 for a more detailed discussion of the technological issues.

a domain name server so that the original Internet Protocol address is replaced with another, with the effect of rendering the original site inaccessible or diverting users to a bogus version.

All three examples primarily involve serious digital effects, although physical consequences may also arise, such as lost revenue from system interference. While the effects do not obviously resemble in form the damage to persons or property flowing from the use of military force they may nevertheless involve significant disruption and harm to a particular State whose system has been attacked and be worthy of prohibition on this basis. Inclusion of such attacks within the concept of illegal force may also deter States from lending assistance to or acquiescing in such conduct.

It must however be acknowledged that some State practice is required before a clear view can be reached on the question whether an attack with almost entirely digital effects is an unlawful use of force.

C. State-Sanctioned Computer Network Attack: Unlawful Intervention?

An alternative argument in customary international law against State-supported cyber attacks against another State would be to classify them as unlawful intervention in the target State's sovereignty. It is clear that customary international law recognizes a duty on States not to intervene in the sovereignty of others and that this duty stands independently of the duty not to use force against another State.[91] If it were found that a computer network attack with predominantly online consequences fell outside the prohibition on the use of force, then an argument could nevertheless be made that such conduct amounted to unlawful intervention.[92] Indeed, the argument may be an easier one to sustain given that the threshold for proving intervention as opposed to "force" would seem to be a lower one.

Moreover, application of the customary norm of non-intervention to cyber attacks may pick up an even wider range of such attacks, in particular those without immediate effects, either physical or digital. An example would be an attack that involves the use of spyware, that is, a program used to observe behaviour at an advanced security site. Such conduct may have adverse effects in the future such as when material obtained is used to harm a State but at the point when the activity itself is being conducted no such effects may have arisen. Nevertheless, a clear intrusion into the

[91] *Nicaragua*, above n 75, 106.
[92] This point is acknowledged by Schmitt at above n 14, 908 and Silver at above n 87, 82, 87, 93.

target State's sovereignty has occurred and one which could be classified as an unlawful intervention.

Another example of a computer network attack without necessary or immediate harmful effects is where a State-sanctioned hacker accesses a site of another State and proceeds to reproduce electronically large amounts of sensitive information. One again while such conduct may cause future harm at the moment the act is performed no effects have manifested themselves. Nevertheless, an encroachment upon the sovereignty of the State has occurred. The introduction of a "worm" into a computer system, that is a program designed to be activated and cause effects in the future, would also fall within this category.

Support for the view that a wide category of computer network attacks may constitute unlawful intervention also may be found in the domestic criminal legislation of many States, which commonly prohibits unauthorized access and interference with computer systems.[93] Such laws are of course almost exclusively directed at the domestic context, such as where a hacker in State A attacks a computer system in State A. However, it is suggested that they may also be relied upon as a form of State practice to support the view that a State-sanctioned computer network attack against a computer system in another State is an unlawful intervention in international law. In other words, States by enacting such domestic laws, can arguably be seen as condemning such conduct whether carried out wholly within their borders or on the international plane against other States.

D. State-Sanctioned Computer Network Attacks and the Right to Self Defence

Customary international law has long recognized the right of a State to use unilateral force in self defence. According to the traditional formulation in the *Caroline* case, the conditions for the exercise of the right are that there is a threat that gives rise to a necessary, instantaneous, unavoidable action of self defence where no time to deliberate is available.[94] By contrast, Article 51 of the UN Charter provides that self defence may only be resorted to by a State where "an armed attack occurs against [it]".

The debate that has proceeded since the adoption of the Charter is whether the pre-1945 customary international law of self defence has survived as a right additional to that contained in Article 51, such that a State may resort to anticipatory or preemptive self defence, without having to show that it faces an armed attack.

[93] Such laws were discussed in section III B above.
[94] (1837) 29 BFSP 1137–1138; 30 BFSP 195–196.

Scholars of the "strict" school[95] argue that the customary law right to self defence is subsumed within and limited to the terms of Article 51. They note the danger of subjectivity[96] and abuse inherent in any preemption doctrine. Writers supporting the anticipatory[97] right to self defence argue in response that a State's capacity to use force in self defence may be completely impaired and rendered practically useless if it were forced to wait until it were the victim of an armed attack before responding.[98] Still other writers have sought to steer a middle ground by arguing that a State should be entitled to use force to "intercept" an armed attack which is at a preliminary, yet irreversible stage.[99]

Ultimately what may be the real difference in practice between the competing views is one of timing: at what stage of an armed attack may a State respond with force—planning, initiation or execution?

It was argued above in the discussion on use of force[100] that an analysis based on the effects of a computer network attack should be used to determine whether the attack amounts to a prohibited use of force. The reason for this view was that otherwise all computer operations would lie outside the scope of Article 2(4), an obviously undesirable conclusion at a time when such attacks are increasing. So too in this section it is suggested that in determining whether a State may resort to force in self defence an analysis of the effects, likely or suffered, of any attack, is required.

There seems to be a clear consensus in the literature on computer attacks and international law that where an attack has caused[101] or is likely to cause[102] physical damage to tangible property and human beings in the physical world then the target State should be entitled to use force in self defence.[103] The more difficult question again is whether purely digital or online harm may also suffice for the exercise of the right. One scholar has argued[104] that an attack causing wholly digital harm may be

[95] See, eg, Brownlie, above n 82, 269–78; L Henkin, *How Nations Behave*, 2nd edn (New York, Colombia University Press, 1979) 141.

[96] Henkin, *ibid*, 295.

[97] See, eg, D Bowett, "Reprisals Involving Recourse to Armed Force" (1972) 66 *American Journal of International Law* 1, 4; MS McDougal and FP Feliciano, *The International Law of War: Transnational Coercion and World Public Order* (Dordrecht, Martinus Nijhoff Publishers, Co-publication with New Haven Press, 1994) 234–40.

[98] O Schachter, "In Defense of International Rules on the Use of Force" (1986) 53 *University of Chicago Law Review* 113, 136.

[99] Y Dinstein, *War Aggression and Self Defence*, 2nd edn (Cambridge, Cambridge University Press, 1994) 187–91 and above n 75, 99, 110–11 approved by Robertson, "Self Defense Against Computer Network Attack under International Law" in Schmitt and O'Donnell (eds), above n 16, 125–26.

[100] See section V B above.

[101] According to the "strict" view of the doctrine.

[102] According to the "anticipatory" view.

[103] Schmitt, above n 14, 935; L Greenberg, *Information Warfare and International Law*, National Defence University Institute for National Strategic Studies, 85–87; Dinstein, above n 75, 105.

[104] Sharp, above n 84, 130.

adequate to trigger the right to self defence where the attack involves the penetration by a State of a highly sensitive computer system of another State. Intrusion into such a system amounts to a "demonstration of hostile intent".

Other scholars have criticized this approach for being far too broad, as well as being subjective and technologically nebulous. The approach also does not appear adequately to distinguish between the degree of force required to fall under the prohibition in Article 2(4) and the generally considered[105] higher standard required to trigger the operation of the right to self defence.

It will be recalled above that computer network attacks with serious online effects were considered to be prohibited uses of force and so arguably something more than this should be required for self defence. Instead of focusing on the sensitivity of the target an alternative approach would be to examine the depth of intrusion of the attack and the hardness or difficulty of penetration of the target system. For example, if a State established sophisticated protective measures in a system, perhaps using firewall or cryptography technology and the system was nevertheless penetrated by another State, then this would suggest a more deliberate and consciously hostile attack. The US Department of Defence has developed a system of levels of protection[106] for computer manufacturers and purchasers in the defence industry to provide guidance as to what security features can be built into systems to protect highly sensitive applications. The standards vary from D or minimal protection all the way up to A1 or verified protection.

It may be argued therefore that where a State's computer system, perhaps with an A1 level of protection, is penetrated by another State, then this would be a key precondition to the exercise of force in self defence. However the penetration of an extremely difficult target would not, by itself, be sufficient to trigger the right. Given the exceptional nature of self defence, the depth of intrusion and degree of degradation of the particular attack should also be considered. An example of a high degree of degradation would be where a system has been "taken down" through an attack. Online harm of a lower level such as the introduction of a malicious code or virus to corrupt large amounts of data may also arguably suffice.

Returning to the issue of whether the anticipatory or strict views of self defence should be applied to computer network attacks, the force of both views must be acknowledged. Those endorsing the strict view are right to say that an anticipatory doctrine opens the way to abuse, particularly

[105] *Nicaragua*, above n 75, 108, 109–110, 126–127; Silver, above n 87, 83.

[106] Trusted Computer System Evaluation Criteria (TCSEC), also known as the "Orange Book" as discussed in Denning, above n 90, 375–377.

given the imprecision in quantifying possible digital effects arising from an hypothetical attack. At the same time, those of the anticipatory school are equally correct in saying that the requirement of an armed attack may render the right practically useless where the target State's systems are effectively destroyed by the offending acts. As mentioned above, a possible solution to the strict/anticipatory dichotomy may be to focus on a point of time between the operation of the two approaches, i.e. the time when a network intrusion is in its preliminary stages but with the requisite harm highly imminent. In this regard, the traditional customary international law requirements for self defence of immediacy and necessity[107] would clearly be satisfied. It is suggested, therefore, that the "interception" approach referred to above[108] would be the most appropriate to adopt in the digital context.

Another matter that needs to be considered in relation to self defence and computer network attacks is the form of response which the target State may take in using force in self defence. The guiding principle in customary international law appears to be proportionality—that whatever response is made represents an approximately equivalent level of force to that which the target State received or was likely to receive.[109] However it is clear that the form of "weapon" used in self defence need not be the same as that employed in the original attack.[110] Applying this reasoning, scholars have argued that a victim of an electronic attack is not obliged to respond solely with digital force but can resort to physical, off line action as well provided that the response is not excessive.[111] Similarly, a victim of an electronic attack that causes wholly physical damage can respond with both digital and physical force, provided that the measures taken as a whole are proportionate. The principle of proportionality would also allow a State to respond to a computer network attack with distributed or dispersed effects (as often occurs) with action in the form of a "single large scale forcible countermeasure".[112]

A final issue that arises in the context of self defence and computer attacks flows from the discussion above on attribution.[113] It was suggested above that given the difficulty of identifying the precise attacker

[107] *Caroline* case, above n 94.
[108] See authors cited at n 99 above.
[109] *Advisory Opinion on the Legality of the Threat or Use of Nuclear Weapons* (8 July 1996) 35 *International Legal Materials* 809, 822.
[110] Dinstein, above n 75, 108.
[111] *Ibid.*
[112] *Ibid*, 109. A "single large scale forcible countermeasure" would possibly take the form of a system or network takedown, the introduction of a malicious code such as a virus or worm into a target system or an infrastructure attack to neutralize a threat. The gravity of such a response would depend on the status of any ongoing threat and the seriousness of preceding attacks.
[113] See section VA above.

and of establishing a link between this person and the State in whose territory such activities originate, a broader notion of responsibility based on presumed knowledge of the attacks by the host State should be adopted, at least where such attacks have been repeated. Recognising that States may have wider responsibility for the acts of individuals or groups in the context of computer network attacks against other States may also have implications for the doctrine of self defence in that it may suggest a greater range of situations in which a target State may respond with force.[114]

Support for such an argument can be found in recent practice of the UN Security Council. In Resolution 1368 the Council describes acts of international terrorism as "a threat to international peace and security"[115] and calls upon member States "to take all necessary steps to respond to . . . and to combat all forms of terrorism".[116] Scholars[117] have argued that the effect of this resolution is to broaden the doctrine of unilateral self defence by equating an attack by a terrorist organization to an act of armed aggression by a State and so enabling the victim State to resort to self defence *against that group*.

Consequently it may be argued that where a terrorist group launches a series of computer network attacks against a neighbouring State the target State may be entitled to use force in self defence against that group without having to establish specific knowledge of or involvement in such acts by the State upon whose territory the acts originated. In this way the expansion of the doctrine of self defence to include responses to terrorist acts would accord with the proposed widening of the scope of State responsibility for computer network attacks. Acceptance of such a doctrine would therefore clearly address the problem mentioned above of a victim State having no means of redress in international law when faced with an attack by a non-State actor which is not attributable to a State.[118]

VI. CONCLUSION

As has been noted in this chapter, cyberterrorism, while not yet a serious problem, is likely to increase in the future, given the dependency of States on technology and the ease with which computer systems can be attacked.

[114] In support of this view, see E Jensen, "Computer Attacks on Critical National Infrastructure: A Use of Force Invoking the Right to Self Defense" (2002) 38 *Stanford Journal of International Law* 207, 235.
[115] UN Doc. S/Res/1368 (2001) available at <http://www.un.org/Docs/sc/unsc_resolutions.html> para 1.
[116] *Ibid*, para 5.
[117] A Cassese, "Terrorism is Also Disrupting Some Crucial Legal Categories of International Law" available at <http://www.ejil.org/forum_WTC/ny-cassese.html>.
[118] See section VA above.

Given the clear, universal threat posed to States by cyberterrorism, an effective response from international law is essential.

In the case of domestic State regulatory practice, there is now a clear trend to enact laws which prohibit attacks on the "architecture" of computer networks, out of a recognition that criminal laws designed to apply to purely physical acts are inadequate.

The increasing harmonization of such laws on cybercrime when accompanied by the strong condemnation of cyberterrorism in international bodies such as the UN General Assembly goes some distance to establishing the crime of cyberterrorism as an emerging norm in customary international law. What is needed however to give further momentum to this process is the adoption of a widely supported convention, with specific provisions imposing compulsory jurisdiction over cyberterrorist offences on State parties. The current absence of such obligations in international law seriously undermines the domestic regulatory consensus on cybercrime by potentially allowing cyberterrorists to evade prosecution.

Another important international law dimension to cyberterrorism arises where computer attacks are performed by or with the acquiescence of States. In this situation the international law rules governing the use of force and the right to self defence do not obviously apply, given the long accepted view that these norms only encompass military force. However, since the effects of cyberterrorism can be as grave as those flowing from military activity, a strong case can be made both for the inclusion of computer attacks within the prohibition on force and as a basis for the exercise of self defence. This argument also receives support from the recent movement in practice and scholarship to widen the scope of State responsibility for terrorist acts. Cyberterrorism is therefore clearly moving from the periphery to the core of international law concern.

Part V

Conclusions

19

Enforcing International Law Norms Against Terrorism: Achievements and Prospects

ANDREA BIANCHI

I. THE ALLEGED INADEQUACY OF INTERNATIONAL LAW TO FACE THE THREAT OF TERRORISM: SOME PRELIMINARY REMARKS

SOME TWO YEARS after the attack against the World Trade Center in New York the time may be ripe to venture into a preliminary assessment of how effectively international law has responded to the reviviscence of international terrorism on such a grand scale.[1] Surely, the threat of international terrorism has had a major impact on a number of issues related to international law. Very many areas have been affected and a panoply of considerations concerning the suitability of either the international regulatory framework or the enforcement processes attached thereto have been made. Indeed, amongst the numerous questions which have arisen, the query of whether international law is well equipped to face the challenges posed by international terrorism stands out as the most recurrent. The concern has been voiced that international terrorism may even bring about the disruption of some crucial legal

[1] It is impossible to account for the vast amount of scholarly work that has been published since 2001 on the subject of international terrorism. Monographs and edited volumes include: International Bar Association Task Force on International Terrorism, *International Terrorism; Legal Challenges & Responses* (New York, 2003); WP Heere (ed), *Terrorism and the Military: International Legal Implications*, (Cambridge University Press, Cambridge, 2003); JP Sterba, *Terrorism and International Justice* (Oxford University Press, Oxford, 2003); PJ Van Krieken (ed), *Terrorism and the International Legal Order: With Special Reference to the UN, the EU and Cross-Border Aspects*, (TMC Asser Press, The Hague, 2002); E Bribosia and A Weyembergh, (eds), *Lutte contre le terrorisme et droits fondamentaux*, (Bruyant and Nemesis, Bruxelles, 2002); K Bannelier *et al* (eds), *Le droit international face au terrorisme*, (Pedone, Paris, 2002). A useful reading on the general subject remains R Higgins and M Flory (eds), *Terrorism and International Law*, (Routledge, London, 1997).

categories of international law[2] and that many of its norms and processes should be re-considered and adapted to an unprecedented reality. The emotional vein of this debate as well as the highly politically charged nature that any discourse on terrorism almost inevitably brings with it have not helped a great deal in framing the real legal issues in their proper context. Short of any ambition to undertake a comprehensive analysis of national and international responses to terrorism, this chapter merely attempts to provide some insights into what can be learnt from these two years of "war against terrorism" and what could be done to improve the efficacy of international law enforcement processes.

In order to address the main question of whether international law possesses adequate tools to effectively fight against international terrorism some preliminary remarks may be apt. First of all it should be emphasized that the dialectical relation of law and politics, which is inherent in any social process within an organized community, becomes an almost inextricable link in the area of terrorism. Few, if any, domains of international law have stirred so much controversy and caused so many political clashes as international terrorism.[3] The often quoted adage "one man's terrorist is another man's freedom fighter" well epitomizes the political and ideological underpinnings to the debate on terrorism.[4] The alleged neglect by the international community of the real causes of terrorism identified with poverty, social injustice and political oppression versus the unconditional condemnation by the Western world of any violent act directed against the civilian population has fuelled even more what has long appeared as an irreconcilable conflict of values. This is all well known and to remind in this context of the predominant political and/or moral connotations of the discourse about international terrorism may appear to many rather futile. However, drawing attention to the need to distinguish the legal dimension from the other components of such a complex social phenomenon as terrorism may turn out to be a fairly useful exercise if one is to avoid misplaced expectations. It would

[2] A Cassese, "Terrorism is Also Disrupting Some Crucial Categories of International Law", (2001) 12 *European Journal of International Law* 993.

[3] This has caused some scholars to express doubts about the utility of the notion. See RR Baxter, "A Sceptical Look at the Concept of Terrorism", (1974) 7 *Akron Law Review* 380: "We have cause to regret that a legal concept of 'terrorism' was ever inflicted upon us. The term is imprecise; it is ambiguous; and above all, it serves no operative legal purpose." Similarly, R Higgins, "The general international law of terrorism", in R Higgins and M Flory (eds), *Terrorism and International Law*, above n 1, at 28: "'Terrorism' is a term without legal significance. It is merely a convenient way of alluding to activities, whether of States or of individuals, widely disapproved of and in which either the methods used are unlawful, or the targets protected, or both."

[4] See RA Friedlander, "Terrorism", in R Bernhard (ed), *Encyclopedia of Public International Law*, IV (2000) 845, at 846.

be highly unrealistic to demand of international law to solve issues, which more properly pertain to the realm of politics. Although it may sound as a truism, to remind that the ultimate responsibility for the eradication of terrorism lies with national and international decision makers rather than with their legal advisers, short of being a disclaimer of responsibility, has the merit of shifting the focus on the proper role that law may perform in this area. This somewhat ancillary role does not take anything away from the fact that international law, by its rules and established processes, is called upon to discharge fundamental functions. On the one hand, it may provide guidance on what normative policies are likely to be perceived as more legitimate than others in the light of past decisions and the existing normative framework. On the other, it may channel the political discourse within the legal boundaries of established and widely accepted international decision-making processes. Finally, international law can provide the technical means by which extant rules can be effectively implemented.

In this respect, it may be opportune to specify that the term "implementation" should be understood in a broad sense to encompass all those elements of a normative, political or of a more broadly social character which by themselves or in combination with one another may ensure respect for the interests and/or values underlying the legal prescriptions which incorporate them. In other words, all those mechanisms and processes which may help ensure compliance with international legal standards and provide redress for their infringement should be considered in their entirety when evaluating the capacity of rules to deploy their intended effects and to ensure respect with their underlying values.[5] Excessive reliance on a narrow interpretation of enforcement processes taken to mean only those mechanisms which may guarantee the actual enforcement of binding rules by way of coercion or under threat of sanctions risks being a simplistic approach to law enforcement and overlooking the current complexities of law abidance inducing factors. Any attempt to evaluate the international legal regime concerning international terrorism and to enhance its effectiveness should thus take into account a variety of factors, which may affect its capacity to implement relevant legal standards.

Against the background of the above preliminary remarks it may now be in order to have a closer look at the international normative framework against terrorism.

[5] This interpretation is reminiscent of, although not limited to, the concept of *garanzia*, used by R Quadri, *Diritto internazionale pubblico*, 5th edn (Liguori editore, Napoli, 1968), at 229 ff, to refer to all the means which the societal body possesses to prevent or punish violations of legal rules and therefore guarantee their effectiveness.

II. THE REGULATORY FRAMEWORK: OLD RULES AND THE THRUST TOWARDS NEW STANDARD SETTING

A. The Treaty Framework

Part of the criticism in relation to the inadequacy of the international legal system to face the threat of international terrorism hinges upon the alleged lack of applicable normative standards. This is a rather misconceived representation of the applicable normative framework, which can be explained on several grounds. The negative perception of the existing regime is partly due to the law-making strategy, which has been developing at international law particularly over the last three decades. As is well known, rather than attempting to conclude a general agreement on the prohibition of terrorism, the adoption of which was prevented by the lack of a common definition of terrorism as such, a number of so called "sectoral treaties" were adopted instead. These treaties prohibit certain particular activities and lay down rules geared towards the punishment of individuals by national jurisdictions.[6] This normative approach prompted by the political difficulties of the time and by the climate of ideological confrontation prevailing in such international fora as the United Nations, has greatly contributed to underestimating the relative importance of developing over time a rather extensive normative framework. The fact that some of the relevant treaties had been adopted in the aftermath of tragic events also contributed to the perception that the response of international law to terrorism was always belated and therefore ineffective.[7]

Some of the above criticism is surely well founded. However, it is worth noticing that the common features of the anti-terror conventions in terms of normative policies — it suffices to think of their jurisdictional clauses — had already produced a fairly consistent pattern of rules applicable to several terrorist activities. The relatively widespread participation in many of the anti-terror conventions by States had also created fertile grounds for customary international law to develop. The persuasive force of the above remarks is only partly affected by the fact that only recently have the two latest universal treaties against terrorism become the object of a wide participation by States.[8] A closer look at the

[6] For comprehensive treatment of the subject see the contribution to this volume by R Kolb, "The Exercise of Criminal Jurisdiction over International Terrorists", ch 11.

[7] A good example is provided by the Convention for the Suppression of Unlawful Acts against the Safety of Maritime Navigation, Rome, 10 March 1988 (entered into force on 1 March 1992), adopted in the aftermath of the *Achille Lauro* affair (see A Cassese, *Terrorism, Politics and Law: The Achille Lauro Affair*, (Blackwell Publishers, Cambridge, 1989)).

[8] See International Convention for the Suppression of Terrorist Bombings, New York, 15 December 1997, UN Doc A/RES/52/164 (1997) (entered in force 23 May 2001).

status of the two conventions reveals that most of the States that are now party to them decided to ratify only in the aftermath of the 11th September attacks. Incidentally, it must be noticed that the US was not a party to the 1997 UN Convention against Terrorist Bombings, which could have been applicable to the attacks against the Twin Towers.[9] Be that as it may, the anti-terror conventions provide a good coverage in terms of regulation of terrorist activities and lay down a series of obligations, which — if properly implemented — are potentially quite effective in enforcing individual responsibility.

It would be nonetheless an incomplete representation of the existing normative framework were one to omit regional treaties. The markedly different approach of the European convention, which mainly focuses on extradition,[10] and some different normative connotations attaching to each convention notwithstanding, the web of international obligations incumbent upon States is rather impressive. The proliferation of normative standards at the regional level has increased in the aftermath of the 11th September attacks, even though at times one legitimately wonders about the efficacy of treaties which add little to the existing rules and provide for no additional enforcement mechanism.[11]

Surely the main reason for the perception of inadequacy of the existing regulatory framework is the failure by the international community to adopt a comprehensive treaty against terrorism. The history of the codification efforts within the United Nations is well known and need not be recounted here.[12] It suffices to mention that negotiations had made remarkable progress lately, although they risk being seriously hampered

As of 12 March 2004, there are 120 States parties. 90 States have become parties since 11 September 2001 and the International Convention for the Suppression of the Financing of Terrorism, New York, 9 December 1999, UN Doc. A/RES/54/109 (1999), (entered into force 10 April 2002). As of 12 March 2004, there are 112 States parties. 106 States have become parties since 11 September 2001.

[9] See Art 2 of the Convention, defining its scope of application: "Any person commits an offence within the meaning of this Convention if that person unlawfully and intentionally delivers, places, discharges or detonates an explosive or other lethal device in, into or against a place of public use, a State or government facility, a public transportation system or an infrastructure facility: a) With the intent to cause death or serious bodily injury; or b) With the intent to cause extensive destruction of such a place, facility or system, where such destruction results in or is likely to result in major economic loss ... ". The United States became a party to the Convention on 26 June 2002.

[10] See the European Convention on the Suppression of Terrorism, Strasbourg, 27 February 1977, ETS No. 90 (entered into force on 4 August 1978), and its amending Protocol, Strasbourg, 15 May 2003 (not yet in force).

[11] See, for instance, the Inter-American Convention Against Terrorism, Bridgetown, 3 June 2002, Treaty Series OAS A-66 (entered into force on 10 July 2003).

[12] For a brief overview see M Halberstam, "The Evolution of the United Nations Position on Terrorism: From Exempting National Liberation Movements to Criminalizing Terrorism Wherever and by Whomever Committed", (2003) 41 *Columbia Journal of Transnational Law* 582.

by the still pending controversy on the text proposed by the member States of the Organization of the Islamic Conference with a view to amending Article 18.[13] In particular, these States demand that the Convention not be applicable to the activities of the parties during an armed conflict "including in situations of foreign occupation". The latter expression, which did not appear in draft Article 18 as circulated by the coordinator of the Ad Hoc Committee for discussion,[14] hardly hides the endemic dispute about the exception to the prohibition of terrorism concerning the activities of people fighting against foreign occupation. Indeed, in the view of the coordinator of the Ad Hoc Committee the "key issue" in order to successfully bring to completion the negotiations on the comprehensive treaty is Article 18.[15] Article 2, which defines terrorist activities, no longer seems an insurmountable obstacle, as all it appears to require is some fine tuning of the language.[16] Convergence of the definitional aspects of terrorism purports that the alleged lack of international consensus is greatly exaggerated and lends support to the view, expressed in this book,[17] that the real dispute is about an alleged exception for the activities of those who fight against foreign occupation. Even though recognition of the exception would have important consequences, it would be simplistic to discard altogether the substantial convergence of view on the general definition. Nor is the consistency clause of draft Article 2 *bis* likely to pose major problems, the prevailing view being that the comprehensive treaty should have a residual scope of application with respect to other treaties "dealing with a specific category of terrorist offence".[18]

[13] See generally, P d'Argent, "Examen du projet de convention générale sur le terrorisme international", in K Bannelier *et al* (eds), *Le droit international face au terrorisme*, above n 1, at 121 ff.

[14] Both texts concerning Art 18 (the one circulated by the Coordinator for discussion and the one proposed by the Member States of the Organization of the Islamic Conference) can be read in their entirety in Annex IV to the "Report of the Ad Hoc Committee established by General Assembly resolution 51/210 of 17 December 1996", Seventh session (28 January–1 February 2002), GAOR, 57th Session, Supplement No. 37 (UN Doc. A/57/37), at 17.

[15] See the conclusions of the coordinator of the informal bilateral discussions concerning a Draft comprehensive convention on international terrorism, reproduced in Annex II to the "Report of the Ad Hoc Committee established by General Assembly resolution 51/210 of 17 December 1996", Seventh session (31 March–2 April 2003), GAOR, 58th Session, Supplement No. 37 (UN Doc. A/58/37), at 10.

[16] *Ibid*.

[17] See A Cassese, "Terrorism as an International Crime", ch 10.

[18] See the text of Art 2 *bis* in the "Report of the Ad Hoc Committee established by General Assembly resolution 51/210 of 17 December 1996", Seventh session (28 January–1 February 2002), above n 14, at 7 and the comments made by the Coordinator of the informal bilateral consultations in the "Report of the Ad Hoc Committee established by General Assembly resolution 51/210 of 17 December 1996", Seventh session (31 March–2 April 2003), above n 15, at 9.

B. Other Applicable Rules of International Law

Commentators have often overlooked the fact that other principles and rules of international law may also lend themselves to be applied to terrorism. At the peak of the debate on whether the international responsibility of Afghanistan could be engaged for its alleged support to the terrorist organization of Al-Qaeda, few considered the applicability of the rules, most of which are of a customary nature, directed to protecting the national security of foreign States. As convincingly argued by scholars in light of a long-established practice, these rules could be aptly classified in three different categories.[19] A first set of rules provides for the duty to abstain from directly organizing activities and sending individuals or groups of individuals to other States to commit hostile acts against the latter's security. In certain circumstances — as is known — such acts may amount to an armed attack and therefore to an act of aggression, if certain requirements are met.[20] Secondly, there exists an obligation not to give support to individuals or groups of individuals who intend to carry out activities against the security of foreign States, which can be characterized, depending on the factual circumstances as either an indirect aggression or as a violation of the principle of non-intervention.[21] Finally, even mere tolerance of activities carried out in its own territory by individuals against the security of foreign States may amount to a breach of international law, if it can be proved that the State has been negligent in failing to prevent or punish such conduct.[22] These rules, which have a firm root in international practice, could have been aptly resorted to in order to

[19] See R Pisillo Mazzeschi, "The Due Diligence Rule and the Nature of the International Responsibility of States", (1992) 35 *German Yearbook of International Law* 9, at 31 ff; and, *amplius, idem, "Due diligence" e responsabilità internazionale degli Stati,* (Giuffré, Milano, 1990), at 289 ff. See also, F Dubuisson, "Vers un renforcement des obligations de diligence en matière de lutte contre le terrorisme?" in K Bannelier *et al* (eds), *Le droit international face au terrorisme,* above n 1, at 141 ff.

[20] See AG Res 3314/1974, Art 3(g); "The sending by or on behalf of a State of armed bands, groups, irregulars or mercenaries, which carry out acts of armed force against another State of such gravity as to amount to the acts listed above or its substantial involvement therein."

[21] See International Court of Justice, *Military and Paramilitary Activities in and against Nicaragua (Nicaragua v United States of America),* Merits, Judgment, ICJ Reports 1986 14, at 127, para 247.

[22] See R Pisillo Mazzeschi, *"Due diligence" e responsabilità internazionale degli Stati,* above n 19, at 337 ff; I Brownlie, "International Law and the Activities of Armed Bands", (1958) 7 *International and Comparative Law Quarterly* 713, at 735. See the interesting opinion rendered by the Legal Service of the Swiss Federal Council in the *Agression contre la Légation de Roumanie à Berne* case, (1959) *Annuaire Suisse de Droit International* 225: *"L'Etat doit prévenir et punir les actes qui sont dirigés de son territoire contre l'intégrité extérieure et intérieure des Etats étrangers...Toutefois, ni l'obligation de prévention ni celle de punition n'ont un caractère absolu. La première ne se réalise que dans le cadre d'un standard général, d'une responsabilité pour négligence...L'Etat doit faire preuve de "due diligence"; il n'est pas tenu d'empêcher n'importe quel incident d'une manière absolue, ce qui serait matériellement impossible ..."*.

invoke the responsibility of Afghanistan, if it could be proved that the conduct of Afghanistan was actually amenable within their scope of application. More generally, a proper characterization of the relevant factual matrix would lead most of the time to the qualification of the conduct of a State which supports international terrorism as unlawful, regardless of any abstract and politically charged discussion about how to define the notion of States supporting terrorism.

Even more importantly, however, one has to consider the binding force of Security Council resolutions adopted under Chapter VII of the UN Charter, which quite remarkably expand the range of obligations incumbent upon States in this area. The Security Council had already taken measures against specific States for their involvement in international terrorism[23] and by way of Resolution 1373 it took up a quasi-legislative role by imposing on States a number of obligations ranging from the prohibition to provide any form of support to terrorist groups and the obligation to criminalize in their domestic legal systems the willful provision or collection of funds to be used for terrorist activities to the obligation of providing safe haven to whoever commits or supports acts of terrorism.[24] Furthermore, by qualifying international terrorism generally and, more recently, even individual acts of terrorism, as a threat to international peace and security,[25] the Security Council has given further political momentum to the consideration of terrorism as a global risk affecting the security of the international community and therefore engaging the responsibility (and the powers) of the Council under the Charter.

Overall one has the impression that the regulatory framework is fairly comprehensive in scope. Lacunae and shortcomings can occasionally be traced, but the whole body of international law rules is fairly satisfactory. This holds true particularly for treaty law, despite the failure to adopt a comprehensive anti-terror treaty. The consistent normative approach adopted by the international community, which focuses on laying down

[23] See resolutions 731 (21 January 1992), 748 (31 March 1992) and 883 (11 November 1993), concerning Libya; resolution 1054 (26 April 1996) concerning Sudan; resolutions 1267 (15 October 1999), and 1333 (19 December 2000) concerning the Taliban and the situation in Afghanistan.

[24] Resolution 1373 (28 September 2001). See also resolution 1269 (19 October 1999): "[u]nequivocally condemn[ing] all acts, methods and practices of terrorism as criminal and unjustifiable, regardless of their motivation, in all their forms and manifestations, wherever and by whomever committed, in particular those which could threaten international peace and security." (para 1).

[25] See the following resolutions: 1368 (12 September 2001), condemning the 11 September attacks; 1438 (14 October 2002) condemning the bomb attacks in Bali; 1440 (24 October 2002), condemning the heinous act of taking hostages in Moscow; 1450 (13 December 2002) condemning the bomb attack and attempted missile attack in Kenya and other recent terrorist acts in various countries; 1465 (13 February 2003), condemning the bomb attack in Colombia; 1516 (20 November 2003), condemning the bomb attacks in Istanbul; and most recently, 1530 (11 March 2004), condemning the bomb attacks in Madrid.

rules geared towards the effective punishment by national jurisdictions of the individuals responsible for the proscribed activities, in principle, provides a suitable framework. Clearly problems lie elsewhere. The alleged lack of efficacy of the anti-terror treaty regime largely depends on national measures of implementation of relevant rules rather than on the latter's content and scope. Having opted for a system which entrusts national authorities with the task of prosecuting individuals presupposes not only that States ratify the treaty, but also that national legal systems effectively and in a timely manner incorporate the treaty within the municipal legal order, enacting such legislation as may be necessary to make the treaty norms self-executing and directly applicable by courts. Internal decision-making processes to determine when to prosecute and when to extradite must be put in place to ensure the smooth implementation of the *aut dedere aut judicare* clause, when applicable, and national legislatures must promptly act to pass legislation whenever the amendment of criminal law and procedure statutes is required.

One may thus conclude by saying that if the proliferation of normative standards is clearly a sign of international cooperation, the efficacy of their underlying policies largely depends on the generality of their acceptance and on their proper implementation.

III. LAW AS AN INTERPRETATIVE ENTERPRISE: THE INTERPRETATION OF NORMS AT A TIME OF POLITICAL DIVISIVENESS

The purposeful character of legal interpretation is no novelty. Nor is it peculiar to international law.[26] The interpretation of legal norms geared towards the achievement of certain ends characterizes the day-to-day activity of lawyers, legal advisers and judges alike.[27] The inherently purposeful nature of legal interpretation should not be understood, as one might tend simplistically to assume, that interpreters are free to take the law to mean whatever suits best their needs. Legal interpretative processes are constrained by a variety of elements, ranging from the rules determining which particular criteria must be used to interpret specific instruments to contextual circumstances and the characterization of the relevant factual matrix. None of these intellectual operations is a neutral

[26] See R Dworkin, *Law's Empire* (Belknap Pr, Cambridge, MA, 1986), at 190 ff.

[27] For an exercise in purposeful interpretation in the area of State immunity, see A Bianchi, "Denying State Immunity to Violators of Human Rights" (1994) 46 *Austrian Journal of Public and International Law* 195–229, and more recently, by the same author, "L'immunité des Etats et les violations graves des droits de l'homme: la fonction de l'interprète dans la détermination du droit international" (2004) 108 *Révue général de droit international public* 59–95.

exercise and whoever is called upon to interpret the law, be it a judge, a scholar or a government official, enjoys a wide measure of discretion. Criteria can be twisted and turned, context may be construed differently depending on which elements one wants to emphasize and facts may be framed in several legal categories. Obviously, considerations of normative policy or mere politics can occasionally play a role, particularly when there is no general consensus on what a desirable outcome of a certain interpretive issue should be. What matters most is whether any given interpretation is sufficiently persuasive. Ultimately, the degree of persuasiveness of interpretive techniques largely depends on the perception of legitimacy of their use and on the social acceptability of the consequences, which may ensue from the application of the rule interpreted in a certain way. However heretical this may sound to orthodox lawyers, this pragmatic consideration accounts for the reality of legal interpretation more than complex theoretical constructs aimed at guaranteeing the alleged neutrality of this intellectual exercise.

A. The Interpretation of Security Council Resolutions

A fairly good example of how much interpretative issues may be affected by political contingencies is given by the uncertainty as to how to interpret Security Council resolutions. With particular regard to terrorism it may be worth recalling that the view was expressed that resolution 1368 of 12 September 2001 entitled the US to act in self-defence against Afghanistan.[28] The argument was set forth that reference in the Preamble of the resolution to the inherent right of States to individual and collective self-defence had to be interpreted to the effect of recognizing that the US, as the victim of a prior armed attack, could legitimately resort to force in conformity with the law of the Charter.[29] Even more strikingly, albeit not with direct reference to terrorism, resolution 1441 on Iraq has been the object of a variety of interpretations with some of the permanent members holding opposite views on what the resolution meant or was supposed to mean. What is clear is that the discrepancy of views on how to interpret the SC's resolution depended on the different

[28] See also the *Statement by the North Atlantic Council*, 12 September 2001, Press Release (2001) 124 (reproduced in 40 *International Legal Materials* 1267 (2001)); the two resolutions, respectively adopted at the 23rd and 24th meetings of consultation of the OAS ministers of foreign affairs on "Strengthening hemispheric cooperation to prevent, combat and eliminate terrorism" (OEA/Ser.F/II.23–RC.23/RES.1/01) and on "Terrorist threats to the Americas" (OEA/Ser.F/II.24–RC.24/RES.1/01) (*ibid*, at p. 1270 and 1273 respectively).
[29] See T Franck, "Terrorism and the Right of Self-Defense" (2001) 95 *American Journal of International Law* at 839.

political agendas of the members and, ultimately, on the purpose they intended to achieve.[30]

Regrettably no clear-cut method of interpretation comes handy to provide a persuasive answer to such an interpretive issue. Plausible arguments can be made both ways if one looks at purpose. On the one hand, it may be argued that it is the purpose of the Charter to outlaw the use of force and that no indirect authorization should be inferred from a Security Council resolution unless the latter clearly and unambiguously provides for it.[31] On the other, one may stress the fairly comprehensive powers of the Security Council and argue that whatever measure is instrumental to achieving the purpose of maintaining and/or restoring international peace and security should be upheld and interpreted in a way which guarantees the maximum of efficacy, including, where appropriate, to the use force against a State which refuses to comply with its international law obligations either under the Charter or under customary law.

To do away with purposeful interpretation and resort to what could be termed as a more formal or objective technique of interpretation is no easy task in this case. Indeed, the idea that different legal texts may be interpreted having regard to different methods depending on what they are and what function they are meant to perform is no novelty and was expressly stated by the International Court of Justice in the *Fisheries Jurisdiction* case (*Spain v Canada*) in 1998 with regard to unilateral declarations of acceptance of the Court's jurisdiction.[32] However, what international law prescribes properly to interpret Security Council resolutions is far from clear. One of the few inspirations one can draw from international case law is the *dictum* of the International Court of Justice in its 1971 Advisory Opinion on Namibia, where the Court identified as relevant factors the "language" of the resolution, "the discussions leading to it", "the Charter provisions invoked" as well as "all circumstances that might assist in determining [its] legal consequences".[33]

[30] See the *Letter dated 24 February 2003 from the Permanent Representatives of France, Germany and the Russian Federation to the United Nations addressed to the President of the Security Council* (UN Doc. S/2003/214) and the two draft resolutions proposed by Spain, United Kingdom of Great Britain and Northern Ireland and United States of America, respectively on 24 February 2003 and 7 March 2003 (UN Doc S/2003/215).

[31] See J Lobel and M Ratner, "Bypassing the Security Council: Ambiguous Authorizations to Use Force, Cease-fires and the Iraqi Inspection Regime" (1999) 93 *American Journal of International Law* 124, at 125.

[32] As is known, the ICJ held that unilateral declaration of acceptance of the jurisdiction of the Court under Art 36 of its Statute should be interpreted "in a natural and reasonable way", having particular regard "to the intention of the State concerned at the time when it accepted the compulsory jurisdiction of the Court." (*Fisheries Jurisdiction (Spain v Canada)*, Judgment of 4 December 1998, para 49).

[33] *Legal Consequences for States of the Continued Presence of South Africa in Namibia South-West Africa Notwithstanding Security Council Resolution 276 (1970)*, Advisory Opinion of 21 June 1971, ICJ Reports 1971 15, at 53.

Scholarly work on the topic remains surprisingly scant and ranges from the suggestion to adopt the outmoded presumption that no restriction on the sovereignty of States should be inferred,[34] to pragmatic approaches which caution against resorting to rules of treaty interpretation and stress a blend of relevant criteria along the lines of those suggested by the ICJ in 1971.[35] In fact, the argument that one could use the rules of the Vienna Convention on the Law of Treaties of 1969 by analogy is not particularly persuasive. To hold that Security Council resolutions, particularly those taken under Chapter VII, can be regarded as international agreements in a simplified form ignores the fact that these resolutions bind all the members of the organization and not just those who happen to be members of the Council at the relevant time. It would thus be odd to use interpretative tools which have developed in the context of *inter partes* obligations. More convincing is the argument whereby Security Council resolutions ought to be interpreted with a view to reconstructing the intent of the organ as such, in the light of the objective it pursues. The collective will of the Security Council need not be regarded as an abstract and unmanageable concept even when the wording of its decisions is not self-evident. When the SC authorized the member States to use "all necessary means" to bring Iraq to comply with its prior resolutions, it was clear that by that expression, in the light of the context and factual circumstances surrounding the resolution, the Council wanted to authorize States to resort to force. It should not come as a surprise that no one challenged the interpretation of resolution 678 at the time.

Different is the case with resolution 1368. Although States largely acquiesced in the use of force against Afghanistan, it remains unclear whether they all were convinced that military intervention had been authorized by the Security Council or, rather, was justifiable under Article 51 of the Charter or international customary law. Be that as it may, no authentic interpretation was available. Presidential statements, which can occasionally help to shed light on the intent of the Council, were equally ambiguous and, arguably, useless.[36] Even more striking is the case with resolution 1441, which was drafted with intentional ambiguity and

[34] See JA Frowein, "Unilateral Interpretation of Security Council Resolutions: A Threat to Collective Security?", in V Götz, P Selmer and R Wolfrum (eds), *Liber Amicorum Günther Jaenicke — Zum 85.Geburtstag* (Springer, Berlin, 1998) 99.

[35] See MC Wood, "The Interpretation of Security Council Resolutions" (1998) 2 *Max Planck Yearbook of United Nations Law* 73, especially at 95.

[36] See the declaration made on 7 October 2001 by the US permanent representative at the United Nations, Ambassador Negroponte (UN Doc. S/2001/1946). See also *Press Statement on Terrorist Threats by Security Council President* of 8 October 2001 (AFG/152; SC/7167), where the President states that "[t]he members of the Council were appreciative of the presentation made by the United States and the United Kingdom ... in which they state that the action [against Afghanistan] was taken in accordance with the inherent right of individual and collective self-defence following the terrorist attacks of 11 September 2001."

allowed for different interpretations, ranging from the authorization to use force either directly on the basis of its wording[37] or, indirectly, by the reviviscence of resolution 678 as a consequence of the material breach of resolution 687,[38] to the outright prohibition of the use of force pending a subsequent decision to be taken by the Security Council, after the inspectors reported back on the situation and the attitude of Iraq.[39] The somewhat extreme example of resolution 1441 attests to the difficulty of interpreting SC resolutions when there is no consensus among its members on what the resolution actually means. At this point one may even wonder whether, with a view to reconstructing the intent of the SC, consensus on interpretative issues by each and every permanent member should be required. The argument is one of logic. If Article 27(3) of the Charter requires the concurring vote of the five permanent members for decisions on non-procedural issues, how could one possibly disregard the interpretation of one or more of them when there is disagreement on such a fundamental issue as the decision of whether or not to authorize force?

The simple truth is that the Security Council as a political organ is subject in its decision-making process to the fluctuations of international politics. If no consensus on a certain course of conduct can be achieved, particularly among the five permanent members, its purported function to maintain international peace and security cannot be discharged and its intentions, however good, are doomed to failure, either because the right of veto or the threat of its exercise will prevent the SC from taking a decision or because the decision will be taken in such an ambiguous way as to lend itself to multiple and even conflicting interpretations. The fact that SC resolutions can make the object of different interpretations depending on political interests is no novelty in the practice of the organization.[40] However, the political divide, which seems to have emerged among the main actors of international politics on how to deal effectively with terrorism and rogue States, has led to stretching legal interpretation well beyond its boundaries. The inability by Security Council members to agree on any given interpretation and, arguably, their deliberate attempt to resort to ambiguous drafting have burdened the lawyers with a task they can hardly accomplish.

[37] See WH Taft Jr and TF Buchwald, "Preemption, Iraq and International Law", (2003) 97 *American Journal of International Law* 557 at 560–61.

[38] See the statement made by the UK Attorney General, Lord Goldsmith, in answer to a parliamentary question on 17 March 2003, available at: <http://news.bbc.co.uk/go/pr/fr/-/1/hi/uk-politics/2857347.stm> (last visited 15 December 2003). See also the Letter of 20 March 2003 addressed from the Permanent Representative of the US to the President of the Security Council (UN Doc. S/2003/351).

[39] In any event the prevailing view within the Security Council's members seemed to be that the matter had to be returned to the SC for discussion (see UN Doc. S/PV.4644).

[40] See S Rosenne, "On Multilingual Interpretation", in J Norton Moore (ed), *The Arab-Israel Conflict. Vol. II: Readings* (Princeton University Press, Princeton, 1974), at 906.

B. International Regulation of the Use of Force

The fact that purposeful interpretation at a time of political divisiveness risks disrupting established rules and practices is clearly attested by the current controversial perception of the international regulation of the use of force. Despite fierce opposition, particularly on the part of European scholars, to admit of the use of force outside the narrow boundaries set by the drafters of the UN Charter,[41] recent international practice shows that force is increasingly resorted to in circumstances in which the legality of its exercise is doubtful. Uncertainties exist as to which decision-making processes one should resort to as well as on the applicable rules.[42] In particular, the extensively relied-on notion of self-defence is the object of different interpretations. Excessive reliance on self-defence as a justification for the use of force is hardly surprising, self-defence allegedly being the only admissible exception to the use of force and armed reprisals being thought to have been stigmatized and outlawed forever. The general prohibition of the unilateral use of force, which in 1986 the International Court of Justice characterized as a peremptory norm of international law, leaves, in principle, little room for further exceptions.[43] In fact, besides the oddity of qualifying a rule that already provides for an exception as non-derogable, the current status of the prohibition of the use of force ought to be seriously reconsidered in the light of recent practice. Unconditional adherence to a formalistic and no longer tenable supremacy of the law of the Charter in this domain ignores the many failures which the system has incurred recently. Attempts to ground military interventions in Kosovo, Afghanistan and Iraq on the UN Charter have proved scarcely persuasive and States have increasingly relied on general international law to provide a justification for resorting to force. Although, as a matter of logic, the argument set forth by the ICJ in 1986 that by invoking exceptions States end up reinforcing the general rule may hold up,[44] it is hard for logic alone to pass the test of a practice in which an increasing number of exceptions might end up swallowing the rule.

[41] See, among others, M Bothe, "Terrorism and the Legality of the Use of Pre-emptive Force" (2003) 14 *European Journal of International Law* 227–40; M Kohen, "The Use of Force by the United States after the End of the Cold War, and its Impact on International Law", in M Byers and G Nolte (eds), *United States Hegemony and the Foundations of International Law* (Cambridge University Press, Cambridge, 2003) 197–231.

[42] See the interesting essay by E Benvenisti, "The US and the Use of Force: Double Edged Hegemony and the Management of Global Emergencies" (2004) 15 *European Journal of International Law* (forthcoming).

[43] See *Military and Paramilitary Activities in and against Nicaragua*, above n 21, at 100, para 190.

[44] *Ibid*, at 98, para 186: "If a State acts in a way prima facie incompatible with a recognized rule, but defends its conduct by appealing to exceptions or justifications contained within the rule itself, then whether or not the State's conduct is in fact justifiable on that basis, the significance of that attitude is to confirm rather than to weaken the rule."

The present writer does not advocate an expansion of the range of exceptions to the use of force. Nor does he believe that the powers of the Security Council under Chapter VII should be circumvented. He simply acknowledges the current state of affairs in which the Security Council, faced with sharp political differences on how to implement global security policies, is often unable to discharge its functions. Furthermore, he warns against the risk of leaving States free to move along the increasingly tenuous borderline between legality and illegality, taking advantage at will of the undetermined character of the applicable normative standards.[45] While waiting for a reform of the collective security system, which may not materialize in the short term,[46] to bring the terms of the debate within general international law, when the Security Council is unable to act, has at least the advantage of providing a normative framework of reference. After all, general international law develops on the basis of the advancement of claims by States, which are either accepted or acquiesced to by other States or rejected and considered as violations of the law. The fact that the military operation against Afghanistan was largely approved of by States, even though its amenability within Article 51 was far from being established, cannot be neglected.[47] By the same token, the circumstance that the large majority of States condemned the military intervention in Iraq carries with it the sense that States are unwilling to uphold exceptions to the use of force, which are grounded on such justifications as preventive self-defence or regime change. The availability of numerous multilateral fora in which States may assert their claims and express themselves makes the task of establishing general *opinio juris* less burdensome than in the past and provides evidence of emerging trends in State practice.[48]

The risk of leaving the situation as it is with the unconditional reliance on the UN Charter on the one hand and the blatant disregard of multilateral fora and generally accepted legal standards on the other, being the two distant poles of an already worn-out spectrum, is self evident. Reciprocal accusations respectively of providing a legal framework far

[45] See B Simma, "NATO, the UN and the Use of Force: Legal Aspects" (1999) 10 *European Journal of International Law* 1; A Cassese, "*Ex Iniuria Jus Oritur*: Are We Moving Towards International Legitimation of Forcible Humanitarian Countermeasures in the World Community?" *ibid* at 23 ff.

[46] See B Fassbender, "All Illusions Shattered? Looking Back on a Decade of Failed Attempts to Reform the Security Council" (2003) 7 *Max Planck Yearbook of United Nations Law* 183.

[47] See UN Doc S/PV.4414 (2001), Resumption 1. See also JM Beard, "America's New War on Terror: The Case for Self-Defense Under International Law" (2002) 25 *Harvard Journal of International Law & Policy* 559, providing an overview of the reaction by States to the military intervention against Afghanistan.

[48] J Charney, "Universal International Law", (1993) 87 *American Journal of International Law* 529.

removed from reality and of disregarding international law altogether are unlikely to lead to a common understanding on the applicable rules. Quite the contrary, they tend to generate counterproductive results and mutually undesirable outcomes. It suffices to mention the mischaracterization of some instances of State practice in order to avoid charges of illegality. Particularly in response to terrorist attacks, States have often resorted to force, justifying themselves on the basis of self-defence, while their actions would more properly be characterized as armed reprisals. Despite some scholarly warnings about the proper qualification of such military operations,[49] the illegality of armed reprisals continue being supported almost unanimously by States. The fact that contemporary international law proscribes armed reprisals is an uncontroversial proposition, codified in international instruments and voiced by the majority of commentators.[50] The paradox is that the notion of armed reprisal surely provides a much more proper legal framing than self-defence for such instances as the bombing of Sudan and Afghanistan in 1998, following the terrorist attacks against American embassies in Africa, or the 1993 bombing against Baghdad, to mention only a handful of cases related to terrorism. The punitive character of the action and its intended deterrent effect to make the wrongdoing State abide by the law is readily recognizable.[51] Despite official statements of condemnation, even by those who undertake such conduct,[52] armed reprisals risk sneakingly making their way back into the reality of international relations if not in its illusive representation.[53]

Once the shackles of legal formalism and orthodoxy are in place, it is difficult to avoid mystification also at the intellectual level. The alleged theoretical underpinnings of the pre-emptive strike doctrine provide a good example of it.[54] The justification of the pre-emptive use of force on

[49] See L Condorelli, "A propos de l'attaque américaine contre l'Irak du 26 juin 1993: Lettre d'un professseur désemparé aux lecteurs du JEDI" (1994) 5 *European Journal of International Law* 136; M Reisman, "Self-defense or Reprisals? The Raid on Baghdad: Some Reflections on Its Lawfulness and Implications", *ibid*, at 120 ff.

[50] But see Y Dinstein, *War, Aggression and Self-Defence*, 3rd ed (Cambridge University Press, Cambridge, 2001) admitting of the legality of defensive armed reprisals somewhat amenable within the scope of self-defence.

[51] See the definition provided by D Bowett, "Reprisals Involving the Use of Force", (1972) 66 *American Journal of International Law* at 3.

[52] See the "categorical position" taken by the United States "that reprisals involving the use of force are illegal under international law." (ML Nash, "Contemporary practice of the United States" (1979) 73 *American Journal of International Law* at 491.

[53] See P Klein, "Vers la reconnaissance progressive d'un droit à des représailles armées?" in K Bannelier *et al* (eds), *Le droit international face au terrorisme*, above n 1, at 249 ff. See also RW Tucker, "Reprisals and Self-Defence: The Customary Law", (1972) 66 *American Journal of International Law* 595 stressing "the little significance of prohibiting armed reprisals while retaining the customary right of self-defence".

[54] See The National Security Strategy of the United States (Washington, September 2002), available at <http://www.whitehouse.gov/nsc/nss.pdf> (last visited 10 August 2003).

the basis of the 1837 *Caroline* case is indeed little persuasive.[55] Besides the oddity of relying on a precedent, which dates back almost two centuries ago when, incidentally, the regulation of the use of force was perceived somewhat differently, it is indeed arguable that, the *Caroline* case be concerned with self-defence. At closer scrutiny, if one looks at the diplomatic correspondence which took place at the time between the United States and Great Britain, it is easy to realize that what Secretary of State Webster wanted to emphasize in his letter of 1842 was merely that only a state of necessity could exempt Her Majesty's Government from the responsibility it had incurred by destroying the *Caroline* in US territory, thus infringing on its territorial sovereignty.[56] The case, which would more properly be characterized as a violation by Great Britain of the international law of jurisdiction, simply purports that no State can carry out an act of enforcement in the territory of another State, in this case an act of self-defence (to be understood in a broad sense and surely not in the technical meaning the expression has acquired in contemporary international law!), unless it can be proved that the latter is "instant, overwhelming, and leaving no choice of means, and no moment for deliberation."[57] Reference by Secretary Ashburton to the "overwhelming necessity" which had prompted the British to act, unchallenged by Webster as the incident was drawn to a close by both parties, further attests to the real legal issue underlying the *Caroline* case. To provide a different interpretation to make a case for the contemporary doctrine of pre-emptive strike is an exercise in purposeful interpretation in itself perfectly legitimate but hardly persuasive from the standpoint of international law. The borderline between self-defence and state of necessity may be tenuous at times and one finds oneself on slippery ground when trying to distinguish them. Even the International Court of Justice in its Advisory Opinion on the *Legality of the Use or Threat of Use of Nuclear Weapons* was confronted with a similar question and fairly unpersuasively opted for self-defence.[58] The two notions, although they both amount to circumstances precluding wrongfulness, remain distinct and their scope of application rather different. The restrictive grounds on which a state of necessity can be invoked are no match for the wide scope of application that an expanded interpretation of the notion of self-defence may present.

The contention that in a world of terrorists and rogue States international law is no longer able to regulate decisions on the use of force is

[55] See, for instance, A Sofaer, "On the Necessity of Pre-emption", (2003) 14 *European Journal of International Law* 209–26.
[56] See Letter from Daniel Webster, US: Secretary of State, to Lord Ashburton, (1857) 29 *British and Foreign State Papers* 1841–42, at 1138.
[57] *Ibid*.
[58] International Court of Justice, Advisory Opinion on the *Legality of the Threat or Use of Nuclear Weapons*, 8 July 1996, ICJ Reports 1996, at 246.

greatly exaggerated,[59] but even the most provoking statements may contain a little truth. Undeniably, some States, including the sole superpower and some of its closest allies, perceive the current international legal regulation of the use of force as too restrictive and by interpretative means they tend to circumvent the limits it imposes on them. Nor can acquiescence in their action be confined to the irrelevant realm of politics as opposed to a neutral and objective *imperium legis*.[60] In order to avoid the above-mentioned risks of misrepresenting the state of the law it would be desirable to bring the discussion back to the level of reality, by acknowledging the difficulties and incongruities of the collective security system and shifting the focus on general international law. After all, the idea that both the UN Charter and customary international law regulate the use of force has been repeatedly stated by the ICJ, most recently in the *Oil Platform* cases between Iran and the United States.[61] This parallel normative track may be troubling as the fact that the UN gathers all the members of the international community makes one wonder how one could possibly distinguish between practice under or outside the Charter by the same States.[62] However, reliance on the dynamic character of general international law-making seems to be a valuable alternative to the current uncertainty about the international regulation of the use of force. Interesting attempts have been made in legal scholarship to provide unconventional frames of analysis. The argument has been raised that States *uti universi* could occasionally resort to force in order to enforce obligations *erga omnes*,[63] an entitlement which legal boundaries they might nonetheless trespass should they act disproportionately[64] or should they depart from their "collective mandate" of law enforcement officers acting on behalf of the international community.[65] If departure from the Charter can pave the way for abuses by States acting unilaterally, sticking to it unconditionally risks jeopardizing the credibility of international law. Limits to the use of force are most needed nowadays to

[59] See MJ Glennon, "The New Interventionism: The Search for a Just International Law", (1999) *Foreign Affairs* (May–June 1999) at 2 ff.

[60] See M Kohen, "The use of force by the United States after the end of the Cold War, and its impact on International Law", above n 41, at 225.

[61] See *Case Concerning Oil Platforms (Iran v United States)*, Judgment of 6 November 2003, para 51.

[62] See G Arangio Ruiz, *The United Nations Declaration on Friendly Relations and the System of the Sources of International Law*, (Kluwer Academic Publishers, Alphen aan den Rijn, 1979), at 44 ff.

[63] See P Picone, "Interventi delle Nazioni Unite e obblighi *erga omnes*", in P Picone (ed), *Interventi delle Nazioni Unite e diritto internazionale* (Cedam, Padova, 1995) at 517 ff.

[64] See P Picone, "La 'guerra del Kosovo' e il diritto internazionale generale" (2000) 83 *Rivista di diritto internazionale* 309 ff.

[65] See P Picone, "La Guerra contro l'Iraq e le degenerazioni dell'unilateralismo", (2003) 86 *Rivista di diritto internazionale* 329.

preserve international peace and security. Where to draw them from may well become an ancillary question if they are generally accepted and reflect a general consensus.

C. International Humanitarian Law

Yet another illustration of how purposeful interpretation may be stretched to its outer borders at a time of divergent political appreciations of the role of law in combating terrorism is given by the different perceptions of how international humanitarian law should be applied. No plausible case has been made about the overall unsuitability of international humanitarian law to be applied in time of armed conflict, the only controversial issue being to what extent the so called "war against terrorism" may trigger its applicability.[66] Be that as it may, no one objected to the applicability of international humanitarian law to the conflict in Afghanistan. In this respect, it is worth noticing that the United States has formally taken the stance of treating humanely the Guantanamo detainees "in a manner consistent with the principles of the Third Geneva Convention" and "to the extent appropriate and consistent with military necessity."[67]

This "pick and choose" approach risks being detrimental to the future application of international humanitarian law, as it leaves one with the impression that States may decide what particular rules to apply in a given circumstance, while discarding altogether other rules and principles which are not perceived by them as either expedient or suitable. In a system of law, which is predominantly based on reciprocity, the departure by one State from generally accepted standards might later backfire on the same State or, in the worst of hypotheses, dismantle the whole edifice of international humanitarian law by insinuating the doubt that rules may change depending on who are the parties to the conflict. At a time when asymmetrical conflicts become more and more numerous in international practice this may well prompt weaker parties to the conflict to depart themselves from accepted standards and resort to prohibited methods of warfare, including acts of terrorism, to offset their comparative

[66] See G Rona, "Interesting Times for International Humanitarian Law: Challenges from the 'War on Terror' ", (2003) 27 *Fletcher Forum of World Affairs* 2; C Greenwood, "International Law and the 'War against Terrorism'", (2002) 78 *International Affairs* 301; SR Ratner, "*Jus ad Bellum* and *Jus in Bello* After September 11", (2002) 96 *American Journal of International* Law 905; L Condorelli, "Les attentats du 11 september et leurs suites: où va le droit international", (2001) 105 *Revue générale de droit international public* 829.

[67] See *White House Fact Sheet on Status of Detainees at Guantanamo* (20 February 2002), available at <http://www.whitehouse.gov/news/releases/2002/02/20020207-13.html> (last visited 11 November 2003).

disadvantages.[68] If international humanitarian law needs to be revised in order to meet the demands of the changing nature and characteristics of contemporary armed conflicts, this has to be done multilaterally and irrespective of political contingencies.[69]

Interestingly enough, the recent judgment of the International Criminal Tribunal for former Yugoslavia (ICTY) Trial Chamber I in the *Galic* case shows how much judicial interpretation can be affected by the climate of political confrontation on the (un)suitability of international humanitarian law to effectively deal with acts of terrorism.[70] As is known, the Trial Chamber found jurisdiction *ratione materiae* on the basis of Article 3 of the ICTY Statute as regards the offence of inflicting terror on a civilian population and on these grounds convicted the former Bosnian Serb General Galic who had been in charge of the military unit which had sniped and shelled on civilians during the siege of Sarajevo in 1992. Among other things, General Galic was found guilty on the count of violations of the laws or customs of war, in particular for acts of violence the primary purpose of which is to spread terror among the civilian population, as set forth in Article 51 of Additional Protocol I to the Geneva Conventions of 1949. After considering that the required distinct material element of "primary purpose of spreading terror" made the crime of terror more specific than the crime of attack on civilians (the factual allegations being the same for both counts), the Trial Chamber decided to convict the defendant for the former count only.[71] While refusing to hold, generally, that the crime of terror has a foundation in customary law, the Chamber, following the *Tadic* jurisprudence,[72] found that the crime found its basis on the 22 May 1992 agreement between the parties to the conflict, "which not only incorporated the second part of 51 (2) by reference", but also "repeated the very prohibition 'Act or threats of violence the primary purpose of which is to spread terror among the civilian population are prohibited' in the agreement proper."[73] Judge

[68] See H Munkler, "The Wars of the 21st Century", 85 (2003) 849 *International Review of the Red Cross* 7; AH Cordesman, *Terrorism, Asymmetric Warfare and Weapons of Mass Destruction* (Praeger, Westport, CT 2002).

[69] See the initiative of the Swiss Government, which in early 2003 hosted an Informal High-Level Expert Meeting on the Reaffirmation and Development of International Humanitarian Law (Harvard University, 27–29 January 2003). The Summary of the Co-Chairs can be read at <http://www.hsph.harvard.edu/hpcr/SummaryFinal.pdf> (last visited, 1 September 2003).

[70] See ICTY (Trial Chamber I), *Prosecutor v Stanislav Galic*, Judgment of 5 December 2003, Case No, IT–98–29–T.

[71] *Ibid*, para 162.

[72] See ICTY, *Prosecutor v Dusko Tadic*, Decision on the Defence Motion for Interlocutory Appeal on Jurisdiction, Decision of 2 October 1995, especially paras 86–94. As is known, under this jurisprudence, also "violations of agreements binding upon the parties to the conflict, considered qua treaty law, i.e. agreements which have not turned into customary international law" entitle the ICTY to take up jurisdiction under Art 3 (para 89).

[73] *Ibid*, para 96.

Nieto-Navia dissenting from the majority on this very point stressed that the agreement would not suffice to establish the jurisdiction of the Trial Chamber and that the offence of inflicting terror among the civilian population was not one which attracts individual criminal responsibility under customary international law.[74]

It is not unreasonable to speculate that the majority of the Trial Chamber intended to send out a clear signal that international humanitarian and criminal law are well suited to punishing acts of terrorism in time of armed conflict. Although the first judicial application by an international tribunal of the relevant provisions of the Geneva Conventions and Protocols are welcome, one would have wished that such a judicial determination came at a less controversial time, with the venomous criticism against international humanitarian law having found a proper antidote in the proper characterization of its function and scope of application.

The above examples attest to the increasing difficulty of providing a generally acceptable interpretation of some of the rules which are most relevant not only to the fight against terrorism but to the cohesion and smooth functioning of the international legal system. Despite the remarkable degree of consensus on the need to fight terrorism, the choice by the sole superpower to make this fight an absolute priority, sometimes to the detriment of other general policy objectives of the international community, and to impose its largely unilaterally determined policy of implementation has exacerbated existing discrepancies of views and created new ones.

IV. THE FIGHT AGAINST TERRORISM AS A CATALYST FOR THE EMERGENCE OF DIFFERENT PERCEPTIONS OF THE INTERNATIONAL LEGAL ORDER AND AS A THREAT TO ITS COHESION

In some ways terrorism has been a catalytic factor, which has brought to the surface latent frictions, which had been lying dormant at times of less political divisiveness. The effects of such circumstances should not be underestimated as they may bear on the overall equilibrium of the international legal system and amount to a serious threat to its cohesion. After the demise of communism, discrepancies have emerged between the United States and other countries, particularly European ones, which the common allegiance to western values during the cold war had confined to the almost irrelevant dimension of different legal approaches and traditions. Once the common ground of shared world political objectives was abandoned, what had long appeared as a mere dissonance between

[74] See the Separate and Partially Dissenting Opinion of Judge Nieto-Navia, para 113.

two allies has started manifesting its practical consequences in a fairly dramatic way. Numerous examples can be made of instances in which the United States and Europe have taken radically different views about how to build a solid international legal order and how to face threats of a global nature. It suffices to mention their different attitudes towards the setting up of emission targets within the framework of the climate change convention[75] and the strong opposition manifested by the United States towards the creation of the International Criminal Court.[76] Differences of views also emerged with respect to such human rights issues as the death penalty[77] or the legality of the exercise of jurisdiction over defendants brought within the jurisdiction in violation of international law.[78] Terrorism has simply caused other discordances to come to the fore, the above-mentioned diverging interpretations on the rules on the use of force and the applicability of international humanitarian law being apt illustrations.

It would be simplistic indeed to dismiss such inconsistencies as contingent and eventually reconcilable. A productive way to deal with them would rather be to understand where they originate and to what extent they can be reduced. It is well beyond the scope of these scattered remarks, mainly focusing on international terrorism, to venture into an in depth analysis of European versus American approaches to international law. However, a few considerations of a general character may be in order. It may be striking and alarming to read that "international law is a threat to democracy and to the hopes of democratic politics all over the world", but the author surely has a point when he stresses that the European tradition of what he calls "international constitutionalism" is fundamentally at odds with "American constitutionalism", which reflects "that nation's fundamental legal and political commitments" and recognizes no role as "a source of legal validation and authority" to international consensus.[79]

[75] See *U.S: Rejection of Kyoto Protocol Process* in: SD Murphy, "Contemporary Practice of the United States", (2001) 95 *American Journal of International Law* 647. See also the alternative plan of action proposed by the Bush Administration to reduce greenhouse gases: *Remarks Announcing the Clear Skies and Global Climate Change Initiatives in Silver Spring, Maryland*, (14 February 2002) 38 *Weekly Comp. Pres. Docs.* 232, at 234–35.

[76] See *U.S. Notification of Intent Not to Become a Party to the Rome Statute*, in SD Murphy, "Contemporary Practice of the United States", (2002) 96 *American Journal of International Law* 724. See also, among others, SB Sewall, C Kaysen (eds.), *The United States and the International Criminal Court: National Security and International Law* (Roman & Littlefield, Lenham, 2000).

[77] For a comprehensive account of international practice see W Schabas, *The Abolition of the Death Penalty in International Law*, 3rd ed (Cambridge University Press, Cambridge, 2002).

[78] Contrast, for instance, *United States v Alvarez Machain* (US Supreme Court, 15 June 1992), reproduced in (1992) 31 *International Legal Materials*, 902 to *State v Ebrahim* (Supreme Court of South Africa, 16 February 1991) reproduced in (1992) 31 *International Legal Materials* 888 and *R v Horseferry Road Magistrate's Court* ex parte *Bennett* [1993] 3 All ER 138 (House of Lords).

[79] J Rubenfeld, "The Two World Orders", (2003) XXVII *The Wilson Quarterly* (Autumn 2003) 22–36.

Despite the harsh criticism that these statements have attracted even in the United States,[80] some stances taken by the United States recently can be fairly ascribed to this strand of legal culture. It suffices to mention that the issues of determining the legality of detention of terrorist suspects as well as the legitimacy of qualifying certain individuals as enemy combatants by the executive are primarily dealt with by reference to US constitutional law, international law rarely and rather immaterially intruding into the core of the debate.[81]

Reliance on national constitutionalism and to its "self-given legal and political commitments" does not alone explain current US attitudes towards international law. First, it is a tendency that manifests itself in some areas only, the US advocating internationalism in economic affairs. Furthermore, it would be unfair to identify US legal scholarship with the above-ascribed attitude. Many scholarly works take the opposite stance, advocating multilateralism and rule of law-oriented approaches to law and policy-making.[82] Undoubtedly, however, the unprecedented terrorist attack in American territory, the ensuing emotional wave and feeling of vulnerability coupled with the sense of an imminent and possibly lethal threat to the nation's security have deeply affected the US legal response and caused the strand of unilateralism illustrated above to re-surge vehemently. Even in academic circles, scholars belonging to different schools of thought ended up providing uncommonly similar outcomes, albeit on the basis of different legal analyses.[83] The counter-response to markedly unilateral policy decisions by the United States and to the stances taken by some segments of international legal scholarship has been equally strong, thus causing the general consensus on the need to fight against international terrorism to be quickly dispersed, different implementation policies being advocated by States and scholars.

[80] See AM Slaughter, "Leading through Law", (2003) XXVII *The Wilson Quarterly* (Autumn 2003) 37–44.

[81] See *Hamdi v Rumsfeld*, 316 F.3d 450 (4th Cir, 2003); *Al Odah v United States*, 321 F.3d 1134 (DC Cir, 2003); *Gherebi v Bush*, No 03–557855, 2003 US App Lexis 25625 (9th Cir 18 December 2003); *Padilla v Rumsfeld*, Docket Nos 03–2235 (L); 03–2438 (Con), 2003 US App Lexis 25616 (2nd Cir, 18 December 2003). At the time of writing the US Supreme Court has yet to pass judgment on the two cases on which it has granted *certiorari*: *Rumsfeld v Padilla*, *cert granted* on 20 February 2004 (157 L Ed 2d 1226) and *Al Odah v United States*, *cert granted* on 10 November 2003 (124 S Ct 534; 157 L Ed 2d 407) limited to the question of "whether United States courts lack jurisdiction to consider challenges to the legality of the detention of foreign nationals captured abroad in connection with hostilities and incarcerated at the Guantanamo Bay Naval Base, Cuba."

[82] B Jentleson, "Though Love Multilateralism", (2003) 27 *The Washington Quarterly* 7–24; J Charney, "The Use of Force Against Terrorism and International Law", (2001) 95 *American Journal of International Law* 835.

[83] See, for instance, WM Reisman, "In Defense of World Public Order", (2001) 95 *American Journal of International Law* 833 and TM Franck, "Terrorism and the Right of Self-Defense", *ibid*, at 839 ff.

Eventually, the debate seems to be hinging upon the different conceptions of the relevance of the rule of law to international affairs. The argument has been made that the rule of law is a valueless myth that international law is doomed never to attain, caught as it is in between the centrifugal forces of world order and national sovereignty. Perhaps only a "culture of formalism" could be used to resist the arguments of realists who see power more than the rule of law as the predominant factor in international relations processes.[84] In fact, the tradition of realism is particularly strong in the United States for historical and cultural reasons, which have been explored by international legal scholarship.[85] Disillusionment with law as a consequence of personal experience and historical contingencies may well have caused such scholars as Morgenthau, once he expatriated to the United States, to revert to a power-based vision of international relations.[86] His influence on American scholarship and US policy is well known. However, his international relations theory found fertile ground on the domestic strand of legal realism and both converged in downplaying the role of law in the conduct of international relations. Indeed, as rightly noted by some commentators, international law has had a minor role to play in the design and implementation of the different national security policies adopted by the various American administrations in recent times.[87] By contrast, the European tradition, in both its most traditional positivistic vein and its more policy or ethics-oriented variants, well epitomized in the works of Hersch Lauterpacht,[88] almost invariably supports the centrality of the rule of law in the conduct of international affairs.

This fundamental difference in approach may reverberate negatively on the overall cohesion of the international legal system and on the further consolidation of the rule of law in international relations. As wisely noted, international law cannot be an "à la carte choice" and "[t]he international community prospers when law and power are in partnership, not in conflict."[89] It would be a twist of fate indeed, should the different

[84] M Koskenniemi, "'The Lady Doth Protest Too Much'. Kosovo and the Turn to Ethics in International Law", (2002) 65 *The Modern Law Review* 159, at 173 ff.

[85] For an extremely thought-provoking and original reconstruction see M Koskenniemi, *The Gentle Civilizer of Nations. The Rise and Fall of International Law 1870–1960*, (Cambridge University Press, Cambridge, 2002), especially ch 6.

[86] See M Koskenniemi, "Carl Schmitt, Hans Morgenthau and the Image of Law in International Relations", in M Byers (ed), *The Role of Law in International Politics* (Oxford University Press, Oxford, 2000) at 17 ff.

[87] Kohen, "The use of force by the United States after the end of the Cold War, and its impact on International Law", above n 41, at 198 ff.

[88] For a sketchy, although effective, representation of Hersch Lauterpacht's work and legacy see the symposium devoted to him in the framework of the "European Tradition in International Law" in (1997) 8 *European Journal of International Law* at 215 ff. with contributions by different authors.

[89] A Watts, "The Importance of International Law", in M Byers (ed), *The Role of Law in International Politics*, above n 86, at 7.

perceptions on how to defend the international community against the threat of terrorism yield to a disruption of the sense of a commonality of interests and to the relinquishment of a collective strategy of response, which reflects the will of the entire community. A pragmatic approach purports that national and international interests do not necessarily need to stand in contradistinction with each other[90] and ought to be regarded as converging in promoting effective law and policy responses to international terrorism.

V. THE COGENCY OF TIMELY ACTION AND THE NEED FOR GENERALLY ACCEPTED STANDARDS: INTERNATIONAL LAW MAKING PROCESSES AND GLOBAL RISKS MANAGEMENT

Another lesson one could learn from the responses given by States and by the international community to the threat of international terrorism is the quest for universal normative standards and the cogency of timely action. This double need is the produce of the exigencies of our time. The global nature of certain risks and threats that affect the international community in its entirety necessarily requires concerted actions and universal responses. Effectively to deal with threats to international peace and security, global environmental risks such as the depletion of the ozone layer or climate change, the transnational spread of infectious diseases and the like compels the international community to develop common normative strategies. The self-evident character of this statement does not dispose of the difficulties in accomplishing such a difficult task. The urge to rely on generally agreed-upon principles and rules often clashes with the equally important need to act promptly to face global threats which could affect fundamental community interests. At the same time, the two requirements have to be met in order to provide regulatory action with a satisfactory degree of efficacy. These problems are not unknown to domestic legal systems, which have different normative tools at their disposal effectively to deal with this issue. This is not the case with international law, which must reconcile the two opposing needs with its peculiar law making processes.

General international law typically comes into being by way of custom. The evidence required to establish custom includes generality of State practice and *opinio juris*, according to a well-known formula, which

[90] See, for instance, the call by the UN Secretary General to expand the sense of the notion of national interest: "...we are living in a world today where the collective interest is almost always invariably the national interest." (UN Doc SG/SM/7312 of 23 February 2000).

has been affirmed by the ICJ on numerous occasions.[91] In spite of the different weight one may give to either factor and the peculiarities of some areas of international law in which one might dispense with or, at least diminish the importance of either requirement, customary law-making processes require time and their outcome need be carefully evaluated by the interpreters, be they judges, government officials or scholars.[92] The somewhat amorphous and rather indeterminate process of law-making may then produce indeterminate standards of conduct or rather general normative prescriptions ill-suited to face the complexity of international regulation.[93] This is particularly true for some areas of international law where detailed rules are necessary if one is to assure effective regulation. The problem is that the international legal system has attained a level of maturity and development that requires a wide array of normative instruments, including norms of general applicability to be produced in a short time. Multilateral treaty-making might theoretically make up for the loss of universally accepted general law-making processes. However, at closer scrutiny this is hardly an alternative to general law-making. The possibility of attaching reservations, the lengthy character of national ratification procedures as well as the varying number of States participating in it often undermine the effectiveness of the treaty. The argument that multilateral fora and their varying normative products "may play a central role" in the creation and shaping of general international law carries some weight with it. It may very well be true that "[t]he augmented role of multilateral forums in devising, launching, refining and promoting general international law has provided the international community with a more formal lawmaking process that is used often."[94] However, this novel trend towards multilateral law and policy-making in heterogeneous international fora is far from having accomplished the task

[91] See the following cases: *North Sea Continental Shelf (Federal Republic of Germany v Denmark; Federal Republic of Germany v Netherlands)*, Merits, Judgment, 20 February 1969, ICJ Reports 1969, paras 76–78; *Continental Shelf (Libyan Arab Jamahiriya/Malta)*, ICJ Reports, 1985, para 27 and *Military and Paramilitary Activities in and against Nicaragua*, above n 21, paras 183–86.
[92] See M Mendelson, "The Subjective Element in Customary International Law", (1995) *British Yearbook of International Law* 177; K Wolfke, *Custom in Present International Law* (Kluwer Academic Publishers, Dordrecht, 2nd ed., 1993); B Stern, "La coutume au coeur du droit international" in *Mélanges Reuter* (Pedone, Paris, 1981) at 479 ff.; M Akehurst, "Custom as a Source of International Law", (1974–1975) *British Yearbook of International Law* 1–53. For criticism of the two requirements (practice and *opinio juris*) theory see the impressive essay by P Haggenmacher, "La doctrine des deux élements du droit coutumier international" (1986) *Révue générale de droit international public* 5–126.
[93] Such difficulty is particularly evident in the law of jurisdiction as it relates to economic transactions. See A Bianchi, "Unity v. Fragmentation: the Customary Law of Jurisdiction in Contemporary International Law", in K Meessen (ed), *Extraterritorial Jurisdiction in Theory and Practice*, (Kluwer Law Publishers, The Hague/London, 1996) at 74 ff.
[94] J Charney, "Universal International Law", above, note 48, at 551.

of providing the international community with a legislative process which be universally accepted and regarded as legitimate.

The difficulties to provide prompt and effective normative responses to global risks management has in all likelihood been the reason for the Security Council taking up a quasi-legislative role by enacting resolution 1373.[95] The resolution has clear law-making features as it imposes on States generally, regardless of any particular situation or circumstances, obligations which partly take up the obligations laid down in the UN Convention for the Suppression of the Financing of Terrorism, thus making them universally applicable, and partly reach out to other fairly sweeping obligations covering different aspects of terrorism prevention and repression. The latter include an obligation to refrain from providing support to entities or persons involved in terrorist acts, a due diligence obligation to prevent the commission of terrorist acts, and a duty to deny safe haven to terrorists and their supporters. The resolution further provides for the obligation to bring to justice the responsible persons and to ensure that terrorist acts are established as serious criminal offences in domestic legal systems and that punishment duly reflects the seriousness of the offence as well as more general obligations concerning mutual assistance in criminal investigations and proceedings and the prevention of the transnational movement of terrorists. The unilateral imposition of legal commands of a general character surely amounts to law-making.[96] This approach is not novel, as the Security Council had already resorted to quasi-legislative enactments in its recent practice.[97] It suffices to recall in this context the creation of two ad hoc criminal tribunals as well as the management of the Iraqi crisis in the "90s, during which the Security Council imposed a disarmament programme and even set up an international quasi-judicial body, the Compensation Commission.[98]

Quasi-legislative acts are hardly compatible with the main responsibility of the Security Council in the maintenance of international peace and security. Although the Council itself has interpreted the latter expression broadly in the past few years, it does remain a fair presumption to assume

[95] SC Resolution 1373 (28 September 2001), reproduced in (2001) 40 *International Legal Materials* 1278.

[96] See the definition given by E Yemin, *Legislative Powers in the United Nations and Specialized Agencies*, (AW Sijthoff, Leyden, 1969): "[L]egislative acts have three essential characteristics: they are unilateral in form, they create or modify some element of a legal norm, and the legal norm in question is general in nature, that is, directed to indeterminate addressees and capable of repeated application in time" (at 6).

[97] On the quasi-legislative acts of the Security Council see FL Kirgis Jr, "The Security Council's First Fifty Years", (1995) 89 *American Journal of International Law* 506, at 520 ff.

[98] See SC Resolution 827, reprinted in (1993) 32 *International Legal Materials* 1203, adopting the Statute of the ICTY as set forth in UN Doc S/25704, annex, reproduced in (1993) 32 *International Legal Materials* 1192; SC Resolution 955, annex, adopting the Statute of the ICTR, reproduced in 33 (1994) *International Legal Materials* 1602; and SC Resolution 692 (1991) setting up the Compensation Commission.

that the Security Council will only enact those measures of a temporary character, which it deems necessary to preserve or restore international peace and security. The shift of focus from characterizing single or particular situations or events as threats to the peace to qualifying as such certain phenomena such as international terrorism and humanitarian crises hardly account for such a drastic change.

The limits inherent in the quasi-legislative activity of the Security Council make one wonder whether this is the appropriate course of action to take at international law to make up for the loss of well-established and effective mechanisms of general law-making. Issues of legitimacy and adequate representation of the general will of the international community are likely to arise. To entrust the power to enact generally applicable rules to an organ in which five permanent members enjoy the privilege of blocking any decision which goes against their interests or those of their allies is not the best guarantee of fairness and equality of treatment. If it is true that Resolution 1373 wisely incorporated in the form of binding provisions prescriptions previously endorsed by the General Assembly,[99] this may not always be the case. The absence of a proper system of judicial review, gracefully turned down by the ICJ in the name of the doctrine of concurrent powers,[100] does not enhance the legitimacy of general law-making by the Security Council. A pragmatic attitude to problem solving and policy making purports that Security Council quasi-legislative resolutions may turn out to be useful instruments to deal with global risks, particularly at a time when prompt action is perceived to be compelling, provided that the Security Council has an adequate political backing by the General Assembly or otherwise enjoys widespread consensus by the international community. What may sound as a truism underscores a simple truth, namely that the legitimacy of the Security Council's decisions as well as the capacity of the UN system of collective security, in the broad sense the latter expression has taken up in recent practice, rests, in the absence of institutional checks and balances, on the consensus of the Member States.

[99] See the remark made in this respect by PC Szasz, "The Security Council Starts Legislating", (2002) 96 *American Journal of International Law* 901, at 903.

[100] See *Questions of Interpretation and Application of the 1971 Montreal Convention Arising from the Aerial Incident at Lockerbie (Libya v UK; Libya v United States of America)*, Provisional Measures, (Orders of 14 April 1992), ICJ Reports, 3, 114, at 22 and 134 respectively: "The Council has functions of a political nature assigned to it, whereas the Court exercises purely judicial functions. Both organs can therefore perform their separate but complementary functions with respect to the same events" (relying on *Case Concerning the Military and Paramilitary Activities in and against Nicaragua (Nicaragua v United States of America)*, Jurisdiction and Admissibility, Judgment, 26 November 1984, ICJ Reports 1985, at 434–35). For comment, see V Gowlland-Debbas, "The Relationship between the International Court of Justice and the Security Council in the Light of the *Lockerbie* Case", (1994) 88 *American Journal of International Law* 643.

VI. THE TWILIGHT ZONE: THE POWER OF STATES IN A STATE OF EMERGENCY AND LIMITS THERETO

As is known the threat of international terrorism to their national security has caused some States to adopt emergency legislation. The power to invoke exceptional circumstances in order either to derogate from international law obligations or to be exempted from international responsibility rests on the assumption that a State is entitled to counter threats to its very existence by resorting to extraordinary means.[101] This also holds true for some human rights treaty regimes, which allow for derogations in the case of war or other public emergency.[102] Given that in such a case the State may strike the balance between individual rights and the community's needs in a way which gives priority to collective interests, the exact characterization of both the factual circumstances in which a derogation can be invoked as well as the legal regime applicable thereto seems compelling. Particularly troubling is the case of those situations that, although falling short of meeting the requirements that trigger the applicability of international humanitarian law, lie at the interface of peacetime and time of armed conflict.[103] State powers, particularly the prerogatives of the executive branch of government, often thrive on the ambiguities surrounding the legal characterization of the situation, and the infringement of human rights may then become the rule.

To stand up for the rule of law and to protect human rights adequately in such twilight zones is no easy task. The perception by States of their security interests bears on the very essence of the social compact between the organized community and its members and at first sight hardly lends itself to be constrained in the narrow boundaries of legal reasoning. On closer scrutiny, however, one realizes that the "inseparable bond between the principle of legality, democratic institutions and the rule of law" makes the protection of fundamental rights an imperative objective for those who are called upon to administer the rule of law in a democratic society.[104] In no way should it sound as a rhetorical artifice to state that

[101] As is well known, also in the law of State responsibility the state of necessity amounts to a circumstance precluding wrongfulness: see Art 25 of the Articles on State Responsibility, adopted by the International Law Commission at its fifty third session (2001): Report of the International Law Commission on the work of its Fifty-third session, *Official Records of the General Assembly, Fifty-sixth session, Supplement No. 10* (A/56/10), chp.IV.E.1 (see J Crawford, *The International Law Commission Articles on State Responsibility. Introduction, Text and Commentaries*, (Cambridge University Press, Cambridge, 2002), especially at 178 ff.).

[102] See R Higgins, "Derogations Under Human Rights Treaties" (1976–1977) 48 *British Yearbook of International Law* 281.

[103] See T Meron, *Human Rights in Internal Strife* (Grotius Publications, Cambridge, 1987).

[104] *Habeas Corpus in Emergency Situations (Arts. 27(2) and 7(6) of the American Convention on Human Rights*, Advisory Opinion OC–8/87, 30 January 1987, Inter-American Court of Human Rights (IACtHR) (Series A) No. 8 (1987), para 24 (referring to IACtHR, *The Word "Laws" in Article 30 of the American Convention on Human* Rights, Advisory Opinion OC–6/86 of 9 May 1986 (Series A) No. 6, para 32).

particularly at times of emergency human rights should be afforded protection and that basic guarantees ought never to be disregarded. The recent practice of international bodies and human rights supervisory organs unconditionally supports this stance.[105]

How to strike the balance between national security interests on the one hand, and human rights on the other and who should do it and by what means are obviously difficult issues to tackle. International law, however, is not unprepared to provide some guidance. In particular, international practice, ranging from the practice of national authorities to the case law of international tribunals and supervisory organs is fairly rich and may help to determine with a sufficient degree of clarity what the contours of the international legal regime of state of emergencies are. Although the international legal regime of states of emergency is primarily treaty-based, the wide participation by States in such instruments as the International Covenant on Civil and Political Rights[106] as well as in such regional treaties as the European and Inter-American Conventions allow for some considerations of a more general character. Incidentally, derogation clauses in all the three instruments, with the exception of the provisions on non-derogable rights, are drafted in similar terms.[107]

Among the threats to the life of the nation, in the terminology of relevant human rights treaties, which may trigger a state of emergency, terrorism ranks high in State practice. Terrorism, particularly in the domestic context, has often been a cause for States to invoke derogation clauses and justify restrictions on their international human rights obligations. States enjoy a fairly wide measure of discretion, even under the jurisprudence of the European Court of Human Rights, which is perhaps the most restrictive in its approach, as to the evaluation of whether a state of emergency exists.[108] National authorities are, in principle, in a better

[105] See, among others, the resolution adopted by the Commission on Human Rights on 25 April 2003 (UN Doc E/CN.4/Res/2003/68); the ministerial declaration attached to SC Resolution 1456 (see UN Doc S/RES/1456 of 20 January 2003); the resolution adopted by the General Assembly of the UN on *Protecting Human Rights and Fundamental Freedoms while Countering Terrorism* (A/Res/57/219, 18 December 2002); the Report of the Policy Working Group on the United Nations and Terrorism, submitted by the UN Secretary General on 6 August 2002 to the GA (A/57/273) and the SC (S/2002/875); the *Guidelines on Human Rights and the Fight against* Terrorism, adopted by the Committee of Ministers of the Council of Europe on 11 July 2002 (Strasbourg, 2002); the joint statement issued on 10 December 2001 by 17 special rapporteurs and independent experts of the Commission on Human Rights on the occasion of the Human Rights Day (UN Doc E/CN.4/2002/75, annex IV): the statement by the UN Committee against Torture of 22 November 2001 (UN Doc. CAT/C/XXVII/Misc 7).

[106] 152 ratifications as of 2 November 2003.

[107] See A Rosas, "Emergency Regimes: a Comparison", in D Gomien (ed), *Broadening the Frontiers of Human Rights: Essays in Honour of Asbjørn Eide* (Scandinavian University Press, Oslo, 1993) at 165 ff.

[108] The relevant case law of the ECHR includes: *Lawless v Ireland*, Ser A, No 3 (1961); *Ireland v United Kingdom*, Ser A, No 25 (1978); *Brogan et al v United Kingdom*, Ser A, No 145–B (1988); *Brannigan and McBride v United Kingdom*, Ser A, No 258–B; *Aksoy v Turkey*,

position to assess the gravity of the threat to their national security and other fundamental interests and, subject to international supervision for those of them who are a party to treaties providing for derogation clauses, may determine that terrorism amounts to a threat to the life of the nation.[109] States' discretion to invoke a state of emergency is not an unfettered one. Notification requirements exist under different treaty-based regimes as well as substantive restrictions on the derogating measures a State may resort to.

Procedural requirements should not be underestimated, as they allow international supervisory bodies to be aware of the exceptional situation existing in a given country at a certain time. By contrast, the applicability of the special regime provided at international law is not dependent on formal notification of its existence by the State concerned. Regrettably, an overview of the Human Rights Committee's practice reveals that States frequently do not comply with notification requirements, by failing to notify internationally a state of emergency which has been internally declared;[110] by not declaring officially a state of emergency while at the same time adopting special legislation on such grounds;[111] by failing to repeal long-established states of emergency thus infringing on the very nature of the regime,[112] under which restrictions must be temporary and aimed at re-establishing a state of normalcy as soon as possible;[113] or, by not disclosing full information about the derogations and a clear explanation of the reasons for their adoption.[114]

Furthermore, State action in states of emergency is subject to a strict proportionality test. Only those measures which are strictly required by

ECHR, 1996–VI; and *Sakik et al v Turkey*, ECHR, 1997–VII. For a comment see: C Warbrick, "The Principles of the European Convention on Human Rights and the Response of States to Terrorism", (2002) *European Human Rights Law Review* 287. See also, O De Schutter, "La Convention européenne des droits de l'homme à l'épreuve de la lutte contre le terrorisme", in E Bribosia and A Weyembergh (dir.), *Lutte contre le terrorisme et droits fondamentaux*, (Bruylant, Brussels, 2002) at 85 ff.

109 See E Crysler, *"Brannigan and McBride v UK*: A New Direction on Article 15 Derogations Under the European Convention on Human Rights?", (1994) 27 *Révue belge de droit international* 603.

110 See the Concluding observations of the HRC on Lebanon, CCPR/C/79/Add 78, 1 April 1997, and Ireland, CCPR/C/79/Add 21, 3 August 1993.

111 See the Concluding observations of the HRC on Mexico, CCPR/C/79/Add 109, 27 July 1999.

112 See the Concluding observations of the HRC in the following cases: Egypt, CCPR/CO/76/EGY, 28 November 2002, Syrian Arab Republic, CCPR/CO/71/SYR, 24 April 2001 and Israel, CCPR/CO/78/ISR, 21 August 2003.

113 See HRC, General Comment No 29 States of Emergency (Article 4) (UN Doc CCPR/C/21Rev.1/Add 11, 31 August 2001), para. 1: "The restoration of a state of normalcy where full respect for the Covenant can again be secured must be the predominant objective of a State party derogating from the Covenant."

114 See *Jorge Landinelli Silva et al*, Communication No 34/1978: Uruguay (08/04/81), CCPR/C/12/D/34/1978.

the exigencies of the situation can be justified, which entails a duty on the part of States to provide justification for the measures they have enacted.[115] In any event no derogation from listed non-derogable rights is ever allowed. As is known, the lists differ from one another with the ECHR mentioning only four of them and the ICCPR and IACHR providing a more extensive list.[116] To hold that a State may not derogate from listed rights may be justified either on the fundamental importance of the right in question or, simply, on the basis that there is usually no need to derogate from other particular rights in a state of emergency.[117] What is clear is that States have pledged not to restrict the enjoyment of listed rights even if the exigencies of the situation require derogation from other human rights. Non-derogable rights listed in human rights treaties do not account for other rights, derogations from which are equally not allowed under international law. This is the case for all human rights rules which have attained the status of peremptory norms (*jus cogens*). No State, regardless of its participation in human rights treaty regimes providing for non-derogable rights, could derogate from the prohibition of torture, which is generally regarded as a rule of *jus cogens*.[118] The Human Rights Committee, mindful of the fact that peremptory norms might extend beyond the list of non-derogable rights under Article 4, proposes to focus on the category of crimes against humanity as codified in the Statute of the International Criminal Court.[119] This approach is not deprived of difficulties, however, Article 7 of the Rome Statute defining as crimes against humanity violations of some human rights regarded in the ICCPR as derogable rights.[120] The argument can be made that such rights have attained a peremptory character in State practice subsequent to the adoption of the Covenant. Be that as it may, determination of the peremptory character of human rights norms and of the intransgressible rules of international humanitarian law,[121] both inderogable in a state of emergency,

[115] See, for instance, the comments submitted by the United Kingdom to the Concluding Observations of the HRC, following the adoption of the Anti-terrorism, Crime and Security Act of 2001 (UN Doc CCPR/CO/73/UK/Add 2 of 4 December 2003).

[116] See respectively Art 15 of the ECHR; Art 4 of the ICCPR and Art 27 of the IACHR.

[117] This may be the case for such non-derogable rights as Articles 11 (prohibition of imprisonment merely on the ground of inability to fulfill a contractual obligation) and 18 (freedom of thought, conscience and religion) under the ICCPR.

[118] For a list of rights which would attain *jus cogens* status see L Hannikainen, *Peremptory Norms (Jus Cogens) in International Law* (Finnjish Lawyers Pub Co, Helsinki, 1988) at 425 ff. and *Restatement (Third) of the Foreign Relations Law of the United* States, (St Paul, Minnesota, 1987), § 702, Comm N, Reporter's note 11. See also T Meron, "On a Hierarchy of International Human Rights", (1986) 80 *American Journal of International* Law 1 and K Teraya, "Emerging Hierarchy in International Human Rights and Beyond: From the Perspective of Non-derogable Rights", (2001) 12 *European Journal of International Law* 917.

[119] See HRC, General Comment No. 29, above n 113, paras 12–13.

[120] *Ibid*, note 7, with particular reference to Articles 9, 12, 26 and 27 of the ICCPR.

[121] See *Legality of the Threat or Use of Nuclear Weapons*, Advisory Opinion, ICJ Reports 1996, para. 79.

should be carefully made on a case by case basis against the background of State practice.

An even more interesting issue is to what extent procedural guarantees, which, with the sole exception of the IACHR, are not listed as inderogable rights are to be regarded as such.[122] The issue is particularly topical as many human rights restrictions adopted by States to face the threat of terrorism concern such procedural safeguards as the writ of *habeas corpus*. The ancillary albeit indispensable character of procedural guarantees to the enjoyment of some inderogable rights, expressly recognized also by municipal tribunals in their recent practice on terrorism,[123] makes the argument that such guarantees should also be considered as inderogable a compelling one. Indeed, as accurately noted by the IACtHR, to suspend or to render ineffective the writ of *habeas corpus* may have the effect of depriving individuals of the only available means of protection vis-à-vis possible violations of such non-derogable rights as the right to life and the right to humane treatment.[124] The view that some basic elements of the right to fair trial, guaranteed also in time of armed conflict by international humanitarian law, must be regarded as inderogable was taken by the HRC in its General Comment No 29 on Article 4 of the ICCPR. Besides the requirement that "[o]nly a court of law may try and convict a person for a criminal offence" and respect of the presumption of innocence, the Committee also referred to "the right to take proceedings before a court to enable the court to decide without delay on the lawfulness of detention".[125] These findings, also supported by the case law of regional human rights tribunals,[126] lend support to the view that the

[122] Art 27 of the IACHR includes among non-derogable rights also "the judicial guarantees essential for the protection of such rights." See also *Judicial Guarantees in States of Emergency (Arts 27(2), 25 and 8 of the American Convention on Human Rights)*, Advisory Opinion OC–9/87, 6 October 1987, IACtHR (Ser A) No 9 (1987) where "[t]he Court holds that the judicial guarantees essential for the protection of the human rights not subject to derogation, according to Article 27(2) of the Convention, are those to which the Convention expressly refers in Article 7(6) and 25(1), considered within the framework and the principles of Article 8, and also those necessary to the preservation of the rule of law, even during the state of exception that results from the suspension of guarantees." (para 38) Besides "*habeas corpus* (Article 7(6)), amparo and any other effective remedy before judges or competent tribunals (Article 25(1)), which is designed to guarantee the respect of the rights and freedoms whose suspension is not authorized by the Convention", also "those judicial procedures, inherent to representative democracy as a form of government (Article 29(c)), provided in the laws of the states Parties as suitable for guaranteeing the full exercise of the rights referred to in Article 27(2) of the Convention and whose suppression or restriction entails the lack of protection of such rights" are not subject to suspension, in the Court's view.

[123] See, for instance, *Al Odah v United States*, above n 81, at 1140, qualifying the writ of *habeas corpus* as a subsidiary procedural right that follows from the possession of constitutional rights.

[124] IACtHR, *Habeas Corpus in Emergency Situations (Arts 27(2) and 7(6) of the American Convention on Human Rights)*, above n 104, para 12.

[125] HRC, General Comment No. 29, above n 113, para 16.

[126] See *Al-Nashif v Bulgaria*, ECHR, Judgment of 20 June 2002: "National authorities cannot do away with effective control of lawfulness of detention by the domestic courts whenever

contours of the non-derogable rights regime in states of emergency have been shaped quite clearly in international practice and that the number of non-derogable rights States must respect is wider than the list provided in conventional instruments.

Yet another essential guarantee in a state of emergency is an independent and impartial judiciary.[127] By this expression reference is not only made to the requirement that the judicial branch of government be formally independent from the executive. What matters is also that judicial organs be not subservient to the latter. This attitude is not uncommon, even in western democracies, where on constitutional or other grounds a deferential attitude towards executive determinations on points of fact or law is rather frequent in a state of emergency. The case law of US and British courts concerning the legality of detention of terrorist suspects in the aftermath of the 11th September attacks bears witness to this tendency.[128] Only recently have courts taken up a more critical stance towards the executive and started challenging the exercise of its powers on the basis of separation of power and fundamental human rights concerns as guaranteed in the Constitution.[129] At the time of writing the US Supreme Court is expected to pass judgment on two important points of law, namely whether the US has jurisdiction over its military base in Guantanamo, Cuba, as maintained by the defence of some of the terrorist suspects therein detained and on whether the executive has the power

they choose to assert that national security and terrorism are involved." (para 94); IACtHR, *Habeas Corpus in Emergency Situations (Arts 27(2) and 7(6) of the American Convention on Human* Rights, above n 113.

[127] The propriety of having military courts trying terrorist suspects has been challenged by the IACtHR in the *Castillo Petruzzi* case, Judgment of 30 May 1999, IACtHR, Ser C, No 52 (see casenote by J Bucherer, (2001) 95 *American Journal of International Law* 171 ff). It seems that the ECHR would also tend to regard wholly military tribunals for the trial of terrorists incompatible with Art 6 (see C Warbrick, "The Principles of the European Convention on Human Rights and the Response of States to Terrorism", above n 108, at 303, speculating on the *Incal v Turkey* case EctHR Reports (1998–IV) at 1547 ff). See also *Öçalan v Turkey*, ECHR, Judgment of 12 March 2003, para 114. For the practice of the HRC see its Concluding observations on Colombia, CCPR/C/79/Add. 76 (1997), para 19 and para 34; Peru, CCPR/C/79/Add. 67 (1996), para 350; Lebanon, CCPR/C/79/Add. 78 (1997), para 14; Egypt, CCPR/CO/76/EGY (2002), para 16 and Uzbekistan, CCPR/CO/71/UZB (2001), para 15.

[128] See *Hamdi v Rumsfeld*, 316 F.3d 450 (4th Cir, 2003): "Once again, however, litigation cannot be the driving force in effectuating and recording wartime detentions. The military has been charged by Congress and the executive with winning a war, not prevailing in a possible court case." (at 470); "The constitutional allocation of war powers affords the President extraordinarily broad authority as Commander in Chief and compels courts to assume a deferential posture in reviewing exercises of this authority." (at 474). See also *Abbasi v Secretary of State for Foreign and Commonwealth Affairs*, UK Court of Appeal (Civil Decision), reproduced in (2003) 42 *International Legal Materials* 355: "While the courts must carefully scrutinise the explanations given by the executive for its actions, the courts must extend the appropriate degree of deference when it comes to judging those actions." (para 44).

[129] See, in particular, *Gherebi v Bush*, above n 81; *Padilla v Rumsfeld*, above n 81.

under the constitution to detain US citizens without an express authorization by Congress.[130] The way the Supreme Court will decide these issues is crucial to determining what the attitude of the judiciary is in the United States at a time of an internally declared state of emergency. In the meantime the executive has restated its conviction that judicial review by courts on issues related to the President's power as Commander-in-Chief must be deferential.[131] Regardless of the contingencies of the fight against terrorism, it is self evident that judicial control by independent and impartial courts remains essential to guaranteeing respect for fundamental human rights in states of emergency. Respect for the principle of legality, democratic institutions and the rule of law requires that restrictions to the enjoyment of human rights be subject to judicial scrutiny. This responsibility lies primarily with domestic courts, international tribunals and/or supervisory organs having a subsidiary and surely ex post facto role in that respect.

The amount of international law norms applicable to states of emergency is quite impressive. Fairly precise standards have been laid down in treaties and their judicial interpretation by courts and supervisory organs has enormously contributed to their refinement. To hold that international law has no clear standards on how to strike the balance between national security interests and human rights in such grey areas as states of emergency when the life of the nation is threatened by terrorist groups or otherwise is at best an unfounded claim. The fact that States may knowingly disregard such standards is little evidence of the alleged inadequacy of international law and more than a clue that what States often do by ratifying human rights treaties is no more than indulging in a rhetorical exercise of self-complacency.

VII. THE QUEST FOR INTERNATIONALLY AGREED UPON POLICIES OF IMPLEMENTATION

The response of the international community to the resurgence of the threat of terrorism on a global scale has not been as effective as one would have expected. In particular, the implementation of international legal standards has been negatively affected by the lack of a common understanding or perception as to what policies should be followed. The unconditional condemnation of the 2001 attacks against the United States by

130 See *Al Odah v United States*, above n 81; *Rumsfeld v Padilla*, above n 81.

131 See *Remarks by Alberto R Gonzales, Counsel to the President, before the American Bar Association Standing Committee on Law and National Security*, Washington, DC, 24 February 2004 (available at <http://www.abanet.org/natsecurity/judge-gonzales.pdf> (last visited 2 March 2004).

virtually all States seemed to have paved the way for a concerted and effective action to be carried out internationally at a multilateral level. Regrettably, universality of consent in international law is a rare and volatile asset. The unfaltering stance taken by the international community as a whole has steadily yielded to a fluctuating consent, occasionally granted or withdrawn depending on political contingencies, and unilateral responses have often been opted for to the detriment of multilateral action. It would be simplistic, however, to infer from the above considerations that no general consensus could be established on the need to fight effectively against international terrorism. The proliferation of normative standards, of a varying nature and scope of application, is evidence of the general will of the international community. No State objects to the need to comply with relevant Security Council resolutions, to bring terrorists to justice and to hold States accountable for their support to terrorist activities. Nor is any State overtly against the need to eradicate the financing of terrorism. What is most needed is consensus on how anti-terror normative policies should be implemented. This issue cannot be confined within the narrow boundaries of the multilateralism versus unilateralism debate. The perception of the legality or illegality of unilateral actions largely depends on the extent to which they can be grounded on internationally agreed upon policies. This holds true even for the highly politicized area of the use of force. Despite the aura of uncertainty currently surrounding the international legal regulation of the use of force, the military operation launched against Afghanistan in 2001 was largely perceived as legitimate, regardless of the different views expressed on its legal basis. By contrast, other instances in which force has been unilaterally used against States allegedly supporting terrorist groups have been the object of general condemnation.

Other examples can be set forth to support the argument that international consensus is the most reliable way to ensure the effective implementation of international rules. A good illustration of how international cooperation in its most traditional manifestation, namely treaty law, can bring about satisfactory outcomes is given by the two treaties signed between the US and the EU on July 2003, on extradition and mutual legal assistance respectively.[132] In many ways, the two treaties can be regarded as supplementing pre-existing bilateral treaties of extradition and judicial cooperation between the United States and the Member

[132] See *Agreement on extradition between the European Union and the United States of America*, OJEU L 181/27 (19 July 2003), and *Agreement on mutual legal assistance between the European Union and the United States*, *ibid*, at 34 ff. For an evaluation of the two agreements, primarily from a UK perspective, see House of Lords, Select Committee on the European Union, *EU/US Agreements on Extradition and Mutual Legal Assistance*, Session 2002–03, 38th Report, HL Paper 153, 15 July 2003.

States of the European Union, which they are not meant to replace in their entirety.[133] As is known, the implementation of bilateral agreements has sometimes been difficult, given that the US and the EU hold divergent views on a number of aspects of international judicial cooperation and extradition law. Most notably, EU members had voiced, even in a formal way, their opposition to surrendering terrorist suspects to the United States where they risked being convicted and sentenced to the death penalty.[134] This stance which seems to be compelled, more than induced, by European human rights law, as developed recently by the additional protocols to the European convention[135] and the jurisprudence of the European Court of Human Rights,[136] risked bringing international cooperation concerning rendition of terrorist suspects to a mutually embarrassing stalemate. In turn, the United States had often complained about its extradition requests not being considered on an equal footing with concurring requests submitted by other EU's members. The new treaty on extradition provides a solution to both issues, on the one hand allowing requested States to make extradition conditional on the death penalty not being imposed on the extraditee or, if imposed, not carried out,[137] and on the other, securing equal treatment

[133] The scope of application of each agreement with respect to bilateral treaties of extradition and mutual legal assistance is spelt out in Art 3 of the two agreements respectively. All the 15 EU Members have bilateral extradition treaties with the United States and 11 of them have also mutual legal assistance treaties with the US. Parties to the Agreements are not prevented from concluding more favourable bilateral arrangements in the future (see Art 18 of the extradition treaty and Art 14 of the mutual legal assistance treaty).

[134] See the statement made by the Minister of Justice of France, reported in Amnesty International, *Death penalty News*, December 2001, at 1, and the declarations to the same effect made by the Spanish authorities: "Spain Sets Hurdles for Extradition", *The New York Times*, 24 November 2001.

[135] See Protocol No. 6 to the European Convention, Concerning the Abolition of the Death Penalty, Strasbourg, 28 April, 1983, ETS No. 114 (in force since March 1985) and Protocol No. 13, Concerning the Abolition of the Death Penalty in All Circumstances, Vilnius, 3 May 2002, ETS No. 187 (in force since July 2003). See also Art 4 of the Protocol amending the 1977 European Convention on the Suppression of Terrorism, Strasbourg, 15 May 2003, ETS No. 190, providing that nothing in the Convention can be interpreted as imposing an obligation on the requested State to extradite an individual to a State which retains the death penalty, unless adequate guarantees are given that the death penalty shall not be imposed or carried out.

[136] See, in particular, the judgment rendered by the ECHR on 12 March 2003 in the case *Öçalan v Turkey*. The Court held that the practice of European States attests to their will "to abrogate, or at the very least modify the second sentence in Article 2 §1 in so far as it permits capital punishment in peacetime." According to the Court, capital punishment has come to be regarded as an unacceptable form of punishment and therefore no longer permissible under Art 2. Moreover, it would amount per se to a violation of Art 3 of the Convention as a form of inhuman and degrading treatment (para 198). For a comment on the *Öçalan* case see A Clapham, "Symbiosis in International Human Rights Law: the Öçalan case and the Evolving Law on the Death Sentence", (2003) 1 *Journal of International Criminal Justice* 475.

[137] See Art 13 of the Agreement on extradition. It is worth noting that, according to Art 3 (1)(j), Art 13 may be applied by the requested State in place of, or in the absence of, bilateral treaty provisions governing capital punishment.

for US extradition requests which will be considered on the same footing as European arrest warrants.[138]

Although nowhere in the text is mention made of terrorism, it is clear that the thrust towards reaching an agreement on these issues was prompted by the need to lay more solid foundations for international cooperation in this area. Several provisions of the agreement on mutual legal assistance can be interpreted along those lines. A legal basis for setting up joint investigative teams is created,[139] parties are required to have video-conferencing facilities for taking testimony,[140] undertake to ascertain if banks located in their territory possess information on whether a person suspected of or charged with a criminal offence is the holder of a bank account[141] and pledge to refuse assistance on data protection grounds only in exceptional cases.[142] Overall, it is not unreasonable to speculate that this concerted effort to bridge past difficulties and to achieve a common understanding on the modalities of judicial cooperation in the broad sense will enhance the effectiveness of international action for the repression of terrorism.

Implementation policies may also be concerted internationally in informal fora by means of soft law. The case of the Financial Actions Task Force on Money Laundering (FATF) is fairly illustrative in this respect.[143] Since the decision to broaden the scope of its mandate to reach out to terrorist financing was taken in 2001, the FATF has elaborated eight special recommendations,[144] occasionally coupled with interpretative notes and best practices papers, with a view to helping States to develop a coherent implementation policy concerning the repression of terrorist financing. The special recommendations complement the existing 40 recommendations on money laundering[145] and provide an easy model for legislative

[138] See Art 10 of the Agreement on extradition.
[139] Art 5.
[140] Art 6.
[141] Art 8. It's a cause for some concern that such action may be taken for the purpose of identifying, inter alia, "information regarding natural or legal persons convicted or *otherwise involved* in a criminal investigation" (Art 4 (1)(b)(emphasis added). It is to be hoped that the expression "otherwise involved", fairly vague in itself, will be interpreted strictly and concern persons subject to actual, official investigations.
[142] Art 9. It is somewhat surprising that no mention is made of the 1981 Council of Europe Convention for the Protection of Individuals with Regard to Automatic processing of Personal Data, Strasbourg, 28 January 1981, ETS No. 108 (in force since 1 October 1985) and its Additional Protocol, regarding supervisory authorities and transborder data flows, Strasbourg , 8 November 2001, ETS No. 181 (to enter into force on 1 July 2004), nor of Directive 95/46/EC on the protection of individuals with regard to the processing of personal data and on the free movement of such data. (OJEC L 281/31 (23 November 1995)).
[143] More generally, on the international legal regime of terrorist financing see I Bantekas, "The International Law of Terrorist Financing", (2003) 97 *American Journal of International Law* 315, giving a detailed account of the different norms and actors involved.
[144] Special Recommendations on Terrorist Financing, (available at <http://www.fatf-gafi.org/SRecsTF_en.htm> (last visited 1 February 2004).
[145] See The Forty Recommendations (2003), available at <http://www.fatf-gafi.org/40Recs_en.htm> (last visited 1 February 2004).

action by those States that wish to comply more effectively with existing international standards against terrorist financing. They do not confine themselves to urging States to cooperate fully with one another or to properly implement their international obligations including the criminalisation of terrorist financing and the freezing of terrorist assets but call upon them also to take effective measures against the use of alternative remittance, wire transfers and non-profit organizations for terrorist financing.[146]

Reliance on a technical body for the development of international standards is no novelty in international law, international environmental and economic law providing numerous examples of this technique. The potential benefit of soft law in this area is apparent. The intricate modalities of terrorist financing and the difficulties inherent in preventing transactions, which may not even be illegal, render the expertise of the FATF invaluable, particularly for those States, whose legislation is not yet sufficiently developed to be brought into compliance with international obligations. The FATF has recently promoted a self-assessment exercise with a view to evaluating the extent to which jurisdictions have in fact implemented the eight special recommendations. The good response rate by States proves that the implementation strategy set up by the FATF is well received and presumably reflects a general consensus on its action.[147]

The means by which consensus is formed and the fora in which the latter may emerge do not appear to be decisive factors. Implementation policies developed within the formal framework of international treaties or Security Council resolutions or in the informal setting of the FATF concur in rendering international action against terrorism more effective. What seems to matter most is that the international community perceives enforcement actions as legitimate. This is much more likely to occur when not just the relevant legal prescriptions which provide for rules of conduct but also their policies of implementation are elaborated internationally on the basis of a general consent.

VIII. OILING THE WHEELS OF INTERACTION BETWEEN DIFFERENT LAYERS OF LEGAL AUTHORITY: THE QUEST FOR A SMOOTH INTERPLAY

What is perhaps most striking about assessing the international legal regime of international terrorism is that it affects very many areas of

146 The FATF has also issued a document, *Guidance for Financial Institutions in Detecting Terrorist Financing* (24 April 2002, available at <http://www.fatf-gafi.org/pdf/ GuidFITF01_en.pdf> (last visited 1 February 2004)), aimed at facilitating the task of financial institutions in detecting the techniques and mechanisms used for the financing of terrorism.

147 See *FATF Self Assessment Exercise for the Eight Special Recommendations on Terrorist Financing: Responses from Jurisdictions* (Status as of 16 September 2003), available at <http://www.fatf-gafi.org/pdf/SATFResponse_en.pdf> (last visited 1 February 2004).

international law. On the one hand, it touches upon rules and principles of a different nature and institutions entrusted with different functions. On the other, it involves both the international legal system and national jurisdictions. The fairly heterogeneous range of normative frameworks which one has to consider is no conclusive reason to argue that the international legal regime concerning terrorism should stand on its own as some sort of self-contained regime derogating from the general principles of international law. The international law of jurisdiction and the regulation of the use of force continue being the backgrounds against which one determines, respectively, whether the prosecution of a terrorist suspect by one particular State or military intervention against a State accused of harbouring terrorist are lawful or unlawful conducts. Along the same lines, international humanitarian law provides fairly clear standards on the treatment of individuals apprehended in the course of an armed conflict and the law of State responsibility provides reliable guidance for establishing when a State can be deemed to have violated international law and what consequences should be attached to the violation. Quite frankly, despite some views to the contrary,[148] one does not have the impression that the unity of international law is in peril because the fight against terrorism demands an *ad hoc* regime.

However, the transectoral impact and the multi-layered dimension of international terrorist activities regulation carry with them some consequences, particularly with regard to implementation. If the effectiveness of international regulation is such a high priority as is the case with terrorism, one must then ensure that the relevant policies effectively reach out to all the concerned normative layers and are properly and consistently implemented. The numerous layers of legal authority involved in the process of implementation range from the international decision-making process to the national implementation process, sometimes through the intermediary of a supranational level as is the case with the European Union.

Oiling the wheels of the interaction among the different layers also implies conceiving appropriate coordination mechanisms. Issues of coordination within the same layer would certainly include the elaboration of appropriate treaty savings or consistency clauses, which should be carefully considered to determine the scope of application of each particular instrument in relation to other treaties. In this respect it is of note that this issue is being attentively assessed by the Ad-Hoc Committee of the General Assembly in its negotiation process on the comprehensive anti-terror convention, with a view to elaborating clear criteria to avoid

[148] A Cassese, "Terrorism is Also Disrupting Some Crucial Categories of International Law", above n 2, note 2; see also, C Gray, "From Unity to Polarization: International Law and the Use of Force against Iraq", (2002) 13 *European Journal of International Law* 1.

conflict between the comprehensive convention and the other anti-terror treaties.[149] Coordination in a vertical sense, namely between different layers, requires considerations of a different kind. Particularly, if one takes terrorism to be a phenomenon the repression of which is to be dealt with primarily at the level of municipal law it becomes crucial that international norms are properly incorporated into municipal legal systems.[150] This may not be sufficient, however, as rules, once they are incorporated, need be interpreted and enforced consistently with the international legal standards from which they emanate.[151] What may sound like a truism to many is likely to be the most important challenge of the foreseeable future. It suffices to think of all those treaty law provisions and Security Council resolutions that demand that States criminalize certain conducts and/or establish in their own legal system heads of jurisdiction that allow for the prosecution of terrorist suspects. Legislative action, encroaching on internal criminal law and procedure, is almost invariably required. If States fail to translate into self-executing domestic law provisions international legal standards, the latter are doomed to remain ineffective.

Particular problems are likely to arise when international standards need to be sifted through an additional layer of legal authority before being implemented into national jurisdictions. Most notably this is the case within the European Union,[152] the latest action of which in the field of terrorism attests to such difficulties. The complex equilibrium of competences between the Union and its Member States in the implementation of Security Council resolutions as well as the somewhat fragmented normative framework of the European Union does not in itself favour smooth enforcement. For example, loopholes and ambiguities may occasionally be traced to the detriment of a consistent implementation of the Security Council resolution 1373.[153] The issue of how to properly

[149] See Report of the Ad Hoc Committee established by General Assembly resolution 51/210 of 17 December 1996, Seventh session (31 March–2 April 2003), GAOR, 58th Sess. Supp. No. 37 (A/59/37), at 9.

[150] On the implementation of international law rules within domestic legal systems see A Cassese, *International Law* (Oxford University Press, Oxford, 2001), ch 8, "Implementation of International Legal Rules within National Systems", 162 ff. As regards the implementation of treaties see M Leigh, MP Blakeslee and LB Ederington, *National Treaty Law and Practice*, (American Society of International Law, Washington, 1999) and F Jacobs and S Roberts, *The Effect of Treaties in Domestic Law* (Sweet and Maxwell, London, 1987).

[151] See B Conforti, *International Law and the Role of Domestic Legal Systems*, (Kluwer Academic Publishers, The Hague, 1993).

[152] For an overview of action taken by the EU see S Peers, "EU Responses to Terrorism", (2003) 52 *International and Comparative Law Quarterly* 227, and for measures taken prior to 11 September 2001 see, by the same author, the account given in (2000) 49 *ibid* 222.

[153] See the critical remarks made by A Reinisch in this volume ("The Action of the European Union to Combat International Terrorism", ch 8) concerning the inadequacies of the EU's action to properly implement international obligations in the field of prevention of terrorist financing.

implement SC's resolutions and how to share the burden of control over supranational and national measures is well known in the context of the EU and has caused problems in the past particularly as regards the protection of individual rights.[154] It would be desirable that some of the built-in safeguards of the system were available, but most recent actions have taken the form of framework decisions, which exclude the involvement of national parliaments and the full array of judicial checks and balances available in other domains of EU law. From a different perspective, the contribution that regional organizations can make is invaluable as they may act as a catalyst for further developments in international law. The action taken by the European Union in respect of judicial cooperation and harmonization of criminal legislation with regard to terrorist offences may pave the way for other States and regional organizations to follow suit and provide a model for more advanced institutional forms of cooperation.[155]

With specific regard to the need to guarantee coordination of action at different normative levels, some remarks on the work of the Counter-terrorism Committee may be apt. As is known, the Committee, established by the Security Council to supervise the proper implementation of Resolution 1373, has set for itself a three stage action plan, which provides for an initial assessment of the adequacy of the state of national legislation in all areas concerned by the obligations laid down in resolution 1373, to a second step consisting of ascertaining that States strengthen their executive machinery to enforce anti-terror legislation and finally to concentrate on the effective implementation by States of their legislation and enforcement mechanisms.[156] Most importantly, the Committee has focused, among other things, on facilitating the providing of technical assistance to bring States' legislation into compliance with international obligations. To this end, it has set up a Technical Assistance Team, a database of available assistance as well as other useful practical arrangements, which are meant to promote technical cooperation on a global scale.[157]

[154] For an example see AR Pavoni, "UN Sanctions in EU and National Law: The Centro-Com Case", (1999) *International and Comparative Law Quarterly* 582.

[155] See in particular the *Council Framework Decision of 13 June 2002 on Combating Terrorism* (2002/475/JHA) (in OJEC, L 164/3 (22 June 2002)) and the *Council Framework Decision of 13 June 2002 on the European arrest warrant and the surrender procedures between Member States* (in OJEC, L 190/1 (18 July 2002)).

[156] The three stages of analysis instituted by the Committee for its work with States can be read at <http://www.un.org/Docs/sc/committees/1373/priorities.html> (last visited 15 January 2004).

[157] The many initiatives undertaken by the Committee in the field of assistance to States for the implementation of resolution 1373 can be found on the Committee's website (<http://un.org/sc/ctc>). The Security Council, in its resolution 1377 of 12 November 2001, has expressly invited the Committee "to explore ways in which States can be assisted, and in particular to explore with international, regional and subregional organizations: the promotion of best-practices in the areas covered by resolution 1373 (2001), including the preparation of model laws as appropriate; the availability of existing technical,

States, which are under a fairly tight reporting schedule, have so far manifested good will in their effort at cooperating with the Committee at this stage,[158] although their "cooperative spirit" might be called into question as the Committee will shift its focus from assessing "whether States have the necessary counterterrorism legislation and executive machinery in place to monitoring what action States are actually taking to combat terrorism".[159] Be that as it may, the Counter-terrorism Committee, with its potential for ensuring the smooth interplay between the international and national levels of legal authority, appears as an indispensable institutional instrument to promote a comprehensive and consistent implementation of international anti-terror normative standards.[160]

Helping decision-makers and law enforcement officers to address properly complex international legal issues and providing them with advice on the required technical assistance is a prerequisite for enhancing the effectiveness of international legal norms at the domestic level. Other functions that the Committee is currently discharging are worth noting. In particular, on the occasion of a special meeting gathering a large number of international, regional and sub-regional organizations, the issue of how to increase cooperation with the Committee was tackled.[161] Participants have committed to sharing data and best practices relevant to global cooperation and have agreed to pursue their mandates and initiatives on the basis of complementarity, focusing on what each organization does best to avoid duplication of effort and waste of resources, under an overall coordination structure.[162] Promoting what in another context

financial, regulatory, legislative or other assistance programmes which might facilitate the implementation of resolution 1373 (2001); the promotion of possible synergies between these assistance programmes."

[158] By 5 January 2004, the Committee had received 461 reports from States and others. They include first reports from 191 Member States and 5 from others, 158 second reports from Member States and 2 from others, 100 third reports from Member States and 5 fourth reports from Member States. As indicated earlier, all States have submitted their first reports (see Work programme of the Counter-Terrorism Committee (1 January–31 March 2004). Annex to the letter dated 12 January 2004 from the Chairman of the Security Council Committee established pursuant to resolution 1373 (2001) concerning counter-terrorism addressed to the President of the Security Council, UN Doc. S/2004/32).

[159] E Rosand, "Security Council Resolution 1373, the Counter-Terrorism Committee, and the fight Against Terrorism" (2003) 97 *American Journal of International Law* 333, at 340.

[160] See the statement by the Secretary General at the Security Council ministerial meeting of 20 January 2003, stressing the central role that the Committee, by its task of ensuring implementation of international law standards, is called upon to play in the global efforts to fight terrorism (see UN Doc. S/PV.4688, at 2.).

[161] The special meeting took place in New York on 6 March 2003, bringing together 57 international, regional and subregional organizations.

[162] See "Outcome document of the special meeting of the Counter-Terrorism Committee with international, regional, and subregional organizations", UN Doc. S/AC.40/2003/SM.1/4*, 31 March 2003. See also the "Counter-Terrorism Committee Follow-up Action Plan" to the special meeting, UN Doc. S/AC.40/2003/SM.1/6/Rev. 1, 3 April 2003.

has been defined as the "strengthening of communication processes"[163] among different institutional actors involved in international legal processes may appear at first sight a relatively sterile exercise. Communication processes are instead very important to prompt consistent law enforcement, as they tend to favour mutual knowledge and enhance mutual trust among institutional participants.

The coexistence of different layers of legal authority entrusted with concurrent law-making and enforcement functions makes their smooth interaction crucial to ensuring the implementation of internationally agreed upon policies.[164] All the more so when such policies, in order to be effective, require uniform and consistent enforcement. The latter is a direct function not only of a general consensus at the international level, but also of the coordinated day-to-day operation of law enforcement within and across jurisdictions at various levels of legal authority. Looking at this phenomenon as part and parcel of contemporary international law enforcement processes may well be a departure from orthodox thinking, but surely represents the best way to ensure that international terrorism is effectively fought against.

[163] A Bianchi, "The Impact of International Trade Law on Environmental Law and Process", in F Francioni (ed), *Environment, Human Rights and the Liberalisation of Trade*, (Oxford, Hart Publishing, 2001) 105–34, at 110. The Security Council has invited the Committee to deepen "its dialogue with international, regional and subregional organizations active in the areas covered by the resolution [Res 1373]" (see Statement by the President of the Security Council, UN Doc S/PRST/2003/17, 16 October 2003).

[164] For an application of this concept in the context of the European Union see A Bianchi, "New Institutional Arrangements and Old Paradigms: Some Remarks on the Nature of the European Union", in *Today's Europe: The Present Situation, Trends in Italy and the Nordic Countries*, 12–21 (Oslo, 1995).

Index